Professional Java™ Development
with the Spring Framework

Professional Java™ Development with the Spring Framework

Rod Johnson
Juergen Hoeller
Alef Arendsen
Thomas Risberg
Colin Sampaleanu

WILEY

Wiley Publishing, Inc.

Professional Java™ Development with the Spring Framework

Published by
Wiley Publishing, Inc.
10475 Crosspoint Boulevard
Indianapolis, IN 46256
www.wiley.com

Published simultaneously in Canada

ISBN-13: 978-0-7645-7483-2
ISBN-10: 0-7645-7483-3

Manufactured in the United States of America

10 9 8 7 6 5 4

1B/RV/QW/QV/IN

Library of Congress Cataloging-in-Publication Data:

Professional Java development with the Spring Framework/Rod Johnson
...[et al.].
  p. cm.
  Includes index.
  ISBN-13: 978-0-7645-7483-2 (paper/website)
  ISBN-10: 0-7645-7483-3 (paper/website)
  1. Java (Computer program language) 2. Application software
–Development. I. Johnson, Rod, Ph.D.
  QA76.73.J38P74585 2005
  005.13'3–dc22

                                        2005013970

For general information on our other products and services please contact our Customer Care Department within the United States at (800) 762-2974, outside the United States at (317) 572-3993 or fax (317) 572-4002.

Trademarks: Wiley, the Wiley logo, Wrox, the Wrox logo, Programmer to Programmer, and related trade dress are trademarks or registered trademarks of John Wiley & Sons, Inc. and/or its affiliates, in the United States and other countries, and may not be used without written permission. Java is a trademark of Sun Microsystems, Inc. All other trademarks are the property of their respective owners. Wiley Publishing, Inc., is not associated with any product or vendor mentioned in this book.

Wiley also publishes its books in a variety of electronic formats. Some content that appears in print may not be available in electronic books.

About the Authors

Rod Johnson is the founder of the Spring Framework and a well-known expert on Java and J2EE.

Rod holds a Ph.D. from Sydney University. Originally from a C/C++ background, he has been involved with Java and J2EE since their releases as a developer, architect, and consultant.

He is the author of two of the most popular and influential books on J2EE: *Expert One-on-One J2EE Design and Development* (Wrox, 2002), and *J2EE without EJB* (Wrox, 2004, with Juergen Hoeller). Both have played a major role in the rise of "agile" J2EE, and the move away from overly complex traditional J2EE architecture.

Rod is co-lead of the Spring Framework. He is a popular conference speaker and regularly appears at leading Java events in the US, Europe, and Asia. He serves in the Java Community Process (JCP) on the expert groups of several JSRs.

He also has wide consulting experience in banking and finance, insurance, software, and media. He is CEO of Interface21 (www.interface21.com), a consultancy devoted to providing expert J2EE and Spring Framework services. He is actively involved with client projects as well as Spring development.

For Kerry.

Juergen Hoeller is co-founder of Interface21, the company providing commercial Spring services from the source. He is a key driver of Spring development and has been release manager since Spring's inception. His special interests and responsibilities in the project cover a wide variety of topics, from the core container to transaction management, data access, and lightweight remoting.

Juergen has a Master's degree in computer science from the University of Linz, specializing in Java, OO modeling, and software engineering. He is co-author of *Expert One-on-One J2EE Development without EJB* (Wiley, 2004) and regularly presents at conferences and other events. He is also active in many community forums, including TheServerSide.

To Eva, for her continuing love and support, and for understanding that there is no separation between working time and spare time in the Spring world.

Alef Arendsen studied computer sciences at the University of Utrecht. Later, also in Utrecht, Alef started his first company. After this turned out to be too little a challenge, Alef went to work for SmartHaven, an Amsterdam-based VC-funded company providing J2EE components for knowledge management applications. He was responsible for streamlining the development process and designing parts of the component infrastructure. In early 2002, together with Joost van de Wijgerd, Alef founded JTeam, a software company providing J2EE development services. Alef is a core Spring committer and, while remaining involved with JTeam, he is now a consultant for Interface21. He is a frequent speaker at public conferences. Alef can be reached by email at alef@interface21.com. You can also read his blog at http://blog.arendsen.net.

To Mas, my nephew, who frequently cheered me up and reminded me of things other than work.

Thomas Risberg is a database developer working for TargetrRx, a pharmaceutical market research company located in Horsham, Pennsylvania. He has many years of experience working with both large and small organizations on various database-related projects ranging from simple data entry programs to large data warehousing implementations. Thomas is a reformed COBOL programmer who came to Java via Xbase, Visual Basic, and PL/SQL. He served as an Oracle DBA for a couple of years but decided that software development was really where his heart was.

Thomas has a B.A. degree in information processing from the University of Stockhom, Sweden. He is a certified Oracle Professional DBA and a Sun Certified Java Programmer and J2EE Architect.

Thomas joined the Spring Framework development team in early 2003 and is mostly involved in evolving the JDBC layer. His non-computer–related interests are soccer, photography, and travel.

Colin Sampaleanu has had a long and varied career spanning almost two decades—after a childhood spent tinkering with computers and software—including experience developing for and managing his own retail software company, other years in the C++ shrinkwrap and enterprise software space, experience with Java since the early days of the language, and a complete focus on enterprise Java since the late nineties.

Colin is a currently a principal partner at Interface21, which specializes in Spring training, consulting, and support. Prior to joining Interface21, Colin was Chief Architect at a software incubator / VC.

As a core Spring developer and Interface21 principal, Colin spends much of his time talking and writing about the benefits of Spring, and promoting agile software development architectures and methodologies in general.

To Nina, for her continued love and support, and for understanding that despite our best intentions, in this field 9–5 is often just the first half of the workday. To Alec and Maia, for their simple innocence and joy, and for reminding me that there are other things in life besides computers.

Credits

Executive Editor
Robert Elliott

Development Editor
Adaobi Obi Tulton

Technical Editors
Peter den Haan
Qi Zhang
Aleksandar Seovic
Erik Janssens

Copy Editor
Nancy Rapoport

Editorial Manager
Mary Beth Wakefield

Vice President & Executive Group Publisher
Richard Swadley

Vice President and Publisher
Joseph B. Wikert

Project Coordinator
Kristie Rees

Graphics and Production Specialists
April Farling
Julie Trippetti

Quality Control Technicians
Leeann Harney
Jessica Kramer
Joe Niesen,
Carl William Pierce

Proofreading and Indexing
TECHBOOKS Production Services

Acknowledgments

Rod Johnson: Many people helped in the writing of this book. In particular, I thank my co-authors, each of whom played a valuable role in ensuring that we were able to achieve coverage of a wide range of Spring's large and growing feature set.

Thanks to Ben Alex, lead developer of Acegi Security for Spring, for contributing most of the material on Spring security. Mark Pollack, Spring developer and lead of Spring.NET, also kindly contributed valuable material relating to Spring's services for JMS. Dmitriy Kopylenko, also a Spring developer, helped with UML diagrams and examples for the AOP chapter.

Finally, thanks to the reviewers—especially Peter den Haan and Aleksander Seovic—for their attention to detail and many valuable suggestions.

Juergen Hoeller: I thank my co-authors, our reviewers, and our editor; it has been a pleasure working with you. A special thank you goes to Peter den Haan for his extraordinarily thorough chapter reviews. Last but not least, I express my gratitude to the entire Spring community: Without your active participation, the Spring project would not be what it is today.

A. Arendsen: I thank all my co-workers at JTeam for their support. Special thanks to Bram Smeets and Arjen Poutsma for providing valuable content on various topics. I also owe a lot to Joost, the chap I originally started JTeam with. Without him I couldn't have found the time to contribute to this book. I also want to express my gratitude to Goof Kerling, who taught me a great deal about programming, how to do it the right way, and life in general. Thanks to Lars for cooking once every month, providing me with a place to stay until my house was finished, and joining me for the occasional beer. Also, thanks to my family for their support and the technical editors for thoroughly reviewing the content and for pointing out that Dutch isn't the most widely used language in the world.

Thomas Risberg: I thank the entire Spring community—without you, neither the project nor this book would be what it is today.

Colin Sampaleanu: I thank my co-authors, my partners at Interface21, and the Spring team for setting the bar so high. It's always a pleasure working with you. I'm grateful for the many colleagues over the years who by being passionate about the art of software development have helped keep my own interest high. I also thank my technical reviewers, Peter den Haan, Qi Zhang, and Jim Leask, who provided much valuable feedback.

Contents

Contents

Contents

Contents

Contents

Contents

Contents

Contents

Contents

Introduction

The Spring Framework is a major open source application development framework that makes Java/J2EE development easier and more productive.

Spring offers services that you can use in a wide range of environments, from applets and standalone clients through web applications running in a simple servlet engine to complex enterprise applications running in a full-blown J2EE application server. Spring enables a POJO programming model that decouples your code from its environment, protecting your investment in the face of change. Spring works on JDK 1.3 and later, taking advantage of JDK 1.4 and 1.5 features if available. Spring's J2EE services run on J2EE 1.2 and later.

This book will show you how you can use all the major parts of Spring to help you develop successful applications. You'll learn not just *what* Spring does, but *why*. You will gain insight into best practices when using the framework, and you will see a complete sample application.

Whom This Book Is For

This book is for Java/J2EE architects and developers who want to gain a deep knowledge of the Spring Framework in order to use it effectively in applications from simple web applications up to complex enterprise applications.

If you're new to Spring, you will still be able to work your way through this book. However, the coverage of advanced topics will ensure that even experienced Spring users will find information to help them use Spring effectively. You will probably want to keep this book on your desk for reference as you develop applications using Spring.

Aims of This Book

This book covers all major parts of the Spring framework, explaining the framework's functionality and motivation. It aims to equip you to implement advanced applications using Spring.

What This Book Covers

This book covers most of the feature set of Spring 1.2.

You will learn:

- ❑ *What* Spring offers. Spring has a large feature set: We guide you through the features and show how they form a coherent whole.

- ❑ *Why* Spring does what it does. We discuss the motivation behind many Spring features and the rationale for Spring's approach.

- ❑ *When* to use Spring features, and about best practices when using Spring.

Introduction

We cover the following areas of Spring, with the background discussion necessary to put the Spring functionality in context:

❑ The core Inversion of Control container and the concept of Dependency Injection that underpins it. Spring's *lightweight container* provides sophisticated configuration management, and a flexible backbone within which other services can be used.

❑ Spring's Aspect-Oriented Programming (AOP) framework and why AOP is important in J2EE development. Together with Spring's Dependency Injection capabilities, Spring AOP enables a POJO programming model, in which application code has minimal dependencies on Spring APIs, even when it enjoys Spring services.

❑ Spring's approach to service abstraction, and the goals it achieves.

❑ Transaction management: Core concepts, Spring's programmatic and declarative transaction management services, and how to use them effectively.

❑ Data access using Spring: You'll see how Spring provides a sophisticated, consistent abstraction over a variety of popular data access technologies. We'll look in detail at how to access data using Spring's JDBC functionality, iBATIS SQL Maps, and the Hibernate O/R mapping framework. You will gain a solid conceptual understanding of Spring data access that is applicable to other supported persistence APIs such as TopLink.

❑ Spring's MVC web framework. Three chapters provide in-depth information about the motivation for Spring's MVC framework, how it compares with other popular web application frameworks such as Struts, and how to use it in scenarios from basic to advanced. You will also see how to use Spring MVC to generate custom content types.

❑ Spring services for exposing and accessing remote services. Spring provides a unique remoting framework that works over a variety of protocols, but is entirely POJO-based.

❑ Spring services for accessing and implementing EJBs.

❑ Spring services relating to JMS.

❑ Spring's integration with the open source Quartz scheduler and other popular open source and commercial products.

❑ How Spring can be used in the design and implementation of a complete application, through our sample application.

❑ Effective testing strategies for Spring applications. One of the major advantages of a sophisticated Dependency Injection container is that it can enable effective unit testing of application code; Spring goes a step further by providing powerful *integration testing* features that also don't require a container, significantly increasing the speed of develop-test cycles.

Throughout, we discuss best practices. Sophisticated frameworks such as Spring inevitably allow multiple ways to achieve the same end; we try to provide guidance as to how to make the best choice.

We also help you understand how Spring can provide a basis for a clean, layered architecture, and how appropriate use of Spring facilitates good OO design and architectural practice.

Assumed Knowledge

This book assumes a working knowledge of core features such as JDBC. Chapters related to J2EE topics such as EJB and JMS assume a basic grounding in those areas. However, we provide suggestions on further reading at appropriate points, so don't worry too much now if you're not sure your knowledge is deep enough.

We assume sound knowledge of OO design and Java language features including reflection, inner classes, and dynamic proxies.

Existing Spring Framework knowledge is not required.

We assume a basic knowledge of SQL and relational database concepts. An understanding of object relational mapping (ORM) is helpful but not essential.

If you've used a MVC web framework such as Struts, you will probably grasp the web content more quickly. However, we begin our coverage of Spring MVC with a discussion of the concepts behind MVC web frameworks.

Recommended Reading

Throughout the book we recommend further reading that will help you get a deeper grasp of concepts important to Spring development, such as Aspect-Oriented programming (AOP).

You may find it helpful to read *J2EE without EJB* (Johnson/Hoeller, Wrox, 2004), which provides a detailed discussion of the architectural rationale for lightweight containers such as Spring. However, this book is *not* purely a sequel to that book and can be understood entirely on its own.

There are many Spring Framework resources online. You should find the following particularly helpful:

- ❏ **The Spring Home page** (www.springframework.org): Portal for most Spring-related information, including the reference documentation and downloads.

- ❏ **Spring Forums** (forum.springframework.org): The place to go to ask questions about Spring. The Spring community is generally very welcoming and helpful.

What You Need to Use This Book

To run the sample application and examples, you will need:

- ❏ The Spring Framework version 1.2 or later.

- ❏ A J2EE web container or/and application server. We used Tomcat 5 where only a web container was required, and WebLogic 8.1 where an application server was required. However, Spring is designed for portability between application servers, and we also tested our code on other products. Thus you do not need to use any particular server product; you can use whatever product you are most familiar and comfortable with.

- ❏ A relational database and appropriate JDBC drivers. You should be able to modify our DDL fairly easily to work with the database of your choice.

❑ The Hibernate O/R mapping framework, version 3.0, available from www.hibernate.org.

❑ Various third-party libraries, including Jakarta Commons Logging. The necessary JAR files are included with the full Spring distribution; see documentation with Spring for details.

❑ The JUnit testing tool, ideally integrated with your IDE.

❑ The popular Jakarta Ant build tool.

All this software is open source or free for developer use.

We recommend a good Java IDE with refactoring support, such as Eclipse or IntelliJ IDEA. Such tools either ship with or can easily be integrated with validating XML editors that provide code assistance. These are helpful when editing Spring XML bean definition documents and other XML artifacts such as Hibernate mapping files, iBATIS SQL Maps definition files, and J2EE deployment descriptors. You should *never* need to edit XML content purely by hand.

The Sample Application

The sample application for this book is an online ticketing application: a web application that works against a relational database. This application uses JSPs to generate web content; Spring's MVC web framework to implement the web tier; Spring to configure middle tier objects and make them transactional; and a mix of Hibernate and JDBC to access and update relational data. We use Spring's data access abstraction to conceal use of Hibernate behind a portable layer of data access interfaces. We have tested with a choice of popular relational databases including MySQL and Oracle.

This application can run in either a web container or on an application server, using either local or global transaction management.

The requirements for the sample application are discussed in Appendix A; the implementation is discussed in Chapter 15.

This problem domain was first used for the sample application in *Expert One-on-One J2EE Design and Development*. It has been rewritten for this book to bring it up to date with the current Spring feature set and current views on best practice for J2EE applications using Spring. If you have the earlier book, you should find the comparison interesting. The past two to three years have seen many developments in the Java framework space, so best practice has moved on significantly (not merely concerning Spring itself).

Conventions

To help you get the most from the text and keep track of what's happening, we've used a number of conventions throughout the book.

Tips, hints, tricks, and asides to the current discussion are offset and placed in italics like this.

As for styles in the text:

❑ We *italicize* important words when we introduce them.

❑ We show keyboard strokes like this: Ctrl+A.

❑ We show filenames, URLs, and code within the text like so: `persistence.properties`

❑ We present code in two different ways:

```
In code examples we highlight new and important code with a gray background.
```

```
The gray highlighting is not used for code that's less important in the present
context, or has been shown before.
```

Source Code

As you work through the examples in this book, you may choose either to type in all the code manually or to use the source code files that accompany the book. All of the source code used in this book is available for download at www.wrox.com. Once at the site, simply locate the book's title (either by using the Search box or by using one of the title lists) and click the Download Code link on the book's detail page to obtain all the source code for the book.

Because many books have similar titles, you may find it easiest to search by ISBN; this book's ISBN is 0-7645-7483-3.

Once you download the code, just decompress it with your favorite compression tool. Alternatively, go to the main Wrox code download page at www.wrox.com/dynamic/books/download.aspx to see the code available for this book and all other Wrox books.

Errata

We make every effort to ensure that there are no errors in the text or in the code. However, no one is perfect, and mistakes do occur. If you find an error in one of our books, like a spelling mistake or faulty piece of code, we would be very grateful for your feedback. By sending in errata, you may save another reader hours of frustration and at the same time help us provide even higher quality information.

To find the errata page for this book, go to www.wrox.com and locate the title using the Search box or one of the title lists. Then, on the book details page, click the Book Errata link. On this page you can view all errata that has been submitted for this book and posted by Wrox editors. A complete book list including links to each book's errata is also available at www.wrox.com/misc-pages/booklist.shtml.

If you don't spot "your" error on the Book Errata page, go to www.wrox.com/contact/techsupport.shtml and complete the form there to send us the error you have found. We'll check the information and, if appropriate, post a message to the book's errata page and fix the problem in subsequent editions of the book.

p2p.wrox.com

For author and peer discussion, join the P2P forums at p2p.wrox.com. The forums are a Web-based system for you to post messages relating to Wrox books and related technologies and interact with other readers and technology users. The forums offer a subscription feature to email you topics of interest of your choosing when new posts are made to the forums. Wrox authors, editors, other industry experts, and your fellow readers are present on these forums.

At `http://p2p.wrox.com` you will find a number of different forums that will help you not only as you read this book but also as you develop your own applications. To join the forums, just follow these steps:

1. Go to `p2p.wrox.com` and click the Register link.

2. Read the terms of use and click Agree.

3. Complete the required information to join as well as any optional information you wish to provide and click Submit.

4. You will receive an email with information describing how to verify your account and complete the joining process.

You can read messages in the forums without joining P2P, but in order to post your own messages, you must join.

Once you join, you can post new messages and respond to messages other users post. You can read messages at any time on the Web. If you would like to have new messages from a particular forum emailed to you, click the Subscribe to this Forum icon by the forum name in the forum listing.

For more information about how to use the Wrox P2P, be sure to read the P2P FAQs for answers to questions about how the forum software works as well as many common questions specific to P2P and Wrox books. To read the FAQs, click the FAQ link on any P2P.

Introducing the Spring Framework

Why Spring?

The Spring Framework is an open source application framework that aims to make J2EE development easier. In this chapter we'll look at the motivation for Spring, its goals, and how Spring can help you develop high-quality applications quickly.

> Spring is an *application framework*. Unlike single-tier frameworks such as Struts or Hibernate, Spring aims to help structure whole applications in a consistent, productive manner, pulling together best-of-breed single-tier frameworks to create a coherent architecture.

Problems with the Traditional Approach to J2EE

Since the widespread implementation of J2EE applications in 1999/2000, J2EE has not been an unqualified success in practice. While it has brought a welcome standardization to core middle-tier concepts such as transaction management, many — perhaps *most* — J2EE applications are over-complex, take excessive effort to develop, and exhibit disappointing performance. While Spring is applicable in a wide range of environments — not just server-side J2EE applications — the original motivation for Spring was the J2EE environment, and Spring offers many valuable services for use in J2EE applications.

Experience has highlighted specific causes of complexity and other problems in J2EE applications. (Of course, not all of these problems are unique to J2EE!) In particular:

❑ **J2EE applications tend to contain excessive amounts of "plumbing" code.** In the many code reviews we've done as consultants, time and time again we see a high proportion of code that doesn't *do* anything: JNDI lookup code, Transfer Objects, try/catch blocks to acquire and release JDBC resources. . . . Writing and *maintaining* such plumbing code proves a major drain on resources that should be focused on the application's business domain.

❑ **Many J2EE applications use a distributed object model where this is inappropriate.** This is one of the major causes of excessive code and code duplication. It's also conceptually wrong in many cases; internally distributed applications are more complex than co-located applications, and often much less performant. Of course, if your business requirements dictate a distributed architecture, you need to implement a distributed architecture and accept the tradeoff that incurs (and Spring offers features to help in such scenarios). But you shouldn't do so without a compelling reason.

❑ **The EJB component model is unduly complex.** EJB was conceived as a way of reducing complexity when implementing business logic in J2EE applications; it has not succeeded in this aim in practice.

❑ **EJB is overused.** EJB was essentially designed for internally distributed, transactional applications. While nearly all non-trivial applications are transactional, distribution should not be built into the basic component model.

❑ **Many "J2EE design patterns" are not, in fact, design patterns, but workarounds for technology limitations.** Overuse of distribution, and use of complex APIs such as EJB, have generated many questionable design patterns; it's important to examine these critically and look for simpler, more productive, approaches.

❑ **J2EE applications are hard to unit test.** The J2EE APIs, and especially, the EJB component model, were defined before the agile movement took off. Thus their design does not take into account ease of unit testing. Through both APIs and implicit contracts, it is surprisingly difficult to test applications based on EJB and many other J2EE APIs outside an application server. Yet unit testing outside an application server is essential to achieve high test coverage and to reproduce many failure scenarios, such as loss of connectivity to a database. It is also vital to ensuring that tests can be run quickly during the development or maintenance process, minimizing unproductive time waiting for redeployment.

❑ **Certain J2EE technologies have simply failed.** The main offender here is entity beans, which have proven little short of disastrous for productivity and in their constraints on object orientation.

The traditional response to these problems has been to wait for tool support to catch up with the J2EE specifications, meaning that developers don't need to wrestle with the complexity noted above. However, this has largely failed. Tools based on code generation approaches have not delivered the desired benefits, and have exhibited a number of problems of their own. In this approach, we might generate all those verbose JNDI lookups, Transfer Objects, and try/catch blocks.

In general, experience has shown that *frameworks* are better than tool-enabled code generation. A good framework is usually much more flexible at runtime than generated code; it should be possible to configure the behavior of one piece of code in the framework, rather than change many generated classes. Code generation also poses problems for round-tripping in many cases. A well-conceived framework can also offer a coherent abstraction, whereas code generation is typically just a shortcut that fails to conceal underlying complexities during the whole project lifecycle. (Often complexities will re-emerge damagingly during maintenance and troubleshooting.)

A framework-based approach recognizes the fact that there is a missing piece in the J2EE jigsaw: the application developer's view. Much of what J2EE provides, such as JNDI, is simply too low level to be a daily part of programmer's activities. In fact, the J2EE specifications and APIs can be judged as far more successful, if one takes the view that they do not offer the developer a programming model so much as provide a solid basis on which that programming model should sit. Good frameworks supply this missing piece and give application developers a simple, productive, abstraction, without sacrificing the core capability of the platform.

> **Using J2EE "out of the box" is not an attractive option. Many J2EE APIs and services are cumbersome to use. J2EE does a great job of standardizing low-level infrastructure, solving such problems as** *how can Java code access transaction management without dealing with the details of XA transactions.* **But J2EE does not provide an easily usable view for application code.**
>
> **That is the role of an** *application framework,* **such as Spring.**

Recognizing the importance of frameworks to successful J2EE projects, many developers and companies have attempted to write their own frameworks, with varying degrees of success. In a minority of cases, the frameworks achieved their desired goals and significantly cut costs and improved productivity. In most cases, however, the cost of developing and maintaining a framework itself became an issue, and framework design flaws emerged. As the core problems are generic, it's much preferable to work with a single, widely used (and tested) framework, rather than implement one in house. No matter how large an organization, it will be impossible to achieve a degree of experience matching that available for a product that is widely used in many companies. If the framework is open source, there's an added advantage in that it's possible to contribute new features and enhancements that may be adopted. (Of course it's possible to contribute suggestions to commercial products, but it's typically harder to influence successful commercial products, and without the source code it's difficult to make equally useful contributions.) Thus, increasingly, generic frameworks such as Struts and Hibernate have come to replace in-house frameworks in specific areas.

The Spring Framework grew out of this experience of using J2EE without frameworks, or with a mix of in-house frameworks. However, unlike Struts, Hibernate, and most other frameworks, Spring offers services for use throughout an application, not merely in a single architectural tier. Spring aims to take away much of the pain resulting from the issues in the list we've seen, by simplifying the programming model, rather than concealing complexity behind a complex layer of tools.

> **Spring enables you to enjoy the key benefits of J2EE, while minimizing the complexity encountered by application code.**
>
> **The essence of Spring is in providing enterprise services to Plain Old Java Objects (POJOs). This is particularly valuable in a J2EE environment, but application code delivered as POJOs is naturally reusable in a variety of runtime environments.**

Lightweight Frameworks

Some parts of J2EE can properly be termed frameworks themselves. Among them, EJB amounts to a framework because it provides a structure for application code, and defines a consistent way of accessing services from the application server. However, the EJB framework is cumbersome to use and restrictive. The work involved in implementing an EJB is excessive, given that the architects of J2EE expected that all business logic in J2EE applications would be implemented in EJBs. Developers must cope with three to four Java classes for each EJB; two verbose deployment descriptors for each EJB JAR file; and excessive amounts of code for client access to EJBs and EJB access to their environment. The EJB component model, up to and including EJB 2.1, fails to deliver on many of its goals, and fails to deliver a workable structure for business logic in J2EE applications. The EJB Expert Group has finally realized this and is attempting an overhaul of the EJB model in EJB 3.0, but we need a solution, right now, and Spring already demonstrates a far superior one in most cases.

Not merely EJB, but the majority of frameworks in the early years of J2EE, proved to have problems of their own. For example, Apache Avalon offered powerful configuration management and other services, but never achieved widespread adoption, partly because of the learning curve it required, and because application code needed to be aware of Avalon APIs.

> **A framework can only be as good as the programming model it provides. If a framework imposes too many requirements on code using it, it creates lock-in and — even more important — constrains developers in ways that may not be appropriate. The application developer, rather than framework designer, often has a better understanding of how code should be written.**
>
> **Yet a framework should provide *guidance* with respect to good practice: *It should make the right thing easy to do*. Getting the right mixture of constraint and freedom is the key challenge of framework design, which is as much art as science.**

Given this history, the emergence of a number of *lightweight* frameworks was inevitable. These aim to provide many of the services of "out of the box" J2EE in a simpler, more manageable manner. They aim to do their best to make the framework itself invisible, while encouraging good practice. Above all, they aim to enable developers to work primarily with POJOs, rather than special objects such as EJBs.

As the name implies, lightweight frameworks not only aim to reduce complexity in application code, but avoid unnecessary complexity in their own functioning. So a lightweight framework won't have a high startup time, won't involve huge binary dependencies, will run in any environment, and won't place obstacles in the way of testing.

While "old J2EE" was characterized by high complexity and a welter of questionable "design patterns" to give it intellectual respectability, lightweight J2EE is about trying to find the "simplest thing that can possibly work": wise advice from the XP methodology, regardless of whether you embrace XP practices overall.

> **While all the lightweight frameworks grew out of J2EE experience, it's important to note that none of them is J2EE-specific. A lightweight container can be used in a variety of environments: even in applets.**
>
> **For example, the *Spring Rich Client* project demonstrates the value of the Spring model outside the server environment, in rich client applications.**

Enter Spring

Spring is both the most popular and most ambitious of the lightweight frameworks. It is the only one to address all architectural tiers of a typical J2EE application, and the only one to offer a comprehensive range of services, as well as a lightweight container. We'll look at Spring's modules in more detail later, but the following are the key Spring modules:

❑ **Inversion of Control container:** The core "container" Spring provides, enabling sophisticated configuration management for POJOs. The Spring IoC container can manage fine or coarse-grained POJOs (object granularity is a matter for developers, not the framework), and work with other parts of Spring to offer services as well as configuration management. We'll explain IoC and *Dependency Injection* later in this chapter.

❑ **Aspect-Oriented Programming (AOP) framework:** AOP enables behavior that would otherwise be scattered through different methods to be modularized in a single place. Spring uses AOP under the hood to deliver important out-of-the-box services such as declarative transaction management. Spring AOP can also be used to implement custom code that would otherwise be scattered between application classes.

❑ **Data access abstraction:** Spring encourages a consistent architectural approach to data access, and provides a unique and powerful abstraction to implement it. Spring provides a rich hierarchy of data access exceptions, independent of any particular persistence product. It also provides a range of helper services for leading persistence APIs, enabling developers to write persistence framework–agnostic data access interfaces and implement them with the tool of their choice.

❑ **JDBC simplification:** Spring provides an abstraction layer over JDBC that is significantly simpler and less error-prone to use than JDBC when you need to use SQL-based access to relational databases.

❑ **Transaction management:** Spring provides a transaction abstraction that can sit over JTA "global" transactions (managed by an application server) or "local" transactions using the JDBC, Hibernate, JDO, or another data access API. This abstraction provides a consistent programming model in a wide range of environments and is the basis for Spring's declarative and programmatic transaction management.

❑ **MVC web framework:** Spring provides a request-based MVC web framework. Its use of shared instances of multithreaded "controllers" is similar to the approach of Struts, but Spring's web framework is more flexible, and integrates seamlessly with the Spring IoC container. All other Spring features can also be used with other web frameworks such as Struts or JSF.

❑ **Simplification for working with JNDI, JTA, and other J2EE APIs:** Spring can help remove the need for much of the verbose, boilerplate code that "doesn't do anything." With Spring, you can continue to use JNDI or EJB, if you want, but you'll never need to write another JNDI lookup. Instead, simple configuration can result in Spring performing the lookup on your behalf, guaranteeing that resources such as JNDI contexts are closed even in the event of an exception. The dividend is that you get to focus on writing code that *you* need to write because it relates to your business domain.

❑ **Lightweight remoting:** Spring provides support for POJO-based remoting over a range of protocols, including RMI, IIOP, and Hessian, Burlap, and other web services protocols.

❑ **JMS support:** Spring provides support for sending and receiving JMS messages in a much simpler way than provided through standard J2EE.

❑ **JMX support:** Spring supports JMX management of application objects it configures.

❑ **Support for a comprehensive testing strategy for application developers:** Spring not only helps to facilitate good design, allowing effective unit testing, but provides a comprehensive solution for integration testing outside an application server.

Spring's Values

To make the most effective use of Spring, it's important to understand the motivation behind it. Spring partly owes its success to its being based on a clear vision, and remaining true to that vision as its scope has expanded.

The key Spring values can be summarized as follows:

❑ **Spring is a *non-invasive* framework.** This is the key departure from most previous frameworks. Whereas traditional frameworks such as EJB or Apache Avalon force application code to be aware of the framework, implementing framework-specific interfaces or extending framework-specific classes, Spring aims to minimize the dependence of application code on the framework. Thus Spring can configure application objects that don't import Spring APIs; it can even be used to configure many legacy classes that were written without any knowledge of Spring. This has many benefits. For example:

    ❑ Application code written as part of a Spring application can be run without Spring or any other container.

    ❑ Lock-in to Spring is minimized. For example, you could migrate to another lightweight container, or possibly even reuse application objects in an EJB 3.0 EJB container, which supports a subset of Spring's Dependency Injection capability.

    ❑ Migration to future versions of Spring is easier. The less your code depends on the framework, the greater the decoupling between the implementation of your application and that of the framework. Thus the implementation of Spring can change significantly without breaking your code, allowing the framework to be improved while preserving backward compatibility.

    Of course in some areas, such as the web framework, it's impossible to avoid application code depending on the framework. But Spring consistently attempts to reach the non-invasive ideal where configuration management is concerned.

❑ **Spring provides a consistent programming model, usable in any environment.** Many web applications simply don't need to run on expensive, high-end, application servers, but are better off running on a web container such as Tomcat or Jetty. It's also important to remember that not all applications are server-side applications. Spring provides a programming model that insulates application code from environment details such as JNDI, making code less dependent on its runtime context.

❑ **Spring aims to promote code reuse.** Spring helps to avoid the need to make some important hard decisions up front, like whether your application will ever use JTA or JNDI; Spring abstractions will allow you to deploy your code in a different environment if you ever need to. Thus

Spring enables you to *defer architectural choices*, potentially delivering benefits such as the need to purchase an application server license only when you know exactly what your platform requirements are, following tests of throughput and scalability.

❏ **Spring aims to facilitate Object Oriented design in J2EE applications.** You might be asking "How can a J2EE application, written in Java — an OO language — not be OO?" In reality, many J2EE applications do not deserve the name of OO applications. Spring aims to remove some of the impediments in place of OO in traditional designs. As one of the reviewers on this book commented, "The code I've seen from my team in the year since we adopted Spring has consistently been better factored, more coherent, loosely coupled and reusable."

❏ **Spring aims to facilitate good programming practice, such as programming to interfaces, rather than classes.** Use of an IoC container such as Spring greatly reduces the complexity of coding to interfaces, rather than classes, by elegantly concealing the specification of the desired implementation class and satisfying its configuration requirements. Callers using the object through its interface are shielded from this detail, which may change as the application evolves.

❏ **Spring promotes pluggability.** Spring encourages you to think of application objects as named services. Ideally, the dependencies between such services are expressed in terms of interfaces. Thus you can swap one service for another without impacting the rest of your application. The way in which each service is configured is concealed from the client view of that service.

❏ **Spring facilitates the extraction of configuration values from Java code into XML or properties files.** While some configuration values may be validly coded in Java, all nontrivial applications need some configuration externalized from Java source code, to allow its management without recompilation or Java coding skills. (For example, if there is a timeout property on a particular object, it should be possible to alter its value without being a Java programmer.) Spring encourages developers to externalize configuration that might otherwise have been inappropriately hard-coded in Java source code. More configurable code is typically more maintainable and reusable.

❏ **Spring is designed so that applications using it are as easy as possible to test.** As far as possible, application objects will be POJOs, and POJOs are easy to test; dependence on Spring APIs will normally be in the form of interfaces that are easy to stub or mock. Unlike the case of JNDI, for example, stubbing or mocking is easy; unlike the case of Struts, for example, application classes are seldom forced to extend framework classes that themselves have complex dependencies.

❏ **Spring is consistent.** Both in different runtime environments and different parts of the framework, Spring uses a consistent approach. Once you learn one part of the framework, you'll find that that knowledge can be leveraged in many others.

❏ **Spring promotes architectural choice.** While Spring provides an architectural backbone, Spring aims to facilitate replaceability of each layer. For example, with a Spring middle tier, you should be able to switch from one O/R mapping framework to another with minimal impact on business logic code, or switch from, say, Struts to Spring MVC or WebWork with no impact on the middle tier.

❏ **Spring does not reinvent the wheel.** Despite its broad scope, Spring does not introduce its own solution in areas such as O/R mapping where there are already good solutions. Similarly, it does not implement its own logging abstraction, connection pool, distributed transaction coordinator, remoting protocols, or other system services that are already well-served in other products or application servers. However, Spring does make these existing solutions significantly easier to use, and places them in a consistent architectural approach.

We'll examine these values later in this chapter and throughout this book. Many of these values are also followed by other lightweight frameworks. What makes Spring unique is that it provides such a consistent approach to delivering on them, and provides a wide enough range of services to be helpful throughout typical applications.

Spring in Context

Spring is a manifestation of a wider movement. Spring is the most successful product in what can broadly be termed *agile* J2EE.

Technologies

While Spring has been responsible for real innovation, many of the ideas it has popularized were part of the *zeitgeist* and would have become important even had there been no Spring project. Spring's greatest contribution — besides a solid, high quality, implementation — has been its combination of emerging ideas into a coherent whole, along with an overall architectural vision to facilitate effective use.

Inversion of Control and Dependency Injection

The technology that Spring is most identified with is *Inversion of Control*, and specifically the *Dependency Injection* flavor of Inversion of Control. We'll discuss this concept in detail in Chapter 2, "The Bean Factory and Application Context," but it's important to begin here with an overview. Spring is often thought of as an Inversion of Control container, although in reality it is much more.

Inversion of Control is best understood through the term the "Hollywood Principle," which basically means "Don't call me, I'll call you." Consider a traditional class library: application code is responsible for the overall flow of control, calling out to the class library as necessary. With the Hollywood Principle, framework code invokes application code, coordinating overall workflow, rather than application code invoking framework code.

Inversion of Control is often abbreviated as IoC in the remainder of this book.

IoC is a broad concept, and can encompass many things, including the EJB and Servlet model, and the way in which Spring uses callback interfaces to allow clean acquisition and release of resources such as JDBC Connections.

Spring's flavor of IoC for configuration management is rather more specific. Consequently, Martin Fowler, Rod Johnson, Aslak Hellesoy, and Paul Hammant coined the name *Dependency Injection* in late 2003 to describe the approach to IoC promoted by Spring, PicoContainer, and HiveMind — the three most popular lightweight frameworks.

> **Dependency Injection is based on Java language constructs, rather than the use of framework-specific interfaces. Instead of application code using framework APIs to resolve dependencies such as configuration parameters and collaborating objects, application classes expose their dependencies through methods or constructors that the framework can call with the appropriate values at runtime, based on configuration.**

Dependency Injection is a form of *push* configuration; the container "pushes" dependencies into application objects at runtime. This is the opposite of traditional *pull* configuration, in which the application object "pulls" dependencies from its environment. Thus, Dependency Injection objects never load custom properties or go to a database to load configuration — the framework is wholly responsible for actually reading configuration.

Push configuration has a number of compelling advantages over traditional pull configuration. For example, it means that:

❑ **Application classes are self-documenting, and dependencies are explicit.** It's merely necessary to look at the constructors and other methods on a class to see its configuration requirements. There's no danger that the class will expect its own undocumented properties or other formats.

❑ For the same reason, **documentation of dependencies is always up-to-date.**

❑ **There's little or no lock-in to a particular framework, or proprietary code, for configuration management.** It's all done through the Java language itself.

❑ As the framework is wholly responsible for reading configuration, **it's possible to switch where configuration comes from without breaking application code.** For example, the same application classes could be configured from XML files, properties files, or a database without needing to be changed.

❑ As the framework is wholly responsible for reading configuration, there is usually **greater consistency in configuration management.** Gone are the days when each developer will approach configuration management differently.

❑ **Code in application classes focuses on the relevant business responsibilities.** There's no need to waste time writing configuration management code, and configuration management code won't obscure business logic. A key piece of application plumbing is kept out of the developer's way.

We find that developers who try Dependency Injection rapidly become hooked. These advantages are even more apparent in practice than they sound in theory.

Spring supports several types of Dependency Injection, making its support more comprehensive than that of any other product:

❑ **Setter Injection:** The injection of dependencies via JavaBean setter methods. Often, but not necessarily, each setter has a corresponding getter method, in which case the *property* is set to be *writable* as well as *readable.*

❑ **Constructor Injection:** The injection of dependencies via constructor arguments.

❑ **Method Injection:** A more rarely used form of Dependency Injection in which the container is responsible for implementing methods at runtime. For example, an object might define a protected abstract method, and the container might implement it at runtime to return an object resulting from a container lookup. The aim of Method Injection is, again, to avoid dependencies on the container API. See Chapter 2 for a discussion of the issues around this advanced form of Dependency Injection.

Uniquely, Spring allows all three to be mixed when configuring one class, if appropriate.

Enough theory: Let's look at a simple example of an object being configured using Dependency Injection.

We assume that there is an interface — in this case, Service — which callers will code against. In this case, the implementation will be called ServiceImpl. However, of course the name is hidden from callers, who don't know anything about how the Service implementation is constructed.

Let's assume that our implementation of Service has two dependencies: an int configuration property, setting a timeout; and a DAO that it uses to obtain persistent objects.

With Setter Injection we can configure ServiceImpl using JavaBean properties to satisfy these two dependencies, as follows:

```
public class ServiceImpl implements Service {
  private int timeout;
  private AccountDao accountDao;

  public void setTimeout(int timeout) {
    this.timeout = timeout;
  }

  public void setAccountDao(AccountDao accountDao) {
    this.accountDao = accountDao;
  }
}
```

With Constructor Injection, we supply both properties in the Constructor, as follows:

```
public class ServiceImpl implements Service {
  private int timeout;
  private AccountDao accountDao;

  public ServiceImpl (int timeout, AccountDao accountDao) {
    this.timeout = timeout;
    this.accountDao = accountDao;
  }
}
```

Either way, the dependencies are satisfied by the framework before any business methods on ServiceImpl are invoked. (For brevity, we haven't shown any business methods in the code fragments. Business methods will use the instance variables populated through Dependency Injection.)

This may seem trivial. You may be wondering how such a simple concept can be so important. While it is conceptually simple, it can scale to handle complex configuration requirements, populating whole object graphs as required. It's possible to build object graphs of arbitrary complexity using Dependency Injection. Spring also supports configuration of maps, lists, arrays, and properties, including arbitrary nesting.

As an IoC container takes responsibility for object instantiation, it can also support important creational patterns such as singletons, prototypes, and object pools. For example, a sophisticated IoC container such as Spring can allow a choice between "singleton" or shared objects (one per IoC container instance) and non-singleton or "prototype" instances (of which there can be any number of independent instances).

Because the container is responsible for satisfying dependencies, it can also introduce a layer of indirection as required to allow custom interception or hot swapping. (In the case of Spring, it can go a step farther and provide a true AOP capability, as we'll see in the next section.) Thus, for example, the container can satisfy a dependency with an object that is instrumented by the container, or which hides a "target object" that can be changed at runtime without affecting references. Unlike some IoC containers and complex configuration management APIs such as JMX, Spring does not introduce such indirection unless it's necessary. In accordance with its philosophy of allowing the simplest thing that can possibly work, unless you want such features, Spring will give you normal instances of your POJOs, wired together through normal property references. However, it provides powerful indirection capabilities if you want to take that next step.

Spring also supports *Dependency Lookup*: another form of Inversion of Control. This uses a more traditional approach, similar to that used in Avalon and EJB 1.*x* and 2.*x*, in which the container defines lifecycle callbacks, such as setSessionContext(), which application classes implement to look up dependencies. Dependency Lookup is essential in a minority of cases, but should be avoided where possible to minimize lock-in to the framework. Unlike EJB 2.*x* and Avalon, Spring lifecycle callbacks are optional; if you choose to implement them, the container will automatically invoke them, but in most cases you won't want to, and don't need to worry about them.

Spring also provides many hooks that allow power users to customize how the container works. As with the optional lifecycle callbacks, you won't often need to use this capability, but it's essential in some advanced cases, and is the product of experience using IoC in many demanding scenarios.

> **The key innovation in Dependency Injection is that it works with pure Java syntax: no dependence on container APIs is required.**
>
> **Dependency Injection is an amazingly simple concept, yet, with a good container, it's amazingly powerful. It can be used to manage arbitrarily fine-grained objects; it places few constraints on object design; and it can be combined with container services to provide a wide range of value adds.**
>
> **You don't need to do anything in particular to make an application class eligible for Dependency Injection — that's part of its elegance. In order to make classes "good citizens," you should avoid doing things that cut against the spirit of Dependency Injection, such as parsing custom properties files. But there are no hard and fast rules. Thus there is a huge potential to use legacy code in a container that supports Dependency Injection, and that's a big win.**

Aspect-Oriented Programming

Dependency Injection goes a long way towards delivering the ideal of a fully featured application framework enabling a POJO programming model. However, configuration management isn't the only issue; we also need to provide declarative *services* to objects. It's a great start to be able to configure our POJOs — even with a rich network of collaborators — without constraining their design; it's equally important to be able to apply services such as transaction management to POJOs without them needing to implement special APIs.

The ideal solution is Aspect-Oriented Programming (AOP). (AOP is also a solution for much more; besides, we are talking about a particular use of AOP here, rather than the be all and end all of AOP.)

AOP provides a different way of thinking about code structure, compared to OOP or procedural programming. Whereas in OOP we model real-world objects or concepts, such as bank accounts, as objects, and organize those objects in hierarchies, AOP enables us to think about *concerns* or *aspects* in our system. Typical concerns are transaction management, logging, or failure monitoring. For example, transaction management applies to operations on bank accounts, but also to many other things besides. Transaction management applies to sets of methods without much relationship to the object hierarchy. This can be hard to capture in traditional OOP. Typically we end up with a choice of tradeoffs:

❑ **Writing boilerplate code to apply the services to every method that requires them:** Like all cut-and-paste approaches, this is unmaintainable; if we need to modify how a service is delivered, we need to change multiple blocks of code, and OOP alone can't help us modularize that code. Furthermore, each additional concern will result in its own boilerplate code, threatening to obscure the business purpose of each method. We can use the **Decorator** design pattern to keep the new code distinct, but there will still be a lot of code duplication. In a minority of cases the **Observer** design pattern is sufficient, but it doesn't offer strong typing, and we must build in support for the pattern by making our objects observable.

❑ **Detype operations, through something like the Command pattern:** This enables a custom interceptor chain to apply behavior such as declarative transaction management, but at the loss of strong typing and readability.

❑ **Choosing a heavyweight dedicated framework such as EJB that can deliver the necessary services:** This works for some concerns such as transaction management, but fails if we need a custom service, or don't like the way in which the EJB specification approaches the particular concern. For example, we can't use EJB services if we have a web application that should ideally run in a web container, or in case of a standalone application with a Swing GUI. Such frameworks also place constraints on our code — we are no longer in the realm of POJOs.

In short, with a traditional OO approach the choices are code duplication, loss of strong typing, or an intrusive special-purpose framework.

AOP enables us to capture the cross-cutting code in modules such as interceptors that can be applied declaratively wherever the concern they express applies — *without imposing tradeoffs on the objects benefiting from the services.*

There are several popular AOP technologies and a variety of approaches to implementing AOP. Spring includes a *proxy-based* AOP framework. This does not require any special manipulation of class loaders and is portable between environments, including any application server. It runs on J2SE 1.3 and above, using J2SE *dynamic proxies* (capable of proxying any number of interfaces) or CGLIB byte code generation (which allows proxying classes, as well as interfaces). Spring AOP proxies maintain a chain of *advice* applying to each method, making it easy to apply services such as transaction management to POJOs. The additional behavior is applied by a chain of advice (usually interceptors) maintained by an *AOP proxy*, which wraps the POJO *target object*.

Spring AOP allows the proxying of interfaces or classes. It provides an extensible *pointcut* model, enabling identification of which sets of method to advise. It also supports *introduction*: advice that makes a class implement additional interfaces. Introduction can be very useful in certain circumstances (especially infrastructural code within the framework itself). Don't worry if AOP terms such as "pointcuts" and "introduction" are unfamiliar now; we'll provide a brief introduction to AOP in Chapter 4, which covers Spring's AOP framework.

Here, we're more interested in the value proposition that Spring AOP provides, and why it's key to the overall Spring vision.

Spring AOP is used in the framework itself for a variety of purposes, many of which are behind the scenes and which many users may not realize are the result of AOP:

❑ **Declarative transaction management:** This is the most important out-of-the-box service supplied with Spring. It's analogous to the value proposition of EJB container-managed transactions (CMT) with the following big advantages:

   ❑ It can be applied to any POJO.

   ❑ It isn't tied to JTA, but can work with a variety of underlying transaction APIs (including JTA). Thus it can work in a web container or standalone application using a single database, and doesn't require a full J2EE application server.

   ❑ It supports additional semantics that minimize the need to depend on a proprietary transaction API to force rollback.

❑ **Hot swapping:** An AOP proxy can be used to provide a layer of indirection. (Remember our discussion of how indirection can provide a key benefit in implementing Dependency Injection?) For example, if an OrderProcessor depends on an InventoryManager, and the InventoryManager is set as a property of the OrderProcessor, it's possible to introduce a proxy to ensure that the InventoryManager instance can be changed without invalidating the OrderProcessor reference. This mechanism is threadsafe, providing powerful "hot swap" capabilities. Full-blown AOP isn't the only way to do this, but if a proxy is to be introduced at all, enabling the full power of Spring AOP makes sense.

❑ **"Dynamic object" support:** As with hot swapping, the use of an AOP proxy can enable "dynamic" objects such as objects sourced from scripts in a language such as Groovy or Beanshell to support reload (changing the underlying instance) and (using introduction) implement additional interfaces allowing state to be queried and manipulated (last refresh, forcible refresh, and so on).

❑ **Security:** Acegi Security for Spring is an associated framework that uses Spring AOP to deliver a sophisticated declarative security model.

There's also a compelling value proposition in using AOP in application code, and Spring provides a flexible, extensible framework for doing so. AOP is often used in applications to handle aspects such as:

❑ **Auditing:** Applying a consistent auditing policy — for example, to updates on persistent objects.

❑ **Exception handling:** Applying a consistent exception handling policy, such as emailing an administrator in the event of a particular set of exceptions being thrown by a business object.

❑ **Caching:** An aspect can maintain a cache transparent to proxied objects and their callers, providing a simple means of optimization.

❑ **Retrying:** Attempting transparent recovery: for example, in the event of a failed remote invocation.

See Chapter 4, "Spring and AOP," for an introduction to AOP concepts and the Spring AOP framework.

> AOP seems set to be the future of middleware, with services (pre-built or application-specific) flexibly applied to POJOs. Unlike the monolithic EJB container, which provides a fixed set of services, AOP offers a much more modular approach. It offers the potential to combine best-of-breed services: for example, transaction management from one vendor, and security from another.
>
> While the full AOP story still has to be played out, Spring makes a substantial part of this vision a reality today, with solid, proven technology that is in no way experimental.

Consistent Abstraction

If we return to the core Spring mission of providing declarative service to POJOs, we see that it's not sufficient to have an AOP framework. From a middleware perspective, an AOP framework is a way of delivering services; it's important to have services to deliver — for example, to back a transaction management aspect. And of course not all services can be delivered declaratively; for example, there's no way to avoid working with an API for data access.

> The third side of the Spring triangle, after IoC and AOP, is a consistent service abstraction.

Motivation

At first glance the idea of Spring providing a consistent "service abstraction" may seem puzzling. Why is it better to depend on Spring APIs than, say, standard J2EE APIs such as JNDI, or APIs of popular, solid open source products such as Hibernate?

The Spring abstraction approach is compelling for many reasons:

❑ **Whether it's desirable to depend on a particular API depends more on the nature of that API than its provenance.** For example, if depending on a "standard" API results in code that is hard to unit test, you are better off with an abstraction over that API. A good example of this is JavaMail. JavaMail is a particularly difficult API to test against because of its use of static methods and final classes.

❑ **You may well end up building such an abstraction anyway; there's a real value in having it off the shelf, in a widely used product.** The reality is that Spring competes with in-house frameworks, rather than with J2EE itself. Most large applications will end up building helper objects and a level of abstraction over cumbersome APIs such as JNDI — as we noted early in this chapter, using J2EE out of the box has generally not proved to be a workable option. Spring provides a well-thought-through abstraction that is widely applicable and requires you to write no custom code.

❑ **Dependency on Spring is limited to a set of interfaces; the dependencies are simple and explicit, avoiding implicit dependencies, which can be problematic.** For example, if you write code that performs programmatic transaction management using JTA, you have a whole range of implicit dependencies. You need to obtain the JTA `UserTransaction` object using JNDI; you thus need both a JNDI and JTA environment. This may not be available in all environments, or at test time. In some important cases, such as declarative transaction management, *no* dependencies on Spring APIs are required to use Spring's abstraction.

❑ **Spring's abstraction interfaces work in a wide range of environments.** If you write code that uses JTA, you are tied to an environment providing JNDI and JTA. For example, if you try to run that code in a web container such as Tomcat, you would otherwise need to plug in a third-party JTA implementation. Spring's transaction infrastructure can help you avoid this need in the majority of cases, where you are working with a single database.

❑ **Spring's abstraction can decouple you from heavy dependence on third-party APIs that may be subject to change, or in case you switch product.** For example, if you aren't 100 percent sure whether you want to use Hibernate or TopLink persistence, you can use Spring's data access abstraction to make any migration a relatively straightforward process. Alternatively, if you need to migrate from Hibernate 2 to Hibernate 3, you'll find that easier if you use Spring.

❑ **Spring APIs are written for use by application developers, rather than merely for usage behind the scenes.** This relates to one of the key points made earlier in this chapter about the value proposition of frameworks in general. Both JTA and JDBC are good counter-examples. JTA was essentially intended to work behind the scenes to enable EJB declarative transaction management. Thus, exception handling using JTA is particularly cumbersome, with multiple exceptions having no common base class and needing individual catch blocks. JDBC is a relatively successful API at providing a consistent view of any relational database, but is extremely verbose and problematic to use directly in application code because of the complex error-handling required, and because of the need to write non-portable code to try to pinpoint the cause of a particular failure and work with advanced scenarios such as working with BLOBs and calling stored procedures.

In keeping with Spring's philosophy of not reinventing the wheel, Spring does not provide its own abstraction over services unless there are proven difficulties, such as those we've just seen, relating to use of that API.

Of course it's important to ensure that the abstraction does not sacrifice power. In many cases, Spring allows you to leverage the full power of the underlying service to express operations, even using the native API. However, Spring will take care of plumbing and resource handling for you.

Exceptions

A consistent exception hierarchy is essential to the provision of a workable service abstraction. Spring provides such an exception hierarchy in several cases, and this is one of Spring's unique features. The most important concerns data access. Spring's `org.springframework.dao.DataAccessException` and its subclasses provide a rich exception model for handling data access exceptions. Again, the emphasis is on the application programming model; unlike the case of `SQLException` and many other data access APIs, Spring's exception hierarchy is designed to allow developers to write the minimum, cleanest code to handle errors.

`DataAccessException` and other Spring infrastructure exceptions are unchecked. One of the Spring principles is that infrastructure exceptions should normally be unchecked. The reasoning behind this is that:

❑ **Infrastructure exceptions are not usually recoverable.** While it's possible to catch unchecked exceptions when one *is* recoverable, there is no benefit in being *forced* to catch or throw exceptions in the vast majority of cases where no recovery is possible.

❑ **Checked exceptions lessen the value of an exception hierarchy.** If Spring's
`DataAccessException` were checked, for example, it would be necessary
to write a `catch (DataAccessException)` block every time a subclass, such as
`IntegrityViolationException`, was caught, or for other, unrecoverable
`DataAccessExceptions` to be handled in application code up the call stack. This cuts
against the benefit of compiler enforcement, as the only useful catch block, for the subclass
that can actually be handled, is not enforced by the compiler.

❑ **Try/catch blocks that don't add value are verbose and obfuscate code.** It is not lazy to want to
avoid pointless code; it obfuscates intention and will pose higher maintenance costs forever.
Avoiding overuse of checked exceptions is consistent with the overall Spring goal of reducing
the amount of code that doesn't do anything in typical applications.

Using checked exceptions for infrastructural failures sounds good in theory, but practice shows differently. For example, if you analyze real applications using JDBC or entity beans (both of which APIs use checked exceptions heavily), you will find a majority of catch blocks that merely wrap the exception (often losing the stack trace), rather than adding any value. Thus not only the catch block is often redundant, there are also often many redundant exception classes.

To confirm Spring's choice of unchecked infrastructure exceptions, compare the practice of leading persistence frameworks: JDO and TopLink have always used unchecked exceptions; Hibernate 3 will switch from checked to unchecked exceptions.

Of course it's essential that a framework throwing unchecked exceptions must document those exceptions. Spring's well-defined, well-documented hierarchies are invaluable here; for example, any code using Spring data access functionality may throw `DataAccessException`, but no unexpected unchecked exceptions (unless there is a lower-level problem such as `OutOfMemoryError`, which could still occur if Spring itself used checked exceptions).

> As with Dependency Injection, the notion of a simple, portable service
> abstraction — accompanied with a rich exception model — is conceptually so simple
> (although not simple to deliver) that it's surprising no one had done it before.

Resource Management

Spring's services abstraction provides much of its value through the way in which it handles resource management. Nearly any low-level API, whether for data access, resource lookup, or service access, demands care in acquiring and releasing resources, placing an onus on the application developer and leaving the potential for common errors.

The nature of resource management differs depending on API and the problems it brings:

❑ JDBC requires Connections, Statements, and ResultSets to be obtained and released, even in the event of errors.

❑ Hibernate requires Sessions to be obtained and released, taking into account any current transaction; JDO and TopLink have similar requirements, for PersistenceManagers and Sessions, respectively.

❑   Correct usage of JNDI requires Contexts to be acquired and closed.

❑   JTA has both its own requirements and a requirement to use JNDI.

Spring applies a consistent approach, whatever the API. While in some cases JCA can solve some of the problems (such as binding to the current thread), it is complex to configure, requires a full-blown application server, and is not available for all resources. Spring provides a much more lightweight approach, equally at home inside or outside an application server.

Spring handles resource management *programmatically*, using callback interfaces, or *declaratively*, using its AOP framework.

Spring calls the classes using a callback approach based on *templates*. This is another form of Inversion of Control; the application developer can work with native API constructs such as JDBC Connections and Statements without needing to handle API-specific exceptions (which will automatically be translated into Spring's exception hierarchy) or close resources (which will automatically be released by the framework).

Spring provides templates and other helper classes for all supported APIs, including JDBC, Hibernate, JNDI, and JTA.

Compare the following code using Spring's JDBC abstraction to raw JDBC code, which would require a try/catch/finally block to close resources correctly:

```
Collection requests = jdbc.query("SELECT NAME, DATE, ...  +
            FROM REQUEST WHERE SOMETHING = 1",
        new RowMapper() {
  public Object mapRow(ResultSet rs, int rowNum) throws SQLException {
        Request r = new Request();
        r.setName(rs.getString("NAME"));
        r.setDate(rs.getDate("DATE"));
        return r;
    }
});
```

If you've worked with raw JDBC in a production environment, you will know that the *correct* raw JDBC alternative is not a pretty sight. Correct resource handling in the event of failures is particularly problematic, requiring a nested try/catch block in the finally block of an overall try/catch/finally block to ensure that the connection and other resources are *always* closed, and there is no potential for connection leaks, which are a severe and common problem in typical JDBC code.

When using Spring JDBC, the developer doesn't need to handle SQLException, although she can choose to catch Spring's more informative DataAccessException or subclasses. Even in the event of an SQLException being thrown, the Connection (which is obtained by the framework) and all other resources will still be closed. Nearly every line of code here *does something*, whereas with raw JDBC most code would be concerned with plumbing, such as correct release of resources.

Many common operations can be expressed without the need for callbacks, like SQL aggregate functions or the following query using Spring's HibernateTemplate:

```
List l = hibernateTemplate.find("from User u where u.name = ?",
new Object[] { name });
```

Spring will automatically obtain a Hibernate `Session`, taking into account any active transaction, in which case a `Session` will be bound to the current thread.

This approach is used consistently within the framework for multiple APIs, such as JDBC, JTA, JNDI, Hibernate, JDO, and TopLink. In all cases, exception translation, as well as resource access, is handled by the framework.

Techniques

As important as the technologies are the techniques that they enable. As we've noted, Spring is partly a manifestation of the movement toward agile processes, and it solves many of the problems that agile practitioners otherwise encounter when working with J2EE.

For example, Test Driven Development (TDD) is one of the key lessons of XP (Extreme Programming) — although of course, the value of rigorous unit testing has long been recognized (if too rarely practiced).

Unit testing is key to success, and a framework must facilitate it. Spring does — as do other lightweight containers such as PicoContainer and HiveMind; recognition of the central importance of unit testing is not unique to Spring, nor is Spring the only product to rise to the challenge.

Unfortunately, J2EE out of the box is not particularly friendly to unit testing. Far too high a proportion of code in a traditional J2EE application depends on the application server, meaning that it can be tested only when deployed to a container, or by stubbing a container at test time.

Both of these approaches have proven problematic. The simple fact is that in-container testing is too slow and too much of an obstacle to productivity to apply successfully in large projects. While tools such as Cactus exist to support it, and some IDEs provide test time "containers," our experience is that it is rare to see an example of a well unit-tested "traditional" J2EE architecture.

Spring's approach — non-invasive configuration management, the provision of services to POJOs, and consistent abstractions over hard-to-stub APIs — makes unit testing outside a container (such as in simple JUnit tests) easy. So easy that TDD is a joy to practice, and an agile process is greatly facilitated.

> **Interestingly, while Spring plays so well with agile approaches, it can also work very well with supposedly "heavyweight" methodologies. We've seen a Spring-based architecture work far better with the Unified Software Development Process than a traditional J2EE architecture because it demands fewer compromises for implementation strategy. (Traditional J2EE approaches often have a problematic gulf between Analysis and Design Models because of the workarounds of "J2EE design patterns.")**

Spring even provides support for integration testing using a Spring context, but out of a container, in the `org.springframework.test` *package. This is not an alternative to unit tests (which should not normally require Spring at all), but can be very useful as the next phase of testing. For example, the test superclasses in this package provide the ability to set up a transaction for each test method and automatically tear it down, doing away with the necessity for database setup and teardown scripts that might otherwise slow things down significantly.*

Relationship to Other Frameworks

As we've noted, Spring does not reinvent the wheel. Spring aims to provide the glue that enables you to build a coherent and manageable application architecture out of disparate components.

Let's summarize how Spring relates to some of the many products it integrates with.

Persistence Frameworks

Spring does not provide its own O/R mapping framework. It provides an abstraction over JDBC, but this is a less painful way of doing exactly the same thing as might otherwise have been done with JDBC.

Spring provides a consistent architectural model, but allows you to choose the O/R mapping framework of your choice (or an SQL-based approach where appropriate). For the many applications that benefit from using O/R mapping, you should integrate an O/R mapping framework with Spring. Spring integrates well with all leading O/R mapping frameworks. Supported choices include:

❑ **Hibernate:** The leading open source O/R mapping tool. Hibernate was the first O/R mapping tool for which Spring offered integration. Spring's Hibernate integration makes Hibernate significantly easier to use, through the `HibernateTemplate` we've briefly discussed and through integration with Spring's transaction management.

❑ **JDO implementations:** Spring provides support for JDO 1.0 and JDO 2.0 standards. Several JDO vendors also ship their own Spring integration, implementing Spring's `JdoDialect` interface, giving application developers access to common capabilities that go beyond the JDO specification without locking into a particular JDO vendor.

❑ **TopLink:** TopLink is the oldest O/R mapping tool on the market, dating back to the mid-1990s. TopLink is now an Oracle product, and Oracle has written a Spring integration that enables Spring users to work as seamlessly with TopLink as with Hibernate or a JDO implementation.

❑ **Apache OJB:** An O/R mapping product from Apache.

❑ **iBATIS:** iBATIS SQL Maps is not, strictly speaking, an O/R mapping product. However, it does offer a convenient way of defining SQL statements in a declarative fashion, mapping objects to statement parameters and result sets to objects. In contrast to full-blown O/R mapping solutions, though, SQL Maps does not aim to provide an object query language or automatic change detection.

All these integrations are consistent in that Spring facilitates the use of DAO interfaces, and all operations throw informative subclasses of Spring's `DataAccessException`. Spring provides helpers such as templates for all these APIs, enabling a consistent programming style. Spring's comprehensive architectural template means that almost any persistence framework can be integrated within this consistent approach. Integration efforts from several JDO vendors — the fact that the Spring/TopLink integration was developed by the TopLink team at Oracle, and that the popular Cayenne open source O/R mapping project itself developed Spring integration for Cayenne — shows that Spring's data access abstraction is becoming something of a de facto standard for consistent approach to persistence in Java/J2EE applications.

Spring's own JDBC framework is suitable when you want SQL-based access to relational data. This is not an alternative to O/R mapping, but it's necessary to implement at least some scenarios in most applications using a relational database. (Also, O/R mapping is not universally applicable, despite the claims of its more enthusiastic advocates.)

Importantly, Spring allows you to mix and match data access strategies — for example Hibernate code and JDBC code sharing the same connection and transaction. This is an important bonus for complex applications, which typically can't perform all persistence operations using a single persistence framework.

Web Frameworks

Again, the fundamental philosophy is to enable users to choose the web framework of their choice, while enjoying the full benefit of a Spring middle tier. Popular choices include:

❑ **Struts:** Still the dominant MVC web framework (although in decline). Many Spring users use Struts with a Spring middle tier. Integration is fairly close, and it is even possible to configure Struts Actions using Spring Dependency Injection, giving them instant access to middle-tier objects without any Java coding.

❑ **WebWork:** Integration with WebWork is particularly close because of WebWork's flexible design and the strong interest in the WebWork community in using WebWork along with a Spring middle tier. It is possible to configure WebWork Actions using Spring Dependency Injection.

❑ **Spring MVC:** Spring's own MVC web framework, which of course integrates particularly well with a Spring middle tier.

❑ **Tapestry:** A component-oriented framework from Apache's Jakarta group, Tapestry integrates well with Spring because declarative page metadata makes it easy for Tapestry pages to access Spring-provided services without any code-level coupling to Spring.

❑ **JSF:** Spring integrates very well with JSF, given that JSF has the concept of "named beans" and does not aim to implement middle-tier services itself.

Spring's approach to web frameworks differs from that to persistence, in that Spring provides its own fully featured web framework. Of course, you are not forced to use this if you wish to use a Spring middle tier. While Spring integrates well with other web frameworks, there are a few integration advantages available only with Spring's own MVC framework, such as the ability to use some advanced features of Spring Dependency Injection, or to apply AOP advice to web controllers. Nevertheless, as Spring integrates well with other web frameworks, you should choose Spring's own MVC framework on its merits, rather than because there's any element of compulsion. Spring MVC is an appealing alternative to Struts and other request-driven frameworks as it is highly flexible, helps to ensure that application code in the web tier is easily testable, and works particularly well with a wide variety of view technologies besides JSP. In Chapter 12 we discuss Spring MVC in detail.

AOP Frameworks

Spring provides a proxy-based AOP framework, which is well suited for solving most problems in J2EE applications.

However, sometimes you need capabilities that a proxy-based framework cannot provide, such as the ability to advise objects created using the new operator and not managed by any factory; or the ability to advise fields, as well as methods.

To support such requirements, Spring integrates well with AspectJ and ApectWerkz, the two leading class weaving–based AOP frameworks. It's possible to combine Spring Dependency Injection with such AOP frameworks — for example, configuring AspectJ aspects using the full power of the Spring IoC container as if they were ordinary classes.

> As of early 2005, the AspectJ and AspectWerkz projects are merging into AspectJ 5.0, which looks set to be the definitive full-blown AOP framework. The Spring project is working closely with the AspectJ project to ensure the best possible integration, which should have significant benefits for both communities.

Spring does *not* attempt to replicate the power of a full-blown AOP solution such as AspectJ; this would produce no benefits to Spring users, who are instead free to mix Spring AOP with AspectJ as necessary to implement sophisticated AOP solutions.

Other Frameworks

Spring integrates with other frameworks including the Quartz scheduler, Jasper Reports, and Velocity and FreeMarker template engines.

Again, the goal is to provide a consistent backbone for application architecture.

All such integrations are modules, distinct from the Spring core. While some ship with the main Spring distribution, some are external modules. Spring's open architecture has also resulted in numerous other projects (such as the Cayenne O/R mapping framework) providing their own Spring integration, or providing Spring integration with third-party products.

Architecting Applications with Spring

Let's now look at how a typical application using Spring is organized, and the kind of architecture Spring promotes and facilitates.

> Spring is designed to facilitate architectural flexibility. For example, if you wish to switch from Hibernate to JDO or vice versa (or from either to the forthcoming JSR-220 POJO persistence API), using Spring and following recommended practice can make that easier. Similarly, you can defer the choice as to whether to use EJB for a certain piece of functionality, confident that you won't need to modify existing code if a particular service ends up implemented by an EJB rather than a POJO.

Let's now look at how a typical Spring architecture looks in practice, from top to bottom.

The architecture described here is referred to as the "Lightweight container architecture" in Chapter 3 of J2EE without EJB (Johnson/Hoeller, Wrox, 2004). As such an architecture is based on OO best practice, rather than Spring, it can be implemented without Spring. However, Spring is ideally suited to making such architectures succeed.

The Big Picture

Figure 1-1 illustrates the architectural layers in a typical Spring application. Although this describes a web application, the concepts apply to most logically tiered applications in general.

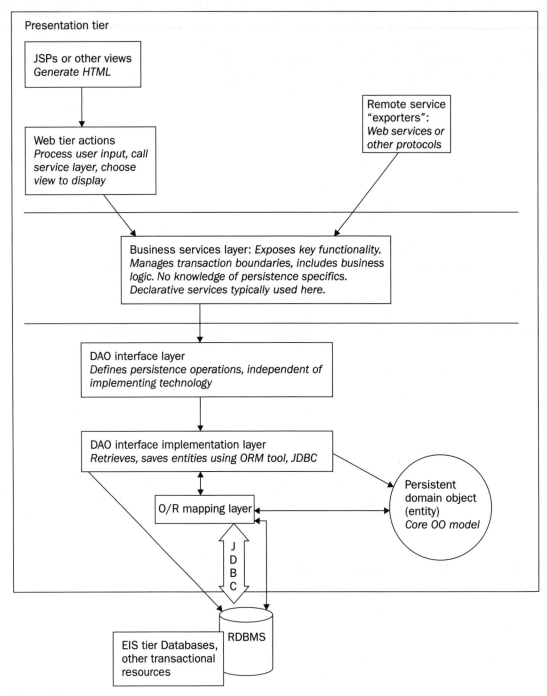

Figure 1-1

Let's summarize each layer and its responsibilities, beginning closest to the database or other enterprise resources:

❑ **Presentation layer:** This is most likely to be a web tier. This layer should be as thin as possible. It should be possible to have alternative presentation layers — such as a web tier or remote web services facade — on a single, well-designed middle tier.

❑ **Business services layer:** This is responsible for transactional boundaries and providing an entry point for operations on the system as a whole. This layer should have no knowledge of presentation concerns, and should be reusable.

❑ **DAO interface layer:** This is a layer of interfaces *independent of any data access technology* that is used to find and persist persistent objects. This layer effectively consists of *Strategy* interfaces for the Business services layer. This layer should not contain business logic. Implementations of these interfaces will normally use an O/R mapping technology or Spring's JDBC abstraction.

❑ **Persistent domain objects:** These model real objects or concepts such as a bank account.

❑ **Databases and legacy systems:** By far the most common case is a single RDBMS. However, there may be multiple databases, or a mix of databases and other transactional or non-transactional legacy systems or other enterprise resources. The same fundamental architecture is applicable in either case. This is often referred to as the *EIS (Enterprise Information System)* tier.

In a J2EE application, all layers except the EIS tier will run in the application server or web container. Domain objects will typically be passed up to the presentation layer, which will display data they contain, *but not modify them,* which will occur only within the transactional boundaries defined by the business services layer. Thus there is no need for distinct Transfer Objects, as used in traditional J2EE architecture.

In the following sections we'll discuss each of these layers in turn, beginning closest to the database.

> Spring aims to decouple architectural layers, so that each layer can be modified as far as possible without impacting other layers. No layer is aware of the concerns of the layer above; as far as possible, dependency is purely on the layer immediately below. Dependency between layers is normally in the form of interfaces, ensuring that coupling is as loose as possible.

Persistence and Integration

Getting data access right is crucial for success, and Spring provides rich services in this area.

Database

Most J2EE (or Java applications) work with a relational database. Ultimately data access will be accomplished using JDBC. However, most Spring users find that they do *not* use the JDBC API directly.

Spring encourages a decoupling of business objects from persistence technology using a layer of interfaces.

Data Access Objects

In keeping with the philosophy that it is better to program to interfaces than classes, Spring encourages the use of *data access interfaces* between the service layer and whatever persistence API the application (or that part of it) uses. However, as the term Data Access Object (DAO) is widely used, we continue to use it.

DAOs encapsulate access to persistent domain objects, and provide the ability to persist transient objects and update existing objects.

By using a distinct layer of DAO objects, and accessing them through interfaces, we ensure that service objects are decoupled from the persistence API. This has many benefits. Not only is it possible to switch between persistence tools more easily, but it makes the code more coherent through separation of concerns and greatly simplifies testing (a particularly important concern when using an agile process). Imagine a business service method that processes a set of orders: If the set of orders is obtained through a method on a DAO interface, it is trivial to supply a test DAO in a JUnit test that supplies an empty set or a particular set of orders, or throws an exception—all without going near a database.

DAO implementations will be made available to objects using them using Dependency Injection, with both service objects and DAO instances configured using the Spring IoC container.

DAO interfaces will typically contain the following kinds of methods:

- ❏ **Finder methods:** These locate persistent objects for use by the business services layer.
- ❏ **Persist or save methods:** These make transient objects persistent.
- ❏ **Delete methods:** These remove the representation of objects from the persistent store.
- ❏ **Count or other aggregate function methods:** These return the results of operations that are more efficient to implement using database functionality than by iterating over Java objects.

Less commonly, DAO interfaces may contain bulk update methods.

> *While Spring encourages the use of the term "DAO" for such interfaces, they could equally well be called "repositories," as they are similar to the Repository pattern described in Eric Evans' Domain-Driven Design (Addison-Wesley, 2003).*

The following interface shows some of the methods on a typical DAO interface:

```
public interface ReminderDao {

  public Collection
      findRequestsEligibleForReminder()   throws DataAccessException;

  void persist(Reminder reminder) throws DataAccessException;

  void countOutstandingRequests() throws DataAccessException;

}
```

Note that all methods can throw Spring's DataAccessException or subclasses, thus wholly decoupling callers from the persistence technology in use. The DAO tier interfaces have become truly persistence technology agnostic.

This interface might be implemented using Hibernate, with Spring's convenience classes, as follows (some methods omitted for brevity):

```
public class HibernateReminderDao extends HibernateDaoSupport implements
ReminderDao {

    public Collection findRequestsEligibleForReminder()
                            throws DataAccessException {
        getHibernateTemplate().find("from Request r where
        r.something = 1");
    }

    public void persist(Reminder reminder)
                            throws DataAccessException {
        getHibernateTemplate().saveOrUpdate(reminder);
    }
}
```

An implementation using another O/R mapping tool, such as TopLink, would be conceptually almost identical, although naturally using a different underlying API (but also benefiting from Spring conveniences). Following the DAO pattern as facilitated by Spring and illustrated in Spring sample applications such as the Spring PetStore ensures a consistent architectural approach, whatever the chosen persistence API.

Our DAO interface could be implemented using Spring's JDBC abstraction as follows:

```
public class JdbcReminderDao extends JdbcDaoSupport
                                    implements ReminderDao {

    public Collection findRequestsEligibleForReminder()
                                throws DataAccessException {
        return getJdbcTemplate().query("SELECT NAME, DATE, ... " +
                                " FROM REQUEST WHERE SOMETHING = 1",
                new RowMapper() {
                public Object mapRow(ResultSet rs, int rowNum) throws SQLException
        {
                    Request r = new Request();
                    r.setName(rs.getString("NAME"));
                    r.setDate(rs.getDate("DATE"));
                    return r;
                }
            });
    }


    public int countRequestsEligibleForReminder()
                                    throws DataAccessException {
        return getJdbcTemplate.queryForInt("SELECT COUNT(*) FROM ...");
    }
}
```

Don't worry if you don't understand the details at this point: we'll discuss Spring's persistence services in detail in Chapter 5, "DAO Support and JDBC Framework." However, you should be able to see how Spring eliminates boilerplate code, meaning that you need to write only code that actually *does something*.

> Although they are typically used with relational databases and O/R mapping frameworks or JDBC code underneath, Spring DAO interfaces are not specific to RDBMS access. Spring's DAO exception hierarchy is completely independent of any persistence technology, so users have contributed support for LDAP and other technologies, and some users have implemented connectivity to products such as Documentum, within the consistent Spring data access architectural approach.

Persistent Domain Objects

Persistent domain objects are objects that model your domain, such as a bank account object. They are persisted, most often using an O/R mapping layer.

Note that the desire to isolate service objects from persistence APIs does *not* mean that persistent objects should be dumb bit buckets. Persistent *objects* should be true objects — they should contain behavior, as well as state, and they should encapsulate their state appropriately. Do not automatically use JavaBean accessor methods, encouraging callers to view persistent objects as pure storage. Likewise, avoid the temptation (as in traditional J2EE architectures using stateless session and entity beans) to move code for navigation of persistent object graphs into the business service layer, where it is more verbose and represents a loss of encapsulation.

> Persistent domain models often represent the core intellectual property of an application, and the most valuable product of business analysis. To preserve this investment, they should ideally be independent of the means used to persist them.

Spring allows the application of Dependency Injection to persistent objects, using classes such as `DependencyInjectionInterceptorFactoryBean`, which enables Hibernate objects to be automatically wired with dependencies from a Spring IoC container. This makes it easier to support cases when domain objects might need, for example, to use a DAO interface. It allows this to be done simply by expressing a dependency via a setter method, rather than relying on explicit "pull" configuration calls to Spring or implementing persistence framework–specific lifecycle methods. (Another, more general, approach to this end is to use a class-weaving AOP solution such as AspectJ.) However, we advise careful consideration before allowing domain objects to access the service layer. Experience shows that it is not usually necessary in typical applications, and it may represent a blurring of the clean architectural layering we recommend.

Persistence Technology

Domain objects are typically persisted with an O/R mapping product such as Hibernate or a JDO implementation.

In certain cases, full-blown O/R mapping may be inappropriate. In this case, the DAO interfaces remain appropriate, but the implementation is likely to use JDBC — through Spring's JDBC abstraction layer, or through iBATIS SQL Maps.

In some applications — and some use cases in nearly any complex application — Spring's JDBC abstraction may be used to perform SQL-based persistence.

Business Service Objects

Depending on your chosen architecture, much of your business logic may reside in persistent domain objects.

However, there is nearly always an important role for a *service layer*. This is analogous to the layer of stateless session beans in traditional J2EE architectures. However, in a Spring-based application, it will consist of POJOs with few dependencies on Spring. The Service Layer provides functionality such as:

❑ **Business logic that is use case–specific:** While it is often appropriate for domain objects to contain business logic applicable to many use cases, specific use cases are often realized in the business services layer.

❑ **Clearly defined entry points for business operations:** The business service objects provide the interfaces used by the presentation layer.

❑ **Transaction management:** In general, although business logic can be moved into persistent domain objects, transaction management should not be.

❑ **Enforcement of security constraints:** Again, this is usually best done at the entry level to the middle tier, rather than in domain objects.

As with the DAO interface layer, the business service layer should expose interfaces, not classes.

> The service layer also represents a valuable investment that — with good analysis — should have a long lifetime. Thus it should also be as independent as possible of the technologies that enable it to function as part of a working application. Spring makes an important contribution here through its non-invasive programming model.
>
> Coupling between architectural layers should be in the form of interfaces, to promote loose coupling.

Presentation

In the recommended architecture using Spring, the presentation tier rests on a well-defined service layer.

This means that the presentation layer will be thin; it will not contain business logic, but merely presentation specifics, such as code to handle web interactions.

It also means that there can be a choice of presentation tiers — or more than one presentation layer — in an application, without impacting lower architectural layers.

> Lower architectural layers should have no knowledge of presentation tier concerns.

Web Tier

In a Spring application, a web tier will use a web application framework, whether Spring's own MVC framework, or an alternative framework such as Struts, WebWork, Tapestry, or JSF.

The web tier will be responsible for dealing with user interactions, and obtaining data that can be displayed in the required format.

The web tier will normally consist of three kinds of objects:

❑ **Controller:** Controller objects, like Spring MVC Controllers and Struts Actions, are responsible for processing user input as presented in HTTP requests, invoking the necessary business service layer functionality, and returning the required model for display.

❑ **Model:** Objects containing data resulting from the execution of business logic and which must be displayed in the response.

❑ **View:** Objects responsible for rendering the model to the response. The mechanism required will differ between different *view technologies* such as JSP, Velocity templates, or conceptually different approaches such as PDF or Excel spreadsheet generation. Views are not responsible for updating data or even *obtaining* data; they merely serve to display Model data that has been provided by the relevant Controller.

This triad is often referred to as an *MVC* (*Model View Controller*) architectural pattern, although such "web MVC" is not the same as the "classic" MVC pattern used in thick client frameworks such as Swing.

Spring's own MVC framework provides a particularly clean implementation of these three elements — the base interfaces have the names `Controller`, `Model`, and `View`. In particular, Spring MVC ensures that not only is the web tier distinct from the business services layer, but web views are completely decoupled from controllers and models. Thus a different type of view can be added without changing controller or model code.

Remote Access Facade

Spring reflects the philosophy that remote access — for example, supporting remote clients over RMI or remote clients over web services — should be viewed as an alternative presentation layer on well-defined middle tier service interfaces.

> **Unlike in traditional J2EE practice, remoting concerns should not cascade throughout an application in the form of Transfer Objects and other baggage.**
>
> **Applications should be internally Object Oriented. As remoting tends to be destructive to true Object Orientation, it should be treated as one view of an application.**

Spring provides a variety of remoting choices, based on exposing POJOs. This is less invasive than traditional J2EE EJB remoting, but it's important to remember that there are inevitable constraints around remoting, which no technology can wholly conceal. There is no such thing as a distributed object. Remoting introduces a range of concerns: not merely the need for serializability, but the depth to which object graphs should be traversed before disconnection, constraints on method granularity ("chatty" calling is ruled out for efficiency reasons), and many other issues.

If you wish to use a traditional EJB-based remoting architecture, you can use one or more Spring contexts inside the EJB container. In such an architecture, EJBs become a facade layer. (They may also be used for transaction management, although Spring's own transaction management is more flexible, and a better choice in Spring-based applications, even when using JTA.)

In such an architecture, we recommend that Transfer Objects and the other paraphernalia of remoting are added *on top of* the basic architecture, rather than used throughout it.

Spring RCP

Another important presentational choice is the Spring Rich Client Project (Spring RCP). This is a framework built around the Spring IoC container that facilitates the building of Swing applications. The use of Spring on the client side is especially compelling when it is necessary to access enterprise services, which are typically remote, as Spring's client-side, as well as server-side, remoting features may be used.

The Future

Spring is a mature, production-ready solution. However, the Spring team has demonstrated a rapid pace of innovation and is committed to further enhancements. While you can be confident of Spring offering backward compatibility, as it has done to this point, you can also expect many enhancements and new capabilities.

Release Schedule

This book covers Spring 1.2, released in early 2005. Spring 1.0 was released in March 2004, Spring 1.1 in September 2004. These two major releases have been close to 100 percent backward compatible, despite adding a significant number of features. Spring continues to evolve and innovate at a rapid rate.

Spring operates on a 4–6 week release schedule. Normally a point release contains bug fixes and minor enhancements. A major release, such as Spring 1.1, contains significant new features (in that case, some IoC container enhancements and the first phase of JMS support). Major releases are normally around 6 months apart.

> A key proof of the value of a non-invasive framework is how Spring's implementation can evolve significantly, and its capabilities increase greatly, while preserving backward compatibility. This is emphatically different from the experience with APIs such as EJB, where every major version has resulted in a substantial migration exercise, or the maintenance of two separate code bases. As we noted earlier, Spring *is* different.
>
> This is also an important benefit for third-party products that integrate with Spring — and, of course, users of those products. For example, Acegi Security System, an external project, is able to provide complex value-added functionality spanning multiple layers, without needing any hooks into Spring.

In general, you should work with the latest production release of Spring. Spring's comprehensive test coverage and excellent record on backward compatibility help make this a workable strategy.

The Evolution of Java and J2EE

J2EE itself is also evolving, so it's natural to ask how Spring will fit into the J2EE ecosystem as J2EE moves forward.

The major changes relevant to Spring development concern the EJB 3.0 specification, currently under development by the JSR-220 Expert Group, and expected to reach final release in early 2006.

EJB 3.0 introduces two major changes relevant to Spring users and Spring's positioning with respect to J2EE:

❑ **It introduces a simplification of the session bean programming model**, which rests partly on the use of Dependency Injection to provide simpler access to the bean's JNDI environment.

❑ **It introduces a new specification for POJO persistence.** Strictly speaking, this is separate from the EJB specification itself, as JSR-220 will in fact produce two deliverables: the EJB 3.0 specification and a POJO persistence specification. The JSR-220 persistence specification is likely to be supported by all major O/R mapping products, including TopLink, Hibernate, and leading JDO products. It also effectively relegates the EJB 2.*x* entity bean model to legacy status, merely formalizing the reality seen among usage trends since 2002.

The introduction of Dependency Injection features in EJB 3.0 is an interesting move from a specification group, indicating that the "lightweight" approach to J2EE popularized by Spring and other projects has become too influential to ignore. (Indeed, the influence of Spring on the EJB 3.0 session bean model is unmistakable.) However, EJB 3.0 offers a very limited form of Dependency Injection, which has different goals, and does not approach the capabilities of Spring or other leading IoC containers. For example, it can inject dependencies only on objects that come from JNDI; it cannot manage objects that are too fine-grained to be placed in JNDI; it cannot easily manage configuration properties such as ints and Strings, which are very important to externalizing configuration from code; and it cannot manage lists, maps, or other complex types that the Spring IoC container can handle. At the time of this writing, it provides no standard way to apply interception or full-fledged AOP capability to injected collaborators, meaning that it misses much of the value-adding possibilities open to a sophisticated IoC container. Finally, it seems capable only of per-*class* Dependency Injection configuration (due to reliance on Java 5.0 annotations for the recommended configuration style), rather than the per-*instance* configuration supported by Spring and other sophisticated IoC containers, which is often necessary in large applications.

After the hype dies down and more technical details emerge, it's unlikely that EJB 3.0 session beans will change things much for Spring users. If you want to use Dependency Injection, you will almost certainly end up using Spring behind an EJB 3.0 facade. The Spring team will ensure that this is easy to do.

If you want to keep your options open regarding an eventual migration to EJB 3.0, a Spring-based approach will give you a production-proven basis for you to implement now, while enabling a far easier migration path than the EJB 2.*x* model, which is effectively deprecated in EJB 3.0. (While you could continue to run EJB 2.*x* beans in an EJB 3.0 container, this isn't attractive in the long run, amounting to a substantial legacy model.) However, it's hard to see any benefit for Spring users in moving from Spring-managed business objects to EJB 3.0 session beans — this would sacrifice many capabilities, reduce the range of environments in which the relevant code could execute, and add little or no functionality.

> *The core benefit of EJB 3.0 Dependency Injection — the ability to inject objects obtained from JNDI such as* `DataSources`, *has been offered by Spring, in the form of the* `JndiObjectFactoryBean`, *since Spring's inception.*

JSR-220 persistence has more significant implications than the EJB 3.0 session bean model (which is essentially playing catch-up with features long offered by lightweight frameworks). JSR-220 persistence adds significantly to the already compelling case for Spring's unique data access abstraction. As we've seen, there is real value in being able to implement a DAO interface using, say, Hibernate or JDO, or JDBC (if it doesn't imply transparent persistence). Today, there is a range of competing O/R mapping products. With the release of the JSR-220 specification for POJO persistence ahead, this value proposition becomes still more compelling. We *know* that persistence is likely to change. Thus it is logical to try to abstract away from the details of your chosen persistence API, and isolate dependence on it behind a layer of interfaces.

Spring's sophisticated persistence infrastructure, and its DAO interface approach, is a perfect candidate to do this — indeed, the *only* candidate at present, the alternative being in-house coding.

Finally, Java is itself evolving. With the release of J2SE 5.0 in September 2004, Java has seen arguably the most significant enhancements in its history. While backward compatibility is essential *internally* for a widely used framework such as Spring, Spring 1.2 offers additional functionality for J2SE 5.0 users: for example, leveraging J2SE 5.0 annotations where appropriate (in particular, for declarative transaction management).

Technology Currents

While the J2EE specifications continue to evolve, they are not evolving fast enough. The Java specification process faces twin dangers: premature standardization, before a technology is well enough understood to choose the correct path; and glacial progress, where standards lag far behind common practice. (For example, although EJB 3.0 is a major overhaul of the session bean model, it will offer *in 2006* a subset of Dependency Injection capabilities available in a production release in Spring and other products *in early 2004.*)

As new paradigms such as AOP and IoC gain further momentum, and experience around their use accumulates, an agile framework such as Spring is far better placed than a specification committee to offer a solid implementation to its user community.

Spring is also well placed to support other emerging areas, such as:

❑ **Scripting:** Java is not the be all and end all of the JVM. Scripting languages — especially Groovy — are enjoying growing popularity. We expect this trend to continue. Spring can provide the same comprehensive IoC and AOP services to objects written in any scripting language as to Java objects, within a consistent programming model. The language in which an object is written — like the particular implementation of an interface — can be concealed from callers. This raises the possibility of writing objects in the most appropriate language. In some cases, language features such as closures offer a much more succinct option than Java.

❑ **A cross-platform programming model:** The Spring programming model is now available for .NET, with the release of Spring.NET. This is particularly interesting for organizations that have an investment in both platforms, and architects and developers who need to work on both platforms.

Standards and Open Source

Of course this touches on another challenge to J2EE orthodoxy, and the belief that Sun "standards" are always the best way forward for the industry.

Chapter 4 of *J2EE without EJB* discusses this issue in more detail. There is a strong argument that while standards have produced real benefit in the case of low level services, such as JNDI and JTA, they have largely failed where (like EJB) they have entered the domain of the application programming model. Specification committees are not best placed to deal with issues in the application programming domain; responsive open source projects with a capable development community and thousands of users are.

The consequences of failed standards, like entity beans, are far worse than the consequences of using good, non-standard, solutions. It's more important to have a working application, delivered on time and budget, than an application that uses only largely unproven standards.

Currently there doesn't seem much likelihood that the JCP will produce anything in the *application programming space* that equals the value of what Spring and other lightweight frameworks provide.

The emergence of non-invasive frameworks such as Spring has also cut against the old assumptions regarding standardization. Framework lock-in *can* be minimized. Where application code depends largely on standard Java constructs (as in the case of Setter and Constructor Injection), there isn't much that needs to be standardized.

Furthermore, it's significant that Spring and other leading lightweight containers are open source. There's an argument that open source reduces the danger of proprietary solutions, as does a non-invasive framework. There's no risk of a greedy vendor cornering the market and fleecing users; the source code is available in any event; and in the case of successful products such as Spring there are many people who understand not just how to use the framework but how it works internally.

Partly for this reason, it seems that infrastructure is inexorably moving toward open source. It's becoming increasingly difficult for commercial products to compete in this space. Spring is a key part of the brave new world of J2EE infrastructure, and application developers are the main beneficiaries.

The Spring Project and Community

Spring is perhaps the only successful software project to have evolved from a book: *Expert One-on-One J2EE Design and Development*, by Rod Johnson (Wiley, 2002). This unusual heritage has proved beneficial, providing Spring with a consistent vision from its outset. From the outset, the Spring team agreed on coding and design conventions, and the overall architecture approach that Spring should enable.

History

Spring initially grew out of Rod Johnson's experience as a consultant on various large Java/J2EE applications from 1997 through 2002. Like most experienced consultants, Rod had written a number of frameworks for various clients. The last, for a prominent global media group, began as a web MVC framework (well before Struts was available), but expanded to include what would now be called a Dependency Injection container (although the name did not exist until late 2003) and data access services.

Thus *Expert One-on-One J2EE Design and Development* included not only a discussion of the problems Rod had encountered doing extensive J2EE development, but 30,000 lines of code, in the form of the "Interface21 framework" demonstrating a practical approach to solving many of them.

The reaction to this code from readers was extremely positive, many finding that it solved problems that they'd seen over and over in their own J2EE experience. Over the next few months, numerous readers sought clarification of the terms of the license so that they could use the code in projects and — far more important — volunteered ideas and practical help to take the framework to the next level.

The most important contribution was made by Juergen Hoeller, who has been co-lead with Rod since the open source framework was founded in February 2003. Juergen immediately began to make a huge contribution to implementation and design. Other developers including co-authors Thomas Risberg, Colin Sampaleanu, and Alef Arendsen also joined early and began to make large contributions in specific areas.

Interestingly, the ideas that Spring is commonly identified with — most notably, Dependency Injection — were also developed independently by other projects. Although it was publicly announced before Spring went public, the PicoContainer project actually began several months after the Spring project.

The ATG Dynamo application server included a Dependency Injection capability in its proprietary functionality, although none of the Spring team was aware of this until Spring was already widely adopted. Proof that an idea so simple, yet powerful, cannot be invented — merely discovered.

The authors of this book include most of the core developers of Spring. Rod and Juergen remain the architects and chief developers of Spring.

The Spring community has also made a huge contribution to the evolution of Spring, through reporting problems based on experience in a wide range of environments, and suggesting many improvements and enhancements. This is a key element in the value proposition of open source infrastructure — indeed, any off-the-shelf infrastructure, as opposed to in-house frameworks. Not only can a large community of talented individuals contribute ideas to the framework itself, but a large body of understanding is available to organizations building applications using Spring.

From its outset, the Spring project has been based around respecting and listening to Spring users. Of course, as any project grows in size, it becomes impossible for any individual to participate in all discussions — even to listen attentively to the details of every discussion. But the Spring developers as a group have been attentive and responsive, and this has helped to build a flourishing community.

Spring is licensed under the Apache 2.0 license — a widely used open source license that is not restrictive.

In August 2004, Rod, Juergen, Colin, and other core Spring developers (including Spring RCP lead, Keith Donald) founded Interface21, a company devoted to Spring consulting, training, and support. This helps to secure the future of Spring, by placing a viable economic model behind it. A sophisticated and wide-ranging framework such as Spring represents a huge amount of effort; it's impossible to continue that effort without a viable economic model. Spring framework itself will always remain open source and free to anybody who wishes to use it. However, the existence of a commercial entity also provides a degree of confidence to more conservative organizations, with the availability of professional services to support the development of Spring-based applications.

Even before the release of Spring 1.0 final in March 2004, Spring had been widely adopted. Today, Spring is one of the most widely used and discussed products in J2EE development, and Spring skills are widely available and sought after on the job market.

Module Summary

Let's now examine the functionality that Spring offers in more detail. It is divided into a number of separate modules.

There are two main categories of functionality in Spring:

- ❑ An IoC container and AOP framework, which handle configuration and application of services to objects.
- ❑ A set of services that can be applied to application objects. These services can be used as a class library, even in a different runtime container.

Each of the modules discussed here fits into one or both of these categories.

Spring is a layered framework with the following core modules:

- ❑ **IoC container:** The core of Spring is the IoC container. This configures objects by Dependency Injection, but also supports a variety of optional callbacks for application objects that have more complex requirements of their environment.

33

❑ **Proxy-based AOP framework:** Spring's AOP framework is the other essential in delivering a non-invasive framework that can manage POJOs. Spring AOP can be used programmatically, or integrated with the IoC container, in which case any object managed by a Spring IoC container can be "advised" transparently.

❑ **Data access abstraction:** This includes:

❑ The DAO exception hierarchy and consistent architectural approach discussed earlier in this chapter.

❑ Template and other integration classes for Hibernate, JDO, TopLink, iBATIS, and other data access APIs.

❑ Spring's own JDBC abstraction framework. While in general Spring's approach to persistence is consistent integration, Spring does provide one persistence API of its own: its JDBC framework. This is an abstraction layer over JDBC that simplifies error handling, improves code portability, and eliminates the potential for many common errors when using JDBC, such as failure to close connections and other valuable resources in the event of errors. Spring's JDBC abstraction is suitable when you want SQL-based persistence, and not O/R mapping: for example, when you have a legacy database that doesn't lend itself to O/R mapping, or you need to make extensive use of stored procedures or BLOB types. Spring's JDBC framework is also a good choice if the persistence needs are limited and you don't want to introduce the learning curve/maintenance cost of an additional persistence framework such as JDO or Hibernate.

❑ **Transaction abstraction:** Spring provides a transaction abstraction that can run over a variety of underlying transaction APIs, including JTA, JDBC, Hibernate, and JDO transactions. Naturally, JTA is the only option for working with multiple transactional resources, as Spring does not provide its own distributed transaction manager. However, many applications work with a single database, and do not require distributed transactions for any other reason (such as working with JMS). However, Spring's transaction abstraction provides a consistent programming model in any environment, from high-end J2EE application servers down to simple web containers and standalone clients: a unique value proposition that does away with the traditional need to choose between "global" and "local" transaction management and commit to one or another programming model early in each J2EE project. Spring provides programmatic declarative management that is much more usable than JTA, which is a fairly cumbersome API, not ideally suited for use by application developers. But most users prefer Spring's sophisticated declarative transaction management, which can provide transaction management for any POJO. Spring transaction management is integrated with all of Spring's supported data access integrations.

❑ **Simplification for working with JNDI, EJB, and other complex J2EE APIs and services:** If you're an experienced J2EE developer, you will have written many JNDI lookups. You may have chosen to move the lookup code to a helper class, but you can't completely conceal the complexity, or hide the implications for testing. If you've worked with EJB, you've needed to write code to look the EJB home up in JNDI before calling the `create()` method to obtain an EJB reference you can use to do work. Chances are, you've done essentially the same thing, over and over, and worked on applications where many developers have done essentially the same thing over and over, but in various different ways. These are routine tasks that are much better done by a framework. Spring's support for JNDI and EJB can eliminate the need to write boilerplate code for JNDI lookups and EJB access or implementation. By eliminating JNDI and EJB API dependencies in application code, it also increases the potential for reuse. For example, you don't need to write code that depends on an EJB home interface or handles EJB exceptions; you merely need to express a dependency on the relevant EJB's *Business Methods Interface*, which is a plain Java interface. Spring can do the necessary JNDI lookup and create an AOP proxy for the EJB that hides the need to work with the EJB APIs. Your code is no longer dependent on EJB — you could choose to implement the Business Methods Interface without using EJB — and another bit of tedious boilerplate is gone.

❑ **MVC web framework:** Spring's own request-driven MVC framework. This is closely integrated with Spring's middle-tier functionality, with all controllers being configured by Dependency Injection, providing the ability to access middle-tier functionality from the web tier without any code. Spring MVC is similar in how it approaches controller lifecycle to Struts, but provides some key benefits over struts, such as:

  ❑ Better support for view technologies other than JSP, such as Velocity and PDF generation libraries

  ❑ Interceptors, in addition to "actions" or "controllers"

  ❑ Ability to use domain objects to back forms, rather than special objects such as Struts `ActionForm` subclasses

  ❑ Interface-based design, making the framework highly customizable, and avoiding the need to subclass framework classes, which is a convenience rather than a necessity

❑ **Integration with numerous third-party products:** This fits into Spring's role as architectural glue. As the Spring IoC container is extensible, it's also easy to "alias" additional services into Spring IoC. The `JndiObjectFactoryBean`, which looks up a named object in JNDI, is a good example.

❑ **Remoting:** Spring provides lightweight remoting support over a variety of protocols, including web services, RMI, RMI over HTTP, IIOP, and Caucho's Hessian and Burlap protocols. Remoting is available for POJOs, in keeping with Spring's emphasis on providing a rich environment for POJOs.

❑ **Simplification for working with EJBs:** This consists of:

  ❑ Support for *implementing* EJBs: EJB 2.1 and earlier have no built-in configuration management. EJB 3.0 looks set to offer a simplistic Dependency Injection capability. In either case, there is a compelling value proposition in using a lightweight container behind an EJB facade. Spring provides support for implementing EJBs that serve as a facade in front of POJOs managed by a Spring application context.

  ❑ Support for *accessing* EJBs, via the "codeless proxying" described earlier.

❑ **Message publication using JMS:** Spring's callback template approach is ideally suited to minimizing the complexity of application code required to publish JMS messages.

❑ **JMX support:** Spring 1.2 provides a powerful JMX layer that can publish any Spring-managed object to JMX, enabling monitoring and management with standard tools.

When you use Spring's AOP framework, a layer of dynamic capabilities is available over the Spring IoC container in Spring 1.3:

❑ Support for scripting languages, with full support both ways for Dependency Injection. This means that any application object can be written in any supported scripting language, depending on other objects written in Java, or vice-versa.

❑ Support for objects backed by a database.

Quite a list! This broad scope sometimes leads people to the misconception that Spring is a big fat blob, which aims to do everything from scratch. It's important to emphasize the following points:

❑ Spring's modular architecture means that you can use any part of Spring in isolation. For example, if you want to use just the IoC container to simplify your configuration management, you can do so, without the need for any other part of Spring. If you want to use Spring AOP, you can do so without the IoC container. You might choose to use Spring's transaction interceptor in another AOP framework, or the Spring JDBC framework as a class library.

❑ Yet there is a consistency in the design of the different Spring modules that is very helpful if you choose to use more of the Spring stack, as you can leverage the same concepts in different areas, making your application more internally consistent and making the whole framework easier to learn than you might expect, given its scope.

❑ Spring is substantially about integrating best-of-breed solutions.

Although the Spring download is quite large, this results mainly from its integration with other products. To run the core IoC container, you need only the Jakarta Commons Logging JAR in addition to the Spring binary. Some advanced features of both IoC container and AOP framework require CGLIB, which is also used by Hibernate and many other products. Beyond that, Spring's dependencies depend on what third-party product you integrate it with. For example, if you use Spring and Hibernate, you need a number of JARs that are required by Hibernate, besides Hibernate's own JAR.

Spring provides a number of JARs itself, offering separate services:

❑ **spring.jar (1.4MB):** Contains all core Spring classes, including all classes from the following JARs except spring-mock.jar.

❑ **spring-core.jar (265K):** The core IoC container and utility classes used elsewhere in the framework.

❑ **spring-context.jar (276K):** More advanced IoC features, JNDI and EJB support, validation, scheduling, and remoting support.

❑ **spring-aop.jar (144K):** Spring's AOP framework.

❑ **spring-dao.jar (241K):** Spring's data access exception hierarchy, JDBC abstraction, and transaction abstraction, including JTA support.

❑ **spring-orm.jar (190K):** Integration with Hibernate, JDO, iBATIS, and Apache OJB.

❑ **spring-web.jar (114K):** `ApplicationContext` implementations for use in web applications (with any web application framework), servlet filters, integration with Struts and Tiles, web data binding utilities, and multipart support.

❑ **spring-webmvc.jar (190K):** Spring's own Web MVC framework.

❑ **spring-mock.jar (40K):** Mock object implementations and superclasses for JUnit testing objects in a Spring container. Includes test superclasses that can begin and roll back a transaction around each test. These superclasses enable JUnit test cases themselves to be configured by Dependency Injection. (Objects to be tested are injected.)

Most users find that using spring.jar is the simplest choice. However, as the file sizes indicate, the core IoC container comes in at little over 200K.

Supported Environments

Spring requires J2SE 1.3 or above. Spring uses J2SE 1.4 optimizations where this will produce significant benefit, but falls back to using J2SE 1.3 APIs if necessary. For example, there are a number of optimizations available to the AOP framework under J2SE 1.4, such as the use of the new `IdentityHashMap` and `StackTraceElement`, which enable Spring's AOP framework to run faster on J2SE 1.4 and above. But it still retains full functionality on J2SE 1.3.

Certain additional features are supported only in Java 5.0. For example, Spring supports Java 5.0 annotations to drive declarative transaction management. However, the implementation of the core framework will remain J2SE 1.4 compatible for the foreseeable future. Our experience is that large enterprise users, in particular, often use older versions of application servers, and tend to be slow in upgrading. (At the time of writing, one of the major users of Spring in London, a global investment bank, is still using J2SE 1.3, with an old version of WebSphere.)

> **The Spring core does not depend on J2EE APIs. The IoC container and AOP frameworks can be used outside the J2EE environment. Even the transaction support can be used with a full J2EE environment (with JTA).**

Summary

Spring is the most popular and comprehensive of the "lightweight" J2EE frameworks that have surged in popularity since 2003.

Spring enables you to streamline your J2EE development efforts, and bring a welcome consistency to application architecture and implementation. Spring will help you deal with the complexity of J2EE APIs, but is also equally at home outside a J2EE environment.

> **Spring is based on supporting an application programming model where code is written in POJOs.**

Spring achieves this through use of two recently proven paradigms, both of which it has played an important role in popularizing:

❑   **Dependency Injection:** An approach to configuration management in which an Inversion of Control container such as that provided by Spring configures application objects via JavaBean properties or constructor arguments. This removes the need for application code to implement framework interfaces, and allows the framework to add value in many areas — for example, supporting hot swapping of objects without affecting other objects that hold references to them.

❑   **AOP:** AOP provides a way of providing services to POJOs without them needing to be aware of framework APIs, or be unduly constrained by framework requirements.

Spring supports its Dependency Injection and AOP capabilities by providing a consistent abstraction in a number of important areas, including:

- ❑ Data access
- ❑ Transaction management
- ❑ Naming and lookup
- ❑ Remoting

We saw how Spring is designed to promote architectural good practice. A typical Spring architecture will be based on programming to interfaces rather than classes, and will facilitate choice between best of breed solutions in areas such as O/R mapping and web framework, within a consistent architecture. It ensures that architectural layers are coupled through well-defined interfaces.

Spring is also designed to facilitate best practice in development process. In particular, applications using Spring are normally easy to unit test, without the need to deploy code to an application server to conduct all tests.

> There is some confusion about whether Spring competes with J2EE. It does not. J2EE is most successful as a set of specifications for low-level services; Spring is essentially an enabler of an application programming model.
>
> Spring does compete with many services provided by *EJB*, but it's important to avoid the mistake of confusing EJB with J2EE. EJB is a component model that enters the application programming domain; J2EE is a *platform* that deals more with consistent provision of low-level services. Spring in fact allows you to use J2EE more effectively. It allows you to dispense with EJB, and the complexity it entails, in many cases, while providing support for implementing and accessing EJBs in case you do choose to use them.
>
> In reality, Spring competes far more with in-house frameworks. As we saw at the beginning of this chapter, trying to develop applications with J2EE out of the box is cumbersome and unwise. For this reason, many companies develop their own proprietary frameworks to simplify the programming model and conceal the complexity of J2EE APIs. Spring provides a far better option, with a powerful, consistent approach that has been tested by tens of thousands of users in thousands of applications.

In the remainder of this book, we'll look in detail at how Spring realizes the vision we've described in this chapter.

2

The Bean Factory and Application Context

At the heart of Spring is its lightweight *Inversion of Control* (IoC) container functionality. One or more instances of a container are used to configure and wire together application and framework objects, and manage their lifecycles. The key principles of IoC ensure that the great majority of these objects do not have to have dependencies on the container itself, and can generally deal with related objects purely in terms of (Java) *interfaces* or abstract *superclasses*, without having to worry about how those other objects are implemented, or how to locate them. The IoC container is the basis for many of the features that will be introduced in the chapters that follow.

In this chapter, you will learn about the configuration and usage of Spring's bean factories and application contexts, as the embodiment of Spring's IoC container functionality. You will learn about the `BeanFactory` and `ApplicationContext` interfaces, along with related interfaces and classes, used when the container needs to be created or accessed in a programmatic fashion. This chapter will focus on the `BeanFactory` and `ApplicationContext` variants configured in a declarative fashion via XML. These generally have the most built-in functionality in terms of configuration and usage, and are the ones used by Spring users in the vast majority of cases. Note however that Spring decouples container configuration and usage. The next chapter will show how you may also access the full power of the containers using programmatic mechanisms for configuration, as well as alternative declarative formats.

We'll be looking at:

- ❑ Inversion of control and *Dependency Injection*
- ❑ Basic object configuration and wiring of objects in the Spring container
- ❑ How dependencies are resolved, and explicit versus automatic wiring of dependencies
- ❑ Handling object lifecycles in the Spring container
- ❑ Abstracting access to services and resources

❑   Bean and bean factory post-processors for customizing bean and container behavior

❑   Programmatic usage of the `BeanFactory` and `ApplicationContext` interfaces

Inversion of Control and Dependency Injection

In Chapter 1, you learned about *Inversion of Control* and why it is important. Let's recap briefly what this term really means, and then look at a few examples as they apply to the Spring container.

Software code is normally broken up into logical components or services that interact with each other. In Java, these components are usually instances of Java classes, or objects. Each object must use or work with other objects in order to do its job. For an object *A*, it can be said that the other objects that object *A* deals with are its *dependencies*. Inversion of Control refers to the generally desirable architectural pattern of having an outside entity (the container in this case) wire together objects, such that objects are given their dependencies by the container, instead of directly instantiating them themselves.

Take a look at some examples.

Most larger examples in this chapter, even when not listed in complete form, are available separately in fully compilable form so that you may experiment with them. See the website.

Assume we have a historical weather data service, coded in a traditional, non-IoC style:

```java
public class WeatherService {

  WeatherDAO weatherDao = new StaticDataWeatherDAOImpl();

  public Double getHistoricalHigh(Date date) {
    WeatherData wd = weatherDao.find(date);
    if (wd != null)
      return new Double(wd.getHigh());
    return null;
  }
}

public interface WeatherDAO {
  WeatherData find(Date date);
  WeatherData save(Date date);
  WeatherData update(Date date);
}

public class StaticDataWeatherDAOImpl implements WeatherDAO {

  public WeatherData find(Date date) {
    WeatherData wd = new WeatherData();
    wd.setDate((Date) date.clone());
    ...
    return wd;
```

```
    }

    public WeatherData save(Date date) {
       ...
    }
    public WeatherData update(Date date) {
       ...
    }
}
```

Following good practice, we will have a test case to verify that this code works. Based on JUnit, it might look as follows:

```
public class WeatherServiceTest extends TestCase {
    public void testSample1() throws Exception {
        WeatherService ws = new WeatherService();
        Double high = ws.getHistoricalHigh(
                new GregorianCalendar(2004, 0, 1).getTime());
        // ... do more validation of returned value here...
    }
}
```

Our weather service deals with a weather data DAO (Data Access Object) in order to get historical data. It deals with the DAO through a WeatherDAO interface, but in this example, the weather service directly instantiates a specific known type of weather DAO that implements that interface, StaticDataWeatherDAOImpl. Additionally, our driver application, WeatherServiceTest, directly uses a specific WeatherService class, with no possibility of specialization. This example is coded in non-IoC style. While the weather service does deal with the weather DAO through an interface, the weather service is directly instantiating a specific DAO type, and is controlling the lifecycle; thus it has a dependency on both the DAO interface and a specific implementation class. Additionally, the test sample representing the client of the service directly instantiates a specific weather service type, instead of dealing with it through an interface. In a real application, further *implicit* dependencies are likely — for example, on a particular persistence framework — and with this approach, they will be hard-coded in the caller code.

Now let's look at a simple example of how a Spring container can provide Inversion of Control. We first rework our weather service so that it is split up into an interface and implementation and allow the specific DAO instance to be set into that implementation object as a JavaBean property:

```
public interface WeatherService {
    Double getHistoricalHigh(Date date);
}
```

```
public class WeatherServiceImpl implements WeatherService {

    private WeatherDAO weatherDao;

    public void setWeatherDao(WeatherDAO weatherDao) {
        this.weatherDao = weatherDao;
    }
```

```
    public Double getHistoricalHigh(Date date) {
      WeatherData wd = weatherDao.find(date);
      if (wd != null)
        return new Double(wd.getHigh());
      return null;
    }
}

// same class as in previous example
public class StaticDataWeatherDAOImpl implements WeatherDAO {
    ...
}
```

We are going to use a Spring application context, specifically ClasspathXmlApplicationContext, to manage an instance of the weather service and ensure that it is given an instance of the weather DAO to work with. First we define a configuration file in XML format, applicationContext.xml:

```
<?xml version="1.0" encoding="UTF-8"?>
<!DOCTYPE beans PUBLIC "-//SPRING//DTD BEAN//EN"
    "http://www.springframework.org/dtd/spring-beans.dtd">

<beans>
    <bean id="weatherService" class="ch02.sample2.WeatherServiceImpl">
        <property name="weatherDao">
            <ref local="weatherDao"/>
        </property>
    </bean>
    <bean id="weatherDao" class="ch02.sample2.StaticDataWeatherDaoImpl">
    </bean>
</beans>
```

We configure a weatherService object using the bean element, and specify that its weatherDao property should be set to an instance of the weatherDao bean, which we also define. Now we just need to modify the test to create the container and obtain the weather service from it:

```
public class WeatherServiceTest extends TestCase {
    public void testSample2() throws Exception {
        ApplicationContext ctx = new ClassPathXmlApplicationContext(
            "ch03/sample2/applicationContext.xml");
        WeatherService ws = (WeatherService) ctx.getBean("weatherService");

        Double high = ws.getHistoricalHigh(
            new GregorianCalendar(2004, 0, 1).getTime());
        // ... do more validation of returned value here...
    }
}
```

The classes are now coded and deployed in an IoC style. The weather service does not know or care about the implementation details of the actual weather DAO, on which it has a dependency solely through the WeatherDAO interface. Additionally, splitting the original WeatherService class into a WeatherService interface and WeatherServiceImpl implementation class shields clients of the weather service from implementation details such as how the weather DAO is provided to the weather service, through a JavaBeans style setter method in this case. It has the added benefit of allowing the actual weather service implementation itself to be transparently changed. At this point we may switch the actual WeatherDAO implementation and/or the WeatherService implementation, with only configuration file changes and clients of these components being unaware of the changes. This is an example of using interfaces when code in one layer uses code from another layer, as mentioned in Chapter 1.

Different Forms of Dependency Injection

The term *Dependency Injection* describes the process of providing a component with the dependencies it needs, in an IoC fashion, because the dependencies can be said to effectively be injected into the component. The form of dependency injection we saw in the previous example is called *Setter Injection* because JavaBean setter methods are used to supply the dependency to the object needing them. Please refer to http://java.sun.com/products/javabeans for more information about JavaBeans and the JavaBeans specification.

Now let's look at a variant of this, called *Constructor Injection*, where dependencies are instead supplied to an object via that object's own constructor:

```java
public interface WeatherService {
    Double getHistoricalHigh(Date date);
}
public class WeatherServiceImpl implements WeatherService {

    private final WeatherDao weatherDao;

    public WeatherServiceImpl(WeatherDao weatherDao) {
        this.weatherDao = weatherDao;
    }

    public Double getHistoricalHigh(Date date) {
        WeatherData wd = weatherDao.find(date);
        if (wd != null)
            return new Double(wd.getHigh());
        return null;
    }
}

// WeatherDAO unchanged
public interface WeatherDAO {
    ...
}
// StaticDataWeatherDAOImpl unchanged
public class StaticDataWeatherDAOImpl implements WeatherDAO {
    ...
}
```

WeatherServiceImpl now has a constructor that takes WeatherDAO, instead of a setter method that takes this value. The application context configuration is modified accordingly. The test class is oblivious to the changes and does not have to be modified at all:

```
<beans>
  <bean id="weatherService" class="ch02.sample3.WeatherServiceImpl">
    <constructor-arg>
      <ref local="weatherDao"/>
    </constructor-arg>
  </bean>
  <bean id="weatherDao" class="ch02.sample3.StaticDataWeatherDaoImpl">
  </bean>
</beans>

// WeatherServiceTest unchanged
public class WeatherServiceTest extends TestCase {
  ...
}
```

Method Injection, the final form of dependency injection we are going to look at, is the most rarely used. In this form, the container is responsible for implementing methods at runtime. For example, an object might define a protected abstract method, and the container might implement it at runtime to return an object resulting from a container lookup. The aim of method injection is, again, to avoid dependencies on the container APIs, and reduce coupling.

One of the best uses of method injection is to handle the case where a singleton, stateless object, needs to use a non-singleton, stateful, or non-threadsafe object. Consider our weather service, of which there is only one instance needed because our implementation is stateless, and as such it is deployed with the default Spring container handling of being treated as a singleton, with only one instance ever being created, which is then cached and reused. What if the weather service needs to use StatefulWeatherDAO, a WeatherDAO implementation that is not threadsafe? On every invocation of WeatherService. getHistoricalHigh(), the weather service needs to use a fresh instance of the weather DAO (or at least make sure no other weather service invocation is using the same DAO at the same time). As you'll shortly see, we can easily tell the container to make the DAO a non-singleton object, so that each request for it returns a new instance, but we have a problem because the one instance of the weather service is injected with its dependencies only once. One option is for the weather service to be aware of the Spring container, and ask for a new DAO whenever it needs one. This, however, couples it to Spring where ideally it would not know anything about Spring at all. Instead, we can rely on Spring's *Lookup Method Injection* support, making the weather service access the weather DAO via a getWeatherDAO() JavaBean method, which can remain abstract or concrete as desired. Then in the factory definition, we tell the container to override this method and provide an implementation that returns the new DAO instance as another bean:

```
public abstract class WeatherServiceImpl implements WeatherService {

  protected abstract WeatherDao getWeatherDao();

  public Double getHistoricalHigh(Date date) {
    WeatherData wd = getWeatherDao().find(date);
    if (wd != null)
      return new Double(wd.getHigh());
    return null;
  }
}

<beans>
  <bean id="weatherService" class="ch02.sample4.WeatherServiceImpl">
    <lookup-method name="getWeatherDao" bean="weatherDao"/>
```

```
        </bean>
        <bean id="weatherDao" singleton="false"
              class="ch02.sample4.StatefulDataWeatherDaoImpl">
        </bean>
    </beans>
```

Note that we have told the container to make the DAO a non-singleton, so that a new instance can actually be returned on each invocation of getWeatherDao(). Otherwise the same cached singleton instance would be returned each time. While this is legal, that's probably almost never what you want because the main benefit of using Lookup Method Injection, as in this case, is to inject prototypes. In this example, the WeatherServiceImpl class and getWeatherDao method are abstract, but we could override any getter method on any JavaBean. (In fact, candidate methods simply need to have no arguments; it is not necessary for them to follow JavaBeans naming conventions, although it's often a good idea.) The important point is that other code must use that getter method to access the DAO, not a field. This is, in any case, a good practice for any JavaBean property.

The use of Method Injection raises the question of how you would test the code without the container being around to inject the method, such as in a unit test. This may seem especially relevant for the case, such as this one, where the implementation class is abstract. One realistic and relatively simple strategy is for the purposes of the unit test to just subclass the abstract class, providing a test-specific implementation of the normally injected method; for example:

```
    ...
    WeatherService ws = new WeatherServiceImpl() {
        protected WeatherDao getWeatherDao() {
            // return a value for the test
            ...
        }
    };
```

The use of some advanced features such as Method Injection should always be subject to scrutiny by Spring users, who ultimately should decide which approach feels cleanest to them, but generally we feel this approach is preferred to putting in a code-level dependency on the container into application code.

Deciding Between Setter Injection and Constructor Injection

When using existing classes, you will sometimes not even have a choice as to whether to use setter injection or constructor injection. If a class has only a multi-argument constructor, and no JavaBean properties, or alternately only a no-arg constructor and simple JavaBean properties, the choice has effectively been made for you. Additionally, some existing classes may actually force you to use both forms in combination, with a multi-arg constructor that needs to be used, followed by the setting of some optional JavaBean properties.

When you do have a choice as to which form to architect for or to use, there are a number of aspects to consider:

❑   Using JavaBean properties generally makes it easier to handle default or optional values, in the case that not all values are actually needed. In the constructor case, this usually leads to multiple constructor variants, with one calling another internally. The many variations or long argument lists can become very verbose and unmanageable.

❏   JavaBean properties (as long as they are not private) are automatically inherited by subclasses, while constructors are never inherited. The latter limitation often leads to the need to create relatively boilerplate constructors in subclasses, which call superclass constructors. Most IDEs, however, do now include code completion aids that make creation of either constructors or JavaBean properties fairly effortless.

❏   JavaBean properties are arguably better at being self-documenting than constructor arguments, at the source level. When adding JavaDocs, properties require less work to document as there is no duplication.

❏   At runtime, JavaBean properties may be used for matching based on name because properties have names visible by reflection. However, in a compiled class file, constructor argument names are not retained, so that automatic matching based on name is not possible.

❏   JavaBean properties allow getting the current state (as well as setting it) if a getter method is provided. This is useful in a number of situations, such as when the state needs to be stored elsewhere.

❏   The JavaBeans `PropertyEditor` mechanism exists for performing automatic type conversion when needed. This is in fact used and supported by Spring.

❏   JavaBean properties can be mutable because a setter method can be called multiple times. This allows changing a dependency if the use case actually supports it. Dependencies passed in via constructors cannot be mutable unless also exposed as properties. If, on the other hand, complete immutability is required, then Constructor Injection allows you to also explicitly declare the field set from a constructor argument as `final`, whereas the best that a setter method can do is throw an exception if it is called more than once; there is no way to make the field storing the value from the setter method `final`, so that other class code may not modify it.

❏   Constructor arguments make it easier to ensure a valid object is constructed because all required values can be declared and thus must be passed in, and the class is free to use them in the order they are needed, in the process of initialization. With JavaBean properties, there is the possibility that some properties have not been set before the object is used, resulting in an invalid state. Additionally, with JavaBean properties, there is no way to specify and enforce that setters must be called in a certain order, which may mean that initialization may need to take place after property setting, via the use of an `init` method. If used, such an `init` method can also verify that all needed properties have been set. Spring can automatically call any declared initialization method after all properties have been set, or alternately beans may implement the `InitializingBean` interface, which declares an `afterPropertiesSet()` method that will automatically be called.

❏   When there are only a few constructors, this can sometimes be less verbose than many JavaBean property accessor methods. Most IDEs, however, do now include code completion aids, which make creation of either constructors or JavaBean properties fairly effortless.

Generally, the Spring team prefers the use of setter injection over constructor injection for most cases in practice, although this decision should not be a hard and fast one. The aspects mentioned should provide most of the factors used to make the decision in each particular situation. Typically, constructor injection seems to work well for simpler initialization scenarios, with perhaps a constructor taking only a few arguments, which are ideally (easier to match) complex types that are not duplicated. As the configuration complexity scales up, setter injection seems to become more manageable and less work. Note that other major IoC containers also support both constructor and setter injection, so the possibility of Spring lock-in should not be a concern when making this choice.

Of course, whatever form is being used, this should really affect only the implementation class and actual configuration of that class. Most other code in the application should be working against interfaces, and should be completely unaffected by configuration concerns.

The Container

The basic IoC container in Spring is called the bean factory. Any bean factory allows the configuration and wiring together of objects using dependency injection, in a consistent and workable fashion. A bean factory also provides some management of these objects, with respect to their lifecycles. The IoC approach allows significant decoupling of code from other code. Additionally, along with the use of reflection to access the objects, it ensures that application code generally doesn't have to be aware of the bean factory, and generally doesn't have to be modified to be used with Spring. Application code needed to configure objects, and to obtain objects using approaches such as singletons or other approaches such as special factory objects, can be completely eliminated or significantly curtailed.

> Typically, only a very small amount of *glue* code in a typical Spring-based application will actually be aware of the Spring container, or use Spring container interfaces. Even this small amount of glue code can often be eliminated by relying on existing framework code to load bean factories in a declarative fashion.

The Bean Factory

Different bean factory implementations exist to support somewhat varying levels of functionality, in practice mostly related to the configuration mechanism, with XML being by far the most common representation. All bean factories implement the `org.springframework.beans.factory.BeanFactory` interface, with instances able to be accessed through this interface if they need to be managed in a programmatic fashion. Sub-interfaces of `BeanFactory` exist that expose extra functionality. A partial listing of the interface hierarchy includes:

- ❏   `BeanFactory`: The basic interface used to access all bean factories. The simple `getBean(String name)` method allows you to get a bean from the container by name. The `getBean(String name, Class requiredType)` variant allows you to specify the required class of the returned bean, throwing an exception if it doesn't exist. Additional methods allow you to query the bean factory to see if a bean exists (by name), to find out the type of a bean (given a bean name), and to find out if there are any aliases for a bean in the factory (the bean is known to the factory by multiple names). Finally, you may find out if a bean is configured as a singleton; that is, whether or not the first time a bean is requested it will be created and then reused for all subsequent requests, as opposed to a new instance being created each time.

- ❏   `HierarchicalBeanFactory`: Most bean factories can be created as part of a hierarchy, such that if you ask a factory for a bean, and it doesn't exist in that particular factory, a parent factory is also asked for the bean, and that parent factory can ask a parent factory of its own, and so on. As far as the client is concerned, the entire hierarchy upwards of and including the factory being used can be considered as one merged factory. One reason to use such a hierarchical layout is to match the actual architectural layers or modules in an application. While getting a bean from a factory that is part of a hierarchy is transparent, the `HierarchicalBeanFactory` interface exists so that you may ask a factory for its parent.

❑ `ListableBeanFactory`: The methods in this sub-interface of `BeanFactory` allow listing or enumeration of beans in a bean factory, including the names of all the beans, the names of all the beans of a certain type, and the number of beans in the factory. Additionally, several methods allow you to get a `Map` instance containing all beans of a certain type in the factory. It's important to note that while methods from the `BeanFactory` interface automatically take part in any hierarchy that a factory may be part of, the `ListableBeanFactory` interface applies strictly to one bean factory. The `BeanFactoryUtils` helper class provides essentially identical methods to `ListableBeanFactory`, which do take into account the entire bean factory hierarchy. These methods are often more appropriate for usage by application code.

❑ `AutowireCapableBeanFactory`: This interface allows you, via the `autowireBeanProperties()` and `applyBeanPropertyValues()` methods, to have the factory configure an existing external object and supply its dependencies. As such, it skips the normal object creation step that is part of obtaining a bean via `BeanFactory.getBean()`. When working with third-party code that insists on creating object instances itself, it is sometimes not an option for beans to be created by Spring, but still very valuable for Spring to inject bean dependencies. Another method, `autowire()`, allows you to specify a classname to the factory, have the factory instantiate that class, use reflection to discover all the dependencies of the class, and inject those dependencies into the bean, returning the fully configured object to you. Note that the factory will not hold onto and manage the object you configure with these methods, as it would for singleton instances that it creates normally, although you may add the instance yourself to the factory as a singleton.

❑ `ConfigurableBeanFactory`: This interface allows for additional configuration options on a basic bean factory, to be applied during the initialization stage.

Spring generally tries to use non-checked exceptions (subclasses of `RuntimeException`) for non-recoverable errors. The bean factory interfaces, including `BeanFactory` and its subclasses, are no different. In most cases, configuration errors are non-recoverable, so all exceptions thrown by these APIs are subclasses of the non-checked `BeansException`. Developers can choose where and when they handle these exceptions, even trying to recover from them if a viable recovery strategy exists.

The Application Context

Spring also supports a somewhat more advanced bean factory, called the *application context*.

> It is important to stress that an application context *is* a bean factory, with the `org.springframework.context.ApplicationContext` interface being a subclass of `BeanFactory`.

Generally, anything a bean factory can do, an application context can do as well. Why the distinction? It comes down mostly to increased functionality, and usage style:

- **General *framework*-oriented usage style:** Certain operations on the container or beans in the container, which have to be handled in a programmatic fashion with a bean factory, can be handled declaratively in an application context. This includes the automatic recognition and usage of special bean post-processors and bean factory post-processors, to be described shortly. Additionally, a number of Spring Framework facilities exist to automatically load application contexts, for example in the Web MVC layer, such that bean factories will mostly be created by user code, but application contexts will mostly be used in a declarative fashion, being created by framework code. Of course, in both cases, most of the user code will be managed *by* the container, and won't know anything *about* the container at all.

- `MessageSource` **support:** The application context implements `MessageSource`, an interface used to obtain localized messages, with the actual implementation being pluggable.

- **Support for application and framework events:** The context is able to fire framework or application events to registered listeners.

- `ResourceLoader` **support:** Spring's `Resource` interface is a flexible generic abstraction for handling low-level resources. An application context itself *is* a `ResourceLoader`, hence provides an application with access to deployment-specific `Resource` instances.

> You may be wondering when it's most appropriate to create and use a bean factory versus an application context. In almost all cases you are better off using an application context because you will get more features at no real cost. The main exception is perhaps something like an applet where every last byte of memory used (or transferred) is significant, and a bean factory will save some memory because you can use the Spring library package, which brings in only bean factory functionality, without bringing in application context functionality. In this chapter and elsewhere, when bean factory functionality is discussed, you can safely assume that all such functionality is also shared by application contexts.

This chapter and most of this book describe container configuration and functionality using examples for the declarative, XML-configured variants (such as `XMLBeanFactory` or `ClassPathXmlApplicationContext`) of the bean factory and application context. It's important to realize that the container functionality is distinct from the configuration format. While the XML configuration format is used in the vast majority of cases by Spring users, there is a full programmatic API for configuring and accessing the containers, and other configuration formats can be built and supported in the same fashion as the XML variants. For example, a `PropertiesBeanDefinitionReader` class already exists for reading definitions in Java Properties file format into a bean factory.

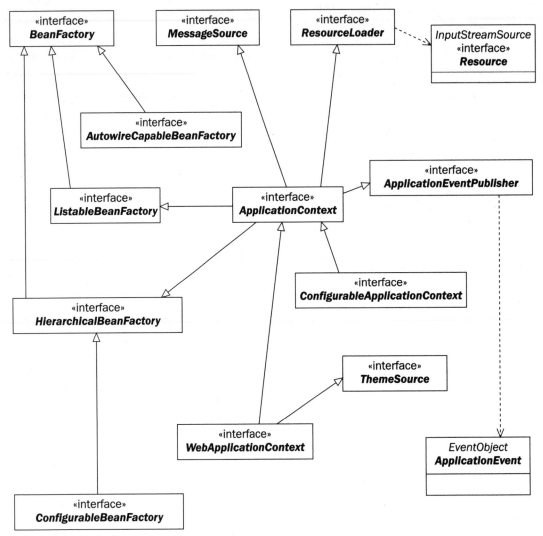

Figure 2-1

Starting the Container

From the previous examples, you already have an idea of how a container is programmatically started by user code. Let's look at a few variations.

We can load an ApplicationContext by pointing to the resource (file) on the classpath:

```
ApplicationContext appContext =
    new ClassPathXmlApplicationContext("ch03/sample2/applicationContext.xml");
// side note: an ApplicationContext is also a BeanFactory, of course!
BeanFactory factory = (BeanFactory) appContext;
```

Or we can point to a file system location:

```
ApplicationContext appContext =
    new FileSystemXmlApplicationContext("/some/file/path/applicationContext.xml");
```

We can also combine two or more XML file fragments. This allows us to locate bean definitions in the logical module they belong to while still producing one context from the combined definitions. As an example in the next chapter will show, this can be useful for testing as well. Here is one of the configuration samples seen before, but split up into two XML fragments:

```
applicationContext-dao.xml:
```

```xml
<?xml version="1.0" encoding="UTF-8"?>
<!DOCTYPE beans PUBLIC "-//SPRING//DTD BEAN//EN"
    "http://www.springframework.org/dtd/spring-beans.dtd">

<beans>
  <bean id="weatherDao" class="ch02.sample2.StaticDataWeatherDaoImpl">
  </bean>
</beans>
```

```
applicationContext-services.xml:
```

```xml
<?xml version="1.0" encoding="UTF-8"?>
<!DOCTYPE beans PUBLIC "-//SPRING//DTD BEAN//EN"
    "http://www.springframework.org/dtd/spring-beans.dtd">

<beans>
  <bean id="weatherService" class="ch02.sample2.WeatherServiceImpl">
    <property name="weatherDao">
      <ref bean="weatherDao"/>
    </property>
  </bean>
</beans>
```

Careful readers will note that compared to a previous example we've slightly changed the way we referred to the weatherDao bean we use as a property of the weather service bean; later we'll describe bean references in much more detail.

Now to load and combine the two (or more) fragments, we just specify all of them:

```
ApplicationContext appContext = new ClassPathXmlApplicationContext(
        new String[] {"applicationContext-serviceLayer.xml", "applicationContext-
dao.xml"});
```

Spring's Resource abstraction, which we will cover in depth later, allows us to use a classpath*: prefix to specify *all* resources matching a particular name that are visible to the class loader and its parents. If, for example, we have an application that is partitioned into multiple jars, all available on the classpath, and each jar contains its own application context fragment that is named applicationContext. xml, we easily specify that we want to create a context made up of all those fragments:

```
ApplicationContext appContext = new
ClassPathXmlApplicationContext("classpath*:ApplicationContext.xml");
```

Creating and loading an XML-configured bean factory is just as simple. The easiest mechanism is to use Spring's `Resource` abstraction for getting at a classpath resource:

```
ClassPathResource res =
    new ClassPathResource("org/springframework/prospering/beans.xml");
XmlBeanFactory factory = new XmlBeanFactory(res);
```

or

```
FilesystemResource res = new FilesystemResource("/some/file/path/beans.xml");
XmlBeanFactory factory = new XmlBeanFactory(res);
```

But we can also just use an `InputStream`:

```
InputStream is = new FileInputStream("/some/file/path/beans.xml");
XmlBeanFactory factory = new XmlBeanFactory(is);
```

Finally, for completeness, we show that we can easily split the step of creating the bean factory from parsing the bean definitions. We will not go into more depth here, but this distinction between bean factory behavior and parsing is what allows other configuration formats to be plugged in:

```
ClassPathResource res = new ClassPathResource("beans.xml");
DefaultListableBeanFactory factory = new DefaultListableBeanFactory();
XmlBeanDefinitionReader reader = new XmlBeanDefinitionReader(factory);
reader.loadBeanDefinitions(res);
```

For application contexts, the use of the `GenericApplicationContext` class allows a similar separation of creation from parsing of definitions. Many Spring applications will never programmatically create a container themselves because they rely on framework code to do it. For example, you can declaratively configure Spring's `ContextLoader` to automatically load an application context at web-app startup. You'll learn about this in the next chapter.

Using Beans from the Factory

Once the bean factory or application context has been loaded, accessing beans in a basic fashion is as simple as using `getBean()` from the `BeanFactory` interface:

```
WeatherService ws = (WeatherService) ctx.getBean("weatherService");
```

or other methods from some of the more advanced interfaces:

```
Map allWeatherServices = ctx.getBeansOfType(WeatherService.class);
```

Asking the container for a bean triggers the creation and initialization of the bean, including the dependency injection stage we've discussed previously. The dependency injection step can trigger the creation of other beans (the dependencies of the first bean), and so on, creating an entire graph of related object instances.

An obvious question might be what to do with the bean factory or application context itself, so that other code that needs it can get at it. As we're currently examining how the container is configured and how it works, we're mostly going to punt on this question here and defer it to later in this chapter.

Remember that excepting a small amount of glue code, the vast majority of application code written and assembled in proper IoC style does not have to be concerned at all with getting at the factory because the container will be hooking up these objects to other objects managed by the container. For the small amount of glue code that is needed to kick things off, the basic strategy is to put the factory in a known location, preferably somewhere that makes sense in the context of the expected usage and what code will actually need access to the factory. Spring itself provides support for declaratively loading an application context for web-app usage and storing it in the ServletContext. Additionally, it provides some quasi-singleton convenience classes that may be used for storing and getting at a factory, when a better fit or strategy does not exist for storing the factory in a particular app.

XML Bean Configuration

We've seen some sample XML format bean factory definition files, but have not gone into much detail so far. Essentially, a bean factory definition consists of just a top-level beans element containing one or more bean elements:

```
<?xml version="1.0" encoding="UTF-8"?>
<!DOCTYPE beans PUBLIC "-//SPRING//DTD BEAN//EN"
    "http://www.springframework.org/dtd/spring-beans.dtd">

<beans>
  <bean id="weatherService" class="ch02.sample2.WeatherServiceImpl">
    <property name="weatherDao">
      <ref local="weatherDao"/>
    </property>
  </bean>
  <bean id="weatherDao" class="ch02.sample2.StaticDataWeatherDaoImpl">
  </bean>
</beans>
```

The valid elements and attributes in a definition file are fully described by the XML DTD (document type definition), spring-beans.dtd. This DTD, along with the Spring reference manual, should be considered the definitive source of configuration information. Generally, the optional attributes of the top-level beans element can affect the behavior of the entire configuration file and provide some default values for individual bean definition aspects, while (mostly) optional attributes and sub-elements of the child bean elements describe the configuration and lifecycle of individual beans. The DTD is included as part of the Spring distribution, and you may also see it online at www.springframework.org/dtd/spring-beans.dtd.

The Basic Bean Definition

An individual bean definition contains the information needed for the container to know how to create a bean, some lifecycle details, and information about the bean's dependencies. Let's look at the first two aspects in this section.

Identifier

For a top-level bean definition, you will almost always want to provide one or more identifiers, or names, for the bean, so that other beans may refer to it, or you may refer to it when using the container programmatically. Try to use the id attribute to supply the ID (or in the case of multiple IDs, the primary one). This has the advantage that because this attribute has the XML IDREF type, when other beans refer to this one, the XML parser can actually help detect whether the reference is valid (exists in the same file), allowing earlier validation of your factory config. However, XML IDREFs have a few limitations with regards to allowed characters, in that they must start with a letter followed by alphanumeric characters or the underscore, with no whitespace. This is not usually an issue, but to circumvent these limitations, you may instead use the name attribute to provide the identifier. This is useful, for example, when the bean identifier is not completely under the user's control and it represents a URL path. Additionally, the name attribute actually allows a comma-separated list of IDs. When a bean definition specifies more than one ID, via the combination of the id attribute and/or the name attribute, the additional IDs after the first can be considered *aliases*. All IDs are equally valid when referring to the bean. Let's look at some examples:

```
<beans>

  <bean id="bean1" class="ch02.sample5.TestBean"/>

  <bean name="bean2" class="ch02.sample5.TestBean"/>

  <bean name="/myservlet/myaction" class="ch02.sample5.TestBean"/>

  <bean id="component1-dataSource"
        name="component2-dataSource,component3-dataSource"
        class="ch02.sample5.TestBean"/>

</beans>
```

The third bean needs an ID that starts with /, so it may not use the id attribute, but must use name. Note that the fourth bean has three IDs, all equally valid. You may be wondering why you would ever want to provide more than one ID for a bean. One valid use case is when you want to split up your configuration by components or modules, such that each component provides one XML file fragment that lists the beans related to that component, and their dependencies. The names of these dependencies can (as one example) be specified with a component-specific prefix, such as was used for the hypothetical DataSource in the previous code sample. When the final bean factory or context is assembled from the multiple fragments (or, as will be described later, a hierarchy of contexts is created), each component will end up referring to the same actual bean. This is a low-tech way of providing some isolation between components.

Bean Creation Mechanism

You also need to tell the container how to instantiate or obtain an instance of the bean, when it is needed. The most common mechanism is creation of the bean via its constructor. The class attribute is used to specify the classname of the bean. When the container needs a *new* instance of the bean, it will internally perform the equivalent of using the new operator in Java code. All the examples we have seen so far use this mechanism.

Another mechanism is to tell the container to use a static *factory-method* to obtain the new instance. Legacy code over which you have no control will sometimes force you to use such a static factory method. Use the `class` attribute to specify the name of the class that contains the static factory method, and specify the name of the actual method itself via the `factory-method` attribute:

```
...
<bean id="testBeanObtainedViaStaticFactory"
      class="ch02.sample4.StaticFactory" factory-method="getTestBeanInstance"/>
...
```

```
public class StaticFactory {
  public static TestBean getTestBeanInstance() {
    return new TestBean();
  }
}
```

The static factory method may return an object instance of any type; the class of the instance returned doesn't have to be the same as the class containing the factory method.

The third mechanism for the container to get a new bean instance is for it to call a non-static factory method on a different bean instance in the container:

```
...
<bean id="nonStaticFactory" class="ch02.sample4.NonStaticFactory"/>

<bean id="testBeanObtainedViaNonStaticFactory"
      factory-bean="nonStaticFactory" factory-method="getTestBeanInstance"/>
...
```

```
public class NonStaticFactory {
  public TestBean getTestBeanInstance() {
    return new TestBean();
  }
}
```

When a new instance of `testBeanObtainedViaNonStaticFactory` is needed, an instance of `nonStaticFactory` is first created, and the `getTestBeanInstance` method on that is called. Note that in this case, we do not specify any value at all for the `class` attribute.

Once a new object instance is obtained, the container will treat it the same regardless of whether it was obtained via a constructor, via a static factory method, or via an instance factory method. That is, setter injection can be used and normal lifecycle callbacks will apply.

Singleton versus Non-Singleton Beans

An important aspect of the bean lifecycle is whether the container treats it as a singleton or not. Singleton beans, the default, are created only once by the container. The container will then hold and use the same instance of the bean whenever it is referred to again. This can be significantly less expensive in terms of resource (memory or potentially even CPU) usage than creating a new instance of the bean on each request. As such, it's the best choice when the actual implementation of the classes in question allow it; that is, the bean is stateless, or state is set only once at initialization time, so that it is *threadsafe*, and may be used by multiple threads at a time. Singleton beans are the default because in practice most services, controllers, and resources that end up being configured in the container are implemented as threadsafe classes, which do not modify any state past initialization time.

A non-singleton, or *prototype* bean as it is also called, may be specified by setting the `singleton` attribute to false. It's important to note that the lifecycle of a prototype bean will often be different than that of a singleton bean. When a container is asked to supply a prototype bean, it is initialized and then used, but the container does not hold onto it past that point. So while it's possible to tell Spring to perform some end-of-lifecycle operations on singleton beans, as we will examine in a subsequent section, any such operations need to be performed by user code for prototype beans because the container will no longer know anything about them at that point:

```
<bean id="singleton1" class="ch02.sample4.TestBean"/>

<bean id="singleton2" singleton="true" class="ch02.sample4.TestBean"/>

<bean id="prototype1" singleton="false" class="ch02.sample4.TestBean"/>
```

Specifying Bean Dependencies

Satisfying bean dependencies, in the form of other beans or simple values the first bean needs, is the meat and potatoes or core functionality of the container, so it's important to understand how the process works. You've already seen examples of the main types of dependency injection, *constructor injection* and *setter injection*, and know that Spring supports both forms. You've also seen how, instead of using a constructor to obtain an initial object instance to work with, Spring can use a factory method. With respect to supplying dependencies to the bean, using a factory method to obtain a bean instance can essentially be considered equivalent to getting that instance via a constructor. In the constructor case, the container supplies (optional) argument values, which are the dependencies, to a constructor. In the factory-method case, the container supplies (optional) argument values, which are the dependencies, to the factory method. Whether the initial object instance comes through a constructor or factory method, it is from that point on treated identically.

Constructor injection and setter injection are not mutually exclusive. If Spring obtains an initial bean instance via a constructor or factory method, and supplies argument values to the constructor or factory method, thus injecting some dependencies, it is still able to then use setter injection to supply further dependencies. This can be useful, for example, when you need to use and initialize an existing class that has a constructor taking one or more arguments, that produces a bean in a known (valid) initial state, but relies on JavaBeans setter methods for some optional properties. Without using both forms of injection, you would not be able to properly initialize this type of object if any of the optional properties needed to be set.

Let's examine how the container initializes and resolves bean dependencies:

❑ The container first initializes the bean definition, without instantiating the bean itself, typically at the time of container startup. The bean dependencies may be explicitly expressed in the form of constructor arguments or arguments to a factory method, and/or bean properties.

❑ Each property or constructor argument in a bean definition is either an actual value to set, or a reference to another bean in the bean factory or in a parent bean factory.

❑ The container will do as much validation as it can at the time the bean definition is initialized. When using the XML configuration format, you'll first get an exception from the XML parser if your configuration does not validate against the XML DTD. Even if the XML is valid in terms of the DTD, you will get an exception from Spring if it is able to determine that a definition is not logically valid; for example two properties may be mutually exclusive, with no way for the DTD to express this.

❑ If a bean dependency cannot be satisfied (that is, a bean dependency is another bean that doesn't actually exist), or a constructor-argument or property value cannot be set properly, you will get an error only when the container actually needs to get a new instance of the bean and inject dependencies. If a bean instance is never needed, then there is the potential that the bean definition contains (dependency) errors you will not find out about (until that bean is eventually used). Partially in order to provide you with earlier error trapping, application contexts (but not bean factories) by default pre-instantiate singleton bean instances. The pre-instantiation stage simply consists of enumerating all singleton (the default state) beans, creating an instance of each including injection of dependencies, and caching that instance. Note that the pre-instantiation stage can be overridden through the use of the default-lazy-init attribute of the top-level beans element, or controlled on an individual bean basis by using the lazy-init attribute of the bean element.

❑ When the container needs a new bean instance, typically as the result of a getBean() call or another bean referring to the first bean as a dependency, it will get the initial bean instance via the constructor or factory method that is configured, and then start to try injecting dependencies, the optional constructor or factory method arguments, and the optional property values.

❑ Constructor arguments or bean properties that refer to another bean will force the container to create or obtain that other bean first. Effectively, the bean that is referred to is a dependency of the referee. This can trigger a chain of bean creation, as an entire dependency graph is resolved.

❑ Every constructor argument or property value must be able to be converted from whatever type or format it was specified in, to the actual type that that constructor argument or property is expecting, if the two types are not the same. Spring is able to convert arguments supplied in string format to all the built-in scalar types, such as int, long, boolean, and so on, and all the wrapper types such as Integer, Long, Boolean, and so on. Spring also uses JavaBeans PropertyEditors to convert potentially any type of String values to other, arbitrary types. A number of built-in PropertyEditors are automatically registered and used by the container. A couple of examples are the ClassEditor PropertyEditor, which converts a classname string into an actual Class object instance, which may be fed to a property expecting a Class, or the ResourceEditor PropertyEditor, which converts a string location path into Spring's Resource type, which is used to access resources in an abstract fashion. All the built-in property editors are described in the next chapter. As will be described later in this chapter in the section "Creating a Custom PropertyEditor," it is possible to register your own PropertyEditors to handle your own custom types.

❑ The XML configuration variant used by most bean factory and application context implementations also has appropriate elements/attributes allowing you to specify complex values that are of various Collection types, including Lists, Sets, Maps, and Properties. These Collection values may nest arbitrarily.

❑ Dependencies can also be implicit, to the extent that even if they are not declared, Spring is able to use reflection to see what constructor arguments a bean takes, or what properties it has, and build up a list of valid dependencies for the bean. It can then, using functionality called *autowiring*, populate those dependencies, based on either *type* or *name* matching. We'll ignore autowiring for the time being, and come back to it later.

Specifying Bean Dependencies, Detailed

Let's look in detail at the specifics of supplying bean properties and constructor arguments in XML format. Each bean element contains zero (0) or more constructor-arg elements, specifying constructor or lookup method arguments. Each bean element contains zero (0) or more property elements, specifying a JavaBean property to set. Constructor arguments and JavaBean properties may be combined if needed, which the following example takes advantage of. It has a constructor argument that is a reference to another bean, and an int property, a simple value:

```
<beans>
  <bean id="weatherService" class="ch02.sample6.WeatherServiceImpl">
    <constructor-arg index="0">
      <ref local="weatherDao"/>
    </constructor-arg>
    <property name="maxRetryAttempts"><value>2</value></property>
  </bean>

  <bean id="weatherDao" class="ch02.sample6.StaticDataWeatherDaoImpl">
  </bean>
</beans>
```

From the XML DTD, we can see that a number of elements are allowed inside a property or constructor-arg element. Each is used to specify some sort of value for a property or constructor argument:

```
(bean | ref | idref | list | set | map | props | value | null)
```

The ref element is used to set the value of a property or constructor argument to be a reference to another bean from the factory, or from a parent factory:

```
<ref local="weatherDao"/>
<ref bean="weatherDao"/>
<ref parent="weatherDao"/>
```

The local, bean, or parent attributes are mutually exclusive, and must be the ID of the other bean. When using the local attribute, the XML parser is able to verify at parse time that the specified bean exists. However, because this relies on XML's IDREF mechanism, that bean must be in the same XML file as the reference, and its definition must use the id attribute to specify the ID being referred to, not name. When the bean attribute is used, the specified bean may be located in the same or another XML fragment that is used to build up the factory definition, or alternately in any parent factory of the current factory. However, Spring itself (not the XML parser) will validate that the specified bean exists, and this will happen only when that dependency actually needs to be resolved, not at factory load time. The much less frequently used parent attribute specifies that the target bean must come from a parent factory to the current one. This may be used in the rare cases when there is a name conflict between a bean in the current factory and a parent factory.

The value element is used to specify simple property values or constructor arguments. As previously mentioned, conversion happens from the source form, which is a string, to the type of the target property or constructor arg, which can be any of the built-in scalar types or related wrapper types, and can also be any type for which a JavaBean PropertyEditor capable of handling it is registered in the container. So for example,

```
<property name="classname">
  <value>ch02.sample6.StaticDataWeatherDaoImpl</value>
</property>
```

will set a `String` property called `classname` to the string literal value `ch02.sample6.StaticDataWeatherDaoImpl`, but if `classname` is instead a property of type `java.lang.Class`, the factory will use the built-in (automatically registered) `ClassEditor` `PropertyEditor` to convert the string value to an actual `Class` object instance.

It is easy to register your own `PropertyEditor`s to handle string conversion to any other custom types that need to be handled in the container config. One good example of where this is useful is for entering dates in string form, to be used to set Date properties. Because dates are very much locale sensitive, use of a `PropertyEditor` that expects a specific source string format is the easiest way to handle this need. How to register custom `PropertyEditor`s will be demonstrated in the description of `CustomEditorConfigurer`, a bean factory *post-processor*, later in this chapter. Also, it is a little-known fact that the JavaBeans `PropertyEditor` machinery will automatically detect and use any `PropertyEditor`s that are in the same package as the class they are meant to convert, as long as they have the same name as that class with "Editor" appended. That is, for a class `MyType`, a `PropertyEditor` called `MyTypeEditor` in the same package would automatically be detected and used by the JavaBeans support code in the Java library, without having to tell Spring about it.

Properties or constructor arguments that need to be set to Null values require special treatment because an empty `value` element is treated as just an empty string. Instead, use the special `null` element:

```
<property name="optionalDescription"><null/></property>
```

The `idref` element is a convenient way to catch errors when specifying the name of another bean as a string value. There are some Spring-specific helper beans in the framework that as property values take the name of another bean and perform some action with it. You would typically use the form

```
<property name="beanName"><value>weatherService</value></property>
```

to populate these properties. It would be nice if typos could somehow be caught, and in fact this is what `idref` does. Using the form

```
<property name="beanName"><idref local="weatherService"/></property>
```

allows the XML parser to participate in validation, as it will catch references to beans that don't actually exist. The resulting property `value` will be exactly the same as if the first value tag had been used.

The `list`, `set`, `map`, and `props` elements allow complex properties or constructor arguments of type `java.util.List`, `java.util.Set`, `java.util.Map`, and `java.util.Properties` to be defined and set. Let's look at a completely artificial example, in which a JavaBean has a List, Set, Map, and Properties property set:

```
<beans>
  <bean id="collectionsExample" class="ch02.sample7.CollectionsBean">
    <property name="theList">
      <list>
        <value>red</value>
        <value>red</value>
        <value>blue</value>
```

```
                <ref local="curDate"/>
                <list>
                    <value>one</value>
                    <value>two</value>
                    <value>three</value>
                </list>
            </list>
        </property>
        <property name="theSet">
            <set>
                <value>red</value>
                <value>red</value>
                <value>blue</value>
            </set>
        </property>
        <property name="theMap">
            <map>
                <entry key="left">
                    <value>right</value>
                </entry>
                <entry key="up">
                    <value>down</value>
                </entry>
                <entry key="date">
                    <ref local="curDate"/>
                </entry>
            </map>
        </property>
        <property name="theProperties">
            <props>
                <prop key="left">right</prop>
                <prop key="up">down</prop>
            </props>
        </property>
    </bean>

    <bean id="curDate" class="java.util.GregorianCalendar"/>
</beans>
```

List, Map, and Set values may be any of the elements

```
(bean | ref | idref | list | set | map | props | value | null)
```

As shown in the example for the list, this means the collection types can nest arbitrarily. One thing to keep in mind is that the properties or constructor arguments receiving Collection types must be of the generic types `java.util.List`, `java.util.Set`, or `java.util.Map`. You cannot depend on the Spring-supplied collection being of a specific type, for example `ArrayList`. This presents a potential problem if you need to populate a property in an existing class that takes a specific type because you can't feed a generic type to it. One solution is to use `ListFactoryBean`, `SetFactoryBean`, and `MapFactoryBean`, a set of helper *Factory Beans* available in Spring. They allow you to specify the collection type to use, for instance a `java.util.LinkedList`. Please see the Spring JavaDocs for more info. We will discuss factory beans shortly.

The final element allowed as a property value or constructor argument, or inside one of the collection elements, is the `bean` element. This means a bean definition can effectively nest inside another bean definition, as a property of the outer bean. Consider a variation of our original setter injection example:

```
<beans>
  <bean id="weatherService" class="ch02.sample2.WeatherServiceImpl">
    <property name="weatherDao">
      <bean class="ch02.sample2.StaticDataWeatherDaoImpl">
        ...
      </bean>
    </property>
  </bean>
</beans>
```

Nested bean definitions are very useful when there is no use for the inner bean outside of the scope of the outer bean. In the preceding example, the weather DAO, which is set as a dependency of the weather service, has been moved to be an inner bean. No other bean or external user will ever need the weather DAO, so there is no use in keeping it as a separate outer-scope bean definition. Using the inner bean form is more concise and clearer. There is no need for the inner bean to have an ID, although it is legal. *Note*: Inner beans are always prototypes, with the singleton flag being ignored. In this case, this is essentially irrelevant; because there is only one instance of the outer bean ever created (it's a singleton), there would only ever be one instance of the dependency created, whether that dependency is marked as singleton or prototype. However if a prototype outer bean needs to have a singleton dependency, then that dependency should not be wired as an inner bean, but rather as a reference to a singleton external bean.

Manual Dependency Declarations

When a bean property or constructor argument refers to another bean, this is a declaration of a dependency on that other bean. You will sometimes have a need to force one bean to be initialized before another, even if it is not specified as a property of the other. The most typical case for this is when a class does some static initialization when it is loaded. For example, database drivers typically register themselves with the JDBC `DriverManager`. The `depends-on` attribute may be used to manually specify that a bean is dependent on another, triggering the instantiation of that other bean first when the dependent bean is accessed. Here's an example showing how to trigger the loading of a database driver:

```
<bean id="load-jdbc-driver" class="oracle.jdbc.driver.OracleDriver "/>

<bean id="dataBaseUsingBean" depends-on="load-jdbc-driver" class="..." >
  ...
</bean>
```

Note that most database connection pools and Spring support classes such as `DriverManagerDataSource` trigger this kind of loading themselves, so this is for example only.

Autowiring Dependencies

We've so far seen explicit declarations of bean dependencies through property values and constructor arguments. Under many circumstances, Spring is able to use introspection of bean classes in the factory and perform *autowiring* of dependencies. In autowiring, you leave the bean property or constructor argument undeclared (in the XML file), and Spring will use reflection to find the type and name of the property, and then match it to another bean in the factory based on type or name. This can potentially save a significant amount of typing, at the possible expense of some loss of transparency. You may control autowiring at both the entire container level and the individual bean definition level. Because autowiring may have uncertain effects when not used carefully, all autowiring is off by default. Autowiring at the bean level is controlled via the use of the `autowire` attribute, which has five possible values:

❑ no: No autowiring at all for this bean. Bean properties and constructor arguments must be explicitly declared, and any reference to another bean must be done via the use of a `ref` element. This is the default handling for individual beans when the default is not changed at the bean factory level. This mode is recommend in most circumstances, especially for larger deployments, as explicitly declared dependencies are a form of explicit documentation and much more transparent.

❑ byName: Autowire by property name. The property names are used to find matching beans in the factory. If a property has the name "weatherDao," then the container will try to set the property as a reference to another bean with the name "weatherDao." If there are no matching beans, then the property is left unset. This handling treats unmatched properties as optional. If you need to treat unmatched properties as an error case, you may do so by adding the `dependency-check="objects"` attribute to the bean definition, as described later.

❑ byType: Autowire by matching type. This is similar to the approach of PicoContainer, another popular dependency injection container. For each property, if there is exactly one bean in the factory of the same type as the property, the property value is set as that other bean. If there is more than one bean in the factory matching the type, it is considered a fatal error and an exception is raised. As for byName autowiring, if there are no matching beans, then the property is left unset. If this needs to be treated as an error case, the `dependency-check="objects"` attribute may be used on the bean definition, as described later.

❑ constructor: Autowire the constructor by type. This works in essentially identical fashion to how byType works for properties, except that there must be exactly one matching bean, by type, in the factory for each constructor argument. In the case of multiple constructors, Spring will try to be greedy and satisfy the constructor with the most matching arguments.

❑ autodetect: Choose byType or constructor as appropriate. The bean is introspected, and if there is a default no-arg constructor, byType is used, otherwise, constructor is used.

It is possible to set a different default autowire mode (than the normal no) for all beans in the factory by using the `default-autowire` attribute of the top-level `beans` element. Note also that you may mix autowiring and explicit wiring, with explicit `property` or `constructor-arg` elements specifying dependencies always taking precedence for any given property.

Let's look at how autowiring could work for our weather service and weather DAO. As you can see, we remove the `weatherDao` property definition in the bean definition, turn on autowiring by name, and Spring will still populate the property based on a name match. We could also have used autowiring by type because the property is of a type `WeatherDao`, and only one bean in the container matches that type:

```
<beans>
  <bean id="weatherService" autowire="byName"
        class="ch02.sample2.WeatherServiceImpl">
    <!-- no more weatherDao property declaration here -->
  </bean>

  <bean id="weatherDao" class="ch02.sample2.StaticDataWeatherDaoImpl">
  </bean>
</beans>
```

It may be tempting to try to use autowiring extensively to try to save typing in the factory configurations, but we would caution you to be very careful when using this feature.

> Removing explicitly declared dependencies also removes a form of documentation of those dependencies. Additionally, when using byType or even byName, there is the potential for surprises when more than one bean matches, or no bean matches. For larger, more complicated deployments especially, we recommend you stay away from autowiring, or use it very judiciously, as you may otherwise find you have actually increased the complexity even though you have reduced the amount of XML. Most IDEs now have DTD-aware XML editors built-in or available as plugins, which can save most of the typing when creating bean configurations, so the verbosity of explicit dependency declarations is not as much of a concern as it once would have been. What may work well in some situations is to rely on autowiring for simple low-level plumbing — say, a DataSource — and to use explicit wiring for more complicated aspects. This tends to reduce clutter without causing surprises or sacrificing much explicitness.

Constructor Argument Matching

As a general rule, you should almost always use the optional index or type attributes with constructor-arg elements you specify. While these attributes are optional, without one or the other, the list of constructor arguments you specify is resolved to actual constructor arguments based on matching of types. When the arguments you specify are references to different types of complex beans, or complex types such as a Map, it's easy for the container to do this matching, especially if there is only one constructor. However, when specifying multiple arguments of the same type, or using the value tag, which can be considered to be (in source string form) an untyped value, trying to rely on automatic matching can produce errors or unexpected results.

Consider a bean that has a constructor taking a numeric error code value and a String error message value. If we try to use the <value> tag to supply values for these arguments, we need to give the container a hint so it can do its job. We can either use the index attribute to specify the correct (0-based) argument index, matching the actual constructor:

```
<beans>
  <bean id="errorBean" class="ch02.sampleX.ErrorBean">
    <constructor-arg index="0"><value>1000<value></constructor-arg>
    <constructor-arg index="1"><value>Unexpected Error<value></constructor-arg>
  </bean>
</beans>
```

or alternately, we can give the container enough information that it can do proper matching based on type, by using the type attribute to specify the type of the value:

```
<beans>
  <bean id="errorBean" class="ch02.sampleX.ErrorBean">
    <constructor-arg type="int"><value>1000<value></constructor-arg>
    <constructor-arg type="java.lang.String">
      <value>Unexpected Error<value>
    </constructor-arg>
  </bean>
</beans>
```

Validating Bean Dependencies

Often, some JavaBean properties on an object are optional. You're free to set them or not as needed for the particular use case, and there would be no easy way for the container to try to help you in catching errors due to a property that needs to be set but isn't. However, when you have a bean in which all properties, or all properties of a certain nature, need to be set, the container's dependency validation feature can help out. When enabled, the container will consider it an error if properties are not supplied either by explicit declaration or through autowiring. By default, the container will not try to validate that all dependencies are set, but you may customize this behavior with the `dependency-check` attribute on a bean definition, which may have the following values:

❑ `none`: No dependency validation. If a property has no value specified, it is not considered an error. This is the default handling for individual beans when the default is not changed at the bean factory level.

❑ `simple`: Validate that primitive types and collections are set, considering it an error if they are not set. Other properties may be set or not set.

❑ `objects`: Validate that properties that are not primitive types or collections are set, considering it an error if they are not set. Other properties may be set or not set.

❑ `all`: Validate that all properties are set, including primitive types, collections, and complex types.

It is possible to set a different default dependency check mode (than the normal `none`) for all beans in the factory by using the `default-dependency-check` attribute of the top-level `beans` element.

Note also that the `InitializingBean` callback interface described in the next section may also be used to manually verify dependencies.

Managing the Bean Lifecycle

A bean in the factory can have a very simple or relatively complex lifecycle, with respect to things that happen to it. Since we're talking about POJOs, the bean lifecycle does not have to amount to anything more than creation and usage of the object. However, there are a number of ways that more complex lifecycles can be managed and handled, mostly centering around bean lifecycle callbacks that the bean and that third-party *observer* objects called *bean post-processors* can receive at various stages in the initialization and destruction phases. Let's examine the possible container-driven actions (described in the following table) that can happen in the lifecycle of a bean managed by that container.

Action	Description
Initialization begins as bean is instantiated	The new bean is instantiated via a constructor, or by calling a factory method, which is considered equivalent. This happens as a result of a `getBean()` call on the factory, or the fact that another bean that was already being instantiated had a dependency on this one, triggering the creation of this one first.
Dependencies injected	Dependencies are injected into the instance, as previously discussed.

`setBeanName()` called	If the bean implements the optional interface, `Bean NameAware`, then that interface's `setBeanName()` method is called to provide the bean with its primary ID as declared in the bean definition.
`setBeanFactory()` called	If the bean implements the optional `BeanFactoryAware` interface, then that interface's `setBeanFactory()` method is called to provide the bean with a reference to the factory it is deployed in. Note that since application contexts are also bean factories, this method will also be called for beans deployed in an application context, however passing in the bean factory internally used by the context.
`setResourceLoader()` called	If the bean implements the optional `ResourceLoader Aware` interface, and it is deployed in an application context, then that interface's `setResourceLoader()` method is called, with the application context as the `ResourceLoader`. (To be discussed in the next chapter.)
`setApplicationEventPublisher` called	If the bean implements the optional `ApplicationEventPublisherAware` interface, and it is deployed in an application context, then that interface's `setApplicationEventPublisher()` method is called, with the application context as the `ApplicationEvent Publisher`. (To be discussed in the next chapter.)
`setMessageSource()` called	If the bean implements the optional `MessageSourceAware` interface, and it is deployed in an application context, then that interface's `setMessageSource()` method is called, with the application context as the `MessageSource`. (To be discussed in the next chapter.)
`setApplicationContext()` called	If the bean implements the optional `ApplicationContext Aware()` interface, and is deployed in an application context, then that interface's `setApplicationContext()` method is called to provide the bean with a reference to the context.
Bean post-processors get "before-initialization" callback with bean	Bean post-processors, which will be discussed shortly, are special handlers that applications may register with the factory. Post-processors get a pre-initialization callback with the bean, which they may manipulate as needed.
`afterPropertiesSet()` called	If the bean implements the `InitializingBean` marker interface, then `afterPropertiesSet()` from this interface is called to allow the bean to initialize itself.
Declared `init` method called	If the bean definition defines an initialization method via the `init-method` attribute, then this method is called to allow the bean to initialize itself.

Table continued on following page

Bean post-processors get "after-initialization" callback with the bean instance as argument	Any bean post-processors get a post-initialization callback with the bean instance, which they may manipulate as needed, as an argument.
Bean is used	The bean instance is actually used. That is, it's returned to the caller of `getBean()`, used to set a property on the other bean that triggered its creation as a dependency, and so on. **Important note:** Only singleton beans are tracked past this point, with prototype beans being considered as owned by the client using the bean. As such, the container will orchestrate only the subsequent lifecycle events for singleton beans. Any prototype beans have to be fully managed by the client past this point, including calling any needed destroy method.
Bean destruction begins	As part of the bean factory or application context shutdown process, all cached singleton beans go through a destruction process, consisting of the actions following this one. Note that beans are destroyed in appropriate order related to their dependency relationship, generally the reverse of the initialization order.
Bean post-processors get "destroy" callback with bean	Any bean post-processors implementing the `DestructionAwareBeanPostProcessors` interface get a callback to manipulate the singleton bean for destruction.
`destroy()` called	If a singleton bean implements the `DisposableBean` marker interface, then that interface's `destroy()` method is called to allow the bean to do any needed resource cleanup.
Declared destroy method called	If the bean definition of a singleton bean defines a destroy method via the `destroy-method` attribute, then this method is called to allow the bean to release any resources that need to be released.

Initialization and Destruction Callbacks

The initialization and destroy methods mentioned previously may be used to allow the bean to perform any needed resource allocation or destruction. When trying to use an existing class with uniquely named init or destroy methods, there is not much choice other than to use the `init-method` and `destroy-method` attributes to tell the container to call these methods at the appropriate time, as in the following example, where we need to call `close()` on a DBCP-based `DataSource`:

```
<bean id="dataSource" class="org.apache.commons.dbcp.BasicDataSource" destroy-method="close">
  <property name="driverClassName">
    <value>oracle.jdbc.driver.OracleDriver</value>
  </property>
  <property name="url">
    <value>jdbc:oracle:thin:@db-server:1521:devdb</value>
  </property>
  <property name="username"><value>john</value></property>
  <property name="password"><value>password</value></property>
</bean>
```

Generally, even for new development we recommend the use of the `init-method` and `destroy-method` attributes to tell the container about init methods or destroy methods, as opposed to the other alternative of having the bean implement the Spring-specific interfaces `InitializingBean` and `DisposableBean`, with their corresponding `afterPropertiesSet()` and `destroy()` methods. The latter approach is more convenient as the interfaces are recognized by Spring and the methods are called automatically, but you are at the same time unnecessarily tying your code to the Spring container. If the code is tied to Spring for other reasons, then this is not as much of a concern, and use of the interfaces can make life simpler for the deployer. Spring Framework code intended to be deployed as beans in the container uses the interfaces frequently.

As mentioned, non-singleton, prototype beans are not kept or managed by the container past the point of initialization. As such, it's impossible for Spring to call destroy methods on non-singleton beans, or involve the bean in any container-managed lifecycle actions. Any such methods must be called by user code. Additionally, bean post-processors do not get a chance to manipulate the bean at the destruction stage.

BeanFactoryAware and ApplicationContextAware Callbacks

A bean that wants to be aware of and access its containing bean factory or application context for any sort of programmatic manipulation may implement the `BeanFactoryAware` and `ApplicationContextAware` interfaces, respectively. In the order listed in the lifecycle actions table earlier in the chapter, the container will call into the bean via the `setBeanFactory` and `setApplicationContext()` methods of these interfaces, passing the bean a reference to itself. Generally most application code should not need to know about the container, but this is sometimes useful in Spring-specific code, and these callbacks are used in many of Spring's own classes. One situation when application code may want a reference to the factory is if a singleton bean needs to work with prototype beans. Because the singleton bean has its dependencies injected only once, the dependency injection mechanism would not appear to allow the bean to get new prototype instances as needed. Therefore, accessing the factory directly allows it to do so. However, we feel that Lookup Method Injection, already mentioned, is a better mechanism to handle this use case for most situations because with that solution the class is completely unaware of Spring or the prototype bean name.

Abstracting Access to Services and Resources

While there are a number of more advanced bean factory and application context features we have not yet touched on, at this point we've seen almost all the lower-level building blocks necessary for successful IoC-style programming and deployment. We've seen how application objects can do their work purely with other objects that have been provided to them by the container, working through interfaces or abstract superclasses, and not caring about the actual implementation or source of those objects. You should already know enough to be off and running in typical usage scenarios.

What is probably not very clear is how those other collaborators are actually obtained, when they can be configured and accessed in such a diverse fashion. Let's walk through some examples, to see how Spring lets you avoid some potential complexity and manage things transparently.

Consider a variation of our weather DAO, which instead of working with static data, uses JDBC to access historical data from a database. An initial implementation might use the original JDBC 1.0 `DriverManager` approach to get a connection; shown here is the `find()` method:

```
public WeatherData find(Date date) {
    // note that in the constructor or init method, we have done a
    // Class.forName(driverClassName) to register the JDBC driver
    // The driver, username and password have been configured as
```

```
  // properties of the bean
try {
  Connection con = DriverManager.getConnection(url, username, password);
  // now use the connection
  ...
```

When we deploy this DAO as a bean in a Spring container, we already have some benefits, as we can easily feed in whatever values are needed for the JDBC driver url, username, and password, via Setter or Constructor Injection. However, we're not going to get any connection pooling, either in a standalone or J2EE container environment, and our connection is not going to be able to participate in any J2EE container-managed transactions, which work only through container-managed connections.

The obvious solution is to move to JDBC 2.0 DataSources for obtaining our connections. Once the DAO has a DataSource, it can just ask it for a connection, and not care how that connection is actually provided. The theoretical availability of a DataSource is not really a problem; we know that there are standalone connection pool implementations such as DBCP from Apache Jakarta Commons that can be used in a J2SE or J2EE environment, exposed through the DataSource interface, and that in most J2EE container environments a container-managed connection pool is also available, which will participate in container-managed transactions. These are also exposed as DataSources.

However, trying to move to obtaining connections through the DataSource interface introduces additional complexity because there are different ways to create and obtain a DataSource. A DBCP DataSource is created as a simple JavaBean, which is fed some configuration properties, while in most J2EE container environments, a container-managed DataSource is obtained from JNDI and used, with a code sequence similar to the following:

```
try {
  InitialContext context = new InitialContext();
  DataSource ds = (DataSource) context.lookup("java:comp/env/jdbc/datasource");
  // now use the DataSource
  ...
}
catch (NamingException e) {
  // handle naming exception if resource missing
}
```

Other DataSources might have a completely different creation/access strategy.

Our DAO could perhaps know itself how to create or obtain each type of DataSource, and be configured for which one to use. Because we've been learning Spring and IoC, we know this is not a great idea, as it ties the DAO to the DataSource implementation unnecessarily, makes configuration harder, and makes testing more complicated. The obvious IoC solution is to make the DataSource just be a property of the DAO, which we can inject into the DAO via a Spring container. This works great for the DBCP implementation, which can create the DataSource as a bean and inject it into the DAO:

```
public class JdbcWeatherDaoImpl implements WeatherDAO {

  DataSource dataSource;

  public void setWeatherDao(DataSource dataSource) {
    this.dataSource = dataSource;
  }
```

```
    public WeatherData find(Date date) {
      try {
        Connection con = dataSource.getConnection();
        // now use the connection
        ...
      }
      ...
    }
```

```xml
<bean id="dataSource" class="org.apache.commons.dbcp.BasicDataSource"
      destroy-method="close">
  <property name="driverClassName">
    <value>oracle.jdbc.driver.OracleDriver</value>
  </property>
  <property name="url">
    <value>jdbc:oracle:thin:@db-server:1521:devdb</value>
  </property>
  <property name="username"><value>john</value></property>
  <property name="password"><value>password</value></property>
</bean>

<bean id="weatherDao" class="ch02.sampleX.JdbcWeatherDaoImpl">
  <property name="DataSource">
    <ref bean="dataSource"/>
  </property>
</bean>
```

Now how do we manage to swap out the use of the DBCP `DataSource` with the use of a `DataSource` obtained from JNDI? It would not appear to be that simple, given that we need to set a property of type `DataSource` on the DAO, but need to get this value to come from JNDI; all we know how to do so far in the container configuration is define JavaBean properties as values and references to other beans. In fact, that's still all we have to do, as we leverage a helper class called `JndiObjectFactoryBean`!

```xml
<bean id="dataSource" class="org.springframework.jndi.JndiObjectFactoryBean">
  <property name="jndiName">
    <value>java:comp/env/jdbc/datasource</value>
  </property>
</bean>

<bean id="weatherDao" class="ch02.sampleX.JdbcWeatherDaoImpl">
  <property name="DataSource">
    <ref bean="dataSource"/>
  </property>
</bean>
```

Examining Factory Beans

`JndiObjectFactoryBean` is an example of a *Factory Bean*. A Spring factory bean is based on a very simple concept: Essentially it's just a bean that on demand produces another object. All factory beans implement the special `org.springframework.beans.factory.FactoryBean` interface. The "magic" really happens because a level of indirection is introduced. A factory bean is itself just a normal JavaBean. When you deploy a factory bean, as with any JavaBean, you specify properties and constructor arguments needed for it to do its work. However, when another bean in the container refers to the factory bean, via a `<ref>` element, or when a manual request is made for the factory bean via `getBean()`, the container does not return the factory bean itself; it recognizes that it is dealing with the factory bean (via the marker interface), and it returns the output of the factory bean. So for all intents and purposes, each factory bean can, in terms of being used to satisfy dependencies, be considered to *be* the object it actually produces. In the case of `JndiObjectFactoryBean`, for example, this is the result of a JNDI lookup, specifically a `DataSource` object in our example.

The `FactoryBean` interface is very simple:

```
public interface FactoryBean {

    Object getObject() throws Exception;

    Class getObjectType();

    boolean isSingleton();

}
```

The `getObject()` method is called by the container to obtain the output object. The `isSingleton()` flag indicates if the same object instance or a different one will be returned on each invocation. Finally, the `getObjectType()` method indicates the type of the returned object, or null if it is not known. While factory beans are normally configured and deployed in the container, they are just JavaBeans, so they are usable programmatically if desired.

> **This raises the question of how a deployed factory bean may be obtained via a** `getBean()` **call, if asking for a factory bean actually returns its output. This is possible using an "escaping" mechanism to tell the container that you want the factory bean, and not its output. This is to prepend an** `&` **to the bean ID, as follows:**
>
> ```
> FactoryBean facBean = (FactoryBean) appContext.getBean
> ("&dataSource");
> ```

It's easy to create your own factory beans. However, Spring includes a number of useful factory bean implementations that cover most of the common resource and service access abstractions that benefit from being handled in this manner. Just a partial list of these includes:

❑ `JndiObjectFactoryBean`: Returns an object that is the result of a JNDI lookup.

❑ `ProxyFactoryBean`: Wraps an existing object in a proxy and returns it. What the proxy actually does is configured by the user, and can include interception to modify object behavior, the performance of security checks, and so on. The usage of this factory bean will be described in much more detail in the chapter on Spring AOP.

❑ `TransactionProxyFactoryBean`: A specialization of the `ProxyFactoryBean` that wraps an object with a transactional proxy.

❑ `RmiProxyFactoryBean`: Creates a proxy for accessing a remote object transparently via RMI. `HttpInvokerProxyFactoryBean`, `JaxRpcPortProxyFactoryBean`, `HessianProxyFactoryBean`, and `BurlapProxyFactoryBean` produce similar proxies for remote object access over HTTP, JAX-RPC, Hessian, and Burlap protocols, respectively. In all cases, clients are unaware of the proxy and deal only with the business interface.

- ❑ `LocalSessionFactoryBean`: Configures and returns a Hibernate `SessionFactory` object. Similar classes exist for JDO and iBatis resource managers.

- ❑ `LocalStatelessSessionProxyFactoryBean` **and** `SimpleRemoteStatelessSessionProxyFactoryBean`: Create a proxy object used for accessing local or remote stateless Session Beans, respectively. The client just uses the business interface, without worrying about JNDI access or EJB interfaces.

- ❑ `MethodInvokingFactoryBean`: Returns the result of a method invocation on another bean. `FieldRetrievingFactoryBean` returns the value of a field in another bean.

- ❑ A number of JMS-related factory beans return JMS resources.

Key Points and the Net Effect

In previous sections, we saw how easy it is to hook up objects in an IoC fashion. However, before getting to the stage of wiring up objects to each other, they do have to be able to be created or obtained first. For some potential collaborators, even if once obtained and configured they are ultimately accessed via a standard interface, the fact that they are normally created or obtained through complicated or non-standard mechanisms creates an impediment to even getting the objects in the first place. Factory beans can eliminate this impediment. Past the initial object creation and wiring stage, the products of factory beans, as embodied in proxies and similar wrapper objects, can serve in an adapter role, helping in the act of abstracting actual resource and service usage, and making dissimilar services available through similar interfaces.

As you saw, without the client (`weatherDao`) being at all aware of it or having to be modified, we swapped out the original DBCP-based `DataSource`, created as a local bean, to a `DataSource` that came from JNDI. Ultimately, IoC enabled this swapping, but it was necessary to move resource access out of the application code, so that it could be handled by IoC.

> We hope that one of the main things this will impress upon you is that when you can easily abstract service and resource access like this, and switch from one mechanism to the other at will, there is really no reason to use deployment scenarios and technologies that don't make sense at the particular time you put them into effect. In any case, the client should be agnostic to the actual deployment and implementation scenario.

If you can transparently (to the client) access remote services via RMI, RPC over HTTP, or EJBs, why should you not deploy the solution that makes the most sense, and why would you couple the client to one implementation over another when you don't have to? J2EE has traditionally pushed the idea of exposing some resources such as `DataSources`, JMS resources, JavaMail interfaces, and so on via JNDI. Even if it makes sense for the resources to be exposed there, it never makes sense for the client to do direct JNDI access. Abstracting via something like `JndiObjectFactoryBean` means that you can later switch to an environment without JNDI, simply by changing your bean factory config instead of client code. Even when you do not need to change the deployment environment or implementation technology in production, these abstractions make unit and integration testing much easier, as they enable you to employ different configurations for deployment and test scenarios. This will be shown in more detail in the next chapter. It is also worth pointing out that using `JndiObjectFactoryBean` has removed the need for some non-trivial code in the DAO—JNDI lookup—that has nothing to do with the DAO's business function. This demonstrates the de-cluttering effect of dependency injection.

Reusing Bean Definitions

Considering the amount of Java code related to configuration and object wiring that they replace, XML bean definitions are actually fairly compact. However, sometimes you will need to specify a number of bean definitions that are quite similar to each other.

Consider our `WeatherService`:

```
<bean id="weatherService" class="ch02.sample2.WeatherServiceImpl">
  <property name="weatherDao">
    <ref local="weatherDao"/>
  </property>
</bean>
```

In a typical application scenario where the backend is a database, we need to use service objects like this transactionally. As you will learn in detail in Chapter 6, "Transaction and DataSource Management," one of the easiest ways to accomplish this is to declaratively wrap the object so that it becomes transactional, with a Spring factory bean called `TransactionProxyFactoryBean`:

```
<bean id="weatherServiceTarget" class="ch02.sample2.WeatherServiceImpl">
  <property name="weatherDao">
    <ref local="weatherDao"/>
  </property>
</bean>

<!-- transactional proxy -->
<bean id="weatherService"
  class="org.springframework.transaction.interceptor.TransactionProxyFactoryBean">

  <property name="target"><ref local="weatherServiceTarget"/></property>

  <property name="transactionManager"><ref local="transactionManager"/></property>
  <property name="transactionAttributes">
    <props>
      <prop key="*">PROPAGATION_REQUIRED</prop>
    </props>
  </property>
</bean>
```

Don't worry for now about the exact details of how `TransactionProxyFactoryBean` is configured or how it actually does its work. What is important to know is that it's a `FactoryBean` that, given a target bean as input, produces as its output a transactional proxy object, implementing the same interfaces as the target bean, but now with transactional usage semantics. Because we want clients to use the wrapped object, the original unwrapped (non-transactional) bean has been renamed to `weatherServiceTarget`, and the proxy now has the name `weatherService`. Any existing clients using the weather service are unaware that they are now dealing with a transactional service.

Being able to wrap objects declaratively like this is very convenient (especially compared to the alternative of doing it programmatically at the code level), but in a large application with dozens or hundreds of service interfaces that need to be wrapped in an almost similar fashion, it seems somewhat wasteful to have so much essentially identical, boilerplate XML. In fact, the container's ability to allow both *parent* and *child* bean definitions is meant exactly for this sort of situation. Taking advantage of this, we can now use the approach of having an abstract parent, or *template*, transaction proxy definition:

```
<bean id="txProxyTemplate" abstract="true"
  class="org.springframework.transaction.interceptor.TransactionProxyFactoryBean">
  <property name="transactionManager">
    <ref local="transactionManager"/></ref>
  </property>
  <property name="transactionAttributes">
    <props>
      <prop key="*">PROPAGATION_REQUIRED</prop>
    </props>
  </property>
</bean>
```

Then we create each real proxy as a child definition that has only to specify properties that are different from the parent template:

```
<bean id="weatherServiceTarget" class="ch02.sample2.WeatherServiceImpl">
  <property name="weatherDao">
    <ref local="weatherDao"/>
  </property>
</bean>
```

```
<bean id="weatherService" parent="txProxyTemplate">
  <property name="target"><ref local="weatherServiceTarget"/></ref></property>
</bean>
```

In fact, it's possible to get an even cleaner and somewhat more compact form. Because no client will ever need to use the unwrapped weather service bean, it can be defined as an inner bean of the wrapping proxy:

```
<bean id="weatherService" parent="txProxyTemplate">
  <property name="target">
    <bean class="ch02.sample2.WeatherServiceImpl">
      <property name="weatherDao">
        <ref local="weatherDao"/>
      </property>
    </bean>
  </property>
</bean>
```

Another service that needs to be wrapped can just use a bean definition that derives from the parent template in a similar fashion. In the following example, the `transactionAttributes` property from the parent template is also overridden, in order to add transaction propagation settings that are specific to this particular proxy:

```
<bean id="anotherWeatherService" parent="txProxyTemplate">
  <property name="target">
    <bean class="ch02.sampleX.AnotherWeatherServiceImpl">
    </bean>
  </property>
```

```
<property name="transactionAttributes">
  <props>
    <prop key="save*">PROPAGATION_REQUIRED </prop>
    <prop key="*">PROPAGATION_REQUIRED,readOnly</prop>
  </props>
</property>
</bean>
```

> AOP "autoproxying" can provide an even simpler way of capturing commonality between AOP advice on different bean definitions. See Chapter 4, "Spring and AOP," for more information.

Child Bean Definition Specifics

A child bean definition inherits property values and constructor arguments defined in a parent bean definition. It also inherits a number of the optional attributes from the parent definition (if actually specified in the parent). As seen in the previous example, the `parent` attribute in the child bean definition is used to point to the parent.

The child bean definition may specify a class, or leave it unset to inherit the value from the parent. If the child definition does specify a class (that is different from the parent), the class must still be able to accept any constructor arguments or properties specified in the parent definition because they will be inherited and used.

From the parent, child definitions inherit any constructor argument values, property values, and method overrides, but may add new values as needed. On the other hand, any `init-method`, `destroy-method`, or `factory-method` values from the parent are inherited, but completely overridden by corresponding values in the child.

Some bean configuration settings are never inherited, but will *always* be taken from the child definition. These are: `depends-on`, `autowire`, `dependency-check`, `singleton`, and `lazy-init`.

Beans marked as abstract using the `abstract` attribute (as used in our example) may not themselves be instantiated. Unless there is a need to instantiate a parent bean, you should almost always specifically mark it as abstract. This is a good practice because a non-abstract parent bean, even if you do not specifically ask the container for it or refer to it as a dependency, may possibly still be instantiated by the container. Application contexts (but not bean factories) will by default try to pre-instantiate non-abstract singleton beans.

> Note also that even without an explicit `abstract` attribute, bean definitions can be considered implicitly abstract if they do not specify a class or factory-method because there is not enough information to be able to instantiate them. Any attempt to instantiate an (explicitly or implicitly) abstract bean will result in an error.

Using Post-Processors to Handle Customized Beans and Containers

Bean *post-processors* are special *listeners,* which you may register (either explicitly or implicitly) with the container, that receive a callback from the container for each bean that is instantiated. Bean factory post-processors are similar listeners that receive a callback from the container when the *container* has been instantiated. You will periodically come across a need to customize a bean, a group of beans, or the entire container configuration, which you will find is handled most easily by creating a post-processor, or using one of the number of existing post-processors included with Spring.

Bean Post-Processors

Bean post-processors implement the `BeanPostProcessor` interface:

```
public interface BeanPostProcessor {
  Object postProcessBeforeInitialization(Object bean, String beanName)
    throws BeansException;
  Object postProcessAfterInitialization(Object bean, String beanName)
    throws BeansException;
}
```

The `DestructionAwareBeanPostProcessor` extends this interface:

```
public interface DestructionAwareBeanPostProcessor extends BeanPostProcessor {
  void postProcessBeforeDestruction(Object bean, String name)
    throws BeansException;
}
```

The bean lifecycle table shown previously listed at which points in the bean lifecycle each of these callbacks occurs. Let's create a bean post-processor that uses the `postProcessAfterInitialization` callback to list to the console every bean that has been initialized in the container.

```
public class BeanInitializationLogger implements BeanPostProcessor {

  public Object postProcessBeforeInitialization(Object bean, String beanName)
    throws BeansException {
    return bean;
  }

  public Object postProcessAfterInitialization(Object bean, String beanName)
    throws BeansException {

    System.out.println("Bean '" + beanName + "' initialized");
    return bean;
  }
}
```

This example doesn't do very much; a real-life post-processor would probably manipulate the actual bean instance, and would write to a log file, not the console.

> In an application context, bean post-processors are automatically recognized and
> used by the container, when deployed like any other bean:
>
> ```xml
> <beans>
>   <bean id="weatherService"
> class="ch02.sample2.WeatherServiceImpl">
>     <property name="weatherDao">
>       <ref local="weatherDao"/>
>     </property>
>   </bean>
>   <bean id="weatherDao"
> class="ch02.sample2.StaticDataWeatherDaoImpl"/>
>   <bean id="beanInitLogger"
> class="ch02.sample8.BeanInitializationLogger"/>
> </beans>
> ```

When the context specified by this configuration is loaded, the post-processor gets two callbacks and
produces the following output:

```
Bean 'weatherDao' initialized
Bean 'weatherService' initialized
```

Using bean post-processors with a simple bean factory is slightly more complicated because they must
be manually registered with the factory (in the spirit of the bean factory's more programmatic usage
approach) instead of just being added as a bean in the XML config itself:

```
XmlBeanFactory factory = new XmlBeanFactory(
        new ClassPathResource("ch03/sample8/beans.xml"));
BeanInitializationLogger logger = new BeanInitializationLogger();
factory.addBeanPostProcessor(logger);
// our beans are singletons, so will be pre-instantiated, at
// which time the post-processor will get callbacks for them too
factory.preInstantiateSingletons();
```

As you can see, `BeanFactory.preInstantiateSingletons()` is called to pre-instantiate the singleton
beans in the factory because only application contexts pre-instantiate singletons by default. In any case,
the post-processor is called when the bean is actually instantiated, whether as part of pre-instantiation,
or when the bean is actually requested, if pre-instantiation is skipped.

Bean Factory Post-Processors

Bean factory post-processors implement the `BeanFactoryPostProcessor` interface:

```java
public interface BeanFactoryPostProcessor {
  void postProcessBeanFactory(ConfigurableListableBeanFactory beanFactory)
        throws BeansException;
}
```

Here's an example bean factory post-processor that simply gets a list of all the bean names in the factory
and prints them out:

```
public class AllBeansLister implements BeanFactoryPostProcessor {

  public void postProcessBeanFactory(ConfigurableListableBeanFactory factory)
      throws BeansException {

    System.out.println("The factory contains the followig beans:");
    String[] beanNames = factory.getBeanDefinitionNames();
    for (int i = 0; i < beanNames.length; ++i)
      System.out.println(beanNames[i]);
  }
}
```

Using bean factory post-processors is relatively similar to using bean post-processors. In an application context, they simply need to be deployed like any other bean, and will be automatically recognized and used by the context. With a simple bean factory on the other hand, they need to be manually executed against the factory:

```
XmlBeanFactory factory = new XmlBeanFactory(
        new ClassPathResource("ch03/sample8/beans.xml"));
AllBeansLister lister = new AllBeansLister();
lister.postProcessBeanFactory(factory);
```

Let's now examine some useful bean post-processors and bean factory post-processors that come with Spring.

PropertyPlaceholderConfigurer

Often when deploying a Spring-based application, most items in a container configuration are not meant to be modified at deployment time. Making somebody go into a complex configuration and change a few values that *do* need to be customized can be inconvenient. It can also potentially be dangerous because somebody may make a mistake and invalidate the configuration by accidentally modifying some unrelated values.

PropertyPlaceholderConfigurer is a bean factory post-processor that when used in a bean factory or application context definition allows you to specify some values via special *placeholder* strings, and have those placeholders be replaced by real values from an external file in Java Properties format. Additionally, the configurer will by default also check against the Java System properties if there is no match for the placeholder string in the external file. The systemPropertiesMode property of the configurer allows turning off the fallback, or making the System Properties have precedence.

One example of values that would be nice to externalize are configuration strings for a database connection pool. Here's our previous DBCP-based DataSource definition, now using placeholders for the actual values:

```
<bean id="dataSource" class="org.apache.commons.dbcp.BasicDataSource" destroy-
method="close">
  <property name="driverClassName"><value>${db.driverClassName}</value></property>
  <property name="url"><value>${db.url}</value></property>
  <property name="username"><value>${db.username}</value></property>
  <property name="password"><value>${db.password}</value></property>
</bean>
```

The real values now come from an external file in Properties format: `jdbc.properties`.

```
db.driverClassName=oracle.jdbc.driver.OracleDriver
db.url=jdbc:oracle:thin:@db-server:1521:devdb
db.username=john
db.password=password
```

To use a `PropertyPlaceholderConfigurer` instance to pull in the proper values in an application context, the configurer is simply deployed like any other bean:

```
<bean id="placeholderConfig"

class="org.springframework.beans.factory.config.PropertyPlaceholderConfigurer">
    <property name="location"><value>jdbc.properties</value></property>
</bean>
```

To use it with a simple bean factory, it must be manually executed:

```
    XmlBeanFactory factory = new XmlBeanFactory(
            new ClassPathResource("beans.xml"));
PropertyPlaceholderConfigurer ppc = new PropertyPlaceholderConfigurer();
ppc.setLocation(new FileSystemResource("db.properties"));
ppc.postProcessBeanFactory(factory);
```

PropertyOverrideConfigurer

`PropertyOverrideConfigurer`, a bean factory post-processor, is somewhat similar to `PropertyPlaceholderConfigurer`, but where for the latter, values *must* come from an external Properties files, `PropertyOverrideConfigurer` allows values from the external Properties to *override* bean property values in the bean factory or application context.

Each line in the Properties file must be in the format:

```
beanName.property=value
```

Where `beanName` is the ID of a bean in the container, and `property` is one of its properties. An example Properties file could look like this:

```
dataSource.driverClassName=oracle.jdbc.driver.OracleDriver
dataSource.url=jdbc:oracle:thin:@db-server:1521:devdb
dataSource.username=john
dataSource.password=password
```

This would override four properties in the bean "dataSource." Any properties (of any bean) in the container, not overridden by a value in the Properties file, will simply remain at whatever value the container config specifies for it, or the default value for that bean if the container config does not set it either. Because just looking at the container config will not give you an indication that a value is going to be overridden, without also seeing the Properties file, this functionality should be used with some care.

CustomEditorConfigurer

`CustomEditorConfigurer` is a bean factory post-processor, which allows you to register custom JavaBeans `PropertyEditors` as needed to convert values in String form to the final property or constructor argument values in a specific complex object format.

Creating a Custom PropertyEditor

One particular reason you might need to use a custom `PropertyEditor` is to be able to set properties of type `java.util.Date`, as specified in string form. Because date formats are very much locale sensitive, use of a `PropertyEditor`, which expects a specific source string format, is the easiest way to handle this need. Because this is a very concrete problem that users are likely to have, rather than present some abstract example we're just going to examine how Spring's own existing `CustomDateEditor`, a `PropertyEditor` for Dates, is coded and how you may register and use it. Your own custom `PropertyEditors` would be implemented and registered in similar fashion:

```java
public class CustomDateEditor extends PropertyEditorSupport {

    private final DateFormat dateFormat;
    private final boolean allowEmpty;

    public CustomDateEditor(DateFormat dateFormat, boolean allowEmpty) {
        this.dateFormat = dateFormat;
        this.allowEmpty = allowEmpty;
    }

    public void setAsText(String text) throws IllegalArgumentException {
        if (this.allowEmpty && !StringUtils.hasText(text)) {
            // treat empty String as null value
            setValue(null);
        }
        else {
            try {
                setValue(this.dateFormat.parse(text));
            }
            catch (ParseException ex) {
                throw new IllegalArgumentException("Could not parse date: " +
                        ex.getMessage());
            }
        }
    }

    public String getAsText() {
        return (getValue() == null ? "" : this.dateFormat.format((Date) getValue()));
    }
}
```

For full JavaDocs for this class, please see the Spring distribution. Essentially though, to implement your own `PropertyEditor`, the easiest way is, as this code does, to start by inheriting from the `java.beans.PropertyEditorSupport` convenience base class that is part of the standard Java library. This implements most of the property editor machinery other than the actual `setAsText()` and `getAsText()` methods, the standard implementations of which you must normally override. Note that `PropertyEditors` have state, so they are not normally threadsafe, but Spring does ensure that they are used in a threadsafe fashion by synchronizing the entire sequence of method calls needed to perform a conversion.

`CustomDateEditor` uses any implementation of the `java.text.DateFormat` interface to do the actual conversion, passed in as a constructor argument. When you deploy it, you can use a `java.text.SimpleDateFormat` for this purpose. It can also be configured to treat empty strings as null values, or an error.

Registering and Using the Custom PropertyEditor

Now let's look at an application context definition in which CustomEditorConfigurer is used to register CustomDateEditor as a PropertyEditor to be used for converting strings to java.util.Date objects. A specific date format string is provided:

```
<bean id="customEditorConfigurer"
      class="org.springframework.beans.factory.config.CustomEditorConfigurer">
   <property name="customEditors">
     <map>

       <-- register property editor for java.util.Date -->
       <entry key="java.util.Date">
         <bean class="org.springframework.beans.propertyeditors.CustomDateEditor">
           <constructor-arg index="0">
             <bean class="java.text.SimpleDateFormat">
               <constructor-arg><value>M/d/yy</value></constructor-arg>
             </bean>
           </constructor-arg>
           <constructor-arg index="1"><value>true</value></constructor-arg>
         </bean>
       </entry>

     </map>
   </property>
</bean>

<-- try out the date editor by setting two Date properties as strings -->
<bean id="testBean" class="ch02.sample9.StartEndDatesBean">
   <property name="startDate"><value>10/09/1968</value></property>
   <property name="endDate"><value>10/26/2004</value></property>
</bean>
```

The CustomEditorConfigurer can register one or more custom PropertyEditors, with this sample registering only one. Your own custom PropertyEditors for other types might not need any special configuration. CustomDateEditor, which has a couple of constructor arguments in this sample, took a SimpleDateFormat with a date format string as the first, and a Boolean indicating that empty strings should produce null values, as the second.

The example also showed how a test bean called "testBean" had two properties of type Date set via string values, to try out the custom property editor.

BeanNameAutoProxyCreator

BeanNameAutoProxyCreator is a bean post-processor. The AOP chapter will talk in more detail about how it's used, but it's worth knowing that it exists. Essentially, given a list of bean names, BeanNameAutoProxyCreator is able to wrap beans that match those names in the factory, as they are instantiated, with proxy objects that intercept access to those original beans, or modify their behavior.

DefaultAdvisorAutoProxyCreator

This bean post-processor is similar to BeanNameAutoProxyCreator, but finds beans to wrap, along with the information on how to wrap them (the Advice), in a more generic fashion. Again, it's worth reading about it in the AOP chapter.

Summary

This chapter has given you a good feel for what the terms *Inversion of Control* and *Dependency Injection* really mean, and how they are embodied in Spring's bean factories and application contexts. We've examined and used most of Spring's fundamental container functionality. It's upon the IoC container as a foundation that the rest of Spring builds, and good knowledge of how it works and is configured, along with all of its capabilities, is the key to effectively utilizing all of Spring.

You have seen how:

❑ Using the container allows the use of one consistent, predictable mechanism to access, configure, and wire together objects, instead of using programmatic or ad hoc mechanisms that couple
classes to each other and make testing harder. Generally, application or class-specific custom
factories and singletons can be completely avoided.

❑ The container encourages and makes easy the generally desirable practice of separating interface and implementation in application code.

❑ Post-processors add the ability to customize bean and container behavior in a flexible, externalized fashion.

❑ IoC principles, combined with the factory bean, afford a powerful means to abstract the act of
obtaining or accessing services and resources.

❑ IoC and the container provide a powerful base upon which Spring and application code can
build higher value-adding functionality, without generally being tied to the container.

The next chapter looks at some more advanced capabilities of the application context, and will offer some advanced usage scenarios of the container in general.

3

Advanced Container Concepts

In the previous chapter, we focused on the core functionality of the Spring bean factory and application context, as well as the concepts of *Inversion of Control* and *Dependency Injection* that they are based on. You now know how to configure, initialize, and use a Spring container well enough to handle a number of development use cases and scenarios.

In this chapter we are going to examine some additional, more advanced container capabilities. We are also going to discuss a number of advanced container configuration and usage strategies. A good understanding of most of the content of this chapter is a key to using the Spring container in the most efficient and effective way possible.

This chapter examines:

- ❑   Spring's `Resource` abstraction for accessing low-level resources
- ❑   How the application context can act as a source for localized messages
- ❑   The simple eventing mechanism supported by the application context
- ❑   A number of tips and strategies for creating and managing the container
- ❑   Some handy factory beans that make it much easier to handle some configuration requirements
- ❑   Strategies for handling testing concerns
- ❑   Alternatives to XML as the definition format for container configurations, including definitions in Properties format and programmatic definitions

Abstractions for Low-Level Resources

Spring contains a useful abstraction for describing various types of simple resources, as found on the filesystem or classpath, or accessed via a URL. This is the `Resource` interface, with a number of actual implementations available:

```
public interface Resource extends InputStreamSource {

  boolean exists();

  boolean isOpen();

  URL getURL() throws IOException;

  File getFile() throws IOException;

  Resource createRelative(String relativePath) throws IOException;

  String getFilename();

  String getDescription();
}
```

```
public interface InputStreamSource {

  InputStream getInputStream() throws IOException;
}
```

Given a `Resource`, you may obtain an `InputStream` from it, see if it actually exists, try to get a `URL` or `File` handle from it, and do some name-related operations. It may not be obvious why this interface is really needed, with a normal `java.net.URL` potentially being directly used instead. You may in fact think of a `Resource` as a somewhat more capable version of a URL, able to handle extra types of resources that a URL cannot uniquely describe (such as those on a classpath, or those relative to a `ServletContext`), with methods that behave appropriately for the actual resource type. For example, for a `ClasspathResource`, `getInputStream()` will ask a `ClassLoader` for the stream; for a `FilesystemResource`, the underlying `File` will produce the stream; and for a `UrlResource`, the underlying `URL` will open the stream.

The Application Context as a ResourceLoader

Every application context implements the `ResourceLoader` interface:

```
public interface ResourceLoader {
  Resource getResource(String location);
}
```

There's not very much to it, obviously. You can ask the `ResourceLoader` (the context in this case) for a resource as a String location and get back an object implementing the `Resource` interface. What is interesting (and useful) though is that the actual type of `Resource` you get back will depend on a combination of an optional *prefix* that the location string has, and the actual type of application context. If you ask for a location starting with a normal URL prefix (for a URL type known to the Java Virtual Machine, or JVM):

```
Resource mailMessage = ctx.getResource("file:/data/emails/error.email");
```

```
Resource mailMessage = ctx.getResource("http://mydomain.com/emails/error.email");
```

you will get back an instance of `UrlResource`, a `Resource` type backed by a real URL, which will be used for actual operations such as obtaining a stream. If the location string has the special Spring-recognized `classpath:` prefix:

```
Resource mailMessage = ctx.getResource("classpath:error.email");
```

you will get back an instance of `ClasspathResource`, a `Resource` that accesses resources from a classpath, in this case the classpath associated with the `ClassLoader` of the application context. Finally, if the location string has no prefix, as shown here,

```
Resource mailMessage = ctx.getResource("data/emails/error.email");
```

the actual `Resource` implementation returned is dependent on the actual application context implementation being used (and is appropriate to that context). From a `ClasspathXmlApplicationContext`, the location would be interpreted as a classpath location, and you would get back a `ClasspathResource`. From a `FilesystemXmlApplicationContext`, the location would be interpreted as a relative filesystem location, and you would get back a `FilesystemResource`. From an `XmlWebApplicationContext`, the location would be interpreted as being relative to the web-app root, and you would get back a `ServletContextResource`.

> *As an aside, note that depending on the servlet engine implementation, the actual physical resource file for the latter could be on the filesystem, in a packed WAR file, or conceivably even in a database, but handling is transparent.*

A bean that wants to use the application context as a resource loader can just implement the `ResourceLoaderAware` interface, and will automatically be called back by the application context at initialization time with a reference to the application context as the `ResourceLoader`. In this example, an HTML page generator class obtains `Resources` to use as headers and footers for the page:

```java
public class HtmlPageGenerator implements ResourceLoaderAware {

  private ResourceLoader resourceLoader;
  private String headerLocation;
  private String footerLocation;
  private Resource header;
  private Resource footer;

  public void setResourceLoader(ResourceLoader resourceLoader) {
    this.resourceLoader = resourceLoader;
    // properties are set before this callback so are safe to use
    header = resourceLoader.getResource(headerLocation);
    footer = resourceLoader.getResource(footerLocation);
  }
  public void setHeaderLocation(String headerLocation) {
```

```
      this.headerLocation = headerLocation;
    }
    public void setFooterLocation(String footerLocation) {
      this.footerLocation = footerLocation;
    }

    public String generate(String bodyData) {
      //
    }
  }
}
```

Of course, because `ApplicationContext` is a sub-interface of `ResourceLoader`, an application class that already has an instance of the context (which it got by implementing `ApplicationContextAware`, or by any other means) can just use the context as a `ResourceLoader` directly. However, for a new class that needs to do resource loading but doesn't need to programmatically manipulate the context in other ways, it's cleaner to implement `ResourceLoaderAware` rather than `ApplicationContextAware`, as the former is the more specific interface. Among other benefits, this looser coupling makes it easier to mock for testing.

When the `Resources` to be loaded are going to be dynamically selected at runtime (consider for example an emailing service object, which loads email templates as `Resources`), then using the context as a `ResourceLoader` is convenient. However, if there are only a few `Resources` and their locations are known from the beginning, it would be nice to get rid of the dependency on `ResourceLoader` or `ApplicationContext`, as well as reduce the amount of code, by just being able to set the `Resources` directly as properties.

In fact, this is quite possible, and happens transparently, as demonstrated in this variant of the page generator and an application context configuration that populates an instance of it:

```
public class HtmlPageGenerator {

  private Resource header;
  private Resource footer;

  public void setFooter(Resource footer) {
    this.footer = footer;
  }
  public void setHeader(Resource header) {
    this.header = header;
  }

  public String wrapPage(String pageData) {
    return null; //
  }
}
```

```
<bean id="pageGenerator" class="ch04.sampleX.HtmlPageGenerator">
  <property name="header">
    <value>webcontent/templates/footer.txt</value>
  </property>
  <property name="footer">
    <value>webcontent/templates/footer.txt</value>
  </property>
</bean>
```

You are able to specify properties of type `Resource` as string values because the application context automatically self-registers a JavaBean `PropertyEditor` called `ResourceEditor`. The application context itself is set as the `ResourceLoader` to be used by this property editor to produce the output `Resource` objects from the input string locations. The net effect is exactly the same as would be obtained by manually calling `getResource()` on the context with the same location strings.

This ability to directly set `Resource` properties on a bean as text string values when wiring the bean in an application context, along with the general flexibility and usefulness of the `Resource` abstraction, makes it very convenient to use the `Resource` type for all general references to low-level resources in application code.

While using the `Resource` interface and implementations is indeed coupling the application code to a Spring interface, keep in mind that this is not coupling it to the container in any way, just to a very small set of utility classes in Spring, which can be easily separated from the rest of the Spring library if there is a need, and put in its own JAR.

The Application Context as a Message Source

Applications often need to obtain string-form messages, as defined in an external file. These are typically used for UI elements and logging, and often the ability to handle internationalization concerns, with resolution of messages appropriate to a specific locale, is a necessity.

In Spring, the `MessageSource` interface, which is implemented by all application contexts, exists to serve this need:

```
public interface MessageSource {
   String getMessage(String code, Object[] args, String defaultMessage,
                     Locale locale);
   String getMessage(String code, Object[] args, Locale locale)
         throws NoSuchMessageException;
   String getMessage(MessageSourceResolvable resolvable, Locale locale)
         throws NoSuchMessageException;
}
```

When requesting a message via the first two `getMessage()` variants, the message to retrieve is identified by a string code, along with a locale. If the message is not found, the default supplied is returned (first variant) or an exception is thrown (second variant). In standard Java `java.text.MessageFormat` fashion (please see the JavaDocs for the latter class for more info), the message string that is resolved from the code may have placeholders in the {n} format, which get replaced with values supplied by the client requesting the message, before the message is returned. Following is an example where a default string is supplied:

```
String msg = messageSource.getMessage("error.duplicate.username",
      new Object[] {username},
      "Invalid username, as it already exists: {0}", locale);
```

The third `getMessage()` variant() simply passes in the message code, array of arguments, and default message string as an object implementing the `MessageSourceResolvable` interface. This variant is mostly used in concert with other parts of Spring. For example, the validation portion of the framework will return a `FieldError` class that implements this interface to describe a validation error. You can then pass this `FieldError` instance directly to `getMessage()` to get an appropriate error message.

A bean that wishes to use the application context as a message source may implement the `MessageSourceAware` interface, as shown here:

```
public interface MessageSourceAware {
   void setMessageSource(MessageSource messageSource);
}
```

Then, the bean will automatically be called back by the application context at initialization time with a reference to the application context as the `MessageSource`. Of course, because `ApplicationContext` is a sub-interface of `MessageSource`, an application class that already has an instance of the context (which it got by implementing `ApplicationContextAware`, or by any other means) can just use the context as a `MessageSource` directly. However, for a new class that needs to load messages, but doesn't need to programmatically manipulate the context in other ways, it's cleaner to implement `MessageSource Aware` rather than `ApplicationContextAware`, as the former is the more specific interface. Among other benefits, this makes it easier to mock for testing.

The actual implementation of `MessageSource` functionality is pluggable, as the context just delegates `MessageSource` method calls to an internal provider. Configuration of this provider is very simple; the context on startup will look for an application-deployed bean within it, which must have the special name `messageSource` and must implement the `MessageSource` interface, and will treat this bean as the `MessageSource` provider:

```
<bean id="messageSource"
      class="org.springframework.context.support.ResourceBundleMessageSource">
   <property name="basename"><value>applicationResources</value></property>
</bean>
```

Note that `MessageSources` can be hierarchical. A message source in an application context that is the child of another context will be the child of the message source in the parent context. When the message source cannot resolve a message code, it will ask its parent, which will ask its parent on failure, and so on. Because it sometimes makes sense to split up contexts into a hierarchy, this feature allows messages to be associated with their related context, but still be resolved by a request from a child. Note that this also means a message resolved in a child will override any message resolved from the same code in a parent. A child context does not have to actually define a message source for delegation to happen to a parent.

One implementation of `MessageSource`, which is included with Spring, is `ResourceBundleMessageSource`, shown in the preceding example. This is essentially a wrapper around a normal `java.util.ResourceBundle`. The `basename` property specifies the base name of the bundle. Please see the `ResourceBundle` JavaDoc for full details for how resource bundles work, but the bundle will normally look for messages in Properties files with names that are variations of the specified base name depending on the locale; for example, for the base name in the example, an optional `applicationResources_en.properties` would match an English locale, `applicationResources_fr.properties` a French one, and so on. The bundle would fall back to `applicationResources.properties` as a default, so at a minimum the latter file would have to exist. Instead of using the `basename` property, the `basenames` property may be used to specify multiple base names. In this case, message resolution happens against multiple resource bundles, in a sequential fashion. This allows, for example, message files to be split up by functionality.

Resource bundles are normally cached permanently by the resource bundle handling code in Java. Especially while doing development, it's sometimes desirable to be able to pick up changes to the underlying message Properties files without restarting the application. For this reason, an alternative message source implementation exists, `ReloadableResourceBundleMessageSource`. This message source works in a similar fashion to `ResourceBundleMessageSource`, but can be configured to cache values for a specific period of time, instead of permanently like the latter. Additionally, it allows more flexible resolution of message Properties files, not just from the classpath. The JavaDocs for this class should be consulted for more information.

A note on deploying and accessing the message source: As mentioned, the message source is just another bean in the context, deployed under the special name `messageSource`. If you do not wish to tie application code to the `MessageSourceAware` interface, there is nothing stopping you from just setting the message source as another property of your application bean(s), with the value being a reference to the `messageSource` bean. Unless you use autowiring for the message source property (which makes sense since there should only ever be one message source), this is more verbose because you'll have to explicitly do this for any bean that needs it, but has no other disadvantages. All message source functionality will still work, including participation in any hierarchy with message sources in parent contexts.

Users interested in exploiting message sources should also look at the `MessageSourceAccessor` class, which can make working with message sources a bit simpler in terms of default locale handling. See the related JavaDoc for more info.

Application Events

Spring application contexts support a simple form of event publishing and subscription. Spring-specific and application-specific events may be broadcast to any interested beans. This functionality is essentially an implementation of the well-known *Observer* pattern. While simple is the operative word (the eventing mechanism is certainly not meant to be a competitor to the likes of JMS), this functionality is still useful for a number of use cases.

All events to be published and received with the event framework must extend the `ApplicationEvent` class, which is itself a subclass of the standard `java.util.EventObject` class. In order to automatically receive events, a bean must simply implement the `ApplicationListener` interface and be deployed into the application context. It will be recognized by the context, and receive all events that are published through the context:

```
public interface ApplicationListener extends EventListener {
  void onApplicationEvent(ApplicationEvent event);
}
```

Spring includes three standard events:

❑ `ContextRefreshEvent`: This event will be published when the application context gets initialized or refreshed, specifically after all bean definitions have been loaded, and any pre-instantiation of singletons is completed, including injection of dependencies. Essentially, the context is ready for use.

❏ ContextClosedEvent: This event will be published when the context has been closed, typically as a result of a close() call. It will actually be called after the destroy method has been called on all singletons.

❏ RequestHandledEvent: This event will be published within a WebApplicationContext by the FrameworkServlet from Spring's web MVC code *after* a request has been handled by the web MVC code. This event is fairly agnostic to web layer technology, so could also be fired by application code, if desired, when using another web framework.

Publishing custom events is straightforward. Application contexts implement the ApplicationEventPublisher interface, whose publishEvent() method may be called for this purpose. A bean that wants to use the application context as an event publisher may implement the ApplicationEventPublisherAware interface, and will automatically be called back by the application context at initialization time with a reference to the application context as the ApplicationEventPublisher. For new code which doesn't already use the context for other purposes, publishing events through the ApplicationEventPublisher interface, as opposed to ApplicationContext directly, is preferred because it will reduce coupling to the context.

Let's look at an example of publishing and receiving events. Consider a Spring-based deployment in which there is a need for a remote monitoring agent to receive a periodic heartbeat signal from the Spring-based app to know that it's still running. We decide to use a timer task to create the heartbeat. Because it's likely there will be multiple parties interested in using the heartbeat, we decide to publish it as an event, for which any interested parties can listen, including in this case a bean that notifies the remote monitoring agent.

First we create the heartbeat timer task as a subclass of java.util.TimerTask. When it executes, it publishes a HeartBeat event. As the class implements ApplicationEventPublisherAware, it automatically receives the context it is deployed into as the event publisher:

```
public class HeartbeatTask extends TimerTask implements
ApplicationEventPublisherAware {

  private ApplicationEventPublisher eventPublisher;

  public void run() {
    HeartbeatEvent event = new HeartbeatEvent(this);
    eventPublisher.publishEvent(event);
  }

  public void setApplicationEventPublisher(ApplicationEventPublisher
eventPublisher) {
    this.eventPublisher = eventPublisher;
  }
}
```

This can be configured very simply, as shown below:

```
<bean id="heartbeatTask" class="ch04.sample1.HeartbeatTask"/>
```

Now we use Spring's convenient ScheduledTimerTask and TimerFactoryBean to schedule the task to run every second after the application context starts up:

```xml
<bean id="scheduledTask"
      class="org.springframework.scheduling.timer.ScheduledTimerTask">
  <property name="timerTask"><ref local="heartbeatTask"/></property>
  <property name="period"><value>1000</value></property>
</bean>

<bean id="timerFactory"
      class="org.springframework.scheduling.timer.TimerFactoryBean">
  <property name="scheduledTimerTasks">
    <list>
      <ref local="scheduledTask"/>
    </list>
  </property>
</bean>
```

Note that the `heartBeatTask` bean is shown standalone for clarity, but you would probably want to make it an inner bean of `timerFactory` because it is needed there only. Please see the JavaDocs of these classes for more information, but essentially, the initialization of the `TimerFactoryBean` (which will happen when singletons are pre-instantiated) triggers it to start the specified scheduled tasks.

> *Note also that Spring allows much more comprehensive scheduling via the third-party Quartz library.*

At this point, we are publishing heartbeat events once a second. We now need to catch them and forward them to the remote agent. We create an event listener for this purpose:

```java
public class HeartbeatForwarder implements ApplicationListener {

  public void onApplicationEvent(ApplicationEvent event) {
    if (event instanceof HeartbeatEvent) {
      // now tell the remote monitoring agent that we're alive
      ...
    }
  }
}
```

The forwarder implements `ApplicationListener`, so all that has to be done for it to receive the heartbeat events is to deploy it as a bean in the context:

```xml
<bean id="heartbeatForwarder" class="ch04.sample1.HeartbeatForwarder"/>
```

As you can see, publishing and receiving Spring or application events is quite easy.

Managing the Container

You've learned the basics of creating and using bean factories and application contexts. There are a number of more advanced capabilities and strategies for real-world usage of the container. We're going to examine some of the most common ones.

Resource Location Paths in ApplicationContext Constructors

Both `ClasspathXmlApplicationContext` and `FilesystemXmlApplication` context have constructors that take one or more string locations pointing to XML resources that should be merged as the context definition. When the location paths fed to these class constructors are unqualified by any prefix, they will be interpreted as `ClasspathResource` and `FilesystemResource` locations by the respective contexts.

However, for either context class, it's actually legal to use any valid URL prefix (such as `file:` or `http://`) to override this and treat the location string as a `UrlResource`. It's also legal to use Spring's own `classpath:` prefix to force a `ClasspathResource`, although this is redundant with the `ClasspathXmlApplicationContext`:

```
ApplicationContext ctx = new ClasspathXmlApplicationContext(
        "http://myserver.xom/data/myapp/ApplicationContext.xml");
```

You would probably expect that the two following definitions should work identically with the first treating the path as a `FileSystemResource`, and the second treating the path as a `UrlResource` with a `file:` URL:

```
ApplicationContext ctx = new FileSystemXmlApplicationContext(
        "/data/data/myapp/ApplicationContext.xml");
```

```
ApplicationContext ctx = new FileSystemXmlApplicationContext(
        "file:/data/data/myapp/ApplicationContext.xml");
```

However, for backward compatibility reasons, `FilesystemXmlApplicationContext` treats `FileSystemResources` used in the constructor and `getResource()` calls as being relative to the current working directory, not absolute, even if they start with a slash, `/`. If you want true absolute paths, you should always use the `file:` prefix with `Resources` location strings fed to `FileSystemXmlApplicationContext`, which will force them to be treated as `UrlResources`, not `FilesystemResources`.

The Special classpath*: Prefix

In a location string used to create an XML-configured application context, you may also use the special `classpath*:` prefix:

```
ApplicationContext ctx = new ClasspathXmlApplicationContext(
        "classpath*:applicationContext.xml");
```

The `classpath*:` prefix specifies that *all* classpath resources matching the name after the prefix, as available to the `ClassLoader`, should be obtained, and then merged to form the final context definition. (Internally, this would resolve to `ClassLoader.getResources("applicationContext.xml")` to find all matching resources.) Note that you can't use a `classpath*:` prefix to create an actual `Resource` because the latter always refers to just one file.

Ant-Style Paths

In a location string used to create file-based, XML-configured application contexts, you may also use ant-style patterns (containing the * and ** wildcards):

```
ApplicationContext ctx = new FilesystemXmlApplicationContext(
        "file:/data/myapp/*-context.xml");
```

The preceding example would match 0 or more files in the specified directory and merge their contents as the definition for the application context. Note that ant-style wildcards are really usable only where directory locations can actually be resolved to a `File` because that location then needs to be searched for matches to the wildcards. The following

```
ApplicationContext ctx = new ClasspathXmlApplicationContext(
        "/data/myapp/*-context.xml");
```

will work in environments where the classpath resolves to actual filesystem locations, but will fail where it is actually the contents of a JAR, so it should not be relied upon.

Declarative Usage of Application Contexts

Following IoC principles, as little application code as possible should know about the application context. We've mentioned that in spite of these principles, it is sometimes necessary for a small amount of glue code to know about the context. For a Spring-enabled J2EE web-app, it is possible to reduce or completely eliminate even this small amount of code by using Spring code to declaratively specify that an application context should be loaded at web-app startup.

Spring's `ContextLoader` is the class that provides this capability. However, it must actually be instigated by using another helper class. In a Servlet 2.4 environment, or a Servlet 2.3 environment that follows the 2.4 guarantee of executing servlet context listeners before any load-on-startup servlets, the preferred mechanism to kick off `ContextLoader` is via the use of a servlet context listener, called `ContextLoaderListener`. For all other environments, a load-on-startup servlet called `ContextLoaderServlet` may be used instead for this purpose.

At this time, containers known to work with the listener approach are Apache Tomcat 4.x+, Jetty 4.x+, Resin 2.1.8+, JBoss 3.0+, WebLogic 8.1 SP3+, and Orion 2.0.2+. Containers known to not work with the listener approach, and which need the servlet approach, are BEA WebLogic up to 8.1 SP2, IBM WebSphere up to 5.x, and Oracle OC4J up to 9.0.x.

Let's look at how `ContextLoaderListener` is configured via a `<listener>` element in the standard J2EE `web.xml` file that is part of every web-app:

```
...
<listener>
  <listener-class>org.springframework.web.context.ContextLoaderListener</listener-
class>
</listener>
...
```

Setting up `ContextLoaderServlet` instead is done via the `<servlet>` element in the `web.xml` file:

```
<servlet>
  <servlet-name>context</servlet-name>
  <servlet-class>org.springframework.web.context.ContextLoaderServlet</servlet-
class>
  <load-on-startup>1</load-on-startup>
</servlet>
```

It's important that the servlet is set as the first to load, or at least has a higher precedence than any other load-on-startup servlet that uses the application context.

When the web-app starts up, the listener or servlet will execute `ContextLoader`, which initializes and starts an `XmlWebApplicationContext` based on one or more XML file fragments that are merged. By default, the following file is used:

```
/WEB-INF/applicationContext.xml
```

but you may override this to point to one or more files in an alternate location by using the `contextConfigLocation` servlet context param in the `web.xml` file as in the following two examples:

```
<context-param>
  <param-name>contextConfigLocation</param-name>
  <param-value>WEB-INF/myApplicationContext.xml</param-value>
</context-param>
```

```
<context-param>
  <param-name>contextConfigLocation</param-name>
  <param-value>classpath:services-applicationContext.xml,
               classpath:dao-applicationContext.xml
  </param-value>
</context-param>
```

While unqualified locations will be considered to be files relative to the web-app's context root location, you can use the resource location prefixes and ant-style paths as previously described in this chapter for location strings in application context constructors (as shown in the second example). Multiple XML fragments may be specified, as in the last example, to be merged to form the definition, with white space, commas (,), and semicolons (;) used as delimiters in the location list.

When the application context has been loaded, it is bound to the J2EE `ServletContext` for the web-app. Effectively it's a singleton, although keyed to the `ServletContext`, not stored inside a static class field. On destruction of the web-app, the context will automatically be closed. Any application code that needs to access the application context may do so by calling a static helper method from the `WebApplicationContextUtils` class:

```
WebApplicationContext getWebApplicationContext(ServletContext sc)
```

For most applications using Spring MVC, there is not actually any need for application code to get the context in this fashion, however. The framework itself, when processing a request, obtains the context from this location, gets appropriate request handlers, and kicks off request handling, with all objects having been configured in an IoC fashion. The same is possible when using Spring's Struts integration mechanism. Please see the web MVC sections of the book for more information in this area. Note that this is a very lightweight process in use; almost all the work is done at servlet initialization time, and after that the mechanism is generally as efficient as hardwiring your application.

When integrating another web layer technology, you'll have to create a small amount of glue code equivalent to the preceding. All it needs to do, when a request is received, is to obtain the application context using the previously listed method. It may then get any needed objects, and kick off the request handling to them, or with them. Try to architect the application code so that as little code as possible is aware of this mechanism, though, to reduce coupling to Spring and maintain inversion of control. For example, when integrating a traditional style *action*-based web MVC framework, as opposed to each action object using the preceding method call to get services and objects it needs to work with, it's cleaner to get these collaborators via a method call, which is handled in a superclass, so that the superclass is the only place that knows about Spring. It's cleaner yet to hook into whatever mechanism exists in the web framework for obtaining action objects, and make that code look up the actions directly from the context, and then just call them normally. The actions will already have had dependencies injected, and will be used in a pure IoC fashion, without knowing about Spring at all. The exact approach used depends on the particular architecture of the framework that Spring needs to be integrated with. Although integration is not incredibly complicated, you can probably also benefit by searching mailing lists and forums for information on how other people have done the same thing. Besides looking in Spring itself for integration code for a particular framework, also look for Spring-related code in that framework itself.

Splitting Up Container Definitions into Multiple Files

There is real value to be found in splitting up bean factory or application context definitions into multiple files. As a container definition grows as one file, it becomes harder to understand what all the bean definitions within it are for, and harder to manage, including making changes.

Generally we recommend splitting up a context either by vertical architectural layer within the application, or horizontally, by module or component. In the latter case, the definitions in each file fragment make up a narrow vertical slice, which encompasses multiple layers. It can make sense to split using a combination of both of these strategies.

Combining the File Fragments Externally

You've already seen in the ContextLoader example that when using the ContextLoader for declarative context creation, it's legal to specify multiple fragments that should all be used to create one context. For programmatic creation of a context from multiple fragments, simply use the constructor variant that takes multiple locations:

```
ApplicationContext ctx = new ClasspathXmlApplicationContext(new String[] {
        "applicationContext-web.xml",
        "applicationContext-services.xml",
        "ApplicationContext-dao.xml" } );
```

Another effect of splitting up the context definition is that it can make testing easier. For example, it is relatively common to be using Spring's JTATransactionManager (as described in Chapter 6, "Transaction and DataSource Management") and a DataSource coming from JNDI for the deployed application in the appserver, but for integration or unit tests running outside of the appserver, you need to use a local transaction manager (such as HibernateTransactionManager) and local DataSource (such as one created with DBCP). If the transaction manager and DataSource are in their own separate XML fragment, then it is easy to handle tests by setting up the classpaths for tests so that a version of the file specific to the tests is first on the classpath, and overrides the normal deployment variants. You might even want to wire up an in-memory database such as HSQLDB.

Combining File Fragments with the Import Element

We normally prefer to combine multiple XML files into one definition from an external point of control, as described previously. This is because the files themselves are unaware of being combined, which feels cleanest in some respects. Another mechanism exists, however, and this is to import bean definitions into one XML definition file from one or more external XML definition files by using one or more instances of the import element. Any instances of import must occur before any bean elements.

Here's an example:

```
<beans>

  <import resource="data-access.xml"/>

  <import resource="services.xml "/>

  <import resource="resources/messgeSource.xml"/>

  <bean id="..." class="..."/>

  ...
</beans>
```

In this case, three external files are being imported. Note that all files being imported must be in fully valid XML configuration format (including the top-level beans element), according to the XML DTD. The external definition file to merge in is specified as a location path with the resource attribute. All location paths are relative to the location of the definition file doing the importing. In this case, definition files data-access.xml and services.xml must be located in the same directory or classpath package as the file performing the import, while messageSource.xml must be located in a resource directory or package below that.

Combining File Fragments Programmatically

When programmatically creating a bean factory or application context using bean definition readers, you may combine multiple XML file fragments by simply pointing the reader at multiple files, as shown in the following example:

```
DefaultListableBeanFactory factory = new DefaultListableBeanFactory();
XmlBeanDefinitionReader reader = new XmlBeanDefinitionReader(factory);
ClassPathResource res = new ClassPathResource("beans.xml");
reader.loadBeanDefinitions(res);
res = new ClassPathResource("beans2.xml");
reader.loadBeanDefinitions(res);
// now use the factory
```

Strategies for Handling Components

There are a few different strategies for handling Spring-based components or modules. As the words *component* and *module* are somewhat nebulous, let's clarify first what we mean when we use them. We are essentially talking about a relatively coarse-grained physical bundling or logical separation of code that handles related functionality. While a JAR file could be a component or module, so could be all the code underneath a certain package in a larger package tree. The fundamental idea is that the code is related somehow, and can be used as a library to provide certain services.

When trying to build an app in a component-oriented style (i.e., the app assembles and uses components), one workable strategy with respect to handling the container definition is to not have components care at all about the definition. Components, when using this strategy, simply provide Java code. It is considered the responsibility of the main application to define a bean factory or application context configuration, whether in one file or multiple files, which wires together all the object instances for classes provided by the components, including providing them with their dependencies. This strategy is quite viable because code should be written to be utilized in an IoC fashion anyway, and should not care about container initialization or its definition. Because the application using the component needs to do all the wiring, what is required, however, is a full and thorough documentation of all the component classes that need to be wired together for the externally visible component classes to be used, even if external users of the component don't care about many of these classes. This is a disadvantage of using this approach. While this is not a disadvantage on the level of code coupling or something of that nature (after all, we're just talking about an easily changed configuration file), it's not ideal that configuration concerns for a component are not handled in the component itself.

A nicer strategy is to try to have components bundle together with their code, one or more XML file fragments that define how to wire together some or all of the component classes. In the final app, an application context definition is assembled from all the XML fragments provided by all the components, along with one or more XML fragments defining objects needed by the application itself, or objects needed by the components, which the component fragments do not define. To avoid bean name collisions, bean names in component XML fragments should use some sort of simple namespace scheme, such as by adding `componentname-` or `componentname:` as a prefix on all bean names.

One question is how two or more components that do not know about each other can refer to the same external bean (consider, for example, a `DataSource`), which they do not themselves provide, but have a dependency on. Because each component does not know about the other, they cannot use a common name. The solution is for each component to use a component-specific name for the external bean, and then have the application provide the definition for this bean, making sure to add aliases to the bean name that match the name(s) expected by the component(s).

Let's look at an example. Consider a "devices" module, which provides *mappers* (i.e., DAOs for handling persistence for some device-related domain objects). These mappers are internally implemented with Spring's JDBC convenience classes, so they need a `DataSource` fed to them when they are initialized. An XML fragment for wiring up the mappers could look like the following:

```
<beans>

  <bean id="devices:deviceDescriptorDataMapper"
        class="ch04.sampleX.devices.DeviceDescriptorDataMapperImpl">
    <property name="dataSource"><ref bean="devices:dataSource"/></property>
  </bean>
```

```
        <bean id="devices:deviceMapper"
              class="ch04.sampleX.devices.DeviceMapperImpl">
          <property name="dataSource"><ref bean="devices:dataSource"/></property>
        </bean>

      </beans>
```

An external user (the application) of this module simply needs to combine this fragment along with others, and refer to the mappers by their bean names, as needed. It also needs to ensure that a DataSource with the bean name devices:dataSource is available.

Let's look at another component, a "user" module:

```
<beans>

    <bean id="users:userMapper"
          class="ch04.sampleX.users.userMapperImpl">
      <property name="dataSource"><ref bean="users:dataSource"/></property>
    </bean>
    <bean id="users:roleMapper"
          class="ch04.sampleX.users.DeviceMapperImpl">
      <property name="dataSource"><ref bean=" users:dataSource "/></property>
    </bean>

</beans>
```

This module provides DAOs for mapping users and roles. These also need to be initialized with a DataSource. Now consider that we have an application using these components. It will create an application context using the XML fragments from the components, along with one or more fragments defined for the application itself, used at a minimum for tying things together. Here's an XML fragment for the application, showing how a service object refers to the mappers, and how a DataSource is defined so both component definitions can see it:

```
  ...

    <--- UserDeviceService works with both user and device mappers -->
    <bean id="app:userDeviceService"
          class="ch04.sampleX.users.UserDeviceServiceImpl">
      <property name="userMapper"><ref bean="users:userMapper "/></property>
      <property name="deviceMapper"><ref bean="devices:deviceMapper "/></property>
    </bean>

    <bean id="app:dataSource" name="users:dataSource,devices:dataSource"
          class="org.apache.commons.dbcp.BasicDataSource" destroy-method="close">
      ...
    </bean>
  ...
```

As you can see, while the DataSource instance has the primary ID app:dataSource, it is also aliased as users:dataSource and devices:dataSource, so that the references in the XML fragments coming from the components can be resolved.

This approach to component handling obviously requires discipline in some respects. There is no built-in namespace protection, so the developer is required to manage all bean names carefully, by using the distinct component-specific prefixes on bean names and generally trying to avoid name conflicts. In practice, however, this approach has proven to be usable and effective.

Another general strategy for mixing code from multiple components is to use multiple application contexts in some fashion. One Spring user has reported employing a Factory Bean deployed in one context, which exposed just one bean (via an interface) from another context that it instantiated. In this way, the mixing of beans was tightly controlled.

Singletons for Accessing the Container

We have already emphasized that most code should never have to know about the container when it's written and deployed in an IoC style. For some architectural scenarios, however, there is no avoiding the fact that some glue code (ideally a very small amount of it) in the application does have to have access to the container so that it may get one or more populated objects out of it and initiate a sequence of method calls.

One example is when using EJBs. Because the J2EE AppServer is responsible for creating actual EJB objects, if the EJB wants to delegate to one or more POJOs managed by the Spring container, to actually implement the EJB method's functionality, the EJB (or a common base class) effectively has to have some knowledge of the container so it can get these objects from it, normally on creation of the EJB. One strategy is for each EJB instance to create its own copy of the Spring container. This is potentially problematic in terms of memory usage if there are a large number of objects in the Spring container, and is problematic if creating the context or bean factory is expensive in terms of time, for example if a Hibernate SessionFactory needs to be initialized.

For both the EJB scenario, and for some non-EJB scenarios as well, it may make sense to keep a shared instance of the Spring container in some sort of singleton object for access by the glue code that needs it. Spring provides such a singleton access mechanism via the `SingletonBeanFactoryLocator` and `ContextSingletonBeanFactoryLocator` classes. The use of these classes also allows for creation and usage of a container hierarchy such that one or more *demand-loaded* application contexts are parents to individual web-app application contexts. As a more concrete example, inside a J2EE Application (EAR file), a service-layer (and lower layer) shared application context could be the parent of one or more web-app application contexts for web-apps also deployed in the EAR. Chapter 11, "Spring and EJB," contains a full description of how to use the singleton container access classes, and we direct readers to that content if these classes are of interest, even if there is no need to use Spring and EJBs. The relevant section in that chapter is titled "ContextSingletonBeanFactoryLocator and SingletonBeanFactoryLocator."

Some Convenience Factory Beans

Spring includes a number of factory beans we have not described yet, which can make some container configurations much simpler, or even possible. Note that the usefulness of these factory beans will decrease when Spring implements built-in support of an expression language in the application context, as is scheduled to be completed for Spring 1.3.

PropertyPathFactoryBean

`PropertyPathFactoryBean` is a very useful factory bean that can be used to return the result of evaluating a property path on a target object. While you can set a bean property or constructor argument to the value of another bean in the container via a direct bean reference (`ref` element), this doesn't help when you need a property of that bean, or a property of a property. `PropertyPathFactoryBean` lets you get at those nested properties. Let's look at some examples.

In this example, the result of the factory bean is the `city` property of the `address` property of the `person` bean that is pointed to:

```
<bean id="person"
    ...
</bean>
<bean id="theCity"
        class="org.springframework.beans.factory.config.PropertyPathFactoryBean">
    <property name="targetObject"><ref local="person"/></property>
    <property name="propertyPath"><value>address.city</value></property>
</bean>
```

The following example is equivalent, except that the target bean on which the property is being evaluated has been moved to be an inner bean:

```
<bean id="theCity"
        class="org.springframework.beans.factory.config.PropertyPathFactoryBean">
    <property name="propertyPath"><value>address.city</value></property>
    <property name="targetObject">
      <!-- person bean has been moved to be an inner bean -->
      <bean class="... ">
        ...
      </bean>
    </property>
</bean>
```

Here we refer to the target bean by name:

```
<bean id="person"
    ...
</bean>
<bean id="theCity"
        class="org.springframework.beans.factory.config.PropertyPathFactoryBean">
    <property name="targetBeanName"><value>person</value></property>
    <property name="propertyPath"><value>address.city</value></property>
</bean>
```

And finally, there is a very convenient shortcut form, where the name of the `PropertyPathFactoryBean` instance is used as the actual property path. Of course, you no longer have any choice in the bean name. This form is very useful for an inner bean:

```
<bean id="person"
    ...
</bean>

<bean id="person.address.city"
        class="org.springframework.beans.factory.config.PropertyPathFactoryBean"/>
```

Note that nesting can go to arbitrary levels, not just two deep as in these examples.

FieldRetrievingFactoryBean

This factory bean retrieves the value of a static or non-static class field. The most useful use case is when you need to get a static constant from a class:

```xml
<bean id="max-long"
      class="org.springframework.beans.factory.config.FieldRetrievingFactoryBean">
  <property name="staticField">
    <value>java.lang.Long.MAX_VALUE</value>
  </property>
</bean>
```

There is a short form that uses the name of the bean as the static field name. This variant will produce the same output, although of course there is no longer any choice as to the bean name:

```xml
<bean id="java.lang.Long.MAX_VALUE"
      class="org.springframework.beans.factory.config.FieldRetrievingFactoryBean"/>
```

You may also get a non-static field from another bean:

```xml
<bean id="address"
      class="org.springframework.beans.factory.config.FieldRetrievingFactoryBean">
  <property name="targetObject"><ref local="person"/></property>
  <property name="targetField"><value>address</value></property>
</bean>
```

MethodInvokingFactoryBean

`MethodInvokingFactoryBean` is a factory bean that returns the result of a method invocation as its output. This is useful in two scenarios.

In one scenario, a bean property or constructor argument needs to be set to the result of a method invocation on another bean in the container, or a static method call on some arbitrary class. Spring's factory method support (used via the `factory-method` attribute as described in the previous chapter) is actually the best way to handle this need for most situations. Factory methods were described in the "Bean Creation Mechanism" section of Chapter 2. You'll still sometimes see `MethodInvokingFactoryBean` used for this purpose, instead of the factory method mechanism, as the former has been around longer.

The other scenario where this factory bean is useful is when a static method on some arbitrary class needs to be called in order to initialize some component, and that method doesn't have any return value. In this case, the `factory-method` mechanism is not usable, as it expects the factory method to return a value to be used as the bean. One example of such an initialization scenario is JDBC 1.0 style creation of a `DataSource` via JDBC's `DriverManager..getConnection()`. Before using this method, you need to ensure that the JDBC driver has been registered, by calling `Class.forName(<db-driver class>)`, which triggers the JDBC driver to register itself with the `DriverManager`, as part of its static initialization block. Here's an example of how `Class.forName()` could be called in this fashion:

```xml
<bean id="load-oracle-jdbc-driver"
      class="org.springframework.beans.factory.config.MethodInvokingFactoryBean">
  <property name="staticMethod">
    <value>java.lang.Class.forName</value>
```

```
      </property>
      <property name="arguments">
        <list><value>oracle.jdbc.driver.OracleDriver</value></list>
      </property>
    </bean>
```

To ensure that this method call is invoked before another bean is initialized, that other bean can refer to this one via the `depends-on` attribute.

Property Editors Provided by Spring

JavaBeans property editors, as mentioned in the last chapter when explaining dependency resolution, are the basis for Spring's ability to automatically convert string values to complex object types in bean factory and application context definition. Additionally, they are heavily used for form binding in the Spring MVC web UI layer. Knowing which `PropertyEditors` are used automatically, as well as which others are also available for use, is valuable in using Spring effectively.

A class called `BeanWrapperImpl`, implementing the `BeanWrapper` interface, is the basic engine in Spring for performing `PropertyEditor`-based conversions in the containers and web MVC layer. `BeanWrapper` automatically registers and uses a number of property editors:

❑ `ByteArrayPropertyEditor`: Two-way conversion between a string and its corresponding byte representation.

❑ `ClassEditor`: Two-way conversion of a string class name to an instance of `java.lang.Class`.

❑ `CustomBooleanEditor`: Customizable two-way conversion between a string and a Boolean value. While this is registered by default, it can be overridden to be appropriate for a particular locale by registering a custom instance of it as a custom editor.

❑ `CustomNumberEditor`: Customizable two-way conversion of a string to any of the subclasses of `Number`, including `Integer`, `Long`, `Float`, and `Double`. While this is registered by default, it can be overridden by registering a custom instance of it as a custom editor.

❑ `FileEditor`: Two-way conversion of a string to a `File` object.

❑ `InputStreamEditor`: Conversion of a string to an `InputStream` object, via an intermediate `Resource` and `ResourceEditor`. Note that the user must close the stream.

❑ `LocaleEditor`: Two-way conversion of a string to a `Locale` object. See the JavaDoc for exact string format.

❑ `PropertiesEditor`: Two-way conversion of a string to a `Properties` object. See JavaDoc for exact string format.

❑ `ResourceEditor`: Convert location strings to `Resource` objects. This is actually not manually registered but is found automatically by the JavaBeans support code, as it is in the same package as the `Resource` class.

❑ `ResourceArrayPropertyEditor`: Convert wildcard location strings (for example, `file: c:/my*.txt` or `classpath*:myfile.txt`) to `Resource` arrays. This is not registered by BeanWrapper itself, but only by application contexts.

❑ `StringArrayPropertyEditor`: Two-way conversion of a string containing comma-delimited items to a String[].

❑ `URLEditor`: Two-way conversion of a string to a `URL` object.

Application contexts, but not bean factories, override the normal instances of `InputStreamEditor`, `ResourceEditor`, and `URLEditor` with customized versions, which behave appropriately for the context type in terms of resource resolution. With a `ClasspathApplicationContext`, for example, location strings would default to resolving as classpath resources.

Two additional property editors are available to be registered (as described in Chapter 2 in the section "Creating a Custom PropertyEditor") and used as needed by users:

❑ `CustomDateEditor`: Customizable two-way conversion of a string to a `Date` object. May be registered as a custom editor as needed. An example for this class was shown in the last chapter.

❑ `StringTrimmedEditor`: `PropertyEditor` that trims Strings. Optionally allows transforming an empty string into a null value.

Strategies for Testing

The topic of testing application code and the application itself, in all its incarnations, is a large one. It can and has filled numerous books on the subject. All we can reasonably discuss in the scope of this chapter are some testing strategies as they relate to Spring itself. The following text assumes you have at least a basic familiarity with JUnit (`www.junit.org`).

Unit Tests

The most important point that can be made with regards to unit testing classes that are used in a Spring container is that the majority of the time, the Spring container does not have to be used and should not be used for this type of test. One of the main benefits of IoC is that code is unaware of the container, so in terms of a unit test, even if the container is lightweight like Spring, it's usually faster and easier to use Java code to create and wire together the class being tested, along with its dependencies.

Let's review a test from the previous chapter:

```xml
<?xml version="1.0" encoding="UTF-8"?>
<!DOCTYPE beans PUBLIC "-//SPRING//DTD BEAN//EN"
    "http://www.springframework.org/dtd/spring-beans.dtd">

<beans>
  <bean id="weatherService" class="ch02.sample2.WeatherServiceImpl">
    <property name="weatherDao">
      <ref local="weatherDao"/>
    </property>
  </bean>
  <bean id="weatherDao" class="ch02.sample2.StaticDataWeatherDaoImpl">
  </bean>
</beans>
```

```
public class WeatherServiceTest extends TestCase {
  public void testSample2() throws Exception {
    ApplicationContext ctx = new ClassPathXmlApplicationContext(
        "ch03/sample2/applicationContext.xml");
    WeatherService ws = (WeatherService) ctx.getBean("weatherService");

    Double high = ws.getHistoricalHigh(
        new GregorianCalendar(2004, 0, 1).getTime());
    // ... do more validation of returned value here...
  }
}
```

In the last chapter, we were demonstrating container functionality, so it was appropriate to have the test do its work through the container. However, if your main interest is in testing WeatherServiceImpl, you are better off doing everything as Java code:

```
public class WeatherServiceTest extends TestCase {

  public void testWithRealObjects () throws Exception {

    WeatherServiceImpl ws = new WeatherServiceImpl();
    ws.setWeatherDao(new StaticDataWeatherDaoImpl());

    Double high = ws.getHistoricalHigh(
        new GregorianCalendar(2004, 0, 1).getTime());
    // ... do more validation of returned value here...
  }
}
```

This is an artificially simple test, in that there is only one collaborator for the main class, and even so, we are not actually validating as much as we would like to; we don't know that the weather service is actually calling the weather DAO and using the result returned by the latter. Because we are working against interfaces, why don't we just create a mock object implementing the weather DAO interface, just for the purpose of the test? This will allow us to not worry about test data, as we would when testing with the real StaticDataWeatherDaoImpl:

```
public void testWithMock() throws Exception {

  WeatherServiceImpl ws = new WeatherServiceImpl();

  ws.setWeatherDao(new WeatherDao() {
    public WeatherData find(Date date) {

      WeatherData wd = new WeatherData();
      wd.setDate(date);
      wd.setLow(10);
      wd.setHigh(20);
      return wd;
    }

    // 2 methods not needed for test
    public WeatherData save(Date date) { return null; }
    public WeatherData update(Date date) { return null; }
```

```
        });

        Double high = ws.getHistoricalHigh(new GregorianCalendar(2004, 0, 1).getTime());
        assertTrue(high.equals(new Double(20)));
    }
```

In this case the mock object was created inline as an anonymous class. Many times, it is useful to define a separate static mock class that can be reused. Additionally, if more than one test is going to need the mock object, it's useful to create it in the JUnit setup() method. Spring actually includes some mock classes, including, among others, MockHttpSession, MockHttpServletRequest, and MockHttpServletResponse, to mock the HttpSession, HttpServletRequest, and HttpServletResponse classes, respectively. These are used for internal Spring unit tests, and you may use them yourself when testing your web layer controllers.

It is sometimes painful to try to mock as a normal class a complicated interface with many operations. EasyMock (www.easymock.org) is an extension library that can dynamically create a mock object for a specified interface (and with a small add-on, also for a specified class). Let's look at a version of the previous test that uses a weather DAO mock generated by EasyMock:

```
public void testWithEasyMock() throws Exception {

    // create test data
    Date date = new GregorianCalendar(2004, 0, 1).getTime();
    WeatherData wd = new WeatherData();
    wd.setDate(date);
    wd.setLow(10);
    wd.setHigh(20);

    // create mock weather dao with EasyMock, returning test data on find() call
    MockControl control = MockControl.createControl(WeatherDao.class);
    WeatherDao weatherDao = (WeatherDao) control.getMock();
    // set the method we expect called on the mock, and return value
    weatherDao.find(date);
    control.setReturnValue(wd);

    WeatherServiceImpl ws = new WeatherServiceImpl();
    ws.setWeatherDao(weatherDao);

    // turn on the mock
    control.replay();
    Double high = ws.getHistoricalHigh(date);
    // verify the mock actually received a find() call
    control.verify();

    assertTrue(high.equals(new Double(20)));
}
```

In the example, we create some test data, ask EasyMock to create for us a mock object implementing the weather DAO interface, register a method call on the mock object, specify that the mock should return the test data, and then feed the mock to the weather service, which is what we actually test. Afterwards, we can ask EasyMock to verify that the method we registered actually got called. There are a number of optional features, such as the ability to specify the minimum and maximum number of times a method is called, and verifying the order of method calls.

While this sample actually ends up longer than the one using a simple class-based mock, you can see how simple it is to create a mock object for an arbitrary interface, and how this approach can save significant time and effort for some mocking scenarios. When considering the use of EasyMock, you should also take a look at jMock (`www.jmock.org`), which is another dynamic mock library. We prefer the somewhat different approach used by jMock, for some scenarios.

For each unit test, you should carefully consider which approach to mocking makes the most sense, and in fact whether mocking makes sense at all, as opposed to state-based testing as in our first example, where real objects are used.

Tests That Use the Spring Container

For a relatively small percentage of unit tests, it may make sense to use a Spring container to do object wiring and configuration, as it is the least amount of work.

For most integration tests, on the other hand, it will make sense to use the container. The term *integration test* is somewhat nebulous, but it generally means a test that tries to use a number of classes or components working together, usually in the same fashion as for normal application usage. Often, especially if the container definition is split up into multiple files, it's possible to use the same or most of the same container definition as is used when the application is run normally. If the Spring-based app needs to be deployed in an appserver for normal usage, the integration test can run inside or outside of the appserver, but it's preferable if possible to run it outside the appserver because eliminating the deployment step can reduce a build-deploy-test, as an example, from 2 minutes to 2 seconds, increasing productivity greatly. Whether it's possible to run the integration test outside of the appserver really depends on what set of classes or components of the application is being tested, and whether there are dependencies on the appserver that cannot be removed, or would make the test irrelevant if removed. One advantage to running the test inside the appserver is that the execution environment and deployment scenario is more similar to the final execution environment, reducing the potential surprise of having an integration test work, but having the same classes or components fail when used normally in the deployed app. Except for the view layer or EJBs, this is not usually a great concern, but a reasonable approach is to try to do most integration testing outside of the appserver, but also to do some in-appserver testing.

When the test is run outside of the appserver, it may simply be a normal JUnit test. When the test is run inside the appserver, then some sort of mechanism is actually needed to kick it off inside the appserver after the application is deployed. One of the most convenient approaches is something like Jakarta Apache Cactus (`http://jakarta.apache.org/cactus/`), which allows a command-line ant build to transparently run a normal JUnit test remotely, inside the deployed test application in the appserver. The other approach is to simply do integration testing by driving the view layer itself, with a tool like Canoo WebTest (`http://webtest.canoo.com/webtest/manual/WebTestHome.html`) to use view layer functionality that will stress the classes that need to be tested. While tests of the view layer itself are very useful, if in-appserver integration testing of lower-layer code is actually needed, an approach similar to that afforded by Cactus is much more convenient, as normal JUnit tests, which directly drive the relevant code, may be used.

Let's focus on using JUnit to drive integration tests.

Managing the Container Configuration in a Test

You've seen a number of JUnit test samples already where the test method itself loads the application context (or bean factory). For a real-life integration test it is generally more appropriate to load the context in the JUnit `setUp()` method (and closed in the `tearDown()`), so that each test method does not have to repeat this step. One concern is that while this will avoid code duplication, the context will still be created once for each test method, as calls to setup()/teardown() surround each test method invocation. JUnit does this to ensure fresh base test data, but when using a context that has an initialization operation that is time-intensive, such as creating a Hibernate SessionFactory, this is less than ideal, especially if, as in most cases, the same context instance could be reused for all test methods.

Inside the spring-mock.jar add-on JAR, Spring includes a convenience base test case class, AbstractDependencyInjectionSpringContextTests, which makes it easy to load and reuse just one context instance for all the test methods in a test case. As an additional benefit, the base class is capable of triggering the direct injection of dependencies into the test case class, via setter injection (autowired by type), or field injection matching by name. Let's examine how the test case from the beginning of this section would look, as implemented via the use of AbstractDependencyInjectionSpringContextTests:

```
public class WeatherServiceTest extends
    AbstractDependencyInjectionSpringContextTests {

  private WeatherService weatherService;

  public void setWeatherService(WeatherService weatherService) {
    this.weatherService = weatherService;
  }

  protected String[] getConfigLocations() {
    return new String[]{"ch03/sample3/applicationContext.xml"};
  }

  public void testWeatherService() throws Exception {
    Double high = weatherService.getHistoricalHigh(
        new GregorianCalendar(2004, 0, 1).getTime());
    // ... do more validation of returned value here...
  }
}
```

There is no longer any explicit loading of the application context by the test. The template method getConfigLocations() is implemented to simply return one or more location strings for XML fragments that make up the context definition. The WeatherService instance is now directly injected into the test as a property, instead of the test having to ask for it. After the initial load, the context is actually cached based on a key, which is normally the config locations. This means that all test methods, and even other tests that use the same locations, will all share the same context instance. On the other hand, the property (or field) injection will still happen before each test method. If a test knows that it will modify or has modified the context (for example, it has replaced a bean definition), and wants to force the context to be reloaded before the next text method is executed, it may call the setDirty() method.

Another set of base test case classes provided by Spring, AbstractTransactionalSpringContextTests and AbstractTransactionalDataSourceSpringContextTests, can be very useful for testing database-related code. When testing this type of code, including DAOs/Mappers, a common problem or inconvenience is how to handle the fact that the database state is modified by a test of this type. Typically, this is handled by one of several approaches. Tests can try to ensure that only data that doesn't interfere with other data is produced or modified. Alternately, the program driving the test (such as an ant build script) can initialize the database to a known state before and/or after the test. Alternately, the test itself can try to take care of database initialization or cleanup.

The approach offered by these base test case classes is, using Spring's transaction abstraction (which will be fully described in subsequent chapters), to automatically create (in the JUnit `setUp()` method) a database transaction before the test is executed, and when the test is done, to automatically roll back the transaction (in the `teardown()` method). The test is free to insert or delete any data in the database as needed, without affecting other tests, as the state will be reset afterwards by the rollback. If there is a need to leave the data as-is after a test, this can be done by calling a `setComplete()` method. This approach is quite usable for a number of test scenarios, with only a few caveats. One is that the test itself must make sure to flush data as appropriate for the particular data access technology. Spring's Hibernate integration support, for example, ensures that all data in the Hibernate session is flushed (if needed) when a transaction commits. Because a test using these base classes will never end up committing the transaction, it's important for the test to manually, as a last step, tell Hibernate to flush all data out to the database so that any problems such as database constraint violations are still caught.

In-Appserver Tests

Chapter 11, "Spring and EJB," demonstrates how to use Apache Cactus to execute test code inside an application deployed in an appserver. While it does this in order to test EJBs, this technique is valid for testing *any* code inside an appserver, so we direct you to that chapter to learn how to use Cactus in this fashion.

Alternatives to XML

The previous chapter and most of this one have focused on XML as the configuration format for Spring bean factories and application contexts. This is appropriate because this is the format used in the great majority of cases to configure the containers. However, the capabilities of the containers, and the configuration format used to read in bean definitions, are really two separate things; there are, in fact, two other existing ways you can get definitions into the containers, along with the possibility of rolling your own.

Definitions from Properties Files

An alternative declarative definition format is the use of Java `Properties` files, and their close cousins, `ResourceBundles`. The `Properties` definition format is not as expressive as XML; there are a number of container capabilities that cannot be expressed using this format, including constructor-injection, method-injection, nested beans, or setting of complex collection types. However, for simple basic bean definitions with Setter Injection, it's fairly concise, and it might also be useful in an environment where it's not desirable to bring in an XML parser. An example might be an applet using only basic BeanFactory functionality, and trying to keep code size and memory use down. One Spring class that uses this format itself is `ResourceBundleViewResolver`, part of Spring's web MVC layer. The use there is well-suited because view definitions are fairly simple, with no nesting needed, and the class is able to take advantage of `ResourceBundles` to load views appropriate to various locales.

Let's see how our Setter Injection configuration sample from the previous chapter would look in `Properties` format. The XML variant:

```xml
<?xml version="1.0" encoding="UTF-8"?>
<!DOCTYPE beans PUBLIC "-//SPRING//DTD BEAN//EN"
    "http://www.springframework.org/dtd/spring-beans.dtd">

<beans>
  <bean id="weatherService" class="ch02.sample2.WeatherServiceImpl">
    <property name="weatherDao">
      <ref local="weatherDao"/>
    </property>
  </bean>
  <bean id="weatherDao" class="ch02.sample2.StaticDataWeatherDaoImpl"/>
</beans>
```

translated to `Properties` format would be:

```
weatherService.class=ch02.sample2.WeatherServiceImpl
weatherService.weatherDao(ref)=weatherDao

weatherDao.class=ch02.sample2.StaticDataWeatherDaoImpl
```

Even taking out the XML header, which is needed only once, this is obviously more concise than the XML format. However, this has to be traded off against the lack of some capabilities. For the `Properties` file format, there is no one-step bean factory or application context constructor; initializing the container becomes a multistep process, using the `PropertiesBeanDefinitionReader` to actually parse this format. Here's a test case for a bean factory, showing the steps:

```java
public void testBeanFactoryLoadedFromProperties() throws Exception {

    DefaultListableBeanFactory bf = new DefaultListableBeanFactory();
    PropertiesBeanDefinitionReader bdReader =
        new PropertiesBeanDefinitionReader(bf);
    Resource def = new ClassPathResource("ch03/sample4/beans.properties");
    bdReader.loadBeanDefinitions(def);
}
```

Here's an equivalent test for an application context. Note that `refresh()` must be called on the `GenericApplicationContext` to fully initialize it after all definitions have been loaded:

```java
public void testApplicationContextLoadedFromProperties() throws Exception {

    GenericApplicationContext ctx = new GenericApplicationContext();
    PropertiesBeanDefinitionReader bdReader =
        new PropertiesBeanDefinitionReader(ctx);
    Resource def = new ClassPathResource("ch03/sample4/beans.properties");
    bdReader.loadBeanDefinitions(def);
    ctx.refresh();
}
```

We'll direct you to the JavaDoc for `PropertiesBeanDefinitionReader` for an actual description of the exact syntax in Properties format, which is fairly simple.

Programmatic Bean Definitions

The functionality of the containers, and the XML and Properties definition formats, are built on a programmatic API for creating and using bean definition metadata, which is fully user accessible. There are a number of classes involved in specifying definition metadata, including:

- ❑ `RootBeanDefinition`: Used to specify a definition for a bean with no parent bean
- ❑ `ChildBeanDefinition`: Allows definitions for beans that inherit settings from their parents
- ❑ `MutablePropertyValues`: Allows simple manipulation of properties, as used in a definition
- ❑ `ConstructorArgumentValues`: Holder for constructor argument values for a bean

Here's a test case showing the previous bean factory definition, handled completely programmatically:

```java
public void testBeanFactoryLoadedProgrammatically() throws Exception {

    DefaultListableBeanFactory bf = new DefaultListableBeanFactory();

    MutablePropertyValues mpv = new MutablePropertyValues();
    mpv.addPropertyValue("weatherDao", new RuntimeBeanReference("weatherDao"));
    RootBeanDefinition weatherService =
        new RootBeanDefinition(WeatherServiceImpl.class, mpv);
    bf.registerBeanDefinition("weatherService", weatherService);

    mpv = new MutablePropertyValues();
    RootBeanDefinition weatherDao =
        new RootBeanDefinition(StaticDataWeatherDaoImpl.class, mpv);
    bf.registerBeanDefinition("weatherDao", weatherDao);
}
```

Other Formats

At the time of the writing of this book, the Spring team is already thinking about how to simplify bean configuration even further. This may include specialized XML dialects to handle specialized concerns such as AOP, smaller tweaks to the existing generic XML format, or the inclusion of completely alternate mechanisms such as definition builders for the Groovy JVM scripting language. However, regardless of the format of the container definition and how it's parsed, clients of the containers are generally unaware of any of these aspects. They deal with the container via the `BeanFactory` and `ApplicationContext` interfaces, and their sub-interfaces, to obtain configured objects in a consistent and predictable manner. Only a small amount of code needs to know or care about how the container is configured. Just as importantly, the containers themselves are unaware of the configuration format; the internal use of bean definition readers, which use the programmatic API to configure the container, is what actually makes it possible to implement other formats relatively easily.

References

This chapter has only touched upon the large subject of testing, which has many excellent books devoted to it. Among others, the authors recommend *JUnit Recipes* by J. B. Rainsberger (Manning, 2004), which offers cookbook-style examples for handling almost any testing concern.

Summary

In this chapter you've built on the base knowledge picked up in the previous chapter to learn about a number of more advanced capabilities of and usage strategies for the Spring container. You should now know how to configure, initialize, and manage the container, as well as handle testing concerns as you put core Spring bean factory and application context functionality to use in your own applications.

You are now ready to learn how other layers in Spring build upon and rely upon the base container capabilities to provide a large number of value-added functionality. In the next chapter, you'll learn about Spring's powerful Aspect-Oriented Programming (AOP) capabilities. AOP is a natural complement to Inversion of Control. You'll see how the AOP portion of the framework can be used to handle additional crosscutting concerns, which normal programming styles have difficulty handling in a nonredundant, decoupled fashion.

Spring and AOP

Aspect-Oriented Programming (*AOP*) is an important technology, well-suited to solving many common problems. Spring offers AOP features to complement its IoC features and ensure that enterprise service code does not pollute your application objects.

In keeping with Spring's layered architecture, Spring's AOP features are separate from the core IoC container. You are not forced to use AOP with Spring. However, most users choose to do so, if only to leverage valuable out-of-the-box services provided by Spring, which are delivered using AOP.

Spring takes a pragmatic approach to AOP. You can use as little AOP as you want, or integrate with AspectJ to harness the power of AOP extensions to the Java language. While learning how to exploit the full power of AOP is likely to take the industry years, Spring enables *incremental* adoption of AOP without the risk of dragging projects to the bleeding edge. We recommend that you take the time to understand the basic concepts of this important technology, which can help you solve practical problems today.

Goals

Enterprise applications often face *crosscutting* concerns — concerns that might potentially affect code in many objects. Consider the following requirements:

❑ Every operation on the `AccountManager` interface should be performed within a transaction.

❑ The return values of certain expensive methods should be cached for a specified period of time.

❑ Whenever an instance field is modified in a domain object, the object should be marked as dirty. All domain objects should implement an `IsModified` interface, exposing whether they're dirty.

❑ A company is conducting a one-month marketing campaign and wants to analyze its effect on user activity. The temporary analysis code is better externalized from the service layer.

By definition, such crosscutting or orthogonal concerns are not well addressed by traditional OOP. For example, the *Decorator* design pattern can help with the first requirement (creating transactions around methods), but it leads to much code duplication. It will result in boilerplate code to begin and end transactions in every `AccountManager` method. If we add a new method, it won't automatically be transactional until we cut and paste that boilerplate code. There's no way to control which methods are transactional besides modifying the `AccountManager` class itself. The only other option has been specific middleware models such as EJB, in which the component model itself applies crosscutting behavior to handle well-known aspects such as transaction management. However, this is invasive—it works only if you jump through the hoops imposed by the particular component model—and it isn't extensible. The services in question are tied to the component model, and you can't add support for your own arbitrary service or behavior.

The second requirement (caching) also results in code duplication. Such *per method* operations can't easily be modularized using OOP alone.

The third requirement (dirty checking domain objects) will need to be addressed through keeping a dirty flag in every affected class, and setting it to true on every data change. If you remember using server-specific optimizations in EJB 1.1 entity beans, you'll remember how error-prone this approach is. It's not just a question of code bloat. We can't solve this problem using inheritance; the dirty flag could be held in an abstract base class that implemented the `IsModified` interface, but the crucial thing is *updating* that flag, and that can't be modularized using OO.

To address such problems, minimizing code duplication, we need a new way to think about program structure. AOP provides this, enabling us to target additional behavior at sets of methods or other points in our application structure using *pointcuts*. In this chapter, we'll see when, and how, to use this capability effectively.

Spring provides support for both proxy-based and class weaving AOP (the latter through integration with products such as AspectJ). This enables us easily to address requirements such as those mentioned—and many others.

Assumptions

This is not a complete introduction to AOP. We assume knowledge of basic AOP concepts. We will not be making the case for AOP. In 2005, we believe that should no longer be necessary.

You should be able to understand the examples in this chapter without deep knowledge of AOP. You can use Spring's AOP capabilities to address common problems such as transaction management without detailed knowledge of AOP. However, we recommend that you increase your understanding of AOP to enable you to make the most of this powerful feature of Spring.

Please see the "References" section later in this chapter for recommended reading. For a discussion of AOP that helps to explain the motivation for Spring's AOP framework, see Chapter 8 of *J2EE without EJB* (Wrox, 2004).

Example

Let's start with an example of how we can use Spring's AOP support to provide a simple, effective solution to a common problem.

Let's assume that we have a business interface called `AccountManager`, and that one of the non-functional requirements is "Email the system administrator when any exception is thrown by a business method, letting the exception propagate to the layer above to handle it."

Thanks to Spring developer Dmitriy Kopylenko for contributing the following example and some of the UML diagrams in this chapter.

Let's take a look at the implementation of this requirement without the help of AOP. Following OO best practice, we'll have an `AccountManager` interface, but as it can easily be deduced from the following implementation class, we won't show it. The implementation class is configured by Setter Injection:

```java
public class AccountManagerImpl implements AccountManager {
    private MailSender mailSender;
    private SimpleMailMessage message;
    private AccountDao accountDao;
    public void setMailSender(MailSender mailSender) {
        this.mailSender = mailSender;
    }

    public void setMessage(SimpleMailMessage message) {
        this.message = message;
    }

    public void setAccountDao(AccountDao accountDao) {
        this.accountDao = accountDao;
    }

private void sendMail(Exception ex) {
        SimpleMailMessage msg = new SimpleMailMessage(this.message);
        msg.setText("Encountered exception " + ex.getMessage());
        this.mailSender.send(msg);
}

    public Account getAccount(String accountId) throws AccountNotFoundException,
DataAccessException {
        try{
            return this.accountDao.findAccount(accountId);
        }
        catch(AccountNotFoundException ex){
            sendMail(ex);
            throw ex;
        }
        catch (DataAccessException ex) {
            sendMail(ex);
            throw ex;
        }
    }

    public void createAccount(Account account) throws DataAccessException,  {
            try{
                if (isInvalid(account)) {
                    throw new InvalidAccountException(account);
    }
                this.accountDao.saveAccount(account);
            }
        catch (IOException ex) {
            sendMail(ex);
```

115

```
            throw ex;
        }

        catch (DataAccessException ex) {
            sendMail(ex);
            throw ex;
        }

    }
}
```

As you can see, the "boilerplate" code of the try-catch block to send email is scattered throughout the code base in different business methods such as getAccount() and createAccount(). Although the actual sending of email can be extracted into the sendMail() method, the invocation of this method crosscuts numerous methods.

The notification functionality is not the main responsibility of the class and is effectively a "crosscutting" behavior, yet it has a major impact on how the class is implemented. The solution is also inelegant. Consider the following problems:

❑ **What if we add more methods requiring exception logging?** We would need to remember to add the boilerplate code to them also. It is no longer possible to add or maintain code in this class without considering the exception notification concern.

❑ **We need a distinct catch block for every checked exception subclass.** Although we really are interested only in the fact that an exception was thrown, not the class of the exception, we need a distinct block for each type of exception to preserve method signatures. While we could catch Exception or even Throwable with a single catch block, we could not rethrow to propagate them to callers without breaking the throws clause of each method signature.

❑ **What if business requirements change, so that exception notification is not required, or a completely different strategy is required?** As exception notification is baked into this class, this could be problematic.

These problems are likely to be magnified many times, as the exception notification policy will need to be enforced not just in one business object, but across the entire code base.

In short, we have a serious problem for code quality and maintainability, which pure OO cannot solve.

The solution is AOP, which enables us to modularize the crosscutting exception notification concern and apply it to any number of methods on any number of objects.

Let's refactor the preceding email notification code into a modular aspect and apply it to our AccountManager using Spring AOP. We begin by writing an aspect class that implements the exception notification policy:

```
public class EmailNotificationThrowsAdvice implements ThrowsAdvice {

private MailSender mailSender;

    private SimpleMailMessage message;

    public void setMailSender(MailSender mailSender) {
        this.mailSender = mailSender;
```

```
    }

    public void setMessage(SimpleMailMessage message) {
        this.message = message;
  }

      public void afterThrowing(Exception ex) throws Throwable {
         SimpleMailMessage msg = new SimpleMailMessage(this.message);
         msg.setText("Encountered exception " + ex.getMessage());
         this.mailSender.send(msg);
      }

    }
```

We can then apply this advice to multiple objects. Following normal Spring practice, we define the advice itself as an object in a Spring IoC container, using Dependency Injection:

```
<bean id="emailNotificationThrowsAdvice"
      class="com.mycompany.EmailNotificationThrowsAdvice">
      <property name="mailSender"><ref bean="mailSender"/></property>
      <property name="message"><ref bean="mailMessage"/></property>
</bean>
```

We can then apply the advice to any number of other objects managed by the Spring container, as follows:

```
<bean id="accountManagerBeanNameProxyCreator"
     class="org.springframework.aop.framework.autoproxy.BeanNameAutoProxyCreator">
     <property name="beanNames"><value>accountManagerTarget</value></property>
     <property name="interceptorNames">
          <list>
               <value>emailNotificationThrowsAdvice</value>
          </list>
     </property>
</bean>
```

Don't worry too much about the details, which we'll explain later. This is one of several ways Spring offers to apply advice to multiple managed objects.

Now we have the pleasant task of removing all the crosscutting code in `AccountManagerImpl` concerned with exception notification:

```
public class AccountManagerImpl implements AccountManager {

    private AccountDao accountDao;

    public void setAccountDao(AccountDao accountDao) {
        this.accountDao = accountDao;
    }

    public Account getAccount(String accountId)
                   throws AccountNotFoundException, DataAccessException {
        return this.accountDao.findAccount(accountId);
    }

    public void createAccount(Account account) throws DataAccessException {
```

117

```
                    this.accountDao.saveAccount(account);
            }
        }
```

The result is a major improvement. The `AccountManager` is purely responsible for account management, making the code much simpler and easier to read and maintain. The exception notification mechanism is cleanly modularized so that it can be maintained separately from business logic. For example, one developer can now revise the exception notification policy without the need to modify large numbers of files that would be affected in the traditional approach.

There is some complexity in setting up the AOP framework, but the payoff is an even greater return if there are more crosscutting concerns to consider. For example, what if any of these methods should be transactional? With the AOP infrastructure in place, it's easy to add a transaction aspect.

We hope you can now see the value proposition in AOP and Spring's integration of AOP with its IoC container. In the rest of this chapter, we'll look at the capabilities of Spring AOP in detail and how you can use other AOP frameworks with Spring.

Spring's AOP Framework

Let's begin by looking at Spring's own AOP framework — a proxy-based framework that works in pure Java. You can use it in any application server and all the required classes are included in the Spring distribution. Although many users think of Spring AOP largely as a powerful middleware alternative to much EJB functionality, Spring AOP can be used in any environment. You can use it in a web container, inside an EJB container behind an EJB facade, in a rich client application — even in an applet.

The Interceptor Chain

Like most proxy-based AOP implementations, Spring AOP is based around the concept of an *interceptor chain*. Invocations are notionally directed toward a *target object*. In AOP terminology, this object contains the *join point*. Each interceptor in the chain provides *around* advice — that is, has the ability to interpose additional behavior before or after the invocation, or short circuit the invocation altogether, returning its own chosen value. Each interceptor controls whether the invocation *proceeds* down the interceptor chain toward the target object, and what the return value should be. So it's possible for an interceptor to chain the arguments or return value, and interpose custom behavior before or after the method on the target object executes.

The target object is said to be *advised* by the AOP framework by the addition of crosscutting behavior.

We'll look at the `org.aopalliance.intercept.MethodInterceptor` interface in detail later in this chapter.

Pros and Cons

The notion of a distinct *target* object is central to understanding Spring AOP.

This concept is different to that seen in some other AOP solutions, such as AspectJ. In those solutions, the byte codes of either the caller or the callee are modified and the advice becomes part of the compiled code at runtime.

The idea of a separate target object has many consequences, both positive and negative. It's a good tradeoff for the intended usage of Spring AOP to address common problems in enterprise applications, some of which were traditionally addressed in a far less flexible way using EJB.

This separation has the following advantages:

❑ **There is no need to perform a special compilation step or instrument the class loader at runtime.** Thus the build and deployment process is that of a plain Java application.

❑ **It's possible to proxy any object,** regardless of what language it is implemented in. Thus you can use Spring's support for scripting languages to implement any managed object in any language, yet still apply the full power of Spring AOP to your scripted objects.

❑ **It enables the use of different advice for multiple instances of the same class, even in the same class loader.** This is difficult or impossible with byte code modification approaches, but is sometimes very useful. For example, imagine that an application uses two `DataSources` of the same class, and we want to apply different exception handling policies to each.

❑ **It is easy to understand** in terms of the Proxy and Decorator design patterns.

❑ **It does not affect the target object.** The target object itself will behave the same way; it has not been altered.

❑ **It's possible to create a proxy programmatically,** in class library style.

The negative consequences are that:

❑ **Spring AOP is limited to method interception.** While Spring's API design, like the AOP Alliance APIs it uses, would allow for other types of join point to be advised, Spring AOP is likely to remain focused around delivering its core value proposition well. For example, it is not possible to advise field access or object creation.

❑ **It's possible only to proxy explicitly.** Objects will not automatically be proxied when created by the `new` operator; proxies must be created programmatically or obtained from a Spring context through Dependency Injection or explicit lookup. This is the most significant of the limitations in practice. However, as Dependency Injection provides such compelling advantages in general, your enthusiasm for the `new` operator is likely to wane significantly when working with an IoC container such as Spring, PicoContainer, or HiveMind.

❑ **Targets are not aware of being proxied.** This is usually a good thing, but it does mean that if a target object calls a method on itself, the call will not be advised. Similarly, if the target passes a collaborator a reference to itself using `this`, calls on that reference will not be advised. We'll discuss how to address this issue when required later in this chapter.

Advice

Let's now move on to some definitions.

The first essential to AOP is *advice*.

> **Advice specifies what to do at a join point. In the case of Spring, this is the additional behavior that Spring will inject around a method invocation. It is most often defined in a *method interceptor*, which will be invoked as part of an interceptor chain wrapping the method invocation.**

The AOP Alliance

Spring's AOP framework is based on the AOP Alliance API. This is a small set of interfaces specifying the signatures required to implement method interception code that can run in multiple AOP frameworks — most important, the `org.aopalliance.intercept.MethodInterceptor` interface. The AOP Alliance was founded in early 2003 by Rod Johnson, Jon Tirsen (creator of Nanning Aspects and a pioneer of proxy-based AOP), and Bob Lee (author and creator of the jAdvise and DynAOP AOP frameworks).

The AOP Alliance interfaces do not presently specify pointcuts. However, they do provide the ability to use interceptors such as Spring's `org.springframework.transaction.interceptor.TransactionInterceptor` in multiple AOP frameworks. This is valuable, as it allows the building of libraries of reusable aspects. Instead of the old EJB model where all services were provided by the container vendor, it's possible to select best-of-breed services for use in any compliant aspect framework — a different way of thinking about assembling exactly the infrastructure required by each application.

> **AOP provides a powerful way of modularizing and, hence, componentizing services such as transaction management. As this becomes reality, monolithic containers aiming to provide all services, such as EJB containers, seem quite literally like dinosaurs, unable to compete with smaller, more agile competitors.**

Besides Spring, DynAOP and JAC implement the AOP Alliance interfaces. AspectJ also provides support for invoking AOP Alliance method interceptors. While if using AspectJ, you'd probably choose the more powerful AspectJ AOP model in general, it's still valuable to be able to use existing method interceptors in AspectJ code.

Method Interceptors

AOP Alliance method interceptors implement the following interface:

```
public interface org.aopalliance.intercept.MethodInterceptor extends Interceptor {

    Object invoke(MethodInvocation invocation) throws Throwable;
}
```

The `MethodInvocation` argument to the `invoke()` method exposes the method being invoked, the target joinpoint, the AOP proxy, and the arguments to the method. The `invoke()` method should return the invocation's result: the return value of the join point.

A simple `MethodInterceptor` implementation might look as follows:

```
public class DebugInterceptor implements MethodInterceptor {

    public Object invoke(MethodInvocation invocation) throws Throwable {
        System.out.println("Before: invocation=[" + invocation + "]");
        Object rval = invocation.proceed();
        System.out.println("Invocation returned");
        return rval;
    }
}
```

The `proceed()` method on the `MethodInvocation` interface is used to invoke the next interceptor in the chain. If the interceptor invoking `proceed()` is the last in the chain, the target method on the target object will be invoked by calling `proceed()`, and control will flow back down the chain as shown in Figure 4-1.

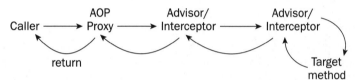

Figure 4-1

If you're familiar with Servlet filters, or any of the many other special-purpose APIs using a similar interception concept, you already understand the key concept here. The only difference is that this is a general-purpose approach that can be used with any POJO, whatever the method signatures involved.

Spring Advice Types

Besides the AOP Alliance `MethodInterceptor`, Spring provides several advice types of its own. These are implemented under the covers using AOP Alliance `MethodInterceptors`, but they offer a slightly different programming model.

Around advice such as a `MethodInterceptor` can be used to achieve anything that other advice types can. However, it's not always best to use the most powerful construct available. Often we want to expose the minimum amount of power to get the job done. Also, thinking of AOP purely in terms of interception is not always the best approach.

Spring's additional advice types are inspired by those offered by AspectJ, which also provides the choice of around advice and more restricted advice types, and which has demonstrated its value.

The UML class diagram shown in Figure 4-2 illustrates the different advice types supported out of the box by Spring. Note that all are descended from the tag interface `org.aopalliance.aop.Advice`, which is taken as an argument by many Spring AOP framework methods, enabling consistent manipulation of all advice types.

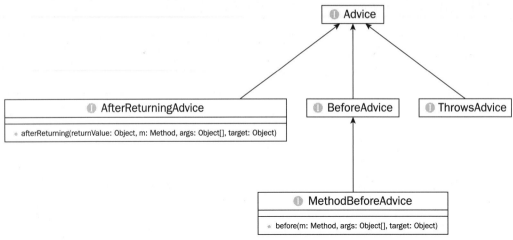

Figure 4-2

> Using a Spring-specific advice type, such as `MethodBeforeAdvice` or `ThrowsAdvice`, **may be the simplest and most natural way of expressing a particular construct. It also minimizes the potential for errors, as there's no need to call** `MethodInvocation.proceed()`.
>
> **If you choose to use Spring-specific advice types, you can still easily use the code in another AOP framework supporting the AOP Alliance interfaces by wrapping the Spring-specific advice in the relevant Spring wrapper, such as** `org.springframework.aop` `.framework.adapter.MethodBeforeAdviceInterceptor`. **To facilitate use outside Spring, these wrapper classes do not depend on any other Spring framework classes.**

Let's look at the other advice types offered by Spring.

Before Advice

Before advice, as its name implies, executes *before* the join point. While Spring offers a generic `org.springframework.aop.BeforeAdvice` interface that could be used with any kind of join point, the `org.springframework.aop.MethodBeforeAdvice` subinterface is always used for method interception. You will always implement `MethodBeforeAdvice`.

The signature of a before advice exposes the target method and arguments. The `before()` method returns void, meaning that before advice cannot change the return value. However, it can throw any throwable, to break the interceptor chain:

```
public interface MethodBeforeAdvice extends BeforeAdvice {

    void before(Method m, Object[] args, Object target) throws Throwable;
}
```

Let's look at a simple implementation that counts method invocations:

```
public class CountingBeforeAdvice implements MethodBeforeAdvice {
    private int count;
    public void before(Method m, Object[] args, Object target) {
        ++count;
    }

    public int getCount() {
        return count;
    }
}
```

Before advice is particularly useful for auditing style operations, and security checks.

> Sharp-eyed readers will note that this advice, like the advice in the next few examples, is not entirely threadsafe. Although ints are atomic, and the advice's state cannot become corrupted, the count may not be entirely accurate under heavy load (which may or may not matter). In this case, synchronization would easily solve the problem without excessive impact on throughput. However, it does bring up an important point: Advice instances are most often shared among threads, so we need to consider thread safety issues, exactly as with service objects. Typically — as with service objects — advices are naturally threadsafe, so this is not a problem. (Consider the Spring transaction interceptor, which does not need to hold read-write instance variables, as its behavior depends on per-invocation state such as the method being invoked.)

After Returning Advice

After returning advice is invoked when a method returns successfully, without throwing an exception. As with before advice, the return type is void; after returning advices are not intended to change the return value.

The interface again contains a single method. Again, it's not possible to change the return value — this is reserved to `MethodInterceptor` around advice:

```
public interface org.springframework.aop.AfterReturningAdvice extends Advice {

    void afterReturning(Object returnValue, Method m,
            Object[] args, Object target)
            throws Throwable;
}
```

We could implement our count as an after returning advice as follows:

```
public class CountingAfterReturningAdvice implements AfterReturningAdvice {
    private int count;

    public void afterReturning(Object returnValue, Method m, Object[] args,
```

```
                            Object target) {
            ++count;
        }

        public int getCount() {
            return count;
        }
    }
```

Although there might not seem to be much difference in effect on such a simple count from the before advice shown earlier (merely counting invocations after, rather than before, the method invocation), in fact there is: This advice will count only successful method invocations, not those that throw an exception.

Throws Advice

Spring's *throws advice* differs from other advice types in that it is more strongly typed (in terms of method arguments), yet has a less well-defined interface.

The `org.springframework.aop.ThrowsAdvice` interface does not contain any methods; it is a tag interface identifying that the given object implements one or more typed throws advice methods. These methods should be of the following form:

```
afterThrowing([Method, args, target,] Throwable)
```

Only the last argument is required. Thus each `afterThrowing()` method must take either one or four arguments, depending on whether the implementation is interested in the method and arguments. Unlike the case of other advice types, where there is a single strongly typed method to implement, a throws advice may implement any number of overloaded `afterThrowing()` methods to handle different exceptions.

A counting throws advice, reacting to any exception, might look as follows:

```
public class CountingThrowsAdvice implements ThrowsAdvice {
    private int count;

    public void afterThrowing(Exception ex) throws Throwable {
        ++count;
    }

    public int getCount() {
        return count;
    }
}
```

The following advice will be invoked if a `RemoteException` is thrown. It will also react to any subclass of `RemoteException` being thrown:

```
public class RemoteThrowsAdvice implements ThrowsAdvice {

    public void afterThrowing(RemoteException ex) throws Throwable {
        // Do something with remote exception
    }
}
```

The following advice is invoked if a `ServletException` or a `RemoteException` is thrown. Unlike the previous examples, this class implements an `afterThrowing()` method taking all four arguments, so it has access to the invoked method, method arguments, and target object:

```
public static class ServletThrowsAdviceWithArguments implements ThrowsAdvice {

    public void afterThrowing(Method m, Object[] args, Object target,
ServletException ex) {
        // Do something with all arguments
    }

    public void afterThrowing(RemoteException ex) throws Throwable {
        // Do something with remote exception
    }
}
```

Throws advice is perhaps the most useful of the specialized Spring advices. While it is, of course, possible to react to exceptions using interception around advice, throws advice is clearer. And, as our initial example in this chapter showed, it's often important to apply consistent, crosscutting policies in the event of failures.

Other Advice Types

The Spring AOP framework is also extensible to allow the implementation of custom advice types. This is a rarely used advanced feature and beyond the scope of this chapter. If you would like to see an example, look at the `org.springframework.aop.SimpleBeforeAdvice` class in the Spring test suite, and the `org.springframework.aop.SimpleBeforeAdviceAdapter` class that extends the AOP framework to support it, without any modification to existing Spring code.

This extensibility allows support for other flavors of AOP such as the concept of *typed advice*, introduced by Rickard Oberg and originally called *abstract schema advice*. This kind of advice involves an abstract class that implements those methods whose behavior should be advised, while retaining the ability to proceed through a special method invocation. Typed advice represents a significantly different approach to AOP than other advice types. However, the fact that it can be accommodated within Spring's advice support—without changing the core of Spring AOP—indicates the flexibility of the Spring AOP framework. Typed advice is likely to be supported by Spring out of the box post–Spring 1.2.

Pointcuts

As noted at the beginning of this chapter, the key to AOP is providing a different way of thinking about application structure.

This structural thinking is captured in the form of *pointcuts*. Pointcuts are predicates determining which joinpoints a piece of advice should apply to. It's more intuitive—although not entirely accurate—to think of a pointcut as a *set of joinpoints:* for example, a set of methods that might be targeted by an advice.

> **Pointcuts identify where advice should apply. The magic of AOP lies more in the specification of *where* action should be taken (pointcuts) than *what* action to apply (advice).**

Spring Pointcut Concepts

Spring pointcuts are essentially ways of identifying method invocations that fit a certain criteria. Often this means identifying methods; sometimes it means identifying methods in a certain context. A pointcut might select a set of method invocations such as:

❑   All setter methods.

❑   All methods in a particular package.

❑   All methods returning void.

❑   All method calls with one argument, where that argument is passed a null value. This last is an example of a pointcut that identifies methods in a certain context. Whether or not this pointcut is satisfied can't be known until runtime.

As the possibilities are limitless, Spring provides a programmable pointcut model.

The Pointcut Interface and Friends

Spring expresses pointcuts through the `org.springframework.aop.Pointcut` interface, shown as follows:

```
public interface Pointcut {
 ClassFilter getClassFilter();
 MethodMatcher getMethodMatcher();
 }
```

You can implement the `Pointcut` interface yourself, but it's nearly always best to use one of the convenient pointcut implementations Spring provides, which include base classes for implementing custom pointcuts.

The `Pointcut` interface is broken into two dependent interfaces because class filtering and method matching are occasionally used independently — for example, *introduction* (discussed later in this chapter) requires only class filtering.

The `MethodMatcher` is the most important of the two interfaces returned by a `Pointcut`. As its name suggests, it tests methods (and, optionally, arguments) for matching. We'll discuss this important interface shortly.

The `ClassFilter` interface is used to limit which target classes the pointcut applies to:

```
public interface ClassFilter {

    boolean matches(Class clazz);

    ClassFilter TRUE = TrueClassFilter.INSTANCE;

}
```

For example, we might want to limit matches to all classes in a particular package, all classes derived from a particular class, or all classes implementing a particular interface. By "target class" we mean the class of the target object, not the interface or class the invoked method is declared on. For example, it will be a class like `DefaultAccountManager` or `AccountManagerImpl`, rather than the interface `AccountManager`.

The canonical instance ClassFilter.TRUE will match all classes. This is commonly used, as custom class matching is rarer than custom method matching.

> *The* Pointcut *interface could be extended to address matching fields and other joinpoints. However, there are no plans to add such support in Spring.*

Static and Dynamic Pointcuts

The terms *static* and *dynamic* are given varying meanings in AOP usage.

Spring uses *static* to refer to a pointcut that can be evaluated when a proxy is created. Such a pointcut will be evaluated based on criteria that can't change afterwards, such as the method invoked, any annotations on the method, or the interface the method is invoked on.

In Spring terminology, a *dynamic* pointcut is one that not only may have static criteria, but also relies on information known only when an invocation is made, such as the argument values or the call stack.

Dynamic pointcuts are slower to evaluate than static pointcuts and allow less potential for optimization. It's always necessary to evaluate them on each invocation to which they might apply, although some dynamic pointcuts can be excluded in advance, if they cannot possibly match particular methods.

In Spring, both static and dynamic pointcuts are captured in a single interface, org.springframework.aop.MethodMatcher:

```
public interface MethodMatcher {

    boolean matches(Method m, Class targetClass);

    boolean isRuntime();

    boolean matches(Method m, Class targetClass, Object[] args);

}
```

A dynamic pointcut will return true in the isRuntime() method; a static pointcut false. If the isRuntime() method returns false, the 3-argument dynamic matches() method will never be invoked.

The method argument to the matches() methods will be the declaring method on the class or interface the proxy invokes. Thus if there is an AccountManager interface and the advised instance is of class AccountManagerImpl, the 2-argument matches() method will be invoked with the first argument being the invoked method on AccountManager and the second argument being class AccountManagerImpl.

Pointcuts Shipped with Spring

While it's easy enough to implement any of these interfaces yourself, there's usually no need. Spring provides concrete pointcuts and abstract base classes for your convenience.

Pointcut Constants

If you want to do certain common matching operations, you can use the constants defined in the org.springframework.aop.support.Pointcuts class.

❑   GETTERS is a constant Pointcut object matching any getter method in any class.

❑   SETTERS is a constant Pointcut object matching any setter method in any class.

NameMatchMethodPointcut

The simple concrete `org.springframework.aop.support.NameMatchMethodPointcut` class is useful for programmatic proxy creation, as well as configuration in a Spring factory via Setter Injection. It includes the following methods:

```
NameMatchMethodPointcut addMethodName(String methodName)
void setMappedName(String methodName)
void setMappedNames(String methodName)
```

For convenience, the `addMethodName()` method returns `this`, so you can add multiple method names in one line as follows:

```
Pointcut pc = new
NameMatchMethodPointcut().addMethodName("setAge").addMethodName("setName");
```

The two JavaBean properties are for use with Setter Injection.

`NameMatchMethodPointcut` is intended for simple uses. All methods with the given name will be advised in the event of method overloading. This may or may not be what you want, but provides a simple API.

Regular Expression Pointcuts

For more sophisticated out-of-the-box pointcuts, regular expressions provide a good way of selecting methods.

Regular expression pointcuts are ideally suited to configuration via XML or other metadata, and thus fit well into typical usage of Spring.

Both Jakarta ORO and the Java 1.4 regular expression API are supported, so this functionality is available even on Java 1.3. `org.springframework.aop.support.Perl5RegexpMethodPointcut` uses Jakarta ORO; and `org.springframework.aop.support.JdkRegexpMethodPointcut` uses Java 1.4 regular expression support. As both these classes share a common base class, usage is identical.

Configuration is done through the following properties:

❑   **patterns:** Array of regular expressions for methods that the pointcut will match

❑   **pattern:** Convenient `String` property when you have just a single pattern and don't need an array

Matching takes place against the fully qualified method name, such as `com.mycompany.mypackage` `.MyClass.absquatulate`. This means that you must remember to consider the package: This method could be matched by the regular expression `.*absquatulate`, but *not* by `absquatulate`, which doesn't match the package prefix.

If you are not familiar with regular expression syntax, please refer to documentation on regular expression syntax for information about wildcards and other capabilities of Java 1.4 or ORO "Perl" regular expressions.

The following example shows XML configuration of a regular expression pointcut:

```
<bean id="settersAndAbsquatulatePointcut"
  class="org.springframework.aop.support.JdkRegexpMethodPointcut">
```

```
        <property name="patterns">
                <list>
                        <value>.*get.*</value>
                        <value>.*absquatulate</value>
                </list>
        </property>
</bean>
```

ControlFlowPointcut

Another out-of-the-box pointcut is dynamic, rather than static, and concerns the call stack that led to the current invocation.

This is similar to the AspectJ *cflow* construct, although much less powerful. However, it is powerful enough to address some important requirements: for example, applying a special security check if a business method was invoked from a web GUI, rather than a web services client.

Control flow pointcuts perform significantly better on J2SE 1.4 and above because of the availability of the new StackTraceElement *API that avoids the need to parse an exception stack trace String.*

You can configure control flow pointcuts programmatically or declaratively (using setter injection). However, programmatic definition, in a custom pointcut or advisor, is most common. The following control flow pointcut will match any method invocation under the scope of a method from MyWebTierObject:

```
Pointcut pc = new
org.springframework.aop.support.ControlFlowPointcut(MyWebTierObject.class)
```

Pointcut composition works best programmatically. It's easy to create pointcut instances or pointcut factory methods that can then be used in Spring metadata.

StaticMethodMatcherPointcut Base Class

Most likely when you implement a custom pointcut it will be static. Most likely you won't bother with a custom ClassFilter element. In this case, you are best to extend Spring's convenient StaticMethodMatcherPointcut class, as follows:

```
public static Pointcut myStaticPointcut = new StaticMethodMatcherPointcut() {
 public boolean matches(Method m, Class targetClass) {
        // implement custom check
 }
};
```

As the example shows, you can then create a pointcut by implementing a single method. This is especially useful if you want to create a pointcut in an anonymous inner class, as shown.

DynamicMethodMatcherPointcut Base Class

This is an analogous base class for use when you want to implement a custom dynamic pointcut, where you need to implement the 3-argument matches() method as well. Again, it's useful when an anonymous inner class is appropriate. Use it as follows:

```
public static Pointcut myDynamicPointcut = new DynamicMethodMatcherPointcut() {

 public boolean matches(Method m, Class targetClass) {
```

129

```
            // implement custom check
    }

    public boolean matches(Method m, Class targetClass, Object[] args) {
            // implement custom check
    }

    }
```

The 2-argument matches() method will be invoked exactly as in the static pointcut example we've just seen. It will be evaluated when the proxy is created, identifying the set of methods (for which it returns true) which *might* match the dynamic criteria.

The 3-argument matches() method is invoked only on methods that match the 2-argument method, and allows custom argument-based checks.

Operating on Pointcuts

The org.springframework.aop.support.Pointcuts class provides static methods for manipulating pointcuts:

```
public static Pointcut union(Pointcut a, Pointcut b)
   public static Pointcut intersection(Pointcut a, Pointcut b)
```

The union of two pointcuts is the pointcut matching any method matched by either pointcut. The intersection matches only methods matched by both pointcuts.

This enables convenient pointcut composition. This is normally more convenient in Java than in XML. However, it's easy to create Java classes that will then be configured in XML bean definition files.

Advisors

In order to pull pointcuts and advice together, we need an object that contains both: that is, containing the *behavior that should be added* (advice) and *where that behavior should apply* (pointcut).

Spring introduces the concept of an *Advisor*: an object that includes both advice and a pointcut specifying where that advice should apply. Unlike advice and pointcut, an advisor is not an established AOP concept, but a Spring-specific term.

> **The purpose of an Advisor is to allow both advice and pointcuts to be reusable independently.**

If an advice is used without a pointcut, a pointcut will be created that will match all method invocations. Spring uses the canonical instance Pointcut.TRUE in this case. Thus it is normally possible to use an advice instead of an advisor if you want the advice to apply to all proxied methods.

Advisor Implementations

Besides the case of introductions (discussed later in this chapter), which don't require a MethodMatcher, Advisors are instances of PointcutAdvisor.

DefaultPointcutAdvisor

`org.springframework.aop.support.DefaultPointcutAdvisor` is the most commonly used `Advisor` class. It is a generic `Advisor` that can contain any pointcut and advice. It can be used in the majority of cases where an `Advisor` is required; there is seldom any need to implement a custom Advisor. (On the other hand, you will quite often implement custom pointcuts if you make sophisticated use of Spring AOP.)

A `DefaultPointcutAdvisor` instance can be created programmatically as follows:

```
Advisor myAdvice = new DefaultPointcutAdvisor(myPointcut, myAdvice);
```

It can also be configured using Dependency Injection, via either setter or constructor injection. The following illustrates the use of Setter Injection to achieve the same result declaratively:

```
<bean name ="myAdvisor"
class="org.springframework.aop.support.DefaultPointcutAdvisor">
    <property name="pointcut"><ref local="myPointcut" /></property>
    <property name="advice"><ref local="myAdvice" /></property>
</bean>
```

Of course you may choose to user inner bean definitions for pointcut and advice properties. If these objects are not referenced elsewhere in configuration, this can be regarded as best practice.

Regular Expressions, Take 2

Often we want to create an advisor using a regular expression pointcut. Spring provides a concrete advisor for this common case.

```
<bean id="settersAndAbsquatulateAdvisor"
   class="org.springframework.aop.support.RegexpMethodPointcutAdvisor">
        <property name="advice"><ref local="myAdvice"/></property>
        <property name="patterns">
                <list>
                        <value>.*set.*</value>
                        <value>.*absquatulate</value>
                </list>
        </property>
</bean>
```

Configuration properties are the same as defined in `AbstractRegexpMethodPointcut`, with the addition of a `perl5` property, which determines whether to use Jakarta ORO Perl5 regular expressions.

Wrapping

The publicly visible Spring invocation chain consists of advisors. This representation is optimized internally to minimize the need for pointcut evaluation at runtime, but that's not visible to the application developer. Thus any advice you add *without specifying an advisor* (as an `Advisor` subclass) will be wrapped in an advisor. This is important to remember. Thus if you want to programmatically query an advice you added, the `getAdvisors[]` method of the `Advised` interface (discussed shortly) will return a `DefaultPointcutAdvisor` that wraps your advice, but matches any method.

Integration with the Spring IoC Container

Spring's AOP framework does not aim to be the most powerful AOP framework. It aims to provide a good solution to common problems faced in J2EE development, and a close integration with Spring's IoC container.

To this end:

❑　Any object created by the IoC container can easily be advised.

❑　All AOP framework objects, such as pointcuts and advices, can be configured using Spring IoC.

This means that all AOP objects are first-class parts of the application. For example, a dynamic pointcut could match methods at runtime depending on the state of other application objects — for example, a security check could be applied based on comparing certain method arguments to a `Limit` object.

Basic Proxy Configuration

To create a Spring proxy, it's necessary to use a proxy factory, or configure a context to "autoproxy" objects it manages.

All proxy factories are derived from `org.springframework.aop.ProxyConfig`. This provides common configuration properties that can be set programmatically or by Setter Injection.

When an AOP proxy is created, it holds a reference to the configuration object that created it. A configuration object may create many proxies.

Subclasses of `ProxyConfig` normally double as *proxy factories*. While it is possible for a proxy configuration to become divorced from a factory — for example, as a result of serialization and deserialization — normally subclasses of `ProxyConfig` know how to create proxies.

Note that all configuration parameters discussed in this section will affect all AOP proxies created by a configuration object.

The UML class diagram shown in Figure 4-3 illustrates the hierarchy below `ProxyConfig`.

It's important to understand the function of each class in this diagram:

❑　`ProxyConfig` is the base class for all objects than can create AOP proxies.

❑　`AdvisedSupport` holds configuration for objects with a single `TargetSource` and set of interfaces.

❑　`ProxyFactoryBean` is used to define proxies in XML or other metadata configuration. As its name indicates, it is a `FactoryBean`, as discussed in Chapter 3 on Spring's IoC container.

❑　`ProxyFactory` is used to create proxies programmatically, without an IoC container.

❑   `AbstractAutoProxyCreator` and subclasses handle "autoproxying," discussed later. They inherit basic configuration from `ProxyConfig`, but do not extend from `AdvisedSupport`, as `TargetSource`, interfaces, and other `AdvisedSupport` configuration parameters are relevant to a single proxy type, rather than generic proxy creation.

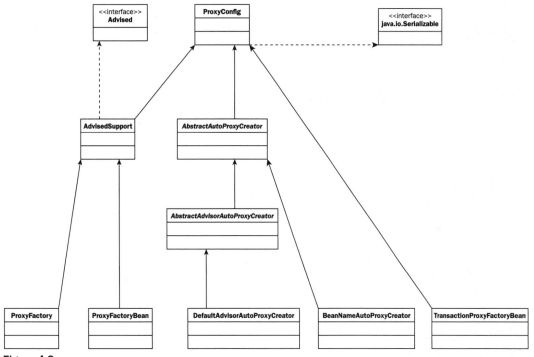

Figure 4-3

> **A quick summary:** `ProxyConfig` **defines configuration relating to the creation of proxies in general, such as whether to proxy the target class.**
>
> `AdvisedSupport` **extends** `ProxyConfig` **to define configuration relating to the creation of one or more instances** *of the same type of proxy.* **For example,** `AdvisedSupport` **defines interfaces to be proxied.**
>
> **Thus "autoproxy creators" or other objects that can create many proxies of different types extend** `ProxyConfig`, **not** `AdvisedSupport`.

All configuration objects inherit the behavior shown in the following table from `ProxyConfig`.

Property	Purpose	Default	Notes
proxyTargetClass	Cause the proxy to extend the target class — making public methods on the class available, as well as methods on all interfaces implemented by the class — rather than implement only the interfaces implemented by the target class, or the subset identified. Setting this property to true forces the use of CGLIB proxies, rather than J2SE dynamic proxies, which can implement interfaces only.	False	Setting this value to true requires CGLIB on the classpath. We recommend the use of J2SE dynamic proxies rather than CGLIB. It's simpler, only marginally slower, and avoids problems with final variables and some other quirks of CGLIB. It's good practice to program to interfaces, rather than classes, anyway, so using CGLIB this way should seldom be necessary. However, it is sometimes unavoidable when you need to proxy legacy classes.
exposeProxy	Expose the AOP proxy as a thread local on each AOP invocation.	False	This property defaults to false because the thread local binding has a small performance impact.
optimize	Tells the framework to apply optimizations if possible.	False	Effect depends on the AOP proxy created. As of Spring 1.1, the optimize flag doesn't have a significant effect and shouldn't normally be used.
frozen	To allow advice to be fixed, preventing changes at runtime.	False	Setting frozen to true may allow for optimization, with a gain in runtime performance in some cases. It may also be appropriate for security: for example, to prevent a user from removing a security interceptor or transaction interceptor. Note that the frozen field does not prevent a user querying for advice and possibly changing the state of any advice in the advice chain; it's just not possible to *change* the advice chain, for example by replacing an advice or adding or removing an advice.

Property	Purpose	Default	Notes
opaque	To prevent proxies being cast to Advised, preventing querying or modifying advice.	False	Provides a higher-level of security than the frozen flag. When this property is true, it's impossible to cast a proxy created by the configuration to the Advised interface, meaning that advice cannot be queried or changed.
aopProxyFactory	Provides an extension point, allowing for customization of how proxies are created.	Instance of DefaultAop ProxyFactory, which knows how to create J2SE dynamic proxies and CGLIB proxies	Not serialized. There should be no need for user code to modify this property; it allows for extensions to the framework.

AdvisedSupport is the superclass of ProxyFactory and ProxyFactoryBean. It adds the properties shown in the following table, defining a single type of proxy, with a particular set of interfaces and TargetSource.

Name	Type	Purpose	Default	Notes
targetSource	Bean property	Allows the framework to obtain the target object on each invocation	EmptyTarget Source, containing a null target	The TargetSource interface is discussed in detail later. The application developer usually sets a target, rather than a TargetSource. You might set this property to use a pooling or other "dynamic" TargetSource.
target	Writable bean property of type java.lang.Object	Sets the target	No target. Setting the target Source property is an alternative to setting this property.	This property is not readable, as the target object will be wrapped in a Singleton TargetSource.

Table continued on following page

Name	Type	Purpose	Default	Notes
interfaces	Bean property with additional config methods	Sets the proxied interface	The default is for the AOP framework to automatically proxy all interfaces implemented by the target, or to use CGLIB to proxy the target class if the target implements no interfaces, and thus J2SE dynamic proxies are not usable.	Configure using `setInterfaces (Class[])` property setter or using `addInterface (Class)`.
listeners	Configured via methods	Adds listeners that receive notifications of changes to advice (such as adding or removing advice)		Not serialized. Primarily intended for framework use.
advisorChain Factory	Bean property			Not for end-user use.
addAdvice/ removeAdvice	Allows advice to be added or removed			Most of these configuration methods are inherited from the `Advised` interface.
addAdvisor/ removeAdvisor	Allows Advisors to be added or removed			The add*XXXX* methods are typically used when constructing a proxy programmatically with `ProxyFactoryBean`, not when configuring a proxy using XML or other bean definitions.

ProxyFactoryBean adds the properties shown in the following table.

Property	Purpose	Default	Notes
singleton	Indicate whether there should be a single shared instance of the proxy, or whether a new instance should be created for each getBean() call or distinct object dependency	true	Is the ProxyFactoryBean intended to create a shared instance, or should it create a new instance for each call to its getObject() method? This is a common concept to factory beans. If the singleton property is true, a single proxy instance will be cached in ProxyFactoryBean.
interceptor Names	Establish interceptor chain	Empty interceptor chain (not valid unless a custom TargetSource is set)	This method can be used to specify the name of Advice or Advisor beans in the current factory.
advisor Adapter Registry	Allow extension of Spring AOP to recognize new advice type	A default implementation that understands the Spring advice types beyond the AOP Alliance Method Interceptor: before, after returning, and throws Advice.	Not intended for use by application developers. Allows control over custom advice type conversion.

Using ProxyFactoryBean

ProxyFactoryBean is the lowest-level and most flexible way of creating proxies in a Spring IoC environment. However, it is also the most verbose. Nevertheless, it is important to understand it, as it directly exposes the core concepts of Spring AOP.

Basic Concepts

Let's look at the XML-based configuration most commonly used to configure AOP proxies.

Note that ProxyFactoryBeans can be defined using any supported Spring configuration format, not just XML.

This requires the following configuration steps:

1. Define beans for any Advisors you wish to use (possibly including separate Advice and Pointcut bean references), and any Interceptors or other Advices you wish to use that aren't contained in Advisors.

2. Define a `ProxyFactoryBean` bean definition with the public name you want your proxy to have. The most important properties to set here are:

    a.   proxyInterfaces

    b.   interceptorNames

    c.   target

The following example shows the use of `ProxyFactoryBean` with an `Advisor` and an `Advice` (an interceptor):

```xml
<bean id="myAdvisor" class="com.mycompany.MyAdvisor">
    <property name="someProperty"><value>Custom string property
value</value></property>
</bean>

<bean id="debugInterceptor"
class="org.springframework.aop.interceptor.DebugInterceptor">
</bean>

<bean id="person"
    class="org.springframework.aop.framework.ProxyFactoryBean">
    <property name="proxyInterfaces"><value>com.mycompany.Person</value></property>

    <!-- Use inner bean, not local reference to target -->
    <property name="target">
        <bean class="com.mycompany.PersonImpl">
            <property name="name"><value>Tony</value></property>
            <property name="age"><value>51</value></property>
        </bean>
    </property>

    <property name="interceptorNames">
        <list>
            <value>myAdvisor</value>
            <value>debugInterceptor</value>
        </list>
    </property>
</bean>
```

You should be familiar with most of these properties.

The most important property on `ProxyFactoryBean` is `interceptorNames`. This is a list of names of advice or advisors that together build up the interceptor chain. Ordering is important. We need to use a list of bean names here, rather than advice or advisor bean references, as there may be singleton or non-singleton advices.

The bean names in the `interceptorNames` properties need not only be interceptors; they can be any advice or advisor. The "interceptor" part of the name is retained largely for backward compatibility.

Note the use of an "inner bean" for the target. We could equally use a `<ref>` element instead of an inline inner bean definition in the preceding target element. In fact, this usage is common:

```xml
<bean id="personTarget" class="com.mycompany.PersonImpl">
    . . .
```

```
    </bean>

    ...

    <bean id="person"
        class="org.springframework.aop.framework.ProxyFactoryBean">
        <!--Other configuration omitted -->
        <property name="target"><ref local="personTarget"/></property>
    ...
```

This usage — with a top-level "target" object — has the disadvantage that there are now two beans of type `Person`: `personTarget` and `person`. We're most likely interested only in person (the AOP proxy): other beans will express a dependency on that using Dependency Injection. If autowiring by type is used to resolve dependencies, having an extra bean of this type will be a problem, as it will be impossible to resolve a dependency of type `Person` unambiguously. With an inner bean as in the first example, there is a single bean. It's impossible to get access to the unadvised object.

> We recommend using an inner bean to define the target for a `ProxyFactoryBean` in most cases.

Simplifying Configuration When Using ProxyFactoryBean

Clearly if you have multiple proxies that are set up identically, using multiple, very similar `ProxyFactory Bean` definitions might become verbose. Worse still, you'd have duplication in your XML configuration files and would need to change multiple elements to make a consistent change such as adding a new advisor.

There are several solutions to this problem. One is to use "autoproxy creators," discussed later, rather than `ProxyFactoryBean`. But you can also use the bean definition inheritance features of the Spring IoC container to help. This can enable you to capture shared definitions such as interceptor names, `proxy TargetClass`, or any other proxy configuration flags you may set, *once* in an abstract base definition, extended by each child definition. The child definition will typically add only a unique name, and the "target" property: the object that is to be proxied, along with any properties that that inner bean definition requires.

The following example, refactoring the "Person" example shown earlier, illustrates this approach and shows best practice for using `ProxyFactoryBean` consistently across multiple application objects:

```
    <bean id="proxyTemplate"
        class="org.springframework.aop.framework.ProxyFactoryBean"
        abstract="true">

        <property name="interceptorNames">
            <list>
                <value>myAdvisor</value>
                <value>debugInterceptor</value>
            </list>
        </property>
    </bean>


    <bean id="person"
        parent="proxyTemplate">
```

```
        <property name="proxyInterfaces"><value>com.mycompany.Person</value></property>

        <!-- Use inner bean, not local reference to target -->
        <property name="target">
            <bean class="com.mycompany.PersonImpl">
                <property name="name"><value>Tony</value></property>
                <property name="age"><value>51</value></property>
            </bean>
        </property>

    </bean>
```

The `proxyTemplate` bean definition specifies the interceptor chain. This bean definition is abstract and cannot be instantiated. (It is incomplete and does not identify a target.) Any number of child bean definitions can "extend" the `proxyTemplate` definition, specifying a target. They can optionally add further properties, such as proxy interfaces.

Duplication is error-prone and nearly always worth eliminating. When you have several proxies defined, there can also be a significant saving in the total volume of configuration data.

> **Remember the option of dedicated proxies such as** `TransactionProxyFactoryBean` **and** `LocalStatelessSessionProxyFactoryBean`**. These provide less control over AOP configuration but are simpler to use when you're primarily interested in the aspect they specialize in. You will typically use these, too, with the common parent approach to avoiding code duplication. Look at the transactional bean definitions in the Spring PetStore example for an illustration of best practice for** `TransactionProxyFactoryBean` **usage.**

Understanding the Lifecycle of Objects

As with everything you do with Spring IoC, you should consider the lifecycle of AOP proxies and the objects they reference.

Any AOP framework object can be configured via Spring IoC. This means that we can choose whether we want to define the necessary beans with *singleton* or *prototype* (non-singleton) scope.

Let's see why this is important and useful.

In simple cases, all objects will be singletons. For example, a transactional proxy might wrap a threadsafe singleton service object by using a singleton instance of a threadsafe `TransactionInterceptor`.

However, what if an advice needs to hold state on behalf of the target? For example, what if it needs to guard the target based on whether a lock is activated? In this case the advice and/or containing advice can be said to be stateful. Of course in this case, there is a greater overhead to creating a proxy, as a new advice instance needs to be created when the interceptor chain is created. Of course, it will be cached for the life of that proxy.

You can mix and match singleton and non-singleton advices in the same proxy definition. Normally, for efficiency reasons, you will want to minimize the number of stateful advices you have.

If you need stateful advice, you must remember to set the `singleton` property of `ProxyFactoryBean` to false. Otherwise the `ProxyFactoryBean` will assume singleton usage and cache a single proxy instance as an optimization.

There is no point using a prototype `ProxyFactoryBean` unless your target is also a prototype.

> "Enterprise-level" generic advice, such as transaction interceptors, will typically be singleton scoped.
>
> Pointcuts will typically be singleton-scoped, as they're unlikely to hold per-proxy state.
>
> However, if it's necessary for some aspects to hold state on behalf of an advised target, Spring AOP fully supports this.

Autoproxying

`ProxyFactoryBean` provides a powerful way of specifying exactly how each proxy is created. The downside is that with one `ProxyFactoryBean` for each proxy instance, there's quite a bit of configuration for each bean.

Autoproxying means that depending on some configuration, proxying is applied consistently to a number of objects.

Autoproxying is built on the IoC container's *bean post processor* mechanism, discussed in Chapter 3. This enables objects implementing the `org.springframework.beans.factory.config.BeanPostProcessor` interface to wrap or otherwise replace the raw objects resulting from bean definitions. In the case of AOP autoproxying, various "autoproxy creator" implementations use different approaches and configuration data to wrap the raw POJO resulting from a bean definition in an AOP proxy.

Thus an infrastructure team may be responsible for setting up the autoproxy definitions while application developers simply implement POJOs and write regular bean definitions — without any AOP information — as they focus on the application domain.

There are two main types of autoproxy creator:

❑ `BeanNameAutoProxyCreator`: This wraps a number of raw bean definitions in an AOP proxy with the same config, applying AOP advice.

❑ `DefaultAdvisorAutoProxyCreator`: This causes bean definitions to be proxied regardless of their bean name. Proxying will add any advisors whose pointcuts can match any method on the target bean instance.

BeanNameAutoProxyCreator

The simplest form of autoproxy creator, this basically amounts to a more concise take on `ProxyFactoryBean`. It's always obvious what advice will apply to a given bean.

Configuration is via:

❑ The properties inherited from `ProxyConfig`, discussed previously.

❑ The `interceptorNames`.

❑ The `beanNames` property. This can contain multiple values. It supports both literal bean names for exact matching, and a simple wildcard mechanism, where an * character matches any number of characters.

The following simple example will apply a consistent interceptor chain to beans with the name `accountManager`, `inventoryManager`, and `inventoryDao`:

```
<bean id="myBeanNameProxyCreator"
    class="org.springframework.aop.framework.autoproxy.BeanNameAutoProxyCreator">

    <property name="beanNames"><value>accountManager,inventory*</value></property>
    <property name="interceptorNames">
        <list>
            <value>auditAdvisor</value>
            <value>securityInterceptor</value>
        </list>
    </property>
</bean>
```

Both advisors and advices can be used in the `interceptorNames` list.

DefaultAdvisorAutoProxyCreator

`DefaultAdvisorAutoProxyCreator` provides a more sophisticated model, driven by `Advisors` defined in the current context.

Like `BeanNameAutoProxyCreator`, this is transparent to bean definitions, which don't need to declare any AOP configuration but may end up being proxied.

> A `DefaultAdvisorAutoProxyCreator` **examines all** `Advisors` **defined in the current context or ancestor contexts. Any** `Advisors` **whose pointcut can match one or more methods on a target object will result in that object being autoproxied.**

Thus, different target objects can be given quite different advice chains by an advisor autoproxy creator. This is more magical than bean name autoproxying, but still more powerful, as you don't need to keep a list of bean names up to date.

Note that pointcuts are required for such matching; thus advisors are required, not just advices.

Defining a `DefaultAdvisorAutoProxyCreator` can be as easy as including a bean definition, without setting any configuration properties:

```
<bean id="aapc"
class="org.springframework.aop.framework.autoproxy.DefaultAdvisorAutoProxyCreator"/
>
```

The behavior of a `DefaultAdvisorAutoProxyCreator` will be determined by the advisors it finds in the current context. As with any autoproxy creator, the bean name of the autoproxy creator itself is usually unimportant; an autoproxy creator bean definition is intended to change the effect of other bean definitions, not for access by application code or other framework objects.

Configuration Options

`AbstractAutoProxyCreator` is the base class for all Spring autoproxy creators and defines a number of common configuration options, shown in the following table. Note that as it extends `ProxyConfig`, all `ProxyConfig` parameters are inherited.

Property	Purpose	Default	Notes
Order	Allow control over ordering of this autoproxy creator relative to other `Bean PostProcessors` in the same context. It is possible, although unusual, to have a chain of `BeanPostProcessors` that each modify the bean instance, and thus make ordering important.	`Integer.MAX_ VALUE`: means after all post processors with a lower order value, and in no guaranteed order among unordered post processors	Spring uses the `org. springframework. core.Ordered` interface as an optional interface that can be implemented by many classes to control behavior when Spring manages a group of the same objects.
Interceptor Names	Set the advisors or advices for "common interceptors."		Analogous to the same named property on `ProxyFactoryBean`. Provides the ability to have a common interceptor chain in addition to bean-specific advisors.
applyCommon Interceptors First	Should common interceptors be applied before bean-specific interceptors (advisors matching the given bean)?	true	
customTarget SourceCreators	List of `TargetSource Creators` that should be used to try to create a custom `TargetSource` for this bean instance. The first `TargetSource Creator` returning non-null from its `get TargetSource()` method will "win." If the list is empty, or all `Target SourceCreators` return `null`, a `SingletonTarget Source` will be used.	Empty list	Used to customize `TargetSource` creation, in cases where it isn't sufficient to wrap the target in a `Single tonTargetSource` (the default). The `TargetSourceCreator` interface is discussed later in this chapter. This is an advanced configuration setting that is used to provide instance pooling and other special-ized services.

Like `ProxyFactoryBean`, autoproxy creators work only in a `BeanFactory` (including its subclass `ApplicationContext`). They cannot be used without a Spring context. Like all post processors, they run automatically only in an `ApplicationContext`.

The ordering of advisors matching a particular autoproxied bean is controlled by whether those advisors implemented the `Ordered` interface.

If no advisors match a bean and no custom target source is created by a `TargetSourceCreator`, the bean instance is not proxied by the AOP framework. A normal bean reference will result from `getBean()` calls for that bean, or dependencies expressed on that bean.

Attribute-Driven Autoproxying

An important special case of autoproxying concerns pointcuts that are driven by source-level attributes. This simply involves static pointcuts that are aware of metadata attributes or annotations associated with source elements. Typically we are most interested in method and class level attributes when using Spring AOP.

> **Source-level metadata will become increasingly important in Java as J2SE 1.5 reaches the mainstream. Spring already supports attributes.**

Attributes are usable out of the box for transaction management, as you see in Chapter 6, "Transaction and Resource Management."

Advanced Autoproxy Creation

The `org.springframework.aop.framework.autoproxy.TargetSourceCreator` interface is required to help autoproxy creators work with target sources. As you'll see in more detail later, a `TargetSource` implementation is used to obtain the instance of the "target" object to invoke at the end of the interceptor chain. Usually, there is only one target object, so the `TargetSource` interface performs a simple function of returning that instance.

An object such as a `ProxyFactoryBean` works with a single `TargetSource`. However, autoproxy creators may affect multiple bean definitions with different target objects, and hence must be able to work with multiple `TargetSources`.

In general, you don't need to concern yourself with this. A `SingletonTargetSource` will be created by the autoproxy creator as needed. However, if you need more sophisticated `TargetSource` features such as pooling, you need to be able to control `TargetSource` creation.

The `TargetSourceCreator` interface defines the following method:

```
TargetSource getTargetSource(Object bean, String beanName, BeanFactory factory);
```

This method should return `null` if this `TargetSourceCreator` is not interested in the bean, or a custom `TargetSource` (such as pooling `TargetSource`) if it is.

An `AbstractAutoProxyCreator` maintains a list of `TargetSourceCreators`. By default, this list is empty. When each bean is analyzed, this method is called on each `TargetSourceCreator` in turn. The first `TargetSourceCreator` to return non-null will win. If all `TargetSourceCreators` return `null`, or the list of `TargetSourceCreators` is empty, a `SingletonTargetSource` will be used to wrap the bean.

The `TargetSourceCreator` interface is useful for infrastructure requirements. Inside Spring, for example, the `TargetSourceCreator` mechanism is used to handle pooling and hot swapping. In this case, there must be a distinct `TargetSource` instance for each autoproxied bean definition, although the autoproxy mechanism provides a single means of configuration. The `TargetSourceCreator` implementation will use some strategy to determine whether or not a pooling or other special target source should be used for a given bean definition. (The `BeanDefinition` can be found from the factory if necessary.)

You should understand the mechanism, but are unlikely to need to implement your own `TargetSourceCreator` in normal application development.

Making a Choice

You may be feeling a little confused right now. Why does Spring provide so many different ways of creating AOP proxies? Why not just standardize on one?

Spring's flexibility is arguably a strength rather than a weakness. It's partly a consequence of the fact that Spring uses a consistent configuration mechanism across the entire framework; anything can be defined using XML bean definitions because the IoC container can manage an arbitrarily fine-grained object. However, Spring also provides higher-level constructs to achieve simplification in some cases, and it's important to understand them.

The following guidelines on proxy creation may be helpful:

❑ `ProxyFactoryBean` is a dependable way of creating proxies, allowing control over every aspect of the proxy, but using it often results in more verbose configuration. However, this can be offset by using the inheritance mechanism of Spring's IoC container.

❑ `BeanNameAutoProxyCreator` is a good half-way house that can reduce verbosity somewhat without excessive magic. It's ideal for replacing a number of `ProxyFactoryBean` configurations that are identical with the exception of the target, with a single definition.

❑ `DefaultAdvisorAutoProxyCreator` is the most powerful AOP configuration option. It more closely approaches "true" AOP solutions such as AspectJ, where advice is applied to objects automatically based on pointcuts. But there's also more magic involved, which can be confusing at times. One of the main strengths of advisor-based autoproxy creation is that it can be put in place by developers specializing in the AOP framework, with the rest of the team able subsequently to write POJO bean definitions, yet have their objects benefit from crosscutting code.

Examining and Manipulating Proxy State at Runtime

Spring allows us to examine and even change the advice applying to any AOP proxy at runtime.

It's easy to find whether an object is an AOP proxy. Use the static `isAopProxy(Object o)` method in the `org.springframework.aop.support.AopUtils` class.

You can also use the `isJdkDynamicProxy()` method to find whether an object is a JDK proxy and the `isCglibProxy()` method in the same class to find whether an object is a CGLIB proxy.

Any AOP proxy can be cast to the `org.springframework.aop.framework.Advised` interface, which enables advice to be examined and changed. The methods are as follows:

```java
public interface Advised {
    TargetSource getTargetSource();
    void setTargetSource(TargetSource targetSource);
    boolean getExposeProxy();
    boolean getProxyTargetClass();
    Advisor[] getAdvisors();
    Class[] getProxiedInterfaces();
    boolean isInterfaceProxied(Class intf);
    void addAdvice(Advice advice) throws AopConfigException;
    void addAdvice(int pos, Advice advice) throws AopConfigException;
    void addAdvisor(Advisor advisor) throws AopConfigException;
    void addAdvisor(int pos, Advisor advisor) throws AopConfigException;
    boolean removeAdvisor(Advisor advisor) throws AopConfigException;
    void removeAdvisor(int index) throws AopConfigException;
    boolean removeAdvice(Advice advice) throws AopConfigException;
    boolean isFrozen();
    // Other methods omitted: finding and replacing advices and advisors
}
```

It can be useful to be able to *examine* proxy state at runtime — particularly when testing. The `getAdvisors[]` method can be used to find the current `Advisors`.

The `getTargetSource()` method is particularly useful, as you can use it to obtain a reference to the target object in the commonest case, where `SingletonTargetSource` is in use. This means that given a reference to an advised object, it is possible to find the target object it is proxying as well.

It is sometimes useful to *manipulate* proxy state at runtime, but there's potential danger in doing so, as well as a conceptual question mark. Do we really want to change the structure of an application at runtime?

Spring's AOP framework is threadsafe in normal operation, but, for performance reasons, does not synchronize to protect against race conditions in adding or removing advice. Thus, if you add an advice while one or more method invocations are underway, the effect might be a concurrent modification exception. As with the core Java Collections, you are responsible for ensuring thread safety in your application code.

Programmatic Proxy Creation

While the integration with Spring's IoC container is usually the main focus of use of Spring AOP, it's easy to create proxies programmatically. This can be very useful, and is used in several places in the Spring framework itself. For example:

❑ You might want to add auditing behavior around a particular object on the fly, removing it when the operation needing auditing is complete.

❑ You might want to add a set of interceptors to a particular object based on the user identity, rather than configuration known in advance.

❑ You might want to make an introduction (to be discussed shortly) in Java code at runtime, rather than in configuration written before the application is running.

❑ You might be writing some infrastructure elements that benefit from interception.

It is possible to create AOP proxies programmatically using the `org.springframework.aop.framework.ProxyFactory` class. The following simple example demonstrates the approach. We need to set the target or `TargetSource`, add any advisors or advice we choose, and then call the `getProxy()` method to obtain an AOP proxy, as follows:

```
PersonImpl personTarget = new PersonImpl();
ProxyFactory pf = new ProxyFactory();
pf.setTarget(personTarget);
pf.addInterface(Person.class);
pf.addAdvisor(myAdvisor);
pf.addAdvice(myAdvice);
Person person = (Person) pf.getProxy();
```

`ProxyFactory`, like `ProxyFactoryBean`, is a subclass of `org.springframework.aop.framework.AdvisedSupport`, so its properties should be familiar. `ProxyFactory` adds no new properties, merely convenient constructors: one taking a target object (from which interfaces will be deduced if none are specified) and one taking an array of `Class` specifying the interfaces to proxy. The no-arg constructor, as used in the preceding code, leaves the caller to specify target or `TargetSource` and interfaces to proxy.

The preceding example could be rewritten as follows using the constructor that takes a target object:

```
PersonImpl personTarget = new PersonImpl();
ProxyFactory pf = new ProxyFactory(personTarget);
pf.addAdvisor(myAdvisor);
pf.addAdvice(myAdvice);
Person person = (Person) pf.getProxy();
```

This would have the same effect as the preceding code, assuming that the `PersonImpl` class implemented only the `Person` interface. The interfaces to proxy would automatically be found using reflection. If the target object implemented no interface, Spring would try to create a CGLIB proxy.

It's not possible to automatically proxy an object created using the new *operator using Spring AOP. If you need to do this — for example, to advise large numbers of fine-grained objects — consider using AspectJ or AspectWerkz as alternatives to Spring's own AOP framework.*

Using Advanced Features of Spring's AOP Framework

Let's now look at some more advanced uses of Spring's AOP framework.

TargetSources

Typically, the interceptor chain concludes by using reflection to invoke the appropriate method on the target object. This is the target object's implementation of the method. Typically, there is a target object that is known when the proxy is constructed. The point of using Spring AOP is normally to add declarative behavior around a target object.

However, the way in which Spring actually terminates the interceptor chain is a bit more sophisticated. Spring obtains the target object reference just before it invokes the appropriate method. The target object is obtained from an implementation of the `TargetSource` interface. This interface is as follows:

```
public interface TargetSource {

    Class getTargetClass();

    boolean isStatic();

    Object getTarget() throws Exception;

    void releaseTarget(Object target) throws Exception;

}
```

In the simplest, commonest case, where there's a target object known in advance, Spring creates an implementation of the `TargetSource` interface without the developer needing to be aware of it. This implementation (`SingletonTargetSource`) will return the same instance in all cases, when the `getTarget()` method is invoked.

However, the `TargetSource` interface also allows for more sophisticated behavior. For example, the target instance can be obtained from a pool or a factory.

Spring comes with a number of `TargetSource` implementations out of the box, and you can easily implement your own `TargetSource`.

HotSwappableTargetSource

The most important `TargetSource` implementation — other than the default implementation used for "singleton" targets — is `HotSwappableTargetSource`. This enables us to switch the target object under a proxy in a threadsafe manner. This capability is particularly important in a Dependency Injection framework. Let's suppose that object A expresses a dependency on interface B via Dependency Injection. How do we retain the option of changing the implementation of B in a manner transparent to A? To do this, the implementation of B supplied by the container to satisfy the dependency must be a proxy — and the logical approach is for it to be a proxy created by Spring's AOP framework, enabling the option of using other AOP capabilities. Such proxies will use `HotSwappableTargetSource`.

> By default, hot swapping is not enabled, and Spring will satisfy dependencies with an unadorned POJO. This provides optimum performance and is appropriate in most cases. Explicit configuration is required to enable hot swapping.

The `HotSwappableTargetSource` class offers one new method:

```
Object swap(Object o);
```

This returns the old target object.

Typical use of the `HotSwappableTargetSource` will be as follows. We define an object to be the initial target, and construct a proxy using the `HotSwappableTargetSource`. We can then swap programmatically at any time.

```xml
<bean id="target1" class="com.mycompany.MyInterfaceImpl">
</bean>


<bean id="target2" class="com.mycompany.MyInterfaceImpl">
</bean>


<bean id="swapper"
 class="org.springframework.aop.target.HotSwappableTargetSource">
 <constructor-arg><ref local="target1"/></constructor-arg>
</bean>



<bean id="swappable"
    class="org.springframework.aop.framework.ProxyFactoryBean"
>

    <property name="targetSource"><ref local="swapper"/></property>
</bean>
```

Programmatic swapping is shown here:

```java
MyInterface target1 = (MyInterface) beanFactory.getBean("target1");
MyInterface target2 = (MyInterface) beanFactory.getBean("target2");

MyInterface proxied = (MyInterface) beanFactory.getBean("swappable");
// Invocations on proxied now hit target1

HotSwappableTargetSource swapper = (HotSwappableTargetSource)
beanFactory.getBean("swapper");
Object old = swapper.swap(target2);
// old will be target1

// Invocations on proxied now hit target2
```

In this case, both targets come from bean definitions. It's quite likely that the initial target would come from a bean definition and that a new target might come from another source.

> **The `HotSwappableTargetSource` is ideal for building infrastructure — for example, to support dynamic reconfiguration of certain application objects that change frequently.**

Pooling Target Source

Another important use of the `TargetSource` interface is to support pooling. In this case, you don't want a single target — you want a pool of targets, with the actual call at the end of the interceptor chain going to a free target. Note that the interceptor instances will normally be shared. This is appropriate; typically the interceptors will be threadsafe, such as transaction interceptors.

The proxy itself will be a singleton instance, and stands in front of a pool of target objects.

Use Out of the Box

Out of the box, Spring supports Apache Commons Pool (http://jakarta.apache.org/commons/pool/). This is an open source pool implementation with acceptable performance, which is robust under load.

You can configure a pool for any POJO as follows:

```
<bean id="prototypeTest" class="org.springframework.aop.interceptor.SideEffectBean"
  singleton="false">
 <property name="count"><value>10</value></property>
</bean>

<bean id="poolTargetSource"
class="org.springframework.aop.target.CommonsPoolTargetSource">
 <property name="targetBeanName"><value>prototypeTest</value></property>
 <property name="maxSize"><value>25</value></property>
</bean>


<bean id="pooled"
          class="org.springframework.aop.framework.ProxyFactoryBean"
>
 <property name="targetSource"><ref local="poolTargetSource"/></property>
 <property name="interceptorNames"><value>whatever...</value></property>

</bean>
```

Note that while `pooled` is a singleton bean definition, the target `prototypeTest` *must* be a non-singleton definition, to allow the pool that Spring will configure to instantiate independent instances as necessary.

There are no constraints on the actual classes that can be pooled; while the pooling model is similar to that for stateless session EJBs, it applies to any POJO.

Use with Your Own Choice of Pooling Implementation

Like everything else in Spring, the pooling `TargetSource` support allows for customization. You can extend `org.springframework.aop.target.AbstractPoolingTargetSource` to use a pool provider other than Commons Pool. It's necessary to implement the following methods:

```
protected final void createPool(BeanFactory beanFactory);
```

This method should be used to create the pool. As usual, dependencies can be specified using Dependency Injection.

```
public Object getTarget() throws Exception;
```

This method should return an object obtained from the pool.

```
public void releaseTarget(Object target) throws Exception;
```

This method should return an object to the pool after an invocation has finished with it.

```
public void destroy();
```

This method should shut down the pool before the `TargetSource` is destroyed.

Any pool API will normally require a callback to construct a new object for the pool. This should be implemented using the inherited `newPrototypeInstance()` method, as shown in the following example from the Commons Pool implementation:

```
public Object makeObject() {
    return newPrototypeInstance();
}
```

Basic pool configuration parameters such as `maxSize` are inherited from `org.springframework.aop.target.AbstractPoolingTargetSource`; you should add properties for any pool-specific configuration.

When Should You Use Pooling?

Spring's AOP-based pooling capability is most often used as an alternative to local stateless session EJBs. It provides the same basic model: a pool of stateless service objects, any of which may be invoked by a given method invocation. However, stateless service objects are typically easy to make threadsafe; there's usually no need for read-write instance variables — or at least instance variables that are read-write after configuration is complete. And it's usually more convenient to have a single instance of an object than a pool; consider the case in which you want to maintain a cache of objects.

> **Don't be too eager to use pooling. It's often unnecessary. See Chapter 12 of *J2EE without EJB* for a discussion of the tradeoffs involved in pooling. Pooling is an overvalued idea in J2EE architecture, given the efficient garbage collection of modern JVMs.**

Exposing Pool Statistics

If you want to expose information about pool statistics for a pooled object, you can do so as follows:

```
<bean id="poolConfigAdvisor"
class="org.springframework.beans.factory.config.MethodInvokingFactoryBean">
 <property name="targetObject"><ref local="poolTargetSource" /></property>
 <property name="targetMethod"><value>getPoolingConfigMixin</value></property>
</bean>

<bean id="pooled"
 class="org.springframework.aop.framework.ProxyFactoryBean"
>
 <property name="targetSource"><ref local="poolTargetSource"/></property>

 <property name="interceptorNames"><value>poolConfigAdvisor</value></property>

 <!-- Necessary as have a mixin and want to avoid losing the class,
         because there's no target interface -->
 <property name="proxyTargetClass"><value>true</value></property>

</bean>
```

This uses an introduction (discussed later in this chapter) to cause the AOP proxy in front of the pool to implement the `PoolingConfig` interface.

You can now cast any object obtained from the pool to `PoolingConfig` and interrogate its statistics as follows. We assume that the `pooled` object is a reference to the AOP proxy in front of the pool:

```
PoolingConfig conf = (PoolingConfig) pooled;
assertEquals(1, conf.getInvocations());
assertEquals("Correct target source", 25, conf.getMaxSize());
```

This is an interesting example of the potential of *introduction*, discussed in the next section.

Custom TargetSources

You are also free to implement your own `TargetSource`.

Consider a recent question that came up in one of the Spring lists. A user needed to use several datasources, selecting one at runtime based on the context.

The traditional OO way to address this would be to implement a `DataSource` decorator that delegated to one or the other `DataSource`, depending on the state. As there aren't a huge number of methods on the `DataSource` interface, this wouldn't be too painful. However, it's verbose and a good example of crosscutting.

You could meet this requirement by implementing a `TargetSource` that chose the correct `DataSource` based on context — the state of other application objects (which the custom `TargetSource` could access through Dependency Injection), the current user, or any other contextual information. Any interception chain would be shared, whatever the target the `TargetSource` chose at runtime.

> *You could also address this problem using the Method Injection feature of the core Spring IoC container. That approach would have the advantage that the object could itself invoke a* `getDataSource()` *method. You would need to implement a custom* `MethodReplacer` *in this case (see Chapter 2).*

Programmatic Access to the TargetSource

It's possible to obtain, and even modify, the `TargetSource` from any AOP proxy by casting to `Advised` and using the `TargetSource` property. This is most useful with `TargetSource` implementations such as `HotSwappableTargetSource` that permit programmatic configuration changes.

In most cases, you won't have set the `TargetSource` explicitly, and the `TargetSource` will be of type `SingletonTargetSource`.

> The `TargetSource` **will never be** `null`**, even in the special case when there is no target object.**

Doing Without a Target Object

Occasionally, there will be *no* target object. In this case, an interceptor will be responsible for returning the result. The `TargetSource` will be the canonical instance of `org.springframework.aop.target` `.EmptyTargetSource`, which always returns `null` from its `getTarget()` method.

You can dispense with a target in cases when all behavior is supplied by interceptors—possibly including `IntroductionInterceptors`, which often themselves hold a target. The most common case is when a terminal interceptor uses a strategy other than reflective invocation of a target object to call out of the interceptor stack. The Spring EJB proxies, such as `org.springframework.ejb.access.LocalSlsbInvoker Interceptor`, illustrate this approach: Instead of calling `proceed()`, which would cause the AOP infrastructure to reflectively invoke a target obtained from the `TargetSource` in the case of the last interceptor in the chain, they invoke the method specified in the `MethodInvocation` on a local or remote EJB. The same technique is used for remoting technologies.

> **Remember that an interceptor designed to call out of the interceptor chain, rather than call proceed, should normally be the last in the interceptor chain.**

It's also possible, but more unusual, to have interceptors themselves implement methods. Any interceptor in the chain can choose to return a value (or throw an exception) rather than invoke the `proceed()` method.

You cannot dispense with a target object when using CGLIB proxying. See the discussion of proxy types later in this chapter.

Terminating the Interceptor Chain Early

When you do without a target—or for any other reason—you may want an advice in the chain to terminate early. This can happen in two ways: through throwing an exception or returning a value instead of calling `proceed`. Any advice can throw an exception, which will be reported to the client. Only `Method Interceptors` can return rather than call `proceed()`. Other advice types such as `MethodBeforeAdvice` don't have the ability to alter the return value.

> **What happens if a `MethodInterceptor` or other advice throws an exception? If it's not a checked exception, the exception will be seen by the client. If it's a checked exception on the signature of the method, the client will see that exception. If it's a checked exception *not* on the signature of the method, it will be wrapped in `java.lang.reflect.UndeclaredThrowableException` and reported to the client.**

Using Introduction

Introduction means making an advised object (in this case, the Spring AOP proxy) implement additional interfaces, which are not implemented by the target object. It's even possible to create a proxy that consists solely of introductions, with no target object.

Introduction has many uses:

❑   To create a *mixin*, adding to the state held in the object. This is probably the most important use.

❑   To expose additional states associated with a special `TargetSource`. This is used within Spring, for example with scripting support.

❑   To expose an object or object graph in a different way—for example, making an object graph implement the XML DOM interfaces.

> **Introduction is known as "intra-type declarations" in AspectJ terminology.**

Spring provides two ways of making introductions:

- ❏ **The** `IntroductionInfo` **interface:** Any advice can implement this to indicate that it introduces one or more interfaces. Such advices can be used with any pointcut, or even without a pointcut.

- ❏ **The** `IntroductionAdvisor` **interface:** A special advisor type for introductions that doesn't include a `MethodMatcher`, which is not relevant for introductions. This actually extends the `IntroductionInfo` interface.

The first is the simpler approach and has been recommended since its introduction in Spring 1.1.1. (In earlier versions of Spring an `IntroductionAdvisor` was always required in order to make an introduction.)

Let's now look at a realistic example. Suppose we want to make any object "lockable," making it implement a Lockable interface to expose and control the locking state, and disabling all its setter methods when its state is locked.

The `Lockable` interface might look as follows:

```
public interface Lockable {
    void lock();
    void unlock();
    boolean locked();
}
```

We now need an advice that makes the introduction. This must implement the `IntroductionInfo` interface, which contains the following method:

```
Class[] getInterfaces()
```

This method is implemented to return the interfaces that are introduced by the advisor or advice.

Typically, we will extend Spring's convenient `DelegatingIntroductionInterceptor` class when implementing an introduction advice. This class automatically detects any interface that a subclass implements and returns that in the `IntroductionInfo.getInterfaces()` method.

Thus our simple introduction can look like this:

```
public class LockMixin extends DelegatingIntroductionInterceptor
            implements Lockable {

    private boolean locked;

    public void lock() {
        this.locked = true;
    }

    public void unlock() {
        this.locked = false;
```

```
        }

        public boolean locked() {
            return this.locked;
        }

        public Object invoke(MethodInvocation invocation) throws Throwable {
            if (locked() &&
                    invocation.getMethod().getName().indexOf("set") == 0)
                throw new LockedException();
            return super.invoke(invocation);
        }
    }
```

Not much code, considering that we can use this to enable locking on any object! But this is actually a fairly complex example of a `DelegatingIntroductionInterceptor` subclass. It overrides the `invoke()` method to add a guard to setter methods *that are not covered by the introduction*. Because an introduction is normally made by an interceptor, it has the ability to perform around advice also. A simpler `DelegatingIntroductionInterceptor` subclass would not override the `invoke()` method implemented by `DelegatingIntroductionInterceptor` but would merely implement the interfaces to be introduced.

> *It is possible to use* `DelegatingIntroductionInterceptor` *with an arbitrary delegate without concrete inheritance by setting its delegate property to any object. The default value is* `this`, *meaning the subclass.*

We can now add this advice to a proxy configuration, in an interceptor chain (using the `interceptorNames` property) or programmatically, as shown here:

```
ProxyFactory pc = new ProxyFactory(new Class[] {Target.class });
pc.setTarget(myTarget);
pc.addAdvice(new LockMixin());
```

We will now have a `LockMixin` instance associated with the target object.

In our second approach, using an `IntroductionAdvisor`, we need an advisor wrapper for this mixin. This gives us the opportunity to specify a `ClassFilter` to target the introduction, although we don't in this simple example:

```
public class LockMixinAdvisor extends DefaultIntroductionAdvisor {

    public LockMixinAdvisor() {
        super(new LockMixin(), Lockable.class);
    }
}
```

`DefaultIntroductionAdvisor` *is concrete, so it can also be used declaratively in the same way as* `DefaultPointcutAdvisor`.

We can use this advisor as follows:

```
ProxyFactory pc = new ProxyFactory(new Class[] {Target.class });
pc.setTarget(myTarget);
pc.addAdvisor(new LockMixinAdvisor());
```

> The only reasons for using an introduction advisor, rather than simply an introduction advice, are to apply a `ClassFilter` to limit where the introduction applies, or to narrow the number of interfaces that an advice implementing `IntroductionInfo` introduces. If neither of these applies, you should just use an introduction advice.

Let's look beyond the mechanics and think about the effect of our use of introduction in the example we've just seen. We have modularized an important crosscutting concern. We can now add locking behavior to any object without the need to modify that object. This is stateful advice; we need one advice instance per advised object.

> It's possible to build applications using introductions. However, there's a danger here of recreating multiple inheritance in Java. Mixins are probably best restricted to infrastructure, such as the locking aspect we've just seen, or security aspects.

While Spring provides good support for introductions, in some cases you should consider using AspectJ to perform introductions. AspectJ can actually add fields to the advised classes, eliminating the need for a distinct mixin object for each instance for which the introduction applies.

Exposing the Current Proxy

You may have figured by this point that because of Spring's distinction between target object and AOP framework, the target object doesn't know anything about the AOP framework. While this is a good thing in many cases, it does have one unfortunate consequence: If a target object invokes a method on itself, it doesn't get advised unless the programmer takes special care. For example, if we have an object called `AccountManager`, and any other object has a reference to `AccountManager` via Spring IoC, the methods will be advised appropriately. If, however, an advised `AccountManager` implementation invokes a method on itself, it will simply be invoking a method on an unmodified class. It won't be advised. This situation might arise, for example, if a coarse-grained method in an `AccountManager` implementation requires several transactions and attempts to use declarative transaction management through calling multiple transactional methods.

This is exactly the same as the situation with EJBs, which must use the `getEJBObject()` method on the `javax.ejb.SessionContext` interface if they want to invoke methods on themselves.

To be able to invoke the target object through the advice chain, you must:

- ❑ Configure the proxy factory to set the `exposeProxy` flag to true. The default is false, as the necessary ThreadLocal binding adds a small performance hit.

- ❑ Use the `AopContext.currentProxy()` method to obtain the current proxy.

Then you will write code like this, to invoke the `doSomething()` method on the current object *through the advice chain*:

```
((MyObject) AopContext.currentProxy()).doSomething();
```

The downside here is that we have a dependence on Spring. In general we want to avoid dependencies on the framework. You will typically want to refactor the dependence on the AopContext class into a protected method so that you can override it at test time. This way you can unit test without always making invocations through the Spring AOP framework.

You might be thinking that it's inelegant that Spring forces you to explicitly access the proxy. It is, but it's a consequence of the tradeoffs in Spring's AOP implementation. If this is a real problem for you, it may be an indication to consider AspectJ or AspectWerkz to address the requirement in question.

Exposing the Current MethodInvocation

While the need to expose the AOP proxy is uncommon, it does arise from time to time. More rarely, we need to expose the MethodInvocation to objects within an AOP invocation that don't have access to it. Normally the only objects that need access to the MethodInvocation are AOP Alliance MethodInterceptors. As interceptors are passed the MethodInvocation in the arguments to the invoke method, they don't have a problem. However, what if a target object needs to see the invocation, or a pointcut? This isn't a common requirement, but it's not unheard of. For example, a target object may need to know how it's being used in an AOP context; a pointcut may need to access information available only through the MethodInvocation.

In this case, add the canonical instance of org.springframework.aop.interceptor .ExposeInvocationInterceptor to the beginning of the interceptor chain to expose the invocation, and use its static currentInvocation() method to obtain the current MethodInvocation. This value will be set correctly in the event of nested invocations.

If you're using programmatic proxy creation, or modifying an existing Advised object, configuration is trivial:

```
advised.addAdvice(ExposeInvocationInterceptor.INSTANCE);
```

It's a little harder when using XML configuration. Because ExposeInvocationInterceptor enforces the singleton pattern through exposing an INSTANCE field containing the canonical instance, you can't create an instance using new, as a normal Spring bean definition would do.

You need to use the FieldRetrievingFactoryBean (see Chapter 3) to get a reference to the canonical instance of ExposeInvocationInterceptor, as follows:

```
<bean id="exposeInvocation"
    class="org.springframework.beans.factory.config.FieldRetrievingFactoryBean">
    <property name="targetClass">

 <value>org.springframework.aop.interceptor.ExposeInvocationInterceptor</value>
    </property>
    <property name="targetField"><value>INSTANCE</value></property>
</bean>
```

You can name this bean anything you like and use the name (exposeInvocation in the preceding example) in the interceptorNames list.

Try to avoid exposing the MethodInvocation **if at all possible. It creates a dependence on the Spring AOP framework, and it's seldom necessary.**

Understanding Proxy Types

Spring decouples the implementation of an AOP proxy from the rest of the framework using the `AopProxyFactory` interface. This defines the following method, to create an AOP proxy given proxy configuration data:

```
AopProxy createAopProxy(AdvisedSupport advisedSupport) throws AopConfigException;
```

Proxy configuration objects such as `AdvisedSupport` control how one or more proxies should be created. Created proxies will normally contain a reference to the configuration object that created them, but this reference can be broken on serialization to allow the proxy to stand alone.

The `AopProxyFactory` interface enables the Spring AOP API to support proxies implemented with a range of technologies. For example, Spring could use a code generation approach to generate proxy classes, rather than using a reflection-based mechanism. Additional proxy types are currently being considered, but won't change the public API of Spring AOP. The flexibility of the design is shown by the fact that the .NET port of the Spring Framework uses a virtually identical AOP API, despite the very different proxy generation strategies required in a CLI environment.

It's worth understanding the contract of a Spring AOP proxy before we go further:

❑ It must implement all interfaces that the configuration indicates should be proxied.

❑ It must implement the `Advised` interface, discussed earlier.

❑ It must implement the `equals()` method to compare proxied interfaces, advisors, and target.

❑ It must be serializable if advisors and target are serializable.

❑ It must be threadsafe if advisors and target are threadsafe.

Spring 1.1 provides two `AopProxy` implementations out of the box:

❑ `JdkDynamicAopProxy`: An implementation using a J2SE dynamic proxy. This allows only methods on interfaces to be proxied.

❑ `Cglib2AopProxy`: An implementation using the CGLIB byte code generation library. This enables methods on interfaces or classes to be proxied. CGLIB works by subclassing the target class. Thus you can use CGLIB proxies only if you *have* a target class. CGLIB cannot override `final` methods. Spring's CGLIB proxies can implement any number of additional methods besides the methods on the target class.

The type of proxy created is controlled by the `AopProxyFactory` implementation held in an `AdvisedSupport` object creating a proxy. The default implementation will use a dynamic proxy where possible (that is, if it hasn't been asked to proxy a target class). There should be no need in normal usage to implement the `AopProxyFactory` interface; however, Spring, as usual, provides a host of extension points.

You can force the use of CGLIB proxy — even when proxying interface methods only — by setting the `proxyTargetClass` flag on `ProxyConfig` (the superclass of all proxy creators) to `true`.

> If you use CGLIB proxying, the CGLIB JAR file must be on the classpath. Hibernate depends on CGLIB, and some environments, such as the Geronimo application server, use it, so many Spring users already have the required binaries on their classpath. However, users who don't understand the distinction between the two proxy types are often caught out by missing class exceptions relating to CGLIB.

Apart from the fact that CGLIB proxies can proxy methods on classes as well as interfaces, you should notice no difference between the two types of proxies. A few tips for making a choice:

❑ If you're still running in a JDK 1.3 environment (for example, because of an old application server version), CGLIB proxies will give much better performance than JDK proxies, which were significantly optimized in 1.4 JVMs. Use CGLIB if the performance overhead of AOP proxying is an issue. It usually isn't, even on JDK 1.3.

❑ If you have many methods to which no advice will apply, CGLIB proxies will be significantly faster, as using CGLIB allows greater potential for optimization than dynamic proxies.

❑ Besides this special case, you will find very little performance difference between the two types of proxy. CGLIB proxies may be marginally faster overall.

❑ If you use only J2SE dynamic proxies, you do not need CGLIB binaries on your classpath, unless they are required by other frameworks. (CGLIB is required to use Spring IoC's Method Injection features, but not otherwise required in Spring itself.)

It's okay to let the framework decide on the proxy type to use in most cases. However, if you can use dynamic proxies, you should probably do so, as they are simpler than CGLIB proxies, and it's a good idea in general to adopt the simplest possible solution.

Debugging and Testing

What are the implications of using Spring AOP for debugging?

Essentially you'll see a few extra lines in the call stack for advised invocations, produced by the Spring AOP infrastructure. Some of these concern the use of reflection to invoke the target object; others result from the AOP framework itself, in which a proxy (in this case `JdkDynamicAopProxy`) invokes the `proceed()` method of a `MethodInvocation`. Each interceptor in turn will invoke `proceed()` to continue down the interceptor chain:

```
Thread [main] (Suspended (breakpoint at line 103 in BusinessObject))
  BusinessObject.someMethod(String) line: 103
  NativeMethodAccessorImpl.invoke0(Method, Object, Object[]) line: not available
[native method]
  NativeMethodAccessorImpl.invoke(Object, Object[]) line: not available
  DelegatingMethodAccessorImpl.invoke(Object, Object[]) line: not available
  Method.invoke(Object, Object[]) line: not available
  AopProxyUtils.invokeJoinpointUsingReflection(Object, Method, Object[]) line: 59
  ReflectiveMethodInvocation.invokeJoinpoint() line: 151
  ReflectiveMethodInvocation.proceed() line: 120
  TransactionInterceptor.invoke(MethodInvocation) line: 57
```

```
ReflectiveMethodInvocation.proceed() line: 140
JdkDynamicAopProxy.invoke(Object, Method, Object[]) line: 153
$Proxy1.setName(String) line: not available
```

```
Caller.callingMethod()
```

Essentially you can skip through the AOP elements in the stack trace to interpret them.

There's nothing magic about this at runtime. We can set breakpoints in Spring or custom advice, as well as in advised code.

If you are puzzled about the behavior of an AOP proxy, you can cast it to `Advised` and call the `toProxyConfigString()` method. The output will look like this example from the Spring test suite:

```
org.springframework.aop.framework.ProxyFactory:
    1 interfaces=[org.springframework.beans.ITestBean];
    2 advisors=[{DefaultPointcutAdvisor: pointcut=Pointcut.TRUE;
advice=org.springframework.aop.interceptor.NopInterceptor@10ab78a},
    {DefaultPointcutAdvisor:
pointcut=org.springframework.aop.support.NameMatchMethodPointcut@98062f;
advice=org.springframework.aop.framework.CountingBeforeAdvice@be0446}];
    targetSource=[SingletonTargetSource: target=(name=null; age=0; touchy=null;
spouse={null})];
    proxyTargetClass=false; optimize=false; exposeProxy=false; frozen=false;
```

```
aopProxyFactory=org.springframework.aop.framework.DefaultAopProxyFactory@10aa282;
    advisorChainFactory=org.springframework.aop.framework
.HashMapCachingAdvisorChainFactory@1332109
```

From the output of `toProxyConfigString()` you can see the proxied interfaces, the advisors, and their ordering (both pointcut and advice are shown); the `TargetSource`, which in the case of `Singleton TargetSource` will call `toString()` on the target; and a range of AOP configuration parameters. Of course you can also cast to `Advised` and query programmatically — perhaps even using a scripting language such as Groovy.

Examining AOP configuration and debugging advised objects, however, is really only a matter for integration testing and later stages of testing. In general, you should run unit tests *without* running the AOP framework.

It's important to remember that with AOP, as with other Spring features, it's possible to run many integration tests outside an application server, even when the code is intended for a J2EE environment. You should normally use the `org.springframework.test` package, shipped in `spring-mock.jar`, for this; your Spring AOP configuration will execute just as in production with this approach to integration testing. The PetClinic sample application shipped with Spring illustrates use of this testing package in conjunction with transactional proxying.

> In general, *appropriate* use of Spring AOP should make debugging easier. AOP serves to keep the framework (and orthogonal concerns) out of your application code; you should reap the rewards.

Understand implications for unit testing. This means that you can — and *should* — unit test target objects without the AOP framework, as well as perform integration tests.

For example, if we use Spring AOP for transaction management, the contract for application classes is narrowly defined and easily testable. Through the use of *rollback rules* (discussed in Chapter 6), we need only test that the application classes either succeed or throw the appropriate exceptions to cause rollback in the event of failure. There is no need to start an actual transaction.

> Aspects can decouple application code from its environment. While EJB offered a limited kind of AOP to address a fixed set of concerns such as transaction management and security, it came at the price of an awareness of the code on its environment. With AOP we can avoid this problem. This is beneficial in many scenarios. One of the most important is testing.

Miscellaneous

Let's conclude by covering some miscellaneous questions that come up on the Spring user lists.

Changing Method Arguments

It's possible for an interceptor to change method arguments by modifying the contents of the array returned by the `MethodInvocation getArguments()` method. Such a change will affect later interceptors in the chain before the target is invoked, the arguments with which the target object is invoked, and any interceptors interested in arguments as the chain returns after the target is invoked.

It is of course trivial for any interceptor to change the return value, by returning a value other than that returned by the `MethodInvocation proceed()` method.

Double Proxying

It's possible to proxy a proxy — except, at present, when using two CGLIB proxies, because of a limitation of CGLIB that may well have been removed by the time you read this. However, it's best avoided, as it will complicate stack traces and add overhead. There should rarely if ever be any need for double proxying, as it's normally possible to add all required advice to a single proxy. One potentially valid use would be to make the "outer" proxy work with multiple "inner proxy" targets using a `TargetSource`.

Implementing Multiple AOP Framework Interfaces

A Spring AOP advice should implement only one advice interface. For example, a single class should not implement both `MethodBeforeAdvice` and `AfterReturningAdvice`. While it's legal Java (Spring can't prevent application classes implementing whatever interfaces they choose), the effect of deploying such a class within the Spring AOP framework is undefined. Only one of the interfaces will be picked up: There is no guarantee which.

Fortunately, there's a simple and superior alternative: If one class needs to implement more than one advice type, it should just implement `MethodInterceptor` and be an around advice, giving it total control over the invocation of the join point.

Serializing AOP Proxies

As of Spring 1.1, AOP proxies are serializable if the TargetSource is serializable and all Advisors are serializable. (The latter condition means that both Advice and Pointcut contained in the Advisor must be serializable.) Unless the developer has specified a TargetSource, Spring will automatically use SingletonTargetSource, which is serializable if the target object is serializable.

On deserialization, the proxy will have the same interceptor chain, with all Advisors having been serialized. The deserialized proxy will implement the same interfaces. The TargetSource (including the target) will have been serialized.

Serialization disconnects the AOP proxy from the factory that created it. This means that even if a proxy was created by a ProxyFactoryBean, which depends on its owning BeanFactory, which is probably not serializable, the proxy itself *is* serializable so long as its advice satisfies these criteria. Disconnection of proxies on serialization is achieved by cloning the basic configuration held in the AdvisedSupport class and its ProxyConfig superclass. State held lower down the inheritance hierarchy than AdvisedSupport (such as ProxyFactoryBean) is ignored, as it relates to how to create more proxies, rather than the supporting data for a working proxy.

Most Spring AOP framework classes — pointcuts, interceptors, and TargetSource implementations — are serializable. Thus, for example:

❑ You can serialize an AOP proxy that uses a HotSwappableTargetSource. You can continue to work with the HotSwappableTargetSource on deserialization.

❑ You can serialize regular expression pointcuts such as org.springframework.aop.support .Perl5RegExpMethodPointcut, assuming that you have all the necessary regular expression libraries on the client side.

❑ You can serialize ControlFlowPointcuts.

❑ Transactional AOP proxies are serializable if both the PlatformTransactionManager and TransactionAttributeSource implementation they use are serializable. In practice, this means that transactional proxies are serializable if they use JtaTransactionManager and both client and server environments support access to the JTA UserTransaction.

❑ "Prototype based target sources" — subclasses of org.springframework.aop.target .AbstractPrototypeBasedTargetSource such as PrototypeTargetSource and pooling target sources — are serializable, but serialization results in disconnecting a single target object instance from the pool or other dynamic source of target objects. On deserialization, the TargetSource will be a simple SingletonTargetSource wrapping an object obtained from the TargetSource before serialization.

The AOP proxy serialization infrastructure is designed to minimize the amount of state that has to be carried across the wire. However, advised objects will be more expensive to serialize than plain Java objects, and there may also be some cost to rebuild state on deserialization. As usual, avoid remoting if possible.

There is no guarantee that the serialized form of AOP proxies will be compatible across different versions of Spring.

The onus is on the application developer to choose whether an interceptor or other AOP framework class is serializable. If so, it should be marked as Serializable. Framework interfaces such as Pointcut and MethodInterceptor do not themselves extend java.io.Serializable. However, framework classes such as DefaultPointcutAdvisor, which are designed for use without subclassing, *do* implement Serializable, so they do not prevent serializable application classes being serialized.

Invoking proceed() More Than Once

What if you want to retry invocation of the relevant method on the target object — for example, if you want to retry in the event of failure, or if you simply want to invoke the method more than once?

It's not possible for an interceptor to call proceed() more than once on its MethodInvocation argument, because invoking proceed() will exhaust the interceptor chain held in the MethodInvocation. A MethodInvocation holds a list of interceptors and maintains the position of the current interceptor; once all interceptors have been run, it is illogical to call the proceed() method.

However, multiple calls on the rest of the interceptor chain can be achieved using the invocableClone() method of org.springframework.aop.framework.ReflectiveMethodInvocation, which was added for this reason. It's possible to cast the MethodInvocation argument to the MethodInterceptor.invoke() method to ReflectiveMethodInvocation whenever using Spring's AOP framework, as the MethodInvocation instance will be of class ReflectiveMethodInvocation or a subclass. You can call proceed() on each copy (including the original object), as shown in this example:

```
MethodInterceptor doubleInvoker = new MethodInterceptor() {
public Object invoke(MethodInvocation mi) throws Throwable {
  // Clone the invocation to proceed twice
  MethodInvocation clone = ((ReflectiveMethodInvocation) mi).invocableClone();
  clone.proceed();
  return mi.proceed();
}
```

There are some implications to consider here. If using a custom TargetSource, the target will be obtained when the original MethodInvocation is created. The copy will use the same TargetSource. So, for example, if the target comes from a pool, all calls to proceed() on MethodInvocation clones will hit the same target instance.

If you've chosen to expose the MethodInvocation using a ThreadLocal, and the target relies on it, the target will see the original method invocation in all cases, not the clones. However, this shouldn't normally matter, and, as we've seen, exposing the MethodInvocation is best avoided.

The invocableClone() method does a shallow copy of the invocation except for the arguments array. The arguments array is deep copied, meaning that it's possible to change the arguments independently when making multiple invocations.

Integration with Other AOP Frameworks

Spring AOP provides a good, simple solution to typical crosscutting concerns in J2EE applications. However, if you want to make more adventurous use of AOP — for example, to advise fine-grained objects created using new, to advise domain objects, or to advise fields — or when you absolutely need to minimize the overhead of advice, you may need a more powerful AOP solution.

To address such requirements, Spring integrates well with specialized AOP frameworks.

Goals

It's important to note here that integrating Spring with a more powerful AOP framework benefits the AOP framework as much as Spring.

The use of Dependency Injection brings as many benefits to aspects as it does to objects. Aspects can also depend on a range of objects—infrastructure objects as well as application objects—and, as with objects, it's better for those dependencies to be resolved through pushing than pulling. It's also often useful to be able to pass in simple parameterization to objects. For example, AspectJ doesn't let us add or remove advice at runtime; however, we can enable or disable an aspect using Dependency Injection, using configuration properties or interaction with injected collaborators.

AspectJ Integration

AspectJ is an extension to the Java language that elevates aspects and pointcuts to language-level constructs. AspectJ is mature and powerful. It is more difficult to use effectively for simple AOP tasks than Spring AOP. However, its capabilities far exceed those of Spring or other proxy-based frameworks where we need to make more advanced use of AOP.

This is not the place for a full discussion of AspectJ's capabilities. Please refer to the "References" section near the end of this chapter to help find more material on AspectJ. For the moment, let's note some key points:

❑ AspectJ expresses pointcuts in source code, not XML or another metadata format. A common idiom uses an abstract base aspect to define the advice, leaving subclasses to implement abstract pointcuts.

❑ Although compile-time weaving is not intrinsic to the AspectJ model, it's normal to use the AspectJ compiler rather than `javac` to compile AspectJ code. This changes the build process. There may also be performance implications if using AspectJ IDE integration. (However, the Eclipse integration, AJDT, offers an impressive feature set for working with aspects.)

❑ Advice is compiled into classes. It's not added by runtime weaving as with Spring. Thus it's impossible to add or remove advice.

❑ Unlike Spring, AspectJ implicitly uses singletons. Most advice is scoped per class loader.

❑ AspectJ does not use interception as an implementation strategy.

To use AspectJ best, you'll need to think about AOP at a higher, more conceptual level than method interception. While you can get a fair (if incomplete) grasp of the capabilities of Spring AOP by thinking of it as a sophisticated means of targeted method interception, this type of thinking is inappropriate where AspectJ is concerned.

Using Dependency Injection to Configure AspectJ Aspects

Despite the difference of the model, it's possible to integrate AspectJ aspects into a Spring context using Dependency Injection almost as smoothly as Spring AOP classes such as pointcuts and advice.

The approach will vary depending on the scope of the aspect—"aspect association" in AspectJ terminology—but it's based on defining AspectJ aspects as beans in a Spring context.

Singleton Aspects

In the most common case, aspects are singletons that can advise multiple objects. Thus by configuring an aspect instance using Dependency Injection, we can affect the advice applying to many objects.

Let's look at an example. The following AspectJ aspect applies a security check on every change to the value of the balance instance variable in the `Account` class. Such a field-level check cannot be performed using Spring's own AOP framework, although it would be possible to apply the security check to every method that might result in a change to the value of the field. But the key capability here that cannot easily be replicated using a proxy-based AOP framework is that *all* `Account` *instances will be advised, regardless of how they are created.* We don't need to manage instances of the `Account` class using Spring AOP to leverage this advice.

The code in the aspect is pure AspectJ, with the only difference from conventional AspectJ usage being the use of Setter Injection to populate the value of the `securityManager` instance variable before the aspect is used. The pointcut is defined in AspectJ code as usual, meaning that it is checked at compile time:

```
public aspect BalanceChangeSecurityAspect {

    private SecurityManager securityManager;


    public void setSecurityManager(SecurityManager securityManager) {
        this.securityManager = securityManager;
    }

    private pointcut balanceChanged() :
        set(int Account.balance);

    before() : balanceChanged() {
        this.securityManager.checkAuthorizedToModify();
    }

}
```

We must now configure the aspect using Setter Injection, as though it was any other object:

```
<bean id="securityAspect"
    class="org.springframework.samples.aspectj.bank.BalanceChangeSecurityAspect"
    factory-method="aspectOf"
>
    <property name="securityManager">
        <ref local="securityManager"/>
    </property>
</bean>
```

The magic parameter is the `factory-method` parameter. It's impossible to instantiate AspectJ aspects using constructors, as we can instantiate classes. So Spring cannot instantiate aspects using a no-arg constructor, in the case of JavaBean conventions, and it's impossible to use Constructor Injection. What we can do is use a feature introduced in Spring 1.1 — partly for AspectJ integration — in which Spring uses a factory method to obtain the object to configure.

Every singleton aspect has a static method called `aspectOf()`. We specify this factory method in the bean definition we've just seen. We can then configure the aspect using JavaBean properties, as though it was any object.

Configuration using Dependency Injection has important benefits when using AspectJ. Traditionally, it was difficult to configure aspects in a consistent way. Also, it could be difficult to integrate aspects into an application—for example, by giving them access to application objects or services such as the security manager in the example just shown. I, and no doubt others, considered these serious objections to usage of ApsectJ.

Configuring aspects using Dependency Injection gives them access to all the services Spring IoC offers—and taps into a powerful, consistent approach to application configuration.

You may be wondering: what happens if the construction of an aspect advises the creation of another singleton bean in the factory? As by default Spring doesn't guarantee the order in which singleton beans are instantiated, this could pose a problem.

By default, Spring eagerly instantiates singleton beans. It's possible to turn this off, or to control ordering. Thus there are three ways to address this:

❑   **Use the optional depends-on attribute of beans whose construction may be advised**, specifying the names of relevant aspects. This works, but has the disadvantage that advised object configurations need knowledge of the aspects that will affect them. The Spring configuration duplicates some of what is expressed in AspectJ code, and of course the two definitions may be out of synch.

❑   **Mark beans that may be advised as lazy-init**, but ensure that aspects are always eagerly instantiated (the default).

❑   **Define your aspects in an ancestor factory**. This uses the fact that Spring will always instantiate beans in an ancestor factory before descendant factories.

All these approaches work, but the third is probably the best in most cases. It clarifies exactly what's happening, encouraging the collection of aspects in one place. It's also a natural idiom once you begin.

This doesn't apply to our aspect, as balance changes are made only after the aspect is configured.

What if we had an aspect that added every object that was created to a tracker? In this case, we could write a pointcut to advise the new *operator.*

More Advanced Usages

This simple example demonstrates the advantages of Spring/AspectJ integration. However, there are a number of subtle issues to consider.

Scoping Issues

When we configured the `BalanceChangeAspect`, we configured it across the entire class loader, not just this application context. This differs from the norm in Spring. In Spring, nothing is ever per-class loader level. Spring aims to free developers from the use of the singleton design pattern—often an antipattern, used for lookup rather than because the number of instances needs to be limited to one. In AspectJ, most aspects are per class loader.

This means that should multiple Spring IoC containers attempt to configure the same aspect in the same class loader, the results will be undefined. Whichever of the contexts is instantiated last will win and reconfigure the singleton aspect that has already been configured by other contexts. This consideration is particularly important if the aspect holds a reference to the "owning" application context—for example, by implementing the `BeanFactoryAware` interface.

Thus, if another application context also constructs `Account` objects, those objects will also be advised by the aspect we configured earlier. This might be desirable, but it might not be. (Consider if the aspect depended on its context, or if there should be a different security policy within each context.)

We have a choice in how to approach this issue:

❑ Avoid it in practice. Recognize that advice has global scope, and accept the implications.

❑ Use the class loader scope to separate differently advised objects. The downside of this approach is that it complicates build and deployment, and may reduce portability between application servers.

Essentially, we're dealing with the downside of AOP based on class weaving, rather than proxying as in Spring's own framework, and the flip side of the added power. This is one reason that we recommend using Spring's own AOP framework if there's a choice of AOP technologies to meet a particular requirement.

"Singleton" aspects probably account for 90 percent of typical usage of AspectJ. As we've seen, singleton aspects are easy to configure using Spring 1.1 and above.

Understanding Aspect Association

AspectJ provides other aspect scopes—called *aspect association* types—besides singleton aspects. The complete range of options is:

❑ **Per virtual machine:** Singleton aspect. The default, as discussed above.

❑ **Per object:** An aspect instance is created for each advised object when the specified pointcut first matches at runtime. The aspect survives thereafter.

❑ **Per control flow:** The aspect scope is that of the control flow associated with the association specification. The aspect instance is released at the end of the control flow.

Aspects using association types other than per JVM need to be defined with an *association specifier*, like this:

```
aspect MyAspect perthis(pointcutName())
```

Presently there is no out-of-the-box support for configuring such aspects using Spring. However, it is possible, and this may have changed by the time you read this. The Spring and AspectJ communities are working together to improve integration between the two products. If you are interested in this advanced feature, you may want to check the AspectJ section of the Spring Reference Manual for an update.

Choosing Between Spring AOP and AspectJ

Spring AOP integrates well with AspectJ. There is no conflict between the two approaches. We can use both in the same application.

Nevertheless, sometimes we will have the choice between using Spring AOP and AspectJ for the same ends. How do we then choose between the two approaches?

Using AspectJ brings much more of a paradigm shift than using Spring AOP. Not only is using such a capable AOP solution likely to change how you think about code, there are some clashes between AspectJ and Spring concepts that you should be aware of.

AspectJ has some significant potential advantages:

- ❑ **Negligible performance overhead.** AspectJ imposes no overhead itself; it should offer performance as good as writing the crosscutting code manually. Nevertheless, it's important to recognize that the interception overhead is insignificant in recommended use of Spring AOP.

- ❑ **It is particularly good for introduction.** Introduction in a proxy-based framework such as Spring requires usually maintaining a distinct object instance for each introduction, as well as the target, because the introduction is holding part of the state. With AspectJ, the additional fields and method implementations can be added to the byte code of the advised class.

- ❑ **It's well suited to advising fine-grained objects.** Not only is overhead low, but objects can be constructed using new, unlike with a proxy-based approach. The fact that objects don't need to be managed by the Spring IoC container to be advised is probably the biggest advantage of a "full-blown" AOP framework.

- ❑ **Non-public methods can be advised.**

- ❑ **Fields can be advised.**

- ❑ **AspectJ is well suited to type-safe advice.** If your advice needs to work directly with the types of objects it is advising, AspectJ is likely to prove more economical to code and less error-prone than AOP Alliance-style code. (Such aspects tend to be application-specific. Middleware aspects, such as transaction management aspects, do *not* normally benefit from type safety. In fact, they are often easier to code using AOP Alliance method interception than AspectJ pointcuts and advice.)

However, there are some costs and complexities associated with AspectJ that mean the decision is not straightforward:

- ❑ **Using AspectJ complicates the build process.** It will have a noticeable effect on build time.

- ❑ **AspectJ syntax is not particularly intuitive.** If you or your project team are already skilled with AspectJ, this is not a concern. Once the learning curve is surmounted, AspectJ is uniquely powerful.

- ❑ **You will require tool support**, and this may constrain your choice of IDE. AspectJ tools are still not perfect, although they are improving rapidly.

- ❑ **AspectJ does not presently allow externalizing pointcuts into configuration files**, which may be appropriate when working with generic middleware aspects.

It's possible to use both Spring's own AOP framework *and* AspectJ in the same application. They do not conflict, and this is perfectly legitimate. Consider the case where we address transaction management using Spring's `TransactionProxyFactoryBean`, but need to apply advice to fine-grained objects such as objects persisted with JDO. Spring provides the simplest solution for transaction management. But no proxy-based framework is well suited to advising fine-grained objects, and AspectJ is simply a better fit in such cases. The Spring/AspectJ integration means that it's possible to apply AOP incrementally, turning to the more powerful and complex solution — AspectJ — only when there is no good alternative.

Of course, many of these advantages and disadvantages apply to other AOP frameworks as well, such as AspectWerkz.

> **We believe that AOP will become increasingly important, and that Spring's AspectJ integration will also become increasingly important.**

AspectWerkz

Because of the flexibility of its IoC framework, which enables a variety of approaches to instantiating objects, Spring can easily integrate with other AOP frameworks besides AspectJ.

Besides AspectJ, the most important dedicated AOP framework is AspectWerkz (`http://aspectwerkz.codehaus.org/`).

AspectWerkz differs from AspectJ in that it does not extend the Java language but uses XML metadata to bind aspects at runtime.

AspectWerkz offers a flexible approach to aspect instantiation, which means that it integrates well with Spring. As with AspectJ, both products gain by the combination.

As a starting point, please see "Spring and AspectWerkz — A Happy Marriage" (`http://blogs.codehaus.org/people/jboner/archives/000826_spring_and_aspectwerkz_a_happy_marriage.html`) by Jonas Boner, the creator of AspectWerkz.

> **It was announced in early 2005 that AspectJ and AspectWerkz are merging to form AspectJ 5.0. We believe that this is good news for the AOP community as a whole, and expect that AspectJ 5.0 will become the definitive full-featured AOP technology. Both the Spring and AspectJ teams are committed to delivering the best possible integration between the two products, and believe that this is important to both communities.**

References

This chapter has provided a thorough description of Spring's AOP infrastructure. However, the following books and articles provide useful background on AOP and its applications:

❑ *J2EE without EJB.* Chapter 8 is a pragmatic discussion of AOP in J2EE applications. The chapter discusses the motivation for the Spring AOP framework at length.

❑ *AspectJ in Action* by Ramnivas Laddad (Manning, 2003). Excellent AspectJ text, which also explains AOP concepts very well.

❑ *Eclipse AspectJ: Aspect-Oriented Programming with AspectJ and the Eclipse AspectJ Development Tools* by Adrian Colyer, AspectJ lead (Addison-Wesley, 2005).

Summary

AOP complements Dependency Injection to enable Spring to provide a non-invasive programming model. The two technologies complement each other perfectly.

Spring offers two flavors of AOP support: its own proxy-based AOP framework, which works in standard Java; and integration with specialized AOP technologies, especially AspectJ, the most mature AOP technology available.

We recommend using Spring AOP for most AOP requirements. It is particularly well suited for applying crosscutting behavior to business objects.

We recommend the following best practices:

❑ Code duplication is a code smell. Avoid it. AOP can be a powerful tool to help avoid code duplication.

❑ Remember that used correctly, AOP can significantly simplify application objects, and enable them to focus on their core responsibilities.

❑ Minimize dependency on Spring framework APIs when using Spring AOP, as when using Spring in general.

❑ If something clearly benefits from AOP, yet it's hard to do using Spring AOP (like advising fine-grained objects), consider using AspectJ.

❑ When using `ProxyFactoryBean`, in most cases use an "inner bean" to ensure that autowiring works correctly and your factory namespace isn't polluted by two beans (proxy and target) when you really want just one (the proxy).

❑ Familiarize yourself with the Spring "autoproxy" infrastructure. Particularly if you need to advise a large number of objects, this can produce significant simplification in application configuration.

❑ Use bean definition "inheritance" as another technique to eliminate duplication of interceptor chain definitions and other AOP configuration.

❑ If you can, use J2SE dynamic proxies rather than CGLIB, and access proxied objects only through their interfaces.

You can use AOP with confidence in your Spring applications: Many users already do, and AOP is the enabling technology for much of Spring's infrastructure functionality, such as declarative transaction management and lightweight remoting.

5

DAO Support and JDBC Framework

This chapter introduces Spring's support for the Data Access Object (DAO) pattern. This is followed by an in-depth discussion of Spring's JDBC framework.

The DAO pattern is one of the most important patterns commonly used in J2EE applications, and Spring's data access architecture provides uniquely sophisticated yet straightforward support for it.

The Spring JDBC framework is built on top of the core J2SE JDBC API, and it is the lowest level data access technology that Spring supports. Other, higher level technologies are iBATIS SQL Maps, Hibernate, JDO, and other O/R mapping tools. These technologies also use JDBC as their underlying API for accessing a relational database but they all provide their own higher level abstraction API that you work with. In Chapter 7 we will discuss these other technologies in detail.

To begin with, we'll spend some time looking at JDBC itself. We will briefly look at what works well and what does not work so well with a traditional JDBC approach. We assume that you have some experience using JDBC. If you don't, you should start with a basic JDBC tutorial before continuing with this chapter. Sun provides a JDBC tutorial on their Java website at `http://java.sun.com/docs/books/tutorial/jdbc/index.html`.

We will then introduce the core functionality of Spring's JDBC framework. The focus of Spring's approach is to make it easier to use the strengths present in the JDBC API while abstracting away the rough spots. We will then cover the JDBC framework in more detail and conclude with a discussion of when it is appropriate to use Spring JDBC rather than an Object/Relational mapping tool.

The Data Access Object Pattern

The Data Access Object (DAO) pattern is a well-established J2EE pattern discussed in many J2EE books including *Core J2EE Patterns*, by Deepak Alur, John Crupi, and Dan Malks (`http://java.sun.com/blueprints/corej2eepatterns/Patterns/DataAccessObject.html`).

The primary purpose of the DAO pattern is to separate persistence-related issues from general business rules and workflows. We don't want the business or workflow logic to depend on or have any knowledge of what data access technology is actually used.

The DAO pattern introduces an interface for defining the persistence operations that the business layer can access, hiding the actual implementation. (This approach represents the *Strategy* Design Pattern.) The implementation for this interface will vary depending on the persistence technology being used, but the DAO interface can largely remain the same. Chapter 10 in *Expert One-on-One J2EE Development without EJB*, by Rod Johnson and Juergen Hoeller (Wiley, 2004), contains some more in-depth discussion on the DAO pattern itself and why it is not always possible or even desirable to try to define a DAO interface that would remain static regardless of persistence technology used. There are many subtle issues, such as managing access over object lifecycles and explicit save operations.

> We recommend using the DAO pattern to separate business logic from the persistence code. The exception to this rule is when the application's business logic consists of data access operations and not much else. In this case it makes sense to include the data access code in the business operations themselves.

Let's see what this looks like in practice, before digging deeper into API and other details.

Spring provides abstract DAO base classes that provide easy access to common database resources. There are implementations available for each data access technology supported by Spring.

For JDBC there is `JdbcDaoSupport` and it provides methods to access the `DataSource` and a pre-configured `JdbcTemplate`. You simply extend the `JdbcDaoSupport` class and provide a reference to the actual `DataSource` in your application context configuration. Here is a brief example:

```
public class TestJdbcDao extends JdbcDaoSupport {
    private final static String TEST_SQL = "select count(*) from dual";

    public int getTestCount() {
        return getJdbcTemplate().queryForInt(TEST_SQL);
    }
}
```

And here is the corresponding entry in `dataAccessContext.xml`:

```
<bean id="dao" class="TestJdbcDao">
  <property name="dataSource">
    <ref local="dataSource" />
  </property>
</bean>
```

Spring also provides an abstract DAO support class for each O/R mapping technology it supports. For example, Hibernate has `HibernateDaoSupport`, iBATIS SQL Maps has `SqlMapClientDaoSupport`, JDO has `JdoDaoSupport`, and OJB has `PersistenceBrokerDaoSupport`. We will look at the configuration for a Hibernate DAO that is part of the sample application:

```
public class HibernateBoxOfficeDao extends HibernateDaoSupport
                                implements BoxOfficeDao {
    ...

    public Show getShow(long id) {
        Show s = (Show) getHibernateTemplate().get(Show.class, new Long(id));
        return s;
    }

    ...

}
```

And here is the bean configuration from `dataAccessContext.xml`:

```
<!-- The Hibernate DAO class -->
<bean id="dao"
    class="org.springframework.prospring.ticket.dao.hibernate.HibernateBoxOfficeDao">
    <property name="sessionFactory">
        <ref local="sessionFactory"/>
    </property>
</bean>
```

The configuration for the other data access technologies is similar; simply replace the `sessionFactory` property with a reference to the corresponding factory type.

Introducing Spring's JDBC Framework

Before going into detail about the various parts of Spring's JDBC support, let's look at some common issues encountered while writing code using the JDBC API directly. After that we'll see how Spring can help and we'll take a quick look at a brief example of using Spring for solving one specific problem — how to populate a table with test data using Java and SQL.

Motivation: Issues with Direct Use of JDBC

JDBC has been available since Java 1.1 and it was one of the most important early APIs that made Java's advances in server-side development possible. Today it is hard to imagine accessing a database from Java without using JDBC either directly or indirectly. Without it we would have to use proprietary APIs specific to a certain database, and these APIs from different vendors would all be significantly different from each other. The JDBC API consists of a number of interfaces that must be implemented by each provider of a JDBC driver. This is how the usage across various databases is unified into a single API. There are some differences between the various JDBC implementations, but overall they are not too difficult to work around.

Managing the Connection, Statements, and ResultSets

The primary JDBC interfaces include `Connection`, `DataSource`, `Statement`, `PreparedStatement`, `CallableStatement`, and `ResultSet`. To go along with these interfaces we have the class `SQLException`. The major obstacles you encounter working with JDBC are usually related to the exception and connection management. These are areas, as we will see later, where Spring's JDBC framework shines.

When you open a connection to the database, you must also close it. This forces you to always provide a try-finally set of blocks where the closing of the `ResultSets`, the `Statements`, and the `Connection` must take place in the `finally` block. On top of this, each call to the `close()` method can itself throw an `SQLException`, forcing you to nest additional try-catch blocks within the `finally` block. If you miss this, which is easy when you are new to JDBC, the connection will remain open. Leaving connections open means that you will sooner or later run out of connections for your application to use — a common cause of operational problems.

Handling SQLExceptions

If there is a problem accessing the database, all JDBC implementations throw an `SQLException`. This is the only exception used and it has proven difficult to manage exceptions in a way that works well across a variety of database products. To begin with, you end up writing lots of error-prone code in try-catch blocks. The exception itself is not very informative, even when we consider the error codes provided as part of the exception. There are two sets of codes provided — an error code and an SQL state code for each exception.

The error code is vendor-specific: for example, in the case of Oracle it will correspond to an ORA code, such as ORA-942 (table or view does not exist). This is informative but not portable. We need to write database-specific code to check it — although *conceptually*, of course, errors (like our example) are not usually database-specific.

The SQL state code is theoretically more portable, as it is supposed to be a generic code defined in the Open Group's XOPEN SQL specification. In reality, however, you will receive different SQL state codes from different implementations for seemingly similar errors. As an example, reading the X/Open specification for SQL version 2.0, it appears that the code for "table not found" should be 42S02. However, running a query selecting from a nonexistent table produced the following SQL state codes:

Oracle	42000
DB2	42704
HSQLDB	S0002
MySQL	S1000
PostgreSQL	42P01

Beginning with JDBC 3.0, the provider of the JDBC implementation can now follow either the XOPEN SQLState conventions or the SQL 99 conventions for the SQL state code. All of this clearly indicates that we need some kind of error code mapping to find the true cause of the problem.

Thus writing portable, self-documenting code that needs to react to specific errors — rather than merely know that "something went wrong" — is problematic using raw JDBC.

Lookup of Resources

The `javax.sql.DataSource` interface is part of JDBC 2.0 API and defines a standard way for interacting with a connection factory without having to provide database-specific parameters such as JDBC driver class name or connection URL. All of these configuration details are managed through some other means of configuration, allowing the code that uses the connection to remain unaware of this detail. Normally you would need to look up the `DataSource` using a naming service such as JNDI or use a local implementation such as Jakarta Common's DBCP from Apache. This leads to a different approach compared to the traditional way of using the JDBC `DriverManager`. You would have to maintain multiple sets of code depending on how the runtime environment was configured.

> Spring's JDBC framework is designed to obtain connections using the standard JDBC 2.0 `DataSource` interface. This is particularly appropriate in J2EE environments, but works well in any environment.

JDBC Strengths

There are a number of features that work well in JDBC. Let's examine some of them.

Implementations Provided by Vendors

The JDBC specification largely specifies interfaces, rather than classes. These interfaces define the core functionality, leaving the actual implementation to JDBC driver vendors. This makes it possible to switch from one database or JDBC driver to another without having to modify your code, in most cases.

Using SQL

With JDBC, we can use regular SQL for querying and modifying the database. SQL is proven to work well for manipulating relational data. Many developers already know it and it is fairly easy to learn the basics if you don't. There are many resources available for learning SQL. The availability of JDBC drivers for almost any relational database is another strength for JDBC. This allows us to write code that can be used against a variety of databases as long as we don't use any esoteric features that may not be portable.

Cross Database Escape Syntax

To make cross-product coding easier, JDBC provides an SQL escape syntax consisting of keywords specified within curly braces. An example of this is `{ fn user() }`, which will retrieve the current user name, and `{d '2004-01-28' }` for a cross-database date format. The JDBC driver is supposed to either map these expressions to the appropriate database feature or provide its own implementation. You can read up on this feature at `http://java.sun.com/j2se/1.3/docs/guide/jdbc/spec/jdbc-spec.frame11.html`.

How Spring Can Help

The main aim of Spring's JDBC framework is to leverage the features of JDBC that work well and to abstract away problem areas. This focuses primarily around connection and exception handling problems we mentioned earlier. This is done by providing an abstraction layer on top of JDBC. The abstraction layer manages connections as well as translates `SQLExceptions` into more meaningful exceptions.

Spring provides its own exception hierarchy for data access errors and the same hierarchy is used both when you use JDBC and when you use an O/R mapping tool such as Hibernate or JDO. This means that all your Data Access Objects (DAO) will throw the same type of errors regardless of the underlying data access implementation. All of this makes your data access code much easier to write and use. An added benefit is that it makes your database code more portable as well.

A Simple Example

We want to be able to populate a database table with some test data that we will be using for some tests. This brief example will set the stage for the more detailed discussion of each concept that follows. The main class used in this example is the `JdbcTemplate`. This is the central framework class that manages all the database communication and exception handling. Under the covers, it uses a `java.sql` `.Connection` that is obtained from a `java.sql.DataSource`. The `JdbcTemplate` provides some convenience methods for running simple SQL statements. One of these convenience methods is `execute()`, which just takes an SQL statement as the only parameter. Let's say you already have a table that was created using the following SQL:

```
create table mytable (id integer, name varchar(100))
```

Now you want to add some test data that can be used for one of your unit tests. Here is a minimal test case that you would write to accomplish this:

```
package org.springframework.prospring.ticket.db;

import junit.framework.TestCase;

import org.springframework.jdbc.core.JdbcTemplate;
import org.springframework.jdbc.datasource.DriverManagerDataSource;

public class MinimalTest extends TestCase {
  private DriverManagerDataSource dataSource;

  public void setUp() {

    dataSource = new DriverManagerDataSource();
    dataSource.setDriverClassName( "org.hsqldb.jdbcDriver");
    dataSource.setUrl( "jdbc:hsqldb:hsql://localhost:");
    dataSource.setUsername( "sa");
    dataSource.setPassword( "");

    JdbcTemplate jt = new JdbcTemplate(dataSource);
    jt.execute("delete from mytable");
    jt.execute("insert into mytable (id, name) values(1, 'John')");
    jt.execute("insert into mytable (id, name) values(2, 'Jane')");

  }

  public void testSomething() {

    // the actual test code goes here

  }
}
```

In this example we first set up one of Spring's `DataSource` implementations that are designed for use in a test environment. Normally we would use Dependency Injection for the `DataSource`, but to show everything in one code snippet, we create the `DataSource` programmatically here. Next, we create a `JdbcTemplate`, passing in the `DataSource` as the only parameter for the constructor. Next, we call the `JdbcTemplate`'s execute() method with the SQL insert statements we need.

As you can see, there is no exception handling in this code. The `JdbcTemplate` will catch any `SQLExceptions` and translate them to a subclass of `DataAccessException`, which is the top-level class in Spring's data access exception hierarchy. These exceptions are unchecked, and because we assume that for this program there is nothing we can do about any database errors, we just let the run-time exception get propagated to the top of the call stack and the whole program execution will fail.

You can also see that there is no need for a try-finally block for closing the connection. This is unnecessary because the `JdbcTemplate` will manage the connection for us and this makes the code we write much more concise and easy to follow. All the unwieldy "plumbing" code has been relegated to the framework classes.

Building the Data Access Layer for the Sample Application

After this simplistic example we will build parts of the data access layer for the sample application that is discussed in Appendix A. As we move along we will introduce the various features of the framework used in the example and explain how to use them.

Data Model for the Sample Application

Let's start this by looking at the data model for the sample application. We won't cover the entire data model to begin with, but we will gradually include the classes and tables that we will be using for the rest of this chapter. To begin with we have three tables that we will be writing some data access classes for: Show, Genre, and Seating_Plan. The data model in Figure 5-1 shows the relationships between these tables.

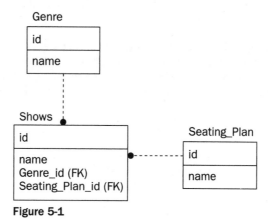

Figure 5-1

We have a `Shows` associated with both a `Genre` and a `Seating_Plan`. Each `Genre` can have a number of `Shows` associated with it. Seating plans can vary between shows because of physical setup limitations. Some shows require room for a choir, for example, so some seating would not be available because of this fact.

The DDL (data definition language) needed to create these tables is as follows:

```
CREATE TABLE Genre (
  id INTEGER NOT NULL,
  name VARCHAR(50),
  PRIMARY KEY(id));

CREATE TABLE Seating_Plan (
  id INTEGER NOT NULL,
  name VARCHAR(50),
  PRIMARY KEY(id));

CREATE TABLE Shows (
  id INTEGER NOT NULL,
  name VARCHAR(50),
  Genre_id INTEGER,
  Seating_Plan_id INTEGER,
  PRIMARY KEY(id));

ALTER TABLE Shows
  ADD CONSTRAINT fk_Genre
  FOREIGN KEY (Genre_id)
  REFERENCES Genre (id)
  ON DELETE CASCADE;

ALTER TABLE Shows
  ADD CONSTRAINT fk_Seating_Plan
  FOREIGN KEY (Seating_Plan_id)
  REFERENCES Seating_Plan (id);
```

This is a generic script that should work for most SQL databases. Note that the table name for the `Show` entity is the plural form — `Shows`. This is because the word "SHOW" is a reserved word in MySQL. If you are using MySQL then you should append `TYPE = InnoDB` to all the table definitions in the script. This will allow you to use transactions.

The next step is to create these tables using your preferred database. We have used HSQL, MySQL, PostgreSQL, and Oracle to test the sample code and we provide database scripts for the sample application for all of these databases. (See Appendix A for more information on the sample application and how to create the sample tables.) Once we have the tables created, we are ready to move on.

DataSource

You might be used to calling `DriverManager.getConnection` to get a JDBC `Connection` object. JDBC 2.0 introduced a new interface, `javax.sql.DataSource`, that acts as a factory for connections. This is now the preferred method for obtaining a connection as it allows the use of connection pooling and avoids hard coding the connection properties. Spring's JDBC framework is built with this in mind, and a `DataSource` is the only thing Spring uses to get a connection to the database.

Normally you would look up the `DataSource` using a naming service like JNDI, or you could alternatively configure a basic `DataSource` locally. In the case of a non-web application or a unit test, you could use a `DataSource` implementation provided by Jakarta Commons DBCP. This is also the case for a web application that connects to a single database only and that does not need support for distributed transactions (see the "DataSource Declarations" section in Chapter 6 for more in-depth discussion). The most commonly used `DataSources` are `org.apache.commons.dbcp.BasicDataSource` and `org.apache.commons.dbcp.PoolingDataSource`.

You could also use a `DataSource` implementation provided by Spring. The `DriverManagerDataSource` implementation will create a new connection each time the framework calls the `getConnection` method. This works well for unit testing, but is not a good choice when you have an application that makes multiple calls to the database. For applications where you want to acquire the connection only once and hold on to it, Spring provides the `SingleConnectionDataSource`. With this implementation, you should make a call to the `destroy` method when you are done with you database processing. This call will allow Spring to close the physical connection. If you use dependency injection with an `ApplicationContext` or `BeanFactory`, then this method will be called automatically when the application is shut down.

It is important to note that while the various `DataSource` implementations are threadsafe, the `SingleConnectionDataSource` is not because it holds on to the connection until the `destroy` method is called. This is not a problem for single-threaded applications, but web applications should allocate a new instance of this class for each request.

> For web applications and other applications, we recommend using a `DataSource` that is threadsafe and one that provides connection pooling. This includes the implementations provided by Apache Commons DBCP and the c3p0 project.

For your data access objects, you normally declare a `DataSource` variable and have it set using Dependency Injection. Your program does not care whether the `DataSource` being used is a pooled or a basic one. When it comes to your unit tests, you have a choice whether you want to create the `DataSource` programmatically or whether you want to use Dependency Injection. The programmatic way would be the following:

```
BasicDataSource ds = new BasicDataSource();
ds.setDriverClassName("org.hsqldb.jdbcDriver");
ds.setUrl("jdbc:hsqldb:hsql://localhost");
ds.setUsername("sa");
ds.setPassword("");
```

If you prefer to use an application context, then this is what you would need:

```
ApplicationContext ac = new ClassPathXmlApplicationContext("ticket-context.xml");
DataSource ds = (DataSource) ac.getBean("dataSource", DataSource.class);
```

Alternatively, you could extend `AbstractTransactionalDataSourceSpringContextTests` in the `org.springframework.test` package, in which case your test will extend a `DataSource` provided by the super class — which obtains it by Dependency Injection from your application context. This is normally best practice for integration testing.

The application context `ticket-context.xml` (see Chapter 2 for more detail about application contexts) should be placed on the classpath and has the following content:

```xml
<?xml version="1.0" encoding="UTF-8"?>
<!DOCTYPE beans PUBLIC "-//SPRING//DTD BEAN//EN"
 "http://www.springframework.org/dtd/spring-beans.dtd">

<beans>

  <bean id="dataSource"
    class=" org.apache.commons.dbcp.BasicDataSource ">
  <property name="driverClassName">
    <value>org.hsqldb.jdbcDriver</value>
  </property>
  <property name="url">
    <value>jdbc:hsqldb:hsql://localhost</value>
   </property>
  <property name="username">
    <value>sa</value>
  </property>
  <property name="password">
    <value></value>
  </property>
  </bean>

</beans>
```

Exception Translation

Spring will catch and translate any `SQLExceptions` that might be thrown during the JDBC processing. The base class for Spring's exception hierarchy is `org.springframework.dao.DataAccessException`. This is an abstract class that inherits from `NestedRuntimeException`. The advantage of using `NestedRuntimeException` is twofold. Firstly, it is a `RunTimeException` so you don't have to catch it if you don't want to. In practice, data access exceptions are usually unrecoverable. If you don't think that your code can recover from a database failure, then you can let the exception propagate to the surrounding class without catching it. Secondly, it is able to wrap the original `SQLException` so that you can get to the root cause of the failure.

By using an exception hierarchy, Spring allows you to catch exceptions at the right level. If you think that you can recover from an `OptimisticLockingException`, then you can easily catch this exception and handle it. Figure 5-2 shows a graph of the entire `DataAccessException` exception hierarchy.

Figure 5-2

The concrete exceptions that inherit from the `DataAccessException` and that are directly related to JDBC usage are the following:

- ❑ `BadSqlGrammarException`: This exception indicates a problem with the SQL issued by your application — such as an invalid table or view name as conveyed by ORA-942. However, in this case, code that catches this Spring exception will be self-documenting — there is no risk of a check against a magic number — and it will no longer be Oracle-specific. There is a gain in both maintainability and portability.

- ❑ `DataIntegrityViolationException`: There is a data integrity problem. You might have tried to insert a duplicate key or no data was supplied for a column that requires a value to be specified.

- ❑ `DataRetrievalFailureException`: A problem was encountered retrieving expected data.

- ❑ `CannotAcquireLockException`: When you update the database, someone else might have a lock on the row you are trying to update. If you have configured your database access to not wait for blocking locks, then this would be the appropriate exception to be thrown. This would happen if you used Oracle and executed a `SELECT ... FROM mytable FOR UPDATE NOWAIT` statement.

- ❑ `DataAccessResourceFailureException`: Exception thrown when there is a problem connecting to the database.

Spring's data access exception hierarchy consists of exceptions that are independent not just of a specific database, such as Oracle, *but of the use of JDBC altogether*. For example, DataAccessResourceFailureException can be thrown by Spring's TopLink integration as well as JdbcTemplate, meaning that code that handles it is less dependent on the specific persistence API in use. JDBC-specific exceptions, such as BadSqlGrammarException, extend the most informative possible generic exception — in this case, InvalidDataAccessResourceUsageException. (Thus it is a sibling of HibernateQueryException, which is thrown on issuing an ill-formed HQL query string.)

Which exception is thrown for a specific SQL error code is controlled by a configuration file named sql-error-codes.xml. This file is loaded when the JdbcTemplate is configured. It contains error codes for the most commonly used databases. The following code shows the entry for Oracle:

```
<beans>

...

    <bean id="Oracle" class="org.springframework.jdbc.support.SQLErrorCodes">
      <property name="badSqlGrammarCodes">
        <value>900,903,904,917,936,942,17006</value>
      </property>
      <property name="dataIntegrityViolationCodes">
        <value>1,1400,1722,2291</value>
      </property>
      <property name="cannotAcquireLockCodes">
        <value>54</value>
      </property>
    </bean>

...

</beans>
```

The error code from the SQLException is matched up with the set of codes provided in this file. Which set of codes that is used depends on the name of the database product that is returned from a call to getDatabaseMetaData on the JDBC connection. If you would like to use a different translation, you can supply your own configuration file with the same name. This file must be placed on the classpath so that the SQLErrorCodesFactory can find it.

If the error code from the SQLException can't be found in the list of error codes, then the translation will fall back on using the SQL state as provided in the SQLException. This fallback translation is done by the class SQLStateSQLExceptionTranslator.

Operations with JdbcTemplate

The central class in the JDBC framework is JdbcTemplate, found in the org.springframework.jdbc.core package. This is the class that manages all the database communication and exception handling using a java.sql.Connection that is obtained from the provided javax.sql.DataSource (see below for more detail on the DataSource).

> JdbcTemplate **is a stateless and threadsafe class and you can safely instantiate a single instance to be used for each DAO.**

Use of Callback Methods

JdbcTemplate is based on a template style of programming common to many other parts of Spring. Some method calls are handled entirely by the JdbcTemplate, while others require the calling class to provide callback methods that contain the implementation for parts of the JDBC workflow. This is another form of Inversion of Control. Your application code hands over the responsibility of managing the database access to the template class. The template class in turn calls back to your application code when it needs some detail processing filled in. These callback methods are allowed to throw a java.sql.SQLException, since the framework will be able to catch this exception and use its built-in exception translation functionality.

We'll look at an example of a callback method for a query method that takes an SQL statement, an object array with parameter values, and a callback implementation to handle the rows returned by the query. We have chosen to implement this callback implementation as an *anonymous inner class*. This is a common practice in code developed with Spring, and idiomatic Java. The advantages are that the code is more compact and the callback implementation has access to variables and parameters from the surrounding method. This is true as long as the variables and parameters are declared as final. A drawback is that the code can be hard to read if the callback implementation is lengthy. In that case it is better to refactor code into a separate method, or use a named, rather than anonymous, inner class. A good IDE will make this type of programming much easier. (It also has the significant advantage versus raw JDBC coding with try/catch blocks that the compiler will detect errors, rather than the errors appearing at runtime in the form of connection leaks.) Here is the code for our query example:

```
JdbcTemplate jt = new JdbcTemplate(dataSource);
String sql = "select id, name from genre where id < ?";
final List myResults = new ArrayList();
List l = jt.query(sql, new Object[] {new Integer(4)},
    new RowCallbackHandler() {
      public void processRow(ResultSet rs) throws SQLException {
        // do something with the rowdata - like create a new
        // object and add it to the List in the enclosing code
        Genre g = new Genre();
        g.setId(rs.getLong("id"));
        g.setName(rs.getString("name"));
        myResults.add(g);
      }
    }
  );
```

The callback implementation is of type RowCallbackHandler, which is an interface requiring the implementation of a single method: processRow. This method gets called once for each row. Most of the time you would implement a method that stores the data in a final variable declared in the enclosing method. This final variable is usually a List or sometimes a Map. We will see examples of this and of other callback methods later in the "Advanced Use of JdbcTemplate" section. For more details on how to use anonymous inner classes, see Chapter 5 of *The Java Programming Language,* Third Edition, by Ken Arnold, James Gosling, and David Holmes (Addison-Wesley, 2000).

JdbcTemplate Convenience Methods

There are several convenience methods on JdbcTemplate that provide an easy interface for accessing and manipulating data in the database. These convenience methods lend themselves to direct use without the need to create or use additional framework objects. They provide basic options for executing queries and updating the database.

We have query methods with four different return types in two variations: one where you pass in static SQL, and one where you pass in SQL with placeholders for your parameters along with an object array containing the values for your parameters.

- ❑ int queryForInt(String sql)
- ❑ int queryForInt(String sql, Object[] args)
- ❑ long queryForLong(String sql)
- ❑ long queryForLong(String sql, Object[] args)
- ❑ Object queryForObject(String sql, Class requiredType)
- ❑ Object queryForObject(String sql, Class requiredType, Object[] args)
- ❑ List queryForList(String sql)
- ❑ List queryForList(String sql, Object[] args)

The return type is indicated in the name of the query method. The ones that return an Object take an additional parameter that indicates the required type that should be returned. If there is no match between the requested data type and the type returned by the database, then the appropriate conversion is attempted. In the case where this conversion fails, a TypeMismatchDataAccessException is thrown. Any type can be converted to a String and any numeric type should be able to be converted to any class that extends java.lang.Number. There might be some rounding issues or truncation, so you should select a type that matches the database value as closely as possible. The appropriate type mappings are defined in the JDBC specification.

The List that is returned by queryForList contains a Map for each row returned by the query. The Map's entries are keyed by the column name and the value is the column value returned from the database. The value's type depends on the database type and it follows the regular JDBC mapping rules.

In addition to the query methods there is an execute method that takes a static SQL statement as the only parameter:

```
void execute(String sql)
```

We used this method in the first example in this chapter where we executed a DDL statement to create a table.

The next group of convenience methods is the update methods. There is one where you pass in static SQL, one where you pass in SQL with placeholders and an object array with the parameter values, and finally one like the previous one except that you also pass in an array of integers containing the SQL types of your parameters. This can be helpful for making sure that the prepared statement is populated with the correct data type rather than relying on the default mappings.

- ❑ `int update(String sql)`
- ❑ `int update(String sql, Object[] args)`
- ❑ `int update(String sql, Object[] args, int[] argTypes)`

All these update methods return an `int` indicating the number of rows that were affected, as reported by the JDBC driver.

`JdbcTemplate` also has a number of methods for more advanced processing requirements where the caller provides callback interfaces for preparing statements and for processing returned results. We will take a closer look at these methods later in this chapter.

Basic Queries Using the JdbcTemplate

The easiest way to query the database is to use some of the previously mentioned convenience methods of `JdbcTemplate`. We already talked about these earlier and now we will see additional examples of how to use them. One very useful method is `queryForInt`, which returns a single integer returned by the SQL statement passed in. The following example shows you how to do this:

```
JdbcTemplate jt = new JdbcTemplate(ds);
int count = jt.queryForInt("select count(*) from Genre");
```

The SQL statement must, of course, return a single row with a single numeric column for this to work properly. If your query uses placeholders for parameters, then you would use a second parameter consisting of an object array with one element for each placeholder. We should note that the use of parameter placeholders will allow the framework to always use a prepared statement. This will allow the application server and the database server to optimize caching and reuse of your query statement. This can provide a significant boost in performance. The mapping between the object passed in and the SQL data type is the same as for regular JDBC usage:

```
JdbcTemplate jt = new JdbcTemplate(ds);
Object[] parameters = new Object[] {"M"};
int count = jt.queryForInt("select count(*) from Genre where name > ?",
  parameters);
```

If your query returns a very large number that exceeds the capacity of an `int`, then you can use `queryForLong` in the same way as `queryForInt`. Any other return type is covered by `queryForObject`. Here you pass in the Class for the object you expect to get returned in addition to the SQL and the optional object array for parameters:

```
JdbcTemplate jt = new JdbcTemplate(ds);
Object[] parameters = new Object[] {new Integer(2)};
Object o = jt.queryForObject("select name from Genre where id = ?",
   parameters, String.class);
```

So far the queries we have looked at have been limited to returning a single value. We also need a method for returning several column values for multiple rows. The method that provides this is `queryForList`. It returns a List of `Map` objects, one `Map` object for each row returned by the query. The `Map` holds the column values with the column name as the key for the entry:

```
JdbcTemplate jt = new JdbcTemplate(ds);
Object[] parameters = new Object[] {new Integer(1)};
List l = jt.queryForList("select id, name from Genre where id > ?",
   parameters);
```

This would return something like the following based on the data in the previous example for our unit test:

```
[{NAME=Circus, ID=2}, {NAME=Rock Concert, ID=3}]
```

These query methods work well for simple queries, but if you have more complex ones or you need to map the data returned to actual business objects rather than a list, then you would be better off using a `MappingSqlQuery`. This query is described later in this chapter.

Basic Updating with JdbcTemplate

It's not enough to just be able to read the data. We also want to be able to modify it. One way of running simple update statements is the `update()` method of the `JdbcTemplate`. We can just pass in an SQL statement, or if we use parameter placeholders in the SQL, then we also pass in an object array with the actual parameters. Here is a more complete example using all the methods we have discussed thus far:

```
JdbcTemplate jt = new JdbcTemplate(ds);
 jt.execute("truncate table Genre");
int x = jt.update("insert into Genre (id, name) values(1, 'Opera')");
x += jt.update("insert into Genre (id, name) values(2, 'Circus')");
x += jt.update("insert into Genre (id, name) values(3, 'Rock Concert')");
x += jt.update("insert into Genre (id, name) values(4, 'Symphony')");
System.out.println(x + " row(s) inserted.");
x = jt.update("update Genre set name = 'Pop/Rock' where id = ?",
   new Object[] {new Integer(3)});
System.out.println(x + " row(s) updated.");
x = jt.update("delete from Genre where id = 2");
System.out.println(x + " row(s) deleted.");
List l = jt.queryForList("select id, name from Genre");
System.out.println(l);
```

You might wonder what the difference between the `execute` and `update` methods is. The update method returns a count of the number of rows affected and it will use a `java.sql.PreparedStatement` if you pass in parameters. The `execute` method always uses a `java.sql.Statement`, does not accept parameters, and it will not return a count of rows affected. The `execute` method is more appropriate for statements where you create and drop tables while the `update` method is more appropriate for insert, update, and delete operations.

Advanced Use of JdbcTemplate

We saw previously some examples of queries where the return type was of a type defined by the type of query you used. What if you wanted to create one of your own domain objects as the output from a query? There are several `JdbcTemplate` methods that will allow you to do that and we will show you some examples of this. We will also show you some examples of how you can create prepared statements and set the parameter values through some framework callback methods.

In addition to the query methods of the `JdbcTemplate` there is a set of RDBMS Operation classes that has similar functionality and at the same time allows you to write JDBC code in a more object-oriented manner. We will cover these classes later in this chapter.

Back to the `JdbcTemplate`. First we'll look at `query(PreparedStatementCreator psc, RowCallbackHandler rch)` which takes a callback interface of type `PreparedStatementCreator` as the first parameter and a `RowCallbackHandler` as the second parameter. The `PreparedStatementCreator` interface allows you to create a prepared statement given a connection that the `JdbcTemplate` provides. You must implement the `createPreparedStatement` method and the framework will handle all the exception and connection management as usual. The `RowCallbackHandler` interface is designed to handle the data return for each row of the `ResultSet`. The method you must implement is `processRow` and it does not have a return value. If you need to return data, then you should choose the `ResultReader` interface, which is what we did for this example. The `ResultReader` extends the `RowCallbackHandler` interface and adds a method called `getResults` for retrieving the locally maintained data. Here is an example of a method that uses both callback methods for a query. Note the use of the final keyword in the method signature to allow the callback method to reference this parameter:

```
public List aPreparedStatementCreatorQuery(final int id) {
    JdbcTemplate jt = new JdbcTemplate(dataSource);
    final String sql = "select id, name from genre where id < ?";
    List results = jt.query(
        new PreparedStatementCreator() {
          public PreparedStatement createPreparedStatement(Connection con)
              throws SQLException {
            PreparedStatement ps = con.prepareStatement(sql);
            ps.setInt(1, id);
            return ps;
          }
        },
        new ResultReader() {
          List names = new ArrayList();
          public void processRow(ResultSet rs) throws SQLException {
            names.add(rs.getString("name"));
          }
          public List getResults() {
            return names;
          }
        }
    );
    return results;
}
```

If the callback methods are long, code may become hard to read. To avoid this, delegate to a method in the enclosing class for the additional logic, or use a top-level, rather than anonymous, inner class.

An alternative to the `PreparedStatementCreator` is the `PreparedStatementSetter`. With this interface, you need to set only the parameter values, so it is easier to use. The framework will create the actual prepared statement for you. This is appropriate if you don't need to control the creation of the prepared statement. Here is the same query using a `PreparedStatementSetter`:

```java
public List aPreparedStatementSetterQuery(final int id) {
JdbcTemplate jt = new JdbcTemplate(dataSource);
final String sql = "select id, name from genre where id < ?";
List results = jt.query(sql,
    new PreparedStatementSetter() {
      public void setValues(PreparedStatement ps)
          throws SQLException {
        ps.setInt(1, id);
      }
    },
    new ResultReader() {
      List names = new ArrayList();
      public void processRow(ResultSet rs) throws SQLException {
        names.add(rs.getString("name"));
      }
      public List getResults() {
        return names;
      }
    }
  );
  return results;
}
```

The only difference in this example, except for the callback method change, is that we pass in the SQL statement along with the `PreparedStatementSetter` as the first two parameters to the `query` method.

Support for RowSet

The `RowSet` interface was introduced as part of the JDBC Optional Package features for JDBC 2.0. It provides a JavaBeans-compliant way to interact with tabular data retrieved from the database. It gives you a more flexible interface than the `ResultSet` and it also provides the ability to detach the data and disconnect from the active database connection while still being able to access the data.

The `RowSet` interface has not been in widespread use until recently because it was part of the JDBC Optional Package. This meant that it was not part of standard J2SE distributions as recent as JDK 1.4. JSR-114 was started to try to popularize the `RowSet` interface and to provide some reference implementations. These implementations are now part of J2SE 5.0.

The `RowSet` implementation that Spring provides support for is the `CachedRowSet`, which is a *disconnected* rowset. Even though this `RowSet` implementation is disconnected, any method call can still result in an `SQLException` being thrown. To work around this limitation, Spring provides an `SqlRowSet` class that wraps a `CachedRowSet` and provides exception translation from any `SQLException` thrown to Spring's own informative, portable data access exception hierarchy.

The `javax.sql.RowSet` interface allows you to update the data and apply the changes back to the database. This is a feature that we consider to be of limited value and there isn't currently any support for this in Spring. You write queries for Spring's RowSet support in the same way that you write queries that retrieve a List. Just use the queryForRowSet methods the same way as you would use the queryForList methods. Here is the queryForList example presented previously rewritten to return an SqlRowSet:

```
JdbcTemplate jt = new JdbcTemplate(ds);
Object[] parameters = new Object[] {new Integer(1)};
SqlRowSet srs = jdbcTemplate.queryForRowSet(
    "select id, name from Genre where id > ?",
    parameters);
```

To access the data returned in the SqlRowSet, you would just navigate and retrieve the column values the same way you would with a regular java.sql.ResultSet:

```
while (srs.next()) {
  System.out.println(srs.getString("id") + " - " + srs.getString("name"));
}
```

You should check that the JDBC driver you are using provides support for the latest RowSet implementations. We have tested successfully with the most recent MySQL, PostgreSQL, and Oracle drivers.

If you are not using J2SE 5.0, you will need to download the JDBC RowSet Implementations available as a separate download from Sun's Java website. To read more about the JDBC RowSet Implementations, refer to the tutorial available at http://today.java.net/pub/a/today/2004/10/15/jdbcRowsets.html.

Using the RDBMS Operation Classes

JdbcTemplate is ideal for simple queries and updates, and when you need to build SQL strings dynamically, but sometimes you might want a higher level of abstraction, and a more object-oriented approach to database access. This is provided by the org.springframework.jdbc.object package. It contains the SqlQuery, SqlMappingQuery, SqlUpdate, and StoredProcedure classes that are intended to be the central classes used by most Spring JDBC applications. These classes are used together with a DataSource and the SqlParameter class. Each of the RDBMS Operation classes is based on the RDBMSOperation class and they all use a JdbcTemplate internally for database access. As a user of these classes you will have to provide either an existing JdbcTemplate or you can provide a DataSource and the framework code will create a JdbcTemplate when it needs one.

> Spring's RDBMS Operation classes are parameterized operations that are threadsafe once they are prepared and compiled. You can safely create a single instance for each operation that you define. The preparation consists of providing a datasource and defining all the parameters that are needed for the operation. We just mentioned that they are threadsafe once they are compiled. This means that we have to be a little bit careful when we create these operations. The recommended method is to define the parameters and compile them in the constructor. That way there will not be any risk for thread conflicts.

SqlQuery and MappingSqlQuery

We have looked at some methods available for JdbcTemplate that make running simple queries and updates possible. There are, however, situations where you want a more complete solution as well as one that is more object oriented. These classes are part of the org.springframework.jdbc.object package. For running queries and mapping the results to Java classes, there is a class called MappingSqlQuery. It is easy to use and should give you enough power for the most demanding mappings. Let's look at a short example. Again, we will use an example table from our sample application. This time the example is based on the Performance table. We have added a few tables to our data model, and it now looks like Figure 5-3.

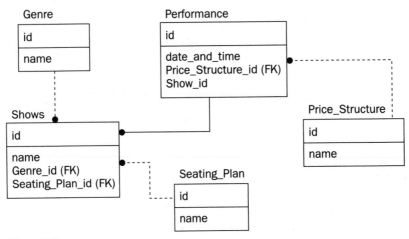

Figure 5-3

The additional DDL for these two new classes is as follows:

```
CREATE TABLE Performance (
    id INTEGER NOT NULL,
    date_and_time DATETIME,
    Price_Structure_id INTEGER,
    Show_id INTEGER,
    PRIMARY KEY(id));

CREATE TABLE Price_Structure (
    id INTEGER NOT NULL,
    name VARCHAR(80),
    PRIMARY KEY(id));

ALTER TABLE Performance
    ADD CONSTRAINT fk_Price_Structure
    FOREIGN KEY (Price_Structure_id)
    REFERENCES Price_Structure (id)

ALTER TABLE Performance
    ADD CONSTRAINT fk_Shows
    FOREIGN KEY (Show_id)
    REFERENCES Shows (id)
```

We will start by creating a very simple mapping of just the Performance table. The class we are mapping to is also called Performance and Figure 5-4 is the class diagram with just setters and getters defined to start out with. We will most likely add some behavior as we develop the application further.

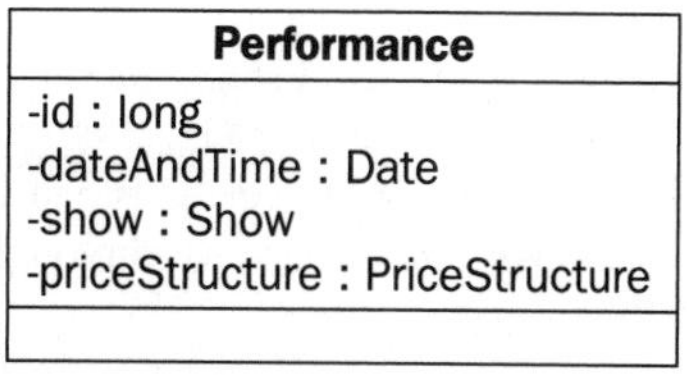

Performance
-id : long
-dateAndTime : Date
-show : Show
-priceStructure : PriceStructure

Figure 5-4

Mapping the table data to this class is straightforward, so it gives us an opportunity to focus on the basics involved in using MappingSqlQuery. We first create a class named PerformanceQuery and this class extends MappingSqlQuery which is provided by the framework. We create a constructor that accepts the DataSource, which together with the static SQL statement gets passed to a constructor of the super class. Next we declare the single parameter we included a placeholder for in the SQL statement. We do this by passing in an SQLParameter to the declareParameter method. The SQLParameter is given a name, which usually is the name of the property, and a type, which is the data type from java.sql.Types for the column parameter. Once we are done declaring parameters, we call compile to finalize the setup of this RDBMS Operations class. Here is the beginning of our PerformanceQuery class:

```
package org.springframework.prospring.ticket.db;

import java.sql.ResultSet;
import java.sql.SQLException;

import org.springframework.jdbc.object.MappingSqlQuery;
import org.springframework.prospring.ticket.bus.Performance;


class PerformanceQuery extends MappingSqlQuery {
  private static String SQL_PERFORMANCE_QUERY =
      "select id, date_and_time from Performance where id = ?";

  public PerformanceQuery(DataSource ds) {
    super(ds, SQL_PERFORMANCE_QUERY);
    declareParameter(new SqlParameter("id", Types.INTEGER));
    compile();
  }


  public Object mapRow(ResultSet rs, int rowNumber) throws SQLException {
    Performance performance = new Performance();
    performance.setId(rs.getInt("id"));
    performance.setDateAndTime(rs.getTimestamp("date_and_time"));
    return performance;
  }

}
```

The `MappingSqlQuery` is an abstract class and there is one method that you must implement: the `mapRow` method, which performs the actual mapping from the result set that gets passed in. In our example, the first thing we do in this method is to create a new instance of `Performance`. Then we populate it with data extracted from the result set. This result set is a regular `java.sql.ResultSet` so we can access all methods available for this interface. We should not do any `ResultSet` navigation like calling `next()` since this is all handled by the framework. We set the two instance variables and we ignore the references to `Show` and `PriceStructure` for now. The last task is to return the object we just created. This method is called once for each row in the result set, so the number of all the objects returned should be the same as the number of rows that were returned. All the returned objects will be put in a list that will be returned to the class using the query.

Let's take a quick look at an example of how the `PerformanceQuery` that we just built can be used:

```
public void setUp() {
  jt.execute("delete from Performance");
  jt.execute("insert into Performance (id, date_and_time)" +
    " values(3, {d '2005-01-31'})");
}

public void testGetPerformance() {
  PerformanceQuery performanceQuery = new PerformanceQuery(ds);
  List perfList = performanceQuery.execute(3);
  assertEquals("list contains one entry", 1, perfList.size());
}
```

First of all, you need to have a data source available. Next you create a new instance of the `PerformanceQuery` passing in the data source to the constructor. This can also be done using setters, but we prefer to use the constructor as we do in this example. Finally you need to execute the query. There are several methods for executing the query and all of them will return a list of objects retrieved. In our example we are doing a unique lookup for a specific ID, so we can use an `execute` method that takes a single `int` as its parameter. If we need to pass in several parameters we can use an object array like we did for the query methods of `JdbcTemplate`.

Note the use of an escape sequence used to specify the date in the `setUp` method. This makes it possible to execute this code against most databases regardless of their specific date representation syntax. The JDBC driver is required to make the translation.

Inserts and Updates with SqlUpdate

Next we will look at the class from the RDBMS Operation group of classes that is used for updating the database. This class is `SqlUpdate` and it is fairly straightforward to use. Here we are updating one column in the Performance table containing the date-and-time for a specific performance:

```
SqlUpdate updatePerformance = new SqlUpdate();
updatePerformance.setDataSource(ds);
updatePerformance.setSql("update Performance set date_and_time = ? where id = ?");
updatePerformance.declareParameter(
  new SqlParameter("date_and_time", Types.TIMESTAMP));
updatePerformance.declareParameter(new SqlParameter("id", Types.INTEGER));
updatePerformance.compile();
Object[] parameters = new Object[] {new Timestamp(System.currentTimeMillis()),
  new Integer(3)};
int count = updatePerformance.update(parameters);
```

In the next example you'll see what an insert statement would look like. It is basically the same approach as for the update statement: Provide the SQL, and if you provide parameter placeholders, then you must declare the parameters and pass in an object array containing the parameters for each execution. The order in which you declare the parameters is important because JDBC relies on them being set by position rather than name. The name is not strictly necessary here, but you are encouraged to provide a name because that makes the code self-documenting:

```
SqlUpdate insertPerformance = new SqlUpdate();
insertPerformance.setDataSource(ds);
insertPerformance.setSql(
  "insert into Performance (id, date_and_time) values(?, ?)");
insertPerformance.declareParameter(new SqlParameter("id", Types.INTEGER));
insertPerformance.declareParameter(
  new SqlParameter("date_and_time", Types.TIMESTAMP));
insertPerformance.compile();
Object[] parameters = new Object[] {new Integer(1),
  new Timestamp(System.currentTimeMillis())};
int count = insertPerformance.update(parameters);
parameters = new Object[] {new Integer(2),
  new Timestamp(System.currentTimeMillis())};
count = count + insertPerformance.update(parameters);
```

Updating a ResultSet Using UpdatableSqlQuery

Sometimes you have to update a large number of rows and it would be convenient to just iterate over an updatable ResultSet and make your updates as you go along. Spring provides a class named UpdatableSqlQuery for just this purpose. The alternative would be to use an SqlQuery and then issue update statements for the rows that needed to be updated. We have found the latter approach to be better performing against an Oracle database, if you use batch updates. For other databases we have not noticed this performance difference and the UpdatableSqlQuery approach has performed just as well.

The UpdatableSqlQuery works just like a MappingSqlQuery except that you provide a method named updateRow instead of mapRow in your implementation. The updateRow method is passed the ResultSet, the row number, and a Map named context that can contain any data you deem necessary for the update. You pass this context in to the execute method along with any parameters. Here is an example where we update the price for any bookings made after a certain date:

```
public class UpdateBookings extends UpdatableSqlQuery {

  public UpdateBookings(DataSource dataSource, String sql) {
    super(dataSource, sql);
    declareParameter(new SqlParameter("date_made", Types.DATE));
    compile();
  }

  public Object updateRow(ResultSet rs, int rowNum, Map context)
      throws SQLException {
    BigDecimal price = rs.getBigDecimal("price");
    price = price.add((BigDecimal)context.get("increase"));
    rs.updateBigDecimal("price", price);
    return null;
  }
}
```

Parameters and the return value follow the same usage as `MappingSqlQuery`, except that sometimes it does not make sense to return anything. In our case we simply return `null` since this is purely an update operation. We can call this class the following way:

```java
Map context = new HashMap(1);
context.put("increase", new BigDecimal(10.00));
final String sql = "select id, price from Booking where date_made > ?";
UpdateBookings query = new UpdateBookings(dataSource, sql);
java.util.Date dateMade = null;
SimpleDateFormat df = new SimpleDateFormat("yyyy-MM-dd");
try {
  dateMade = df.parse("2004-06-01");
} catch (ParseException e) {
  throw new InvalidDataAccessApiUsageException(e.getMessage(),e);
}
Object[] parameters = new Object[] {new java.sql.Date(dateMade.getTime())};
query.execute(parameters, context);
```

Generating Primary Keys

When it comes to inserting data into your database, one issue you always face is how to generate primary keys. There is no single solution that is best in all cases, as databases use different approaches. Instead, there are a couple of strategies and you have to pick the one that suits the way you work with the database. You can rely on a database sequence to generate them for you but then you have to make an extra call to first retrieve the key before you insert the data. Another strategy is to use identity columns that automatically generate the next key when you insert the date. This means that you don't know what key was generated unless you make an additional call to retrieve the value. Also, some databases only provide one of these methods so this limits your options.

JDBC 3.0 introduced a standard way to retrieve generated keys that has yet to be implemented by many of the database vendors. The next section shows how to use Spring's support for this feature when it is available. Another strategy is to generate globally unique identifiers (GUIDs) before inserting into the database. This requires that you have control over all applications that create new rows to ensure that this strategy works for all applications.

Now, let's look at Spring's support for handling key generation for JDBC 2.0. The most common support among databases is support for either true sequences or a pseudo-sequence where you use a separate table with an identity column to generate the unique primary key. Spring provides implementations that support retrieving a sequence value for several popular databases. Let's start by looking at the table we will be using. It is a table that will contain `Booking` entries and its primary key is a plain `INTEGER` column named *id*:

```sql
CREATE TABLE Booking (
   id INTEGER NOT NULL,
   date_made DATE,
   reserved_until TIMESTAMP,
   price DECIMAL(15, 2) NOT NULL,
   Purchase_id INTEGER,
   PRIMARY KEY(id))
```

We will show an example for HSQL and one for Oracle. For HSQL you must first create the sequence table. The following SQL creates a table with an identity column named *value* and sets it to zero (0):

```
create table booking_seq (value identity);
insert into booking_seq values(0);
```

To retrieve the next value from this table you would use a class called `HsqlMaxValueIncrementer`. Here is an example of how this is used:

```
HsqlMaxValueIncrementer incr =
    new HsqlMaxValueIncrementer(dataSource, "booking_seq", "value");

public int getNewBookingId() {
  return incr.nextIntValue();
}
```

The data source parameter is followed by the name of the sequence table and the name of the identity column. This class will attempt to cache a batch of values to limit the number of roundtrips that are necessary for retrieving new key values. The cache size can be set using the `setCacheSize` method with a parameter indicating the number of keys to retrieve in a batch.

For Oracle, the usage is similar except that Oracle uses true sequences and this eliminates the need for a column name in the setup.

To create a sequence you can use the following SQL:

```
create sequence booking_seq
  start with 1
  increment by 1
  nomaxvalue;
```

Finally we will look at the code we need to get the next value from the sequence:

```
OracleSequenceMaxValueIncrementer incr =
    new OracleSequenceMaxValueIncrementer(dataSource, "booking_seq");

public int getNewBookingId() {
  return incr.nextIntValue();
}
```

Retrieving Database-Generated Keys

Another option is to have the database generate the keys using an identity column and then retrieve the generated key after the insert completes. This is supported in the JDBC 3.0 specification, so if you have a database and a JDBC driver that supports this you are in luck.

The following example uses MySQL as the database. MySQL is a database that implements support for retrieving the generated key value. We will use a slightly modified `Booking` table for this example:

```
CREATE TABLE Booking (
    id INTEGER NOT NULL AUTO_INCREMENT,
    date_made DATE,
    reserved_until TIMESTAMP,
    price DECIMAL(15, 2) NOT NULL,
    Purchase_id INTEGER,
    PRIMARY KEY(id))
```

Note the addition of AUTO_INCREMENT to the declaration of the primary key. This will cause MySQL to generate a new key if one is not provided in an insert statement.

Now we can create an update object where we don't have to provide a value for the id column. We can execute this statement with some test values. In addition to the array holding the parameter values, we pass in an object implementing the KeyHolder interface. We are using the GeneratedKeyHolder implementation that is provided as part of Spring. This key holder object will be populated with the generated key. Most of the time there is only one key value generated and we use the getKey method to retrieve the generated key. It is returned as a Number object:

```
SqlUpdate su = new SqlUpdate();
su.setDataSource(dataSource);
su.setSql(
        "insert into booking(date_made, reserved_until, price) " +
        "values (?, ?, ?)");
su.declareParameter(new SqlParameter(Types.TIMESTAMP));
su.declareParameter(new SqlParameter(Types.TIMESTAMP));
su.declareParameter(new SqlParameter(Types.DECIMAL));
su.compile();

Object[] parameters = new Object[] {dateMade, reservedUntil, price};
KeyHolder keyHolder = new GeneratedKeyHolder();
su.update(parameters, keyHolder);
long key = keyHolder.getKey().longValue();
```

Some databases and the JDBC API allow for multiple columns to have their value generated automatically. If that is the case, then you should use the getKeys method to retrieve the generated keys. This method returns a Map with an entry for each generated value keyed by the column name returned from the JDBC API.

Calling a Stored Procedure

The last major class of the RDBMS Operation group is the StoredProcedure class, used for calling stored procedures. Support for stored procedures is not part of the core SQL standard and is not provided by all SQL databases. It is, however, offered by several major databases, and stored procedures play a part in many enterprise applications. Hence, Spring provides sophisticated stored procedure support. Because HSQL does not provide the necessary support for a realistic example, we will be using Oracle as the database for the examples.

Let's take a look at a simple example, based on the expanded data model shown in Figure 5-5. The procedure we are going to call is used to reserve seats for a performance. We need to first expand our data model to include some new tables. We need to add Seat, Seat_Status, Booking, and Price_Band.

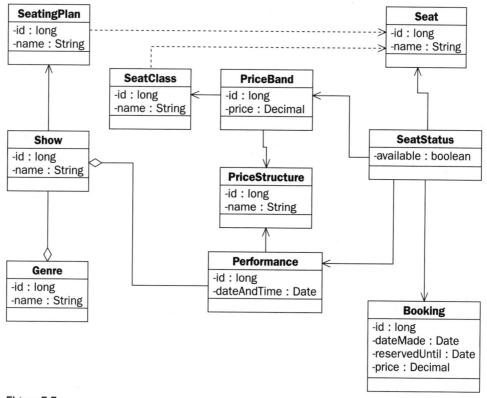

Figure 5-5

The stored procedure gets a `performanceId`, `seatId`, `price`, and `reservedUntilDate` passed in. It inserts a new row into the Booking table and updates the Seat_Status table for the seat. It looks as follows:

```
create or replace
procedure reserve_seat(in_performance_id in number,
            in_seat in number,
            in_price number,
            in_reserved_until date,
            out_new_booking_id out number)
is
begin
  -- Get a new pk for the booking table
  select booking_seq.nextval into out_new_booking_id from dual;

  -- Create a new booking
  insert into booking(id, date_made, price, reserved_until)
     values (out_new_booking_id, sysdate, in_price, in_reserved_until);

  update seat_status set REF_Booking_id = out_new_booking_id
    where REF_Seat_id = in_seat
    and in_performance_id = in_performance_id;

end;
```

To call this procedure we need to create a class that extends the abstract class `StoredProcedure`. You are required to extend this class and provide code necessary for supporting the call to the stored procedure. Syntax varies between implementations, but the JDBC specification provides an escape syntax that makes it possible to call stored procedures from different vendors using the same syntax. The `StoredProcedure` class will build the call statement using this escape syntax and the only thing you have to provide is the name of the stored procedure. You are also required to declare any parameters that are passed in or out to the procedure.

The `StoredProcedure` has an `execute` method that takes a `Map` of input parameters as its only argument. The results are also returned using a `Map` with one entry per output parameter. We normally define an `execute` method, in the class that extends `StoredProcedure`, with a calling signature that matches the stored procedure itself. This class then creates the input parameter `Map` and populates it with the parameters passed in. The final step is then to take the `Map` of output parameters and map that to an object structure or primitive value that is the return value for the `execute` method. Here is an example that calls the stored procedure `reserve_seat` that we saw in the preceding text:

```
public class CallReserveSeat extends StoredProcedure {
    private static final String RESERVE_SEAT_SQL = "reserve_seat";

    public CallReserveSeat(DataSource dataSource) {
        super(dataSource, RESERVE_SEAT_SQL);
        declareParameter(new SqlParameter("performance_id", Types.INTEGER));
        declareParameter(new SqlParameter("seat", Types.INTEGER));
        declareParameter(new SqlParameter("price", Types.DECIMAL));
        declareParameter(new SqlParameter("reserved_until", Types.DATE));
        declareParameter(new SqlOutParameter("new_booking_id", Types.INTEGER));
        compile();
    }

    public int execute(int performanceId, int seatId, BigDecimal price,
            java.util.Date reservedUntil) {
        Map inParams = new HashMap(4);
        inParams.put("performance_id", new Integer(performanceId));
        inParams.put("seat", new Integer(seatId));
        inParams.put("price", price);
        inParams.put("reserved_until", new java.sql.Date(reservedUntil.getTime()));
        Map outParams = execute(inParams);
        if (outParams.size() > 0)
            return ((Integer)outParams.get("new_booking_id")).intValue();
        else
            return 0;
    }
}
```

Most of the code is in the `CallReserveSeat` class itself, so it is very easy to use it. Just create a new class and call the `execute` method with a set of parameters:

```
CallReserveSeat proc = new CallReserveSeat(dataSource);
Map result = proc.execute(1, 2, new BigDecimal("44.12"),
        new java.util.Date(System.currentTimeMillis()+ 864000000L));
```

When you specify the name of the stored procedure in the class that extends stored procedures, you are creating a class that is specifically tailored for a single stored procedure. By providing a customized execute with a method signature that maps to the parameter signature of the stored procedure, you are essentially providing a one-to-one mapping between the stored procedure and a Java class and its execute method.

> **Like other RDBMS operation objects, StoredProcedure subclasses are threadsafe, unless your subclass implementation introduces read-write instance variables. You should normally avoid doing so.**

Advanced Concepts

If you have made it this far, then you should have a good understanding of the basic functionality of the Spring JDBC framework, and you should already be productive with it. It is primarily based on abstraction shielding the calling code from having to deal with the technical details of database access, and allowing you to concentrate on accessing the actual data.

However, there are some details that we have not yet covered. In the pages that follow, we will cover advanced topics such as custom exception translation, LOB support, and returning result sets from stored procedures.

Running Spring JDBC in an Application Server

Running JDBC in general inside an application server provides a few challenges. Using Spring does not change this, but Spring provides valuable help in addressing these issues.

Connection Pooling

Most application servers provide some kind of connection pooling. The reason for this is that establishing the physical connection to the database can take a long time and it is preferable to have connections that are ready to use available. If your application server does not provide connection pooling, then you should use a third-party connection pool like Apache Commons DBCP. Usually the database connection is provided via a DataSource that is bound to a specific JNDI name. If you use an application context, then you should configure the DataSource lookup with a JndiObjectFactoryBean (see Chapters 2 and 3 for more details about configuring an application context). Here is an example of how you can specify this in the configuration files:

```
<bean id="ticketDataSource"
      class="org.springframework.jndi.JndiObjectFactoryBean">
   <property name="jndiName">
     <value>java:comp/env/jdbc/ticketdb</value>
   </property>
</bean>
```

If you are not using a Spring application context, you could use DataSourceUtils for the lookup directly from your application code. We do recommend the use of an application context, but the utility methods are available if you need them. If the `DataSource` is declared in a `resource-ref` in web.xml, then you should use this method:

```
DataSource ds = DataSourceUtils.getDataSourceFromJndi("jdbc/ticketdb");
```

The `java:comp/env` part will automatically be added if you don't provide it in the JNDI name. If you don't want this to be added, then your call should look as follows:

```
DataSource ds = DataSourceUtils.getDataSourceFromJndi("jdbc/ticketdb", false);
```

After you are done with your processing, the connection is returned to the pool to be reused by a future request for a connection. This is handled by the framework using `DataSourceUtils.getConnection` and `DataSourceUtils.closeConnectionIfNecessary` behind the scenes, and you don't have to worry about these details in your application code.

Connection and Statement Wrappers

Application server vendors typically need to provide extra hooks for managing transactions and other container-related concerns. They often do that by wrapping the connection and statement objects with their own special proxy classes. This can lead to problems when the database feature that you want to use requires the use of the native object as it was provided by the database. This is the case for handling LOBs and other special Types using Oracle. Spring provides a number of implementations of `NativeJdbcExtractorAdapter`. The `SimpleNativeJdbcExtractor` works for many servers and connection pools, but there are also specific implementations for WebLogic, WebSphere, JBoss, CommonsDBCP, and XAPool.

To use these extractors, you should pass the one you need to the `JdbcTemplate` you are using. This can best be done in the application context configuration:

```xml
<bean id="ticketDataSource"
        class="org.springframework.jndi.JndiObjectFactoryBean">
  <property name="jndiName">
    <value>java:comp/env/jdbc/ticketdb</value>
  </property>
</bean>

<bean id="nativeJdbcExtractor"
 class="org.springframework.jdbc.support.nativejdbc.CommonsDbcpNativeJdbcExtractor"
 lazy-init="true"/>

<!-- JdbcTemplate -->
<bean id="jdbcTemplate"
 class="org.springframework.jdbc.core.JdbcTemplate"
 lazy-init="true">
  <property name="dataSource">
    <ref local="ticketDataSource"/>
  </property>
  <property name="nativeJdbcExtractor">
    <ref local="nativeJdbcExtractor"/>
  </property>
</bean>
```

The programmatic way to do this is:

```
jdbcTemplate.setNativeJdbcExtractor(new CommonsDbcpNativeJdbcExtractor
);
```

Using Custom Exception Translations

If you have special needs in terms of exception translation, then you have a few options. The easiest one is to supply your own version of sql-error-codes.xml accessible on the classpath. This still only allows you to use any of the six categories defined for Spring's SQLErrorCodesSQLExceptionTranslator class, but in most cases this does provide enough customization. Additional options will be discussed shortly. Here is a summary of the translation sequence provided by Spring's JDBC framework:

1. Call to customTranslate overridden method provided by a user-supplied implementation of SQLErrorCodeSQLExceptionTranslator.

2. Custom translations to either your own exception extending DataAccessException or to one of Spring's data access exceptions. This is specified in a customized sql-error-codes.xml.

3. Translation of error codes to one of the standard six exception categories provided in a customized sql-error-codes.xml.

4. Standard translation of codes in sql-error-codes.xml provided in the Spring distribution.

5. Fallback on SQL state translation using SQLStateSQLExceptionTranslator.

> **Why might you want to perform custom exception translation?** Perhaps your database is reporting an unusual error condition that is not supported by Spring's default mappings. Or perhaps you have an advanced requirement, such as an Oracle trigger that throws an application-specific PL/SQL exception, and which should be reported to an application code with an appropriate exception class, providing elegant communication between PL/SQL and Java code.

Providing a CustomSQLErrorCodesTranslation

If you need an additional exception or you have your own exception that inherits from DataAccessException, then you can add a customTranslations entry to the sql-error-codes.xml. The format for this entry is shown in the following example:

```xml
<bean id="customSqlErrors" class="org.springframework.jdbc.support.SQLErrorCodes">
  <property name="badSqlGrammarCodes">
    <value>11,24,33</value>
  </property>
  <property name="dataIntegrityViolationCodes">
    <value>1,12,17,22</value>
  </property>
  <property name="customTranslations">
    <list>
      <bean
        class="org.springframework.jdbc.support.CustomSQLErrorCodesTranslation">
        <property name="errorCodes">
```

```
              <value>942</value></property>
          <property name="exceptionClass">
              <value>com.mycompany.test.MyCustomException</value>
          </property>
        </bean>
      </list>
    </property>
  </bean>
```

You need to provide the error codes that you want translated and a concrete exception class that must be a subclass of `DataAccessException`. An example of a custom exception might look like this:

```
public class MyCustomException extends DataAccessException {

  public MyCustomException(String msg) {
    super(msg);
  }

  public MyCustomException(String msg, Throwable ex) {
    super(msg, ex);
  }
}
```

For the most part, exceptions have little or no custom code in them. It is the class itself that carries the information we need about what type of exception it is.

The exception class provided must have one of the following constructors accessible: `(String)`, `(String, Throwable)`, `(String, SQLException)`, `(String, String, Throwable)`, or `(String, String, SQLException)`. If there is a problem loading or instantiating this exception, then the translation will fall back on the regular SQL error code translation and a warning message will be logged.

Implementing an SQLErrorCodeSQLExceptionTranslator

If this still is not enough, then you can implement your own error code translator that will handle only some specific cases. You might, for instance, want to throw different exceptions based on the type of statement that failed. Maybe you have one exception for DDL statements and another one for all other statements. There is no need to handle all exception cases in your custom translator. You need to translate only the ones that are truly custom and delegate all other exceptions to the regular framework implementation by returning a `null`.

The recommended way of implementing custom translations is to create a new translator class that extends the `SQLErrorCodeSQLExceptionTranslator` class. The method that you should override is `customTranslate`. This method is passed three parameters. The first one is called "task" and it contains a short description of the task that failed. This description is provided by the framework class, which caught the exception. The second parameter contains the SQL statement that the framework was using at the time of the exception. If this was not available, then this parameter will be `null`. The third and last parameter is the actual `SQLException` that was caught. Using these parameters as a base, you should be able to determine if your special custom translation applies to this exception. If it does, you return the specific runtime exception that you want to use. This exception must inherit from the `DataAccessException` to make it easier for any calling classes to catch this exception. If the exception at hand was not one that you provide custom translation for, then you should simply return `null` and let the default translation implementation take care of it.

The following is an example of a custom exception translator where an error code of –12 for a select statement is translated to a MyCustomException:

```
public class CustomErrorCodesTranslator
        extends SQLErrorCodeSQLExceptionTranslator {

    protected DataAccessException customTranslate(String task, String sql,
        SQLException sqlex) {
      if (sll != null && sqlex.getErrorCode() == -12 &&
          sql.toUpper().startsWith("SELECT")) {
        return new MyCustomException(task, sql, sqlex);
      }
      return null;
    }
}
```

To use this custom translator we need to prepare a JdbcTemplate that has this implementation set as its translator. You do this by using the setExceptionTranslator method of JdbcTemplate. You now have a prepared JdbcTemplate, and if you usually pass in a DataSource to your data access objects, now you should instead pass in this prepared JdbcTemplate. If you set the DataSource instead of the JdbcTemplate, then each data access object will create its own instance of JdbcTemplate and this instance will not know anything about your custom translation. It is important to set the DataSource for the custom translator instance. This DataSource is used for the fallback translation of any codes not handled explicitly by your custom translation. The fallback is the standard translation that uses the DataSource to get the database metadata and look up a set of error codes specific for the current database. Here is a simple example of this configuration:

```
CustomErrorCodesTranslator customTranslator = new CustomErrorCodesTranslator();
customTranslator.setDataSource(dataSource);
jdbcTemplate = new JdbcTemplate(dataSource);
jdbcTemplate.setExceptionTranslator(customTranslator);
SqlUpdate operation = new SqlUpdate();
operation.setJdbcTemplate(jdbcTemplate);
operation.setSql("SELECT THAT IS NO GOOD");
try {
  operation.update();
}
catch (DataAccessException dae) {
  System.out.println(dae);
}
```

Reading and Writing LOB Data

Most databases support reading and writing large chunks of data. We commonly refer to one of these chunks as a large object or a LOB. A LOB that contains binary data is called a BLOB (Binary Large Object) and one that contains character data is called a CLOB (Character Large Object). Spring lets you handle these large objects both via the JdbcTemplate directly and also through a higher abstraction via the RDBMS Objects support. Both these approaches use an implementation of the LobHandler interface for the actual management of the LOB data. The LobHandler provides the following support for LOB input and output:

- ❏ BLOB

  - ❏ `byte[]`: `getBlobAsBytes` and `setBlobAsBytes`

  - ❏ `InputStream`: `getBlobAsBinaryStream` and `setBlobAsBinaryStream`

- ❏ CLOB

  - ❏ `String`: `getClobAsString` and `setClobAsString`

  - ❏ `InputStream`: `getClobAsAsciiStream` and `setClobAsAsciiStream`

  - ❏ `Reader`: `getClobAsCharacterStream` and `setClobAsCharacterStream`

Using the JdbcTemplate for LOB Access

We will first look at an example of writing a BLOB to the database using a `JdbcTemplate` directly. The table is one that will hold the image of a poster used for a specific show. The table also includes a date for the first performance date because the show might have different posters at different times. Here is the SQL to create this `Show_Poster` table:

```
CREATE TABLE Show_Poster(
    id INTEGER PRIMARY KEY NOT NULL,
    first_performance DATE,
    poster_image BLOB,
    REF_Show_id INTEGER)
```

Now we will look at the Java code we need to insert a row into this table:

```
DataSource dataSource;
LobHandler lobHandler;

...

JdbcTemplate jt = new JdbcTemplate(dataSource);

int newId = 1;
Date firstPerformance = new Date(System.currentTimeMillis());
File in = new File("spring2004.jpg");
InputStream is = null;
try {
  is = new FileInputStream(in);
} catch (FileNotFoundException e) {
  e.printStackTrace();
}

insertBlob(db, newId, firstPerformance, is, (int) in.length(), showId);

...

private void insertBlob(JdbcTemplate jt, final int newId,
    final Date firstPerformance, final InputStream is,
    final int blobLength, final int showId) {
  jt.execute(
    "INSERT INTO Show_Poster " +
    "(id, first_performance, poster_image, REF_Show_id) " +
    "VALUES (?, ?, ?, ?)",
```

```
      new AbstractLobCreatingPreparedStatementCallback(this.lobHandler) {
        protected void setValues(PreparedStatement ps, LobCreator lobCreator)
          throws SQLException {
          ps.setInt(1, newId);
          ps.setDate(2, new java.sql.Date(firstPerformance));
          lobCreator.setBlobAsBinaryStream(ps, 3, is, blobLength);
          ps.setInt(4, showId);
        }
      }
    );
  }
```

Let's take a closer look at what this code does. In addition to the `DataSource` and `JdbcTemplate`, we need an instance of a `LobHandler` implementation. For this example we can use the `DefaultLobHandler` that works with any database and JDBC driver that supports the standard LOB methods as they are defined in the JDBC specification. This includes drivers for MySQL, MS SQL Server, and the most recent Oracle 10g driver. For the earlier Oracle 9i driver, there is a custom `OracleLobHandler` implementation available.

Next we take advantage of the `JdbcTemplate execute(String sql, PreparedStatementCallback action)` method. This method will let us pass in an implementation of the `AbstractLobCreatingPreparedStatetementCallback` class. The only method we need to implement is `setValues` where we have access to the `PreparedStatement` and can use regular JDBC `setXxx` methods to set the values. We use the `setBlobAsBinaryStream` method from the `LobHandler` interface because this gives us the flexibility to rely on a custom implementation of the `LobHandler` interface if we need to. The `DefaultLobHandler` implementation just delegates to the regular JDBC method `setBinaryStream`, but the `OracleLobHandler` implementation provides more complex code to be able to support Oracle-specific LOB handling issues.

Next we will show an example of how to read the same BLOB from the database and write it to a file:

```
DataSource dataSource;
LobHandler lobHandler;

...

  JdbcTemplate jt = new JdbcTemplate(dataSource);

  int id = 1;
  File out = new File("copy-of-spring2004.jpg");
  OutputStream os = null;
  try {
    os = new FileOutputStream(out);
  }
  catch (FileNotFoundException e) {
    e.printStackTrace();
  }

  streamBlob(jt, id, os);

...

  private void streamBlob(JdbcTemplate jt, final int id, final OutputStream os)
    throws DataAccessException {
```

```
    jt.query(
        "SELECT poster_image FROM Show_Poster WHERE id = ?",
        new Object[] {new Integer(id)},
        new AbstractLobStreamingResultSetExtractor() {
            public void streamData(ResultSet rs) throws SQLException, IOException {
                FileCopyUtils.copy(lobHandler.getBlobAsBinaryStream(rs, 1), os);
            }
        }
    );
}
```

We are again making use of an anonymous inner class in the call to the query method of JdbcTemplate. This time we pass in an implementation of the AbstractLobStreamingResultSetExtractor class, which has one method we must implement. This is the streamData method, which utilizes the getBlobAsBinaryStream method of the DefaultLobHandler to get the BLOB as a stream and write it to the OutputStream that is passed in.

The AbstractLobStreamingResultSetExtractor class has two additional methods: handleNoRowFound and handleMultipleRowsFound. These methods can be used to provide custom error messages.

Using the JdbcTemplate directly gives you low-level control over the JDBC processing, but sometimes you want to work at a higher extraction level. The RDBMS Operation classes allow just that, and in the following section we will show an example of how the preceding code would look using this higher abstraction layer.

Using the RDBMS Operation LOB Support

Let's start by inserting a BLOB value into the Show_Poster table. For this task we will use the SqlUpdate class that we are familiar with already. The new feature that we will see is how we use an SqlLobValue class to pass in the BLOB content and a LobHandler:

```
DataSource dataSource;
LobHandler lobHandler;

...

JdbcTemplate jt = new JdbcTemplate(dataSource);

SqlUpdate su = new SqlUpdate(dataSource,
    "INSERT INTO Show_Poster  " +
    "(id, first_performance, poster_image, REF_Show_id) " +
    "VALUES (?, ?, ?, ?)" );
su.declareParameter(new SqlParameter("id", Types.INTEGER));
su.declareParameter(new SqlParameter("first_performance", Types.DATE));
su.declareParameter(new SqlParameter("poster_image", Types.BLOB));
su.declareParameter(new SqlParameter("REF_Show_id", Types.INTEGER));
su.compile();

Object[] parameterValues = new Object[4];
parameterValues[0] = new Integer(1);
parameterValues[1] = new Date(System.currentTimeMillis());
```

```
    File in = new File("spring2004.jpg");
    InputStream is = null;
    try {
      is = new FileInputStream(in);
    } catch (FileNotFoundException e) {
      e.printStackTrace();
    }
    parameterValues[2] = new SqlLobValue(is, (int) in.length(), lobHandler);
    parameterValues[3] = new Integer(3);

    su.update(parameterValues);
```

The `SqlLobValue` class will use the `LobHandler` to write the BLOB data to the database so the difference is that you don't provide an anonymous class to set the parameter values. Instead you declare the parameter values and rely on the `SqlUpdate` implementation to do the work.

Now it is time to read the BLOB data from the table. Let's first define a new class that we would like to map the data to. We can call this class `Poster`:

```
public class Poster {
  int id;
  Date firstPerformance;
  byte[] posterImage;

  public Poster(int id, Date firstPerformance, byte[] posterImage) {
    this.id = id;
    this.firstPerformance = firstPerformance;
    this.posterImage = posterImage;
  }

  ...

}
```

Next we need to define a `MappingSqlQuery` implementation and call it to retrieve a single poster from the database:

```
private class PosterQuery extends MappingSqlQuery {
  private static final String POSTER_QUERY =
    "SELECT id, first_performance, poster_image FROM Show_Poster WHERE id = ?";
  private LobHandler lobHandler;

  PosterQuery(DataSource dataSource) {
    super(dataSource, POSTER_QUERY);
    declareParameter(new SqlParameter("id", Types.INTEGER));
    compile();
  }

  public Object mapRow(ResultSet rs, int rowNumber) throws SQLException {
    Poster p = new Poster(
        rs.getInt(1),
        rs.getDate(2),
        lobHandler.getBlobAsBytes(rs, 3));
```

```
        System.out.println(p);
        return p;
    }

    ...

}
```

Again, we use a `LobHandler` to retrieve the BLOB data from the database. This time we use the `getBlobAsBytes` method, which returns a byte array.

This query can be created and executed using the following code:

```
PosterQuery pq = new PosterQuery(dataSource);
List posterList = pq.execute(1);
```

Using LobHandler and JdbcExtractor Together

If you need to use a `JdbcExtractor` for your application, then you also need to specify it for the `LobHandler`. For more on the `JdbcExtractor`, see the earlier section introducing this support.

```
<bean id="nativeJdbcExtractor"
 class="org.springframework.jdbc.support.nativejdbc.WebLogicNativeJdbcExtractor "
 lazy-init="true"/>

<!-- LobHandler for Oracle JDBC drivers -->
<bean id="oracleLobHandler"
 class="org.springframework.jdbc.support.lob.OracleLobHandler"
 lazy-init="true">
  <property name="nativeJdbcExtractor">
    <ref local="nativeJdbcExtractor"/>
  </property>
</bean>
```

Or if you prefer to do it programmatically:

```
oracleLobHandler.setNativeJdbcExtractor(new WebLogicNativeJdbcExtractor);
```

Batch Updates

If you perform a large number of updates, you will benefit from JDBC batching support. This allows you to group a number of statements together and have them sent together to the database for processing. This could be very beneficial for certain types of operations and with certain databases. Let's assume that we need to insert a large number of rows of data read from a flat file or an XML document. We will look at an example where we pass in a list of names and email addresses that we want to insert to the table. The table looks like this:

```
create table Contact_List
    (id integer,
     name varchar(100),
     email varchar(100),
     added date)
```

The data for each row, passed in to the method that will perform the insert, is in the form of a `Map` with the key being the name of the column. All these `Map` objects are then added to a `List`, making up the entire set of data to be inserted.

We will look at two solutions for batch updates. The first one uses the `JdbcTemplate` directly and the second one relies on the RDBMS Operation support provided in `BatchSqlUpdate`. Here is the first solution:

```java
private void insertBatch(JdbcTemplate db, final List data) {
    int[] actualRowsAffected = db.batchUpdate(
        "insert into contact_list (id, name, email, added) " +
        "values(?, ?, ?, ?)",
        new BatchPreparedStatementSetter() {
            public void setValues(PreparedStatement ps, int i)
                throws SQLException {
                Map entry = (Map)data.get(i);
                ps.setInt(1, ((Integer)entry.get("id")).intValue());
                ps.setString(2, (String)entry.get("name"));
                ps.setString(3, (String)entry.get("email"));
                ps.setDate(4, (Date)entry.get("added"));
            }
            public int getBatchSize() {
                return data.size();
            }
        });
}
```

The RDBMS Operation version is similar but instead of providing a callback implementation of the `BatchPreparedStatementSetter`, you create a `BatchSqlUpdate` object and declare all the parameters. Each call to `update` adds an item to the batch and the batch will be written once the batch size has been reached. It defaults to 5000 and can be overridden by a call to `setBatchSize`. Once you are done it is important to call `flush` to write the last batch because the batch size most likely has not been reached yet:

```java
private void insertBatch(DataSource dataSource, List data) {
    BatchSqlUpdate update = new BatchSqlUpdate(dataSource,
        "insert into contact_list (id, name, email, added) " +
        "values(?, ?, ?, ?)");
    update.declareParameter(new SqlParameter("id", Types.INTEGER));
    update.declareParameter(new SqlParameter("name", Types.VARCHAR));
    update.declareParameter(new SqlParameter("email", Types.VARCHAR));
    update.declareParameter(new SqlParameter("added", Types.DATE));

    for (int i = 0; i < data.size(); i++) {
        Map entry = (Map)data.get(i);
        Object[] values = new Object[4];
        values[0] = entry.get("id");
        values[1] = entry.get("name");
        values[2] = entry.get("email");
        values[3] = entry.get("added");
        update.update(values);
    }
    update.flush();
}
```

Advanced Use of Stored Procedures

Things get a little bit more complicated when you start using some of the more advanced features of the stored procedure support. (Although they're a lot simpler than performing the same task with raw JDBC, especially if you have any interest in portability.) Advanced features include support for stored procedures that return a result set and the use of arrays as both input and output parameters. We will look at some examples of this in this section.

Passing in a Complex Type as a Parameter

We saw earlier an example of a stored procedure that reserves a seat. If you wanted to reserve more than one seat then you had to make multiple calls to the procedure. We would like to be able to reserve a group of seats using a single call to the stored procedure. To be able to do this, we will enhance the procedure to accept an array of seat IDs as part of the input.

We are making use of a user-defined type called NUMBERS in this example. It is defined to be an array of numbers, and the SQL to create it is CREATE TYPE numbers AS TABLE OF NUMBER.

The new procedure looks as follows:

```
CREATE OR REPLACE procedure SPRING.RESERVE_SEATS(in_performance_id in number,
            in_seats in numbers,
            in_price number,
            in_reserved_until date,
            out_new_booking_id out number)
is
begin
  -- Get a new pk for the bookin
g table
  select booking_seq.nextval into out_new_booking_id from dual;

  -- Create a new booking
  insert into booking(id, date_made, price, reserved_until)
     values (out_new_booking_id, sysdate, in_price, in_reserved_until);

  for i in 1..in_seats.count loop
  insert into seat_status (REF_seat_id, REF_performance_id)
       values(in_seats(i), in_performance_id);
  update seat_status set REF_Booking_id = out_new_booking_id
             where REF_Seat_id = in_seats(i)
             and REF_performance_id = in_performance_id;
  end loop;
end;
```

To call this procedure we need to create an instance of oracle.sql.ARRAY because Oracle does not support simply using setObject with a java.sql.Array object. In order to create an oracle.sql.ARRAY object, we need to first create an oracle.sql.ArrayDescriptor and then use this descriptor to create the ARRAY class. Both these steps require the use of the active connection to the database. This is something that we normally don't have when we use Spring's abstraction layer. The connection is always managed by the framework code behind the scenes. Luckily, there is a ParameterMapper interface that provides just the functionality that we need. The interface specifies a method with createMap that takes a connection as the only argument and then returns a Map containing the values that the framework should use to set the parameters for the `execute` call to the callable statement. Typically, we just call `execute(Map inParams)`, but now we would call `execute(ParameterMapper myMapper)` and let the `ParameterMapper` implementation take care of creating the `Map` for us:

```
private class CallReserveSeats extends StoredProcedure {
  private static final String RESERVE_SEATS_SQL = "reserve_seats";
  public CallReserveSeats(DataSource dataSource) {
    super(dataSource, RESERVE_SEATS_SQL);
  }

  public Map execute(final Integer id, final BigDecimal price,
      final java.sql.Date reservedUntil) {
    return execute(new ParameterMapper() {
      public Map createMap(Connection conn) throws SQLException {

        HashMap inpar = new HashMap(4);
        inpar.put("performance_id", id);
        ArrayDescriptor desc = new ArrayDescriptor("numbers", conn);
        Integer[] numarr = {new Integer(2), new Integer(3)};
        //params.remove("seats");
        ARRAY nums = new ARRAY(desc, conn, numarr);
        inpar.put("seats", nums);
        inpar.put("price", price);
        inpar.put("reserved_until", reservedUntil);

        System.out.println(inpar);

        return inpar;
      }
    });
  }
}
```

Returning a ResultSet

In addition to the common data types we have seen so far, stored procedures can return one or more result sets to the calling Java class. This can be done either as an implicit return value, as is the case for Sybase and Microsoft SQL Server, or it can be done as an explicitly declared parameter that returns a reference to a database cursor object, as is the case for PostgreSQL and Oracle. We will look at an example of each in this section. We will start off looking at a Microsoft SQL Server procedure that returns a result set and also returns an `out` parameter containing the timestamp when the process was executed:

```
CREATE PROCEDURE get_genres
  @rundate datetime OUTPUT
AS
BEGIN
  select @rundate = getdate()
  select id, name from Genre
END
```

In order to tell the `StoredProcedure` class to expect a result set, we provide a new type of parameter declaration. This new declaration is `SqlReturnResultSet` and it takes a name and an implementation of the `RowMapper` interface as parameters. The `RowMapper` is another example of Spring using a callback interface to carry out some database operations. The implementation you supply here is responsible for generating an object for each row returned, and these objects will be put in a List and returned in the output Map using the name declared in the SqlReturnResultSet as the key. The result set must be processed before any other out parameters in order to provide maximum portability between databases. In order to do this, the SqlReturnResultSet parameters must be declared before any other parameters of type SqlParameter or SqlOutParameter. Here is an example of how to call the get_genres stored procedure:

```java
public void doTest() {

    ...

    GetGenresCall proc = new GetGenresCall(dataSource);
    Map out = proc.executeGetGenre();

    System.out.println("Run: " + out.get("rundate"));
    List genres = (List) out.get("genre");
    for (int i = 0; i < genres.size(); i++) {
        Genre g = (Genre) genres.get(i);
        System.out.println(g.getId() + " " + g.getName());
    }
}

class GetGenresCall extends StoredProcedure {
    private static final String GET_GENRES_SQL = "get_genres";

    public GetGenresCall(DataSource dataSource) {
        super(dataSource, GET_GENRES_SQL);
        declareParameter(new SqlReturnResultSet("genre", new MapGenre()));
        declareParameter(new SqlOutParameter("rundate", java.sql.Types.TIMESTAMP));
        compile();
    }

    Map executeGetGenre() {
        Map out = execute(new HashMap());
        return out;
    }

}

class MapGenre implements RowMapper {

    public Object mapRow(ResultSet rs, int rowNum) throws SQLException {
        Genre genre = new Genre();
        genre.setId(rs.getInt("id"));
        genre.setName(rs.getString("name"));
        return genre;
    }
}
```

As you can see, the mapping is done the same way as when MappingSqlQuery is used. Just create a new object and populate the properties with data retrieved from the result set.

The Oracle version is very similar except that Oracle passes the result set back using a regular out parameter. This parameter must be declared being of the type `oracle.jdbc.OracleTypes.CURSOR` and it must also get a `RowMapper` implementation passed in as a third parameter. Because this is a regular `SqlOutParameter` out parameter, it should be declared in the same order as if it were any other type of out parameter:

```
CREATE OR REPLACE PROCEDURE get_genres (
  refcur OUT Types.refcurtype,
  rundate OUT DATE)
IS
  refsql VARCHAR(255);
BEGIN
  refsql := 'select id, name from genre';
  OPEN refcur FOR refsql;
  SELECT sysdate INTO rundate FROM DUAL;
END;
```

We reference a type called `Types.refcurtype` for the reference to the cursor that is going to be passed back to the calling code. This type is declared in a separate package called `Types`. Here is the content of this package:

```
CREATE OR REPLACE PACKAGE Types AS
  TYPE refcurtype IS REF CURSOR;
END;
```

The Java code for the Oracle version code looks almost exactly the same: The only difference is the declaration of the out parameter as mentioned previously:

```
public void doTest() {

  ...

  GetGenresCall proc = new GetGenresCall(dataSource);
  Map out = proc.executeGetGenre();

  System.out.println("Run: " + out.get("rundate"));
  List genres = (List) out.get("genre");
  for (int i = 0; i < genres.size(); i++) {
    Genre g = (Genre) genres.get(i);
    System.out.println(g.getId() + " " + g.getName());
  }
}

class GetGenresCall extends StoredProcedure {
  private static final String GET_GENRES_SQL = "get_genres";

  public GetGenresCall(DataSource dataSource) {
    super(dataSource, GET_GENRES_SQL);
    declareParameter(new SqlOutParameter("genre",
      oracle.jdbc.OracleTypes.CURSOR, new MapGenre()));
    declareParameter(new SqlOutParameter("rundate", java.sql.Types.TIMESTAMP));
    compile();
  }
```

```
    Map executeGetGenre() {
      Map out = execute(new HashMap());
      return out;
    }

  }

  class MapGenre implements RowMapper {

    public Object mapRow(ResultSet rs, int rowNum) throws SQLException {
      Genre genre = new Genre();
      genre.setId(rs.getInt("id"));
      genre.setName(rs.getString("name"));
      return genre;
    }
  }
```

This feature of returning a reference to a database cursor can come in handy at times. You just have to remember that you tie yourself to the database platform you are currently using and it makes your code less portable.

Additional Considerations

There are still some issues that you will have to consider before you can successfully implement a JDBC-based solution using Spring's JDBC abstraction framework.

Performance

So how does Spring's JdbcTemplate with all of its callback methods perform? Compared to using straight JDBC, we have not found any difference that is worth noting when executing queries and regular updates. This is not that surprising because we would expect object creation, query execution, and the transfer of the serialized data to take most of the processing time. A few extra callbacks are not going to impact this very much. This includes the RDBMS Operation classes that perform queries and updates.

One area where there is a slight performance penalty is with the batch updates. This is because we create new objects that we hold on to for the entire batch, and then write them all at once when the batch is flushed. Doing it this way limits the time we have to keep the connection to the database open, but it incurs a slight performance penalty. However, we have seen Spring JDBC batch updates used in extreme situations (one million updates per transaction) and showing excellent performance.

Another item to note for performance tuning: If you are retrieving a large number of rows, you can change the number of rows that the JDBC driver will fetch from the database when more rows are needed. This cuts down on the number of roundtrips that are made to the database:

```
JdbcTemplate jt = new JdbcTemplate(ds);
jt.setFetchSize(100);
```

You just have to be careful not to set it too high, or you might run out of memory.

When to Use JDBC Versus O/R Mapping

What are the factors that determine when you choose different data access technologies? Let's first assume that the database solution is limited to a relational database. The access choices would then be straight JDBC, Spring's JDBC framework, TopLink, iBATIS, and Hibernate or JDO. The straight JDBC solution would, in our opinion, be the solution of choice only when you are not allowed to use any framework besides what is delivered in J2SE or J2EE.

If your project has only a few persistent classes or you have to map to an existing database with several stored procedures, then a Spring JDBC solution makes sense. There is very little to configure and if you have only a few classes to map to a Java class, then the MappingSQLQuery makes mapping straightforward. The StoredProcedure class makes working with stored procedures easy.

If you have many classes that map to an existing database or you don't have control over the database design, then you have to look at the mapping options between the tables and your Java classes. If the mapping is mostly one table per Java class, then Hibernate or JDO makes for a good option. If you have a group of tables mapping to a single Java class, you will have an easier time mapping using iBATIS SQL Maps. Both iBATIS and Hibernate/JDO will allow you to use Spring's JDBC layer for the few instances where the mapping is not appropriate, or where you have to use stored procedures for interacting with the database. In most applications with complex persistence requirements using an ORM tool, there will be corner cases that are best addressed using an SQL-oriented approach.

JDBC Versions and J2EE Versions

One issue you face when using an application framework combined with an application server is the supported version of various APIs. The J2EE specification that is currently supported by the majority of application servers is J2EE 1.3. The JDBC specification that is part of this specification is JDBC 2.1. There is now a JDBC 3.0 specification that is part of J2SE 1.4 and J2EE 1.4, but it is not yet widely supported by application servers and also not fully supported by most database vendors.

The Spring JDBC support is based on the JDBC 2.1 specification, which means that you can use almost all the features of Spring's JDBC support in older application servers. The option to retrieve generated keys and RowSet support are the two features that do require JDBC 3.0 support.

Summary

We have covered a lot of ground in this chapter. We introduced Spring's JDBC framework, including the use of a DataSource to obtain connections, and the translation of uninformative SQLExceptions to a number of subclasses of Spring's DataAccessException.

We looked at the following:

❑ How to use JdbcTemplate, Spring's central class for JDBC database access. You saw examples using JdbcTemplate for querying and updating data.

❑ The RDBMS Operations abstraction layer, which is a higher abstraction than the JdbcTemplate. We looked at MappingSqlQuery for querying, and how to perform updates and inserts with the SqlUpdate class.

❑ The UpdatableSqlQuery, as an alternative way to update data, which can be appropriate if you want to iterate through data as you update it.

❑ Strategies for generating and capturing primary keys during database inserts — a common challenge.

❑ The StoredProcedure class, Spring's sophisticated approach to simplifying stored procedure invocation.

After this, we felt we were ready to tackle some more advanced issues:

❑ We considered some issues you might encounter running JDBC code in an application server.

❑ We saw how to provide customized SQLException translation by overriding the default exception translator provided by Spring.

❑ We saw how to handle large objects such as BLOBs and CLOBs using both JdbcTemplate and RDBMS Operations support.

❑ We looked at batch updates.

❑ We saw how to handle a stored procedure that returns a ResultSet.

Spring's JDBC support enables you to write far less code than in traditional JDBC usage. That code is typically less error prone — for example, connection leaks can no longer result from buggy application code — and more portable. Instead of wrestling with the mechanics of resource management and JDBC's incidental API complexity, you can focus on the SQL you wish to execute. Thus, Spring JDBC is a good example of the Spring value proposition: taking care of plumbing to allow you to focus on your domain.

6

Transaction and Resource Management

This chapter discusses general issues relating to resource and transaction management. We will start with a basic overview of the subject, followed by a discussion of how Spring's transaction management features fit into the bigger picture.

You will see examples of how to configure and use the transactional features that Spring provides in a variety of environments. We will cover *local* transactions with a single database and *distributed* "global" transactions in a J2EE system.

We will see how Spring provides powerful declarative and transaction management services, and offers a consistent programming model in all environments.

Background

Transaction processing in J2EE applications is a large topic that merits an entire book for thorough coverage. For a more in-depth discussion we recommend *Java Transaction Processing: Design and Implementation* by Mark Little, Jon Maron, and Greg Pavlik (Prentice Hall PTR, 2004).

The following discussion will give you enough background to be able to understand Spring's transaction support.

What Is a Transaction?

For the discussion here, we will define a transaction as a *unit of work* that is made up of a set of operations, against one or more resources, that must be completed in its entirety. One example of a transaction is when you go to the bank and transfer money from your savings account to your checking account. First your savings account is debited and then your checking account is credited. If the credit to your checking account failed for some reason, you would want the debit to the savings account undone. If this did not happen, then you would have lost the transferred amount. The entire transfer should take place as a single unit of work, which we call a transaction.

The ACID Properties

For a Java application, transactions behave in a similar manner. All individual steps of the transaction must complete. If one step fails, they must all fail or be undone. This is referred to as the rule that a transaction must be *atomic*.

Transactions must also leave any affected resources in a *consistent* state. The consistent state is defined as a set of rules for the resource that you are interacting with and they should also be enforced by the resource. One example could be that if you transfer funds between two accounts, the deposit to one account can't be more or less than the amount that you withdrew from the other account.

When you withdraw money from an account, it could be bad for the bank if your spouse were allowed to withdraw money at the same time because that could leave you with insufficient funds in the account. Each transaction should operate *isolated* from each other and also in the required sequence. If your withdrawal happened first, then your spouse's withdrawal transaction should be required to recheck the balance of the account.

Finally, we want the transactions to be *durable*. If you deposit money into your account, you expect the balance of your account to be maintained until you perform another transaction against the same account. Even if your bank experiences a hardware failure, you would expect them to keep track of every single transaction.

In combination, these four central requirements for a transaction are referred to as the *ACID (Atomic, Consistent, Isolated, Durable)* properties.

Which problems do transactions solve for the application developer? The two aspects of the ACID rule that most commonly relate to application development are *Atomicity* and *Isolation*. Consistency and Durability are more related to the actual transactional resource. They are necessary for a complete transactional environment, but they don't really affect how we code our application.

Let's look at what this means for us as Java developers.

Atomicity

We need to guarantee that all steps complete or none of them complete. This is done by first declaring the start of a transaction, and then making a decision whether to commit all changes or roll them back. The sequence in your code would look something like this:

```
//start the transaction
begin work

// do your work
read ...
update ...
read ...
update ...
   ...
```

```
// decide on the outcome
if (everythingIsOk())
    commit
else
    rollback
```

Here we included explicit transaction handling statements in our code. It is also possible to use *declarative transaction management*, where you declare which methods should be surrounded by transaction management, and how specific events would trigger a commit or rollback of the transaction. The J2EE platform provides *container-managed transactions* (CMT) for EJBs where a runtime or system exception would trigger a rollback and any other outcome would trigger a commit. Spring expands on this concept and provides its own version of declarative transactions for POJOs. It has the same basic features as the J2EE CMT, but it also adds more control for when the transactions should be rolled back. You can specify in detail which exceptions should trigger a rollback. We will see much more of this later in this chapter.

Isolation

We need to make sure our changes are not affected by other concurrent changes. Transactions are one way of solving this. Optimistic concurrency control using a version number (defined in the next section) can help here, too. You effectively span transactions, but avoid *lost updates*. Isolation is one area where we usually don't achieve 100 percent success. To guarantee isolation, you have to restrict processing and not allow multiple processes to operate on the same data simultaneously. This is usually achieved by locking resources, which sooner or later will lead to some process being blocked for a period of time. This blocking will reduce the throughput and make your application less scalable. One way to solve this problem is to relax the isolation requirement. Maybe we allow certain types of concurrent access to avoid excessive locks. It comes down to a tradeoff. Most database resources allow you to specify a number of different isolation levels:

❑   **SERIALIZABLE:** This is the most restrictive level. Transactions should appear to run as if they were executed one by one after each other. This means that two transactions are not allowed to read or write a piece of data that the other one has changed or will change during the entire life span of the transactions. This is the isolation level that gives you the best protection against interference by concurrent changes. It is also the level that is the most expensive to maintain in terms of resource usage.

❑   **REPEATABLE READ:** Now we have to guarantee that we will not see any updates made by other transactions to any data that we have accessed within a transaction. If we read the data again, it should always be unchanged. There could, however, be additional data that has been added by another transaction. This is called a *phantom read*.

❑   **READ COMMITTED:** Here we relax the isolation a bit further. We will not see any changes made by other transactions while they are active. Once they finish and commit their work we will be able to see the changes. This means that we can't guarantee repeatable reads; instead we get unrepeatable reads — data we have already read can change while our transaction is running and a later read or update could operate on modified data.

❑   **READ UNCOMMITTED:** All bets are off. There is practically no isolation. Any transaction can see changes made by other transactions even before they are committed. These types of reads of uncommitted data are called *dirty reads*. You are, however, not able to update data that has been modified by another transaction until the other transaction has completed.

❑   **NONE:** This level indicates that there is no transaction support. This level is not provided by most databases.

Most database systems are delivered with READ COMMITTED as the default isolation level. HSQLDB supports only READ UNCOMMITTED, so any use of HSQLDB is fine in terms of providing atomic changes, but for transaction isolation it is not the best choice. This is why we use MySQL/Oracle for all examples in this chapter.

Concurrency Control

When multiple processes are accessing the same transactional resource concurrently, we need a way to control the access to this resource. To provide the required isolation, we need to ensure that the same object is not updated by two processes running concurrently.

Pessimistic Locking

The most common way of doing this is by locking the data to prevent others from updating or accessing it for as long as the lock is held. The amount of time that we hold on to this lock will affect the performance of our applications because it limits how many processes can access the data concurrently. This strategy is referred to as *pessimistic locking* because we make the pessimistic assumption that another transaction *will* try to modify the resource.

Optimistic Locking

One way to avoid the need to lock resources is to check at update time whether the object that is being changed is in the same state as it was when we started our transaction. We are hoping that the object has not changed, so this is called *optimistic locking*. This means we need some way of detecting changes. The most common way this is done is via a timestamp or a version number. If none of these is available, then we would have to check the entire object against a copy made when the object was read the first time.

Transactions and J2EE

Transactions for J2EE are addressed by the Java Transaction Service (JTS) and Java Transaction API (JTA) specifications. The JTS specification defines five distinct players involved in transaction processing:

❑   A **transaction manager** that provides services for transaction demarcation, resource management, synchronization, and transaction context propagation.

❑   A **resource manager** that provides access to the underlying transactional resources. Examples of this are a database server, a message queue, or legacy systems.

❑   An **application server** or **TP monitor** that provides the runtime environment for the applications and also manages the state of the transactions.

❑   An **application** that operates in either a standalone mode or within the environment of an application server.

❑   A **communication resource manager** (CRM) that will facilitate propagation of transaction context between multiple transaction managers.

We will break down the discussion of transactions in this environment into two distinct approaches — *local* versus *global* transactions.

Local Transactions

If your transaction involves only a single transactional resource manager, then you have a local transaction. This is often the case when you are retrieving and modifying data in one database or when you send messages to one messaging queue. The transaction semantics are greatly reduced, as there is no need to coordinate the transaction with other resources. One option for local transactions is to use a database transaction rather than a JTA transaction. This is simpler and also involves less overhead. The database server has transaction support built in and this support is exposed via JDBC. All we need is to turn off auto-commit and call commit or rollback to complete the transaction. Later in this chapter, you will see how this can be leveraged without having to tie your code to the JDBC API.

Global/Distributed Transactions

A distributed or global transaction typically involves multiple resource managers and it also involves a transaction manager that coordinates the resources involved to make sure that the transaction is completed successfully by all involved resources. The transaction manager should use a two-phase commit protocol to make this reliable. The first phase consists of asking all the involved resources to prepare to commit. If the first phase completes and all resources are able to commit, then the second phase can continue with all resources committing the changes. If any resource failed to prepare in the first phase, then all resources will roll back any changes during the second phase.

Transaction Propagation

Each transaction has some attributes associated with it, like its status. This information is stored in what is called the *transaction context*. This context must be made available to any transaction manager that handles this transaction. The transaction context is associated with the thread that is executing. In the case where there is a remote call when a transaction is active, the transaction context is passed along, propagated, to the remote process. This allows the remote process to participate in the same transaction.

The propagation of the transactional context is covered by JTS, which specifies the Java implementation of the OMG Object Transaction Service (OTS). A JTS transaction manager supports the JTA specification as the interface that application programs and application servers interact with. Some J2EE servers provide a JTS/JTA implementation that supports remote transaction propagation, but this is not a feature that is required by the J2EE specification.

Transaction Demarcation

Whether you use local or global transactions, you must somehow inform the transaction manager when your transaction begins and when it ends. This is called transaction demarcation and there are two ways to accomplish this. You can either do it programmatically by using the JTA or JDBC APIs, or you can take advantage of declarative transaction management that is offered by an EJB container as well as by the Spring Framework.

Programmatic Transaction Management

In your application program, you can programmatically demarcate transactions. This is possible both using direct transaction management with JDCB and using JTA directly. One drawback with this approach is that you tie your code to a specific strategy. You also tie your code to a specific transaction API. This reduces your options for future reuse of your code.

Declarative Transactions

Declarative transactions provide a very attractive alternative to the programmatic solutions. Your code can now be transaction agnostic and you can allow a framework to demarcate the transactions. Not having to include transaction management in your code makes your code much more readable and easier to maintain. It also allows you to switch transaction strategy or implementation without changing your code. The EJB specification defines a number of transaction attributes that you specify in the deployment descriptor. The EJB transaction attributes for container-managed transaction demarcation are:

❑ **REQUIRED:** This means that the method must participate in a transaction. A new transaction will be started if one is not already active.

❑ **REQUIRES NEW:** A new transaction will always be started for this method. If there is an active transaction for the calling component, then that transaction is suspended until this method has completed.

❑ **NOT SUPPORTED:** The method will not take part in any transactions. If there is one active in the calling component, then it is suspended while this method is processing. The suspended transaction is resumed once this method has completed.

❑ **SUPPORTS:** There is no requirement that this method should be executed in a transaction. If one is already started, then this method will take part in that transaction.

❑ **MANDATORY:** The calling component must already have an active transaction that this method will take part in.

❑ **NEVER:** This method is not participating in a transaction and it is also required that there is not an active transaction for the calling component.

Later in this chapter, we will see the same attributes used by Spring's declarative transaction implementation as well.

An Example of Spring's Transaction Support

Now that we have covered some background material regarding transactions from a general J2EE perspective, it is time to look at what Spring has to offer. Before we go into detail about Spring's support for transaction management, let's just take a quick look at a brief example using programmatic transaction management with Spring's DataSourceTransactionManager.

The task that we need to wrap in a transaction is updating the price of all rows in the Price_Band table. We will update the price using the current price to determine the size of the increase. If there is an error while the updates are performed, the transaction should be rolled back.

This example starts with some setup work; we create a DataSource instance and also an instance of the DataSourceTransactionManager. Both these instances are passed into a new instance of the MassUpdate class. We could have done all this using Dependency Injection, instead of doing it in the main method of our example. The doUpdate method starts by creating the TransactionDefinition and then the transaction status is obtained by a call to getTransaction on the TransactionManager instance. This action starts the transaction.

The updates take place inside of a try/catch block to allow us to determine the outcome of the updates. If an exception is thrown, then we call rollback and re-throw the exception; otherwise everything went fine and we can call commit. The updates are performed using Spring's JDBC framework and you can read more about this in Chapter 5.

```java
public class MassUpdate {
  DataSource dataSource;
  PlatformTransactionManager transactionManager;

  public static void main(String[] args) {
    // setup environment
    BasicDataSource ds = new BasicDataSource();
    ds.setDriverClassName("com.mysql.jdbc.Driver");
    ds.setUrl("jdbc:mysql://localhost:3306/spring");
    ds.setUsername("spring");
    ds.setPassword("t1cket");
    DataSourceTransactionManager tm = new DataSourceTransactionManager();
    tm.setDataSource(ds);
    // create update instance and set dependencies
    MassUpdate update = new MassUpdate();
    update.setDataSource(ds);
    update.setTransactionManager(tm);
    // execute
    update.doUpdate();
  }

  public void setDataSource(DataSource dataSource) {
    this.dataSource = dataSource;
  }

  public void setTransactionManager(
      PlatformTransactionManager transactionManager) {
    this.transactionManager = transactionManager;
  }

  public void doUpdate() {
    DefaultTransactionDefinition td = new DefaultTransactionDefinition(
        TransactionDefinition.PROPAGATION_REQUIRED);
    td.setIsolationLevel(TransactionDefinition.ISOLATION_SERIALIZABLE);
    td.setTimeout(10);
    TransactionStatus status = transactionManager.getTransaction(td);

    try {
      updatePrices();
    } catch (DataAccessException e) {
      transactionManager.rollback(status);
      throw e;
    }
    transactionManager.commit(status);
  }

  private void updatePrices() throws DataAccessException {
    UpdateQuery query = new UpdateQuery();
    query.execute();
```

```
    }

    private class UpdateQuery extends SqlQuery {
      // update logic omitted to keep this example brief - see code download
      // for the JDBC code used to update the table
    }
  }
```

This is an example of direct programmatic use of the `DataSourceTransactionManager` that works with a single `DataSource` without complicating things with a JTA implementation. Using a single resource transaction manager gives us the option of running the application standalone or deploying it to a standard Tomcat server with full transaction support. If we needed to deploy in an application server using JTA, then all we would have to do would be to replace the `DataSourceTransactionManager` with a `JTATransactionManager`. If we use Dependency Injection with a Spring application context, then this is a one-minute change.

Introducing Spring's Transaction Abstraction

Spring includes a lightweight transaction infrastructure that provides a rich set of options for transaction management in a wide range of environments. Traditional Java programming using transactions involves making a choice whether to code for local transactions, like JDBC transactions, or to code for global transactions using JTA. This choice has to be made up front, and if you later decide to switch to a different strategy, then you are facing a significant effort in rewriting the transaction management code.

The EJB specification provides container-managed transactions (CMT) that eliminate the need to include code to explicitly manage the transactions. All transaction demarcation is done via deployment descriptors. It works well and is probably the most popular feature provided by EJBs. The downside is that you are now tied to the EJB container. You cannot run your code within a standalone application and still take advantage of the transaction demarcation provided by CMT.

Spring's transaction abstraction framework eliminates these problems by providing the same semantics for local and global transaction managements, within an application server or running in a standalone environment. It also provides the option for declarative transaction management via Spring's AOP framework. The AOP framework — and the IoC container it is typically used in conjunction with — can be used in any runtime environment.

Spring's transaction management capabilities — and especially its declarative transaction management — significantly change traditional thinking as to when a J2EE application requires a full application server rather than a simple servlet engine. It's not necessary to use an application server just to have declarative transactions via EJB.

If you need to use multiple transactional resources or non-database resources, then you will need an application server's JTA capability. This does not mean that you have to use EJBs because most JTA features are exposed to the web tier via a JNDI lookup. If you need only JTA, then you could also consider an open source JTA add-on such as JOTM. However, high-end application servers provide more robust support for XA at present. (You should always check your application server's transaction management capabilities, if intending to use distributed transactions, as QOS varies significantly.)

Using Spring's transaction framework reduces the choice of transaction management strategy to a configuration and deployment issue that can be made even after a significant portion of the application is already coded. There are no code changes necessary if you switch the transaction environment from a local one to JTA.

The following list highlights the most important features. Each will be covered in more detail later in this chapter.

- ❑ Programmatic transaction demarcation through direct use of a subclass of `PlatformTransactionManager`

- ❑ A template style approach using a `TransactionTemplate` that will handle most of the transaction demarcation

- ❑ Declarative transaction demarcation for POJOs using AOP in the form of a `ProxyFactoryBean` combined with a `TransactionInterceptor`

- ❑ Simplified declarative transaction demarcation for POJOs with the one-stop-shop `TransactionProxyFactoryBean`

- ❑ Automatic proxying of business interfaces using the `BeanNameAutoProxyCreator` or the `DefaultAdvisorAutoProxyCreator`

- ❑ Demarcating transactions and specifying transaction attributes using source-level metadata with annotations

Overview of Choices for Transaction Control

When you work with Spring's transaction framework, there are two distinct choices that you have to make.

First you have to pick a strategy for demarcating the transactions in your application. There are two ways of interacting with the transaction manager. You can do this programmatically, either through direct use of the API exposed by the `PlatformTransactionManager` interface, or through a template approach using the `TransactionTemplate`. A less intrusive approach is to take advantage of Spring's AOP support and use declarative transaction management with either a `ProxyFactoryBean`/ `TransactionInterceptor` combination or the more convenient `TransactionProxyFactoryBean`.

Next, you have to pick a transaction management strategy in the form of an implementation of `PlatformTransactionManager`. If you have only a single transactional resource, then you can choose from one of the "single-resource" `PlatformTransactionManager` implementations: `DataSourceTransactionManager`, `HibernateTransactionManager`, `JdoTransactionManager`, `PersistenceBrokerTransactionManager`, and `JmsTransactionManager`. The choice at this point depends on what underlying technology you are using. For J2EE applications running in a server with JTA support, the `PlatformTransactionManager` implementation to use would be the `JtaTransactionManager`, unless you have only a single resource, in which case you could still choose one of the "single-resource" transaction managers mentioned previously. The `JtaTransactionManager` will delegate all transaction management to your application server's JTA implementation.

Following is a table outlining the data access technologies supported by Spring's transaction infrastructure, the appropriate transaction manager implementation, and the framework classes that will automatically enable transaction participation if the application is configured to use declarative transaction management or if it uses Spring's transaction framework programmatically.

Technology	Transaction Manager	Built-in Transaction Support
JDBC	`DataSourceTransactionManager` `JtaTransactionManager`	`JdbcTemplate` and all classes in `org.springframework.jdbc.object` package
IBATIS	`DataSourceTransactionManager` `JtaTransactionManager`	`SqlMapClientTemplate` and `SqlClientTemplate`
Hibernate	`HibernateTransactionManager` `JtaTransactionManager`	`HibernateTemplate` and `HibernateInterceptor`
JDO	`JdoTransactionManager` `JtaTransactionManager`	`JdoTemplate` and `JdoInterceptor`
Apache OJB	`PersistenceBrokerTransactionManager` `JtaTransactionManager`	`PersistenceBrokerTemplate`
JMS	`JmsTransactionManager`	`JmsTemplate`

> **Transaction demarcation strategy and choice of transaction manager are independent of each other—a unique Spring capability. Both programmatic and declarative transaction demarcation work equally well with any of the transaction manager choices. You should pick the demarcation strategy that works best with the application you are writing and the transaction management strategy based on the operating environment and data access technology used for your application.**

A key distinguishing feature of Spring's transaction abstraction layer is that you don't have to change your application code if you switch your transaction manager. You need only to modify your configuration files. This is a great advantage as your code can be deployed unchanged in both an application server environment and as part of a standalone application.

Figure 6-1 shows an overview of Spring's transaction management features.

Transaction Definition

When you configure your transaction environment, there are several items that you might want to configure differently from what the defaults are. For programmatic transaction management, you use the `DefaultTransactionDefinition` class that implements the `TransactionDefinition`. If you are using declarative transaction management, then you will use the `DefaultTransactionAttribute` that also implements the `TransactionDefinition` interface in addition to the `TransactionAttribute` interface. The latter allows you to specify which exceptions will cause a rollback and which ones should result in a commit.

The transaction attributes that you can configure are propagation behavior, isolation level, timeout value, and read-only flag. We will cover each one of these attributes in the sections that follow.

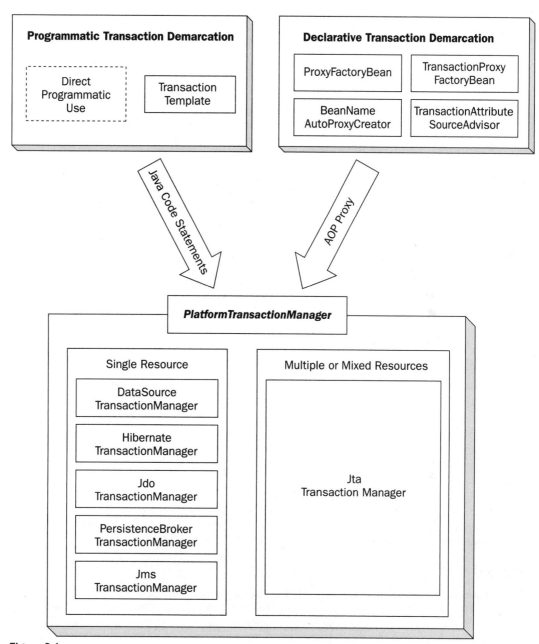

Figure 6-1

Propagation Behavior

The propagation behavior is the attribute that can be used to define the scope of your transactions and how multiple transactions will interact with each other. The default behavior is defined as PROPAGATION_ REQUIRED. The following table describes the different options and you will recognize most of them from the EJB specification.

Propagation Constant	Description
PROPAGATION_REQUIRED	Support a current transaction, create a new one if none exists. Analogous to EJB transaction attribute of the same name. This is typically the default setting of a transaction definition.
PROPAGATION_SUPPORTS	Support a current transaction, execute non-transactionally if none exists. Analogous to EJB transaction attribute of the same name.
PROPAGATION_MANDATORY	Support a current transaction, throw an exception if none exists. Analogous to EJB transaction attribute of the same name.
PROPAGATION_REQUIRES_NEW	Create a new transaction, suspending the current transaction if one exists. Analogous to EJB transaction attribute of the same name.
PROPAGATION_NOT_SUPPORTED	Execute non-transactionally, suspending the current transaction if one exists. Analogous to EJB transaction attribute of the same name.
PROPAGATION_NEVER	Execute non-transactionally, throw an exception if a transaction exists. Analogous to EJB transaction attribute of the same name.
PROPAGATION_NESTED	Execute within a nested transaction if a current transaction exists, or behave like PROPAGATION_REQUIRED otherwise. There is no analogous feature in EJB.

The PROPAGATION_NESTED option is the only one that does not correspond to an attribute in the EJB specification. Nested transactions are not supported by EJBs and because support for them is optional in the JTS specification, most JTA/JTS implementations do not provide support for nested transactions. Spring's support for nested transactions is limited to single resource transaction managers, and you also need a database and JDBC driver that supports the JDBC 3.0 Save Point feature. If a nested transaction is rolled back, it is rolled back only to the save point where the nested transaction started. This includes any transactions that are nested within the transaction that is rolled back.

Isolation

The isolation attribute allows you to override the default isolation setting of your data source. The default varies between data sources but the most common one is READ_COMMITTED. Change this if you need to adjust the level of isolation that your transaction requires. All settings are not valid for all resources. Oracle for instance, supports only READ_COMMITTED and SERIALIZABLE. The EJB specification doesn't provide any means of setting the isolation level for CMT but some application servers provide their own proprietary configuration options for this. The complete set of possible isolation attribute values is shown in the following table.

Isolation Constant	Description
ISOLATION_DEFAULT	Use the default value of the underlying data source.
ISOLATION_READ_UNCOMMITTED	Dirty reads, non-repeatable reads, and phantom reads can occur.
ISOLATION_READ_COMMITTED	Dirty reads are prevented; non-repeatable reads and phantom reads can occur.
ISOLATION_REPEATABLE_READ	Dirty reads and non-repeatable reads are prevented; phantom reads can occur.
ISOLATION_SERIALIZABLE	Dirty reads, non-repeatable reads, and phantom reads are prevented.

Timeout

The number of seconds the transaction is allowed to run. After the timeout value has been reached, the transaction manager will cancel the transaction and roll back all changes. The options are TIMEOUT_ DEFAULT or any positive number of seconds. Some resources will not support this, but JTA and various JDBC drivers do support timeouts.

Read-Only

This flag can be set to true to indicate that the transaction does not modify any persistent state. This is more of a hint because not all transactional resources can take advantage of this setting. It's particularly useful when using Hibernate because it tells Hibernate not to detect and flush changes within a read-only transaction.

Transaction Status

The Spring TransactionStatus interface defines a way for transactional code to control transaction execution and query transaction status. You use this interface mostly when using programmatic transaction demarcation, but it can also be used with declarative transaction management. In the latter case it's advisable to avoid using this interface because it creates a dependency on the transaction framework. It's normally better to use exceptions to indicate transaction rollbacks.

```
public interface TransactionStatus {
  boolean isNewTransaction();
  void setRollbackOnly();
  boolean isRollbackOnly();
}
```

Transaction Demarcation Strategies

Defining what portions of your program are participating in a transaction and if or how these transactions interact are critical decisions that can affect the reliability and scalability of your application. You will also have to decide whether a programmatic strategy is beneficial. Programmatic demarcation makes your code dependent on the transaction framework whether you are using Spring, JTA, or JDBC transactions. It also tends to pollute your business objects with code that has nothing to do with its core responsibility. Declarative transactions have proven very popular in the case of EJB CMT. Spring gives you the option of using declarative transactions regardless of your choice of using POJOs or EJBs, making the benefits of declarative transaction management available in a wider range of environments, and imposing far less onerous requirements on application code.

Where to Demarcate Transactions

Before we get into the different demarcation strategies, it is important to consider where we should apply transactions in our applications. We recommend applying transactions at the business layer. This allows the business layer to catch any exceptions that caused a rollback and issue the appropriate business-level application exceptions.

We don't want to apply them at the data access level because that would limit the opportunity to reuse data access code with varying transaction requirements. Data access code should not delimit transaction boundaries because it doesn't implement business logic, and atomicity is a business-level concept. Let's say we apply a transaction on a data access method that updates the balance of an account. This would prevent us from reusing this method in a task that transferred data between two accounts. If the subtraction from the first account was already committed, then we could not roll back all changes in the case of the addition to the second account failing. We should instead apply the transaction at the higher business operation level. This would in our case be the "deposit," "withdraw," and "transfer" business method.

One issue with applying transactions in the business layer is that for local transactions that are controlled programmatically, the business logic becomes dependent on the data access technology. If we use JDBC for the data access, then the business logic layer must control the connection object. This is undesirable because we prefer to decouple the business logic from the data access logic. The most commonly applied solution to this dilemma is to use declarative transactions like EJB container-managed transactions (CMT) or Spring's declarative transaction support. An alternate solution is to use a transaction management framework that will encapsulate the transaction logic and hide the detail from the business logic. An example of this is Spring's programmatic transaction management support using a `TransactionTemplate`.

Programmatic Transaction Demarcation

Although declarative transactions are (deservedly) more popular and decouple your code from the transaction infrastructure, there are times when we want to use a programmatic approach. You might write a conversion program that is not going to be maintained beyond a few months, so the coupling with the transaction framework is not terribly important. In this case it might be simpler to keep everything in the Java code rather than creating a number of configuration files containing the transaction definitions in addition to the Java program. Otherwise, your transaction management might be integrated with business logic, and not best externalized as an aspect.

Direct Programmatic Use of PlatformTransactionManager

We have already seen an example of direct use of the `PlatformTransactionManager`, but we will show one more example for completeness. This time we use IoC to configure the business class. This allows us to use an implementation that fits the environment we will be running in. For a single data source, `DataSourceTransactionManager` is the choice, but for a JTA environment we would choose the `JtaTransactionManager`. It's important to note that the choice of transaction manager does not force us to change the actual code at all. This is one of the advantages of using Spring for this type of processing.

First we'll look at the configuration of our sample:

```xml
<!-- The DBCP DataSource -->
<bean id="dataSource" class="org.apache.commons.dbcp.BasicDataSource"
      destroy-method="close">
  <property name="driverClassName">
    <value>${jdbc.driverClassName}</value>
  </property>
  <property name="url"><value>${jdbc.url}</value></property>
  <property name="username"><value>${jdbc.username}</value></property>
  <property name="password"><value>${jdbc.password}</value></property>
</bean>

<!-- The DAO class -->
<bean id="dao"
    class="org.springframework.prospring.ticket.dao.jdbc.JdbcBoxOfficeDao">
  <property name="dataSource">
    <ref local="dataSource"/>
  </property>
</bean>

<!-- The transactionmanager to use for regular non JTA datasource -->
<bean id="transactionManager"
  class="org.springframework.jdbc.datasource.DataSourceTransactionManager">
  <property name="dataSource">
    <ref local="dataSource"/>
  </property>
</bean>

<!-- Business Object -->
<bean id="boxOffice"
    class="org.springframework.prospring.ticket.service.BoxOfficeImpl">
  <property name="boxOfficeDao">
    <ref local="dao"/>
  </property>
  <property name="transactionManager">
    <ref local="transactionManager"/>
  </property>
</bean>
```

Next, take a look at the code that will perform the transactional processing. This time we will use the default settings for the DefaultTransactionDefinition, which are PROPAGATION_REQUIRED and no timeout, and the isolation level is the default for the resource:

```java
Reservation reservation = null;
TransactionDefinition td = new DefaultTransactionDefinition();
TransactionStatus tranStatus = transactionManager.getTransaction(td);
try {
  //... some business processing
  reservation = bookSeats(performance, reserve, request.getHoldUntil(), cost);
}
catch (ApplicationException e) {
  //... handle exception
```

```
      transactionManager.rollback(tranStatus);
      throw e;
   }
   transactionManager.commit(tranStatus);
   return reservation;
```

This is equivalent to using JTA directly in your code by obtaining a `UserTransaction` object reference.

TransactionTemplate

It's usually preferable to apply some IoC principles to your transaction processing very much the same way we saw them applied to JDBC processing via the `JdbcTemplate` class. The `TransactionTemplate` allows you to execute code within a transaction without having to code the entire transactional workflow with a try/catch block. The `TransactionTemplate` will take care of initializing the transaction and also the proper outcome whether it is a rollback or a commit. Your transactional code will run within the `TransactionCallback.doInTransaction` callback method. The transaction outcome is determined based on how the callback method completes. If your code throws a runtime exception, then the transaction is rolled back. It is also rolled back if your code calls `setRollbackOnly` on the `TransactionStatus` object that is passed in to the callback method. Otherwise the transaction is committed. Here is an example using the same application context as in the previous example:

```
Reservation reservation = null;

TransactionTemplate transactionTemplate =
    new TransactionTemplate(transactionManager);
// alter any transaction characteristics for the template here if necessary
reservation =
  (Reservation) transactionTemplate.execute(new TransactionCallback() {
    public Object doInTransaction(TransactionStatus status) {
      //... some business processing
      Reservation result;
      try {
        result = bookSeats(performance, reserve,
          request.getHoldUntil(), cost);
      }
      catch (RequestedSeatNotAvailableException e) {
        throw new WrappedException(e);
      }
      return result;
    }
  });

return reservation;
```

One thing to note about the `TransactionTemplate` is that we can't throw any checked exceptions from inside the `doInTransaction` method. We have to use an exception wrapper technique and throw unchecked exceptions because the `TransactionTemplate` doesn't have a `throws` clause. This wrapped exception can later be un-wrapped and the original exception re-thrown.

Declarative Transaction Demarcation

The focus from here on will be on declarative transaction demarcation. It provides many benefits and allows you to eliminate any dependencies on the transaction framework from your Java code. It should be regarded as the default approach, unless you have unusual requirements.

There are four specific participants that must be configured to properly interact and provide transaction support. This functionality builds on Spring's AOP features, covered in Chapter 4. The four participants are transaction manager, proxy factory, transaction interceptor, and a set of transaction attributes. The diagram in Figure 6-2 shows their relationships and how they interact with your regular objects used in a typical application.

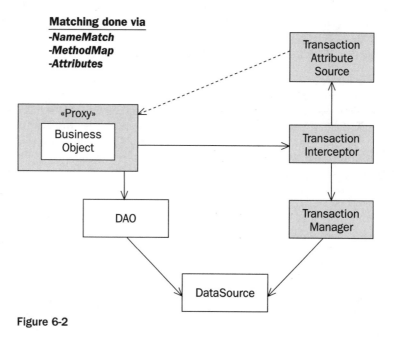

Figure 6-2

These participants each come in different flavors that can be combined in many ways to tailor your transaction demarcation strategy to your specific needs. The following sections show and explain the most commonly used variations.

ProxyFactoryBean/Transaction Interceptor

Using the generic Spring AOP `ProxyFactoryBean` (discussed in Chapter 4) and a transaction interceptor is an appropriate solution when you want as much control over the transaction processing as possible. Because this solution uses a regular AOP `ProxyFactoryBean`, it allows us to use additional interceptors for other purposes. In the following example, the business object is named `boxOfficeTarget` to indicate that it is the target object for a proxy object. This is a commonly used naming convention that makes it clear what roles the different objects are playing. If we look at the `ProxyFactoryBean` that is named `boxOffice`, we can see that its target is the `boxOfficeTarget`.

The interceptor is specified as a bean named `transactionInterceptor`. This interceptor bean has a property called `transactionAttributeSource` that specifies a `MethodMapTransactionAttributeSource` containing the fully qualified method names of the target class and the transaction attributes that should be in effect for this transaction. The method names can contain an * as a wildcard either at the end or the beginning of the name. After the method name you can specify propagation behavior, isolation level, timeout value, and a `readOnly` flag in any order. A timeout value is specified with a special `timeout_x` syntax where *x* should be replaced by the positive number of seconds for the timeout. Isolation level and propagation behavior are specified with the constants specified in the `TransactionDefinition` class. They were also listed in the sections covering these settings earlier.

In addition to the mentioned transaction attributes, you can also specify additional rollback and no-rollback attributes based on an exception class. These attributes indicate the desired behavior in terms of transaction commit/rollback when the specified exception is thrown during the transaction processing. The default rule is to roll back on a runtime exception and commit on any checked exception. This matches the behavior of EJB CMT, but it can easily be changed by specifying rollback attributes (known as *rollback rules*).

> **Rollback rules are a unique — and important — Spring capability that has no counterpart in EJB CMT. They are particularly valuable because they limit the need to call a `setRollbackOnly()` method to force rollback, which implies dependencies on a transaction management API. Thus they are an essential for a "non-invasive" framework.**

The following complete example illustrates the use of rollback rules in the sample application to specify the rollback behavior of the `BoxOffice` instance in configuration, rather than Java code:

```xml
<!-- The DBCP DataSource -->
  <bean id="dataSource" class="org.apache.commons.dbcp.BasicDataSource"
        destroy-method="close">
    <property name="driverClassName">
      <value>${jdbc.driverClassName}</value>
    </property>
    <property name="url"><value>${jdbc.url}</value></property>
    <property name="username"><value>${jdbc.username}</value></property>
    <property name="password"><value>${jdbc.password}</value></property>
  </bean>

  <!-- The DAO class -->
  <bean id="dao"
class="org.springframework.prospring.ticket.dao.jdbc.JdbcBoxOfficeDao">
    <property name="dataSource">
      <ref local="dataSource"/>
    </property>
  </bean>

  <!-- The transactionmanager to use for regular non JTA datasource -->
  <bean id="transactionManager"
     class="org.springframework.jdbc.datasource.DataSourceTransactionManager">
    <property name="dataSource">
      <ref local="dataSource"/>
```

```
        </property>
    </bean>

    <!-- TransactionInterceptor -->
    <bean id="transactionInterceptor"
        class="org.springframework.transaction.interceptor.TransactionInterceptor">
        <property name="transactionManager">
            <ref bean="transactionManager"/>
        </property>
        <property name="transactionAttributeSource">
            <value>
org.springframework.prospring.ticket.service.BoxOffice.get*=PROPAGATION_SUPPORTS,re
adOnly
org.springframework.prospring.ticket.service.BoxOffice.allocate*=PROPAGATION_REQUIR
ED
            </value>
        </property>
    </bean>

    <!-- Transactional proxy for the primary business object -->
    <bean id="boxOffice"
            class="org.springframework.aop.framework.ProxyFactoryBean">
        <property name="target">
            <ref local="boxOfficeTarget"/>
        </property>
        <property name="proxyInterfaces">
            <value>org.springframework.prospring.ticket.service.BoxOffice</value>
        </property>
        <property name="interceptorNames">
            <value>transactionInterceptor</value>
        </property>
    </bean>

    <!-- Business Object -->
    <bean id="boxOfficeTarget"
        class="org.springframework.prospring.ticket.service.BoxOfficeImpl">
        <property name="boxOfficeDao">
            <ref local="dao"/>
        </property>
    </bean>
```

TransactionProxyFactoryBean

This Factory Bean is a good choice for general use. It is easy to configure and provides the functionality most often needed. There are only two beans to define. First there is the transaction manager and second there's the TransactionProxyFactoryBean that contains the proxy, transaction interceptor, and transaction attribute definitions in a single bean definition.

For the transaction attributes, we are using the property transactionAttributes, which takes the form of a property bundle. This translates to a NameMatchTransactionAttributeSource that is similar to the MethodMapTransactionAttributeSource that we saw in the previous section. The biggest difference is that we don't have to use fully qualified method names. We need to specify only the method name itself with or without a leading or trailing * as a wildcard character. Because this attribute source is tied to the proxied class, there really is no need to specify the fully qualified method names anyway. We are dealing with a single class only.

We are defining the bean for the proxied class BoxOfficeImpl inside the target property as an inner bean. This makes this bean definition pretty much self contained and very compact. The interfaces to be proxied are automatically determined. It is also possible to proxy a class via CGLIB by setting the proxyTargetClass property to true:

```xml
<!-- The DBCP DataSource -->
<bean id="dataSource" class="org.apache.commons.dbcp.BasicDataSource"
        destroy-method="close">
  <property name="driverClassName">
    <value>${jdbc.driverClassName}</value>
  </property>
  <property name="url"><value>${jdbc.url}</value></property>
  <property name="username"><value>${jdbc.username}</value></property>
  <property name="password"><value>${jdbc.password}</value></property>
</bean>

<!-- The DAO class -->
<bean id="dao"
class="org.springframework.prospring.ticket.dao.jdbc.JdbcBoxOfficeDao">
    <property name="dataSource">
      <ref local="dataSource"/>
    </property>
</bean>

<!-- The transactionmanager to use for regular non JTA datasource -->
<bean id="transactionManager"
    class="org.springframework.jdbc.datasource.DataSourceTransactionManager">
    <property name="dataSource">
      <ref local="dataSource"/>
    </property>
</bean>

<!-- Transactional proxy and the primary business object -->
<bean id="boxOffice"
  class="org.springframework.transaction.interceptor.TransactionProxyFactoryBean">
    <property name="transactionManager"><ref bean="transactionManager"/></property>
    <property name="target">
      <bean class="org.springframework.prospring.ticket.service.BoxOfficeImpl">
        <property name="boxOfficeDao">
          <ref local="dao"/>
        </property>
      </bean>
    </property>
    <property name="transactionAttributes">
      <props>
        <prop key="get*">PROPAGATION_SUPPORTS,readOnly</prop>
        <prop key="allocate*">PROPAGATION_REQUIRED</prop>
      </props>
    </property>
</bean>
```

BeanNameAutoProxyCreator

If you have a large number of beans that need to have transactions declared, then the `BeanNameAuto ProxyCreator` comes in handy. It allows you to rely on the framework automatically providing the proper proxy based on your configuration. You configure your transaction settings once and then all you need to do is to provide the name of the bean to the proxy creator. This is convenient because for each additional bean you need only to add it to the list of `beanNames`:

```xml
<!-- The DBCP DataSource -->
<bean id="dataSource" class="org.apache.commons.dbcp.BasicDataSource"
    destroy-method="close">
  <property name="driverClassName">
    <value>${jdbc.driverClassName}</value>
  </property>
  <property name="url"><value>${jdbc.url}</value></property>
  <property name="username"><value>${jdbc.username}</value></property>
  <property name="password"><value>${jdbc.password}</value></property>
</bean>

<!-- The DAO class -->
<bean id="dao"
class="org.springframework.prospring.ticket.dao.jdbc.JdbcBoxOfficeDao">
    <property name="dataSource">
      <ref local="dataSource"/>
    </property>
</bean>

<!-- The transactionmanager to use for regular non JTA datasource -->
<bean id="transactionManager"
    class="org.springframework.jdbc.datasource.DataSourceTransactionManager">
    <property name="dataSource">
      <ref local="dataSource"/>
    </property>
</bean>

<!-- TransactionInterceptor -->
<bean id="transactionInterceptor"
        class="org.springframework.transaction.interceptor.TransactionInterceptor">
    <property name="transactionManager">
      <ref bean="transactionManager"/>
    </property>
    <property name="transactionAttributeSource">
      <value>
org.springframework.prospring.ticket.service.BoxOffice.get*=PROPAGATION_SUPPORTS
,readOnly
org.springframework.prospring.ticket.service.BoxOffice.allocate*=
PROPAGATION_REQUIRED
      </value>
    </property>
</bean>

<!-- BeanNameAutoProxyCreator -->
```

```
<bean id="autoProxyCreator"
    class="org.springframework.aop.framework.autoproxy.BeanNameAutoProxyCreator">
  <property name="interceptorNames">
    <value>transactionInterceptor</value>
  </property>
  <property name="beanNames">
    <list>
      <idref local="boxOffice"/>
    </list>
  </property>
</bean>

<!-- Business Object -->
<bean id="boxOffice"
    class="org.springframework.prospring.ticket.service.BoxOfficeImpl">
  <property name="boxOfficeDao">
    <ref local="dao"/>
  </property>
</bean>
```

Source-Level Metadata Using Commons Attributes

This is a feature inspired by XDoclet and the .NET framework. It allows us to specify transaction attributes directly in the Java code as part of the comment block preceding any class or method definition.

Starting with J2SE 5.0, source-level metadata annotations will be a built-in language feature. The section following this one explains how to use this new feature for transaction demarcation. Currently, the majority of application servers are still using J2SE 1.4 or earlier so we will first provide an example using Jakarta Commons Attributes that can be used with these earlier Java versions.

Start off by annotating the class definition and the method that performs a database update:

```
/**
 * @@DefaultTransactionAttribute (
 *       propagationBehavior=TransactionDefinition.PROPAGATION_SUPPORTS,
 *       readOnly=true )
 */
public class BoxOfficeImpl implements BoxOffice {
  private BoxOfficeDAO boxOfficeDao;

...

  /**
   * @@RuleBasedTransactionAttribute (
   *       propagationBehavior=TransactionDefinition.PROPAGATION_REQUIRED )
   * @@RollbackRuleAttribute (
   *       org.springframework.prospring.ticket.service.ApplicationException.class )
   */
  public Reservation allocateSeats(ReservationRequest request)
      throws RequestedSeatNotAvailableException, NotEnoughSeatsException,
             InvalidSeatingRequestException {
  }
```

```
    ...

    public Booking[] getAllBookings() {
            return boxOfficeDao.getAllBookings();
    }
}
```

Next we need to add a metadata compilation step to our build script. Here is an example for Ant:

```xml
<property name="commons.attributes.tempdir" value=".atts"/>
<path id="attribute-compiler-classpath">
  <fileset dir=".">
    <include name="commons-collections.jar"/>
    <include name="commons-attributes-compiler.jar"/>
    <include name="xjavadoc-1.0.jar"/>
  </fileset>
</path>
<target name="compileattr"
    description="Compile attributes with Jakarta Commons Attributes">
  <!-- Bring in Jakarta Commons attribute compilation -->
  <taskdef resource="org/apache/commons/attributes/anttasks.properties">
    <classpath refid="attribute-compiler-classpath"/>
  </taskdef>
  <!-- Compile to a temp directory:
      Commons Attributes will place Java source there. -->
  <attribute-compiler destdir="${commons.attributes.tempdir}"
      attributepackages=
        "org.springframework.transaction;
         org.springframework.transaction.interceptor">
    <fileset dir="${src.dir}" includes="**/*.java"/>
  </attribute-compiler>
</target>
```

The directory defined to hold the Java source generated by Commons Attributes (`${commons.attributes.tempdir}`) must later be included in the build task that compiles all the Java code for the project. By including the `attributepackages` attribute specifying the package names of any classes used as attributes, we avoid having to use fully qualified names in the attribute specifications. This makes the attributes much more readable.

Finally, let's look at the application context configuration. We can now remove the transaction demarcation bean declarations from the application context and instead include additional configuration in a separate file; in this example it is named `declarativeServices.xml`. It makes sense to keep this file separate because it is generic and can be reused in other configurations:

```xml
<?xml version="1.0" encoding="UTF-8"?>
<!DOCTYPE beans PUBLIC "-//SPRING//DTD BEAN//EN"
"http://www.springframework.org/dtd/spring-beans.dtd">

<beans>

  <!--
    This bean is a postprocessor that will automatically apply relevant advisors
    to any bean in child factories.
```

```
    -->
    <bean id="autoproxy" class=
        "org.springframework.aop.framework.autoproxy.DefaultAdvisorAutoProxyCreator">
    </bean>

  <bean id="transactionAttributeSource"
      class=
  "org.springframework.transaction.interceptor.AttributesTransactionAttributeSource"
      autowire="constructor">
  </bean>

  <bean id="transactionInterceptor"
      class="org.springframework.transaction.interceptor.TransactionInterceptor"
      autowire="byType">
  </bean>

  <!--
    AOP advisor that will provide declarative transaction management
    based on attributes.
  -->
  <bean id="transactionAdvisor"
      class=
  "org.springframework.transaction.interceptor.TransactionAttributeSourceAdvisor"
      autowire="constructor" >
  </bean>

  <!--
    Commons Attributes Attributes implementation. Replace with another
    implementation of org.springframework.metadata.Attributes to source
    attributes from a different source.
  -->
  <bean id="attributes"
    class="org.springframework.metadata.commons.CommonsAttributes"
  />

</beans>
```

The power of this approach is more apparent when you have many transactional business objects, not just one as in this simple example. You can just add more business objects to the context with no additional configuration needed, beyond the attributes in the business object source.

Our application context definition is now shorter without the specific transaction demarcation declarations. Note that the preceding declarations use the auto wire feature, so all we need to supply in the application context is a PlatformTransactionManager implementation:

```
<!-- The DBCP DataSource -->
<bean id="dataSource" class="org.apache.commons.dbcp.BasicDataSource"
      destroy-method="close">
  <property name="driverClassName">
    <value>${jdbc.driverClassName}</value>
  </property>
  <property name="url"><value>${jdbc.url}</value></property>
  <property name="username"><value>${jdbc.username}</value></property>
```

```
    <property name="password"><value>${jdbc.password}</value></property>
</bean>

<!-- The DAO class -->
<bean id="dao"
    class="org.springframework.prospring.ticket.dao.jdbc.JdbcBoxOfficeDao">
    <property name="dataSource">
        <ref local="dataSource"/>
    </property>
</bean>

<!-- The transactionmanager to use for regular non JTA datasource -->
<bean id="transactionManager"
    class="org.springframework.jdbc.datasource.DataSourceTransactionManager">
    <property name="dataSource">
        <ref local="dataSource"/>
    </property>
</bean>

<!-- Business Object -->
<bean id="boxOffice"
    class="org.springframework.prospring.ticket.service.BoxOfficeImpl">
    <property name="boxOfficeDao">
        <ref local="dao"/>
    </property>
</bean>
```

Finally, to specify that we want to use both the `applicationContext.xml` and the
`declarativeServices.xml`, we include the following in `web.xml`:

```
<context-param>
    <param-name>contextConfigLocation</param-name>
        <param-value>
            /WEB-INF/applicationContext.xml
            /WEB-INF/declarativeServices.xml
        </param-value>
</context-param>
```

Source-Level Metadata Using J2SE 5.0 Annotations

Support for Java 5.0 annotations is currently being added to Spring, and should be available by the time
you read this.

Spring configuration is very similar to that for Commons Attributes, with the same use of an autoproxy
creator. However, there is no additional attribute compilation step, as annotations are a core feature of
Java 5.0.

Thus, only the Java source would change. (Unfortunately, it would no longer compile with Java 1.4 or
earlier.) Our example might look like this:

```
@TxAttribute(propagationType=PropagationType.SUPPORTS, readOnly=true)
public class BoxOfficeImpl implements BoxOffice {
    private BoxOfficeDAO boxOfficeDao;
```

```
...

@TxAttribute(propagationType=PropagationType.REQUIRED,
rollbackFor=ApplicationException.class)
  public Reservation allocateSeats(ReservationRequest request)
      throws RequestedSeatNotAvailableException, NotEnoughSeatsException,
            InvalidSeatingRequestException {
  }

  ...

  public Booking[] getAllBookings() {
        return boxOfficeDao.getAllBookings();
  }
}
```

Performance Implications

In case you're wondering, the performance overhead of Spring declarative transaction management is small — usually significantly smaller than that of even a local EJB invocation. See Chapter 15 of *J2EE without EJB* for some benchmarks against EJB CMT.

Transaction Demarcation Best Practices

We have seen many ways to demarcate transactions, and a common question is "Which approach should I use for my application?"

A good starting point for a small application with a couple of transactional business objects is the `TransactionProxyFactoryBean`. This option is easy to configure and provides enough flexibility for most needs.

For applications with several business classes that need transaction demarcations, we recommend using a parent/child setup as discussed in Chapter 2 in the "Reusing Bean Definitions" section. You specify a `TransactionProxyFactoryBean` as an abstract parent bean that has the base definitions. You can then easily reference this parent bean for any class that needs to have transactions applied without repeating all the configuration settings for all the classes.

If you have a really large application with many business objects, then you should consider using an auto-proxying solution. This includes both the `BeanNameAutoProxyCreator` and the `DefaultAdvisorAutoProxyCreator` mentioned earlier.

Annotations are going to see increased use once J2SE 5.0 is in widespread use. We believe that at that point, the annotation solutions discussed earlier in this chapter often will replace the other solutions entirely based on external bean configuration files.

Transaction Management Strategies

The choice of transaction management strategy is fairly straightforward. If you access only a single database resource and you don't have any other transactional resources involved, then you can use one of the "single-resource" `PlatformTransactionManager` implementations. Which one you choose depends on your data access technology. There are a few conventions you have to follow and they are covered in the following section under the respective transaction manager. Using a single resource transaction manager keeps your configuration simpler and you don't need to use an application server that provides a JTA implementation. If at a later point you need to make use of JTA, simply change your configuration files.

Single Resource Transaction Managers

The single-resource transaction managers rely on a Spring utility class to register any application use of a transactional resource. This is necessary to allow transaction managers to manage and synchronize use of the resource within an execution thread. The utility class, responsible for this registration, varies for the different transaction managers and it is described for each individual manager in the sections that follow.

DataSourceTransactionManager

The `DataSourceTransactionManager` can be used for code that accesses a single database via JDBC. The connection to the database gets associated with the thread and the transaction manager will take care of any commit, rollback, and close calls. As long as the connection is obtained via the `DataSourceUtils` class, the connection will be bound to the thread for the duration of the transaction.

The `JdbcTemplate` and all classes in the `org.springframework.jdbc.object` package automatically use the `DataSourceUtils` behind the scenes, so any data access using these classes is automatically participating in any Spring-controlled transactions as well as any potential JTA transactions.

Application code not using the Spring classes mentioned should make a call to `DataSourceUtils` `.getConnection` to obtain a connection and make a call to `DataSourceUtils` `.closeConnectionIfNecessary` to close or return the connection to the connection pool. If there is an active transaction, the framework code will manage the connection and call commit or rollback as required. The following example illustrates this usage:

```
public class MyDataAccessObject {
  private void DataSource dataSource;
  public void setDataSource(DataSource ds) {
    this.dataSource = ds;
  }
  public void myDataAccessMethod() {
    Connection con = DataSourceUtils.getConnection(this.dataSource);
    try {
      ...
    }
    finally {
      DataSourceUtils.closeConnectionIfNecessary(con, this.dataSource);
    }
  }
}
```

If you use Spring's `JdbcTemplate`, you don't have to apply this usage pattern because it is always applied by the `JdbcTemplate` itself. This is also true if you use any of the RDBMS Operation classes that are built on top of the `JdbcTemplate`.

Examples of bean declarations for the data access class, the transaction manager, and the data source are as follows:

```
<beans>
    ...
    <bean id="myDataSource"
        class="org.apache.commons.dbcp.BasicDataSource">
      <property name="driverClassName"> ... </property>
      <property name="url"> ... </property>
      <property name="username"> ... </property>
      <property name="password"> ... </property>
    </bean>
    <bean id="myTransactionManager"
        class="org.springframework.jdbc.datasource.DataSourceTransactionManager">
      <property name="dataSource">
        <ref bean="myDataSource"/>
      </property>
    </bean>
    <bean id="myDataAccessObject" class="mypackage.MyDataAccessObject">
      <property name="dataSource">
        <ref bean="myDataSource"/>
      </property>
    </bean>
</beans>
```

Both the transaction manager and the data access class have a reference to the data source, and this allows the transaction management to take place as long as the previously mentioned connection lookup pattern is employed.

An alternative to this connection lookup pattern for legacy code that cannot be modified is the use of a TransactionAwareDataSourceProxy class. This class wraps the data source in use and intercepts the getConnection call. It also wraps the connection in a wrapper class to be able to detect any calls to close the connection. This allows this proxy class to provide the functionality of the DataSourceUtils class to check for an active transaction before obtaining a new connection from the data source. Here is an example of how this proxy class would be configured:

```
<beans>
    ...
    <bean id="myDataSource"
        class="org.springframework.jdbc.datasource.TransactionAwareDataSourceProxy">
      <property name="targetDataSource">
        <ref bean="myDataSourceTarget"/>
      </property>
    </bean>
    <bean id="myDataSourceTarget"
        class="org.apache.commons.dbcp.BasicDataSource">
      <property name="driverClassName"> ... </property>
      <property name="url"> ... </property>
      <property name="username"> ... </property>
      <property name="password"> ... </property>
    </bean>
    ...
</beans>
```

The real data source is defined as the target data source and the application will get a reference to the proxy data source.

HibernateTransactionManager

Just as a `DataSourceTransactionManager` worked with a single `DataSource`, a `HibernateTransactionManager` can provide transaction support with a locally defined Hibernate `SessionFactory` outside of a J2EE environment.

When using Hibernate, the utility class that provides the transaction-aware lookups is `SessionFactoryUtils`. Use the `getSessionFactory` method to obtain a new Hibernate session that is associated with a current transaction if one is attached to the thread. When you want to close a session, call the `closeSessionIfNecessary` method. The `HibernateTemplate` will handle this lookup pattern, so all this additional code won't be necessary. The code sample that follows shows an example of the lookup that you would have to do if you did not take advantage of the `HibernateTemplate`:

```
public class MyDataAccessObject {
    private void SessionFactory sessionFactory;
    public void setSessionFactory(SessionFactory sf) {
    this.sessionFactory = sf;
    }
    public void myDataAccessMethod() {
      Session session = SessionFactoryUtils.getSession(this.sessionFactory);
      try {
        ...
      }
      finally {
        SessionFactoryUtils.closeSessionIfNecessary(session, this.sessionFactory);
      }
    }
}
```

The following bean definition file shows how this example could be configured. In this example, we are using a `LocalSessionFactoryBean`, which will allow us to use a single database as the data source:

```
<beans>
  ...
  <bean id="myDataSource"
     class="org.apache.commons.dbcp.BasicDataSource">
    <property name="driverClassName"> ... </property>
    <property name="url"> ... </property>
    <property name="username"> ... </property>
    <property name="password"> ... </property>
  </bean>

  <bean id="mySessionFactory"
     class="org.springframework.orm.hibernate.LocalSessionFactoryBean">
    <property name="mappingResources">
      <list>
        <value>mypackage/hibernate/sample.hbm.xml</value>
      </list>
    </property>
```

```
          <property name="hibernateProperties">
            <props>
              <prop key="hibernate.dialect">
               net.sf.hibernate.dialect.MySQLDialect
              </prop>
            </props>
          </property>
          <property name="dataSource">
            <ref bean="myDataSource"/>
          </property>
        </bean>

        <bean id="myTransactionManager"
           class="org.springframework.orm.hibernate.HibernateTransactionManager">
          <property name="sessionFactory">
           <ref bean="mySessionFactory"/>
          </property>
        </bean>
        <bean id="myDataAccessObject" class="mypackage.MyDataAccessObject">
          <property name="sessionFactory">
            <ref bean="mySessionFactory"/>
          </property>
        </bean>
      </beans>
```

Starting from the bottom, we have the `MyDataAccessObject` with a reference to the `SessionFactory`.
The `SessionFactory` in turn has a reference to the `DataSource`, which is also referenced by the
`TransactionManager`.

JDOTransactionManager

The `JDOTransactionManager` is very similar to the Hibernate version. You must use the
`getPersistenceManager` method from `PersistenceManagerFactoryUtils` to get the
`PersistenceManager` that will take part in a, potentially existing, transaction and that will allow the
`JDOTransactionManager` to provide all of the transaction management for the `PersistenceManager`.
Once the processing is done, call the `closePersistenceManagerIfNecessary` method of the same
utility class. If you are using the `JDOTemplate`, then this lookup pattern will automatically be handled
by the framework code.

```java
public class MyDataAccessObject {
  private void PersistenceManagerFactory persistenceManagerFactory;
  public void setPersistenceManagerFactory(PersistenceManagerFactory pmf) {
    this.persistenceManagerFactory = pmf;
  }
  public void myDataAccessMethod() {
    PersistenceManager pm =
        PersistenceManagerFactoryUtils.getPersistenceManager(
          this.persistenceManagerFactory);
    try {
      ...
    }
    finally {
```

```
            PersistenceManagerFactoryUtils.closePersistenceManagerIfNecessary(
                pm, this.persistenceManagerFactory);
        }
    }
}
```

The following is an example of the bean configuration that would provide the base for the preceding example:

```
<beans>
    ...
    <bean id="myPersistenceManagerFactory"
      class="org.springframework.orm.jdo.LocalPersistenceManagerFactoryBean">
      <property name="jdoProperties">
        <props>
          ...
        </props>
      </property>
    </bean>

    <bean id="myTransactionManager"
      class="org.springframework.orm.jdo.JdoTransactionManager">
      <property name="persistenceManagerFactory">
        <ref bean="myPersistenceManagerFactory"/>
      </property>
    </bean>

    <bean id="myDataAccessObject" class="mypackage.MyDataAccessObject">
      <property name="persistenceManagerFactory">
        <ref bean="myPersistenceManagerFactory"/>
      </property>
    </bean>
</beans>
```

The data access class has a reference to the `PersistenceManagerFactory` and so does the `JDOTransactionManager`.

TopLinkTransactionManager

The Spring/TopLink integration, implemented by the Oracle TopLink team, provides a `TopLinkTransactionManager` that allows local transactions to be applied with TopLink. (Of course, TopLink can be used with JTA global transactions as well.) The details should be familiar.

See the following article by Jim Clark for further information: `www.oracle.com/technology/products/ias/toplink/preview/spring/SpringTopLink.html`.

PersistenceBrokerTransactionManager

The last single resource transaction manager that we will cover is the one provided for Apache Object relational Bridge (OJB). OJB provides three different APIs: Persistence Broker, Object Transaction Manager, and ODMG. The Persistence Broker is the lowest level API and that is the API that Spring currently provides support for. Spring provides a `PersistenceBrokerTransactionManager` that works together with the `OjbFactoryUtils` for coordinating and managing transactions. To obtain a `PersistenceBroker`, you should call the `getPersistenceBroker` method of `OjbFactoryUtils`. When your processing is done, you should call `closePersistenceBrokerIfNecessary`. Here is an example of this usage:

```
public class MyDataAccessObject {
  private void PBKey pbKey;
  public void setPbKey(PBKey pbk) {
    this.pbKey = pbk;
  }
  public void myDataAccessMethod() {
    PersistenceBroker pb =
        OjbFactoryUtils.getPersistenceBroker(this.pbKey, false);
    try {
      ...
    }
    finally {
      OjbFactoryUtils.closePersistenceBrokerIfNecessary(
          pb, this.pbKey);
    }
  }
}
```

Configuration follows along the same lines as JDO and Hibernate where the data access class and the transaction manager both need access to the OJB specific configuration, which is in a class named `PBKey`:

```
<beans>
  ...
  <bean id="myPbKey" class="org.apache.ojb.broker.PBKey">
    <constructor-arg index="0">
      <value>mykey</value>
    </constructor-arg>
    <constructor-arg index="0">
      <value>user</value>
    </constructor-arg>
    <constructor-arg index="0">
      <value>passwd</value>
    </constructor-arg>
  </bean>

  <bean id="myTransactionManager"
    class="org.springframework.orm.ojb.OjbTransactionManager">
    <property name="pbKey">
      <ref bean="myPbKey"/>
    </property>
  </bean>

  <bean id="myDataAccessObject" class="mypackage.MyDataAccessObject">
    <property name="pbKey">
      <ref bean="myPbKey"/>
    </property>
  </bean>
</beans>
```

JtaTransactionManager

So far we have looked only at transaction manager implementations that work with a single database resource. Many applications have to work with other types of resources like JMS queues, or they have to work with multiple resources within a single transaction. For these types of access you must use the JtaTransactionManager, which works with your application server's JTA implementation. You must also use resources that are enabled to work with a JTA implementation. If you have multiple resources for a transaction, then these resources must support the XA interface as well.

Here is a sample configuration for the JtaTransactionManager:

```
<beans>
  ...
  <bean id="myTransactionManager"
     class="org.springframework.transaction.jta.JtaTransactionManager"/>

  <bean id="myDataAccessObject" class="mypackage.MyDataAccessObject">
     ... // properties expecting references to transactional container resources
  </bean>

</beans>
```

There are a few features that you can use with a single resource transaction manager that are not always available in a J2EE environment using a JTA implementation. Here is a summary of Spring/JTA compatibility:

When using Spring's JtaTransactionManager within EJB BMT or web tier components:

❑ Everything but transaction suspension will work properly on any J2EE server, as it just touches the JTA UserTransaction, which is covered by standard J2EE and required to be available to application programs.

❑ Transaction suspension (REQUIRES_NEW, NOT_SUPPORTED) requires the JTA TransactionManager, which is not a public component of standard J2EE. It is, however, a standard JTA interface, defined by the JTA specification. Most application servers make this interface available, and many combine implementations of the TransactionManager and UserTransaction interfaces in the same implementation class.

❑ Suspend and resume via the JTA TransactionManager has been tested to work on various J2EE servers. Currently known to work are

    ❑ Resin

    ❑ JBoss 3.*x*

    ❑ Orion

    ❑ Oracle OC4J

    ❑ JOnAS/JOTM

    ❑ WebSphere 4.0 and 5.*x*

    ❑ WebLogic 7.0 and 8.1

When using Spring's `JtaTransactionManager` within EJB CMT:

❏   Using direct JTA within EJB CMT is not allowed by the J2EE specification. This applies to Spring's `JtaTransactionManager` within EJB CMT. To follow the J2EE specification, you should rely on the EJB CMT configuration for all transaction definitions in this environment. In spite of this, we have successfully used Spring-managed transactions in an EJB CMT environment. Alternatively use BMT combined with Spring's transaction framework.

Application Server–Specific JTA Configuration

Vendor-specific lookup of JTA `TransactionManager` is necessary, as J2EE does not define a standard location for it. By default, we autodetect whether the `UserTransaction` object implements the `TransactionManager` interface, which is the case for a surprisingly large number of J2EE servers. If you do not want this behavior, it can be turned off by explicitly setting the `autodetectTransactionManager` property to `false`.

WebLogic 7.0 and 8.1 officially supports lookup of both JTA `UserTransaction` and `TransactionManager` for EJB BMT and web components. The `WebLogicJtaTransactionManager` should be used to properly handle resuming a suspended transaction that has been marked for rollback. If you don't need this feature, then the regular `JtaTransactionManager` will work just as well. For WebLogic 7.0, you should use the `WebLogicServerTransactionManagerFactoryBean` to look up the `TransactionManager`. This factory looks up the `TransactionManager` using an internal WebLogic class to avoid problems related to the implementation returned via the regular JNDI lookup. This workaround is not necessary for WebLogic 8.1.

```
<!-- WebLogic 7.0 transaction manager -->
<bean id="wls7TM"
class="org.springframework.transaction.jta
.WebLogicServerTransactionManagerFactoryBean"/>
<bean id="transactionManager"
    class="org.springframework.transaction.jta.WebLogicJtaTransactionManager">
    <property name="transactionManager">
      <ref local="wls7TM"/>
    </property>
</bean>

<!-- WebLogic 8.1 transaction manager -->
<bean id="transactionManager"
    class="org.springframework.transaction.jta.WebLogicJtaTransactionManager">
</bean>
```

WebSphere 4.0, 5.0, and 5.1 use different locations for the `TransactionManager` lookup. The `WebSphereTransactionManagerFactoryBean` will check the WebSphere version in use and use the correct lookup. Here is a sample configuration:

```
<!-- WebSphere transaction manager -->
<bean id="webSphereTM"
class="org.springframework.transaction.jta.WebSphereTransactionManagerFactoryBean"/
>
<bean id="transactionManager"
    class="org.springframework.transaction.jta.JtaTransactionManager">
    <property name="transactionManager">
```

```
              <ref local="webSphereTM"/>
          </property>
      </bean>
```

Considerations for JTA and O/R Mapping

In order for Spring's `JtaTransactionManager` to coordinate JTA transactions and O/R mapping tool resource access, the O/R mapping tool has to register with the JTA implementation. For Hibernate, this is done by using Hibernate's JCA Connector. Other O/R mapping solutions such as JDO will have the same type of configuration options and they must be configured for proper participation in the JTA transactions. Check the manual for the respective implementation and for instructions on how to install this.

DataSource Declarations

A data source declaration is a critical part of the transaction infrastructure. Traditionally this is done in J2EE via a JNDI lookup of a `javax.sql.DataSource` object. The `DataSource` is pre-configured by the server administrator and enabled to support JTA transactions if necessary. If you are running outside of a J2EE environment, then the data source configuration is up to the application developer and is typically done via some kind of factory object that obtains a `java.sql.Connection` through the `java.sql.DriverManager` interface. This leaves us with two very different and incompatible approaches for data source configuration.

Spring provides a solution for this problem by always using a `javax.sql.DataSource` for any framework code accessing a database. To avoid the factory/lookup problem, Spring's IoC framework allows us to easily configure a data source that will be provided to the application without any messy lookup code. The following examples show configurations for local configurations as well as for J2EE configurations obtained via JNDI. The application program is not aware of the type of data source used. All that is needed for your program to access the database is a reference to the common interface `javax.sql.DataSource`.

Local Unpooled

For code running outside a J2EE environment, Spring provides a couple of `DataSource` implementations that don't rely on any pre-configured server resources. Instead, these implementations use the `DriverManager` internally to present the connection wrapped in a `javax.sql.DataSource` interface.

> These implementations are primarily intended to be used for unit and integration testing and they are not intended for production use. We recommend using one of the solutions providing connection pooling mentioned in the following section for any production use.

The first data source we will look at is the `DriverManagerDataSource`. We need to supply the name of the JDBC driver class, the connection URL, as well as a username and password combination that lets us connect to the database. Here is an example of this configuration:

```
<bean id="dataSource"
    class="org.springframework.jdbc.datasource.DriverManagerDataSource">
  <property name="driverClassName">
    <value>org.hsqldb.jdbcDriver</value>
  </property>
  <property name="url">
    <value>jdbc:hsqldb:hsql://localhost:9001</value>
  </property>
  <property name="username"><value>sa</value></property>
  <property name="password"><value></value></property>
</bean>
```

`DriverManagerDataSource` does not provide any pooling of the connection resources. It does provide a new connection each time the `getConnection` method is called. This is not ideal and Spring provides an implementation named `SingleConnectionDataSource` that will keep the connection open for multiple uses:

```
<bean id="dataSource"
    class="org.springframework.jdbc.datasource.SingleConnectionDataSource"
    destroy-method="destroy">
  <property name="driverClassName">
    <value>org.hsqldb.jdbcDriver</value>
  </property>
  <property name="url">
    <value>jdbc:hsqldb:hsql://localhost:9001</value>
  </property>
  <property name="username"><value>sa</value></property>
  <property name="password"><value></value></property>
</bean>
```

As long as this data source is accessed via Spring's `JdbcTemplate` or `DataSourceUtils` `getConnection` and `closeConnectionIfNecessary` methods, then the connection will be kept open. If you use legacy code that accesses the connection directly and calls the connection's `close` method, then you must set the `supressClose` property to `true` for the `SingleConnectionDataSource`:

```
<property name="supressClose"><value>true</value></property>
```

It is important to note that you don't want to leave this connection open forever. In order for the connection to really be closed, you should invoke the `destroy` method after all processing is done. Also, this `DataSource` is not threadsafe and it is best to get a new instance for each use via a *method-injection* `lookup-method`. See Chapter 2 for more on this configuration option.

Local Pooled

Spring does not provide a connection pool implementation because several open source projects already do so. We recommend using a data source configuration based on the pool implementation from the Apache Commons DBCP or SourceForge c3P0 projects. Here is a sample configuration using the `BasicDataSource` from Apache Commons DBCP. Aside from usage in production, this connection pool is quite lightweight and is also quite easy to use even for testing. There are no common scenarios where you would be at a disadvantage in using it instead of `DriverManagerDataSource` or `SingleConnectionDataSource`, while there are some advantages, because using a pooling

`DataSource` even for integration testing will simulate production environments more accurately, and the tests will perform better:

```
<bean id="dataSource" class="org.apache.commons.dbcp.BasicDataSource"
    destroy-method="close">
  <property name="driverClassName">
    <value>${jdbc.driverClassName}</value>
  </property>
  <property name="url"><value>${jdbc.url}</value></property>
  <property name="username"><value>${jdbc.username}</value></property>
  <property name="password"><value>${jdbc.password}</value></property>
</bean>
```

JNDI

Most application servers include a connection pool implementation and they also let you configure data sources that can be bound to the server's JTA implementation. This enables you to use Spring's JTA support for the transaction framework that we already covered earlier in this chapter. We recommend using the connection pooling that is included with your application server or a configuration based on one of the open source implementations mentioned previously.

The connection pooling implementations provided by an application server allow you to bind a data source using the pool to a JNDI name. This is the preferred way to obtain the data source in a J2EE environment. To avoid having to code the JNDI lookup, you should use Spring's `JndiObjectFactoryBean` to obtain the reference to the `DataSource` object. Here is a sample configuration using the JNDI lookup name of `java:comp/env/jdbc/mydb`:

```
<bean id="dataSource" class="org.springframework.jndi.JndiObjectFactoryBean">
  <property name="jndiName"><value>java:comp/env/jdbc/mydb</value></property>
</bean>
```

The J2EE server appends a `java:comp/env/` prefix to the JNDI name and you can either specify the full name as we did in the previous example or you can set the `resourceRef` property of `JndiObjectFactoryBean` to `true`. Here is an example of this style:

```
<bean id="dataSource" class="org.springframework.jndi.JndiObjectFactoryBean">
  <property name="jndiName"><value>jdbc/mydb</value></property>
  <property name="resourceRef"><value>true</value></property>
</bean>
```

Choosing Between Local and JNDI DataSource

Should you always use a JNDI `DataSource` that is provided by your application server or are there advantages to using a locally defined pooled `DataSource`?

A `DataSource` implementation that is provided by your application server vendor will always be better supported by this vendor. This is an important consideration if you are using their paid support offering. Additionally, this type of `DataSource` can be shared by several applications accessing the same database. This can be important if you must limit the number of open connections for the database. Most databases have a configurable limit for how many connections can be open at a time. Even if the connection is not actively used, it is still open while it is in the pool, and it uses resources on the database side.

The locally defined DataSource makes it much easier to deploy your application. There isn't any configuration necessary on the application server side. The entire configuration is part of your application. This is a considerable advantage if your application is going to be deployed to many different application servers. This is especially true if you also have full and exclusive control over the database your application accesses.

As you can see, both solutions have their advantages and you will have to weigh the advantages of the two solutions based on your requirements and other limiting factors.

> **Spring completely abstracts this choice away from application code. It is reduced to a configuration issue. Spring enables a consistent, simple programming model and allows you additional options.**

Summary

We have seen that Spring's transaction support gives us several advantages over a more traditional J2EE approach. We can easily replace a full-fledged JTA implementation with one that runs against local JDBC transactions without modifying the application code. This is true as long as we are accessing only a single database resource. There is no difference in the programming model regardless of the underlying transaction technology.

Spring's transaction management makes working with JTA transactions just as easy as working with local JDBC transactions. This is especially true if you configure all the transaction components with Spring's IoC framework.

Declarative transactions provided by Spring have several advantages over EJB CMT. They can work without using EJBs and the code can be tested outside of a J2EE container. They provide the option of being configured to roll back automatically on any checked exceptions declared for this purpose.

The additional propagation option of PROPAGATION_NESTED provides the ability to nest a transaction within an existing one allowing for more control and the possibility of restarting a failed transaction from a certain save point. This nested transaction support is available only for single database resources, but it provides a real benefit for applications that can make use of it.

Spring's ability to work equally well with single database resources and JTA resources opens up declarative transactions to a much larger group of applications. There is no specific need to use an application server with JTA support. A plain vanilla Tomcat servlet engine can be used just as well.

Finally, the most important benefit of Spring's transaction framework is that any POJO can be enabled to take advantage of transactions without special requirements or deployment steps. Any existing business service object can be provided with transaction semantics by defining it in a Spring application context and adding a transactional proxy to it. There is no need to modify or rewrite the application like you would have to do to deploy it as an EJB.

7

Object/Relational Mapping

We saw in the previous chapter how Spring supports transaction strategies and JTA transaction synchronization for a variety of *Object-Relational mapping (O/R mapping)* tools. Rather than providing its own O/R mapping implementation, Spring integrates with popular third-party solutions:

❑ **iBATIS SQL Maps (1.3 and 2.0):** A simple but powerful solution for externalizing SQL statements into XML files, including result mappings and parameter mappings for JavaBeans. Does not aim to provide an object query language or automatic change detection.

❑ **Hibernate (2.1 and 3.0):** A very popular open source O/R mapping tool, featuring its own textual object query language called HQL and dedicated support for detached objects. Uses snapshot comparisons for automatic change detection.

❑ **JDO (1.0 and 2.0):** The JCP specification for general object persistence, focusing on byte code modification for on-the-fly change detection, in combination with a strict lifecycle for persistent objects. JDO 2.0 is about to introduce standard support for relational databases and detached objects.

❑ **Apache OJB (1.0):** O/R mapping platform with multiple client APIs: `PersistenceBroker`, ODMG, and (through a plugin) JDO. Spring includes dedicated support for the `PersistenceBroker` API, which offers full-fledged mapping capabilities but does not aim to provide automatic change detection.

❑ **Oracle TopLink:** Mature O/R mapping tool, originally from The Object People, now owned by Oracle. Offers very flexible mapping capabilities through the TopLink Workbench GUI. Uses snapshot comparisons for change detection on explicitly registered objects.

In this chapter, we will concentrate on iBATIS SQL Maps 2.0 and Hibernate 2.1 — two very popular persistence solutions, but with quite different approaches. While previous knowledge about those tools is not required, comprehensive coverage of either of them is outside of the scope of this chapter. We will instead introduce the basic principles and focus on usage in a Spring environment, as illustrated by our sample applications.

We will also discuss Spring's JDO integration, discussing the basic model and pointing out important similarities and differences to the Hibernate support, and Spring's TopLink support, to highlight the conceptual consistency within Spring's support for different O/R mapping frameworks. This conceptual basis shows how Spring will support JSR-220 persistence—the POJO persistence standard to be defined by the EJB 3.0 expert group—which is to be independent of the EJB 3.0 specification proper.

A full discussion of Apache OJB and Oracle TopLink is outside the scope of this book. The basic approach is similar to Hibernate and JDO, although there are differences in both semantics and features. Please refer to http://db.apache.org/ojb and www.oracle.com/technology/products/ias/toplink for further information on OJB and TopLink, respectively, and to the Spring reference documentation for information on how to integrate them into a Spring environment.

Note that all these strategies work within Spring's consistent DAO abstraction approach, allowing for mixed usage with Spring's own JDBC framework, and as far as possible also allowing for mixed usage of multiple O/R mapping strategies in the same application.

Background

For an extensive discussion of persistence strategies, focusing on O/R mapping strategies and DAO interface design, please refer to Chapter 10 of *J2EE without EJB*. In this section, we will give only a brief overview, to outline the basic concepts and clarify where the O/R mapping tools fit in terms of common O/R mapping concepts.

Basic O/R Mapping

Data entities in database tables are often mapped to persistent Java objects that make up a *Domain Model*, so that business logic can be implemented to work with these object representations rather than the database tables and fields directly. Object-relational mapping (O/R mapping) is the general term for such strategies: It aims to overcome the so-called *Impedance Mismatch* between object-oriented applications and relational databases.

> The object-relational *Impedance Mismatch* is a popular term for the gulf between the relational model, which is based around normalized data in tables and has a well-defined mathematical basis, and the world of object-orientation, which is based on concepts such as classes, inheritance, and polymorphism.

In its simplest form, O/R mapping is about mapping JDBC query results to object representations and in turn mapping those object representations back to JDBC statement parameters (for example, for insert and update statements). Database columns are usually mapped to JavaBean properties or instance fields of domain objects.

This basic level can be achieved through custom JDBC usage, for example with the RowMapper interface of Spring's JDBC framework (see Chapter 5). The common pattern is to delegate the actual mapping to *data mappers*, such as a set of DAOs, to keep the persistence logic out of the domain model.

Beyond such basic table-to-object mapping, data mappers are often required to provide more sophisticated mapping capabilities, such as automatic fetching of associated objects, lazy loading, and caching of persistent objects. Once such requirements come in, it is preferable to adopt an existing O/R mapping solution instead of implementing your own mapper based on JDBC. There are very good tools available, which offer far more sophistication than custom in-house development can sensibly achieve.

iBATIS SQL Maps is a good example of a persistence solution working at the level described in the previous paragraphs. It offers reasonably sophisticated mapping capabilities, including support for associated objects, lazy loading, and caching. It still works at the SQL level: DAOs trigger the execution of so-called *mapped statements*, which are defined in an XML file — specifying SQL statements with parameter placeholders and result mapping. The tool never generates SQL statements; it rather relies on the application developer to specify the SQL for each operation.

The advantage of the SQL Maps strategy is that the developer is in full control over the SQL, which allows for full customization for a specific target database (by the application developer or a database administrator). The disadvantage is that there is no abstraction from database specifics like auto-increment columns, sequences, select for update, and so on. The mapped statements need to be defined for each target database if they are supposed to leverage such database-dependent features.

Object Query Languages

Full-blown O/R mapping solutions (or what most people refer to when they say "O/R mapping" without further qualification) usually do not work at the SQL level but rather feature their own object query language, which gets translated into SQL at runtime. The mapping information is usually kept in metadata, for example in XML files, which defines how to map each persistent class and its fields onto database tables and columns.

With such an abstraction level, there is no need to specify separate statements for select, insert, update, and delete. The tool will automatically generate the corresponding SQL from the same centralized mapping information. Database specifics are usually addressed by the tool rather than the application developer, through configuring an appropriate database "dialect." For example, the generation of IDs is usually configured in metadata and automatically translated into auto-increment columns or sequences or whatever identity generation strategy is chosen.

This level is provided by Hibernate, JDO, TopLink, and Apache OJB: sophisticated mapping capabilities with an object query language. Hibernate, JDO, TopLink, and OJB's ODMG API actually go beyond it in that they provide automatic change detection, while the OJB PersistenceBroker API purely provides the mapping plus object query level. The advantage of the latter approach is less complexity for the application developer to deal with. Storing of changes will happen only on explicit save, update, or delete, as with iBATIS SQL Maps — there is no automatic change detection "magic" working in the background.

The syntax of object query languages varies widely. Hibernate uses HQL, which is an SQL-like textual query language working at the class/field level, while JDO and the OJB PersistenceBroker use different flavors of query APIs with criteria expressions. The TopLink *expression builder* and Hibernate *criteria queries* are also API-based approaches. JDO 2.0 introduces the concept of textual querying, as an alternative to the classic JDOQL query API; OJB also has pluggable query facilities. The query language is still an important differentiator, as it is the most important "face to the application developer" aside from the mapping files.

Transparent Persistence

So-called *transparent persistence* tools do not just allow for mapped objects to be retrieved through object queries; they also keep track of all loaded objects and automatically detect changes that the application made. A *flush* will then synchronize the object state with the database state: that is, issue corresponding SQL statements to modify the affected database tables accordingly; this usually happens at transaction completion.

Such change detection just applies to changes made within the *original transaction* that loaded the objects. Once an object has been passed outside that transaction, it needs to be explicitly reattached to the new transaction. In Hibernate, this corresponds to a saveOrUpdate call; in JDO 2.0, to a reattach operation. Compare this behavior to tools such as iBATIS SQL Maps or the OJB PersistenceBroker, which never do automatic change detection and therefore always require explicit store calls, no matter if within the original transaction or outside of it.

Persistence operations often just deal with *first-class domain objects*; dependent objects are implicitly addressed via cascading updates and deletes (*persistence by reachability*). With such sophisticated operations, there is no need for explicit save or delete calls on dependent objects because the transparent persistence tool can automatically and efficiently handle this.

To perform such automatic change detection, the persistence tool needs to have a way to keep track of changes. This can either happen through snapshots made at loading time (as done by Hibernate) or through modifying the persistent classes to make the tool aware of modified fields — like JDO's traditional byte code modification strategy. This either incurs the memory overhead of snapshots or the additional compilation step for JDO byte code enhancement. It also incurs a somewhat strict lifecycle for persistent objects, as they behave differently within or outside a transaction.

The advantage of "transparent persistence" is that the application developer does not have to track any changes applied with the original transaction because the tool will automatically detect and store them. The disadvantage is that the persistence tool needs to have quite complex background machinery to perform such change detection, which the application developer has to be aware of. In particular, such change detection machinery introduces side effects in terms of lifecycle: for example, when the same persistent object should participate in multiple transactions.

When to Choose O/R Mapping

O/R mapping can have many benefits, but it is important to remember that not every application fits the O/R mapping paradigm.

Central issues are heavy use of set access and aggregate functions, and batch updates of many rows. If an application is mainly concerned with either of those — for example, a reporting application — and does not allow for a significant amount of caching in an object mapper, set-based relational access via Spring JDBC or iBATIS SQL Maps is probably the best choice.

Because all O/R mapping frameworks have a learning curve and setup cost, applications with very simple data access requirements are also often best to stick with JDBC-based solutions. Of course, if a team is already proficient with a particular O/R mapping framework, this concern may be less important.

Indicators that O/R mapping *is* appropriate are:

❏ A typical load/edit/store workflow for domain objects: for example, load a product record, edit it, and synchronize the updated state with the database.

❏ Objects may be possibly queried for in large sets but are updated and deleted individually.

❏ A significant number of objects lend themselves to being cached aggressively (a "read-mostly" scenario, common in web applications).

❏ There is a sufficiently natural mapping between domain objects and database tables and fields. This is, of course, not always easy to judge up front. Database views and triggers can sometimes be used to bridge the gap between the OO model and relational schema.

❏ There are no unusual requirements in terms of custom SQL optimizations. Good O/R mapping solutions can issue efficient SQL in many cases, as with Hibernate's "dialect" support, but some SQL optimizations can be done only via a wholly relational paradigm.

O/R Mapping Support in Spring

Spring's support for specific O/R mapping strategies covers two main areas: design and implementation of data access objects, and convenient transaction management. The basic patterns apply to all of the O/R mapping tools mentioned.

> **In general, Spring provides a consistent usage model for persistence: common DAO design and implementation, common setup style in a Spring context, and common transaction management. As you will see, Spring's O/R mapping support basically follows the design of the JDBC support. It provides as much conceptual commonality as possible, while still retaining the full power of the concrete underlying tool.**

Data Access Objects

You have already learned about Spring's generic `DataAccessException` hierarchy, which facilitates the design of implementation-agnostic DAO interfaces, in Chapter 5. All of the O/R mapping integration classes that come with the Spring distribution follow the same pattern: That is, they allow for being used behind application-specific DAO interfaces that consistently throw `DataAccessExceptions`. Thus, callers do not usually need to be aware of the implementation strategy used by a DAO. As you will see, this is important if there is a possibility that you might ever want to switch between O/R mapping technologies.

All of Spring's O/R mapping integration classes aim to provide sophisticated exception translation as far as possible. They will convert O/R mapper exceptions to proper `DataAccessException` subclasses such as `DataIntegrityViolationException` or `OptimisticLockingFailureException`, and translate underlying `SQLExceptions` via a Spring `SQLExceptionTranslator`. This allows callers to catch specific subclasses of `DataAccessException`, without special regard to the chosen persistence tool.

As discussed in detail in Chapter 10 of *J2EE without EJB*, it is usually *not* feasible to design DAO interfaces that are supposed to be used with either plain JDBC or a full-blown O/R mapping tool. DAO interfaces for Hibernate and JDO usually just operate on first-class objects, relying on cascading to dependent objects, and just require store calls for reattaching persistent objects to new transactions—in contrast to JDBC-oriented DAOs, which tend to offer fine-grained operations without implicit cascading.

DAO interfaces designed for a transparent persistence backend have the choice to offer *loosely typed operations* (such as store and delete operations that take java.lang.Object) or *strongly typed operations* (such as store and delete operations on application-specific, first-class domain objects). While the former reduce the number of exposed operations, they do not clearly indicate which persistent objects are supposed to be created, updated, or deleted. Therefore, we recommend designing such DAO interfaces as strongly typed, even if the implementation delegates to loosely typed Hibernate or JDO operations.

> **The DAO pattern usually offers clear benefits even with O/R mapping tools underneath. It conceals the use of database-specific query optimizations or vendorspecific JDO extensions, and allows for easy mock implementations of the application-specific DAO interfaces. We recommend designing such DAO interfaces as strongly typed, to make the available operations and their target classes immediately obvious, and to ease mocking of specific operations.**

For all supported O/R mapping strategies, Spring provides pre-built template classes to ease DAO implementations, analogous to the JdbcTemplate class for JDBC. Any kind of work can be performed via the native API of the underlying tool through custom callback implementations, without having to care about resource opening/closing, transaction participation, and exception conversion. Furthermore, these template classes offer a wide variety of convenience operations, which reduce typical DAO method implementations to one-liners, as you will see below.

Transaction Management

Spring provides two kinds of transaction support for O/R mapping tools:

❑ Automatic synchronization of local O/R mapper contexts such as a Hibernate Session or a JDO PersistenceManager with global JTA transactions, usually demarcated via Spring's JtaTransactionManager. This is an alternative to deploying special JCA connectors for your O/R mapping tool, which achieve a similar goal.

❑ Local transaction strategies for single databases, in the form of one implementation of Spring's PlatformTransactionManager interface per particular O/R mapping tool (for example, HibernateTransactionManager or JdoTransactionManager). Such a strategy will work completely without JTA, for example in Tomcat or a standalone application.

With proper setup, neither the DAO implementations nor the transaction demarcation code has to change when switching between global and local transactions—a simple configuration change is enough. Usually, this has to coincide with the backend JDBC DataSource choice: In the global transaction case, these will be J2EE container DataSources; in the local transaction case, these will often be local DataSources such as a Commons DBCP BasicDataSource or a C3P0 ComboPooledDataSource.

For general details on Spring's transaction infrastructure and setup of global transactions or local transactions, including appropriate choices for JDBC DataSources, see Chapter 6.

iBATIS SQL Maps

The basic idea of SQL Maps is simple: Statements are defined in an XML file, specifying an SQL string with parameter placeholders (optionally specifying SQL types and other details for the parameters). On execution, the placeholders are resolved to given parameter values, either from a *parameter map*, a JavaBean with *bean properties*, or a *simple parameter object*. In case of an SQL query, the definition maps result columns to a result object, supporting the same kinds of values as for parameters.

Beyond plain statement mapping, SQL Maps provides support for *caching query results*, with pluggable cache strategies. Various out-of-the-box implementations are provided, including a default memory cache and a strategy for OpenSymphony's *OSCache*. Cache models are applied per mapped query statement; it's possible to specify insert/update/delete statements that should cause flushing of the particular cache (for example to flush the accountCache cache if an updateAccount statement is executed). There is no support for evicting specific object instances from the cache; if a single Account gets updated, all Account instances will be evicted.

For detailed information on SQL Maps capabilities and configuration, please refer to Clinton Begin's excellent *iBATIS SQL Maps Developer Guide* (available from www.ibatis.com). We will concentrate on Spring integration in this section, showing examples from the Spring JPetStore — which builds on the original iBATIS JPetStore, for example reusing its SQL Maps definition files. We will refer to the Spring 1.2 version of JPetStore here, which uses iBATIS SQL Maps 2.0, rather than SQL Maps 1.3, as used by the original JPetStore.

iBATIS SQL Maps is available from www.ibatis.com, under the Apache license 2.0. SQL Maps 2.0 final was released in June 2004, providing the new (non–backward-compatible) SqlMapClient API as successor of the original SqlMap API, and featuring a revised mapping file format. The iBATIS project applied for Apache membership in late 2004, so future releases are likely to be offered under the Apache umbrella.

Mapping File

An SQL Maps mapping file contains *mapped statements*, including parameter and result mapping. For example, JPetStore's Account domain object is mapped as follows (omitting a couple of further statements from the actual JPetStore Account.xml file for simplicity's sake):

```
<sqlMap namespace="Account">

  <typeAlias alias="account"
      type="org.springframework.samples.jpetstore.domain.Account"/>

  <resultMap id="accountResult" class="account">
    <result property="username" column="USERID"/>
    <result property="email" column="EMAIL"/>
    <result property="firstName" column="FIRSTNAME"/>
    <result property="lastName" column="LASTNAME"/>
    <result property="status" column="STATUS"/>
    <result property="address1" column="ADDR1"/>
    <result property="address2" column="ADDR2"/>
    <result property="city" column="CITY"/>
    <result property="state" column="STATE"/>
```

```xml
        <result property="zip" column="ZIP"/>
        <result property="country" column="COUNTRY"/>
        <result property="phone" column="PHONE"/>
        <result property="languagePreference" column="LANGPREF"/>
        <result property="favouriteCategoryId" column="FAVCATEGORY" />
        <result property="listOption" column="MYLISTOPT" />
        <result property="bannerOption" column="BANNEROPT" />
        <result property="bannerName" column="BANNERNAME" />
    </resultMap>

    <select id="getAccountByUsername" resultMap="accountResult"
        parameterClass="string">
        select
            SIGNON.USERNAME as USERID,
            ACCOUNT.EMAIL,
            ACCOUNT.FIRSTNAME,
            ACCOUNT.LASTNAME,
            ACCOUNT.STATUS,
            ...
            PROFILE.LANGPREF,
            PROFILE.FAVCATEGORY,
            PROFILE.MYLISTOPT,
            PROFILE.BANNEROPT,
            BANNERDATA.BANNERNAME
        from ACCOUNT, PROFILE, SIGNON, BANNERDATA
        where ACCOUNT.USERID = #value#
          and SIGNON.USERNAME = ACCOUNT.USERID
          and PROFILE.USERID = ACCOUNT.USERID
          and PROFILE.FAVCATEGORY = BANNERDATA.FAVCATEGORY
    </select>

    <insert id="insertAccount" parameterClass="account">
      insert into ACCOUNT (EMAIL, FIRSTNAME, LASTNAME, STATUS, ADDR1, ADDR2,
      CITY, STATE, ZIP, COUNTRY, PHONE, USERID)
      values (#email#, #firstName#, #lastName#, #status#, #address1#,
      #address2:VARCHAR#, #city#, #state#, #zip#, #country#, #phone#, #username#)
    </insert>

    <insert id="insertProfile" parameterClass="account">
      insert into PROFILE (LANGPREF, FAVCATEGORY, MYLISTOPT, BANNEROPT, USERID)
      values (#languagePreference#, #favouriteCategoryId#, #listOption#,
      #bannerOption#, #username#)
    </insert>

    <insert id="insertSignon" parameterClass="account">
      insert into SIGNON (PASSWORD,USERNAME) values (#password#, #username#)
    </insert>

    ...

</sqlMap>
```

The most important parts of an SQL Maps mapping file are:

❑ **Result maps:** Mapping result set columns to JavaBean properties of the Account domain class. A result map can be reused for multiple query statements. Alternatively, bean property names can also be specified inline in the statement, as column aliases (not shown in the preceding sample).

❑ **Query statements:** Defining SQL select statements, referring to a result map for mapping the result columns onto an Account domain object. The result of executing such a statement via the SQL Maps API will be one or more instances of the Account domain class.

❑ **Update statements:** Defining SQL insert/update/delete statements, using an Account domain object as parameter. Each # . . . # placeholder refers to a bean property of the Account class, using its value as column value in the database table.

This is already a typical, fully functional mapping file for iBATIS SQL Maps. Of course, there are further options, such as specifying a cache model. However, the basic principle is illustrated in the preceding sample: mapped SQL statements with result maps and parameter maps. For further details, please refer to the *iBATIS SQL Maps Developer Guide*.

Note that such mapped statements can leverage any specific database SQL constructs, for example on Oracle; you are in full control over the SQL issued. If you need multiple versions of a statement to support multiple databases, simply define different statement IDs for them and let your DAO choose a specific statement to execute. Whether the DAO detects the database and chooses an appropriate statement or has special subclasses for specific databases is up to you; iBATIS does *not* provide any prebuilt database abstraction.

Usage of iBATIS SQL Maps in Spring does not impose any special requirements. The mapping files are usually completely independent from the actual usage style; they can be seamlessly used with plain iBATIS API or with Spring's iBATIS support.

> iBATIS SQL Maps works at the SQL statement level. The application developer defines mapped SQL statements with results and parameters. In contrast to such a statement-based approach, full-blown O/R mapping tools such as Hibernate map persistent classes to database tables and columns, generating the SQL statements under the hood.

DAO Implementation

Spring provides prebuilt convenience classes for accessing iBATIS SQL Maps according to Spring conventions, that is, in DAOs that throw Spring's generic DataAccessException and are usually set up as Spring beans in a Spring application context.

The template class for data access operations is org.springframework.orm.ibatis .SqlMapClientTemplate, working with iBATIS 2.0's SqlMapClient API underneath. It is typically used through the base class org.springframework.orm.ibatis.support.SqlMapClientDaoSupport, which takes an SqlMapClient instance as bean property and provides an SqlMapClientTemplate instance for it. (This is not a requirement, however: SqlMapClientTemplate can also be instantiated directly, just like JdbcTemplate.)

For example, the DAO for account domain objects in JPetStore looks as follows, when leveraging
`SqlMapClientDaoSupport`:

```
public class SqlMapAccountDao extends SqlMapClientDaoSupport
    implements AccountDao {

  public Account getAccount(String username) throws DataAccessException {
    return (Account) getSqlMapClientTemplate().queryForObject(
        "getAccountByUsername", username);
  }

  public void insertAccount(Account account) throws DataAccessException {
    getSqlMapClientTemplate().update("insertAccount", account);
    getSqlMapClientTemplate().update("insertProfile", account);
    getSqlMapClientTemplate().update("insertSignon", account);
  }

  ...
}
```

Without the provided convenience base class, the implementation could implement its own
`setSqlMapClient` method, preferably creating a shared `SqlMapClientTemplate` instance for
the DAO:

```
public class SqlMapAccountDao implements AccountDao {

  private SqlMapClientTemplate sqlMapClientTemplate;

  public void setSqlMapClient(SqlMapClient sqlMapClient) {
    this.sqlMapClientTemplate = new SqlMapClientTemplate(sqlMapClient);
  }

  public Account getAccount(String username) throws DataAccessException {
    return (Account) this.sqlMapClientTemplate.queryForObject(
        "getAccountByUsername", username);
  }

  public void insertAccount(Account account) throws DataAccessException {
    this.sqlMapClientTemplate.update("insertAccount", account);
    this.sqlMapClientTemplate.update("insertProfile", account);
    this.sqlMapClientTemplate.update("insertSignon", account);
  }

  ...
}
```

As you have come to expect, Spring takes care of all resource management "plumbing" and cleanup
issues — you just need to specify the required persistence operations.

Alternatively, a DAO implementation could also use the provided `SqlMapClient` instance directly,
without Spring's `SqlMapClientTemplate`. However, this would involve manual exception translation
and checks for existing Spring transactions; therefore, it is usually advisable to stick with
`SqlMapClientTemplate`.

Essentially, each `SqlMapClient` operation refers to a statement name as defined in the mapping file. The input parameters must correspond to the defined input parameters in the statement mappings (`String`, `Account` object). The result values, if any, can be cast to the defined result type (an `Account` object in the query case).

All convenience operations defined on `SqlMapClientTemplate` correspond one-to-one to operations on `com.ibatis.sqlmap.client.SqlMapExecutor`, but they throw Spring's `DataAccessException` rather than JDBC's checked `SQLException`, and participate in Spring transactions (if any). Please refer to the iBATIS docs for details on the semantics of those operations.

As an alternative to invoking such operations on `SqlMapClientTemplate` itself, there is the option to implement an `org.springframework.orm.ibatis.SqlMapClientCallback` that works directly on a given `SqlMapExecutor` resource, via `SqlMapClientTemplate`'s generic `execute` method. However, this is rarely necessary for typical one-line operations. One use case for such a callback is working with batches, for example.

All such a DAO needs to be able to work is an iBATIS 2.0 `SqlMapClient` instance via the `setSqlMapClient` method. In the next section, you will see how to set up such an instance in a Spring context.

Setup in a Spring Context

In a Spring application context, an iBATIS SQL Maps instance is usually set up via Spring's `SqlMapClientFactoryBean`, referring to an SQL Maps configuration file and the JDBC `DataSource` to use:

```
<bean id="sqlMapClient"
    class="org.springframework.orm.ibatis.SqlMapClientFactoryBean">
  <property name="configLocation">
    <value>classpath:sql-map-config.xml</value>
  </property>
  <property name="dataSource">
    <ref bean="dataSource"/>
  </property>
</bean>
```

The `sql-map-config.xml` file enumerates the mapping files to load for this `SqlMapClient` instance:

```
<sqlMapConfig>

  <sqlMap resource="org/springframework/samples/jpetstore/dao/ibatis/Account.xml"/>
  <sqlMap resource="org/springframework/samples/jpetstore/dao/ibatis/Product.xml"/>
  ...

</sqlMapConfig>
```

The SQL Maps configuration file may also contain further configuration such as a JDBC connection pool and transaction configuration; however, this is not common when used within Spring. Instead, the `SqlMapClientFactoryBean` refers to a Spring-configured `DataSource` bean, and typically this `DataSource` is backed by a connection pool. Note that iBATIS lazy loading will still work properly, even if the JDBC configuration is managed by Spring.

The account DAO can now receive a reference to the `SqlMapClient` instance via a Spring bean reference, just as a JDBC-based DAO receives a reference to a JDBC `DataSource`:

```
<bean id="accountDao"
    class="org.springframework.samples.jpetstore.dao.ibatis.SqlMapAccountDao">
  <property name="sqlMapClient">
    <ref bean="sqlMapClient"/>
  </property>
</bean>
```

Whether the `sqlMapClient` property, corresponding to the `setSqlMapClient` method, is defined by the provided `SqlMapClientDaoSupport` base class or implemented by the DAO class itself is not relevant here. The same configuration would work in both scenarios.

Transaction Management

While iBATIS does provide its own API for transaction management, this API is not normally used in a Spring environment. Instead, transaction management is delegated to Spring's generic transaction facilities, with the generic `TransactionTemplate` or `TransactionProxyFactoryBean` used for demarcation. See Chapter 6 for details on Spring transaction management.

There is no special transaction backend implementation for iBATIS, as SQL Maps do not involve special resource handling. Rather, any transaction strategy suitable for JDBC will work with iBATIS too; DAOs based on `SqlMapClientTemplate` will simply participate in such JDBC-based transactions. In particular, the following choices are available:

❑ `org.springframework.jdbc.datasource.DataSourceTransactionManager`: Allows the execution of transactions on a single JDBC `DataSource` — that is, a single target database — using the local transaction methods on the JDBC `Connection` interface. Both JDBC-based and iBATIS-based DAOs can seamlessly participate in such transactions. This strategy is usually sufficient as long as there is no need for transactions that span multiple transactional resources.

❑ `org.springframework.transaction.jta.JtaTransactionManager`: Delegates transaction execution to a JTA implementation — usually a J2EE server's JTA subsystem. `SqlMapClientTemplate`-based DAOs will automatically participate in such transactions, as long as the JDBC `DataSource` is JTA-aware — that is, defined as XA `DataSource` in the J2EE server. This strategy allows for performing transactions across multiple transactional resources, for example across multiple database systems. See Chapter 6 for details on when to choose JTA.

Note that no special attention is required for iBATIS *lazy loading*. If loading within a transaction, it will participate in it; if loading outside a transaction, it will fetch a non-transactional JDBC connection for that particular operation. This is in sharp contrast to Hibernate and JDO, which have special lifecycle requirements for lazy loading.

For example, a transactional proxy for the account DAO defined previously could look as follows. Of course, it is usually preferable to define transactional proxies at the service facade level rather than at the DAO level; we will just use this example for simplicity's sake. The actual Spring JPetStore uses a proxy at the `PetStoreFacade` level rather than the DAO level.

```
<bean id="transactionManager"
    class="org.springframework.jdbc.datasource.DataSourceTransactionManager">
  <property name="dataSource">
    <ref bean="dataSource"/>
  </property>
</bean>

<bean id="accountDaoTarget"
    class="org.springframework.samples.jpetstore.dao.ibatis.SqlMapAccountDao">
  <property name="sqlMapClient">
    <ref bean="sqlMapClient"/>
  </property>
</bean>

<bean id="accountDao"
    class="org.springframework.transaction.interceptor.TransactionProxyFactoryBean">
  <property name="transactionManager">
    <ref bean="transactionManager"/>
  </property>
  <property name="target">
    <ref bean="accountDaoTarget"/>
  </property>
  <property name="transactionAttributes">
    <props>
      <prop key="insert*">PROPAGATION_REQUIRED</prop>
      <prop key="*">PROPAGATION_REQUIRED,readOnly</prop>
    </props>
  </property>
</bean>
```

Please refer to Chapter 6 for details on transaction proxy definitions. This configuration example uses Spring's standard JDBC `DataSourceTransactionManager`, which is, as explained in its description, perfectly suitable for iBATIS-based DAOs.

iBATIS Summary

iBATIS SQL Maps is a straightforward data access tool, working at the SQL level like JDBC code, but externalizing SQL statements and their result and parameter mappings into an XML file. It does not aim to abstract specific databases but rather gives full control over the SQL issued, allowing the developer to leverage the full power of the target database, including proprietary SQL syntax.

The SQL Maps approach is particularly suitable for read-only reference data, where database tables or views are read into domain object representations, but not necessarily with a direct relationship between table and domain class. Such query statements can share the same result map; property to column mappings are defined only once. As such, reference data won't be changed from within that kind of application; a tool that does not track changes in the first place is a good match.

However, a complex read-write domain model is *not* a good fit for SQL Maps, as this would require many definitions for insert and update statements, with repeated property to column mappings. Furthermore, it is usually desirable to store at the level of primary persistent objects in such a scenario, rather than call `store` for each fine-grained persistent object in a graph. For such an application with a complex domain model, a full-blown O/R mapping tool such as Hibernate is recommended.

Usage of iBATIS in Spring is straightforward. Essentially, all you need is an `SqlMapClient` instance, populated with mapping files, to be accessed by your DAOs. Transaction management is exactly the same as in a JDBC scenario, using Spring's `DataSourceTransactionManager` or `JtaTransactionManager`.

Mixing Spring's JDBC support and iBATIS SQL Maps is seamless. Some DAOs could work with the former, some with the latter, sharing the same JDBC `DataSource` and the same JDBC-based transactions. While externalizing SQL statements is usually a good idea, Spring's JDBC support is particularly appropriate for applying complex parameters, analyzing complex results, and handling BLOB/CLOB access. So an application could use iBATIS SQL Maps for most of its data access, but still leverage Spring's JDBC support for special operations: for example, streaming binary content from a BLOB.

> **The beauty of iBATIS SQL Maps is its simplicity. Externalizing SQL statements and their result and parameter mappings into an XML file is a simple but nevertheless powerful concept. In contrast to Hibernate or JDO, there is no special query language to learn and no automatic change detection working in the background, which means that there is less complexity to deal with.**

Hibernate

Hibernate is probably the most popular O/R mapping tool in early 2005. Its two key features are the query language HQL and automatic change detection through snapshot comparisons. In contrast to iBATIS SQL Maps, Hibernate *does* abstract the underlying database and its data model, generating SQL under the hood rather than letting the user work at the SQL level. In combination with Hibernate's very lenient lifecycle for persistent objects, the resulting programming model is very convenient, while still being able to adapt to existing data models as far as possible.

Hibernate's query language, *HQL*, offers important relational concepts such as joins and aggregate functions. In general, HQL is closer to SQL than to other object query languages, with the important difference from SQL that queries are expressed in terms of domain object properties rather than database column values, thus decoupling from the database schema. In many respects, HQL allows developers to leverage SQL's power at the domain object level. It is also relatively easy to learn for developers already familiar with SQL.

Hibernate performs change detection via *snapshot comparisons*. With its optimized reflection usage via CGLIB — creating runtime proxies for persistent objects through dynamic byte code generation — the performance overhead of such comparisons is not as high as might be assumed. The advantage of Hibernate's model over JDO-style change notifications is that Hibernate does not need to modify persistent objects to observe their state.

Working with *detached objects* is easy because of Hibernate's lenient lifecycle for persistent objects. A persistent object will seamlessly switch from managed to non-managed when a Hibernate `Session` gets closed, without an explicit detachment step. An object can then get modified outside of a Hibernate `Session`, for example in a form workflow in a web application, and subsequently become reattached to a new Hibernate `Session` (through a `saveOrUpdate` operation), which will store the current state of the object.

Hibernate supports *pluggable cache strategies*, providing out-of-the-box implementations for EHCache, OSCache, SwarmCache, and JBoss TreeCache. Hibernate applies fine-granular caching of individual objects per ID and optionally also of query results. Modifications performed via Hibernate will automatically update affected objects and affected query results in the cache; timeouts are necessary only if other processes are also modifying the database.

For detailed information on Hibernate mapping options, query syntax, and so on, please refer to the excellent documentation in the Hibernate distribution and/or to Gavin King and Christian Bauer's *Hibernate in Action* (Manning, 2004) or another book on Hibernate. Hibernate is a very powerful tool with a wide variety of features; it is beyond the scope of this book to cover it in a comprehensive fashion. Rather, we will concentrate on integration into a Spring environment and on added value provided by Spring.

Hibernate is available from `www.hibernate.org`, licensed under the LGPL. At the time of this writing, the stable branch was Hibernate 2.1, which all examples refer to. Hibernate 3.0 is scheduled for early 2005; because of a package name change from `net.sf.hibernate` to `org.hibernate`, Spring will provide separate support for it in the `org.springframework.orm.hibernate3` package. In most respects, Hibernate3 support will be an exact mirror of the Hibernate 2.1 support, but in the `orm.hibernate3` package rather than the `orm.hibernate` package. Thus the following discussion is equally relevant to Hibernate 3 as Hibernate 2 — only the package name changes.

Mapping File

A Hibernate mapping file contains definitions for classes, mapping them to database tables, with each property in the persistent class corresponding to a column in the database table. At runtime, Hibernate will generate SQL statements from those mappings; the same mapping definition is used for creating query, insert, update, and delete statements. All mapped classes are in principle assumed to be read-write; non-mutable objects can be marked as such, but are in many respects treated just like mutable objects.

The following is an excerpt from a simple Hibernate mapping file, taken from the PetClinic sample application:

```
<class name="org.springframework.samples.petclinic.Vet" table="vets">
  <id name="id" column="id" unsaved-value="-1">
    <generator class="identity"/>
  </id>
  <property name="firstName" column="first_name"/>
  <property name="lastName" column="last_name"/>
  <set name="specialtiesInternal" table="vet_specialties">
    <key column="vet_id"/>
    <many-to-many column="specialty_id"
        class="org.springframework.samples.petclinic.Specialty"/>
  </set>
</class>

<class name="org.springframework.samples.petclinic.Specialty" table="specialties">
  <id name="id" column="id" unsaved-value="-1">
    <generator class="identity"/>
  </id>
  <property name="name" column="name"/>
</class>
```

Essentially, each class mapping contains properties that map to database columns, and association properties that interpret a database column as a foreign key. Such associations will be resolved into objects at load time. The persistent objects do not need to hold foreign key IDs or the like, but can be designed for pure object-to-object associations, no matter whether 1:1, 1:n, or m:n. Properties can either be accessed through JavaBean property setters and getters or through direct access to the instance fields.

ID generation is abstracted by Hibernate. The mapping file defines the generation strategy to use. Among the supported strategies are native database features such as auto-increment columns (for example on MySQL) and sequences (for example on Oracle), but also various flavors of UUID generation (in the JVM). To make database-specific strategies work, a Hibernate "dialect" needs to be configured. This is done at the `SessionFactory` level, not in the mapping file, as we will discuss later.

Usage of Hibernate in Spring does not impose any special requirements. The mapping files are usually completely independent from the actual usage style; they can be seamlessly used with a plain Hibernate API or with Spring's Hibernate support.

> **As a full-blown O/R mapping tool, Hibernate works at the persistent class level, rather than at the statement level. The corresponding SQL statements are generated under the hood. Database specifics such as identity generation are abstracted through a configurable database "dialect."**

DAO Implementation

Direct Hibernate usage involves a resource factory, `net.sf.hibernate.SessionFactory`, which is used to open a single-threaded resource, `net.sf.hibernate.Session`, for each transaction or sequence of operations. This is roughly analogous to a `javax.sql.DataSource` and a `java.sql.Connection`, respectively, in the case of JDBC. Non-Spring Hibernate code usually manages such `Sessions` in a manual fashion, associating them with the scope of a transaction or the scope of a web request.

In a Spring environment, application code does *not* usually manage Hibernate `Sessions` manually — a major boon for developers. Spring provides convenience classes that remove the burden of resource management from the application developer. Most important, Hibernate `Sessions` will automatically be synchronized with Spring transactions. In other respects, the usual conventions apply: DAO operations will throw Spring's generic `DataAccessException`, and DAOs are usually set up as beans in a Spring context.

The template class for data access operations is `org.springframework.orm.hibernate.HibernateTemplate`, working with Hibernate's `Session` API underneath. It is typically used through the base class `org.springframework.orm.hibernate.support.HibernateDaoSupport`, which takes a Hibernate `SessionFactory` instance as a bean property and provides a `HibernateTemplate` instance for it. (This is not a requirement, though: `HibernateTemplate` can also be instantiated directly, just like `JdbcTemplate`.)

For example, the following is a Hibernate-based DAO from the PetClinic sample application:

```
public class HibernateClinic extends HibernateDaoSupport implements Clinic {

    public Collection getVets() throws DataAccessException {
```

```
        return getHibernateTemplate().find(
            "from Vet vet order by vet.lastName, vet.firstName");
    }

    public Collection getPetTypes() throws DataAccessException {
        return getHibernateTemplate().find("from PetType type order by type.name");
    }

    public Collection findOwners(String lastName) throws DataAccessException {
        return getHibernateTemplate().find(
            "from Owner owner where owner.lastName like ?", lastName + "%");
    }

    public Owner loadOwner(int id) throws DataAccessException {
        return (Owner) getHibernateTemplate().load(Owner.class, new Integer(id));
    }

    public Pet loadPet(int id) throws DataAccessException {
        return (Pet) getHibernateTemplate().load(Pet.class, new Integer(id));
    }

    public void storeOwner(Owner owner) throws DataAccessException {
        getHibernateTemplate().saveOrUpdate(owner);
    }

    public void storePet(Pet pet) throws DataAccessException {
        getHibernateTemplate().saveOrUpdate(pet);
    }

    public void storeVisit(Visit visit) throws DataAccessException {
        getHibernateTemplate().saveOrUpdate(visit);
    }
}
```

Without the provided convenience base class, the implementation could implement its own
setSessionFactory method, preferably creating a shared HibernateTemplate instance for the DAO:

```
public class HibernateClinic implements Clinic {

    private HibernateTemplate hibernateTemplate;

    public void setSessionFactory(SessionFactory sessionFactory) {
        this.hibernateTemplate = new HibernateTemplate(sessionFactory);
    }

    public Collection getVets() throws DataAccessException {
        return this.hibernateTemplate.find(
            "from Vet vet order by vet.lastName, vet.firstName");
    }

    public Collection getPetTypes() throws DataAccessException {
        return this.hibernateTemplate.find("from PetType type order by type.name");
    }
```

```
public Collection findOwners(String lastName) throws DataAccessException {
  return this.hibernateTemplate.find(
      "from Owner owner where owner.lastName like ?", lastName + "%");
}

  ...

}
```

Alternatively, a DAO implementation could also use the provided `SessionFactory` instance directly, without Spring's `HibernateTemplate`. However, this would involve manual handling of Hibernate `Sessions`, manual exception translation, and manual synchronization with Spring transactions; therefore, it is usually advisable to go through `HibernateTemplate`. If necessary, helpers for manual DAO implementations can be found in the `org.springframework.orm.hibernate.SessionFactoryUtils` class:

```
public class HibernateClinic implements Clinic {

  private SessionFactory sessionFactory;

  public void setSessionFactory(SessionFactory sessionFactory) {
    this.sessionFactory = sessionFactory;
  }

  public Collection getVets() throws DataAccessException {
    Session session = SessionFactoryUtils.getSession(this.sessionFactory, true);
    try {
      return session.find("from Vet vet order by vet.lastName, vet.firstName");
    }
    catch (HibernateException ex) {
      throw SessionFactoryUtils.convertHibernateAccessException(ex);
    }
    finally {
      SessionFactoryUtils.closeSessionIfNecessary(session, this.sessionFactory);
    }
  }

  ...

}
```

The operations defined on `HibernateTemplate` basically correspond to operations on `net.sf.hibernate.Session`, but throw Spring's `DataAccessException` rather than Hibernate's checked `HibernateException` and participate in Spring transactions (if any). Please refer to the Hibernate documentation for details on the semantics of those operations. `HibernateTemplate` defines a wide variety of convenience versions of those methods. Many of them are not available on a plain Hibernate `Session`, so `HibernateTemplate` has a significant convenience value, besides its other benefits.

As an alternative to invoking such operations on `HibernateTemplate` itself, there is the option to implement an `org.springframework.orm.hibernate.HibernateCallback` that works directly on a given Hibernate `Session` resource, via `HibernateTemplate`'s generic execute method. This is rarely necessary for typical one-line operations; however, complex Hibernate queries or processing operations should be implemented in a `HibernateCallback`, in particular if they rely on getting executed on the same Hibernate `Session`. The callback approach should be familiar from Spring's approach to JDBC and other APIs:

```
public class HibernateClinic extends HibernateDaoSupport implements Clinic {

    public Collection getVets() throws DataAccessException {
        return getHibernateTemplate().executeFind(
            new HibernateCallback() {
                public void doInHibernate(Session session) throws HibernateException {
                    Query query = session.createQuery
                        "from Vet vet order by vet.lastName, vet.firstName");
                    // further customization of the query object
                    return query.list();
                }
            });
    }

    ...
}
```

Note that Hibernate has a special requirement for *lazy loading*. The Hibernate `Session` that originally loaded the affected persistent objects needs to still be open to make lazy loading work. As `HibernateTemplate` by default closes the Hibernate `Session` at the end of each operation, returned objects are *not* capable of lazy loading. It is recommended to execute such operations within transactions, which will keep the same Hibernate `Session` open for the lifetime of the entire transaction. If you need lazy loading beyond the scope of your transactions — for example in web views — you need to resort to the *Open Session in View* pattern, discussed later in this chapter.

All such a DAO needs to be able to work is a Hibernate `SessionFactory` instance via the `setSessionFactory` method. In the next section, we will see how to set up such an instance in a Spring context.

Setup in a Spring Context

In a Spring application context, Hibernate is usually set up via Spring's `LocalSessionFactoryBean`, referring to the JDBC `DataSource` to use and the Hibernate mapping files to load. Typically, there are also a couple of Hibernate properties defined: Most important, the database "dialect" to use:

```xml
<bean id="sessionFactory"
    class="org.springframework.orm.hibernate.LocalSessionFactoryBean">
  <property name="dataSource">
    <ref bean="dataSource"/>
  </property>
  <property name="mappingResources">
    <value>petclinic.hbm.xml</value>
  </property>
  <property name="hibernateProperties">
    <props>
      <prop key="hibernate.dialect">net.sf.hibernate.dialect.OracleDialect</prop>
    </props>
  </property>
</bean>
```

The `"mappingResources"` entry in the preceding code refers to a classpath resource. Other ways of loading mapping files are `"mappingLocations"`, accepting any Spring location string, for example to load from the WEB-INF directory of a web application:

```
<bean id="sessionFactory"
    class="org.springframework.orm.hibernate.LocalSessionFactoryBean">
  <property name="dataSource">
    <ref bean="dataSource"/>
  </property>
  <property name="mappingLocations">
    <value>/WEB-INF/petclinic.hbm.xml</value>
  </property>
  <property name="hibernateProperties">
    <props>
      <prop key="hibernate.dialect">net.sf.hibernate.dialect.OracleDialect</prop>
    </props>
  </property>
</bean>
```

Further options to load mapping files from include `"mappingJarLocations"` and `"mappingDirectoryLocations"`, loading all mapping files contained in given JAR files or in given directories. These correspond to operations on `net.sf.hibernate.Configuration`, as documented in the Hibernate reference manual.

Alternatively, you can also use a standard `hibernate.cfg.xml` file to configure your `SessionFactory`, specifying the location as `"configLocation"`. Mapping files and Hibernate properties are usually defined in that separate file in such a scenario, although those could also be mixed with `LocalSessionFactoryBean` properties.

```
<bean id="sessionFactory"
    class="org.springframework.orm.hibernate.LocalSessionFactoryBean">
  <property name="dataSource">
    <ref bean="dataSource"/>
  </property>
  <property name="configLocation">
    <value>/WEB-INF/hibernate.cfg.xml</value>
  </property>
</bean>
```

An advantage of defining properties in the Spring context is that you can use placeholders for certain properties, linking in values from configuration properties files (via Spring's `PropertyPlaceholderConfigurer` mechanism, see Chapter 2). So even when loading configuration from a `hibernate.cfg.xml` file, it is advisable to define such administrative properties on `LocalSessionFactoryBean` in the Spring context.

When using Hibernate in a Spring environment, resource and transaction management is usually the responsibility of Spring. Hibernate configuration should therefore not contain any transaction-related properties. In particular, the choice between local transactions and JTA transactions should be deferred to the Spring transaction manager. We will discuss transactions further in the next section.

The DAO can now receive a reference to the Hibernate `SessionFactory` instance via a Spring bean reference, just like a JDBC-based DAO receives a reference to a JDBC `DataSource`.

```
<bean id="clinicDao"
    class="org.springframework.samples.petclinic.hibernate.HibernateClinic">
  <property name="sessionFactory">
    <ref bean="sessionFactory"/>
  </property>
</bean>
```

Whether the `sessionFactory` property, corresponding to the `setSessionFactory` method, is defined by the provided `HibernateDaoSupport` base class or implemented by the DAO class itself is not relevant here. The same configuration would work in both scenarios.

Setup as a JCA Connector

As an alternative to setting up a `LocalSessionFactoryBean` in a Spring context, a `SessionFactory` can also be set up as a server-wide resource in a J2EE environment, shared by multiple applications. Such a global `SessionFactory` can be linked in as a JNDI resource, replacing a `LocalSessionFactoryBean` definition, using Spring's standard JNDI lookup Factory Bean, as follows:

```
<bean id="sessionFactory"
    class="org.springframework.jndi.JndiObjectFactoryBean">
  <property name="jndiName">
    <value>java:/mySessionFactory</value>
  </property>
</bean>

<bean id="clinicDao"
    class="org.springframework.samples.petclinic.hibernate.HibernateClinic">
  <property name="sessionFactory">
    <ref bean="sessionFactory"/>
  </property>
</bean>
```

While it is possible to use a server-specific startup class to register such JNDI resources, this is not portable. The only standard J2EE way to set up such a shared resource is through a *JCA connector*: that is, by deploying a connector that follows the *J2EE Connector Architecture*. Such resources can then usually be managed centrally in the J2EE server's management console, including fine-grained settings if they expose JMX properties.

JCA connectors are an appropriate way to plug drivers for non-relational backend resources into a J2EE server, especially if they require connection pooling and are supposed to participate in global transactions. However, we do not feel that JCA is an appropriate way to deploy an O/R mapping resource such as a Hibernate `SessionFactory`, for the following reasons:

❑ Mappings between database tables and *domain objects of a particular application* should be considered as part of the application, not as a shared resource in the server.

❑ Hibernate `Sessions` are not pooled separately; pooling of the underlying JDBC Connections is perfectly sufficient.

❑ Hibernate `Sessions` do not represent physical resources that need to participate in the XA protocol for global transactions; this just applies to the underlying JDBC Connections.

The Hibernate JCA connector does not leverage specific features of the JCA container, and inappropriately moves domain-specific mapping logic out of the application. Furthermore, deployment of a JCA connector involves server-specific parameterization and extra deployment steps — for little benefit.

> **We recommend defining a Hibernate** `SessionFactory` **as a local resource within the application — where it logically belongs — using Spring's** `LocalSessionFactoryBean`. **Note that the choice between a local JDBC** `DataSource` **and a shared** `DataSource` **from JNDI is a separate decision. A local Hibernate** `SessionFactory` **can work with a shared J2EE server** `DataSource`, **using either JTA or local transactions.**

Transaction Management

While the Hibernate `Session` API provides methods for transaction management, they are not normally used in a Spring environment (and are not intended for use in a J2EE environment). Instead, transaction management is delegated to Spring's generic transaction facilities, with the generic `TransactionTemplate` or `TransactionProxyFactoryBean` used for demarcation.

The following choices are available as backend transaction strategies for Hibernate. As with iBATIS and other data access APIs, we essentially have the choice between Spring's dedicated transaction manager for that API and the global JTA transaction manager:

❑ `org.springframework.orm.hibernate.HibernateTransactionManager`: Allows transaction execution on a single Hibernate `SessionFactory` that is associated with a single target database, using native Hibernate facilities. Hibernate-based DAOs can seamlessly participate in such transactions. JDBC-based DAOs can join in, provided that the JDBC `DataSource` is available to the transaction manager (it is auto-detected when specified on `LocalSessionFactoryBean`). This strategy is usually sufficient as long as there is no need for transactions that span multiple transactional resources.

❑ `org.springframework.transaction.jta.JtaTransactionManager`: Delegates transaction execution to a JTA implementation: that is, to a J2EE server's JTA subsystem or a JTA implementation such as ObjectWeb's JOTM. `HibernateTemplate`-based DAOs will automatically participate in such transactions, as long as the JDBC `DataSource` is JTA-aware (usually defined as XA `DataSource` in the J2EE server). This strategy allows the execution of transactions across multiple transactional resources, for example across multiple database systems. See Chapter 6 for details on when to choose JTA.

In both cases, Hibernate `Sessions` will automatically be associated with transactions: one Hibernate `Session` for the entire scope of a transaction. Data access code will automatically receive the transactional `Session` if executing within a transaction; otherwise, a short-lived `Session` will be opened for each operation. The only exception to this rule is when applying the Open Session in View pattern in single session mode (see the upcoming "Session Lifecycle" section for a further discussion of the `Session` lifecycle).

In the case of suspended transactions, each transaction will be associated with its own Hibernate `Session`. So when a new inner transaction starts, the Hibernate `Session` of the outer transaction will be suspended and a new one will be created. On completion of the inner transaction, the inner Hibernate `Session` will be closed and the outer one will be resumed. This will work with both `HibernateTransactionManager` and `JtaTransactionManager`, leveraging Spring's transaction synchronization mechanism.

> **If there is a need to perform transactions across multiple resources, choose** `JtaTransactionManager`, **which delegates to the J2EE server's JTA subsystem (or a locally defined transaction coordinator such as JOTM). However, for transactions on a single target database,** `HibernateTransactionManager` **is perfectly sufficient — and will work in any environment, whether a J2EE web application, a standalone application, or a test suite.**

For example, a transactional proxy for the DAO as previously defined could look as follows:

```xml
<bean id="transactionManager"
    class="org.springframework.orm.hibernate.HibernateTransactionManager">
  <property name="sessionFactory">
    <ref bean="sessionFactory"/>
  </property>
</bean>

<bean id="clinicDaoTarget"
    class="org.springframework.samples.petclinic.hibernate.HibernateClinic">
  <property name="sessionFactory">
    <ref bean="sessionFactory"/>
  </property>
</bean>

<bean id="clinicDao"
   class="org.springframework.transaction.interceptor.TransactionProxyFactoryBean">
  <property name="transactionManager">
    <ref bean="transactionManager"/>
  </property>
  <property name="target">
    <ref bean="clinicDaoTarget"/>
  </property>
  <property name="transactionAttributes">
    <props>
      <prop key="store*">PROPAGATION_REQUIRED</prop>
      <prop key="*">PROPAGATION_REQUIRED,readOnly</prop>
    </props>
  </property>
</bean>
```

Please refer to Chapter 6 for details on transaction proxy definitions. This configuration example uses Spring's `HibernateTransactionManager`, which is sufficient for accessing a single database via Hibernate.

JTA Synchronization

As outlined previously, Spring's `JtaTransactionManager` — Spring's `PlatformTransactionManager` implementation for JTA — works well with Hibernate, using Spring's own transaction synchronization facility to associate a Hibernate `Session` with each transaction. This is the recommended usage style for Spring on JTA: *Spring-driven transactions*, demarcated via the generic `TransactionTemplate` or `TransactionProxyFactoryBean`, with `JtaTransactionManager` as the backend strategy. No further configuration is necessary here; in particular, there is usually no need for JTA-related properties in Hibernate configuration.

As a special feature of Spring's Hibernate support, Hibernate `Sessions` can also be associated with *plain JTA transactions* or *EJB-driven transactions*, without Spring transaction demarcation being involved. (Essentially, such transactions are always managed by JTA underneath, even when demarcated via EJB CMT.) This allows the use of `HibernateTemplate`-based DAOs behind EJB facades (with EJB-demarcated transactions) or with plain JTA, still benefiting from transaction-scoped `Sessions` managed in the background by Spring's Hibernate integration.

> Spring's **HibernateTemplate** is able to synchronize with either Spring-driven transactions or JTA transactions, which includes EJB-driven transactions. A DAO that uses **HibernateTemplate** does not have to be modified or reconfigured for the actual strategy: It will automatically participate in whatever transaction it encounters.

Direct JTA synchronization will work only if the Hibernate `SessionFactory` is associated with a JTA `TransactionManager` (`javax.transaction.TransactionManager`). This requires a `TransactionManagerLookup` class specified in Hibernate configuration, which is specific to the application server (or the standalone JTA implementation). In contrast to the JTA `UserTransaction`, there is unfortunately no standard JNDI location for the JTA `TransactionManager`.

```
<bean id="sessionFactory"
    class="org.springframework.orm.hibernate.LocalSessionFactoryBean">
  <property name="dataSource">
    <ref bean="dataSource"/>
  </property>
  <property name="mappingLocations">
    <value>/WEB-INF/petclinic.hbm.xml</value>
  </property>
  <property name="hibernateProperties">
    <props>
      <prop key="hibernate.dialect">
        net.sf.hibernate.dialect.OracleDialect
      </prop>
      <prop key="hibernate.transaction.manager_lookup_class">
        net.sf.hibernate.transaction.WeblogicTransactionManagerLookup
      </prop>
    </props>
  </property>
</bean>
```

Alternatively, you can also specify the `javax.transaction.TransactionManager` as a bean reference, passing it into `LocalSessionFactoryBean`'s `jtaTransactionManager` property. The `TransactionManager` reference can be obtained from a server-specific JNDI location (for example, `"javax.transaction.TransactionManager"` in the case of WebLogic) or defined as a special Factory Bean (for example, `org.springframework.transaction.jta.WebSphereTransactionManagerFactoryBean`).

```
<bean id="jtaTransactionManager"
    class="org.springframework.jndi.JndiObjectFactoryBean">
  <property name="jndiName">
    <value>javax.transaction.TransactionManager</value>
  </property>
</bean>

<bean id="sessionFactory"
    class="org.springframework.orm.hibernate.LocalSessionFactoryBean">
  <property name="dataSource">
    <ref bean="dataSource"/>
  </property>
  <property name="jtaTransactionManager">
    <ref bean="jtaTransactionManager"/>
  </property>
  <property name="mappingLocations">
    <value>/WEB-INF/petclinic.hbm.xml</value>
  </property>
  <property name="hibernateProperties">
    <props>
      <prop key="hibernate.dialect">net.sf.hibernate.dialect.OracleDialect</prop>
    </props>
  </property>
</bean>
```

Such a `jtaTransactionManager` bean can, for example, be shared with Spring's `JtaTransactionManager` (the Spring's `PlatformTransactionManager` implementation for JTA), which needs the `javax.transaction.TransactionManager` reference to perform transaction suspension. This allows for setting up the special location of the JTA `TransactionManager` once and sharing it, rather than specifying it multiple times (once in Hibernate configuration, once as a Spring bean for other purposes).

Spring's `HibernateTemplate` will then automatically detect the JTA `TransactionManager` and register appropriate synchronizations for flushing and closing transaction-scoped Hibernate `Sessions` on transaction completion. Association of an individual Hibernate `Session` per transaction in case of suspended transactions will work too; usually, such suspension happens through EJB CMT (for example, with propagation code `REQUIRES_NEW`), as the JTA `UserTransaction` does not support transaction suspension.

Specifying the JTA `TransactionManager` for Hibernate is not necessary when solely using Spring-driven transactions; Spring's own transaction synchronization mechanism will then be used to properly close the Hibernate `Session` after completion. However, some J2EE servers are very strict in what kind of JDBC operations they allow after transaction completion. If encountering warnings in your log, specifying a `TransactionManagerLookup` will help, as it leads to internal JTA synchronization of the Hibernate `Session` itself (which should *never* interfere with the J2EE server's resource handling).

> With Spring-driven transactions, it is usually not necessary to specify JTA-related properties in Hibernate configuration, as Spring will automatically care for proper transaction completion (including correct handling of a transactional second-level cache). However, it might still add value to make Hibernate aware of the JTA `TransactionManager`, to avoid warnings on J2EE servers with strict transactional connection pools.

Session Lifecycle

Understanding the lifecycle of a Hibernate `Session` and the side effects of its behavior can be very important for tracking down problems in data access operations. While Spring does manage `Sessions` implicitly, with a variety of options, application code still needs to respect the side effects.

As discussed, Spring usually associates `Sessions` with transactions. Each transaction will use its own Hibernate `Session`. More specifically, each transaction will use *one transactional Hibernate `Session` per `SessionFactory`*, that is, one `Session` per target database. So in the case of a JTA transaction, multiple `Sessions` might be involved in a single transaction — one per `SessionFactory`.

A Hibernate `Session` effectively serves as a transactional cache for persistent objects. It holds references to all loaded objects in order to wire them correctly in case of bidirectional associations, and to check them for changes on transaction commit when *flushing* the `Session`. On flush, SQL statements will be issued to synchronize the in-memory state with the database state. A flush can also be triggered explicitly, to make other data access code see the changes within the same transaction. (This is particularly useful if it is necessary to mix Hibernate usage with JDBC queries.)

One Hibernate `Session` per transaction is usually a good fit. The `Session` will represent all objects loaded within the transaction, in a consistent fashion. At transaction completion, all changes will be flushed and committed in a single database transaction. In the case of a *transaction rollback*, the Hibernate `Session` will carry modifications that have been rolled back at the database level; this does not matter in case of a transaction-scoped `Session`, which will be closed at transaction completion.

The only common case to extend the `Session` lifecycle beyond the scope of a transaction is the Open Session in View pattern, discussed in its own section later in this chapter. In such a scenario, the Hibernate `Session` will not be closed at transaction completion; therefore, it needs to be cleared in case of a rollback, throwing away all modifications carried by the `Session`. Spring's transaction management will automatically perform such clearing when appropriate.

Reattachment and the Duplicate Object Problem

A common problem when using transaction-scoped `Sessions` is reattaching a persistent object to a new transaction via a `saveOrUpdate` operation, for example coming in from a web session where the object has been edited in a form. This needs to happen as early as possible in the transaction. Otherwise, Hibernate might complain that an object with the given ID has already been loaded in the current `Session` — the *duplicate object problem*. A Hibernate `Session` is a strict cache for persistent objects. It does not allow for replacing an existing persistent object with a different instance that represents the same persistent entity.

Note that `saveOrUpdate` actually serves two purposes. It can be used to reattach a persistent object to a new transaction, but also to persist a *new* instance for the first time. This is very convenient for typical use cases in a web application, where a form controller can often edit both existing and new instances, without special discrimination. A DAO operation can then simply call `saveOrUpdate` for a given instance, without explicit case handling for existing and new instances. Furthermore, `saveOrUpdate` will simply be ignored if the given instance is already attached to the current Hibernate `Session`; this allows for writing DAO store operations that will work both within and outside a transaction.

> When reattaching an object to a new transaction via `saveOrUpdate`, make sure that the operation happens as early as possible. In particular, don't perform other operations that might load a representation of the given persistent entity (for the given id) before — explicitly or implicitly.

Hibernate's `saveOrUpdateCopy` operation addresses the same problem through copying the state over if an object with the given ID already exists, instead of always reattaching the given instance itself. Unfortunately, in general it is not recommended to rely on `saveOrUpdateCopy`: Associated objects reached through cascading can still cause duplicate object exceptions.

HibernateInterceptor

A special feature for controlling the lifecycle of a Hibernate `Session` is `org.springframework.orm.hibernate.HibernateInterceptor`, which can be registered with an AOP proxy to open a Hibernate `Session` for the scope of a given method invocation. This is just necessary for special scenarios, though; in general, relying on transaction-scoped `Sessions` will be sufficient.

One possible use case for `HibernateInterceptor` is to enforce opening a Hibernate `Session` at the beginning of the transaction. The default behavior in a JTA environment is to register transactional resources on first access, for example in the case of JDBC `Connections`. It might sometimes be desirable to strictly enforce opening of a Hibernate `Session` at the beginning of a transaction, which can be configured as a `postInterceptor` on `TransactionProxyFactoryBean`:

```xml
<bean id="clinicDao"
  class="org.springframework.transaction.interceptor.TransactionProxyFactoryBean">
  <property name="transactionManager">
    <ref bean="transactionManager"/>
  </property>
  <property name="target">
    <ref bean="clinicDao"/>
  </property>
  <property name="transactionAttributes">
    <props>
      <prop key="store*">PROPAGATION_REQUIRED</prop>
      <prop key="*">PROPAGATION_REQUIRED,readOnly</prop>
    </props>
  </property>
  <property name="postInterceptors">
    <list>
      <bean class="org.springframework.orm.hibernate.HibernateInterceptor">
        <property name="sessionFactory">
          <ref bean="sessionFactory"/>
        </property>
      </bean>
    </list>
  </property>
</bean>
```

In the preceding code, HibernateInterceptor is registered as an unnamed inner bean. Of course, it could also be defined as a separate bean, with a bean reference pointing to it.

If a HibernateInterceptor is used to enforce early creation of a Hibernate Session, DAOs can be configured to rely on an existing Session rather than implicitly creating a new one if none is found. This also allows for direct Session access via Spring's org.springframework.orm.hibernate. SessionFactoryUtils class instead of HibernateTemplate. It is not necessary to worry about closing the Session in the DAO implementation in such a scenario, even outside a transaction. However, this is not recommended for typical scenarios, as it ties the DAO to HibernateInterceptor usage and still requires manual exception conversion.

See the section on DAO implementation earlier in the chapter; it gives an example for manual DAO implementations based on SessionFactoryUtils. When applying HibernateInterceptor, the finally block with the closeSessionIfNecessary call can be omitted; the rest of the DAO method implementation would remain. It is recommended that you specify false for getSession's allowCreate flag, though, as the code relies on an existing thread-bound Session now.

```
public class HibernateClinic implements Clinic {

  private SessionFactory sessionFactory;

  public void setSessionFactory(SessionFactory sessionFactory) {
    this.sessionFactory = sessionFactory;
  }

  public Collection getVets() throws DataAccessException {
    Session session = SessionFactoryUtils.getSession(this.sessionFactory, false);
    try {
      return session.find("from Vet vet order by vet.lastName, vet.firstName");
    }
    catch (HibernateException ex) {
      throw SessionFactoryUtils.convertHibernateAccessException(ex);
    }
  }

  ...

}
```

Open Session in View

As outlined earlier, lazy loading will just work as long as the Hibernate Session that originally loaded the persistent object is still open. In the case of a transaction-scoped Session, this means that lazy loading will work only until transaction completion. While it is generally advisable to perform data access within transactions, one major use case requires lazy loading outside transactions: model access in web views.

In classic web MVC, a controller prepares model attributes, for example fetching them from the DAO layer, and exposes them to a view. The view in turn renders the given model attributes, displaying parts of their state. In the case of persistent domain objects with lazy loading, certain associations might not have been loaded until rendering happens. Unfortunately, lazy loading won't work in such a scenario if the original transaction has already ended and thus closed the Hibernate Session that loaded the given persistent object.

One solution for the problem would be to process the entire HTTP request, including view rendering, within a single transaction. However, such a solution is not ideal: It would hold database locks until view rendering has been completed, which is dependent on the client and network speed. In the case of a large HTML page as result, this can take dozens of seconds. Keeping transactions open for such a long time increases contention and wastes resources, so this is not a recommended strategy.

The common solution is the Open Session in View pattern. Transactions end in the service layer, but the associated Hibernate `Session` remains open until view rendering has been completed. This releases database locks early but still allows for lazy loading in the view. Spring supports this pattern out of the box, via `org.springframework.orm.hibernate.support.OpenSessionInViewFilter` (for use with any web tier) or `OpenSessionInViewInterceptor` (for use with Spring's web MVC framework).

Single Session Versus Deferred Close

`OpenSessionInViewFilter` and its companion feature two modes of operation: *single session* mode and *deferred close* mode. In single session mode, a single Hibernate `Session` will be used for the entire HTTP request, with transactions operating on the request-scoped `Session`. In deferred close mode, each transaction will use its own `Session` as usual, but each of those `Sessions` will be kept open after transaction completion, to be closed when view rendering has completed.

Single session mode, which is the default, is the most efficient version of the Open Session in View pattern. The request-scoped Hibernate `Session` serves as first-level cache, loading each persistent object only once within the entire request. The main disadvantage is that all objects managed by that `Session` are required to be unique. As discussed in the "Session Lifecycle" section, Hibernate insists on all persistent objects being unique in a `Session`, which can lead to duplicate object exceptions when trying to reattach an object from the `HttpSession` (for example, when storing the result of a form workflow).

In deferred close mode, the duplicate object problem is avoided by using a fresh Hibernate `Session` for each transaction. All such `Sessions` are kept open until view rendering has been completed, to allow for lazy loading on each of them. Unfortunately, this can lead to problems if a single persistent object becomes involved in multiple transactions; Hibernate requires persistent objects (more specifically, their managed collections) to be associated with a specific Hibernate `Session`, not with two `Sessions` at the same time. In such a scenario, single session mode is usually preferable.

> In general, try using single session mode first, in particular if the reattaching of persistent objects is not likely to conflict with other data access operations in the same request. If you encounter issues with your use of Open Session in View in single session mode, consider switching to deferred close mode.

It might also be worthwhile to consider avoiding the Open Session in View pattern in the first place. As long as all your lazy associations get initialized within the original transaction, there is no need to actually perform lazy loading in your views. Unfortunately, such pre-loading of all required associations is often fragile; depending on view state, different associations might need to be loaded, imposing knowledge about view state onto the controller. In many applications, it will be more natural and more convenient to allow arbitrary lazy loading through the Open Session in View pattern.

Configuration Examples

The OpenSessionInViewFilter must to be set up in web.xml as a standard Servlet 2.3 filter. The following configuration will apply it to all requests with a URL path that ends with .do:

```xml
<filter>
  <filter-name>OpenSessionInView</filter-name>
  <filter-class>
    org.springframework.orm.hibernate.support.OpenSessionInViewFilter
  </filter-class>
</filter>

<filter-mapping>
  <filter-name>OpenSessionInView</filter-name>
  <url-pattern>*.do</url-pattern>
</filter-mapping>
```

The filter needs to be able to access the Hibernate SessionFactory, by default, as a bean in the Spring root web application context (where middle tier resources usually reside). The default bean name is sessionFactory; this can be customized through a sessionFactoryBeanName init-param in web.xml.

By default, the filter will operate in single session mode. To configure it for deferred close mode, specify the singleSession init-param as false:

```xml
<filter>
  <filter-name>OpenSessionInView</filter-name>
  <filter-class>
    org.springframework.orm.hibernate.support.OpenSessionInViewFilter
  </filter-class>
  <init-param>
    <param-name>singleSession</param-name>
    <param-value>false</param-value>
  </init-param>
</filter>
```

OpenSessionInViewInterceptor is a HandlerInterceptor for Spring's web MVC, to be registered with a Spring HandlerMapping in a DispatcherServlet context (see Chapter 12 for a discussion of Spring's web MVC):

```xml
<bean id="openSessionInView"
    class="org.springframework.orm.hibernate.support.OpenSessionInViewInterceptor">
  <property name="sessionFactory">
    <ref bean="sessionFactory"/>
  </property>
</bean>

<bean id="myUrlMapping"
    class="org.springframework.web.servlet.handler.SimpleUrlHandlerMapping">
  <property name="interceptors">
    <list>
      <ref bean="openSessionInView"/>
    </list>
  </property>
```

```
        <property name="urlMap">
          <map>
            <entry key="/myUrlPath"><ref bean="myController"/></entry>
          </map>
        </property>
      </bean>
```

The `SessionFactory` is passed in as a bean reference here because a `HandlerInterceptor` can be configured as bean. As the `DispatcherServlet` context is usually a child of the root web application context, a `SessionFactory` bean defined there is visible and can be referenced directly.

As with the filter, the interceptor is by default in single session mode. To configure it for deferred close mode, specify the `singleSession` bean property as `false`:

```
<bean id="openSessionInView"
     class="org.springframework.orm.hibernate.support.OpenSessionInViewInterceptor">
    <property name="sessionFactory">
      <ref bean="sessionFactory"/>
    </property>
    <property name="singleSession">
      <value>false</value>
    </property>
</bean>
```

BLOB/CLOB Handling

Spring ships with several Hibernate `UserType` implementations that map BLOB or CLOB fields in the database to a variety of target property types in persistent classes:

- ❑ `org.springframework.orm.hibernate.support.ClobStringType`: Mapping a CLOB field in the database to a String property in the persistent class

- ❑ `org.springframework.orm.hibernate.support.BlobByteArrayType`: Mapping a BLOB field in the database to a byte array property in the persistent class

- ❑ `org.springframework.orm.hibernate.support.BlobSerializableType`: Mapping a BLOB field in the database to a serializable object property in the persistent class

While Hibernate can, in principle, map BLOBs and CLOBs out of the box, it can do so only with the standard JDBC API. Unfortunately, this has severe limitations on some databases — for example, on Oracle 9i with the Oracle 9i thin driver. For full BLOB and CLOB usage with unlimited content size, native Oracle API has to be used. To allow for handling BLOBs and CLOBs in such database-specific fashions too, the Spring-provided `UserTypes` delegate to a Spring-managed `LobHandler` — an abstraction that allows for multiple implementations. Two `LobHandlers` are provided out of the box:

- ❑ `org.springframework.jdbc.support.lob.DefaultLobHandler`: Delegating to standard JDBC API. Known to work with, for example, MySQL, DB2, MS SQL Server, and Oracle 10g.

- ❑ `org.springframework.jdbc.support.lob.OracleLobHandler`: Delegating to Oracle-specific LOB handling API. Necessary for Oracle 9i; with Oracle 10g, `DefaultLobHandler` will work, too.

See Chapter 5 for a discussion of Spring's `LobHandler` abstraction in the context of JDBC.

All of the Spring-provided LOB `UserTypes` depend on a `LobHandler` being specified on `LocalSessionFactoryBean`. On initialization, each `UserType` object will fetch the `LobHandler` from there:

```
<bean id="lobHandler
    class="org.springframework.jdbc.support.lob.OracleLobHandler"/>

<bean id="sessionFactory"
    class="org.springframework.orm.hibernate.LocalSessionFactoryBean">
  <property name="dataSource">
    <ref bean="dataSource"/>
  </property>
  <property name="lobHandler">
    <ref bean="lobHandler"/>
  </property>
  <property name="mappingLocations">
    <value>/WEB-INF/petclinic.hbm.xml</value>
  </property>
  <property name="hibernateProperties">
    <props>
      <prop key="hibernate.dialect">net.sf.hibernate.dialect.OracleDialect</prop>
    </props>
  </property>
</bean>
```

Additionally, all LOB `UserTypes` depend on being executed within transactions when modifying LOBs, to be able to synchronize the closing of temporary LOBs (if any) with transaction completion. This applies to both writing to LOBs and reading from LOBs. It is not strictly necessary to perform a full database transaction ("`PROPAGATION_REQUIRED`") for this: A Spring-demarcated transaction with "`PROPAGATION_SUPPORTS`" is sufficient, as it offers transaction synchronization even without an existing full database transaction.

If not used with Spring-driven transactions but rather with plain JTA transactions or EJB-driven transactions, the JTA `TransactionManager` needs to be specified on `LocalSessionFactoryBean`. This is the same setting that is necessary for direct JTA synchronization of Hibernate `Sessions` (see the "JTA Synchronization" section earlier in the chapter).

```
<bean id="sessionFactory"
    class="org.springframework.orm.hibernate.LocalSessionFactoryBean">
  <property name="dataSource">
    <ref bean="dataSource"/>
  </property>
  <property name="jtaTransactionManager">
    <ref bean="jtaTransactionManager"/>
  </property>
  <property name="lobHandler">
    <ref bean="lobHandler"/>
  </property>
  <property name="mappingLocations">
    <value>/WEB-INF/petclinic.hbm.xml</value>
```

```
        </property>
        <property name="hibernateProperties">
          <props>
            <prop key="hibernate.dialect">net.sf.hibernate.dialect.OracleDialect</prop>
          </props>
        </property>
      </bean>
```

As with the synchronization of Hibernate `Sessions`, `UserTypes` will automatically adapt to any kind of transaction that they encounter: If Spring's transaction synchronization is active, it will be used; otherwise, direct JTA synchronization will apply.

Hibernate: Summary

Hibernate is a full-fledged O/R mapping tool. Its excellent query facilities are intuitive and convenient. Its lenient lifecycle requirements for persistent objects make it particularly suitable for working with detached objects: in particular, for use in web applications. Portability across databases is impressive: Specifying the correct database dialect is usually all that is necessary.

Hibernate is particularly well-suited for complex domain models with many associations, where convenient querying and automatic change detection show their full benefits. It does incur a certain level of complexity, however, because of the semantics of a Hibernate `Session`: for example, on reassociation of a persistent object with a new transaction. For lazy loading, the `Session` lifecycle needs to be regarded too, for example, through applying Spring's `OpenSessionInViewFilter` in a web environment.

Hibernate was the first third-party persistence tool supported in Spring; the Hibernate support has been heavily battle-tested and refined. The main facilities that Spring offers are:

❑ `org.springframework.orm.hibernate.HibernateTemplate`: A data access class used in DAOs, seamlessly handling Hibernate `Sessions` in the background. Automatically participates in both Spring-driven and EJB-driven transactions. Converts the checked `HibernateException` into Spring's generic `DataAccessException` hierarchy.

❑ `org.springframework.orm.hibernate.LocalSessionFactoryBean`: A convenient way of setting up a local Hibernate `SessionFactory` in a Spring context. `SessionFactory` references can then be passed to DAOs, typically via Spring bean references.

❑ `org.springframework.orm.hibernate.HibernateTransactionManager`: A local transaction strategy, executing transactions on a single target `SessionFactory`. This strategy works in any environment, in contrast to `JtaTransactionManager`, which depends on a J2EE server (or a standalone JTA implementation).

❑ `org.springframework.orm.hibernate.support.HibernateDaoSupport`: A convenient base class for DAO implementations, taking a `SessionFactory` reference and providing a `HibernateTemplate` instance for it.

❑ `org.springframework.orm.hibernate.support.OpenSessionInViewFilter` and `org.springframework.orm.hibernate.support.OpenSessionInViewInterceptor`: A Servlet 2.3 `Filter` and a `HandlerInterceptor` for Spring's web MVC framework, respectively, providing the Open Session in View pattern for Hibernate. Supports two different modes: single session mode and deferred close mode.

❑ org.springframework.orm.hibernate.support.ClobStringType, org.springframework
.orm.hibernate.support.BlobByteArrayType, and org.springframework.orm
.hibernate.support.BlobSerializableType: Hibernate UserType implementations that
delegate to Spring's LobHandler abstraction. Allow for mapping LOB values to properties of
persistent classes, even when database-specific LOB handling is necessary (for example, on
Oracle 9i).

Mixing Hibernate access code with other data access strategies is as straightforward as possible, as long
as all of them access the same JDBC DataSource. Spring's HibernateTransactionManager automatically exposes its transactions to JDBC-based access code. Consequently, adding Spring JDBC or iBATIS
SQL Maps to the mix is easy: for example, for BLOB/CLOB or stored procedure access, or for read-only
reference data.

> **Hibernate is an excellent option for full-fledged O/R mapping. Its greatest
> strengths are the powerful mapping facilities and the SQL-style query language.
> Its disadvantages are mainly drawbacks of full-fledged O/R mapping in general:
> the complexity of automatic change detection, and stricter requirements for lazy load-
> ing. Furthermore, it is not ideally suited for legacy data models or over-normalized
> data models: Spring JDBC and iBATIS SQL Maps are usually better options in such
> scenarios.**

There are many compelling benefits in using Hibernate in conjunction with Spring, rather than alone.
Three major benefits are the elimination of the need for custom resource management code like implementation of thread local session management; the reduced lock in to the Hibernate API, which results
from placing Hibernate usage in the context of Spring's overall data access abstraction; and increased
overall architectural clarity. If you've used Hibernate extensively in the past, you will probably have
noticed these and other benefits already.

JDO

Java Data Objects (JDO) is not strictly a specification for O/R mapping but rather for *general object persistence*, covering any kind of backend data store, among them relational databases and object-oriented
databases. Nevertheless, most JDO implementations do primarily target relational databases and can
thus be classified as O/R mapping solutions.

JDO 2.0 builds on JDO 1.0, adding two important features: *support for detached objects* and *dedicated support for O/R mapping*. Detaching and reattaching objects is a very typical use case in web applications,
which the JDO 1.0 API did not properly allow for (in contrast to other persistence solutions such as
iBATIS SQL Maps and Hibernate). JDO implementations that access relational databases can support a
variety of optional O/R mapping features, among those a common metadata format for mapping files.

JDOQL is a pure object query language in the tradition of ODMG's *OQL*, using a Java query API and
Java-based criteria strings. The query facilities will become significantly extended in JDO 2.0, for example introducing textual queries as alternative style. Many current JDO implementations already support
query extensions, mainly for access to relational databases.

JDO 1.0 implementations perform change detection in persistent objects through enhancing their byte code to make them implement the `javax.jdo.PersistenceCapable` interface. The byte code enhancer needs to be run as part of the application's build process. An enhanced class informs the JDO `StateManager` of any changes to its instance fields within a transaction; JDO always works with the instance fields, never with JavaBean property setters or getters. At transaction commit, the JDO `PersistenceManager` will flush the changes to the database, synchronizing the in-memory state with the database state.

JDO 2.0 downgrades byte code enhancement to one implementation option, removing the requirement for binary compatibility. JDO 2.0 implementations will then be free to choose any other strategy for change detection, such as snapshot comparisons as used by Hibernate and TopLink.

For further information on JDO's design and the current state of JDO, see `www.jdocentral.com`, the official online portal for JDO, which is backed by a large community of JDO vendors and affiliates.

Persistent Object Lifecycle

The most important characteristic of JDO is the strict lifecycle for persistent objects. By default, a persistent object will work only within an active JDO `PersistenceManager`; its instance fields will throw exceptions when accessed after the `PersistenceManager` has been closed. Furthermore, changes to persistent objects can be made only within a JDO transaction; there is no concept of non-transactional modifications. While this allows for very efficient change detection — essentially, every persistent field will notify the JDO `StateManager` of changes, rather than JDO looking for changed fields — it significantly restricts usage styles.

To work with persistent objects outside of an active JDO connection, they need to be made *transient* (JDO 1.0) or *detached* (JDO 2.0) — usually an explicit step. A transient instance has lost its persistent identity, so can never be persisted again; this is the reason why JDO 2.0 introduces the concept of *detachment* and *reattachment*, allowing modification of objects outside of the JDO `PersistenceManager` that loaded them and then persist them in a new transaction (which is a typical use case in a web application).

Further options discussed for JDO 2.0 are *auto-detach-on-close* and *auto-detach-on-serialization*, which aim to remove the burden of explicit detachment. It is still unclear whether either or both of those will be part of the specification; certain JDO implementations already support such options as vendor-specific extensions. Persistent objects will then work in a managed fashion within a `PersistenceManager`, while still being usable outside of the `PersistenceManager` — containing a copy of their current state, without immediate change detection. This is similar to Hibernate's lenient lifecycle, where objects seamlessly turn into a non-managed state as soon as the Hibernate `Session` is closed.

Unlike managed persistent instances, detached objects can be modified outside an active `PersistenceManager` and thus outside a JDO transaction. This will usually happen in a form workflow: for example, in a web application or in a rich client. Such an object will then be passed back into the persistence layer again, getting *reattached to a new JDO transaction*, which will persist the current state as contained in the given instance. This corresponds to a `saveOrUpdate` operation in Hibernate.

Later, we will discuss a further area affected by the JDO lifecycle model: lazy loading.

DAO Implementation

Traditional JDO usage involves a resource factory, `javax.jdo.PersistenceManagerFactory`, which is used to open a single-threaded resource, `javax.jdo.PersistenceManager`, for each transaction or sequence of operations. This is roughly analogous to a Hibernate `SessionFactory` and a Hibernate `Session`, respectively; in many respects, Spring's support for Hibernate and JDO is very similar in this area.

In a Spring environment, provided convenience classes remove the burden of resource management from the application developer. Most importantly, JDO `PersistenceManagers` will automatically be synchronized with Spring transactions. In other respects, the usual conventions apply: DAO operations will throw Spring's generic `DataAccessException`, and DAOs are usually set up as beans in a Spring context.

The template class for data access operations is `org.springframework.orm.jdo.JdoTemplate`, working with JDO's `PersistenceManager` API underneath. It is typically used through the base class `org.springframework.orm.jdo.support.JdoDaoSupport`, which takes a JDO `PersistenceManagerFactory` instance as bean property and provides a `JdoTemplate` instance for it. (This is not a requirement, though: `JdoTemplate` can also be instantiated directly, just like `HibernateTemplate`.)

For example, the following is a rough version of a JDO-based implementation of PetClinic's DAO:

```
public class JdoClinic extends JdoDaoSupport implements Clinic {

    public Collection getVets() throws DataAccessException {
      return getJdoTemplate().find(
          Vet.class, null, "lastName ascending, firstName ascending");
    }

    public Collection getPetTypes() throws DataAccessException {
      return getJdoTemplate().find(PetType.class, null, "name ascending");
    }

    public Collection findOwners(String lastName) throws DataAccessException {
      return getJdoTemplate().find(
          Owner.class, "lastName == value", "String value", new Object[] {value});
    }

    ...
}
```

As in the case of iBATIS and Hibernate, the provided convenience base class can easily be avoided: The implementation could implement its own `setPersistenceManagerFactory` method, preferably creating a shared `JdoTemplate` instance for the DAO.

Alternatively, a DAO implementation could also use the provided `PersistenceManagerFactory` instance directly, without Spring's `JdoTemplate`. However, this would involve manual handling of JDO `PersistenceManagers`, manual exception translation, and manual synchronization with Spring transactions; therefore, it is usually advisable to stick with `JdoTemplate`. If necessary, helpers for manual DAO implementations can be found in the `org.springframework.orm.jdo.PersistenceManagerFactoryUtils` class.

The operations defined on `JdoTemplate` basically correspond to operations on `javax.jdo.PersistenceManager`, however throwing Spring's `DataAccessException` rather than

`JDOException`, and participating in Spring-managed transactions (if any). Please refer to the JDO specification for details on the semantics of those operations. Note that `JdoTemplate` defines a variety of convenient `find` methods that are not directly available on a plain JDO `PersistenceManager`. In plain JDO, you always need to go through the JDOQL API.

As an alternative to invoking such operations on `JdoTemplate` itself, there is the option to implement an `org.springframework.orm.jdo.JdoCallback` that works directly on a given JDO `PersistenceManager` resource, via `JdoTemplate`'s generic `execute` method. This is rarely necessary for typical one-line operations; however, complex JDO queries or processing operations should be implemented in a `JdoCallback`, in particular if they depend on getting executed on the same JDO `PersistenceManager`.

Like Hibernate, JDO has a special requirement for lazy loading. The JDO `PersistenceManager` that originally loaded the affected persistent objects needs to still be open to make lazy loading work. As `JdoTemplate` by default closes the JDO `PersistenceManager` at the end of each operation, returned objects are *not* capable of lazy loading. It is recommended that you execute such operations within transactions, which will keep the same JDO `PersistenceManager` open for the lifetime of the entire transaction. If you need lazy loading beyond the scope of your transactions, for example in web views, you need to resort to the Open PersistenceManager in View pattern (as described in detail in the "Open PersistenceManager in View" section).

All such a DAO needs to be able to work is a JDO `PersistenceManagerFactory` instance via the `setPersistenceManagerFactory` method. In the next section, you will see how to set up such an instance in a Spring context.

Setup in a Spring Context

In a Spring application context, a JDO implementation is usually set up via Spring's `LocalPersistenceManagerFactoryBean`, getting configured via specified *JDO properties*. The following is an example for the open source JDO implementation JPOX:

```
<bean id="persistenceManagerFactory"
    class="org.springframework.orm.jdo.LocalPersistenceManagerFactoryBean">
  <property name="jdoProperties">
    <props>
      <prop key="javax.jdo.PersistenceManagerFactoryClass">
        org.jpox.PersistenceManagerFactoryImpl
      </prop>
      <prop key="javax.jdo.option.ConnectionDriverName">
        com.mysql.jdbc.Driver
      </prop>
      <prop key="javax.jdo.option.ConnectionURL">...</prop>
      <prop key="javax.jdo.option.NontransactionalRead">true</prop>
    </props>
  </property>
</bean>
```

Alternatively, you can also use a standard `jdo.properties` file to configure your `PersistenceManagerFactory`, specifying the location as `configLocation`. Such file-based properties could also be mixed with `LocalPersistenceManagerFactoryBean` properties, with the latter taking precedence.

```
<bean id="persistenceManagerFactory"
    class="org.springframework.orm.jdo.LocalPersistenceManagerFactoryBean">
  <property name="configLocation">
    <value>classpath:jdo.properties</value>
  </property>
</bean>
```

An advantage of defining properties in the Spring context is that you can use placeholders
for certain properties, linking in values from configuration properties files (via Spring's
PropertyPlaceholderConfigurer mechanism, see Chapter 2). So even when loading
configuration from a jdo.properties file, it is advisable to define such administrative properties
on LocalPersistenceManagerFactoryBean in the Spring context.

A different configuration style is to set up the PersistenceManagerFactory implementation class *itself*
as a Spring bean. JDO properties can usually be applied as bean properties, using the equivalent bean
property names (which can be checked in the javadoc of your JDO implementation). Furthermore, it is
usually possible to specify a Spring-managed JDBC DataSource as a JDO connection factory, which is
important if you want to share a DataSource for both JDO and JDBC access code. Here's an example,
again using JPOX:

```
<bean id="persistenceManagerFactory"
    class="org.jpox.PersistenceManagerFactoryImpl">
  <property name="connectionFactory">
    <ref bean="dataSource"/>
  </property>
  <property name="nontransactionalRead">
    <value>true</value>
  </property>
</bean>
```

Such a PersistenceManagerFactory implementation instance is a direct replacement for a
LocalPersistenceManagerFactoryBean definition. These are simply two different ways to set up
a JDO PersistenceManagerFactory, which can be chosen according to configuration requirements
and the JDO implementation used.

For special setup requirements, it might also be necessary to use a custom subclass of
LocalPersistenceManagerFactoryBean, overriding the newPersistenceManagerFactory
method with vendor-specific instantiation code. This can be used to pass in a Spring-managed JDBC
DataSource even with properties-driven PersistenceManagerFactory configuration, for example.

Most JDO implementations also provide a JCA connector, just like Hibernate does. As with
Hibernate, it is usually not necessary to use the JCA connector for JTA integration; a locally defined
PersistenceManagerFactory with a properly configured JTA transaction manager lookup is often
sufficient. See "Setup as JCA Connector" earlier in this chapter for a discussion of the value of a JCA
connector in the context of O/R mapping.

The DAO can now receive a reference to the JDO PersistenceManagerFactory instance via a Spring
bean reference, just as a JDBC-based DAO receives a reference to a JDBC DataSource.

```
<bean id="clinicDao"
    class="org.springframework.samples.petclinic.jdo.JdoClinic">
```

```
    <property name="persistenceManagerFactory">
      <ref bean="persistenceManagerFactory"/>
    </property>
  </bean>
```

Whether the `persistenceManagerFactory` property, corresponding to the `setPersistenceManagerFactory` method, is defined by the provided `JdoDaoSupport` base class or implemented by the DAO class itself is not relevant here. The same configuration would work in both scenarios.

Transaction Management

While the JDO `PersistenceManager` API does provide its own means for transaction handling, this is typically not used in a Spring environment. Rather, transaction management is delegated to Spring's generic transaction facilities, with the generic `TransactionTemplate` or `TransactionProxyFactoryBean` used for demarcation (see Chapter 6 for details on Spring transaction management).

The following choices are available as backend transaction strategies for JDO:

❑   `org.springframework.orm.jdo.JdoTransactionManager`: Allows transaction execution on a single JDO `PersistenceManagerFactory`, working on a single target database, using native JDO facilities. JDO-based DAOs can seamlessly participate in such transactions. This strategy is usually sufficient as long as there is no need for transactions that span multiple transactional resources.

❑   `org.springframework.transaction.jta.JtaTransactionManager`: Delegates transaction execution to a JTA implementation, that is, to a J2EE server's JTA subsystem or a local JTA instance like ObjectWeb's JOTM. The JDO instance needs to be properly configured for JTA, which is vendor-specific. This strategy allows transactions to span and be coordinated across multiple transactional resources, for example multiple database systems.

In both cases, JDO `PersistenceManagers` will automatically be associated with transactions: one JDO `PersistenceManager` for the entire scope of a transaction. Data access code will automatically receive the transactional `PersistenceManager` if executing within a transaction; otherwise, a short-lived `PersistenceManager` will be opened for each operation. The only exception to this rule is when applying the Open PersistenceManager in View pattern (as described in the upcoming "Open PersistenceManager in View" section).

In case of suspended transactions, each transaction will be associated with its own JDO `PersistenceManager`. So when a new inner transaction is starting, the JDO `PersistenceManager` of the outer transaction will be suspended and a new one will be created. On completion of the inner transaction, the inner JDO `PersistenceManager` will be closed and the outer one will be resumed. This will work with both `JdoTransactionManager` and `JtaTransactionManager`, leveraging Spring's transaction synchronization mechanism.

Note that there is no support for direct JTA synchronization in Spring's JDO infrastructure. To benefit from transaction-scoped `PersistenceManagers`, you need to use Spring-driven transactions; plain JTA transactions or EJB-driven transactions are *not* sufficient, in contrast to Spring's Hibernate synchronization.

> If there is a need to perform transactions across multiple resources, choose
> `JtaTransactionManager`, which delegates to the J2EE server's JTA subsystem (or
> a local JTA instance such as JOTM). However, for transactions on a single target
> database, `JdoTransactionManager` is perfectly sufficient — and will work in any
> environment, be it a J2EE web application, a standalone application, or a test suite.

PersistenceManager Lifecycle

As discussed, Spring always associates `PersistenceManagers` with transactions. Each transaction will use its own JDO `PersistenceManager`. More specifically, each transaction will use one transactional JDO `PersistenceManager` per `PersistenceManagerFactory`: that is, one per target database. So in the case of a JTA transaction, multiple `PersistenceManagers` might be involved in a single transaction — one per `PersistenceManagerFactory`.

Like a Hibernate `Session`, a JDO `PersistenceManager` effectively serves as transactional cache for persistent objects. It manages all loaded objects, to be able to wire them correctly in case of bidirectional associations, and to get notified of changes to persistent fields. On flush, SQL statements will be issued to synchronize the in-memory state with the database state. In JDO 2.0, a flush can also be triggered explicitly, to make other data access code see the changes within the same transaction.

One JDO `PersistenceManager` per transaction is usually a good fit. The `PersistenceManager` will represent all objects loaded within the transaction, in a consistent fashion. At transaction completion, all changes will be flushed and committed in a single database transaction. In the case of a transaction roll-back, the JDO `PersistenceManager` will still be consistent, because it will have rolled back the state of the in-memory objects too; this is different from Hibernate, where a rollback does not reset the state of persistent objects.

At the time of this writing, the semantics of detaching and reattaching have not been fully clarified yet, as the JDO 2.0 specification is still in the draft phase. The current semantics of the `reattach` operation are different to Hibernate's `saveOrUpdate` operation in some respects, though. Most importantly, `reattach` cannot be used for persisting new instances; `makePersistent` needs to be used for that. Furthermore, `reattach` will fail if the instance is already associated with the current `PersistenceManager`; DAO operations need explicit checks for that case. The `reattach` operation is strictly meant for reattachment of existing instances that have been detached before, in contrast to Hibernate's more lenient `saveOrUpdate`.

> While JDO 2.0's reattach operation appears superficially similar to Hibernate's
> `saveOrUpdate`, it behaves quite differently in the details. JDO-based DAOs need to
> be written more carefully to support all possible scenarios.

For special use cases, Spring provides `org.springframework.orm.jdo.JdoInterceptor`, analogous to `HibernateInterceptor` as discussed in the "Hibernate" section of this chapter. Usage of the `JdoInterceptor` allows the lifecycle of a JDO `PersistenceManager` to be tied to the scope of a method invocation on an AOP proxy. This can, for example, be used to enforce opening of a `PersistenceManager` at the beginning of a JTA transaction, instead of relying on automatic registration of a transactional `PersistenceManager` on first access. See the discussion of `HibernateInterceptor` for a configuration example; setting up and using a `JdoInterceptor` is analogous.

Open PersistenceManager in View

As with Hibernate, Spring supports the Open PersistenceManager in View pattern for JDO. Transactions end in the service layer, but the associated JDO `PersistenceManager` remains open until view rendering has been completed. This releases database locks early but still allows for lazy loading in the view. Spring supports this pattern out of the box, via `org.springframework.orm.jdo.support.OpenPersistenceManagerInViewFilter` (for use with any web tier) or `OpenPersistenceManagerInViewInterceptor` (for use with Spring's web MVC framework).

In principle, the usage patterns of `OpenPersistenceManagerInViewFilter` are similar to `OpenSessionInViewFilter` for Hibernate. JDO has the advantage that a `PersistenceManager` and the objects that it loaded do not become inconsistent in case of a transaction rollback, which effectively removes part of the need for a "deferred close" mode — if lazy loading is required, a single `PersistenceManager` per request is usually appropriate.

However, a single `PersistenceManager` being open for an entire request and being used for multiple transactions does incur side effects on detachment and reattachment, in particular on *auto-detach-on-close*, which unfortunately affect typical usage patterns in web MVC:

- ❑ With transaction-scoped `PersistenceManagers`, auto-detachment would happen on transaction completion. So one could load an object first, modify it outside a transaction (for example populating it with HTTP request parameters), and reattach it to a new transaction.

- ❑ With a single `PersistenceManager` for the entire request, auto-detachment will not happen during the request, so the object stays managed by the `PersistenceManager` — not allowing modifications outside a transaction. Even if the reattach operation accepted already attached objects too, all changes made in the meantime would get lost. This breaks such typical usage models in web MVC.

The only solutions for such a scenario are to either avoid a single PersistenceManager per request in the first place — loading all required data within transactions rather than relying on lazy loading — or to *explicitly detach* all objects to be modified outside a transaction (rather than rely on *auto-detach-on-close*). JDO's strict requirement for modifications to happen within a transaction restricts convenient usage models here.

Deferred close would cause even more severe issues with managed persistent objects. Every persistent instance needs to be registered with at most one `PersistenceManager` at any time. In Hibernate, this affects only managed collections; in JDO, all persistent instances are affected. As each `PersistenceManager` remains open when using deferred close, no auto-detachment would happen, which effectively does not allow any persistent object to be reattached to another transaction — unless having been explicitly detached before.

> The Open PersistenceManager in View pattern involves different tradeoffs in JDO than the corresponding Open Session in View pattern does in Hibernate. On the one hand, JDO avoids inconsistencies in loaded state; on the other hand, it does not allow modifications outside transactions, which effectively breaks typical usage models in web MVC. The exact tradeoffs depend on the final semantics of the JDO 2.0 specification, or on any vendor-specific auto-detachment features you might choose to use.

Configuration Examples

`OpenPersistenceManagerInViewFilter` needs to be set up in `web.xml` as a standard Servlet 2.3 Filter. The following configuration will apply it to all requests with a URL path that ends with `.do`:

```
<filter>
  <filter-name>OpenPersistenceManagerInView</filter-name>
  <filter-class>
    org.springframework.orm.jdo.support.OpenPersistenceManagerInViewFilter
  </filter-class>
</filter>

<filter-mapping>
  <filter-name>OpenPersistenceManagerInView</filter-name>
  <url-pattern>*.do</url-pattern>
</filter-mapping>
```

The filter needs to be able to access the JDO `PersistenceManagerFactory` by default as a bean in the Spring root web application context (where middle tier resources usually reside). The default bean name is `persistenceManagerFactory`; this can be customized through a `persistenceManagerFactoryBeanName` init-param in `web.xml`.

`OpenPersistenceManagerInViewInterceptor` is a `HandlerInterceptor` for Spring's web MVC, to be registered with a Spring `HandlerMapping` in a `DispatcherServlet` context (see Chapter 12 for a discussion of Spring's web MVC):

```
<bean id="openPersistenceManagerInView" class=
    "org.springframework.orm.jdo.support.OpenPersistenceManagerInViewInterceptor">
  <property name="persistenceManagerFactory">
    <ref bean="persistenceManagerFactory"/>
  </property>
</bean>

<bean id="myUrlMapping"
    class="org.springframework.web.servlet.handler.SimpleUrlHandlerMapping">
  <property name="interceptors">
    <list>
      <ref bean="openPersistenceManagerInView"/>
    </list>
  </property>
  <property name="urlMap">
    <map>
      <entry key="/myUrlPath"><ref bean="myController"/></entry>
```

```
        </map>
      </property>
    </bean>
```

The `PersistenceManagerFactory` is passed in as a bean reference here because a `HandlerInterceptor` can be configured as bean. As the `DispatcherServlet` context is usually a child of the root web application context, a `PersistenceManagerFactory` bean defined there is visible and can be referenced directly.

JDO Dialect

`JdoTransactionManager` and `JdoTemplate` support certain advanced features that are not covered by the JDO 1.0 specification, namely:

❑ Applying a **transaction isolation level** and/or a **transaction timeout** — as specified by a Spring transaction definition — to a native JDO transaction.

❑ Access to the **underlying JDBC Connection** of a `PersistenceManager`, to let JDBC access code participate in JDO-managed transactions (working on the same JDBC `Connection`).

❑ Eager **flushing of a JDO transaction**, to make changes visible to JDBC access code within the same transaction (through issuing corresponding SQL statements).

❑ Sophisticated **exception translation**, from `JDOException` to Spring's `DataAccessException` hierarchy. Standard JDO exceptions allow only for limited sophistication in that respect.

Spring handles those features via the `org.springframework.orm.jdo.JdoDialect` SPI, an interface to be implemented for specific JDO vendors, supporting one or more of those features via vendor-specific API. The default implementation, `org.springframework.orm.jdo.DefaultJdoDialect`, simply throws appropriate exceptions when extended functionality is requested. Vendor-specific `JdoDialects` can be derived from that base class, using it as a convenient adapter for the `JdoDialect` interface.

`DefaultJdoDialect` implements exception translation through some standard `JDOException` checks, plus a detection of nested SQLExceptions, which will get translated through a Spring `SQLExceptionTranslator` (just like in the case of Spring JDBC and Spring's Hibernate support). Vendor-specific subclasses might refine translation according to special rules, or detect nested SQLExceptions in special ways.

An example for a vendor-specific `JdoDialect` is the `JPOXJdoDialect` class included in JPOX, a popular open source JDO implementation, which supports all of the previously mentioned advanced features. Other JDO vendors are expected to follow with a corresponding `JdoDialect` implementation for their respective tool.

Once the JDO 2.0 API becomes available, Spring's `DefaultJdoDialect` will be adapted to support the new standard JDO 2.0 ways of accessing the underlying JDBC `Connection` and flushing a JDO transaction. However, a vendor-specific subclass will still be necessary for transaction isolation levels and transaction timeouts, and might add value through more sophisticated exception translation. And of course, a specific `JdoDialect` implementation can still be used to adapt a JDO 1.0–compliant tool accordingly.

Several JDO vendors, including SolarMetric (vendors of the popular Kodo implementation) emphasize Spring integration and ship a `JdoDialect` integration for their product.

> Spring's JDO support offers advanced features beyond the JDO 1.0 specification, most importantly special transaction semantics, access to the underlying JDBC `Connection`, and eager flushing. Spring's `JdoDialect` SPI can be implemented to provide support for those features, using a vendor-specific API. JDO 2.0 will standardize some — but not all — of those features, so the need for a vendor-specific `JdoDialect` should decline.

JDO: Summary

The JDO specification addresses the same level of O/R mapping as Hibernate: object-level querying and transparent persistence through automatic change detection. It uses a different query API style than Hibernate, namely JDOQL's programmatic query objects with sub-expressions, rather than Hibernate's textual HQL. Change detection happens through byte code modification, to receive notifications for each changed field in a managed persistent object, rather than through Hibernate-style snapshot comparisons.

While JDO 1.0 is a reasonably complete standard for general object persistence, it lacks specific support for relational databases and, even more importantly, support for detached objects (including proper reattachment). JDO 2.0 will remedy these deficiencies as far as possible; however, JDO's strict lifecycle requirements still make working with persistent objects harder than with Hibernate's lenient lifecycle handling. This is particularly prominent in typical web MVC usage models, where changes to persistent objects often happen outside transactions.

Of course, some JDO vendors already support a wide variety of extensions and JDO 2.0 preview features. If you require such features now — for example, detachment and reattachment — use appropriate, vendor-specific API behind your DAO facades. Migrating to the standard JDO 2.0 API will be straightforward.

The main JDO support facilities that Spring offers are:

❑ `org.springframework.orm.jdo.JdoTemplate`: A data access class to be used in DAOs, seamlessly handling JDO `PersistenceManagers` in the background. It automatically participates in Spring-driven transactions and converts `JDOExceptions` into Spring's generic `DataAccessException` hierarchy.

❑ `org.springframework.orm.jdo.LocalPersistenceManagerFactoryBean`: A convenient way to set up a JDO `PersistenceManagerFactory` in a Spring context. `PersistenceManagerFactory` references can then be passed to DAOs, typically via Spring bean references. Alternatively, set up an instance of your vendor's `PersistenceManagerFactory` implementation class directly.

❑ `org.springframework.orm.jdo.JdoTransactionManager`: A local transaction strategy, executing transactions on a single target `PersistenceManagerFactory`. This strategy works in any environment, in contrast to `JtaTransactionManager`, which depends on a J2EE server (or a standalone JTA implementation).

❑ `org.springframework.orm.jdo.support.JdoDaoSupport`: A convenient base class for DAO implementations, taking a `PersistenceManagerFactory` reference and providing a `JdoTemplate` instance for it.

❑ `org.springframework.orm.hibernate.jdo.OpenPersistenceManagerInViewFilter` and `org.springframework.orm.hibernate.jdo.OpenPersistenceManagerInViewIntercept or`: A Servlet 2.3 Filter and `HandlerInterceptor` for Spring's web MVC framework, respectively, providing the Open PersistenceManager in View pattern for JDO.

Mixing JDO access code with other data access strategies is possible, as long as all of them access the same JDBC `DataSource`. Spring's `JdoTransactionManager` can expose its transactions to JDBC-based access code, provided that there is an appropriate `JdoDialect` implementation. In such a scenario, adding Spring JDBC or iBATIS SQL Maps to the mix is reasonably easy: for example, for BLOB/CLOB or stored procedure access, or for read-only reference data.

> **Modern JDO implementations such as Kodo JDO or JPOX are powerful tools for full-fledged O/R mapping. The build-time enhancement step that most JDO implementations require is usually less burden than often perceived. However, the lack of support for detached objects in JDO 1.0 is a major issue, which will get addressed in JDO 2.0; many JDO implementations already support detachment and reattachment in a vendor-specific fashion.**
>
> **JDO's main disadvantage is its strict lifecycle for persistent objects, which incurs a certain level of complexity that application developers have to deal with. In a typical web application, Hibernate is significantly more convenient to use, even given JDO extensions for detached objects. As with Hibernate, Spring JDBC and iBATIS SQL Maps are usually better options for legacy data models or over-normalized data models, in particular for read-only access.**

Other O/R Mapping Tools

Spring's data access abstraction as a whole — and hence its support for O/R mapping tools — is designed to be extensible. It's possible to plug in additional persistence APIs, while providing consistent programming models to developers working with Spring. As we have already learned, the two main areas are implementation of data access objects and transaction management: All integration packages are supposed to follow the usual Spring patterns in those respects.

> *In principle, it is possible to implement support for any O/R mapping framework — or arbitrary persistence framework. Implementations can build on generic base classes such as* `org.springframework` `.transaction.support.AbstractPlatformTransactionManager` *and use existing support packages as a starting point. However, sophisticated integration is still a significant effort, which usually requires in-depth knowledge about the semantics of the respective persistence tool.*

Apache OJB

As outlined in the introduction of OJB at the beginning of this chapter, OJB offers multiple data access APIs. Spring just includes dedicated support for OJB's `PersistenceBroker` API; support for OJB's ODMG layer is not planned because ODMG is an old API that predates the Java collections framework and is also dated in other respects. OJB's third API, the JDO plugin, can be used via Spring's JDO support, without special facilities.

The `PersistenceBroker` API offers full-fledged querying and full access to OJB's mapping power. However, it does not perform automatic change detection; it rather relies on explicit store calls for primary persistent objects (which might automatically store dependent objects too). Handling a `PersistenceBroker` is significantly less complex than working with Hibernate or JDO because there are no strict lifecycle requirements imposed by automatic change detection. A `PersistenceBroker` is particularly suitable for detached objects, which need to be explicitly stored in any case.

The facilities offered by Spring's support for the OJB `PersistenceBroker` are:

❑ `org.springframework.orm.ojb.PersistenceBrokerTemplate`: A data access class to be used in DAOs, seamlessly handling OJB `PersistenceBrokers` in the background. It automatically participates in Spring-driven transactions and converts `PersistenceBrokerExceptions` into Spring's generic `DataAccessException` hierarchy.

❑ `org.springframework.orm.ojb.PersistenceBrokerTransactionManager`: A local transaction strategy, executing transactions on a single target database (that is, a single `PersistenceBroker` key). This strategy works in any environment, in contrast to `JtaTransactionManager`, which depends on a J2EE server (or a standalone JTA implementation).

❑ `org.springframework.orm.ojb.support.PersistenceBrokerDaoSupport`: A convenient base class for DAO implementations, taking a `PersistenceBroker` key and providing a `PersistenceBrokerTemplate` instance for it.

❑ `org.springframework.orm.ojb.support.LocalDataSourceConnectionFactory`: An OJB `ConnectionFactory` that allows you to use a Spring-managed `DataSource` bean as a connection pool. Needs to be defined in OJB configuration.

In contrast to Hibernate and JDO, OJB does not use a factory instance as a central configuration point. Instead, it uses a singleton that initializes on first access and enables it to create `PersistenceBrokers` for a specific database configuration. A specific configuration is identified by a `PersistenceBroker` key; this is what the Spring-provided support classes need to work with. The OJB team plans to introduce instance-based configuration in OJB 1.1; in the meantime, OJB configuration is driven by the central `OJB.properties` file even in a Spring environment.

TopLink

Spring's support for TopLink is a recent addition to Spring's O/R mapping support; as of early 2005, it is available from Oracle's OTN. It was largely developed by the TopLink team at Oracle, following Spring's consistent architectural approach, and with the support of the Spring team. At the time of this writing, Oracle plans to donate the code to the Spring project, under Spring's Apache license, so that it can be shipped with Spring 1.2.

TopLink is a sophisticated, full-fledged O/R mapping solution, which dates back to 1997 (for its first Java implementation) and 1994 (for its genesis in Smalltalk). It offers a sophisticated *Mapping Workbench* UI to support development and offers a particularly wide range of object-relational mappings. TopLink is usable either in a J2EE or J2SE environment.

TopLink has some significant semantic differences to both Hibernate and JDO. The biggest differentiator is its change detection mechanism. TopLink uses snapshot comparisons, but only for objects that have been explicitly registered with a TopLink `UnitOfWork`; objects loaded by a plain TopLink `Session` are strictly read-only. While this allows for efficient use of cached persistent objects — sharing a single instance for multiple `Sessions` — it imposes some restrictions on the handling of persistent objects. Application code must take care to modify only references returned by a `UnitOfWork`; accidental modifications to objects returned by a `Session` will lead to side effects and cache corruption. It is possible that future releases of the Spring TopLink integration will conceal this requirement from the application developer, making using TopLink with Spring even more compelling for TopLink users: Please check the TopLink website for details. The upside of this design decision is that TopLink can deal more efficiently than Hibernate with very large numbers of persistent objects in memory, at least as long as only a minority are modified.

> It is beyond the scope of this chapter to discuss TopLink and its capabilities in detail. Please refer to Oracle's documentation (`www.oracle.com/technology/products/ias/toplink/index.html`) for more details.

The facilities offered by Spring's TopLink support are:

❑ `org.springframework.orm.toplink.TopLinkTemplate`: A data access class to be used in DAOs, seamlessly handling TopLink `Sessions` in the background. It automatically participates in Spring-driven transactions and converts TopLink exceptions into Spring's generic `DataAccessException` hierarchy.

❑ `org.springframework.orm.toplink.SessionFactoryBean`: A convenient way to set up a TopLink `SessionFactory` in a Spring context. `SessionFactory` references can then be passed to DAOs, typically via Spring bean references.

❑ `org.springframework.orm.toplink.TopLinkTransactionManager`: A local transaction strategy, executing transactions on a single target `SessionFactory`. This strategy works in any environment, in contrast to `JtaTransactionManager`, which depends on a J2EE server (or a standalone JTA implementation).

❑ `org.springframework.orm.toplink.support.TopLinkDaoSupport`: A convenient base class for DAO implementations, taking a `SessionFactory` reference and providing a `TopLinkTemplate` instance for it.

Essentially, the usage model of the TopLink support closely follows Spring's Hibernate and JDO support. However, as with the differences between Hibernate and JDO, the application needs to be aware of the special semantics involved in TopLink usage, in particular regarding modifications to loaded instances.

For further information, see the page on Spring/TopLink integration on the TopLink website at www.oracle.com/technology/products/ias/toplink/preview/spring/index.html.

TopLink support rounds out Spring's support for leading O/R mapping technologies. TopLink is and is likely to remain an important O/R mapping product, especially among enterprise-class users, and hence it is important for Spring to support it fully. The fact that the TopLink integration was developed at Oracle, in response to requests from TopLink users, is proof that Spring's data access integration is becoming recognized as a significant integration platform.

A key benefit of the Spring data access abstraction is that the consistent approach it offers helps to localize differences between persistence tools in DAO implementation classes. For example, in presentations on Spring, we often find that attendees can quickly come to grips with, say, the TopLink implementation of the PetClinic, even if they have no previous experience with TopLink. This would probably not be the case if they saw an implementation of the same functionality using TopLink without Spring.

Cayenne

During the editing of this book, the developers of the open source Cayenne O/R mapping project (www.objectstyle.org/cayenne/) developed Spring support for their product. Please refer to the Cayenne website for further information. As in the case of TopLink, this resulted from interest within their own community, and both communities benefit from the integration.

JSR-220 Persistence

As you can see, this strong, proven conceptual basis makes it easy for Spring to integrate with additional — or emerging — persistence technologies.

The most important emerging persistence technology is the POJO persistence specification to be delivered by the JSR-220 (EJB 3.0) expert group. Note that this specification will *not* be tied to an EJB container. While the nature of this specification is still not entirely clear, the major inputs to its definition are coming from the developers of Hibernate, TopLink, and some JDO products, and it is clear that Spring's data access abstraction will work with the result, both inside or outside an EJB container.

If you wish to use JSR-220 persistence once it is available, using your O/R mapping framework via the Spring abstraction will ease the migration path. Not only does using Spring's data access abstraction make your job easier, whatever persistence technology you use, it also provides a unique partial decoupling from the underlying persistence API.

Spring will support JSR-220 as soon as final binaries are released. As of early 2005, there is no solid API documentation for JSR-220 yet, and no binaries have officially been released.

Summary

Spring provides highly sophisticated support for a variety of O/R mapping solutions, ranging from iBATIS SQL Maps to full-blown transparent persistence tools such as Hibernate, JDO, and TopLink. The most important areas addressed are *data access object implementation* and *transaction management*; there are also a variety of further support classes for special features of certain tools.

The Spring philosophy, in data access as elsewhere, is that there is no single correct answer for data access. Instead, we aim to provide a consistent overall architectural template, within which you can choose whatever persistence solution best fits your needs.

Spring provides a consistent model for resource and transaction management, no matter which O/R mapping tool you choose. Connections are always managed under the hood, and transactions are always demarcated via Spring's generic transaction demarcation facilities. Furthermore, all resource exceptions are converted to Spring's generic `DataAccessException` hierarchy, allowing DAOs to throw a generic exception rather than a tool-specific one.

While providing many convenience operations for each tool, Spring offers the full power of the underlying resource if you need it, through callbacks that give access to the native Hibernate `Session`, JDO `PersistenceManager`, or TopLink `Session`, respectively. In general, Spring does not aim to abstract the data access operations of the actual tool used: Instead, it separates the transaction management concern from the data access operations and provides implicit connection handling, including transaction synchronization.

All of Spring's O/R mapping support can either work with a corresponding *local* transaction strategy, executing transactions for a single target database, or with *JTA* transactions, delegating to the J2EE server for distributed transaction coordination (potentially spanning multiple resources). The main advantage of the local strategies is that they can work in any environment, that is, both *within* and *outside* a J2EE server — as long as you are accessing a single target database.

As much as possible, Spring's O/R mapping support isolates dependencies on a specific O/R mapping tool within an application's codebase. Neither transaction demarcation nor DAO usage involve dependencies on a concrete tool, as they purely work with Spring concepts. Only DAO implementations depend on a specific persistence API; in principle, those can quite easily be replaced with implementations for a different tool — if you ever need to switch an application from one O/R mapper to another. However, there are semantic differences between the persistence strategies, in particular with respect to the lifecycle of persistent objects. Be aware that callers might rely on specific behavior that might vary between different tools.

> **The main areas addressed by Spring's O/R mapping support are data access object implementation and transaction management. Resources are consistently managed under the hood, and exceptions automatically translated to Spring's** `DataAccessException` **hierarchy.**
>
> **Despite the common handling, DAO implementations can still work with the full power of the underlying persistence tool. Spring does *not* aim to provide an abstraction over the native API of Hibernate or JDO. Instead, it offers a consistent setup and usage style for all supported strategies, while still allowing DAOs to use the native query and operation style of each tool.**

We feel that by using Spring's data access abstraction — whatever your choice of O/R mapping tool — you will gain much convenience, eliminate common causes of errors, yet sacrifice none of the power of the ORM tool itself.

8

Lightweight Remoting

There are two main scenarios where remoting constitutes an important element of the overall architecture:

- **Client-server remoting:** Remote applications that access a backend server, often providing a "rich" user interface, as opposed to a "thin" HTML-based user interface. If such a client application is implemented in Java, it will typically have a Swing user interface and be distributed with Java Web Start. Alternatively, such a client might be implemented in Macromedia Flash or in .NET, talking to backend services implemented in Java. Remote communication in a client-server scenario will usually be HTTP-based because of the ease of setup and to avoid firewall issues.

- **Intra-server remoting:** Communication between various processes within the same server system: for example, for integrating existing backend systems or for distributing workload across multiple machines. The demands and tradeoffs in such a scenario differ significantly from client-server remoting: For example, there are often no firewalls between servers, allowing for non–HTTP-based protocols. Furthermore, the overhead of remote invocations is lower (although always significant).

If none of these scenarios applies, it is likely that your application will not benefit from remoting. However, your requirements might change over time, for example making it necessary to add remoting to an *existing* web application.

Spring mainly focuses on local middle tiers, managing loosely coupled components within the same process. However, it nevertheless provides powerful remoting support, allowing you to export and consume remote services with ease. Spring offers a consistent, POJO-based programming model, whichever of the many supported remoting protocols you choose.

Concepts and Scope

In contrast to traditional component frameworks such as EJB, Spring does *not* build remoting into the *core* component model. We strongly believe that business logic components should *not* be designed with remoting in mind. Instead, a typical Spring middle tier consists of local components with fine-grained interface methods and local invocation semantics, called by user interface controllers in the same process.

However, Spring does support remoting at the component level — not through the core container but through add-on support. If you need to expose a component to a remote process, you can define an *exporter* for that component, making it available through a specific remoting protocol. On the client side, a corresponding *accessor* can be defined to delegate method calls on a given interface to a specific remote service.

In keeping with Spring's overall philosophy, Spring's remoting support is designed to be as *non-intrusive* as possible. Neither service implementers nor callers need to be aware of remoting (at least not unnecessarily); exporters and accessors can be applied in a seamless fashion. Of course, the chosen interface needs to be suitable for remoting — that is, it needs to define coarse-grained methods with serializable arguments and return types. The interface used can still be a *plain Java business interface*, however: There is no need to derive from a base interface or throw a specific checked remoting exception.

You might choose to add a remote facade above a number of local components, to offer a coarser level of granularity to minimize chatty calling, improve performance, and observe the constraints relating to remote arguments and return types.

Thus Spring does not impose any constraints on remoting itself, and Spring's remoting support seamlessly fits into existing applications. For example, in the case of a web application that should be enriched with a remote service that exposes some existing functionality to cooperating applications, remoting can be added within the existing WAR deployment unit — using a lightweight, HTTP-based remoting protocol. There is no need to change the entire application architecture just because of the need to expose a remote service, which would be unavoidable when choosing to extend an existing web application with a remote EJB, for example.

Out of the box, the following remoting solutions are supported, sharing a common access and export style as much as possible:

❑ **Hessian:** A slim binary protocol, based on HTTP. Language-independent but Java-oriented; currently mainly used for Java-to-Java remoting. Available under the Apache license from Caucho, the makers of the Resin application server.

❑ **Burlap:** A slim XML-based protocol, based on HTTP. Like its sibling Hessian, it is language-independent but Java-oriented, and currently mainly used for Java-to-Java remoting. Available under the Apache license from Caucho.

❑ **HTTP invoker:** Java serialization of remote invocations over HTTP. This is Spring's own take on HTTP-based Java-to-Java remoting, combining the strengths of HTTP-based remoting with the full power of Java serialization. Shares common infrastructure with RMI invoker (see the next bullet point).

❑ **RMI (traditional and invoker):** Classic Java remoting infrastructure, using JRMP or IIOP as protocol (not HTTP-based). Can either be used with a traditional RMI service interface or with a plain Java business interface ("RMI invoker"). The latter shares common infrastructure with HTTP invoker.

❏ **WSDL/SOAP through JAX-RPC:** For standard WSDL Web Services with SOAP over HTTP, handled through the standard Java API for Web Services. Can, for example, be used with Apache Axis. Completely language-independent, incurring extra effort for special types. Often used for communication with .NET applications.

Spring also provides support for accessing and implementing remote EJBs, sharing the access style with the lightweight remoting support. However, implementing a remote service as EJB does have some other implications, such as the introduction of a new deployment unit, with its own class loader, to be handled as a completely separate part of the application. Unless the remote services are the only entry points into the system, it is usually preferable to add a lightweight remoting strategy to the existing deployment unit, resulting in less complex overall architecture. See Chapter 11 for a discussion of Spring's EJB support.

Spring's remoting support focuses on *stateless remoting*, not keeping client-specific state on the server in between method invocations. This is usually the preferred strategy because it avoids the need for session state with timeouts and failover and is thus the most scalable option. If you need stateful remoting with client-specific sessions, consider the use of EJB's stateful session beans (which of course introduces a new deployment unit if your application did not use EJB before, as elaborated previously).

Throughout this chapter, we will show code and configuration examples from Spring's JPetStore sample application, which comes with the standard Spring distribution. JPetStore's web application exports its `OrderService` through all five different strategies presented in this chapter. A demo client in turn allows for fetching an order for a given ID, and performing the operation for each protocol. Have a look at JPetStore's `readme` file for deployment instructions. The sample application chapter of *J2EE without EJB* discusses the original Spring 1.0 JPetStore in detail.

Common Configuration Style

All of Spring's remoting support — including the support for remote EJBs — shares a *common access style*, which essentially consists of two parts:

❏ **Proxy factory:** To "import" a remote service into a client-side Spring context, a special factory bean for a specific protocol is defined. Configuration such as the service interface to use and the URL of the target service is defined on the `factory bean`, which in turn exposes a proxy that implements the specified service interface.

❏ **Proxy behavior:** A proxy for a remote service delegates each method invocation on the proxy to the remote service. Any exception thrown by the target service will be propagated through the proxy. If the remote invocation itself failed, a proxy will consistently throw Spring's generic `RemoteAccessException` — no matter which remoting solution is used under the hood.

Spring's `org.springframework.remoting.RemoteAccessException` is a generic, unchecked exception that indicates a remote invocation failure. It does not have to be declared on the service interface because of its unchecked nature. Nevertheless, it can be caught and handled in a consistent fashion by the client — or simply let through if considered fatal.

Spring's remoting support is mainly designed for plain Java business interfaces, not declaring any remoting exception. Handling remote invocation failures through throwing the unchecked `RemoteAccessException` will be managed by the protocol-specific proxies and won't affect the service implementation on the server side at all. This model is seamless with Hessian, Burlap, and HTTP invoker, which have all been designed for plain Java interfaces in the first place.

With Spring's RMI support, either traditional RMI service interfaces or plain Java business interfaces can be used. In the former case, the service interfaces will derive from `java.rmi.Remote` and throw `java.rmi.RemoteException`, as required for traditional RMI interfaces; of course, the client will need to handle the checked `RemoteException` accordingly in such a scenario. In the latter case, the RMI infrastructure will be used for tunneling invocations on plain Java interfaces — the *RMI invoker* mode.

A further option with Spring's RMI, JAX-RPC, and EJB support is to specify a plain Java business interface for the proxy, *despite the target service using a traditional RMI service interface*. In that case, each invocation on the proxy will be converted into a corresponding invocation on the underlying RMI stub for the remote service; checked RMI `RemoteExceptions` thrown will automatically get converted to Spring's unchecked `RemoteAccessException`. Of course, the target service still implements the RMI service interface, without having to implement the Java business interface used by the client — in contrast to when using RMI invoker, where both the client and the server use the same plain Java business interface.

We will show examples for various service interface scenarios in the corresponding sections for each remoting solution.

On the server side, Spring also provides a common style for exporting a service: defining an exporter for an existing Spring-managed bean, exposing it as remote service at a specific URL. The configuration is virtually the same for Hessian, Burlap, and HTTP invoker. The RMI support does not have to run in a servlet container, but is analogous in all other respects. Web Services are usually exported in a tool-specific style; standard JAX-RPC unfortunately does not allow for seamless exporting of an existing service instance.

Spring provides a common configuration style for all supported remoting solutions — as common as possible — both for client-side accessors and server-side exporters.

On the client side, plain Java business interfaces can be used for accessing a remote service with a common proxy definition style. All remoting proxies will throw Spring's unchecked `RemoteAccessException` in a consistent fashion on a remote invocation failure.

On the server side, Spring allows for exporting an existing Spring-managed bean as remote service, under a specific protocol. This is particularly seamless for Hessian, Burlap, and HTTP invoker, but also for RMI when leveraging Spring's RMI invoker mechanism. The same service instance can be exported under multiple protocols at the same time, at different URLs.

This consistency means that once you understand Spring's approach to remoting, you will find it easy to work with whatever remoting protocol is best suited to a particular requirement.

Hessian and Burlap

Caucho Technology, the makers of the Resin application server, have released two lightweight remoting protocols, which are available as standalone distributions under the Apache license: *Hessian*, a slim binary protocol, and *Burlap*, a slim XML-based protocol. Both use HTTP as their transport mechanism. The protocols are defined in concise specifications. While Java-oriented, they allow for implementations in other languages.

Hessian and Burlap use their own serialization algorithms for primitive types, collections, and so on. This avoids the hassle of Java serialization, which requires strictly compatible classes on both sides, while still working efficiently for Java objects. However, it does incur side effects. For example, Hessian and Burlap are not able to deserialize a state that is held in final instance variables, as they need to be able to rebuild an object's fields through reflection. Furthermore, they are not able to detect objects with customized serialization, for example Hibernate collections: Such objects often cause deserialization failures.

> **Hessian's and Burlap's own serialization mechanisms allow for loose coupling (between loosely related Java processes or even different languages) but can incur side effects. If encountering deserialization failures, we recommend switching to the tighter coupling of Spring's HTTP invoker (discussed later in this chapter), which uses standard Java serialization over HTTP.**

Both Hessian and Burlap services are traditionally defined as servlets in web.xml, using Caucho's prebuilt HessianServlet or BurlapServlet class, respectively. The application service to be exported is either implemented as a subclass of such a servlet (being tied to a protocol) or as a plain Java class implementing the service interface. In the latter case, the implementation will simply get instantiated and used; there is no way to wire it with middle tier services other than via JNDI lookups.

On the client side, standard Hessian and Burlap provide proxy factory classes, which can generate a proxy for a specific service interface and target URL. Remote invocation failure will lead to special HessianRuntimeExceptions or BurlapRuntimeExceptions being thrown.

To allow seamless integration of Hessian and Burlap into a Spring-based architecture, Spring provides the following prebuilt support classes:

- ❑ org.springframework.remoting.caucho.HessianProxyFactoryBean and org.springframework.remoting.caucho.BurlapProxyFactoryBean: Proxy factories for Spring-compliant proxies that communicate with backend Hessian or Burlap services, respectively. To be defined in a Spring bean factory or application context, exposing the proxy object for references (through the FactoryBean mechanism). Proxies will throw Spring's generic RemoteAccessException in case of remote invocation failure.

- ❑ org.springframework.remoting.caucho.HessianServiceExporter and org.springframework.remoting.caucho.BurlapServiceExporter: Exporters implemented as Controllers for Spring's web MVC framework. Can take any existing Spring-managed bean and export it at a given HTTP URL, allowing the target bean to be fully configured and wired via Spring. The same target bean can easily be exported through both Hessian and Burlap at the same time, at different URLs.

Note that Spring's Hessian and Burlap support works with standard Hessian and Burlap means underneath; that is, it does not use a special invoker mechanism. Any existing Hessian or Burlap service can be accessed via Spring's accessor classes, even if the target service is not exported via Spring; and any Hessian or Burlap client can access a Spring-managed bean that has been exported via Spring's exporter classes.

> **Hessian and Burlap are compelling choices for HTTP-based remoting — in particular, for Java-to-Java remoting. Spring allows for convenient definition of proxies on the client side and service exporters on the server side, without tying client objects or service implementations to a specific protocol.**
>
> **Setup and maintenance efforts for Hessian and Burlap services are close to negligible. Because of their HTTP-based nature, there are no issues with stale proxies on server restart or the like (that is, none of the traditional headaches of RMI). The simplicity of configuration is matched only by Spring's own HTTP invoker, discussed later in this chapter.**

Accessing a Service

On the client side, a proxy for a target service can easily be created via a Spring bean definition. The configuration needed is the proxy factory class name, the HTTP URL of the target service, and the service interface to expose. For example, for Hessian:

```
<bean id="hessianProxy"
    class="org.springframework.remoting.caucho.HessianProxyFactoryBean">
  <property name="serviceUrl">
    <value>http://localhost:8080/remoting/OrderService-hessian</value>
  </property>
  <property name="serviceInterface">
    <value>org.springframework.samples.jpetstore.domain.logic.OrderService</value>
  </property>
</bean>
```

The service interface can be a plain Java business interface that doesn't have to derive from specific base interfaces or throw special remoting exceptions:

```
public interface OrderService {

  Order getOrder(int orderId);
}
```

For Burlap, only the class name of the proxy factory would have to change. Spring uses consistent property naming across its remote service accessors, as much as possible.

```
<bean id="burlapProxy"
    class="org.springframework.remoting.caucho.BurlapProxyFactoryBean">
  <property name="serviceUrl">
    <value>http://localhost:8080/remoting/OrderService-burlap</value>
```

```
        </property>
        <property name="serviceInterface">
          <value>org.springframework.samples.jpetstore.domain.logic.OrderService</value>
        </property>
    </bean>
```

Such a proxy is then available for bean references; for example:

```
<bean id="myOrderServiceClient" class="example.MyOrderServiceClient">
    <property name="orderService">
      <ref bean="hessianProxy"/>
    </property>
</bean>
```

The `MyOrderServiceClient` class would simply expose a bean property of type `org.springframework` `.samples.jpetstore.domain.logic.OrderService` here, thus the client is not tied to a remote service but rather to a plain Java business interface, which could have a local implementation too.

```java
public class MyOrderServiceClient {

    private OrderService orderService;

    public void setOrderService(OrderService orderService) {
        this.orderService = orderService;
    }

    public void doSomething() {
        Order order = this.orderService.getOrder(...);
        ...
    }
}
```

Note that switching between a Hessian and a Burlap proxy for our `OrderService` would just involve redefining the proxy from `HessianProxyFactoryBean` to `BurlapProxyFactoryBean`. Through using a placeholder, this can even be driven from outside an XML bean definition file:

```
<bean id="myOrderServiceClient" class="example.MyOrderServiceClient">
    <property name="orderService">
      <ref bean="${proxyBeanName}"/>
    </property>
</bean>
```

The actual bean name to be wired to would typically be defined in a Properties file, for example an `admin.properties` file residing in the `WEB-INF` directory of a web application. (See Chapter 2 for details on Spring's placeholder mechanism for bean definitions.)

```
proxyBeanName=hessianProxy
#proxyBeanName=burlapProxy
```

> Switching between a Hessian proxy and a Burlap proxy is a configuration matter; the actual protocol used can be considered a deployment choice. This basically applies to all of Spring's supported remoting strategies: A client object can seamlessly receive a different proxy for the service interface that it expects, as it is not tied to a particular proxy factory.

Both `HessianProxyFactoryBean` and `BurlapProxyFactoryBean` support some customization options, for example specifying `username` and `password` properties for HTTP-based authentication. Such settings apply to the entire service instance; they cannot be customized at a per-invocation level. Furthermore, secure communication via SSL is straightforward: Simply specify an HTTPS URL as service URL.

Exporting a Service

On the server side, exporting an existing Spring-managed bean as Hessian and/or Burlap service is straightforward. Corresponding service exporters need to be defined as Spring `Controller`s in a Spring web MVC context. It is usually advisable to define such exporters in a separate `DispatcherServlet` with its own context. However, defining them in an existing `DispatcherServlet` context will also work.

For example, such `Controller` definitions in a `DispatcherServlet` context could look as follows, relying on the default `BeanNameUrlHandlerMapping` strategy. (See Chapter 12 for details on Spring's `DispatcherServlet` and its strategies.)

```
<bean name="/OrderService-hessian"
    class="org.springframework.remoting.caucho.HessianServiceExporter">
  <property name="service">
    <ref bean="petStore"/>
  </property>
  <property name="serviceInterface">
    <value>org.springframework.samples.jpetstore.domain.logic.OrderService</value>
  </property>
</bean>

<bean name="/OrderService-burlap"
    class="org.springframework.remoting.caucho.BurlapServiceExporter">
  <property name="service">
    <ref bean="petStore"/>
  </property>
  <property name="serviceInterface">
    <value>org.springframework.samples.jpetstore.domain.logic.OrderService</value>
  </property>
</bean>
```

The actual `OrderService` implementation in JPetStore's middle tier is the `PetStoreImpl` object, which also implements the `PetStoreFacade` interface. Therefore, the exporter refers to the `petStore` bean from the root application context.

Those exporters could be defined in the context of a `DispatcherServlet` called `remoting`: that is, in a file `remoting-servlet.xml` in the `WEB-INF` directory of a web application. The corresponding `web.xml` entries would look like this:

```
<servlet>
  <servlet-name>remoting</servlet-name>
  <servlet-class>org.springframework.web.servlet.DispatcherServlet</servlet-class>
  <load-on-startup/>
</servlet>

<servlet-mapping>
  <servlet-name>remoting</servlet-name>
  <url-pattern>/remoting/*</url-pattern>
</servlet-mapping>
```

Assuming that the server is available at http://localhost:8080, the remote `OrderService` would then be available as Hessian service at `http://localhost:8080/remoting/OrderService-hessian` and as Burlap service at `http://localhost:8080/remoting/OrderService-burlap`.

Of course, defining only one exporter — that is, for either Hessian or Burlap — will work too. However, as you can see in the previous example, it is straightforward to define multiple exporters, binding them to different URLs but wiring them with the same target service instance.

> In contrast to classic remoting frameworks, a service instance for use with Hessian or Burlap (or effectively any other remoting strategy supported by Spring) is not tied to a particular endpoint. It can seamlessly be exported through multiple endpoints at the same time. A client can then choose which protocol to use for communication with that service, through talking to the endpoint at a specific URL.

HTTP Invoker

As a direct alternative to Hessian and Burlap, Spring offers the HTTP invoker remoting strategy. Instead of the custom serialization found in Hessian and Burlap, HTTP invoker uses Java serialization — just like RMI. Applications can rely on full serialization power, as long as all transferred objects properly follow Java serialization rules (implementing the `java.io.Serializable` marker interface and properly defining `serialVersionUID` if necessary).

The main classes of Spring's HTTP invoker are:

❑ `org.springframework.remoting.httpinvoker.HttpInvokerProxyFactoryBean`: Proxy factory for Spring-compliant proxies that communicate with backend HTTP invoker services. To be defined in a Spring bean factory or application context, exposing the proxy object for references (through the `FactoryBean` mechanism). Proxies will throw Spring's generic `RemoteAccessException` in case of remote invocation failure.

❑ `org.springframework.remoting.httpinvoker.HttpInvokerServiceExporter`: Exporter implemented as `Controller` for Spring's web MVC framework. Can take any existing Spring-managed bean and export it at a given HTTP URL, allowing the target bean to be fully configured and wired via Spring. The same target bean can easily be exported through HTTP invoker and other protocols (such as Hessian and Burlap) at the same time, at different URLs.

These classes are direct equivalents of `HessianProxyFactoryBean` and `HessianServiceExporter` and `BurlapProxyFactoryBean` and `BurlapServiceExporter`, respectively. They can be considered as drop-in replacements, as they share the same configuration style and behavior.

Because of the nature of HTTP invoker (which is available only in Spring), both the client side and the server side need to be based on Spring—and on Java in the first place because of the use of Java serialization. In contrast to Hessian and Burlap, there is no option for cross-platform remoting. HTTP invoker is clearly dedicated to powerful and seamless Java-to-Java remoting.

A further difference to Hessian and Burlap is the tight coupling of client and server codebases. Java serialization requires strictly matching versions of the involved classes at both ends. If the application versions on the client and server side differ, use of `serialVersionUID` is required. (See the documentation on Java serialization for details.)

> **HTTP invoker is a powerful option for Java-to-Java remoting, which uses Java serialization and offers the same serialization power as RMI.**
>
> **Consider Hessian as a loosely coupled alternative to HTTP invoker. Both are binary and roughly equivalent in terms of efficiency. Their major difference is the serialization mechanism: HTTP invoker uses standard Java serialization; Hessian uses its own serialization mechanism.**
>
> **Setup and maintenance is as easy as with Hessian and Burlap. The only stricter requirement is that the class versions at both ends have to be compatible—a consequence of using Java serialization.**

Accessing a Service

On the client side, a proxy for a target service can easily be created via a Spring bean definition—analogous to Hessian and Burlap. The configuration needed is the proxy factory class name, the HTTP URL of the target service, and the service interface to expose. For example:

```
<bean id="httpInvokerProxy"
    class="org.springframework.remoting.httpinvoker.HttpInvokerProxyFactoryBean">
  <property name="serviceUrl">
    <value>http://localhost:8080/remoting/OrderService-httpinvoker</value>
  </property>
  <property name="serviceInterface">
    <value>org.springframework.samples.jpetstore.domain.logic.OrderService</value>
  </property>
</bean>
```

The service interface is the same plain Java business interface used in the Hessian/Burlap example. It does not derive from specific base interfaces or throw special remoting exceptions:

```
public interface OrderService {

  Order getOrder(int orderId);
}
```

Such a proxy is then available for bean references; for example:

```xml
<bean id="myOrderServiceClient" class="example.MyOrderServiceClient">
  <property name="orderService">
    <ref bean="httpInvokerProxy"/>
  </property>
</bean>
```

The `MyOrderServiceClient` class is the same as in the Hessian/Burlap example. It would simply expose a bean property of type `org.springframework.samples.jpetstore.domain.logic.OrderService` here, so the client is not tied to a remote service but rather to a plain Java business interface:

```java
public class MyOrderServiceClient {

  private OrderService orderService;

  public void setOrderService(OrderService orderService) {
    this.orderService = orderService;
  }

  public void doSomething() {
    Order order = this.orderService.getOrder(...);
    ...
  }
}
```

Switching between an HTTP invoker proxy and a Hessian proxy for our `OrderService` simply involves redefining the proxy from `HttpInvokerProxyFactoryBean` to `HessianProxyFactoryBean`. Through the use of a placeholder, this can even be driven from outside an XML bean definition file; see the example in the "Hessian and Burlap" section for an illustration.

> As outlined in the discussion of Hessian and Burlap, switching between different remoting protocols is a configuration matter. This also applies to HTTP invoker. It can be considered a drop-in replacement for Hessian or Burlap, as long as all transferred objects properly support Java serialization. Configuration-wise, only the class name of the proxy factory will change.

Exporting a Service

On the server side, exporting an existing Spring-managed bean as an HTTP invoker service is straightforward. A corresponding service exporter needs to be defined as Spring `Controller` in a Spring web MVC context. As discussed in the section on Hessian and Burlap, it is usually advisable to define such exporters in a separate `DispatcherServlet` with its own context. For example, the following code exposes the `petStore` bean in the root application context as HTTP invoker service:

```xml
<bean name="/OrderService-httpinvoker"
    class="org.springframework.remoting.httpinvoker.HttpInvokerServiceExporter">
  <property name="service">
    <ref bean="petStore"/>
  </property>
  <property name="serviceInterface">
    <value>org.springframework.samples.jpetstore.domain.logic.OrderService</value>
  </property>
</bean>
```

As with Hessian and Burlap, such an exporter could be defined in the `remoting-servlet.xml` context file of a `DispatcherServlet` called `remoting`. The corresponding `web.xml` entries would look like this:

```xml
<servlet>
  <servlet-name>remoting</servlet-name>
  <servlet-class>org.springframework.web.servlet.DispatcherServlet</servlet-class>
  <load-on-startup/>
</servlet>

<servlet-mapping>
  <servlet-name>remoting</servlet-name>
  <url-pattern>/remoting/*</url-pattern>
</servlet-mapping>
```

Assuming that the server is available at `http://localhost:8080`, the remote `OrderService` would then be available as HTTP invoker service at `http://localhost:8080/remoting/OrderService-httpinvoker`.

The same `DispatcherServlet` could be used for exporting an HTTP invoker service and Hessian and Burlap services. It would simply define one exporter per remoting protocol, each available at a distinct URL. This is effectively the case in the JPetStore sample application, from which all examples in this chapter originate.

> **An HTTP invoker endpoint can seamlessly coexist with Hessian and Burlap endpoints, even in the same dispatcher. The client chooses a specific endpoint through the URL that it talks to, as discussed in the section on Hessian and Burlap.**

Customization Options

HTTP invoker uses Spring's generic remote invocation mechanism underneath, serializing `org.springframework.remoting.support.RemoteInvocation` and `org.springframework.remoting.support.RemoteInvocationResult` objects.

The standard configuration is sufficient for typical needs, where no additional invocation attributes have to be passed along. However, if, for example, a user credential attribute should be included in the invocation, a custom `org.springframework.remoting.support.RemoteInvocationFactory` can be implemented and registered with the `HttpInvokerProxyFactoryBean`. A corresponding custom `org.springframework.remoting.support.RemoteInvocationExecutor`, to be registered with the `HttpInvokerServiceExporter`, will apply such additional attributes on the server side, for example performing authorization checks. This can also be provided out-of-the-box by Spring extension libraries.

Note that the remote invocation infrastructure is shared with the RMI invoker, discussed later in this chapter. A custom `RemoteInvocationFactory` / `RemoteInvocationExecutor` pair can be applied to either HTTP invoker or RMI invoker without changes, transferring the additional attributes over the respective protocol.

Secure communication via SSL is straightforward, as with Hessian and Burlap: Simply specify an HTTPS URL as a service URL. Alternatively, you can also implement your own encryption mechanism as a custom `RemoteInvocationFactory` / `RemoteInvocationExecutor` pair, sharing the encryption mechanism with RMI invoker.

A further customization option is the `org.springframework.remoting.httpinvoker` `.HttpInvokerRequestExecutor` strategy, which is responsible for the actual generation of the HTTP request for a given invocation. The default implementation, `org.springframework.remoting` `.httpinvoker.SimpleHttpInvokerRequestExecutor`, uses a standard `java.net.URLConnection` for sending and receiving. As an alternative, Spring also provides `org.springframework.remoting` `.httpinvoker.CommonsHttpInvokerRequestExecutor`, which delegates to Jakarta's Commons `HttpClient` (`http://jakarta.apache.org/commons/httpclient`), allowing for HTTP-based authentication and other advanced uses of HTTP.

> **HTTP invoker is highly customizable through the `RemoteInvocationFactory`,** `RemoteInvocationExecutor`, and `HttpInvokerRequestExecutor` strategies. **However, for typical needs, you don't have to worry about any of this. The standard configuration of** `HttpInvokerProxyFactoryBean` **and** `HttpInvokerService` `Exporter` **should be perfectly sufficient.**

RMI

Spring includes support for the standard RMI infrastructure as the remoting backend. As much as possible, the usage style is analogous to Hessian, Burlap, and HTTP invoker. Standard RMI-JRMP, included in the JDK, uses Java serialization, like Spring's HTTP invoker. It is a Java-to-Java remoting solution that does not aim for cross-platform remoting.

In contrast to the previously discussed HTTP-based remoting strategies, standard RMI does not work at the HTTP level, but uses a special TCP port for communication: by default, port 1099. Exported services have to be registered with the RMI registry, which can either be started in-process or externally (potentially shared by multiple processes).

> **RMI stubs registered with the RMI registry are connected to a specific endpoint. If you restart the server that hosts the RMI endpoints (your Spring-managed services), you need to re-register the stubs — and clients need to look them up again.**

Traditional RMI involves using RMI service interfaces, that is, interfaces that derive from `java.rmi` `.Remote`, with each method declaring the checked `java.rmi.RemoteException`. On J2SE 1.4 and earlier, the RMI compiler (`rmic`) needs to be run for each service implementation to generate the corresponding stub. On J2SE 5.0 and higher, the RMI runtime infrastructure will generate a dynamic proxy on the fly.

Spring supports the traditional style of RMI, but offers — and recommends — RMI invoker as an alternative, using plain Java business interfaces on top of RMI as the remoting infrastructure. There is no need to run the RMI compiler for an RMI invoker service, on J2SE 1.4 and earlier, or on J2SE 5.0.

Spring's RMI support consists of the following main classes:

❑ `org.springframework.remoting.rmi.RmiProxyFactoryBean`: Proxy factory for Spring-compliant proxies that communicate with backend RMI services. To be defined in a Spring bean factory or application context, exposing the proxy object for references (through the

FactoryBean mechanism). Proxies will either throw RMI's RemoteException or Spring's generic RemoteAccessException in case of remote invocation failure, depending on the type of service interface used.

❏ org.springframework.remoting.rmi.RmiServiceExporter: Exporter that registers a given service — either a traditional RMI service or a plain Java object — with the RMI registry. Can take any existing Spring-managed bean and expose it under a given RMI name in the registry, allowing the target bean to be fully configured and wired via Spring. Creates an in-process RMI registry if none is found at the specified port. The same target bean can easily be exported through other protocols (such as HTTP invoker) at the same time.

These classes are direct equivalents of HttpInvokerProxyFactoryBean and HttpInvokerServiceExporter. While RMI requires a different registry and exposure style, they still share the same configuration style and behavior.

Spring's RMI support will work with standard RMI underneath in the case of a traditional RMI interface; that is, it does not use a special invoker mechanism unless necessary. Any existing RMI service can be accessed via Spring's RmiProxyFactoryBean, even if the target service is not exported via Spring; and any RMI client can access a Spring-managed traditional RMI service that has been exported via Spring's RmiServiceExporter. However, a traditional RMI client will *not* be able to access a Spring-exported POJO with a plain Java business interface; only a Spring-based client will be able to access such a service.

As with HTTP invoker, client and server codebases are tightly coupled. Java serialization requires strictly matching versions of the involved classes at both ends. If the application versions on the client and server side might differ, use of serialVersionUID is required. (See the JDK's documentation on Java serialization for details.)

RMI is the traditional option for Java-to-Java remoting. Spring enhances it through the RMI invoker mechanism, which allows it to use a plain Java business interface on top of the RMI backend infrastructure.

However, consider HTTP invoker as a direct alternative. Both are binary and roughly equivalent in terms of efficiency. The serialization mechanism is the same: standard Java serialization. The main difference is that HTTP invoker is more convenient. It can easily go through firewalls, does not require a registry, and does not need to reconnect in case of a server restart.

Nevertheless, RMI's level of setup and maintenance is often acceptable, in particular with Spring's auto-reconnect feature (see the following section). Note that as with HTTP invoker, the class versions at both ends have to be compatible — a consequence of using Java serialization.

Accessing a Service

On the client side, a proxy for a target service can easily be created via a Spring bean definition — analogous to Hessian, Burlap, and HTTP invoker. The configuration needed is the proxy factory class name, the RMI URL of the target service, and the service interface to expose. For example:

```
<bean id="rmiProxy" class="org.springframework.remoting.rmi.RmiProxyFactoryBean">
    <property name="serviceUrl">
```

```
      <value>rmi://localhost:1099/order</value>
    </property>
    <property name="serviceInterface">
      <value>org.springframework.samples.jpetstore.domain.logic.OrderService</value>
    </property>
  </bean>
```

The service interface can be the same plain Java business interface used in the earlier examples. It does not need to derive from specific base interfaces or throw special remoting exceptions:

```
public interface OrderService {

  Order getOrder(int orderId);
}
```

Such a proxy is then available for bean references; for example:

```
<bean id="myOrderServiceClient" class="example.MyOrderServiceClient">
  <property name="orderService">
    <ref bean="rmiProxy"/>
  </property>
</bean>
```

The MyOrderServiceClient class is the same as in the earlier example. It would simply expose a bean property of type org.springframework.samples.jpetstore.domain.logic.OrderService here, so the client is tied not to a remote service but rather to a plain Java business interface.

```
public class MyOrderServiceClient {

  private OrderService orderService;

  public void setOrderService(OrderService orderService) {
    this.orderService = orderService;
  }

  public void doSomething() {
    Order order = this.orderService.getOrder(...);
    ...
  }
}
```

If the specified service interface is a traditional RMI service interface, RmiProxyFactoryBean will access it as a standard RMI service rather than as a special RMI invoker. This allows access to RMI services that are not exported through Spring, or to services with traditional RMI interfaces that are exported through Spring (for example, for reasons of compatibility). Of course, callers of such a proxy need to deal with the checked RMI RemoteException thrown by each service method.

```
public interface RemoteOrderService extends java.rmi.Remote {

  Order getOrder(int orderId) throws java.rmi.RemoteException;
}
```

If the specified service interface is a plain Java business interface (for example the OrderService interface shown previously) but the RMI stub received represents a traditional RMI service (for example implementing the RemoteOrderService RMI interface), special behavior will apply. Each invocation on the plain Java interface will be delegated to the corresponding method on the RMI proxy. If the underlying RMI proxy throws an RMI RemoteException, it will automatically be converted to Spring's unchecked RemoteAccessException.

> **Spring's** RmiProxyFactoryBean **can access RMI invoker services or traditional RMI services, through a plain Java business interface or RMI service interface, respectively. The actual mode of operation will be determined by the specified service interface. If both ends are managed by Spring, RMI invoker is recommended because it follows Spring's usual remoting conventions (that is, a plain Java business interface plus the unchecked** RemoteAccessException**).**
>
> **As a special feature,** RmiProxyFactoryBean **is able to access a traditional RMI service through a plain Java business interface, delegating all method calls to corresponding methods on the underlying stub and automatically converting checked** RemoteExceptions **to unchecked** RemoteAccessExceptions**. While this involves maintaining two interfaces for the same service, it does allow for accessing existing RMI services in a consistent Spring proxy fashion.**

Stub Lookup Strategies

As indicated, RMI stubs are connected to a specific endpoint, rather than just opening a connection to a given target address for each invocation. Consequently, if you restart the server that hosts the RMI endpoints, you need to re-register the stubs — and clients need to look them up again.

While the re-registration of the target service usually happens automatically on restart, stubs held by clients become stale in such a scenario. Clients won't notice this unless they try to call a method on the stub again, which will fail with a connect exception.

To avoid this scenario, Spring's RmiProxyFactoryBean offers a refreshStubOnConnectFailure setting as a bean property: Set this to true to enforce automatic re-lookup of the stub if a call fails with a connect exception.

```
<bean id="rmiProxy" class="org.springframework.remoting.rmi.RmiProxyFactoryBean">
  <property name="serviceUrl">
    <value>rmi://localhost:1099/order</value>
  </property>
  <property name="serviceInterface">
    <value>org.springframework.samples.jpetstore.domain.logic.OrderService</value>
  </property>
  <property name="refreshStubOnConnectFailure">
    <value>true</value>
  </property>
</bean>
```

A further issue with stub lookup is that the target RMI server and the RMI registry need to be available at the time of lookup. If the client starts before the server and tries to look up and cache the service stub, client startup will fail — even if the remote service is not needed yet.

To enable lazy lookup of the service stub, set RmiProxyFactoryBean's lookupStubOnStartup flag to false. The stub will then be looked up on first access, that is, when the first method invocation on the proxy comes in; it will be cached from then on. The disadvantage is that there will be no validation that the target service actually exists until the first invocation.

```
<bean id="rmiProxy" class="org.springframework.remoting.rmi.RmiProxyFactoryBean">
  <property name="serviceUrl">
    <value>rmi://localhost:1099/order</value>
  </property>
  <property name="serviceInterface">
    <value>org.springframework.samples.jpetstore.domain.logic.OrderService</value>
  </property>
  <property name="lookupStubOnStartup">
    <value>false</value>
  </property>
  <property name="refreshStubOnConnectFailure">
    <value>true</value>
  </property>
</bean>
```

To avoid caching of the stub altogether, RmiProxyFactoryBean's cacheStub flag can be set to false. This forces the proxy to perform a stub lookup for each method invocation. While this is clearly not desirable from a performance perspective, it guarantees that the stub will never be stale. However, it is usually sufficient to activate refreshStubOnConnectFailure, which will cache the stub unless a connection failure occurs on invocation.

```
<bean id="rmiProxy" class="org.springframework.remoting.rmi.RmiProxyFactoryBean">
  <property name="serviceUrl">
    <value>rmi://localhost:1099/order</value>
  </property>
  <property name="serviceInterface">
    <value>org.springframework.samples.jpetstore.domain.logic.OrderService</value>
  </property>
  <property name="lookupStubOnStartup">
    <value>false</value>
  </property>
  <property name="cacheStub">
    <value>false</value>
  </property>
</bean>
```

Spring offers a variety of stub lookup strategies. Instead of looking up the stub on startup and caching it for the lifetime of the proxy, there are options to automatically refresh the stub if a connect failure occurs, lazily look up the stub on first access, and/or not cache the stub in the first place.

While the default early lookup and eternal caching is, strictly speaking, the most efficient strategy because it does not require any synchronization on proxy invocation, it is the default mainly for historical reasons. It is usually advisable to turn on `refreshStubOnConnectFailure`, and also to turn off **lookupStubOnStartup**. The lifecycles of the client and the server are as decoupled as possible in such a scenario.

Exporting a Service

On the server side, exporting an existing Spring-managed bean as an RMI invoker service is straightforward. A corresponding service exporter must be defined in a Spring context — which can be the middle tier context because it does not have to be a web dispatcher context. RMI is not based on HTTP; therefore no `DispatcherServlet` is involved.

For example, such an RMI exporter definition could look as follows, exposing the `"petStore"` bean in the root application context as an RMI invoker service:

```
<bean id="order-rmi" class="org.springframework.remoting.rmi.RmiServiceExporter">
  <property name="service">
    <ref bean="petStore"/>
  </property>
  <property name="serviceInterface">
    <value>org.springframework.samples.jpetstore.domain.logic.OrderService</value>
  </property>
  <property name="serviceName">
    <value>order</value>
  </property>
  <property name="registryPort">
    <value>1099</value>
  </property>
</bean>
```

Assuming that the RMI registry is available on `localhost`, the remote `OrderService` would then be available as an RMI invoker service at `rmi://localhost:1099/order`.

In the JPetStore sample application, the `RmiServiceExporter` definition can be found in the `applicationContext.xml` file in the `WEB-INF` directory, alongside resource and business objects. Alternatively, such exporter definitions can be put into a separate bean definition file, building the root application context from multiple files via a corresponding `contextConfigLocation` entry in `web.xml`.

If the specified service interface is a traditional RMI service interface, `RmiServiceExporter` will automatically expose the service as a traditional RMI service rather than as a special RMI invoker. In such a scenario, any client can access the service in standard RMI style (even if not based on Spring).

> `RmiServiceExporter` **will automatically register the service with the RMI registry. If no existing registry is found, a new in-process one will be created. Note that all services in an RMI registry share a single namespace: You need to choose unique service names.**
>
> **Corresponding to** `RmiProxyFactoryBean`, `RmiServiceExporter` **can expose RMI invoker services or traditional RMI services through a plain Java business interface or RMI service interface, respectively. The actual mode of operation will be determined by the specified service interface.**
>
> **Overall, Spring makes RMI remoting much less painful than you may remember if you have worked with RMI in the past.**

Note that it is not advisable to use the RMI exporter in a process that also runs an EJB container, as RMI uses a shared infrastructure with a central registry, which is likely to cause conflicts if used by both the EJB container and Spring's RMI exporter. Of course, such a setup might nevertheless work, provided that you manage to configure the overall system accordingly to avoid conflicts.

Customization Options

Like HTTP invoker, RMI invoker uses Spring's generic remote invocation mechanism underneath, serializing `org.springframework.remoting.support.RemoteInvocation` and `org.springframework.remoting.support.RemoteInvocationResult` objects. This can be leveraged, for example, to include a custom user credential attribute in the invocation, as illustrated in the HTTP invoker section.

As the remote invocation infrastructure is shared with HTTP invoker, a custom `RemoteInvocation Factory` / `RemoteInvocationExecutor` pair can be applied to either HTTP invoker or RMI invoker without changes, transferring the additional attributes over the respective protocol.

> **Like HTTP invoker, RMI invoker is highly customizable, through the** `RemoteInvocationFactory` **and** **RemoteInvocationExecutor** **strategies. However, for typical needs, you don't have to worry about any of this. The standard configuration of** `RmiProxyFactoryBean` **and** `RmiServiceExporter` **should be perfectly sufficient.**

RMI-IIOP

Spring also supports RMI-IIOP: RMI access via CORBA's IIOP protocol. RMI-IIOP can be used for accessing backend CORBA services, but also as wire protocol for Java-to-Java remoting. The main support classes are:

❑   `org.springframework.remoting.rmi.JndiRmiProxyFactoryBean`: Proxy factory for Spring-compliant proxies that communicate with backend RMI-IIOP services. To be defined in a Spring bean factory or application context, exposing the proxy object for references (through the `FactoryBean` mechanism). Proxies will either throw RMI's `RemoteException` or Spring's generic `RemoteAccessException` in case of remote invocation failure, depending on the type of service interface used.

❑ `org.springframework.remoting.rmi.JndiRmiServiceExporter`: Exporter that registers a given service—a traditional RMI-IIOP service—with an ORB. Can take any existing Spring-managed bean and expose it under a given JNDI name in the ORB, allowing the target bean to be fully configured and wired via Spring.

These classes are direct equivalents of `RmiProxyFactoryBean` and `RmiServiceExporter`. There is no RMI invoker mechanism available here; the target service needs to be a traditional RMI-IIOP service, with a stub generated through the `rmic` tool with the `-iiop` option. Furthermore, the exporter is not able to start an in-process registry on demand; instead, an existing ORB needs to be available, for example the `orbd` executable included in the JDK.

On the client side, either the RMI service interface or a plain Java business interface can be specified. In the case of the latter, each invocation on the plain Java interface will be delegated to the corresponding method on the RMI proxy (analogous to when working with standard RMI). If the underlying RMI proxy throws an RMI `RemoteException`, it will automatically get converted to Spring's unchecked `RemoteAccessException`.

`JndiRmiProxyFactoryBean` supports the same stub lookup strategies as `RmiProxyFactoryBean`: `refreshStubOnConnectFailure`, `lookupStubOnStartup`, and `cacheStub`. See the section "Stub Lookup Strategies," earlier in this chapter, for details.

EJB containers are required to support RMI-IIOP. As a consequence, Spring's `JndiRmiProxyFactoryBean` can be used to access remote EJB home objects, for example for stateful session beans. The main difference from a plain JNDI lookup as performed by Spring's `org.springframework.jndi.JndiObjectFactoryBean` is that the RMI-IIOP access performs narrowing through the `javax.rmi.PortableRemoteObject` class, as required by well-behaved EJB lookups.

Web Services via JAX-RPC

To be able to access and implement Web Services based on WSDL (Web Service Definition Language) and SOAP (Simple Object Access Protocol), Spring integrates with the standard JAX-RPC API.

The JAX-RPC specification defines client access and two service endpoint models: one for servlet containers, and one for EJB containers. JAX-RPC support is required for J2EE 1.4–compliant servers, which have to support both endpoint models. There are also a variety of standalone providers that support JAX-RPC client access and the servlet endpoint model: for example, Apache Axis (`http://ws.apache.org/axis`).

For client access, JAX-RPC uses RMI-style stubs: Service interfaces have to follow traditional RMI conventions, that is, extend `java.rmi.Remote` and throw `java.rmi.RemoteException` on each method. As an alternative, there is also the Dynamic Invocation Interface, which allows invocation of methods by name (similar to Java reflection).

Spring supports both the client and the server side of JAX-RPC: Spring-style client access with service interfaces, and servlet endpoints that can easily delegate to Spring-managed service implementations. The two main components involved are:

❏ `org.springframework.remoting.jaxrpc.JaxRpcPortProxyFactoryBean`: Proxy factory for Spring-compliant proxies that communicate with backend Web Services. To be defined in a Spring bean factory or application context, exposing the proxy object for references (through the `FactoryBean` mechanism). Proxies will either throw RMI's `RemoteException` or Spring's generic `RemoteAccessException` in case of remote invocation failure, depending on the type of service interface used.

❏ `org.springframework.remoting.jaxrpc.ServletEndpointSupport`: Convenient base class for Web Service endpoints, that is, for service classes to be exposed as Web Services via a JAX-RPC–compliant tool. The Web Service tool itself will instantiate and manage such an endpoint class, which needs to implement the corresponding RMI service interface. With standard JAX-RPC, it is not possible to export an existing Spring-managed bean directly as a Web Service; an endpoint adapter is always needed.

Furthermore, there is also a `LocalJaxRpcServiceFactoryBean`, which sets up a JAX-RPC `Service` (`javax.xml.rpc.Service`) instance. Such a `Service` reference can be used, for example, to perform dynamic JAX-RPC invocations instead of method calls on a proxy interface. This is rarely used in typical application code, however.

While client access is as similar to the other remoting protocols supported in Spring as possible (the main difference being that significantly more configuration settings are required), service export is completely different: Rather than defining seamless exporters for existing Spring-managed beans, a special service endpoint class has to be written *for each service*, registered with the chosen Web Service tool in a proprietary fashion. The service endpoint class can in turn delegate to Spring-managed beans, but its lifecycle is not under control of Spring — it is managed by the Web Service tool.

Note that by default, only primitive types and collections can be serialized via JAX-RPC because Web Services and thus JAX-RPC do *not* provide a general serialization mechanism. Application-specific classes such as `Order` and `Product` in Spring's JPetStore sample application need to be addressed in a specific fashion, for example registering custom serializers and deserializers for them. Axis includes such a serializer for JavaBeans, which is useful for typical domain objects.

> **WSDL/SOAP-based Web Services are an obvious choice for cross-platform remoting, for example between J2EE and .NET. However, setup and configuration are significantly more complex than with Hessian or HTTP invoker, and the parsing overhead of SOAP is significantly higher.**
>
> **Hessian and HTTP invoker are usually preferable alternatives for HTTP-based Java-to-Java remoting. In particular, their serialization power makes them attractive for the transfer of complex Java objects. We recommend that you resort to SOAP only if there is a concrete need for it, that is, if there are non-Java clients with existing SOAP support.**
>
> **It is important to note that remoting protocol is not an either/or choice when using Spring. The same target service can be exported via both Hessian and SOAP at the same time, for example, through defining a corresponding exporter for Hessian and referring to the same service from a JAX-RPC servlet endpoint — available at different URLs. Clients can then choose the protocol for talking to the service: Java clients might prefer Hessian, while .NET clients will choose SOAP.**

Accessing a Service

On the client side, a proxy for a target service can easily be created via a Spring bean definition—analogous to RMI. The configuration needed is as follows, assuming Axis as a concrete backend implementation. For details on the parameters, see the JAX-RPC specification or the Axis documentation.

```xml
<bean id="jaxRpcProxy"
    class="org.springframework.remoting.jaxrpc.JaxRpcPortProxyFactoryBean">
  <property name="serviceFactoryClass">
    <value>org.apache.axis.client.ServiceFactory</value>
  </property>
  <property name="wsdlDocumentUrl">
    <value>http://localhost:8080/axis/OrderService?wsdl</value>
  </property>
  <property name="namespaceUri">
    <value>http://localhost:8080/axis/OrderService</value>
  </property>
  <property name="serviceName">
    <value>JaxRpcOrderServiceService</value>
  </property>
  <property name="portName">
    <value>OrderService</value>
  </property>
  <property name="serviceInterface">
    <value>org.springframework.samples.jpetstore.service.RemoteOrderService</value>
  </property>
</bean>
```

The service interface used here is an RMI interface version of the `OrderService` used in the earlier examples. It might have been generated by a Web Service tool that turns a WSDL service description into a Java interface (usually following RMI conventions).

```java
public interface RemoteOrderService extends java.rmi.Remote {

  Order getOrder(int orderId) throws java.rmi.RemoteException;
}
```

Alternatively, the service interface can also be the same plain Java business interface used in the earlier examples, not deriving from specific base interfaces or throwing special remoting exceptions. On remote invocation failure, it will throw Spring's unchecked `RemoteAccessException`.

```java
public interface OrderService {

  Order getOrder(int orderId);
}
```

The corresponding proxy bean definition looks as follows. It defines the plain Java interface as `serviceInterface` and the (potentially generated) RMI interface as JAX-RPC `portInterface`. Each method call on the service interface will be delegated to the corresponding method on the RMI interface, converting the checked RMI `RemoteException` into Spring's unchecked `RemoteAccessException`.

```xml
<bean id="jaxRpcProxy"
    class="org.springframework.remoting.jaxrpc.JaxRpcPortProxyFactoryBean">
  <property name="serviceFactoryClass">
    <value>org.apache.axis.client.ServiceFactory</value>
  </property>
  <property name="wsdlDocumentUrl">
    <value>http://localhost:8080/axis/OrderService?wsdl</value>
  </property>
  <property name="namespaceUri">
    <value>http://localhost:8080/axis/OrderService</value>
  </property>
  <property name="serviceName">
    <value>JaxRpcOrderServiceService</value>
  </property>
  <property name="portName">
    <value>OrderService</value>
  </property>
  <property name="serviceInterface">
    <value>org.springframework.samples.jpetstore.domain.logic.OrderService</value>
  </property>
  <property name="portInterface">
    <value>org.springframework.samples.jpetstore.service.RemoteOrderService</value>
  </property>
</bean>
```

Alternatively, you can also omit the portInterface value, which will turn service invocations into dynamic JAX-RPC calls (using JAX-RPC's *Dynamic Invocation Interface*). Dynamic calls work nicely on Axis, for example, which means you do not need to maintain an RMI port interface. While specifying an RMI port interface might offer advantages on certain JAX-RPC implementations, it is often preferable to stick with a single plain Java business interface instead, using dynamic calls underneath.

> Similar to its RMI support equivalent, JaxRpcPortProxyFactoryBean is able to access a JAX-RPC port through a plain Java business interface, automatically converting checked RemoteExceptions to unchecked **RemoteAccessExceptions**. This enables you to access standard JAX-RPC services in a consistent Spring proxy fashion.

Such a proxy is then available for bean references; for example:

```xml
<bean id="myOrderServiceClient" class="example.MyOrderServiceClient">
  <property name="orderService">
    <ref bean="jaxRpcProxy"/>
  </property>
</bean>
```

The MyOrderServiceClient class is the same as in the earlier example. It would simply expose a bean property of type org.springframework.samples.jpetstore.domain.logic.OrderService here, so the client is tied not to a remote service but rather to a plain Java business interface.

```
public class MyOrderServiceClient {

  private OrderService orderService;

  public void setOrderService(OrderService orderService) {
    this.orderService = orderService;
  }

  public void doSomething() {
    Order order = this.orderService.getOrder(...);
    ...
  }
}
```

Exporting a Service

The biggest difference in setting up a JAX-RPC service is on the server side. In contrast to all other supported remoting strategies in Spring, this is *not* possible through an exporter definition in a Spring context. Instead, the actual deployment is tool-specific; just the *service endpoint model* is standardized by the JAX-RPC specification.

A JAX-RPC servlet endpoint is a plain Java class that implements the RMI-style port interface of the service. It can optionally implement the `javax.xml.rpc.server.ServiceLifecycle` interface, to receive a `javax.xml.rpc.server.ServletEndpointContext` on initialization, which in turn allows access to the `javax.servlet.ServletContext` of the web application. This can be used to access the Spring root application context, in turn delegating to Spring-managed middle tier beans for service operations.

Spring provides the `org.springframework.remoting.jaxrpc.ServletEndpointSupport` class as a convenient base class for such endpoint implementations: It pre-implements the `ServiceLifecycle` interface and the Spring root application context lookup, allowing easy access to context facilities.

In the case of JPetStore's `OrderService`, the endpoint implementation looks as follows. It derives from `ServletEndpointSupport` and implements the plain Java business interface of the service, simply delegating a `getOrder` call to the target `OrderService` in the root application context.

```
public class JaxRpcOrderService extends ServletEndpointSupport
    implements OrderService {

  private OrderService orderService;

  protected void onInit() {
    this.orderService =
        (OrderService) getWebApplicationContext().getBean("petStore");
  }

  public Order getOrder(int orderId) {
    return this.orderService.getOrder(orderId);
  }
}
```

As shown in the earlier examples, the actual `OrderService` implementation in JPetStore's middle tier is the `PetStoreImpl` object, which also implements the `PetStoreFacade` interface. Therefore, the endpoint class looks up the `petStore` bean from the application context.

An endpoint class such as the one in the preceding example, just implementing a business interface, will be accepted by most JAX-RPC implementations, including Axis. However, the JAX-RPC specification requires an endpoint to implement an RMI port interface, so strict JAX-RPC implementations might reject such a plain endpoint class. In that case, simply let your endpoint class implement an RMI port interface, too, mirroring the business interface but complying to RMI conventions.

> **It is good practice to let the endpoint class implement both the RMI service interface and the plain Java business interface, if both are used. Those interfaces will just differ in the remote exception thrown; as the target service is not supposed to throw remote invocation failure exceptions itself, its methods can easily comply to both interfaces (through not throwing any such exception).**

An endpoint class needs to be implemented *for each exported service*, even if just delegating to the corresponding target method of the corresponding Spring-managed bean. It acts as an adapter between the JAX-RPC endpoint model and the plain Java nature of the target service implementation.

As an example of tool-specific deployment of an endpoint class, let's superficially look at how to deploy to Axis. Essentially, you need to add a `service` section to the Axis `server-config.wsdd` file, which resides in the `WEB-INF` directory:

```
<service name="OrderService" provider="java:RPC">
  <parameter name="allowedMethods" value="*"/>
  <parameter name="className" value=
      "org.springframework.samples.jpetstore.service.server.JaxRpcOrderService"/>
</service>
```

The Axis servlet will read this configuration on startup and make the service available under the given port name, instantiating the specified endpoint class and delegating remote calls to it. The Axis servlet itself needs to be defined in `web.xml`:

```
<servlet>
  <servlet-name>axis</servlet-name>
  <servlet-class>org.apache.axis.transport.http.AxisServlet</servlet-class>
  <load-on-startup/>
</servlet>

<servlet-mapping>
  <servlet-name>axis</servlet-name>
  <url-pattern>/axis/*</url-pattern>
</servlet-mapping>
```

We have deliberately omitted custom type mappings here, for simplicity's sake. In the next section, we will look at how to register custom serializers with Axis, on both the server and the client side.

> Even though deployment of a Web Service via Axis is completely different from all other supported remoting strategies in Spring, it can still coexist with other remote exporters. The endpoints deployed via Axis will usually delegate to the same Spring-managed middle tier beans as other remote exporters.
>
> For example, you can define a Spring `DispatcherServlet` for exporting services via Hessian, Burlap, and/or HTTP invoker, while also defining an `AxisServlet` for exporting via SOAP. This is the case in the JPetStore sample application, using the servlet names `remoting` and `axis`, respectively.

Custom Type Mappings

To allow Axis to serialize custom application objects, special type mappings have to be registered. On the server side, this usually happens through `beanMapping` tags nested within the service definition in the `server-config.wsdd` file:

```
<service name="OrderService" provider="java:RPC">
  <parameter name="allowedMethods" value="*"/>
  <parameter name="className" value=
     "org.springframework.samples.jpetstore.service.server.JaxRpcOrderService"/>
  <beanMapping qname="jpetstore:Order" xmlns:jpetstore="urn:JPetStore"
     languageSpecificType=
     "java:org.springframework.samples.jpetstore.domain.Order"/>
  <beanMapping qname="jpetstore:LineItem" xmlns:jpetstore="urn:JPetStore"
     languageSpecificType=
     "java:org.springframework.samples.jpetstore.domain.LineItem"/>
  <beanMapping qname="jpetstore:Item" xmlns:jpetstore="urn:JPetStore"
     languageSpecificType=
     "java:org.springframework.samples.jpetstore.domain.Item"/>
  <beanMapping qname="jpetstore:Product" xmlns:jpetstore="urn:JPetStore"
     languageSpecificType=
     "java:org.springframework.samples.jpetstore.domain.Product"/>
</service>
```

Each mapping defines a specific symbolic name in the WSDL namespace and associates a Java class name with it. When encountering such objects, Axis will automatically serialize them as JavaBeans, as indicated by the `beanMapping` tag.

On the client side, the registration of custom serializers usually happens programmatically. Spring's `JaxRpcPortProxyFactoryBean` offers a specific hook to register such serializers, namely the `JaxRpcServicePostProcessor` interface:

```
public class BeanMappingServicePostProcessor
    implements JaxRpcServicePostProcessor {

  public void postProcessJaxRpcService(Service service) {
    TypeMappingRegistry registry = service.getTypeMappingRegistry();
    TypeMapping mapping = registry.createTypeMapping();
```

```
        registerBeanMapping(mapping, Order.class, "Order");
        registerBeanMapping(mapping, LineItem.class, "LineItem");
        registerBeanMapping(mapping, Item.class, "Item");
        registerBeanMapping(mapping, Product.class, "Product");
        registry.register("http://schemas.xmlsoap.org/soap/encoding/", mapping);
    }

    protected void registerBeanMapping(TypeMapping mapping, Class type, String name){
        QName qName = new QName("urn:JPetStore", name);
        mapping.register(type, qName,
            new BeanSerializerFactory(type, qName),
            new BeanDeserializerFactory(type, qName));
    }
}
```

The corresponding bean definition looks as follows. An instance of the
BeanMappingServicePostProcessor class is registered through JaxRpcPortProxyFactoryBean's
servicePostProcessors property, in this case as an unnamed inner bean:

```
<bean id="jaxRpcProxy"
    class="org.springframework.remoting.jaxrpc.JaxRpcPortProxyFactoryBean">
    <property name="serviceFactoryClass">
      <value>org.apache.axis.client.ServiceFactory</value>
    </property>
    <property name="wsdlDocumentUrl">
      <value>http://localhost:8080/axis/OrderService?wsdl</value>
    </property>
    <property name="namespaceUri">
      <value>http://localhost:8080/axis/OrderService</value>
    </property>
    <property name="serviceName">
      <value>JaxRpcOrderServiceService</value>
    </property>
    <property name="portName">
      <value>OrderService</value>
    </property>
    <property name="serviceInterface">
      <value>org.springframework.samples.jpetstore.domain.logic.OrderService</value>
    </property>
    <property name="servicePostProcessors">
      <list>
        <bean class="org.springframework.samples.jpetstore.service.client.
            BeanMappingServicePostProcessor"/>
      </list>
    </property>
</bean>
```

With both ends properly configured, Order, LineItem, Item, and Product objects can be transferred
through the Web Service. For details on custom type mappings, please refer to the Axis documentation.

> Custom types require special effort with WSDL/SOAP-based Web Services. In contrast to other remoting protocols such as Hessian or HTTP invoker, each custom type needs to be registered with an appropriate serializer/deserializer on both the server and the client side.

Summary

We have seen that Spring supports a wide variety of remoting strategies: from the slim HTTP-based protocol twins Hessian and Burlap over Spring's own HTTP invoker to standard RMI and JAX-RPC. It brings the Spring values of consistency and simplicity, *without sacrificing power*, to a wide variety of remoting scenarios.

As much as possible, Spring offers a common configuration style for all of those strategies. Proxies can consistently use plain Java business interfaces and throw Spring's unchecked `RemoteAccessException`, although there is also the option of exposing traditional RMI service interfaces for RMI and JAX-RPC services. As a special feature, an existing RMI-style service can also be proxied with a plain Java business interface, delegating each method call to the underlying RMI service stub.

On the server side, the export mechanism depends on the actual protocol. The lightweight HTTP-based protocols Hessian, Burlap, and HTTP invoker all allow for exposing an existing Spring-managed bean as a remote service, through defining an exporter for a specific protocol. It is also straightforward to expose the same service instance through multiple protocols at the same time, simply defining multiple exporters for the same target bean and binding them to different URLs.

Using Spring's RMI exporter is usually a seamless process, too — provided that there is no conflicting RMI infrastructure in place. It is in general not advisable to use the RMI exporter in a process that also runs an EJB container, as this might lead to conflicts. Exporting a service via RMI works nicely in a J2EE web container such as Tomcat, Jetty, or Resin, though, and is a particularly convincing option for a process that does not run in a J2EE container.

Exporting a Web Service through JAX-RPC is significantly more complex than exporting a service through one of the other protocols. It involves tool-specific deployment of a special endpoint implementation. Delegation to an existing Spring-managed bean can be achieved, but only through writing a thin endpoint adapter for each service. Accessing a Web Service basically follows Spring style, but requires more configuration than Hessian or HTTP invoker.

This flexibility poses the question: which protocol to choose for which scenario? As outlined, the protocol choice is not an either/or decision with Spring, as the same service can be exported through multiple protocols at the same time. Nevertheless, there has to be a choice of protocol per client. The basic recommendation is as follows:

❑ **Java-to-Java remoting:** If all you need is remote calls from one Java process to another Java process, we strongly recommend that you avoid a cross-platform protocol such as SOAP. Instead, choose a binary strategy such as Hessian, HTTP invoker, or RMI invoker. The former allows for loose coupling without strictly matching codebases, while the latter two impose the restrictions of Java serialization on your objects. Even if your server has to expose a SOAP endpoint for other clients, let your Java clients talk to a (more efficient) Hessian or HTTP invoker endpoint instead.

❑ **Cross-platform remoting:** If non-Java clients need to talk to your server, SOAP via JAX-RPC is an obvious choice, in particular for platforms such as .NET and Delphi, which include native support for SOAP. This is where the configuration complexity of Web Services will pay off, in contrast to a Java-to-Java remoting scenario. However, there is still an alternative: If there is a Hessian or Burlap implementation for the platform in question, you could choose one of them as a lighter alternative to SOAP. Even implementing your own Hessian or Burlap client can be feasible, in particular for platforms without native SOAP support.

A further important criterion is whether you need client-server remoting or intra-server remoting. For the former, an HTTP-based protocol is preferable, to avoid firewall issues and to be able to communicate over the Internet. However, for an intra-server scenario, a non-HTTP solution such as RMI would be appropriate, too, although Hessian and HTTP invoker are roughly equivalent in terms of efficiency (despite being HTTP-based). Most importantly, do not choose SOAP for communication between Java-based servers unless absolutely necessary.

To a large degree, the protocol choice becomes a configuration matter with Spring. Neither client objects nor service implementations are tied to a specific protocol or remoting API. In many cases, the protocol can indeed be switched at deployment time: for example, from RMI invoker to HTTP invoker if facing firewall limitations in a concrete environment. Some of the protocols have specific requirements for serializable objects, but in general even switching between different serialization mechanisms — for example, between Hessian and HTTP invoker — is rather smooth.

> Of course, as with any infrastructure that you depend on, test your application with the remoting protocols of your choice, and test it thoroughly. All deployment scenarios for your application need to be tested, including all potential remoting protocols. Once you have made sure that a certain set of remoting protocols works for your requirements, the actual deployment choice becomes a configuration matter with Spring.

Supporting Services

Let's look now at some of the many features of Spring beyond the core container. These include useful features for implementing enterprise applications—part of Spring's overall service abstraction—and support for implementing objects in languages other than Java.

In this chapter we will focus on the following areas:

- ❑ **Messaging:** Spring provides support for sending JMS messages.
- ❑ **Scheduling:** Spring provides a scheduling abstraction, including integration with the popular Quartz scheduler.
- ❑ **Mail:** Spring provides an abstraction for sending email that simplifies use of JavaMail and makes application code easier to test.
- ❑ **Scripting:** Spring allows you to implement objects in scripting languages such as Groovy and Java. Scripted objects enjoy full IoC and AOP support, and can be reloaded without affecting objects that depend on them.

JMS

Asynchronous messaging is important in many enterprise applications. Spring provides support for consuming JMS messages, which both simplifies the programming model (compared to direct use of the JMS API) and provides a consistent basis for access to advanced features such as dynamic destinations.

Future versions of Spring will provide support for consuming messages comparable to—but simpler than—Message Driven Beans.

Introduction

JMS, the *Java Message Service*, is a messaging standard that allows applications to communicate with each other reliably and asynchronously. Usually referred to as *Message-Oriented Middleware* or *MOM*, messaging middleware had been used extensively in enterprise solutions before the release of the JMS standard in 1999. Similar in spirit to the ODBC standard for database access, the goals of the JMS standardization process were to provide a common API and uniform delivery semantics across different vendors' messaging systems. Areas such as administration, interoperability, and clustering were not addressed by the specification and allow vendors to differentiate themselves.

The asynchronous nature of messaging middleware is the central characteristic that distinguishes it from RPC-based middleware technologies such as RMI/IIOP. Asynchronous behavior is achieved by having a message broker sit between a message producer and message consumer application. JMS supports two categories of messaging, *Point-to-Point* (P2P) and *Publish/Subscribe* messaging (*Pub/Sub*). The true loosely coupled nature of JMS, where applications can still communicate despite not being available at the same time, is an important aspect to consider in deciding to use JMS in your solution.

JMS providers typically provide many language bindings for their products, which reflects the history of using MOM in enterprise application integration solutions across heterogeneous platforms and programming languages. This provides an effective means of interoperability between the .NET, Java, and C/C++ applications. Combined with a way to define the content of messages, for example using XML Schema, JMS can be used directly as an alternative to asynchronous or synchronous Web Services for interoperability solutions. Synchronous request-reply interactions are also possible using JMS by writing synchronous helper classes that are an abstraction on top of the underlying asynchronous message exchange.

There are two major revisions of the JMS specification: JMS 1.0, which was incorporated into J2EE 1.2; and JMS 1.1, incorporated into J2EE 1.4. The 1.1 revision improved the programming model by providing a polymorphic API that could be used easily across both messaging categories, P2P and Pub/Sub. The 1.0 API had modeled these two categories using a repetitive parallel class hierarchy for each domain. This led to code that was difficult to maintain if there was a need to change from using P2P to Pub/Sub delivery. The 1.1 revision also removed functional differences between the two messaging categories such as mixing P2P message consumption and Pub/Sub production within the same JMS transacted session.

The use of JMS is not restricted to an EJB container; it can also be used in web and standalone environments. The EJB container provides the infrastructure for creating message *consumers* through the use of Message Driven Beans (MDBs). In addition, through the use of XA-capable JMS providers, the EJB container provides declarative and programmatic transaction management for enlistment of a JMS resource in a JTS transaction. A common scenario is to perform database access and message production within a distributed transaction.

Like the JDBC API, the JMS API is relatively low level, requiring a large volume of code to do simple tasks. This repetitive and error-prone code begs to be encapsulated in an abstraction layer. Hence, Spring uses a similar approach to the approach it takes for the JDBC API. The Spring Framework provides a template class that simplifies the use of the JMS API for *producing* messages concealing the complexity of doing JNDI lookups and working with multiple JMS API objects. It also shields users from the differences between the 1.0 and 1.1 APIs, ensures proper resource handling, and leverages the managed transaction features of Spring enabling JMS publishing applications to enlist JMS in a distributed transaction without the use of an EJB container.

Creating simple message consumer applications outside the EJB container is a straightforward exercise in the use of the JMS API, which can be an appropriate choice in application scenarios that do not require concurrent processing of messages. Infrastructure for concurrent message consumer applications comparable to the functionality offered by MDBs will be provided in future releases of Spring.

Motivation for Spring's JMS Support

The following code shows the standard usage of the JMS 1.1 API for sending a `TextMessage`. It assumes the JMS `ConnectionFactory` and `Destination` have already been obtained using JNDI or other means. (We assume familiarity with core JMS API concepts: Please consult a reference on J2EE if necessary.)

```
public void testJMS() throws JMSException {

  Connection connection = null;
  Session session = null;

  try {
    connection = connectionFactory.createConnection();
    session = connection.createSession(false, Session.AUTO_ACKNOWLEDGE);
    MessageProducer producer = session.createProducer(null);
    Message message = session.createTextMessage("hello world");
    producer.send(destination, message);

  } finally {
    if (session != null) {
      try {
        session.close();
      } catch (JMSException ex) {
        logger.warn("Failed to close the session", ex);
      }
    }
    if (connection != null) {
      try {
        connection.close();
      } catch (JMSException ex) {
        logger.warn("Failed to close the connection", ex);
      }
    }
  }
}
```

If you are using the JMS 1.0 API, the code inside the `try` block would be changed to the following:

```
connection = queueConnectionFactory.createQueueConnection();
session = connection.createQueueSession(false, session.AUTO_ACKNOWLEDGE);
QueueSender queueSender = session.createSender(null);
Message message = session.createTextMessage("hello world");
queueSender.send(queue, message);
```

As in the case of JDBC, the visibility of intermediate JMS API objects and the addition of correct resource handling introduce a significant amount of code in order to perform the simplest of JMS operations. Adding the retrieval of the connection factory, destination, and configuration of quality-of-service parameters in the JMS session would further increase the length of the code.

JMS Access via a Template

The `JmsTemplate` class located in the `org.springframework.jms.core` package implements the core JMS processing tasks. It follows the same design as the `JdbcTemplate`, providing simple one-liner methods to perform common send and synchronous receive operations, and using callback interfaces for more advanced usage scenarios. As we've noted before, once you master the core Spring concepts, you can leverage them in many areas.

The code shown previously for sending a simple `TextMessage` now is simply as follows:

```
public void testTemplate() {

    JmsTemplate jmsTemplate = new JmsTemplate(connectionFactory);
    jmsTemplate.convertAndSend(destination, "Hello World!");

}
```

As you can see, this is much simpler. There is no need to manage resources in application code.

`JmsTemplate` uses the JMS 1.1 API, and the subclass `JmsTemplate102` uses the JMS 1.0 API. The Boolean property `PubSubDomain` is used to configure the `JmsTemplate` with knowledge of what messaging category is being used, point-to-point or Pub/Sub. This is important when using the `JmsTemplate102`. The default value of this property is `false`, indicating that the point-to-point domain will be used. This flag has no effect on send operations for the 1.1 implementation since the 1.0 API is agnostic to the messaging category.

The `JmsTemplate` increases the level of abstraction in using JMS by providing overloaded `convertAndSend` and `receiveAndConvert` methods, which represent the message data type as a Java object instead of a `javax.jms.Message`. These methods convert between Java objects and JMS messages by delegating the conversion process to an instance of the `MessageConverter` interface. This allows your application code to focus on the business object that is being sent or received with JMS and not the details of how to represent the object as a JMS message. In the previous example, the default message converter is used to convert the string `"Hello world"` to a `TextMessage`. `MessageConverters` are covered in greater detail later in the chapter.

Callback Methods

Many of `JmsTemplate`'s methods use callback interfaces to provide greater control over the message creation process and to expose the JMS `Session` and `MessageProducer` to the user. The callback interfaces let you control the key aspects of using the raw JMS API while letting the template handle correct resource management of JMS connections and sessions.

> **As you should realize, the use of callback methods is consistent with that in Spring's JDBC abstraction, and other Spring libraries such as JNDI and Hibernate and TopLink support. Callbacks are a powerful concept that can be applied to many enterprise (and other) APIs.**

Sending and receiving of `javax.jms.Messages` are performed using `JmsTemplate`'s send and receive methods. These methods use an instance of the callback interface `MessageCreator` shown here:

```
public interface MessageCreator {

    Message createMessage(Session session) throws JMSException;

}
```

The following code uses the template method send(Destination, MessageCreator) and an anonymous inner class to implement the MessageCreator callback:

```
JmsTemplate jmsTemplate = new JmsTemplate(connectionFactory);
jmsTemplate.send(
    destination,
    new MessageCreator() {
      public Message createMessage(Session session) throws JMSException {
        Message m = session.createTextMessage("Hello World!");
        m.setIntProperty("UserID", 46);
        m.setJMSCorrelationID("314-61803");
        return m;
      }
    }
);
```

The MessageCreator callback exposes the JMS session object allowing you to create any of the supported JMS message types. Once the message is created, you can set the property and client-assigned header values as you would in standard JMS code.

While the send and convertAndSend methods cover most usage scenarios, there are cases when you want to perform multiple operations on a JMS Session or MessageProducer. The SessionCallback and ProducerCallback expose the JMS Session and a Session/MessageProducer pair respectively. The execute() methods on JmsTemplate execute these callback methods. If you are using a JMS 1.0 provider, you will need to downcast MessageProducer to point-to-point or Pub/Sub subclasses to access send and publish methods.

Synchronous Receiving

While JMS is typically associated with asynchronous processing, it is straightforward to consume messages synchronously using the receive method on a MessageConsumer. The overloaded receive and receiveAndConvert methods on JmsTemplate provide this functionality. In addition, the receive methods will also start the JMS connection in order to enable the delivery of messages.

> A synchronous receive will block the calling thread until a message becomes available. This can be a dangerous operation because the calling thread can potentially be blocked indefinitely. The property receiveTimeout specifies how long the receiver should wait before giving up waiting for a message.

Quality of Service Parameters

The raw JMS API has two categories of send methods: one that specifies delivery mode, priority, and time-to-live as quality of service (QOS) parameters; and another with no parameters. The no-parameter send method uses the default QOS values specified by the JMS standard. Because there are many overloaded send methods in `JmsTemplate`, the QOS parameters have been exposed as bean properties to avoid duplication in the number of send methods. These properties are named `DeliveryMode`, `Priority`, and `TimeToLive`. Similarly, the timeout value for synchronous receive calls is set using the property `ReceiveTimeout`.

Some JMS providers allow the setting of default QOS values administratively through the configuration of `ConnectionFactory` or `Destination` objects that override client-specified values. In order to raise awareness of this issue for configuring consistent management of QOS values, the `JmsTemplate` must be specifically enabled to use its client-specific QOS values by setting the Boolean property `isExplicitQosEnabled` to `true`.

Exception Handling

The JMS API provides a checked exception hierarchy that effectively captures messaging error conditions. Following the use of unchecked exceptions throughout Spring, the `JmsTemplate` class converts the checked `javax.jms.JMSException` to the unchecked `org.springframework.jms.JmsException`. While the analogy with data access and the DAO patterns is not perfect, the use of unchecked exceptions with JMS does facilitate the use of the Strategy pattern to separate the details of a service interface with a particular implementation as seen in high-level user code.

The package `org.springframework.jms.support` provides `JMSException` translation functionality. Unlike the case with JDBC, the JMS exception translation is considerably less complex and converts the checked `JMSException` hierarchy to a mirrored hierarchy of unchecked exceptions. If there are any provider-specific subclasses of the checked `javax.jms.JMSException`, this exception is wrapped in the unchecked `UncategorizedJmsException`.

ConnectionFactory Management

The `JmsTemplate` requires a reference to a `ConnectionFactory`. The `ConnectionFactory` is part of the JMS specification and serves as the entry point for working with JMS. It is used as a factory to create connections with the JMS provider and encapsulates various configuration parameters, many of which are vendor specific such as SSL configuration options.

When using JMS inside an EJB or web container, the container provides an implementation of the JMS `ConnectionFactory` interface that can participate in declarative transaction management and perform pooling of connections and sessions. In order to use this implementation, containers typically require that you declare a JMS connection factory as a `resource-ref` inside the EJB or servlet deployment descriptors. To ensure the use of these features with the `JmsTemplate` inside an EJB or servlet, the client application should ensure that it references the managed implementation of the `ConnectionFactory`.

Spring provides an implementation of the `ConnectionFactory` interface, `SingleConnectionFactory`, which returns the same `Connection` on all `createConnection` calls and ignores calls to `close`. This is useful for testing and standalone environments so that the same connection can be used for multiple `JmsTemplate` calls that may span any number of transactions. `SingleConnectionFactory` takes a reference to a standard `ConnectionFactory` that would typically come from JNDI.

Message Converters

As mentioned previously, message converters are used to support `JmsTemplate`'s `convertAndSend` and `receiveAndConvert` methods, which represent the JMS message data as a Java object. The

MessageConverter interface is in the `org.springframework.jms.support.converter` package and is defined as

```
public interface MessageConverter {

   Message toMessage(Object object, Session session) throws JMSException,
 MessageConversionException;

   Object fromMessage(Message message) throws JMSException,
 MessageConversionException;

}
```

Spring provides a default implementation, `SimpleMessageConverter`, which supports conversion between `String` and `TextMessage`, `byte[]` and `BytesMesssage`, `java.util.Map` and `MapMessage`, and `Serializable` and `ObjectMessage`. Please note that sending serialized objects via JMS is not a best practice and should be used carefully, if at all, because of the difficulties of keeping producer and consumers synchronized with the same class version.

To accommodate the setting of message content that cannot be generically encapsulated inside a converter class, the interface `MessagePostProcessor` gives you access to the message after it has been converted, but before it is sent. The example that follows shows how to modify a message header and a property after a `java.util.Map` is converted to a JMS message:

```
Map m = new HashMap();
m.put("Name", "Stewie");
m.put("Age", new Integer(1));

jmsTemplate.convertAndSend(destination, m,
     new MessagePostProcessor() {

        public Message postProcessMessage(Message message) throws JMSException {
           message.setIntProperty("AccountID", 1234);
           message.setJMSCorrelationID("314-61803");
           return message;
        }
     }
);
```

This results in a message of the form:

```
MapMessage={
  Header={
    ... standard headers ...
    CorrelationID={314-61803}
  }
  Properties={
    AccountID={Integer:1234}
  }
  Fields={
    Name={String:Stewie}
    Age={Integer:1}
  }
}
```

341

We encourage you to develop more sophisticated implementations that can marshal a broader class of Java objects. One implementation option is to leverage popular XML data marshalling toolkits such as JAXB, Castor, XMLBeans, or XStream to create a JMS `TextMessage` representing the object. The definition of messages exchanged would then leverage standard XML facilities such as XML DTDs or Schemas. Another implementation option would be to use reflection to convert a Java object to a `MapMessage`. A robust implementation based on `MapMessages` and reflection requires the use of nested `MapMessages`, which are not supported by the JMS specification but are a popular vendor extension.

Destination Management

Destinations such as connection factories are JMS-administered objects that can be stored and retrieved in JNDI. When configuring a Spring application context, you can use the JNDI factory class `JndiObject FactoryBean` to perform dependency injection on your object's references.

```
<bean id="queue" class="org.springframework.jndi.JndiObjectFactoryBean">
  <property name="jndiName">
    <value>testQueue</value>
  </property>
</bean>
```

This can then be used to set a `Destination` property on the object that will be performing JMS operations. Alternatively, you can also configure the `JmsTemplate` with a default destination using the property `DefaultDestination`. The default destination will be used with send and receive methods that do not refer to a specific destination.

However, using Dependency Injection can be cumbersome or inappropriate if there are a large number of destinations or if advanced destination management features are offered by JMS provider. Examples of such advanced destination management would be the creation of dynamic destinations or support for a hierarchical namespace of destinations.

Often the destinations used in a JMS application are known only at runtime and cannot be administratively created when the application is deployed. This is often because there is shared application logic between interacting system components that create destinations at runtime according to a well-known naming convention. Although the creation of dynamic destinations is not part of the JMS specification, most vendors support it. Dynamic destinations are created with a name defined by the user that differentiates them from JMS temporary destinations and are often not registered in JNDI.

The API used to create dynamic destinations varies from provider to provider because the properties associated with the destination are vendor specific. However, a simple implementation choice that is sometimes made by vendors is to disregard the warnings in the JMS specification and use the `TopicSession` method `createTopic(String topicName)` or the `QueueSession` method `createQueue(String queueName)` to create a new destination with default destination properties.

The send methods of `JmsTemplate` that take a string argument for a destination name delegate the resolution of that name to a JMS `Destination` object using an implementation of the `DestinationResolver` interface. This interface and related classes are contained in the `org.springframework.jms.support .destination` package.

```
public interface DestinationResolver {
  Destination resolveDestinationName(Session session,
                                     String destinationName,
```

```
                              boolean pubSubDomain)
                        throws JMSException;
    }
```

Spring provides two implementations of this interface. `DynamicDestinationResolver` is the default implementation used by `JmsTemplate` and accommodates resolving dynamic destinations by making calls to a Session's `createQueue` or `createTopic` method as described previously. The `JmsTemplate` property `PubSubDomain` is used by `DestinationResolver` to choose which API call to make when resolving a dynamic destination. A `JndiDestinationResolver` is also provided, which acts as a service locator for destinations contained in JNDI and optionally falls back to the behavior contained in `Dynamic DestinationResolver`.

Transaction Management

Spring provides a `JmsTransactionManager`, which manages transactions for a single JMS `ConnectionFactory`. This allows JMS applications to leverage the managed transaction features of Spring as described in Chapter 6. The `JmsTransactionManager` binds a `Connection` / `Session` pair from the specified `ConnectionFactory` to the thread. In a J2EE environment, the `ConnectionFactory` will pool connections and sessions, so the instances that are bound to the thread depend on the pooling behavior.

This transaction strategy will typically be used in combination with `SingleConnectionFactory`, which uses a single JMS connection for all JMS access to save resources, typically in a standalone application. Each transaction will then use the same JMS `Connection` but its own JMS `Session`.

The `JmsTemplate` can also be used with the `JtaTransactionManager` and an XA-capable JMS `ConnectionFactory` for performing distributed transactions.

Reusing code across a managed and unmanaged transactional environment can be confusing when using JMS API to create a `Session` from a `Connection`. This is because the JMS API has only one factory method to create a `Session` and it requires values relating to the use of JMS local transactions and acknowledgment modes. JMS local transactions provide the ability to group sending or receiving of multiple messages into a single unit of work. In a managed environment, setting these values is the responsibility of the environment's transactional infrastructure, so these values are ignored by the vendor's wrapper to the JMS `Connection`. When using the `JmsTemplate` in an unmanaged environment, you can specify these values through the use of the properties `SessionTransacted` and `SessionAcknowledgeMode`. When using a `PlatformTransactionManager` with `JmsTemplate`, the template will always be given a transactional JMS `Session`.

JmsGatewaySupport

Spring provides a convenient `JmsGatewaySupport` class located in the package `org.spring framework.jms.core.support`, which can be used as a foundation for implementing the Gateway pattern defined in Martin Fowler's *Patterns of Enterprise Application Architecture* (Addison-Wesley, 2001).

> **The Gateway pattern is a wrapper that provides a simple domain-specific API in order to simplify access to external resources that have a complex resource-specific API. Client code that uses the gateway is thereby insulated from the particularities of the resource's API, which would have otherwise obscured the business processing code.**

Implementing the Gateway pattern as a business interface provides a valuable layer of indirection allowing one to easily change the implementation to use a different external resource, for example a Web Service. An added benefit is the improved testability of the application because stub or mock implementations can easily be created to reduce the reliance on external resources that may be difficult to configure or access during testing.

The JmsGatewaySupport class creates a JmsTemplate instance when its ConnectionFactory property is set. By overriding the method createJmsTemplate, a custom instance can be created. Alternatively, the gateway can be configured directly with an instance of a JmsTemplate. JmsGatewaySupport implements the InitializingBean interface and delegates the afterPropertiesSet method to the method initGateway so subclasses can implement custom initialization behavior.

In the following extremely simplified example, we consider a scenario in which a customer relationship management application needs to notify a billing application to reissue a new invoice. The business interface is defined as

```
public interface InvoiceService {

  public void reissue(String accountId, Date billingEndDate);

}
```

The JMS Gateway can then be coded as

```
public class JmsInvoiceService extends JmsGatewaySupport implements InvoiceService
{

  public void reissue(String accountId, Date billingEndDate)
  {
    Map m = new HashMap();
    m.put("accountid", accountId);
    m.put("date", billingEndDate.toGMTString());
    getJmsTemplate().convertAndSend(m);
  }

  protected void initGateway()
  {
    getJmsTemplate().convertAndSend("ServiceNotification",
                         "JmsInvoiceService Started on " +
                                    new Date().toGMTString());

  }
}
```

The following XML configuration segment shows the use of a JmsTemplate instance with a default destination:

```
<bean id="invoiceService" class="example.jms.JmsInvoiceService">
  <property name="jmsTemplate"><ref bean="jmsTemplate"/></property>
</bean>

<bean id="jmsTemplate" class="org.springframework.jms.core.JmsTemplate">
  <property name="connectionFactory"><ref bean="jmsConnFactoryWrapper"/></property>
  <property name="defaultDestination"><ref bean="queue"/></property>
```

```
    </bean>

    <bean id="queue" class="org.springframework.jndi.JndiObjectFactoryBean">
      <property name="jndiName"><value>testQueue</value></property>
    </bean>

    <bean id="jmsConnFactoryWrapper"
          class="org.springframework.jms.connection.SingleConnectionFactory">
      <property name="targetConnectionFactory"><ref bean="jmsConnFactory"/></property>
    </bean>

    <bean id="jmsConnFactory" class="org.springframework.jndi.JndiObjectFactoryBean">
      <property name="jndiName"><value>QueueConnectionFactory</value></property>
    </bean>
```

The Future

We've focused here on publishing messaging, and seen how Spring can make this much easier. Spring 1.3 is scheduled to have sophisticated support for *consuming* JMS messages, with a powerful alternative to Message Driven Beans for asynchronous processing. This will enable Spring to shoulder more of the responsibility formerly associated with EJBs.

Scheduling with Spring

Scheduling is essentially the execution or notification of other software components when a predetermined time is reached. This is important in many enterprise applications. An application might require scheduling in a range of scenarios — for example:

❑ To invoke a batch process on data that has accumulated since the last execution. Many financial applications work like this, even when implemented in modern languages.

❑ To generate periodic reports about application usage and performance.

❑ To execute periodic application maintenance tasks such as archiving or cleaning up temporary data.

The Spring Framework provides support for scheduling. Out-of-the-box integration is included for two scheduling technologies:

❑ **Timers:** Java's built-in scheduling mechanism, expressed in the `java.util.Timer` class and associated classes.

❑ **Quartz scheduling:** Quartz is an open-source solution provided by OpenSymphony (`www.opensymphony.com/quartz`).

In this section, we'll briefly summarize these two scheduling solutions before explaining how you can use them with Spring. We do *not* aim to provide a comprehensive introduction to scheduling, or a manual on use of either of these solutions.

Timers Versus Quartz

J2SE Timers are a simpler approach to scheduling than the more heavyweight Quartz scheduling framework.

However, the Quartz scheduler implementation provides far more functionality than Timers. For example, the following functionality is provided by Quartz implementation, and not supported by J2SE Timers:

❑ **Persistent jobs:** In contrast to a Timer, Quartz provides support for persistent jobs. This enables jobs to maintain state, even between application restarts. This is a very important consideration in many applications.

❑ **Job management:** Quartz allows for more extensive management of scheduled jobs by referencing jobs by their names and group names. This allows the application to trigger and reschedule jobs at will. It even allows the application to change the persistent job details.

❑ **Cron-like timing support:** Through Quartz's `CronTrigger`, Quartz provides more flexible means, in a `cron`-like fashion (`cron` is a scheduled execution facility on Unix and Linux machines), to specify when jobs execute. Timers allow only the specification of the execution time and intervals.

❑ **Threading model:** While Timers are implemented as a single thread, Quartz uses a thread pool for executing jobs. Among others, the size of the thread pool and the thread pool implementation can be specified using the Quartz properties. This allows for more flexible scheduling behavior, as jobs are queued when no free thread is available in the pool.

Quartz also provides a mature event model, allowing listeners on every aspect of the scheduling system (schedulers, triggers, and jobs). It allows for *misfire instructions*: instructions on what to do in cases where a job was not fired correctly (more on this in the Quartz Trigger section). Quartz also provides plug-in support to developers and an initialization servlet, which starts the Quartz scheduler in a J2EE-compliant manner. Finally, Quartz allows for remote job scheduling through an RMI connector and a Web Service, by means of a plug-in that exposes the scheduler interface through XML-RPC.

> **Although JDK Timers are adequate in cases where an application does not require one or more of the features mentioned, use of the Quartz implementation is recommended if non-trivial scheduling requirements seem likely in the future. Even if an application may not initially require persistent jobs, requirements may change to indicate a more sophisticated scheduling system.**

As you would expect, Spring supports these two scheduling mechanisms in a consistent way. Thus many of the configuration concepts are the same, whichever you choose.

Timers

`Timers` offer a simple, lightweight approach to scheduling. Essentially, an instance of `java.util.Timer` can be used to schedule one or more *tasks* of type `java.util.TimerTask`. A `Timer` is responsible for thread management, allowing tasks to execute independently of other application activity. For more information about `Timers`, see `http://java.sun.com/docs/books/tutorial/essential/threads/timer.html`.

The simplest approach to scheduling using `Timers` in a Spring application is using the `Method InvokingTimerTaskFactoryBean` to create a task that invokes a certain method on a bean defined in your context. Let's assume a bean `exampleBusinessObject` with a method `doSomething()` has been defined:

```
<bean id="methodInvokingTask"
    class="org.springframework.scheduling.timer.MethodInvokingTimerTaskFactoryBean">
    <property name="targetObject"><ref bean="exampleBusinessObject"/></property>
    <property name="targetMethod"><value>doSomething</value></property>
</bean>
```

This factory bean creates an instance of `java.util.TimerTask` that will call the method `doSomething()` on a bean with the ID of `exampleBusinessObject`.

We can now ensure that the created task is scheduled to run every 10 minutes through the following bean definition:

```
<bean id="scheduledTask"
      class="org.springframework.scheduling.timer.ScheduledTimerTask">
    <property name="delay">
        <value>60000</value>
    </property>
    <property name="period">
        <value>600000</value>
    </property>
    <property name="timerTask">
        <ref bean="methodInvokingTask"/>
    </property>
</bean>
```

The `ScheduledTimerTask` class holds delay and periodicity information, as well as a reference to the actual `TimerTask`. The configuration shown in the preceding example ensures the created method-invoking task is scheduled to run every 10 minutes after an initial delay of 1 minute. Note that the only timing parameters to be configured are the initial delay and the period between repeated task executions. The `ScheduledTimer Task` also allows the task to be scheduled at a fixed-rate versus fixed-delay, where fixed-rate measures the delay between the start times, while fixed-delay measures the delay between the end time of an execution and the start time of the next.

Now we have declaratively specified *what* should be executed (the `TimerTask`) and *when* (through the `ScheduledTimerTask`). We cause these scheduled tasks to execute using the `TimerFactoryBean`, as follows:

```
<bean id="timerFactory"
class="org.springframework.scheduling.timer.TimerFactoryBean">
  <property name="scheduledTimerTasks">
    <list>
      <ref local="scheduledTask"/>
    </list>
  </property>
</bean>
```

A `TimerFactoryBean` allows us to specify one or more `ScheduledTimerTasks`. The `TimerFactory Bean` is responsible for creating and managing an instance of `java.util.Timer`.

Scheduling using `Timers` allows the definition of your own custom tasks. Consider the following very simple custom task. In order to schedule this task instead of the method-invoking task, change the reference to the `methodInvokingTask` to the `customTask` bean definition.

```
package org.springframework.prospring.scheduling;

public class CustomTask extends TimerTask {
    public void run() {
        // do something
    }
}
```

While the task can be much more complex, the simplest definition looks like the following:

```
<bean id="customTask"
      class="org.springframework.prospring.scheduling.CustomTask"/>
```

Of course, you have the opportunity to use Dependency Injection and AOP here, as in any Spring bean definition.

Quartz

The main difference for the developer between `Timers` and Quartz is that while `Timers` just have a notion of tasks that are scheduled, Quartz has the notion of four entities: a `Scheduler`, a `Trigger`, a `Job`, and a `JobDetail`.

Let's look at how the preceding example would look using Spring's Quartz integration. Remember the `methodInvokingTask` in the `Timer` section. The same job using Quartz would look like this:

```
<bean id="methodInvokingJobDetail"
    class="org.springframework.scheduling.quartz.MethodInvokingJobDetailFactoryBean">
    <property name="targetObject"><ref bean="exampleBusinessObject"/></property>
    <property name="targetMethod"><value>doSomething</value></property>
</bean>
```

So far, there is little difference between the two. Quartz does not allow job details to be scheduled directly; first a Trigger needs to be defined. A Trigger is basically the definition of when to fire a job. Spring defines two predefined triggers: `SimpleTriggerBean` and `CronTriggerBean`. Let's use `SimpleTriggerBean` here, leaving discussion of `CronTriggerBean` until later in this chapter:

```
<bean id="simpleTrigger"
      class="org.springframework.scheduling.quartz.SimpleTriggerBean">
    <property name="startDelay">
        <value>60000</value>
    </property>
    <property name="repeatInterval">
        <value>50000</value>
    </property>
```

```
            <property name="jobDetail">
               <ref bean="methodInvokingJobDetail"/>
            </property>
      </bean>
```

Now that the trigger has been defined, the trigger needs to be scheduled. For this, the Spring Framework provides the `SchedulerFactoryBean`. It initializes a scheduler at startup and handles the scheduler shutdown at application shutdown (more specifically, once the `ApplicationContext` is closed).

```
<bean class="org.springframework.scheduling.quartz.SchedulerFactoryBean">
      <property name="triggers">
            <list>
                  <ref local="simpleTrigger"/>
            </list>
      </property>
</bean>
```

As you can see, the concepts are similar in configuring `Timers` and Quartz scheduling. The following table should clarify the three configuration elements.

Timer Term	Quartz Term	Notes
Timer task	*Job*	What needs to be done
Scheduled timer task		
There is no corresponding object in the J2SE Timer API: merely arguments to the overloaded `schedule()` methods on `java.util.Timer`.	*Trigger*	When it should be done
`TimerFactoryBean`	`SchedulerFactoryBean`	Cause a number of scheduled tasks to be executed

So far, there is very little difference between scheduling using Timers and Quartz. However, the `Scheduler FactoryBean` provides access to the full power of Quartz. For example, it allows you to specify the data source to use and low-level properties of Quartz such as the details of the thread pool to use. For more options, please see the JavaDoc of the `SchedulerFactoryBean`.

However, let's dig a bit deeper into Spring's Quartz support, which, like Quartz itself, is more sophisticated than the Timer integration.

Job

Quartz defines the `Job` interface, which represents a job to be performed. The Spring Framework provides a simple implementation of the interface, the `QuartzJobBean`. This implementation allows the passed-in data map entries, as well as the entries in the `SchedulerContext`, to be applied as property values to the job. Consider implementing a job that uses the job data map to store its last execution date.

```
package org.springframework.prospring.scheduling;

public class ExampleJob extends QuartzJobBean {
    private long lastExecutionDate;

    public void setLastExecutionDate(long lastExecutionDate) {
        this.lastExecutionDate = lastExecutionDate;
    }

    protected void executeInternal(JobExecutionContext context)
    throws JobExecutionException {
        // do something (using the last execution date)

        // store the last execution date in the job data map for the next execution
        JobDataMap map = context.getJobDetail().getJobDataMap();
        map.put("lastExecutionDate", System.currentTimeMillis());
    }
}
```

The `JobExecutionContext` provides a reference to almost all aspects of the Quartz scheduling system. However, as instantiation of jobs is performed by Quartz, the created job must be defined in a job detail definition.

```
<bean id="exampleJobDetail" class="org.springframework.quartz.JobDetailBean">
    <property name="name">
        <value>example</value>
    </property>
    <property name="group">
        <value>examples</value>
    </property>
    <property name="description">
        <value>The example job that retains state by storing its last execution
time in the job detail map.</value>
    </property>
    <property name="jobClass">
        <value>org.springframework.prospring.scheduling.ExampleJob</value>
    </property>

    // any other properties that need to be set
</bean>
```

Note that the example job keeps state between executions, but it does not keep state during system restarts. By default, job details are not persisted between executions. The default Spring implementation of the Quartz scheduling uses an in-memory job store, which subsequently keeps state in memory. Therefore, application restarts (and crashes) result in the loss of state data. Set the data source on the scheduler factory and have your jobs implement the `StatefulJob` interface. Next to enforcing that the job data map is persisted after each job execution, it also enforces that multiple instances of the job will not be executed concurrently. This means that job execution will be delayed in case a trigger fires during a prior execution. Note that when using the `MethodInvokingJobDetailFactoryBean` to create jobs, setting the property `concurrent` to `true` results in the factory creating jobs that implement the `StatefulJob` interface.

> Quartz jobs are not persisted by default. You need to implement the `StatefulJob` interface to have your jobs persisted between executions and between system restarts. You also need to set a data source on the scheduler factory.

Next to the `StatefulJob` job sub interface, Quartz provides an `InterruptableJob`. The implementation of an `InterruptableJob` should allow the job to be interrupted by the scheduler during execution, by means of the `Scheduler interrupt(String, String)` method.

Note that Quartz provides a number of convenience job implementations, with names that should be self-explanatory; for instance: `EJBInvokerJob`, `JMXInvokerJob`, `SendMailJob`, and `NativeJob`.

JobDetail

Quartz defines the notion of a `JobDetail` object, containing all data needed to run a `Job`. Spring defines a `JobDetailBean` to provide sensible defaults and make it aware of the application context it is defined in.

In many cases, jobs need to maintain state between executions and even during application restarts (and crashes), for instance last execution times. Quartz uses a `JobDataMap` to allow the job to store state data between executions. In case of persistent jobs, the data map is serialized into the data store. The `JobDetailBean` provides a convenience method to add data as a map to the underlying `JobDataMap`.

> When using a persistent job, whose job details are stored in a data store, do *not* store references to the `ApplicationContext` or any Spring-managed bean in the job data. This may result in serialization errors and unexpected behavior.

When storing data in the jobs data map to keep state between executions, store only standard Java types, and even better, only primitive wrappers such as `String`, `Integer`, and so on. As the data map is serialized using default Java serialization, deserialization of the stored data fails on changes to the serialized classes if not handled correctly. Storing of non-serializable data will result in runtime exceptions. For storing non-persistent data that needs to be available during job execution, the scheduler context is preferred. The scheduler context holds context/environment data and is available to jobs during execution, through the scheduler.

In addition to the already discussed properties, the job detail has two more properties: volatility and durability. Volatility specifies whether or not to persist the job itself for re-use between system restarts. Durability specifies whether or not the job should be stored after the job becomes orphaned, and no more triggers refer to it.

Trigger

As mentioned in the beginning of this section, jobs need to be associated with a trigger. The `Simple TriggerBean` was already used once, so now consider a cron-based trigger to specify the execution using a cron expression.

```
<bean id="cronTrigger"
    class="org.springframework.scheduling.quartz.CronTriggerBean">
  <property name="jobDetail">
```

```
            <ref bean="exampleJobDetail"/>
        </property>
        <property name="cronExpression">
            <!-- run every morning at 4.15 am on every Monday to Friday -->
            <value>0 15 4 ? * MON-FRI</value>
        </property>
    </bean>
```

The `CronTriggerBean` is a trigger that defines execution timing as Unix "cron-like" expressions. This allows the definition of a more complex execution schedule, such as the one in the preceding example. In short, a cron expression is a string comprising seven fields, where the last option is optional, separated by a white space. The following table lists all fields and possible values they may have.

Field Name	Allowed Values	Allowed Special Characters
Seconds	0-59	, - * /
Minutes	0-59	, - * /
Hours	0-23	, - * /
Day-of-month	1-31	, - * ? / L C
Month	1-12 or JAN-DEC	, - * /
Day-of-week	1-7 or SUN-SAT	, - * ? / L C #
Year (optional)	empty, 1970-2099	, - * /

For more information on cron expressions and the use of the special characters, use the extensive documentation in the JavaDoc of the Quartz `CronTrigger` class.

Both trigger implementations provided by the Spring framework provide the means to specify the misfire instruction of the trigger by its name. A misfire instruction indicates an instruction for the trigger on how to handle a misfire, for instance as a result of downtime. Among others, you can choose to ignore, re-execute, or even delete the trigger on a misfire.

Triggers also allow listeners to be added for listening to the state of a trigger. Normally there's no need to listen to the triggers, as the scheduler manages when triggers fire. It might, however, be useful to some applications, for example to veto a job execution or just to get informed of some job being executed.

Scheduler

The scheduler is the main part of the Quartz scheduling system. It maintains a registry of all job details and associated triggers; it manages job creation and execution when the associated triggers fire and it is responsible for persisting job state data.

In the beginning of this section, a simple scheduler was introduced. Now, have a look further at the most important configuration options for the `SchedulerFactoryBean`:

```
<bean class="org.springframework.scheduling.quartz.SchedulerFactoryBean">
    <property name="name">
        <value>Example</value>
```

```
        </property>
        <property name="schedulerContextAsMap">
            <map>
                <entry key="baseurl"><value>www.springframework.org</value></entry>
                <entry key="businessLogic"><ref bean="exampleBusinessLogic"/></entry>
            </map>
        </property>
        <property name="waitForJobsToCompleteOnShutdown">
            <value>true</value>
        </property>
        <property name="dataSource">
            <ref bean="exampleDataSource"/>
        </property>
        <property name="transactionManager">
            <ref bean="exampleTransactionManager"/>
        </property>
        <property name="configLocation">
            <value>classpath:quartz.properties</value>
        </property>
        <property name="triggers">
            <list>
                <ref local="cronTrigger"/>
            </list>
        </property>
    </bean>
```

First of all, in situations where multiple schedulers are used, always make sure to specify a name for the scheduler in order to actually have multiple scheduler instances. Next, two entries are set in the scheduler context to be available for all jobs during job execution. Remember that the use of the scheduler context is preferred for storing global data that should not be persisted. The scheduler also allows for a property called `waitForJobsToCompleteOnShutdown` that instructs the scheduler to wait for all jobs to complete before shutting down, as otherwise jobs can be terminated during execution. This property will be passed right on to the Quartz `Scheduler` class.

The main configuration items to consider when building an application that requires more complex, persistent jobs are the data source it uses and the location of the Quartz configuration. The first defines where to store the job details data map along with all Quartz related persistent data. The location of the Quartz configuration tells the created scheduler where to obtain its Quartz-specific configuration. A sample configuration file is listed next. More information on Quartz properties can be found in the `example_quartz.properties` file in the Quartz documentation. Note, however, that properties related to the data store should not be specified as they are configured by Spring.

```
# example quartz.properties configuration
org.quartz.threadPool.class=org.quartz.simpl.SimpleThreadPool
org.quartz.threadPool.threadCount=5
org.quartz.threadPool.threadPriority=4
```

Note that specifying a transaction manager on the scheduler factory is not needed because setting a Spring-managed data source should already handle transactions.

Last, as with triggers, schedulers also allow for listeners to be added. Next to adding listeners for scheduler events, it also allows global job and trigger listeners to listen to events all registered jobs and triggers publish.

Some users have commented on the heavy use of the `BeanNameAware` *interface in the Quartz integration code. Many Quartz classes require a name to be set and Spring often exposes name properties to configure one. However, if you do not specify a name yourself, Spring will use the bean name (set by the application context if the bean in question is a* `BeanNameAware` *bean). Be sure to set the bean name (or ID) if you wire, for example,* `JobDetailBeans` *and* `CronTriggerBeans` *as inner beans; if you don't, Spring will use the class name of the bean, which might cause unpredictable situations.*

Sending Email with Spring

Many applications make use of electronic mail. Possible uses include sending content of a contact form and sending periodic reports about application usage and performance to an administrator. Spring facilitates sending of email through the `MailSender` interface, offering two different implementations — one based on JavaMail, and one using Jason Hunter's `MailMessage` class (included in the `com.oreilly` `.servlet` package).

> The JavaMail API in particular is hard to mock or stub, partly because of its use of static methods and final classes. This and the heavy dependency on (system) properties make it hard to test application code that uses the JavaMail API directly. The abstraction layer provided by the Spring Framework allows easy mocking and testing.

The Spring mail framework is centered around the `MailSender` interface. This interface provides the abstraction over the underlying mailing system implementation. It allows for sending of `Simple` `MailMessage` instances. This allows for sending mail messages using the default mail message properties such as from, to, cc, bcc, subject, and text. For more sophisticated email messages, the two implementations provide support for MIME messages.

The complete `MailSender` interface is shown here:

```
public interface MailSender {

  void send(SimpleMailMessage simpleMessage) throws MailException;

  void send(SimpleMailMessage[] simpleMessages) throws MailException;

}
```

`SimpleMailMessage` is a JavaBean that holds what should be sent, and to whom.

Getting Started

To get started, consider a simple example of wiring up a mail sender in a Spring application context:

```
<bean id="mailSender" class="org.springframework.mail.javamail.JavaMailSenderImpl">
  <property name="host"><value>mail.mycompany.com</value></property>
</bean>
```

The preceding bean definition enables sending email from anywhere in your application, by means of the JavaMail implementation. Application code that would send an email using this mail sender would look like the following:

```
package org.springframework.prospring.mail;

import org.springframework.mail.MailSender;
import org.springframework.mail.SimpleMailMessage;
import org.springframework.mail.MailException;

public class BusinessLogicImpl implements BusinessLogic {
    private MailSender mailSender;

    public void setMailSender(MailSender mailSender) {
        this.mailSender = mailSender;
    }

    public void execute(Order order) {
        SimpleMailMessage msg = new SimpleMailMessage();
        msg.setFrom(me@mycompany.com);
        msg.setTo("to@mycompany.com");
        msg.setText("Hello, just sending you this message.");

        try {
            mailSender.send(msg);
        } catch(MailException ex) {
            //log it and go on
            System.err.println(ex.getMessage());
        }
    }
}
```

The preceding code snippet shows how to send a simple message using the mail sender defined in the application context. To wire up the mail sender to the business logic, you will simply use Dependency Injection, as follows:

```
<bean id="businessLogic"
      class="org.springframework.prospring.mail.BusinessLogicImpl">
    <property name="mailSender"><ref bean="mailSender"></property>
</bean>
```

Let's now move on to more detailed examples, including a working mail implementation, using Velocity for email templating.

Reusing an Existing Mail Session

Although it's very useful while testing or running outside of a container, specifying the mail sending details in the application context can be a nuisance because the host and other properties may change on deployment. When running an application inside a container that already provides a mail session, the reuse of that session is preferred. Consider, for instance, running inside a container that exposes a JavaMail session through JNDI under the JNDI name `java:/Mail`. In this case the bean definition for the mail sender looks like this:

```
<bean id="mailSender" class="org.springframework.mail.javamail.JavaMailSenderImpl">
    <property name="session"><ref bean="mailSession"/></property>
</bean>

<bean id="mailSession" class="org.springframework.jndi.JndiObjectFactoryBean">
    <property name="jndiName"><value>java:/Mail</value></property>
</bean>
```

The JndiObjectFactoryBean is used to look up the mail session through JNDI. The retrieved mail session is set as the session in the mail sender. This approach enables the reuse of one mail session for all applications running in the container and therefore allows for a single point of configuration of the mail session.

Mail Sending Using COS

Spring also provides a mail implementation based on the MailMessage class included in COS. This is a very basic implementation of the MailSender interface. It should be used only when there are very simple mailing requirements: for example, no attachments or HTML content. We can change the example from the *Getting started* example earlier in this chapter to use COS mail to send the message as follows:

```
<bean id="mailSender" class="org.springframework.mail.cos.CosMailSenderImpl">
    <property name="host"><value>mail.mycompany.com</value></property>
</bean>
```

Only the class property of the mail sender bean definition needs to be modified. Note that the CosMail SenderImpl class does not support the replyTo and sentDate properties of the SimpleMailMessage. Specifying them will result in an exception being thrown when trying to send the message.

Generic Mail Manager

The remainder of this chapter combines the features of the Spring mail framework and provides a useful working example of a generic mail manager. The mail manager will use Velocity templates to allow for flexible electronic mail functionality. More information on Velocity can be found at http://jakarta .apache.org/velocity. Velocity is a popular choice for generating mail messages, as it can incorporate variables in its templates.

We start by defining a MailManager interface, which defines the business methods needed for a mail manager. The main value add here over Spring's MailSender interface — which of course is used under the covers — is Velocity-based mail templating support:

```
package org.springframework.prospring.mail;

public interface MailManager {
    void send(String senderName, String senderAddress,
              Map from, Map to, Map cc, Map bcc,
              String subject, Map mergeObjects, String template)
        throws MailException;
    void send(Map to, List objects, String template)
        throws MailException;
}
```

Notice that each argument denoting a type of recipient is in the form of a `Map`. This is to allow the user to send an electronic mail message with multiple recipients for each recipient type, while specifying a full name for the recipient alongside the email address. Also note the convenience method to send a message while specifying only the "to" recipient.

The next step is to create a default implementation for our generic mail manager. We start out by setting up the skeleton for the default implementation:

```
package.org.springframework.prospring.mail;

// imports...

public class MailManagerImpl implements MailManager {

    private JavaMailSender javaMailSender;
    private Resource templateBase;
    private VelocityEngine velocityEngine;

    private String defaultFromName;
    private String defaultFromAddress;

    private String textTemplateSuffix = "text.vm";
    private String htmlTemplateSuffix = "html.vm";

    private String overrideToAddress;

    // setters (and optionally getters) for all private instance fields

    public void send(Map to, List objects, String template)
    throws MailException {
        send(null, to, null, null, objects, template);
    }

    public void send(String senderName,
                     String senderAddress,
                     Map to,
                     Map cc,
                     Map bcc,
                     String subject,
                     Map mergeObjects,
                     String templateLocation)
    throws MailException {
        // implementation of the functionality goes here
    }
}
```

Note that in the preceding default implementation, all setters and getters are left out of the listing, as well as the implementation, which will be discussed next. Furthermore, note the override default name and default addresses and names for the "from" and "to" recipients. These will also be discussed in the implementation of the main `send` method. Also, the `templateBase` resource is discussed later. The `JavaMailSender` and `VelocityEngine` are assumed wired up in the application context.

Message Creation

After setting up the skeleton for the implementation of the generic mail manager, it is time to generate a message. The Spring framework provides a helper class for easy implementation of a MIME message. So the first part of the send method implementation creates a message using the mail sender and uses that message to create a helper for it.

```
// create a mime message using the mail sender implementation
MimeMessage message = javaMailSender.createMimeMessage();

// create the message using the specified template
MimeMessageHelper helper;
try {
    helper = new MimeMessageHelper(message, true, "UTF-8");
} catch(MessagingException e) {
    throw new MailPreparationException(
            "unable to create the mime message helper", e);
}
```

Recipients

Next, the handling of the recipients must be implemented. A basic implementation looks like the following:

```
// add the 'from' recipient(s) to the message
// add the sender to the message
helper.setFrom(senderAddress, senderName);

// add the 'cc' recipient(s) to the message
if(cc != null && !cc.isEmpty()) {
    Iterator it = cc.keySet().iterator();
    while(it.hasNext()) {
        String name = (String) it.next();
        String recipient = (String) cc.get(name);
        if(overrideToAddress != null) {
            recipient = defaultToAddress;
        }
        helper.addCc(recipient, name);
    }
}

// add the 'bcc' recipient(s) to the message
if(bcc != null && !bcc.isEmpty()) {
    Iterator it = bcc.keySet().iterator();
    while(it.hasNext()) {
        String name = (String) it.next();
        String recipient = (String) bcc.get(name);
        if(overrideToAddress != null) {
            recipient = defaultToAddress;
        }
        helper.addBcc(recipient, name);
    }
}

// add the 'to' receipient(s) to the message
```

```
if(to != null && !to.isEmpty()) {
    Iterator it = to.keySet().iterator();
    while(it.hasNext()) {
        String name = (String) it.next();
        String recipient = (String) to.get(name);
        if(overrideToAddress != null) {
            recipient = defaultToAddress;
        }
        helper.addTo(recipient, name);
    }
} else {
    // use the default 'to' address
    if(defaultToAddress != null) {
        helper.addTo(defaultToAddress, toName);
    } else {
        helper.addTo(toAddress, toName);
    }
}
```

Note that the code shown here performs little error handling or sanity checking. In the full example source for this chapter, a more extensive implementation is provided. Also note the special handling of the to, cc, and bcc recipients. In case the overrideToAddress has been specified, all recipients' email addresses are replaced with that address. This allows for easy testing and staging configuration of the mail manager, i.e. sending all mail messages to a specific test address. Note also that only one "from" recipient is allowed to be set; specifying more than one results in the last overwriting the others.

Content

The next step is to set the content of the mail message. We use Velocity to merge the list of objects into the specified template. The result is set as the content of the message.

```
StringWriter text = new StringWriter();
VelocityEngineUtils.mergeTemplate(
    velocityEngine, templateLocation + "/" + htmlTemplateSuffix,
    mergeObjects, text);

String html = new StringWriter();
VelocityEngineUtils.mergeTemplate(
    velocityEngine, templateLocation + "/" + htmlTemplateSuffix,
    mergeObjects, text);

text.close();
html.close();

helper.setText(text.toString(), html.toString());

helper.setSubject(subject);
```

Note the use of a base resource for our implementation of the message helper. Depending on the application deployment environment, different resources can be chosen for retrieving the Velocity templates. For instance, a ClassPathResource can be used when templates are not subject to runtime changes. With different needs, a FileSystemResource can be configured to load templates at runtime from disk. Velocity provides the means to cache the templates and handles modifications to the templates to be incorporated without the need to concern oneself with the specifics.

Attachments

In order for our generic mail manager to allow inline images and other attachments, we expand our mail manager by allowing extra files in a folder relative to the template directory to be added as (inline) attachments for the message. The added (inline) attachments are given the filename as the ID for referencing the attachment from the message content. The code snippet that follows implements this functionality:

```
// retrieve contents of the 'attachments' folder and add as attachments
File attachmentsFolder = templateBase.createRelative(
        "mail/" + template + "/attachment").getFile();
File[] attachments = attachmentsFolder.listFiles();
if(attachments != null) {
    for(int i = 0; i < attachments.length; i++) {
        // add the attachment to the message helper
        helper.addAttachment(attachments[i].getName(),
                new FileDataSource(attachments[i]));
    }
}

// retrieve contents of the 'inline' folder and add as inline attachment
File inlinesFolder = templateBase.createRelative(
        "mail/" + template + "/inline").getFile();
File[] inlines = inlinesFolder.listFiles();
if(inlines != null) {
    for(int i = 0; i < inlines.length; i++) {
        // add the attachment to the message helper
        helper.addAttachment(inlines[i].getName(),
                new FileDataSource(inlines[i]));
    }
}
```

Sending

Now that the message is created, its content is set, recipients are handled, and attachments are added, the message is ready to be sent. Using the MailSender wired up to the mail manager implementation, sending the message is easy. Just call the send method with the created and configured mail message as the argument.

```
mailSender.send(message);
```

Note that sending a message by means of the underlying messaging system may take some time to process. A connection to the mail server needs to be established, a handshake protocol needs to be executed, and the message content needs to be sent to the mail server. Depending on application needs, the sending of the mail message can be performed on a different thread. The main advantage of this approach is the client perceives no latency while sending a message. The main disadvantage, however, is that the client will not receive any error messages while sending messages. Of course these messages can be communicated to the client asynchronously, but this may pose some serious challenges. Again, choose the method for sending based on the application requirements.

This concludes the example of creating a generic mail manager by means of the mail functionality provided by the Spring framework. The created mail manager can be wired up in the application context of any application to add electronic mail as an option to communicate with clients. More information and a more detailed listing of the source code discussed in this chapter are provided on the website accompanying this book.

Scripting

As of Spring 1.3, you can use a variety of languages, including Groovy and Beanshell, to implement any object managed by a Spring container. As other objects depend on that object by interface, they are unaware of its implementation language — another example of the benefits of the pluggability that an IoC container provides. You can configure a scripted object using Spring Dependency Injection also, using Setter Injection. (Property support will look different in different languages, but is usually nicer than in Java.) Scripted objects can have simply properties, but depend on other objects written in Java or any other scripting language.

You can also apply the full power of Spring's AOP framework to any scripted object to apply out-of-the-box aspects, such as declarative transaction management, or custom aspects. This is a capability that is possible only with a proxy-based AOP technology such as Spring AOP. Because the target object does not need to be modified, it doesn't matter what language the original object is written in. AspectJ or AspectWerkz, on the other hand, could not weave against a non-Java object — although it might be possible if it directly produced byte code, as in the case of Groovy.

Consistent Model

Whatever the scripting language, the support is consistent. Bean definition isolates the non-Java elements of an application.

You need the following bean definitions:

❑ **A script factory for each language you want to use:** This is where you specify properties affecting all scripts, such as whether scripts should *auto refresh* — that is, poll the definition file to check whether it has changed. (You don't normally need to specify any properties.) One script factory can be used for many scripts.

❑ **A bean definition for each bean that is implemented in that language:** The definition can be inline, or can specify a resource, using Spring's resource abstraction.

Spring does a lot of work behind the scenes to support scripted objects. The support is largely accomplished using Spring AOP. The AOP infrastructure introduces the level of indirection necessary to support reloading

---

Choosing an Implementation Language

Why implement objects in a language other than Java? This decision is yours: Spring merely gives you a choice.

In general, you might choose to implement an object in a scripting language if:

— Doing so makes the code in the object significantly simpler — for example, because of language features such as closures, or because you are not forced to implement methods that can never be called.

— You want to be able to modify the script while your application is running, thus changing its behavior without affecting objects that depend on the script.

— Performance is not critical. Most scripting languages do impose some performance penalty, even if they can be compiled to byte code.

---

of scripted objects without affecting callers and also introduces a special interface that is implemented by all scripted objects: `org.springframework.beans.factory.script.DynamicScript`. This defines methods returning the interface or interfaces supported by the script; the resource location of the script; how many times the script has been reloaded; and a `refresh()` method allowing forcible reloading.

You can cast any scripted object to `DynamicScript` to access these methods.

> *The DynamicScript interface extends the generic* `org.springframework.beans.factory` *`.dynamic.DynamicObject` interface, from which it inherits the* `refresh()` *method and other important methods. Future versions of Spring will use this interface to support a wider range of "dynamic objects," such as objects whose bean definition is sourced from a database and may change without impacting callers.*

Spring supports both singleton and prototype lifecycles for scripted objects.

It's possible to declare scripts *inline*, in the XML or other configuration, by prefixing the script location argument (to be discussed shortly) with `inline`. While you might want to use this as a convenience during rapid prototyping, in general, you should not program in configuration documents. If you declare scripts inline, your gain in convenience will also be offset by the loss of the dynamic reload capability; the script definition is now tied to that of the overall configuration.

One legitimate use for inline declarations — and an important reason for using scripting in some cases in general — is when you don't want to implement all the methods on an interface. In this case, using a scripting language such as Beanshell, you can have Spring cast the script object to one or more interfaces, and the methods you don't want implemented will throw `UnsupportedOperationException` if they are ever called. Especially when prototyping, this may be exactly what you want.

Groovy

Let's look at how we could use a Groovy script in a Spring application.

We'll take our example implementations of the following simple interface:

```
public interface Hello {

String sayHello();

}
```

We will use Setter Injection to parameterize the message returned by implementations, demonstrating how Dependency Injection can be applied to scripted objects.

First we need to define a Groovy Script factory. This will be responsible for instantiating any Groovy scripts we need to use. This can be as simple as the following, which merely specifies the class:

```
<bean id="groovyScriptFactory"
        class="org.springframework.beans.factory.script.groovy.GroovyScriptFactory"
 >
 </bean>
```

This bean definition can have any name. However, that name will need to be referenced whenever we create a new script object:

Next we must make a bean definition for each Groovy-scripted object:

```
<bean id="propertySingleton"
        factory-bean="groovyScriptFactory"
        factory-method="create"
  >
        <constructor-arg
index="0"><value>org/springframework/beans/factory/script/groovy/PropertyHello.groo
vy</value></constructor-arg>

        <property name="message"><value>hello world property</value></property>
  </bean>
```

This uses the factory method feature of the Spring IoC container. The constructor argument is the location argument to the `create()` method of the instance of `GroovyScriptFactory` defined in the `groovy` `ScriptFactory` bean definition. The `create()` method is defined on `AbstractScriptFactory`, the super-class for all script factories, so we will consistently use the same method naming whatever the language, and script factory class, we use.

Properties defined in this bean definition, on the other hand, *apply to the created Groovy script*. We merely use the factory to instantiate scripts; we are free to configure them using Setter Injection.

Other beans can depend on this script object using Dependency Injection, and the script object can also depend on other objects using Dependency Injection. In this case, the `message` property is simply a String, but we could equally use references as in any regular bean definition.

We don't need to specify the interfaces that this script implements. As Groovy can define Java classes, Spring will use CGLIB proxying to ensure that all methods implemented by the Groovy object will be available. Thus all interfaces it implements will be available: It is the Groovy code itself that is responsible for declaring what interfaces it implements, and hence how it can be used by callers.

Let's look at the Groovy script itself:

```
package org.springframework.beans.factory.script.groovy

class Test implements org.springframework.beans.factory.script.Hello {

    property message

    String sayHello() {
            message
    }
}
```

As you can see, Groovy's economic property syntax makes this more concise than the Java equivalent.

Beanshell

Beanshell is a very different language to Groovy. It is interpreted, rather than compiled to byte code, and Beanshell provides only dynamic proxies that implement a single interface. The use of dynamic proxies means that class methods are *not* an option, as in Groovy. Thus we need a different approach to Setter Injection.

Nevertheless, Spring support is very consistent: It allows scripts to implement multiple interfaces (internally, calling several Beanshell evaluations); and it supports property configuration, with a little magic of its own.

We create a Beanshell script factory as follows:

```
<bean id="scriptFactory"
        class="org.springframework.beans.factory.script.bsh.BshScriptFactory"
   >

   </bean>
```

Individual bean definitions will look like this:

```
<bean id="propertySingleton"
  factory-bean="scriptFactory"
  factory-method="create"
   >
        <constructor-arg
index="0"><value>classpath:/org/springframework/beans/factory/script/bsh/SimpleHell
o.bsh</value></constructor-arg>
        <constructor-arg
index="1"><value>org.springframework.beans.factory.script.Hello</value></constructo
r-arg>

        <property name="message"><value>hello world property</value></property>
   </bean>
```

All this looks similar to Spring's Groovy support, enabling a consistent configuration model. However, it works quite differently under the covers.

Note that we must specify a second argument to the `create()` method on `BshScriptFactory`, defining the interface or interfaces implemented by the Script. (This is actually a String array, so we can specify multiple interfaces. But most often we'll want only one.) This argument is optional with Groovy, but mandatory with Beanshell, as Spring has to know up front what interfaces it needs to ask Beanshell to create a dynamic proxy for.

But the real magic happens in the handling of setter methods. These are not part of the interface or interfaces to be exposed by the bean definition, and it would be unreasonable to expect the developer to create a "configuration interface" containing these setter methods. Thus Spring itself *creates* a *configuration interface* containing the necessary setter methods, by first looking at the bean definition. Thus in the preceding example, Spring will create an interface containing a `setMessage()` method. Thus the core Spring IoC container is tricked into thinking that the script really implements this interface, and can invoke the setters normally. The actual interface generation is done using a handling "interface maker" provided by CGLIB.

> The `requiresConfigInterface()` *method in* `AbstractScriptFactory` *must be implemented to return* `true` *for languages such as Beanshell.*

The developer is merely responsible for ensuring that Beanshell scripts implement all setter methods implied by the bean definition, not for implementing them in any interface.

Let's look at the Beanshell definition itself. Note how the `setMessage()` method is implemented:

```
String message;

public void setMessage(String pmessage) {
 message = pmessage;

}

String sayHello() {
    return message;
}
```

Note that this doesn't look like a complete class: We have implemented only the methods we are interested in. In this case, it was the complete `Hello` interface, but in some cases we won't bother to implement all methods. Nor does the script need to declare what interfaces it implements. The developer is responsible for correct configuration, ensuring that the script isn't specified to implement interfaces for which it doesn't support the methods.

Other Scripting Languages

Spring is likely to support additional scripting languages in the future.

It's also possible to implement support for nearly any other scripting language with Java bindings. You need to do the following:

❑   Implement the `Script` interface for your chosen language. The `AbstractScript` class is a useful base class.

❑   Extend `AbstractScriptFactory` to implement a script factory that creates scripts of that type.

While some of the concepts involved are complex, and you should ensure that you thoroughly understand the implementation of Groovy and Beanshell support before trying to implement support for your own favorite language, there is not normally a large amount of code involved.

The Spring scripting infrastructure will automatically introduce the `DynamicScript` interface for any scripting language supported this way; you don't need to add any explicit support.

Summary

Spring is almost a *platform* rather than a framework. It is far beyond the scope of a single chapter to cover all of Spring's integration and other supporting services.

## Chapter 9

In this chapter we've seen:

- ❑ How Spring simplifies working with JMS
- ❑ How Spring can simplify working with scheduling
- ❑ How you can send email with Spring
- ❑ How Spring enables you to define application objects in languages other than Java, within the consistent overall architecture provided by the Spring IoC container

In the next chapter, we'll cover the important topic of security, discussing *Acegi Security for Spring*, a related project that is used in many Spring projects. We will also briefly introduce *Spring RCP*: Spring's sister project for developing thick client and standalone GUI applications.

10

Acegi Security System for Spring

Every enterprise application requires security in one form or another. The problem domain of the application, its intended user base, and importance to the core business are all major influences on the type of security required. For example, there is a major difference in the security requirements of an Internet banking application from those of an internal telephone directory application. This wide range of security requirements between applications has proven a major challenge in the development of generic security frameworks. In this chapter we will explore the major options available for securing Spring-based applications and examine the recommended security framework, *Acegi Security System for Spring*.

Enterprise Application Security Choices

Developers have a wide range of choices in how to implement security within enterprise applications. Let's start by reviewing the typical requirements of such applications and three major security platforms commonly used with Spring.

Typical Requirements

Although Spring provides a highly flexible framework, most of its users leverage its capabilities to deliver robust, multi-tier enterprise applications. Such applications are usually data-centric, have multiple concurrent users, and are of significant importance to the core business. Hence most enterprise applications must provide a robust approach to security.

Let's briefly recap some of the key terms used when discussing computer security. The term *principal* refers to a user, service, or agent who can perform an operation. A principal presents *credentials* such as a password in order to allow *authentication*, which is the process of establishing the identity of a caller. *Authorization* refers to the process of determining whether a principal (authenticated or non-authenticated) is permitted to perform a given operation.

Four main security concerns must be addressed in typical enterprise applications:

❑ **Authentication:** Enterprise applications typically need to access a variety of *authentication reposi- tories.* Often these repositories will be in the form of LDAP directories, CRM systems, enterprise single-sign-on solutions, and autonomous, application-specific databases. Depending on the repository, the server may never expose the credentials (in which case authentication is performed only by binding to the repository with the correct credentials) or the credentials may be in a hashed format. Each authentication repository also must track the authorities granted to a principal. Security frameworks must integrate with these types of repositories, or new ones, sometimes simultaneously. There may also be a range of client types for an enterprise application, including web applications, Swing clients, and web services. The security framework needs to deal consis- tently with authentication requests from any such client type.

❑ **Web request security:** Many enterprise applications are web-based, often using an MVC frame- work and possibly publishing web services. Security is often required to protect URI patterns. In addition, web views often require integration with a security framework so content can be gen- erated based on the authorities held by the principal.

❑ **Service layer security:** Service (business) layers should be secured in all but the simplest of applications. Security is usually best modeled as an *aspect.* Using an AOP-based solution allows service layer implementations to be largely or completely unaware of security. It also eliminates the error-prone and tedious approach of enforcing security in user interface tiers via techniques such as URI pattern filtering. Acegi Security can secure an AOP Alliance `MethodInvocation`, using Spring AOP. It can also secure an AspectJ `JoinPoint`.

❑ **Domain object instance security:** Java applications generally use domain objects to model the problem domain. Different instances of these domain objects may require different security. A principal may have delete permission to one domain object instance but only read permission to a different domain object instance. Permissions are assigned to a *recipient,* which refers to a principal or a role. The list of permissions assigned to different recipients for a given domain object instance is known as an *access control list,* or ACL.

The following common computer security concern is *not* typical of enterprise applications:

❑ **Limited privilege execution:** Some Java applications need to execute with limited privileges, as the user is concerned about the trustability of the application. The most common examples are applets, which run within a web browser, or Java Web Start applications, which can automatically download from the Internet. Enterprise applications are typically trusted by the computer exe- cuting them, such as a corporate server. As such, it is of unnecessary complexity for most enter- prise applications to execute with limited privileges.

Given these requirements, we recommend the *Acegi Security System for Spring* (http://acegisecurity .sourceforge.net; Apache 2 license) to handle the security requirements of Spring-managed applica- tions. We will now briefly explore Acegi Security with reference to the other major security platforms that target enterprise application development.

Acegi Security in a Nutshell

Acegi Security is widely used within the Spring community for providing comprehensive security services to Spring-powered applications. It comprises a set of interfaces and classes that are configured through a Spring IoC container. In the spirit of Spring, the design of Acegi Security allows many applications to implement the four common enterprise application security requirements listed previously solely via declarative configuration settings in the IoC container. Acegi Security is heavily interface-driven, providing significant room for customization and extension.

> **Acegi Security, like Spring, emphasizes *pluggability*. It is based on the assumption that there is no one-size-fits-all approach for security, instead providing a consistent programming model from a security perspective, while allowing a choice between different strategies to implement key security responsibilities.**

We will now briefly examine the four common enterprise application security requirements (authentication, web request security, service layer security, and domain object instance security), and how Acegi Security addresses each. Later in this chapter we will revisit Acegi Security architecture and configuration in more detail, so don't be concerned if you don't follow everything mentioned in the following quick overview.

Authentication

Before the other three security requirements can be addressed, the principal must be authenticated. Acegi Security performs authentication using a pluggable `AuthenticationManager`, which can be defined in a Spring application context as follows:

```xml
<bean id="authenticationManager"
class="net.sf.acegisecurity.providers.ProviderManager">
  <property name="providers">
    <list>
      <ref local="daoAuthenticationProvider"/>
    </list>
  </property>
</bean>

<bean id="daoAuthenticationProvider"
    class="net.sf.acegisecurity.providers.dao.DaoAuthenticationProvider">
  <property name="authenticationDao"><ref local="jdbcDaoImpl"/></property>
</bean>

<bean id="jdbcDaoImpl" class="net.sf.acegisecurity.providers.dao.jdbc.JdbcDaoImpl">
  <property name="dataSource"><ref bean="dataSource"/></property>
</bean>
```

The `authenticationManager` bean will delegate through the list of authentication providers (the preceding code sample shows only one). Authentication providers are capable of authenticating from a given authentication repository. In this case, the `daoAuthenticationProvider` bean will be used for authentication, which uses a data access object to retrieve the user information.

Web Request Security

Acegi Security provides web request security via `FilterSecurityInterceptor` and `Security EnforcementFilter`. The latter class is implemented as a `web.xml` filter, with the filter itself defined in the application context:

```xml
<bean id="securityEnforcementFilter"
    class="net.sf.acegisecurity.intercept.web.SecurityEnforcementFilter">
  <property name="filterSecurityInterceptor">
    <ref local="filterInvocationInterceptor"/>
```

```
      </property>
      <property name="authenticationEntryPoint">
        <ref local="authenticationProcessingFilterEntryPoint"/>
      </property>
    </bean>

    <bean id="authenticationProcessingFilterEntryPoint"

    class="net.sf.acegisecurity.ui.webapp.AuthenticationProcessingFilterEntryPoint">
      <property name="loginFormUrl"><value>/acegilogin.jsp</value></property>
    </bean>

    <bean id="filterInvocationInterceptor"
        class="net.sf.sf.intercept.web.FilterSecurityInterceptor">
      <property name="authenticationManager">
        <ref bean="authenticationManager"/>
      </property>
      <property name="accessDecisionManager">
        <ref local="httpRequestAccessDecisionManager"/>
      </property>
      <property name="objectDefinitionSource">
        <value>
          CONVERT_URL_TO_LOWERCASE_BEFORE_COMPARISON
          PATTERN_TYPE_APACHE_ANT
          /secure/super/**=ROLE_WE_DONT_HAVE
          /secure/**=ROLE_SUPERVISOR,ROLE_USER
        </value>
      </property>
    </bean>
```

Most of the preceding is boilerplate code, with the actual URI patterns to protect being defined in the `filter InvocationInterceptor` bean `objectDefinitionSource` property. As you can see, the `filter InvocationInterceptor` bean uses Apache Ant–style paths to express the URI patterns. In addition to Apache Ant paths, regular expressions are supported. The CONVERT_URL_TO_LOWERCASE_BEFORE_COMPARISON directs the filter to match URI patterns in a case-insensitive manner. These declarations would prevent a principal from accessing the /secure URI unless they held one of the two indicated roles, and would prevent /secure/super being accessed unless the principal held the ROLE_WE_DONT_HAVE role.

Service Layer Security

Comprehensive services layer security is provided by Acegi Security, again using the application context. Here we define an AOP Alliance method interceptor, which is autowired via Spring's `DefaultAdvisor AutoProxyCreator`:

```
    <bean id="autoproxy"
        class="org.sf.aop.framework.autoproxy.DefaultAdvisorAutoProxyCreator"/>

    <bean id="methodSecurityAdvisor"

    class="net.sf.acegisecurityf.intercept.method.aopalliance.MethodDefinitionSourceAdv
    isor"
        autowire="constructor"/>

    <bean id="bankManagerSecurity"
```

```
class="net.sf.acegisecurity.intercept.method.aopalliance.MethodSecurityInterceptor"
>
  <property name="authenticationManager">
    <ref bean="authenticationManager"/>
  </property>
  <property name="accessDecisionManager">
    <ref local="businessAccessDecisionManager"/>
  </property>
  <property name="objectDefinitionSource">
    <value>
      com.acegitech.BankManager.createAccount=ROLE_TELLER
      com.acegitech.BankManager.deposit=ROLE_TELLER
      com.acegitech.BankManager.approveLoan=ROLE_MORTGAGE_CENTRE
      com.acegitech.BankManager.viewAuditTrail=ROLE_INVESTIGATIONS
    </value>
  </property>
</bean>
```

In this example, the `MethodSecurityInterceptor` will intercept any `BankManager` implementation defined in the application context. The syntax of `MethodSecurityInterceptor` is very similar to Spring's transaction support, allowing both fully qualified method names as well as wildcards (for example, `create*=ROLE_TELLER`) to be used. If the indicated roles are not held, `MethodSecurityInterceptor` will throw an `Access DeniedException`. If the principal is not logged in, an `AuthenticationException` will be thrown.

Domain Object Instance Security

Finally, domain object instance security in Acegi Security leverages the services layer security interceptors. Acegi Security also provides a repository, known as an `AclManager`, that can determine the access control list (ACL) that applies for any domain object instance it is passed:

```
<bean id="aclFolderWriteVoter"
class="net.sf.acegisecurity.vote.BasicAclEntryVoter">
  <property name="processConfigAttribute">
    <value>ACL_FOLDER_WRITE</value>
  </property>
  <property name="processDomainObjectClass">
    <value>com.acegitech.Folder</value>
  </property>
  <property name="aclManager"><ref local="aclManager"/></property>
  <property name="requirePermission">
    <list>
      <ref local="net.sf.acegisecurity.acl.basic.SimpleAclEntry.ADMINISTRATION"/>
      <ref local="net.sf.acegisecurity.acl.basic.SimpleAclEntry.WRITE"/>
    </list>
  </property>
</bean>

<bean id="businessAccessDecisionManager"
class="net.sf.acegisecurity.vote.AffirmativeBased">
  <property name="allowIfAllAbstainDecisions"><value>false</value></property>
  <property name="decisionVoters">
    <list>
      <ref local="roleVoter"/>
      <ref local="aclFolderWriteVoter"/>
    </list>
```

```
      </property>
   </bean>

   <bean id="folderManagerSecurity"

   class="net.sf.acegisecurity.intercept.method.aopalliance.MethodSecurityInterceptor"
   >
      <property name="authenticationManager">
        <ref bean="authenticationManager"/>
      </property>
      <property name="accessDecisionManager">
        <ref local="businessAccessDecisionManager"/>
      </property>
      <property name="objectDefinitionSource">
        <value>
          com.acegitech.FolderManager.createFolderWithParent=ACL_FOLDER_WRITE
          com.acegitech.FolderManager.writeFolder=ACL_FOLDER_WRITE
          com.acegitech.FolderManager.readFolder=ROLE_USER
        </value>
      </property>
   </bean>
```

The preceding settings would cause Acegi Security to intercept every method invocation for the listed methods of FolderManager. For the two methods marked ACL_FOLDER_WRITE, the aclFolder WriteVoter would be asked to vote on access. The aclFolderWriterVoter would then query the AclManager (which is not shown in the preceding sample) for the ACL entries applying to the current principal. If that returned list contains a "read" or "administration" permission, the method invocation would be allowed to proceed.

Acegi Security also publishes AuthenticationEvent and SecurityInterceptionEvent objects for authentication and authorization operations respectively to the Spring ApplicationContext. This provides a convenient hook for loosely coupled auditing, logging, and monitoring systems.

Let's now consider the alternative options available for securing Spring-based enterprise applications.

Java Authentication and Authorization Service

The Java Authentication and Authorization Service (JAAS) was introduced as an optional package to the Java 2 SDK version 1.3, being integrated into the SDK from version 1.4. JAAS provides pluggable authentication and authorization services for the Java platform, integrating into the platform layer security via system security policies. Many web and EJB containers provide some form of JAAS support, although, as of early 2005, there are significant compatibility issues between the various containers.

JAAS uses a Subject to represent an actual person or other entity. When authenticated, a range of identities is added to the Subject in the form of Principal objects. A JAAS Principal is used to represent an identity of the Subject, such as its name. Subjects can also contain public and private credentials, such as X.509 certificates.

Authentication is handled by JAAS through a LoginModule, a list of which is typically contained in an external policy file. A LoginModule is responsible for authenticating the principal and populating the Subject. A LoginModule requires a CallbackHandler to collect credentials from the principal.

Acegi Security provides an authentication provider that can delegate to JAAS, allowing integration between the two systems for authentication.

Once authenticated, JAAS's integration with the platform security, via a `SecurityManager`, allows authorization to take place. Authorization is typically defined in an external policy file. The operation of JAAS authorization is involved and beyond the scope of this book, although interested readers can refer to the Java 2 SDK documentation for a detailed background.

The following table briefly discusses some of the reasons commonly provided for using JAAS.

JAAS Benefit	Why It Matters	Mitigating Factors and Alternatives
Range of `LoginModules`	Saves you from having to write a login module for a given authentication repository.	— Most authentication repositories are relatively easy to integrate with in the first place, which means that it is easy to write a new authentication provider for a framework such as Acegi Security. — Acegi Security can use JAAS for authentication, effectively making all its `LoginModules` available to Acegi Security–managed applications.
JVM-level authorization	In a limited privilege execution environment, the JVM can ensure the code itself as well as that the principal is not requesting an unauthorized operation.	— Acegi Security, on the other hand, requires each secure object to be intercepted, typically via a Filter or an AOP "around" advice. — As Acegi Security provides AspectJ support, AOP "around" advices can even be applied to POJOs without any special step such as creating a proxy through an application context. — Rarely is the code of enterprise applications required to execute in a limited privilege environment. — Significant configuration is required for JAAS authorization, often involving JAR deployments in the SDK lib directory and editing of external policy files. — Acegi Security's use of the application context means Spring users find it a natural and convenient approach to configuration, particularly given its similarity (both in terms of security configuration and AOP interception) with Spring transaction management.

Table continued on following page

JAAS Benefit	Why It Matters	Mitigating Factors and Alternatives
		—Many web and application containers are incompatible with JVM-level authorization and cannot, for example, support two web applications using different security policies. —Using JVM-level authorization will limit web and application server portability, whereas using Acegi Security in its recommended configuration delivers complete compatibility and portability. —Even if JVM-level authorization was necessary for an unusual enterprise application, it would only be as secure as the security policy, and as that security policy will likely be provided by the same people who wrote the enterprise application itself, it becomes debatable just how much more security is realistically being derived from JVM-level authorization. Consider using AspectJ with Acegi Security instead, to gain portability and configuration benefits.
Automatic propagation of security identity from a web container to an EJB container, or from one EJB container to a remote EJB container	If you're using EJBs, this means less work for developers.	—Most new Spring applications don't use EJBs. —As most EJB developers are acutely aware, the EJB specification is limited in terms of authorization expressiveness and this typically requires an application to perform authorization itself anyway. —Through container adapters, Acegi Security can provide authentication for EJB containers, and in doing so provide a `Principal` simultaneously acceptable to both the EJB security subsystem as well as the Acegi Security framework. —Acegi Security performs transparent remote propagation of security identity when using Spring's RMI or `HttpInvoker`, effectively delivering an equivalent security propagation benefit as JAAS for remote POJOs.

JAAS Benefit	Why It Matters	Mitigating Factors and Alternatives
JAAS is an official standard	In some cases this is important for funding or buy-in.	— Acegi Security is the de facto and official standard for securing Spring-based applications, and as such has a large and active community with peer design review, implementation patterns, comprehensive documentation, extensions, and support readily available. — JAAS is only occasionally used in enterprise applications for authentication (usually the web or EJB container is relied upon for authentication) and it is rarely used for authorization because of the compatibility constraints. — Acegi Security can use JAAS for authentication if desired, effectively equalling the level of JAAS support available in most practical cases to enterprise application developers who consider the standard issue an important one.

Certainly JAAS is an important standard when developing applications intended for a limited privilege execution environment, such as an applet. However, unless web and EJB container support for JAAS greatly improves, it is unlikely to prove practical for efficiently developing portable, secure enterprise applications.

Servlet Specification

The Servlet Specification provides a simple way of authenticating principals and securing web URIs.

Each web container is responsible for performing authentication. Typically each web container will provide its own interface that authentication providers must implement to perform authentication. After configuring the web container to use a particular implementation of that interface, web.xml is used to finalize the authentication configuration:

```
<login-config>
  <auth-method>FORM</auth-method>
  <realm-name>Servlet Specification Secured Realm</realm-name>
  <form-login-config>
    <form-login-page>/login.jsp</form-login-page>
    <form-error-page>/login.jsp?login_error=1</form-error-page>
  </form-login-config>
</login-config>
```

Because each web container has its own special authentication provider interface, this introduces web container portability constraints. In addition, the web container will often require those authentication providers to be placed in a common library directory (along with support JARs such as JDBC drivers) and this further complicates configuration and classloader operation.

As far as authorization goes, the Servlet Specification provides just one of the three types of authorization areas typically required by enterprise applications: web request security. Again, web.xml is used to specify the roles that are required for given URI patterns:

```
<security-constraint>
  <display-name>Secured Area Security Constraint</display-name>
  <web-resource-collection>
    <web-resource-name>Secured Area</web-resource-name>
    <url-pattern>/secure/*</url-pattern>
  </web-resource-collection>
  <auth-constraint>
    <role-name>ROLE_USER</role-name>
    <role-name>ROLE_SUPERVISOR</role-name>
  </auth-constraint>
</security-constraint>
```

The major limitation with this approach to web request authorization is that authorization decisions cannot take into account anything but roles. For example, they cannot consider in the authorization logic if a request has a particular query parameter. In addition, the specification provides only one way to express the URI patterns to be secured. (Acegi Security interprets two standard formats, with additional formats easily added.)

As mentioned already, the absence of support for services layer security or domain object instance security translates into serious limitations for multi-tiered applications. Typically developers find themselves either ignoring these authorization requirements, or implementing the security logic within their MVC controller code (or even worse, inside their views). There are disadvantages with this approach:

❑   **Separation of concerns:** Authorization is a crosscutting concern and should be implemented as such. MVC controllers or views implementing authorization code make it more difficult to test both the controller and authorization logic, more difficult to debug, and will often lead to code duplication.

❑   **Support for rich clients and web services:** If an additional client type must ultimately be supported, any authorization code embedded within the web layer is non-reusable. It should be considered that Spring remoting exporters export only service layer beans (not MVC controllers). As such, authorization logic needs to be located in the services layer to support a multitude of client types.

❑   **Layering issues:** An MVC controller or view is simply the incorrect architectural layer to implement authorization decisions concerning services layer methods or domain object instances. Though the Principal may be passed to the services layer to enable it to make the authorization decision, doing so would introduce an additional argument on every services layer method. A more elegant approach is to use a ThreadLocal to hold the Principal, although this would likely increase development time to a point where it would become more economical (on a cost-benefit basis) to simply use a dedicated security framework.

❑ **Authorization code quality:** It is often said of web frameworks that they "make it easier to do the right things, and harder to do the wrong things." Security frameworks are the same, because they are designed in an abstract manner for a wide range of purposes. Writing your own authorization code from scratch does not provide the "design check" a framework would offer, and in-house authorization code will typically lack the improvements that emerge from widespread deployment, peer review, and new versions.

> For simple applications, Servlet Specification security may be sufficient. Although when considered within the context of web container portability, configuration requirements, limited web request security flexibility, and non-existent services layer and domain object instance security, it becomes clear why developers often look to alternative solutions.

Acegi Security Fundamentals

Let's now get to grips with the Acegi Security solution.

Authentication

The major interfaces and implementations of Acegi Security's authentication services are provided in Figure 10-1. As shown, the central interface is Authentication, which contains the identity of the principal, its credentials, and the GrantedAuthoritys the principal has obtained. GrantedAuthority is an interface and implementations can have any meaning appropriate to the application. The GrantedAuthorityImpl is typically used, as it stores a String representation of an authority the principal has been granted.

As shown in the figure, the AuthenticationManager is the central interface responsible for processing an Authentication "request" object and determining if the presented principal and credentials are valid. If they are valid, the AuthenticationManager populates the Authentication with the GrantedAuthoritys that apply. The main implementation of AuthenticationManager is known as ProviderManager, which is responsible for polling a list of AuthenticationProviders.

There are many AuthenticationProviders, each devoted to processing a particular Authentication concrete implementation. The implementation supported by different providers is indicated in Figure 10-1. The ProviderManager uses the first AuthenticationProvider capable of processing a given Authentication request object. It should be noted that because of space constraints, not every AuthenticationProvider included with Acegi Security is shown in the figure.

Most of the time the DaoAuthenticationProvider is used to process an authentication request. Figure 10-2 provides a class diagram for this important provider. As shown, DaoAuthenticationProvider will retrieve a UserDetails from an AuthenticationDao. Most developers write their own AuthenticationDao (to use Hibernate or their preferred persistence strategy), although Acegi Security also ships with a production-quality JdbcDaoImpl. DaoAuthenticationProvider also provides other useful features such as caching layer integration and decoding of encoded passwords (for example, SHA or MD5 with salts).

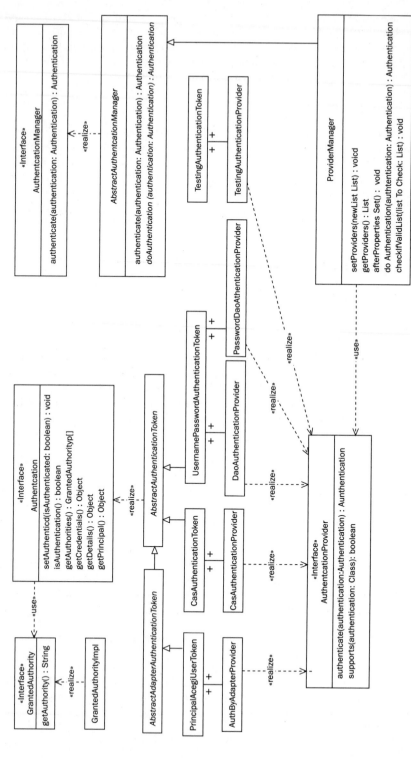

Figure 10-1

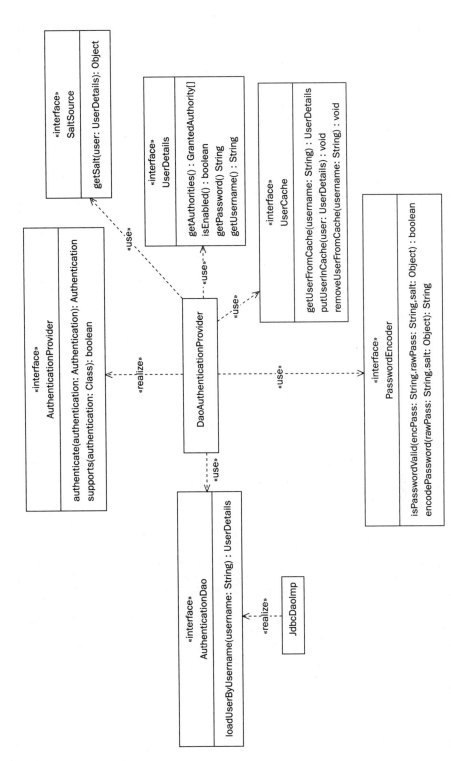

Figure 10-2

Although the preceding text explains how an authentication request is processed into a populated Authentication object, we have not covered how the user interacts with Acegi Security to actually request authentication. This is the role of various *authentication mechanisms*, as shown in the following table.

Module	What It Does	Why and When to Use It
BasicProcessingFilter	Processes BASIC authentication requests in accordance with RFC 1945.	—To publish secured web services —If a simple single sign on approach is desired —Should a simple authentication dialog be desired in the web browser rather than a login form
CasProcessingFilter	Processes Yale University's Central Authentication Service (CAS) tickets	—If your organization already has a CAS server —If you are looking for a comprehensive open source single sign-on solution
AuthenticationProcessingFilter	Processes an HTTP FORM POST similar to the Servlet Specification's j_security_ check	—When single sign-on is not a requirement —Should your web application prefer a form-based login

Each authentication mechanism has two classes. The [Strategy]ProcessingFilter is used to process an authentication request as described in the previous table. The [Strategy]ProcessingFilterEntryPoint implements AuthenticationEntryPoint and is used to cause a web browser to commence the specified authentication mechanism, generally by sending an HTTP redirect message or some browser status code. Each web application also defines a SecurityEnforcementFilter, which is used to catch various Acegi Security exceptions and delegate to the AuthenticationEntryPoint or return a 403 (access denied) as appropriate.

Acegi Security supports multiple authentication mechanisms at the same time. For example, it is possible to handle authentication requests received both from a web form (with AuthenticationProcessingFilter) and from a Web Services client (with BasicProcessingFilter).

Client-server–rich clients are also fully supported. In the client-side application context a RemoteAuthenticationManager is configured. This RemoteAuthenticationManager receives Authentication request objects and passes the contained username and password to a corresponding server-side web service. The server-side web service then builds a new Authentication request object containing the passed username and password, before passing it to a server-side AuthenticationManager. If successful, a list of GrantedAuthoritys is passed back to the RemoteAuthenticationManager. This allows the rich client to make authorization decisions such as the visibility of GUI actions. The rich client will also typically set each remoting proxy factory with the validated username and password.

The authors of Acegi Security recognize that many existing web applications would ideally be modified to leverage Acegi Security's authentication, ACL, and services layer authorization services, yet these apps have an existing investment in taglibs and other web-layer code that depends on the Servlet

Specification's `isUserInRole()`, `getUserPrincipal()`, and `getRemoteUser()` methods. Acegi Security provides two solutions:

❑ `HttpServletRequestWrapper`: Recall that Acegi Security's `ContextHolder` stores an `Authentication`, which is an extension of the `Principal` interface. As such, `ContextHolderAwareRequestWrapper` implements the Servlet Specification methods by delegation to these Acegi Security objects instead of the web server authentication system. The replacement wrapper is enabled simply by adding the `ContextHolderAwareRequestFilter` to `web.xml`.

❑ **Container adapters:** Although use is discouraged in all but very special circumstances, Acegi Security also provides several implementations of proprietary web or application server authentication interfaces. These allow the server to delegate an authentication decision to an Acegi Security `AuthenticationManager`, which returns an Authentication object that is in turn used by both the server and Acegi Security authorization classes. This may be useful if refactoring a large application that uses EJBs to a pure Spring implementation, as the existing EJBs (secured by the application server) can be used in parallel with new Spring POJOs (secured by Acegi Security).

Although `ContextHolderAwareRequestWrapper` is commonly used, container adapters are of very limited usefulness in web servers given that Acegi Security provides a far more extensive and flexible implementation of security functionality than offered by the Servlet Specification. One container adapter for which use is encouraged is `CasPasswordHandler`, which allows an `AuthenticationManager` to be used by an enterprise's CAS server. At the time of this writing CAS does not provide any usable implementations of its `PasswordHandler` interface, so this container adapter makes deployment of CAS much easier.

> **You do not need to "throw away" your existing investment in code and helper classes to move to Acegi Security. Integration hooks have been carefully considered so that you can migrate over time, leveraging the benefit of Acegi Security's additional features and container portability without major refactoring.**

Storing the Authentication Object

All major Acegi Security classes, and many user-specific classes, need to access the currently logged on user. More specifically, they need access to the populated Authentication object that applies to the current principal. Acegi Security ensures any interested class can access the Authentication via the `ContextHolder`, which is a `ThreadLocal` object usually used to hold a `SecureContext`. The `SecureContext` provides a getter and setter for the `Authentication` object, as shown in Figure 10-3.

A `ContextHolder` must be set with the correct `Authentication` for the duration of a given principal's request. For a unit test, that duration is typically a single test case. For a rich client, that duration is typically an entire application execution period. For a web application or web service, that duration is typically a single HTTP request. The `ContextHolder` needs to be made null at the end of a given principal's request; otherwise other principals might reuse the Thread, which would compromise security.

For JUnit tests, the `setUp()` and `tearDown()` methods are often used to configure the `ContextHolder` with an appropriate `Authentication` object. This is of course assuming security actually needs to be tested. Normally, the POJOs making up Spring applications should be unit tested in isolation without transaction, security, and other AOP concerns.

In the case of rich clients, the developer is responsible for setting up the `ContextHolder` for the request duration. With Spring Rich, classes supporting the use of Acegi Security are included in the `org.springframework.richclient.security` package. This package contains a `LoginCommand` and `LogoutCommand`, which hide `ContextHolder` management from developers.

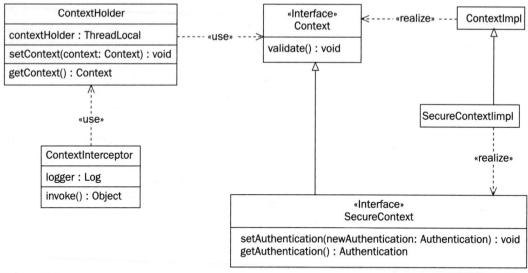

Figure 10-3

For web applications and web services, a Filter is used to address the `ContextHolder` requirement. A series of *authentication integration filters* is provided with Acegi Security, as detailed in the following table.

Module	What It Does	Why and When to Use It
`HttpSessionIntegrationFilter`	Uses the `HttpSession` to store the `Authentication` between requests	— Because container adapters are not recommended, this authentication integration filter is used in almost every situation.
		— `HttpSession` is used to store the Authentication between requests. — It provides a portable and flexible approach that does not depend on container adapters.
`HttpRequestIntegrationFilter`	Obtains the Authentication from `HttpServletRequest.getUserPrincipal()`, but cannot write the Authentication back to this location at the end of a request	— Mandatory if using most container adapters, as this is the only location the Authentication produced by most container adapters is available from.

		—The container is responsible for internally storing the Authentication between requests.
`JbossIntegrationFilter`	Obtains the Authentication from Jboss's `java:comp/env/security/subject` JNDI location, but cannot write the Authentication back to this location at the end of a request	—Mandatory if using the JBoss container adapter. —The container is responsible for internally storing the Authentication between requests. —Do not use the JBoss container adapter if one of the standard web application authentication mechanisms (see the previous table) would suffice.

Authorization

Armed with a solid understanding of how a principal is authenticated and the resulting Authentication is stored between requests and made available through the `ContextHolder`, we can now examine the fundamental objective of security: authorization.

Figure 10-4 provides an overview of the key authorization interfaces and classes. An important interface is `ConfigAttribute`, which represents a configuration setting that applies to a secure object invocation (recall a secure object invocation is any type of object that can have its invocation intercepted and security logic applied). Configuration attributes are similar to Spring's transaction attributes, such as `PROPAGATION_REQUIRED`.

The `AccessDecisionManager` is responsible for making an authorization decision. It is passed the secure object, in case it needs access to properties of the secure object invocation (such as arguments in the case of a `MethodInvocation` or `HttpServletRequest` properties in the case of a `FilterInvocation`). The `AccessDecisionManager` is also passed the configuration attributes that apply to the secure object invocation, along with the validated Authentication object. This information is sufficient to make an authorization decision by returning void or throwing an `AccessDeniedException`.

Similar to the authentication-related `ProviderManager`, the `AbstractAccessDecisionManager` adopts a provider-based approach whereby it will poll a series of `AccessDecisionVoters`. Each voter returns a veto, grant, or deny vote. The final decision based on these votes is left to the specific `AbstractAccessDecisionManager` implementation.

The `RoleVoter` is the most commonly used `AccessDecisionVoter` with Acegi Security. It iterates through each configuration attribute, voting to grant access if one matches a `GrantedAuthority` held by the principal. As such it's a simple way of implementing role-based access control. `BasicAclVoter` is a more complex voter and is discussed in the following "Domain Object Instance Security" section.

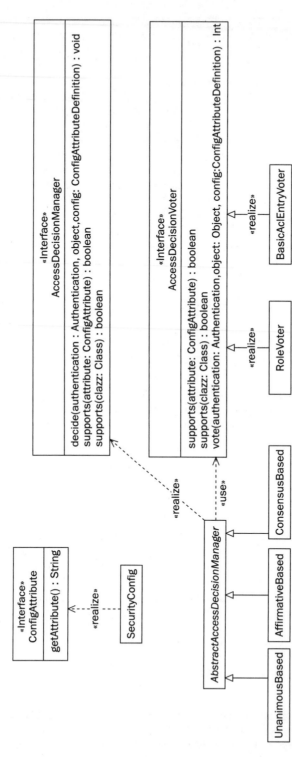

Figure 10-4

In order to actually authorize a secure object invocation, Acegi Security needs to intercept the invocation to begin with. Figure 10-5 shows the key interfaces and classes involved in security interception. As shown, the `AbstractSecurityInterceptor` has a series of subclasses that each handle a specific type of secure object.

The `FilterSecurityInterceptor` is implemented by way of a `<filter>` declaration in `web.xml`. Acegi Security provides a useful `FilterToBeanProxy` class, which allows a `web.xml`-defined Filter to be set up in the Spring bean container. This allows collaborating beans to be easily injected. `MethodSecurityInterceptor` is used to protect beans defined in the bean container, requiring the use of Spring's `ProxyFactoryBean` or `DefaultAdvisorAutoProxyCreator` along with the `MethodDefinitionSourceAdvisor`. The `AspectJSecurityInterceptor` is woven in using AspectJ's compiler.

Upon detection of a secure object invocation, an `AbstractSecurityInterceptor` will look up the configuration attributes that apply to that invocation. If there aren't any configuration attributes, the invocation is deemed to be public and the invocation proceeds. If configuration attributes are found, the `Authentication` contained in the `ContextHolder` is authenticated via the `AuthenticationManager`, and the `AccessDecisionManager` is asked to authorize the request. If successful, the `RunAsManager` may replace the identity of the `Authentication` and then the invocation will proceed. Upon completing the invocation, the `AbstractSecurityInterceptor` will clean up by updating the `ContextHolder` to contain the actual `Authentication` object, and if one is defined, calling the `AfterInvocationManager`.

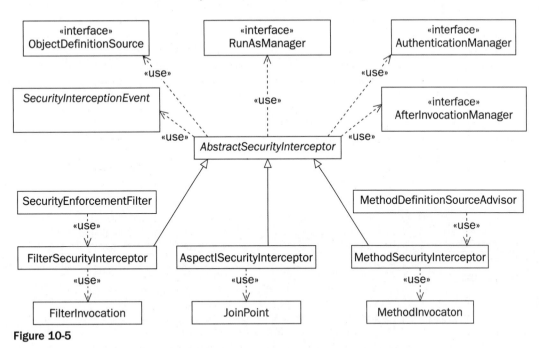

Figure 10-5

The `AfterInvocationManager` is able to modify the object to be returned from the secure object invocation. This is typically used to filter `Collections` only to contained, authorized elements, or mutate instance variables if the information is protected. It can also throw an `AccessDeniedException` if, for example, the principal does not have permission to the object about to be returned.

AfterInvocationManager is similar to AccessDecisionManager. It is passed the Authentication, secure object invocation, applicable configuration attributes, and of course the object to be returned. It is required to return an object, which will then become the result of the secure object invocation. A concrete implementation named AfterInvocationProviderManager is used to poll AfterInvocationProvider instances. The first instance that indicates it can process the after invocation request will be used.

Domain Object Instance Security

Protecting individual domain object instances is a common requirement of large enterprise applications. Often it is necessary to prevent unauthorized principals from accessing certain domain object instances, or preventing services layer methods from being invoked when principals are not authorized for a particular domain object instance. Other times it is desirable to mutate sensitive properties of a domain object instance, depending on the principal retrieving the instance. Acegi Security uses the secure object model discussed previously to enforce this form of ACL security within your applications.

Figure 10-6 illustrates Acegi Security's ACL services. As shown, the AclManager interface allows any Object to be presented and its ACLs obtained. An additional method is provided that allows those ACLs to be filtered to contain only ACLs that apply to the presented Authentication. The AclProviderManager polls AclProviders until one indicates it is capable of retrieving the AclEntrys applying to a given Object.

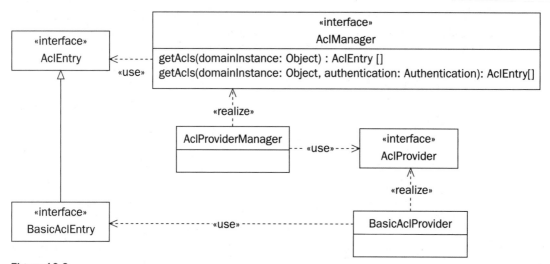

Figure 10-6

Acegi Security provides a BasicAclProvider, which uses integer bit masking and a DAO-based approach to retrieving ACL information. The implementation basically converts the domain Object into an AclObjectIdentity, which is able to uniquely identify the Object. This is then used as a key against a BasicAclDao that can retrieve the BasicAclEntrys for the Object. BasicAclProvider (shown in Figure 10-7) uses a pluggable caching layer to avoid expensive ACL retrievals. Other interfaces are also used by the BasicAclProvider to implement the remainder of the AclProvider contract.

Working in concert with the AclManager are several key classes. These provide the linkage between the AbstractSecurityInterceptor and actual enforcement of ACL security. These are listed in the following table.

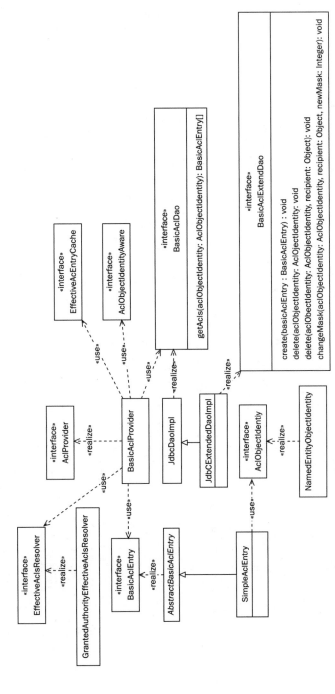

Figure 10-7

Module	What It Does	Why and When to Use It
`BasicAclEntryVoter`	Called by an `AbstractAccessDecisionManager`, looks at method arguments of the secure object invocation and locates one that matches, and then retrieves the ACL details for that `Object` and principal, and votes to grant or deny access based on a list of allowed permissions defined against the `BasicAclEntryVoter`.	— Typically several `BasicAclEntryVoters` are used together. — Different instances respond to different configuration attributes, with each instance typically targeting a different domain object class and/or list of allowed permissions. — Used when you need to deny access *before* a secure object invocation is allowed to proceed.
`BasicAclAfterInvocationProvider`	Called by the `AfterInvocationProviderManager`, looks at the returned `Object`, and then retrieves the ACL details for that `Object` and principal, throwing an `AccessDeniedException` if the principal does not have access according to the list of allowed permissions defined against the `BasicAclAfterInvocationProvider`.	— If you cannot determine *before* a method is invoked whether the principal should be allowed access, such as `getById(int)` methods. — Whenever you do not mind an `AccessDeniedException` being thrown *after* a secure object invocation is allowed to proceed.
`BasicAclEntryAfterInvocation-CollectionFilteringProvider`	Similar to `BasicAclAfterInvocationProvider`, but expects the returned `Object` to be a `Collection` and iterates that `Collection`, locating and removing unauthorized elements (rather than throwing `AccessDeniedException`) based on the list of allowed permissions defined against the `BasicAclEntryAfterInvocation-CollectionFilteringProvider`.	— If you need to filter a `Collection` to remove unauthorized elements. — When the method returns a `Collection` (no other return object types are allowed).

Example Code

We've provided a broad overview of Acegi Security and some of its key capabilities. Let's now look at a sample application that demonstrates the ACL services in detail.

Introducing the Sample

For this sample we are going to assume the role of a developer delivering a domain name system (DNS) administration tool for a major Internet hosting provider. The central function of the new application is to provide the hosting provider's customers with a self-service facility to manage the domain names they have registered. The main customer base comprises Internet entrepreneurs who own multiple domain names, so it is important the new DNS administration tool be able to accommodate each customer having many domain names. It is also a requirement that customers be able to delegate DNS administration responsibility to other people, such as their web designers or branch office IT managers.

It is assumed you have a basic understanding of DNS, in that its main function is to resolve hostnames such as www.springhost.zz into TCP/IP addresses. Each domain name is hierarchical, in that each subdomain falls under a parent domain until eventually reaching a top-level domain (such as an .org or .com or .au). For each domain name, an authoritative DNS server is specified. The role of the authoritative DNS server is to respond to requests for records within the domain.

Returning to our sample, there are a variety of DNS server implementations that could be used to implement the DNS administration tool. In order to promote maximum flexibility and reduce development time, your team has decided to store the DNS data in an RDBMS. With a little searching you discover an open source project called myDns (mydns.bboy.net), which interfaces with Postgres and mySql.

Security Unaware Implementation

After reviewing the myDns schema, for this book we developed a simple core for the new DNS administration tool. The three domain objects and service layer are shown in Figure 10-8. The StartOfAuthority and ResourceRecord objects are both modeled after myDns's soa and rr tables respectively. The Domain object is an addition to allow the hierarchy of the domain to be reflected, as the myDns tables, being focused on a DNS server's requirements, do not provide this support. There is a one-to-one relationship between a given Domain and a StartOfAuthority instance. There is a many-to-one relationship between ResourceRecord and StartOfAuthority. DomainDao provides CRUD operations for the Domain (including its contained StartOfAuthority) and ResourceRecord objects. BasicAclExtendedDao is an Acegi Security class that provides a simple interface to perform CRUD operations for ACL entries.

Also included in the Java package is a DataSourcePopulator class that configures the schema and inserts sample data. The applicationContext-business.xml included with the sample configures the persistence layer and services layer, and adds transaction support.

An in-memory Hypersonic SQL database is also configured in the application context, as it facilitates rapid prototyping and testing. Of course, a production implementation would need to use a database supported by myDns.

The classes, interfaces, and application context just described could be used to provide a basic DNS administration tool in conjunction with myDns.

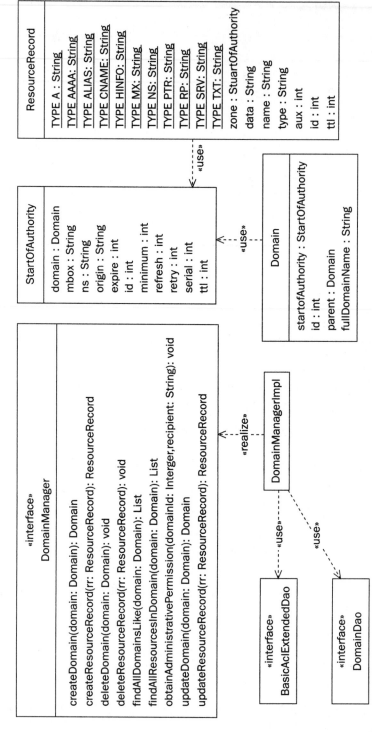

ResourceRecord

TYPE A : String
TYPE AAAA: String
TYPE ALIAS: String
TYPE CNAME: String
TYPE HINFO: String
TYPE MX: String
TYPE NS: String
TYPE PTR: String
TYPE RP: String
TYPE SRV: String
TYPE TXT: String
zone : StuartOfAuthority
data : String
name : String
type : String
aux : int
id : int
ttl : int

StartOfAuthority

domain : Domain
mbox : String
ns : String
origin : String
expire : int
id : int
minimum : int
refresh : int
retry : int
serial : int
ttl : int

«use»

Domain

startofAuthority : StartOfAuthority
id : int
parent : Domain
fullDomainName : String

«interface»
DomainManager

createDomain(domain: Domain): Domain
createResourceRecord(rr: ResourceRecord): ResourceRecord
deleteDomain(domain: Domain): void
deleteResourceRecord(rr: ResourceRecord): void
findAllDomainsLike(domain: Domain): List
findAllResourcesInDomain(domain: Domain): List
obtainAdministrativePermission(domainId: Interger,recipient: String): void
updateDomain(domain: Domain): Domain
updateResourceRecord(rr: ResourceRecord): ResourceRecord

«realize»

DomainManagerImpl

«use»

«use»

«interface»
BasicAclExtendedDao

«interface»
DomainDao

Figure 10-8

Security Approach

The interfaces and classes in Figure 10-8 are unaware of security, except as follows:

❑ When creating `Domains` and `ResourceRecords`, the `DomainManager` implementation needs to create an ACL entry via the `BasicAclExtendedDao`.

❑ When deleting `Domains` and `ResourceRecords`, the `DomainManager` implementation needs to delete all ACL entries via the `BasicAclExtendedDao`.

❑ To allow an administrator to gain full access to a domain (perhaps the owner of that domain revoked the administrator's existing access), `DomainManager` provides an `obtainAdministrativePermission` method that operates via the `BasicAclExtendedDao`.

Though the application does require a small amount of security awareness, this is only to link between the problem domain itself and the Acegi Security ACL services. The remainder of the security requirements of the application are declaratively configured in the Spring bean container. Configuration attributes will be used to tag how we require `ContactManager` methods to be secured. At an implementation level, we'll use `MethodSecurityInterceptor` as the application does not use AspectJ or provide web access that requires URI filtering.

Most of the application will be secured using ACL security. The only method on the `DomainManager` interface that is not secured via ACL security is the `obtainAdministrativePermission` method. For this special method we'll use role-based security, meaning the principal will need to hold a particular `GrantedAuthority`.

Over the following pages we'll be discussing the configuration of a security environment appropriate for integration testing using JUnit. The test cases have been developed to test and demonstrate security integration is functioning correctly for the sample application. Each of the unit tests extends from `AbstractDomainManagerTest`, which extends `AbstractTransactionSpringContextTests` because we leverage the latter's automatic database rollback capability.

Authentication

`AbstractDomainManagerTest` is responsible for providing several methods to assist in handling the `ContextHolder` during our JUnit tests. They allow our tests to simply call `makeActiveUser(String username)` for the `ContextHolder` to be configured with an appropriate `Authentication` request object.

```
protected void makeActiveUser(String username) {
String password = "";
if ("marissa".equals(username)) {
   password = "koala";
 } else if ("dianne".equals(username)) {
   password = "emu";
 } else if ("scott".equals(username)) {
   password = "wombat";
 } else if ("peter".equals(username)) {
   password = "opal";
 }
```

```
Authentication authRequest = new UsernamePasswordAuthenticationToken(
                                  username, password);
  SecureContextImpl secureContext = new SecureContextImpl();
  secureContext.setAuthentication(authRequest);
  ContextHolder.setContext(secureContext);
}

protected void onTearDownInTransaction() {
  ContextHolder.setContext(null);
}
```

Though Acegi Security provides a `TestingAuthenticationToken` and `TestingAuthenticationProvider` that allow you to specify any `GrantedAuthoritys`, principal, and credentials you wish (and they will be automatically accepted), in the DNS administration tool tests we've decided to use the popular `DaoAuthenticationProvider`, which accesses user information using `JdbcDaoImpl`. Key authentication-related XML is listed here:

```xml
<bean id="authenticationManager"
  class="net.sf.acegisecurity.providers.ProviderManager">
  <property name="providers">
    <list>
      <ref local="daoAuthenticationProvider"/>
    </list>
  </property>
</bean>
<bean id="jdbcDaoImpl" class="net.sf.acegisecurity.providers.dao.jdbc.JdbcDaoImpl">
  <property name="dataSource"><ref bean="dataSource"/></property>
</bean>
<bean id="daoAuthenticationProvider"
  class="net.sf.acegisecurity.providers.dao.DaoAuthenticationProvider">
  <property name="authenticationDao"><ref local="jdbcDaoImpl"/></property>
</bean>
```

Authorization

None of the `DomainManager` methods allow anonymous access, meaning every one of them needs to have one or more configuration attributes defined against the `MethodSecurityInterceptor`. The configuration attributes we've used for the DNS administration tool are listed here:

```
DomainManager.createDomain=ACL_DOMAIN_CREATE
DomainManager.createResourceRecord=ACL_RESOURCE_RECORD_CREATE
DomainManager.deleteDomain=ACL_DOMAIN_DELETE
DomainManager.deleteResourceRecord=ACL_RESOURCE_RECORD_DELETE
DomainManager.findAllDomainsLike=ROLE_USER,AFTER_ACL_COLLECTION_READ
DomainManager.findAllResourceRecordsInDomain=ROLE_USER,AFTER_ACL_COLLECTION_READ
DomainManager.obtainAdministrativePermission=ROLE_SUPERVISOR
DomainManager.updateDomain=ACL_DOMAIN_WRITE
DomainManager.updateResourceRecord=ACL_RESOURCE_RECORD_WRITE
```

We suggest a convention when naming configuration attributes to help you understand when they will be used. All configuration attributes that will be processed by an `AfterInvocationManager` should have a name starting with `AFTER_`. No configuration attributes that will be processed by an `AccessDecisionManager` should start with `AFTER_`.

Based on this convention, every method has a configuration attribute indicating an `AccessDecisionManager` will process it. This is because we want to ensure every principal either holds the `ROLE_USER GrantedAuthority` or has a specific ACL for the domain object passed as a method argument. Let's consider several examples.

The `deleteDomain` method uses the `ACL_DOMAIN_DELETE` configuration attribute. The Spring bean container contains the following declaration:

```xml
<bean id="aclDomainDeleteVoter"
class="net.sf.acegisecurity.vote.BasicAclEntryVoter">
  <property
name="processConfigAttribute"><value>ACL_DOMAIN_DELETE</value></property>
  <property
name="processDomainObjectClass"><value>com.acegitech.dns.domain.Domain</value></pro
perty>
  <property name="aclManager"><ref local="aclManager"/></property>
  <property name="requirePermission">
    <list>
      <ref local="net.sf.acegisecurity.acl.basic.SimpleAclEntry.ADMINISTRATION"/>
      <ref local="net.sf.acegisecurity.acl.basic.SimpleAclEntry.DELETE"/>
    </list>
  </property>
</bean>
```

The `SimpleAclEntry.ADMINISTRATION` and `DELETE` references actually relate to a `FieldRetrieveingFactoryBean` that enables the integer values of these static variables to be obtained from the specified class, rather than using integers directly inside the XML.

The `aclDomainDeleteVoter` will vote only when a secure object invocation presents the `ACL_DOMAIN_DELETE` attribute. Based on our earlier list configuration attributes, only `DomainManager.deleteDomain(Domain)` uses this configuration attribute. If voting, the voter will look at the method arguments for the first instance of the `processDomainObjectClass`, which in this case is the Domain object. The `Domain` will then be presented to the `AclManager` defined by the property of the same name, and the `BasicAclEntrys` that apply to the current principal will be obtained. Finally, `aclDomainDeleteVoter` will determine if the principal has any of the ACL permissions listed in the `requirePermission` property. If the principal does not, it will vote to deny access, or vote to grant access otherwise.

An important feature of the `BasicAclProvider` is its support for hierarchical domain object instances. Consider the following unit test:

```java
public void testDeleteAsPeterWhenPermittedViaDeepInheritance() {
  makeActiveUser("peter");
  Domain domain = getDomain("compsci.science.zoo-uni.edu.zz.");
  domainManager.deleteDomain(domain);

  // Ensure it was deleted (transaction will rollback post-test)
  assertNull(getDomain("compsci.science.zoo-uni.edu.zz."));
}
```

In the preceding example, user `peter` has been granted delete permission for domain `science.zoo-uni.edu.zz`. The fact `peter` is authorized to delete this subdomain is only because `BasicAclProvider` delivered the parent object's ACLs.

ACL_DOMAIN_CREATE is an interesting use of the BasicAclEntryVoter class because it demonstrates an additional feature. In this case we do not want to vote on the Domain presented in the method argument, but on whether the principal has create permission for that Domain's parent Domain. To accommodate this we use the internalMethod property, as shown here:

```
<bean id="aclDomainCreateVoter"
class="net.sf.acegisecurity.vote.BasicAclEntryVoter">
  <property
name="processConfigAttribute"><value>ACL_DOMAIN_CREATE</value></property>
  <property
name="processDomainObjectClass"><value>com.acegitech.dns.domain.Domain</value></pro
perty>
  <property name="internalMethod"><value>getParent</value></property>
  <property name="aclManager"><ref local="aclManager"/></property>
  <property name="requirePermission">
    <list>
      <ref local="net.sf.acegisecurity.acl.basic.SimpleAclEntry.ADMINISTRATION"/>
      <ref local="net.sf.acegisecurity.acl.basic.SimpleAclEntry.CREATE"/>
    </list>
  </property>
</bean>
```

Let's consider role-based access control, as used by the DomainManager. obtainAdministrativePermission method. RoleVoter will process the relevant configuration attribute, ROLE_SUPERVISOR. It will simply compare every GrantedAuthority assigned to the principal with the ROLE_SUPERVISOR String. A single RoleVoter is used for all role voting, irrespective of the attribute name (for example, ROLE_USER, ROLE_FOO):

```
<bean id="roleVoter" class="net.sf.acegisecurity.vote.RoleVoter"/>
```

The preceding techniques are used to secure almost every method of DomainManager. The only exceptions are the two find* methods, which use the configuration attribute AFTER_ACL_COLLECTION_READ. The corresponding declaration for this AfterInvocationProvider is:

```
<bean id="afterAclCollectionRead"
class="net.sf.acegisecurity.afterinvocation.BasicAclEntryAfterInvocationCollectionF
ilteringProvider">
  <property name="aclManager"><ref local="aclManager"/></property>
  <property name="requirePermission">
    <list>
      <ref local="net.sf.acegisecurity.acl.basic.SimpleAclEntry.ADMINISTRATION"/>
      <ref local="net.sf.acegisecurity.acl.basic.SimpleAclEntry.READ"/>
    </list>
  </property>
</bean>
```

The afterAclCollectionRead bean will present every element in the Collection to the AclManager, removing that element if the current principal does not hold one of the listed permissions (administration or read). It is used in this case to remove Domains and ResourceRecords the principal is not permitted to access. This is demonstrated by the following JUnit test code:

```
public void testFindAllDomainsLikeAsDianne() {
  makeActiveUser("dianne"); // has ROLE_STAFF
  List domains = domainManager.findAllDomainsLike("");
```

```
        assertNotContainsDomain("scotty.com.zz.", domains);
        assertEquals(8, domains.size()); // all domains except scotty.com.zz.
}
```

As indicated by the comments, user `dianne` has the `ROLE_STAFF` role and is thus granted administrative access to all domains except `scotty.com.zz`. The test demonstrates that `scotty.com.zz` was removed from the `Collection`.

Each `DomainManager` method has a comprehensive suite of JUnit that tests operation using different domain object instances and principals. We recommend you have a look at those tests to gain a fuller understanding of how Acegi Security is being used in this sample application. Acegi Security also provides a sample application that can be used to query the domains. The sample application is a client-server tool that demonstrates the ease at which Acegi Security supports web services clients. A simple command that displays all resource records in the DNS system is shown here:

```
maven -Dusername=marissa -Dpassword=koala
      -Dcommand=findRecordsByDomainName -Ddomain=. run
run:
     [java] Acegi DNS Console Query Tool
     [java] Domain: 10    arts.zoo-uni.edu.zz.
     [java]    10 www      10.1.43.65
     [java] Domain: 11    compsci.science.zoo-uni.edu.zz.
     [java]    12 ssl      10.1.12.88
     [java]    11 www      10.1.12.87
     [java] Domain: 4     jackpot.com.zz.
     [java]     4 www      192.168.0.3
     [java] Domain: 2     petes.com.zz.
     [java]     2 www      192.168.0.1
     [java] Domain: 9     science.zoo-uni.edu.zz.
     [java]     9 www      10.1.12.4
     [java] Domain: 7     tafe.edu.zz.
     [java]     7 www      192.168.0.5
     [java] Domain: 6     zoo-uni.edu.zz.
     [java]     6 www      10.1.0.1
     [java] Domain: 8     zoohigh.edu.zz.
     [java]     8 www      192.168.0.6

maven -o -Dusername=scott -Dpassword=wombat -Dcommand=findAll run
run:
     [java] Acegi DNS Console Query Tool
     [java] Domain: 3     scotty.com.zz.
     [java] Domain: 7     tafe.edu.zz.
```

Finally, Acegi Security itself includes a Contacts sample application that uses domain object instance security and provides a full web layer and web services. This sample also demonstrates form-based, CAS, and container adapter–managed authentication.

Summary

In this chapter we've looked at security within enterprise applications, the most common type of application built with the Spring Framework.

We've seen that enterprise applications typically have four security-related requirements:

- ❑ Authentication
- ❑ Web request security
- ❑ Service layer security
- ❑ Domain object instance security

We briefly considered three common approaches to implementing these requirements:

- ❑ Acegi Security System for Spring
- ❑ JAAS
- ❑ Servlet Specification security

We recommended that Acegi Security be used in all but the simplest of cases, with a simple case being one that does not need any form of services layer or domain object instance authorization, or web container portability.

We examined Acegi Security's architecture, with an emphasis on authentication, authorization, and domain object instance security. We saw how Acegi Security is configured exclusively through the Spring application context, and is similar in many ways to Spring's own transaction services (discussed in Chapter 6). We discussed many of the most commonly used Acegi Security classes in detail.

We saw that Acegi Security supports a wide range of authentication providers, and can not only authorize a web or method invocation before it happens, but also throw an `AccessDeniedException` or modify an `Object` returned from a method invocation. We saw the interface-driven nature of Acegi Security, and we looked at how role-based and access control list (ACL) authorization could be achieved solely using extensible, declarative means.

Following a review of the architecture, we reviewed a DNS application that could be used in a multi-customer Internet hosting provider. The application used Acegi Security — in particular its ACL capabilities — to restrict different customers to their own domains only. The application also leveraged DNS's inherent hierarchical nature so that ACL permissions granted to higher level domains trickled down to subdomains and their contained resource records.

> As we have shown in this chapter, with proper design and an effective security framework, enterprise applications rarely require their own custom security code. Using a high-quality, generic security framework such as Acegi Security can help to free developers to focus on truly domain-specific concerns. The value proposition is just as compelling as with other generic functionality addressed by Spring and other leading frameworks.
>
> As with transactions, security demonstrates the true potential of AOP in delivering transparent crosscutting concerns, and the real-world productivity and quality benefits this delivers.

11

Spring and EJB

This book has so far focused on Spring as a lightweight container, running in a J2EE application server or outside. We have not yet discussed where EJBs come into the picture. Whether by choice, or for legacy reasons, it may make sense to use Spring in concert with EJBs. This chapter will focus on providing you with the information needed for you to do this in the most effective fashion.

We'll cover:

❑ Singleton style access to shared application contexts and bean factories, via Spring's `SingletonBeanFactoryLocator` and `ContextSingletonBeanFactoryLocator`. While EJBs have the most use for a mechanism like this, you may come upon other glue code in your application that also has no other way to get to a common Spring container, and needs to use this approach. Even if you do not read the rest of this chapter, it's worth reading this section.

❑ Deciding on the actual need for EJBs.

❑ Spring's `JndiObjectFactoryBean` for encapsulating Home object lookup.

❑ Spring's local and remote Stateless Session Bean proxies for encapsulating lookup and access of EJB homes and EJB instances, eliminating the need to write EJB API-specific Java code when invoking EJBs.

❑ Spring's abstract convenience base classes for implementing EJBs.

❑ Some high-level strategies for testing EJBs.

Deciding on the Need for EJBs

Given that you are reading a book on lightweight containers, the first question that probably comes to mind at this point is whether EJBs are even still relevant, with or without Spring.

You may not always have a choice in the matter. Many legacy projects already use EJBs. There is a good chance that any attempt to introduce Spring in such an environment means that Spring-related code will have to work with EJBs or run in an EJB container, whether on an ongoing or a transition basis, for a number of reasons. There is usually not enough time to stop delivering new features and do a complete rewrite to new technology. Additionally, even if there is time, it's generally been proven in practice that making changes in shorter iterations is more effective than doing the same thing in longer iterations, in terms of reducing the risk of failure to meet goals or requirements. Finally, there may be political reasons. Regardless of architecture, we have all been in situations where a technology was mandated for reasons beyond our control, and a change is impossible or requires time to effect. In such an environment, where EJBs are actively used, Spring can still be a great benefit, as we explain later in this chapter.

When you do have a choice as to whether to use EJBs or not, that choice is somewhat more complex. This book shows enough of the Spring lightweight container approach that if you are already equally familiar with EJBs, it should be relatively easy to come to an informed opinion about the strengths and weaknesses of each approach, in terms of agility, effort, feature set, and to some extent, performance. It's not within the scope of this book to attempt to answer the lightweight container versus EJB general question in great detail. However, *J2EE without EJB* by Rod Johnson and Juergen Hoeller (Wrox, 2004) devotes a detailed chapter to this topic, and most of that book talks about general architectural concerns and strategies that have a direct or indirect relationship to a decision to use or not use EJBs. Additionally, Chapter 15 in that book presents the results of benchmarks comparing a lightweight Spring-based approach to an EJB-based approach.

Generally, we feel that time has proven that the EJB approach up to version 2.1 of the spec is not agile enough, is too complex, and in most cases does not provide any advantages while having a number of disadvantages compared to a lightweight container approach. One area where EJBs might still wisely be chosen on technical merits is when cluster-safe remoting is needed, perhaps for high-availability, stateful, backend services. Several commercial EJB container implementations have well-implemented, cluster-aware remoting of EJBs, which works very well. However, remoting still has large performance implications compared to local invocations, and the number of applications that actually need this is typically fairly limited. In this chapter, you'll see how to use Spring's EJB access proxies so that you may switch back and forth from a POJO, local EJB, or remote EJB implementation of a service without the client being aware of or coupled to the implementation type. This means that even if there exists the future possibility of needing to use EJB remoting, that is no longer a criterion for choosing to use remote EJBs from the beginning. Even when there is a need to use remoting, this pluggability means that it is possible to use one of the excellent lighter-weight Spring remoting options, and switch to the heavier-weight EJB remoting only if there is an actual need.

The future direction of the EJB spec is actually one of the many reasons that you might want to choose to use a Spring-only approach instead of a Spring + EJB approach at this point. At the time of this writing, the EJB 3.0 working group has released a draft spec for EJB 3.0 that essentially throws away almost everything in EJB 2.1 (keeping the old functionality only in a compatibility layer), in favor of a POJO / lightweight IoC container model that is similar to (but less powerful than) Spring. On the persistence side, the EJB 3.0 persistence spec, which will also run outside of J2EE containers, in normal J2SE apps, appears to be most similar to Hibernate, with influences also from the JDO spec and TopLink ORM product. Based on the direction the EJB specification is moving in, basing your application on a POJO model tied together by the Spring container is actually the best way of ensuring that you'll have the easiest migration path to EJB 3.0, should you want to take that route.

Accessing EJBs

Spring can provide a lot of help to client code that needs to access and use EJBs, both by reducing duplication of boilerplate code used to access EJBs, and also by allowing (stateless) EJBs to be used by clients as if they were any other service accessed via a *business interface*, with configuration happening in an IoC fashion.

Let's briefly review the standard, non-Spring approach to accessing and using an EJB.

The Boilerplate Approach

The standard approach to looking up and using an EJB is well known, if somewhat laborious. Consider the following sequence, for a (remote) Session bean:

Lookups happen via JNDI, so an `InitialContext` is first created:

```
try {
    InitialContext ctx = new InitialContext();
```

In this case, the client code is running inside the appserver, so no configuration of the `InitialContext` needs to be done. However, if the client is remote, then the client-side `InitialContext` needs to be configured so that it can remotely access the server-side JNDI environment. This may be done by passing into the context constructor, as properties in a `Properties` object, values specifying the `InitialContext` factory class, and the URL to access the remote server at:

```
Properties props = new Properties();
props.put(Context.INITIAL_CONTEXT_FACTORY, "com.sun.jndi.cosnaming.CNCtxFactory");
props.put(Context.PROVIDER_URL, "iiop://localhost:2809/");
```

This example uses standard IIOP wire protocol, but some containers, such as WebLogic, have optimized wire protocols that may be preferred. Alternately these values may be specified in a `jndi.properties` file visible on the client classpath.

Once the context has been created, it is used to look up the EJB home object. Calling `create()` on the home object returns the EJB remote proxy or *stub*:

```
SimpleHomeRemote simpleHome = (SimpleHomeRemote) PortableRemoteObject
        .narrow(ctx.lookup("Simple"), SimpleHomeRemote.class);
SimpleRemote simple = simpleHome.create();
```

At this point, the business method may be called on the stub:

```
simple.echo("hello");
```

The client-side invocation on the stub is marshaled to the server side if necessary (even when using remote EJBs, the server may actually internally optimize a remote call to a bean in the same VM to just a local method call), where the EJB server obtains an instance of the Stateless Session bean from the pool of beans it keeps ready, and invokes the actual method on the bean, which is then returned to the pool.

The client then must destroy the stub, by calling `remove()` on it, and also deal with any exceptions during the whole process, most of which are non-recoverable.

```
        simple.remove();
    }
    catch (RemoteException e) {
        ...     // handle
    }
    catch (NamingException e) {
        ...     // handle
    }
    catch (CreateException e) {
        ...     // handle
    }
    catch (RemoveException e) {
        ...     // handle
    }
```

This is a significant amount of code for what is ultimately a single method call on a business interface. Moving to a local EJB doesn't simplify things significantly, as it just removes the need to deal with `RemoteException`.

In a properly designed application, business logic code would of course delegate to some common utility methods in a helper class or superclass to perform some of this work, reducing some of the duplicate code. It is, however, hard to get away from the fact that the EJB client has to know it is dealing with an EJB, which needs to be looked up, and has to deal with some non-recoverable exceptions whether it wants to or not. Managing configuration data is also problematic. The general lookup and usage mechanism does not encourage a coding style that makes it easy or possible to test the EJB client code outside of the EJB container since JNDI access and EJB interfaces are hard to stub or mock. It *is* possible of course, with proper diligence toward separation of concerns, but much harder than it should be. This is a shame because complexity aside, an in-appserver test compared to an outside of the appserver unit test can mean the difference between, for example, a 2-minute build/deploy/test cycle and a 2-second one.

The Spring Approach

Spring provides two mechanisms that can make accessing and using an EJB easier. One is to encapsulate the Home object lookup so it can be handled in a declarative fashion, and the result injected into the client code that needs the Home. The other, usable for Stateless Session Beans, is to encapsulate, via a dynamically generated proxy object, the lookup of both the Home object *and* the EJB stub. This proxy can then be injected into client code to be used by the client, which is unaware that it is calling anything more than a business interface on a POJO service.

Encapsulating the Home Object Lookup

In Chapter 3, you were introduced to the `JndiObjectFactoryBean`, a factory bean that, as its output, returns the result of a JNDI lookup. Use of `JndiObjectFactoryBean` allows an EJB client, which needs a Home object, to be provided with that Home in an IoC fashion. Consider the following EJB client bean:

```
public class SimpleServiceClient {

    private SimpleHomeRemote simpleHome;
```

```
    public void setSimpleHome(SimpleHomeRemote simpleHome) {
      this.simpleHome = simpleHome;
    }

    public void useSimpleService() {

      try {
        SimpleRemote simple = simpleHome.create();
        simple.echo("hello");
      }
      catch (RemoteException e) {
        ...      // handle
      }
      catch (CreateException e) {
        ...      // handle
      }
      finally {
        simple.remove();
      }
    }
  }
}
```

The EJB client deals with the Home only in terms of the remote (or local, as the case may be) Home interface. In a bean factory or application context definition, we configure the client like any other bean, feeding it as the `simpleHome` property, a reference to the `JndiObjectFactoryBean`:

```
<bean id="simpleBeanHome" class="org.springframework.jndi.JndiObjectFactoryBean">
  <property name="jndiName"><value>Simple</value></property>
</bean>

<bean id="simpleServiceClient" class="ch11.sample1.SimpleServiceClient">
  <property name="simpleHome"><ref local="simpleBeanHome"/></property>
</bean>
```

You will sometimes come across a problem related to the particular loading sequence of EJBs versus other artifacts such as web-apps, in some J2EE appservers. The J2EE and EJB specifications do not satisfactorily address this common requirement. `JndiObjectFactoryBean` normally performs the JNDI lookup immediately after instantiation, caching the result. In an application context, which pre-instantiates singletons not marked as *lazy-init*, this will happen when the application context is initialized, and this will normally happen when the web-app starts up. It is possible in some appservers for a web-app to start up before EJBs are all loaded and made available in the JNDI environment. This loading sequence can make it possible for a JNDI lookup to be attempted for a resource that is not yet available! To avoid this problem, it is possible to set `JndiObjectFactoryBean`'s `lookupOnStartup` property to `false`.

```
<bean id="simpleBeanHome2" class="org.springframework.jndi.JndiObjectFactoryBean">
  <property name="jndiName"><value>Simple</value></property>
  <property name="lookupOnStartup"><value>false</value></property>
  <property name="proxyInterface">
  <value>org.springframework.autobuilds.ejbtest.simple.ejb.SimpleHomeRemote</value>
  </property>
</bean>
```

This will force the factory bean to generate a proxy object to stand in for the real JNDI object, which does the actual JNDI lookup only on first use. Note that you do have to specify the interface of the JNDI object (the EJB home in this case) because the proxy has to be generated to match the JNDI object, which has not yet been retrieved. If you need to generate many lazy JNDI proxies like this, remember that, as described in Chapter 3, you may use the parent/child bean definition technique to reduce duplicate configurations by inheriting from an abstract template definition, which sets some properties and attributes that never vary. For example:

```
<bean id="lazyJndiObjectFactoryBean" abstract="true"
      class="org.springframework.jndi.JndiObjectFactoryBean">
  <property name="lookupOnStartup"><value>false</value></property>
</bean>
```

The preceding example did not configure the JNDI environment, assuming the code is run inside an appserver, or the properties are obtained from the classpath in a `jndi.properties` file as mentioned previously as one config option. The `JndiProxyFactoryBean` configuration may, however, specify configuration values for the environment, via the `jndiEnvironment` property.

An alternate solution is to set both the `JndiObjectFactoryBean` and its users (clients) to `lazy-init`. This avoids the need to specify a `proxyInterface` (because there is no proxy needed), but is somewhat unreliable because the whole chain of related beans needs to be marked lazy.

The encapsulation of the Home lookup is useful for client access to both Stateless and Stateful Session beans. For the latter, it is the only client-side help that Spring offers. It would be hard for Spring to do much more because the actual EJB stub needs to be obtained by calling one of the potentially many custom `create()` method variants that an SFSB may define. Additionally, the SFSB instance needs to be used and managed by just one client, potentially over a longer time period, with `remove()` being called on the instance when it is no longer needed.

Encapsulating Stateless Session Bean Lookups

A general EJB best-practice is for clients of Stateless Session Beans to deal with EJBs through a business interface only. Consider an example business interface for a *local* EJB:

```
public interface SimpleService1 {
  public String echo(String input);
  public String echo2(String input);
  public String echo3(String input);
}
```

The following example takes the same approach for a *remote* EJB:

```
public interface SimpleService2 extends java.rmi.Remote {
  public String echo(String input) throws RemoteException;
  public String echo2(String input) throws RemoteException;
  public String echo3(String input) throws RemoteException;
}
```

The client code working against these interfaces may be completely unaware that it is dealing with an EJB. In the case of the remote EJB, it *is* aware that it's dealing with a remote API but doesn't care how that's implemented. This makes testing and changing the implementation much easier.

For the local EJB case, the EJB local interface derives from both the business interface and the standard `EJBLocalObject` interface:

```
public interface SimpleLocal extends EJBLocalObject, SimpleService1 {
}
```

For the remote EJB case, the EJB remote interface derives from both the business interface and the standard `EJBObject` interface:

```
public interface SimpleRemote extends EJBObject, SimpleService2 {
}
```

Aside from the fact that the client code is calling business methods through a business interface only, increasing decoupling and making testing easier, the other benefit of using this pattern is on the EJB implementation side: a normal local or remote EJB implementation class may not implement the local or remote interfaces that the client ends up using. They are meant for client-side use, but with this pattern, implementation classes *can* be forced to implement the business interface, which means that all signatures for methods that will be called by client code will automatically be verified.

> **For these reasons, we recommend that you always use the business interface pattern (see** `http://c2.com/cgi/wiki?BusinessInterface`**) when accessing Session beans. This should be the case with or without Spring.**

If you are willing to use this pattern, when you do use Spring it also means that Spring can be of major help in simplifying lookup and access to Stateless Session beans, as we're going to describe now.

Accessing Local EJBs

Assume that you have EJB client code that deals with a local EJB through a business interface only:

```
public class SimpleServiceClient {

  private SimpleService1 simple;

  public void setSimpleHome(SimpleService1 simple) {
    this.simple = simple;
  }

  public void useSimpleService() {
    simple.echo("hello");
  }
}
```

Spring makes it easy, via a factory bean called `LocalStatelessSessionProxyFactoryBean`, to create and inject into that EJB client, an object implementing the business interface, which actually encapsulates lookup of the EJB Home and EJB. Here's a configuration example:

```
<bean id="simpleBean"
    class="org.springframework.ejb.access.LocalStatelessSessionProxyFactoryBean">
  <property name="jndiName">
    <value>local/Simple</value>
  </property>
  <property name="businessInterface">
    <value>org.springframework.autobuilds.ejbtest.simple.SimpleService1</value>
  </property>
</bean>

<bean id="simpleServiceClient" class="ch11.sample2.SimpleServiceClient">
  <property name="simpleService"><ref local="simpleBean"/></property>
</bean>
```

The `LocalStatelessSessionProxyFactoryBean` instance is configured with the JNDI location of the EJB local home, as well as the business interface, `SimpleService1` in this case. The proxy factory bean produces as its output a proxy object that implements the specified business interface. In a default configuration, at the time the proxy is created, the EJB Home object is looked up and cached. When a client invokes a business interface method on the proxy, it creates an instance of the Session bean by calling `create()` on the cached Home. It then invokes the business method on the Session Bean and returns the result, making sure the Session Bean instance is destroyed first by calling `remove()` on it.

Therefore, as far as the client is concerned, invoking the EJB method in this fashion is no different than if a method on a regular stateless POJO service object were being called. This points out one of the great benefits of this approach. Aside from the reduction in boilerplate access code, it makes it trivial to change the implementation for the service the client is using. Swapping out the EJB implementation and dropping in a POJO version, or vice-versa, can be done without the client being aware.

Note that a number of aspects can be customized by configuring or subclassing the proxy factory bean. As described for the `JndiObjectFactoryBean`, you may want to set the `lookupHomeOnStartup` property to `false`, to have the Home object be lazy loaded on first use, instead of on proxy creation, and avoid potential failure if the particular container running the app loads EJBs after the web-app containing the application context containing the proxy is created. Setting the `cacheHome` property to false will force the proxy to look up the Home object on every invocation, instead of caching it. This is helpful for development scenarios because the client will no longer hold on to a possibly out-of-date Home object after a new version has been deployed into the appserver.

Accessing Remote EJBs

A similar factory bean, `SimpleRemoteStatelessSessionProxyFactoryBean`, exists for producing proxies to look up and access remote Stateless Session Beans. Assuming we are now using the remote `SimpleService2` business interface instead of the local `SimpleService1` interface, the EJB client is (aside from the different interface name introduced in this example for clarity) almost unchanged, except for the fact that it has to deal with `RemoteException`:

```
... // unchanged

public void useSimpleService() {
  try {
    simple.echo("hello");
```

```
        catch {RemoteException e} {
          ...    // handle
        }
      }
    }
}
```

The application context definition is updated to use the remote proxy factory, to specify the appropriate remote `SimpleService` business interface, and to specify the appropriate JNDI location:

```
<bean id="simpleBean"
 class="org.springframework.ejb.access.SimpleRemoteStatelessSessionProxyFactoryBean
">
  <property name="jndiName">
    <value>Simple</value>
  </property>
  <property name="businessInterface">
    <value>org.springframework.autobuilds.ejbtest.simple.SimpleService2</value>
  </property>
</bean>

<bean id="simpleServiceClient" class="ch11.sample2.SimpleServiceClient">
  <property name="simpleService"><ref local="simpleBean"/></property>
</bean>
```

Accessing Remote EJBs, Unifying the Business Interface

The local and remote Session Bean access mechanisms are very useful, and work well, but there remains one annoyance, which would ideally also be resolved by Spring, and this is the fact that the business interface for the local EJB has to be different from that of the remote EJB, which must extend `java.rmi`.`Remote`, and throw `RemoteException` on every method. This makes it impossible for client code directly accessing the EJB to be agnostic to whether the EJB is local or remote. This is also annoying because often remote exceptions are not recoverable by the client code using a business method anyway, and are better handled by an ancestor. (Where methods *are* idempotent, they are better marked as such and retried directly by the appserver, if the appserver is able to do this.)

Spring *can* help. Remember that while the EJB remote interface must have `throws RemoteException` on method signatures, the actual EJB implementation class doesn't extend the remote interface anyway; it extends `SessionBean` and ideally the business interface. This means that instead of having separate local and remote business interfaces, we can have just one business interface (identical to the previous local interface), without any remoting aspects. Then, when creating the remote EJB class, we implement the following (non-remote) business interface:

```
public interface SimpleService {
  public String echo(String input);
  public String echo2(String input);
  public String echo3(String input);
}
```

```
// implement the EJB
public class SimpleEJBWithCmtAndNoSpringTx implements SessionBean, SimpleService {
  ...
}
```

The EJB container is still perfectly happy.

We now have a problem that the remote interface can no longer derive from the business interface, as it still needs to throw RemoteException on every method. The solution is to keep a separate remote interface in synch with the business interface:

```
public interface SimpleRemote extends EJBObject {
    public String echo(String input) throws RemoteException;
    public String echo2(String input) throws RemoteException;
    public String echo3(String input) throws RemoteException;
}
```

The final question concerns how to reconcile the fact that though the client should be dealing with the business interface, the remote interface no longer even extends from it, and the EJB stub with which the client works implements the remote interface, not the business interface. This is where SimpleRemoteStatelessSessionProxyFactoryBean comes in. Without client code having to do anything, if the client works against a business interface and calls a method having the same signature as a method in the remote interface except that RemoteException is not thrown, the proxy will map method invocations from one interface to the other when it internally invokes the method on the EJB stub.

If the EJB container does throw a java.rmi.RemoteException when invoking a method on a remote EJB, Spring will simply re-throw it as Spring's own, non-checked RemoteAccessException. Client code is still free to catch and deal with this, in a similar fashion to how it might want to deal with RemoteException. However, there is the added benefit that because it is a non-checked exception, client code, which cannot deal with the remote exception, doesn't have to add a boilerplate catch clause or throws declaration.

The one negative aspect is the need to keep the business interface in synch with the remote interface, but this is usually easily handled by simple cutting and pasting with the addition of a throws RemoteException on each method. This negative aspect pales in comparison to the advantages of using this approach. (Note that the need to keep in-synch classes with matching method signatures but no common parent is a common problem in EJB, with the need to synchronize component interface and EJB implementation classes. The inelegance here comes from the EJB specification — and RMI — rather than Spring, which allows normal use of interfaces in other cases.)

> This mechanism is very convenient because it means the client can always work against just one business interface used both for local and remote EJBs. The service implementation may be local or remote as initially makes sense, and switched later as needed without client changes.
>
> This mechanism, combined with the general encapsulation of the EJB lookup mechanism described earlier, additionally makes it possible for EJBs to be a completely "use as needed" implementation technology. The client works simply against a business interface, and the actual implementation of the service may be a POJO, remote POJO marshaled via another Spring remoting technology, local EJB, or remote EJB, as makes sense for the particular circumstances.

Implementing EJBs with Spring

Spring provides a number of abstract base classes you may derive from to make it easier to implement Stateless Session Beans, Stateful Session Beans, and Message Driven Beans. Aside from reducing the boilerplate code you have to write, these classes encourage and simplify the generally desirable practice of actually implementing business logic in POJOs to which the EJBs delegate to, as opposed to in the EJBs themselves. These base classes are `AbstractStatelessSessionBean`, `AbstractStatefulSessionBean`, and `AbstractMessageDrivenBean`/`AbstractJmsMessageDrivenBean`.

Stateless Session Beans

Let's look at the absolute simplest Stateless Session Bean possible to be implemented by deriving from `AbstractStatelessSessionBean`:

```
public class SimpleEJB extends AbstractStatelessSessionBean {
}
```

This EJB is, of course, useless, but demonstrates that the classes in the abstract base hierarchy provided by Spring implement all required Session Bean EJB lifecycle methods. If the EJB implementation class needs to hook into any of the lifecycle methods, it generally does so by overriding template methods provided by the base class hierarchy. It's necessary to override template methods and not the actual lifecycle methods because Spring classes in the base class hierarchy implement the lifecycle callback methods themselves to provide configuration management. The actual lifecycle methods would have been made final were it not for EJB restrictions.

Let's look at the superclass template methods and other methods that may be called or have to be implemented by your EJB implementation classes. From `AbstractEnterpriseBean`:

```
/**
 * Subclasses must implement this method to do any cleanup
 * they would otherwise have done in an ejbRemove() method.
 * The BeanFactory will be unloaded afterwards.
 * <p>This implementation is empty, to be overridden in subclasses.
 * The same restrictions apply to the work of this method as to
 * an ejbRemove() method.
 */
protected void onEjbRemove() {
  // empty
}
```

From `AbstractSessionBean`:

```
/**
 * Sets the session context.
 * <p><b>If overriding this method, be sure to invoke this form of it
 * first.</b>
 * @param sessionContext SessionContext context for session
 */
public void setSessionContext(SessionContext sessionContext) {
    this.sessionContext = sessionContext;
}
```

```
/**
 * Convenience method for subclasses.
 * Return the EJB context saved on initialization.
 * @return the SessionContext saved on initialization by this class's
 * implementation of the setSessionContext() method.
 */
protected final SessionContext getSessionContext() {
  return sessionContext;
}
```

From `AbstractStatelessSessionBean`:

```
/**
 * Subclasses must implement this method to do any initialization
 * they would otherwise have done in an ejbCreate() method. In contrast
 * to ejbCreate, the BeanFactory will have been loaded here.
 * <p>The same restrictions apply to the work of this method as
 * to an ejbCreate() method.
 * @throws CreateException
 */
protected abstract void onEjbCreate() throws CreateException;
```

Now let's examine a real EJB:

```java
public class SimpleEJB extends AbstractStatelessSessionBean
        implements SimpleService {

  // --- statics
  public static final String POJO_SERVICE_ID = "simpleService";

  protected SimpleService simpleService;

  protected void onEjbCreate() throws CreateException {
    simpleService = (SimpleService) getBeanFactory().getBean(POJO_SERVICE_ID);
  }

  public String echo(String input) {
    return simpleService.echo(input);
  }
  public String echo2(String input) {
    return simpleService.echo2(input);
  }
  public String echo3(String input) {
    return simpleService.echo3(input);
  }
}
```

This version implements the `SimpleService` business interface. However, rather than actually implementing business method functionality itself, it delegates method calls to a POJO implementation of that interface. While the EJB *could* implement business functionality itself, delegating to a POJO is an option that should be favored because it makes testing much easier. Generally, EJBs are not easily tested inside the application server, while if the real functionality is in a POJO, it can simply be tested with an out-of-server unit or integration test. Additionally, it may make migrating away from EJBs much easier because the client can be hooked up directly to the POJO, instead of going through the intermediary EJB.

> Decoupling business logic from any environmental API — EJB or other — is usually
> desirable to promote reusability and achieve a degree of future proofing. The fact
> that EJB 3.0 will mark a move away from the traditional EJB API — at least in terms
> of the recommended programming model — underlines this point where EJB is
> concerned.

The POJO service implementation is obtained from an application context loaded by the base classes;
application code simply calls `getBeanFactory()` to obtain the application context. How and from
where the application context is loaded, and whether in fact it is a bean factory or application context, is
pluggable, but there is a default behavior, which the class in the preceding code sample relies on. In the
default implementation, the value at the bean-specific JNDI location

```
java:comp/env/ejb/BeanFactoryPath
```

is treated as the classpath location of an XML application context definition to load. Let's look at our EJB
definition from the standard `ejb-jar.xml`:

```
<session>
    <description>Chap11Sample3Simple Session Bean - Stateless Session Bean for
Chapter 11 Sample 30 implementing SimpleService</description>
    <display-name>Chap11Sample3Simple</display-name>
    <ejb-name>Chap11Sample3Simple</ejb-name>
    <local-home>ch11.sample3.ejb.SimpleHomeLocal</local-home>
    <local>ch11.sample3.ejb.SimpleLocal</local>
    <ejb-class>ch11.sample3.ejb.SimpleEJB</ejb-class>
    <session-type>Stateless</session-type>
    <transaction-type>Container</transaction-type>
    <env-entry>
      <env-entry-name>ejb/BeanFactoryPath</env-entry-name>
      <env-entry-type>java.lang.String</env-entry-type>
      <env-entry-value>ch11/sample3/ejb/beans.xml</env-entry-value>
    </env-entry>
</session>
```

In this definition, there is an EJB environment entry defined for the name `ejb/BeanFactoryPath` (which
the bean will access as `java:comp/env/ejb/BeanFactoryPath`), with a value of `ch11/sample3/ejb/`
`beans.xml`, the application context definition classpath location. Here's the actual definition:

```
<?xml version="1.0" encoding="UTF-8"?>
<!DOCTYPE beans PUBLIC "-//SPRING//DTD BEAN//EN"
    "http://www.springframework.org/dtd/spring-beans.dtd">


<beans>
  <bean id="simpleService"
      class="org.springframework.autobuilds.ejbtest.simple.LoggingSimpleService"/>
</beans>
```

In this case, the only bean defined is the POJO implementation of `SimpleService` that the EJB is delegating to.

So in the default setup, each EJB may specify its own unique application context definition location, or use the same definition location as another EJB does. However, regardless of where the *definition* comes from, each actual EJB *instance*—remember that EJBs are pooled by the EJB container—will still have its own unique application context *instance* created when the EJB itself is created. Some readers may be thinking to themselves that this is perfectly workable when the context holds small amounts of configuration data or beans, but has potential issues when some beans that are expensive (in terms of time to initialize or in terms of memory usage) need to be defined in the context and used. In fact, as we mentioned, the bean factory or application context loading mechanism is pluggable, and there is a way to switch to alternate setups, such as one where a common, singleton application context is shared by all the EJBs. We'll investigate this after we finish looking at the other EJB types.

Stateful Session Beans

Let's look at a Stateful Session Bean implemented by deriving from Spring's `AbstractStatefulSessionBean` abstract base class:

```
public class StatefulEJB extends AbstractStatefulSessionBean implements
        StatefulService {
```

The EJB implements a `StatefulService` business interface, with three methods: `clear()`, `addItem()`, and `getItems()`:

```
Collection items = new ArrayList();

public void clear() {
  items.clear();
}
public void addItem(String item) {
  items.add(item);
}
public Collection getItems() {
  return items;
}
```

Finally, as per the Stateless Session Bean specification, we need to implement `ejbActivate()` and `ejbPassivate()`, and define at least one create method:

```
// see javax.ejb.SessionBean#ejbActivate()
public void ejbActivate() {
  super.loadBeanFactory();
}

// see javax.ejb.SessionBean#ejbPassivate()
public void ejbPassivate() {
  super.unloadBeanFactory();
}

public void ejbCreate() {
  super.loadBeanFactory();
}
}
```

At a minimum, the create method(s) and `ejbActivate()` must call `super.loadBeanFactory()`, and `ejbPassivate()` must call `super.unloadBeanFactory()`, to help the Spring base class take care of loading the default application context or bean factory that is loaded for each bean, as per the description in the previous section. Here you should also take care of any of your own state that needs to be handled properly as per normal EJB create method, activation, and passivation semantics.

The `AbstractEnterpriseBean.onEjbRemove()`, and `AbstractSessionBean setSessionContext()` and `getSessionContext()` methods are still available to the Stateful Session Bean, and it may also call `getBeanFactory()` to get the application context or bean factory loaded by the Spring superclasses.

Message Driven Beans

The final EJB type that Spring provides an abstract base class for is the Message Driven Bean. Let's look at an example:

```
public class DispatcherEJB extends AbstractMessageDrivenBean {

  // see org.springframework.ejb.support.AbstractMessageDrivenBean#onEjbCreate()
  protected void onEjbCreate() {
  }

  public void onMessage(Message msg) {
    // do some work here
  }
}
```

In addition to the previously mentioned `AbstractEnterpriseBean.onEjbRemove()` template method, which may be overridden if needed, `AbstractMessageDriveBean` provides a `getMessageDrivenContext()` method:

```
protected final MessageDrivenContext getMessageDrivenContext();
```

to obtain the message driven context, which it has saved in a variable for this purpose. It also forces you to define a create method called `onEjbCreate()`:

```
/**
 * Subclasses must implement this method to do any initialization
 * they would otherwise have done in an ejbCreate() method. In contrast
 * to ejbCreate, the BeanFactory will have been loaded here.
 * <p>The same restrictions apply to the work of this method as
 * to an ejbCreate() method.
 */
protected abstract void onEjbCreate();
```

As with the other bean types, Spring itself implements and uses the real `ejbCreate()` method, and then calls this template method meant for application use. As with other bean types, your code may also call `getBeanFactory()` to get the application context or bean factory loaded by the Spring superclasses.

Spring also provides an `AbstractJmsMessageDrivenBean` abstract superclass. This is simply an `AbstractMessageDrivenBean` subclass whose purpose is simply to force subclasses to implement the `javax.jms.MessageListener` interface:

```
public abstract class AbstractJmsMessageDrivenBean
    extends AbstractMessageDrivenBean implements MessageListener {
    ...
}
```

A Digression into XDoclet

XDoclet (`http://xdoclet.sourceforge.net`) is a code generation tool that is used successfully by many Java developers to automatically generate boilerplate style code dynamically at build time, instead of having to create it by hand. Many people creating EJBs prefer to use XDoclet to generate artifacts such as the EJB deployment descriptors, the local and/or remote interfaces, and so on, by using metadata from JavaDoc tags inside your EJB source file.

If you are not interested in using XDoclet for creating EJB artifacts, you may safely skip the rest of this section. We do generally recommend the use of XDoclet as a timesaver when creating EJBs, although the following text assumes you are already familiar with it. Please see the XDoclet documentation and samples for more information on XDoclet.

Unfortunately XDoclet is a bit dense (as of version 1.2.1) when it comes to working with EJB implementation files, which extend from a base class. If you have such an EJB implementation extending from Spring's `AbstractStatelessSessionBean` or `AbstractStatefulSessionBean`, XDoclet will not realize that the Spring classes already implement the `javax.ejb.SessionBean` interface, and will complain that your code does not implement this interface. Because of this, when using the Spring Session Bean base classes, you must add a redundant `implements SessionBean` declaration even in your own class:

```
public class SimpleEJB extends AbstractStatelessSessionBean
        implements SimpleService, SessionBean {
    ...
```

Similarly, when using XDoclet with an EJB implementation class that derives from Spring's `AbstractMessageDrivenBean`/`AbstractJmsMessageDrivenBean`, you must add a redundant `implements MessageDrivenBean` clause.

Finally, XDoclet is not smart enough to figure out where the Spring superclasses implement `ejbCreate()` themselves (in the case of Stateless Session Beans and Message Driven Beans), and will itself add its own `ejbCreate()` method in the final generated class it puts out. This is completely undesirable and disrupts the normal automatic loading of an application context or bean factory that the Spring version of this method kicks off. This issue is easy to get around; just add in your actual implementation class an instance of `ejbCreate()`, which delegates to the Spring one. XDoclet *will* see this version, and not generate its own.

```
/*
 * This method needed just to make XDoclet happy. As it doesn't see the variant
 * coming from the Spring superclass, it will create an empty ejbCreate() in the
 * subclass it generates from this one, overriding the vital superclass version.
 * @ejb.create-method
 */
public void ejbCreate() throws CreateException {
    super.ejbCreate();
}
```

Singleton Container Access, Good or Evil?

One of the primary goals of Spring as a container is to eliminate the typical singletons and ad hoc factories that most applications end up using for access to objects.

> **Based on experience, we feel that in a properly designed and configured application written in IoC style and running in a sophisticated IoC container such as Spring, almost no application code needs to know about the container, or resort to singletons for access to other code.**

That said, there is no question that in a number of applications, a small amount of glue code that is container aware is often needed to kick things off at some point of execution, typically obtaining one or more configured objects from the Spring container and starting the execution of a chain of related actions. This glue code may come from Spring itself (as in the case of the request handler mechanism in the Spring Web MVC layer), or in the form of application code.

One of the main cases where application code may need to be aware of the Spring container is when the Spring container is not itself responsible for creating objects that then need to work with other objects from the Spring container. In the better (ideal) variant of this scenario, the other entity creating objects can at least be made to pass along an instance of the Spring container to the newly created object. For example, in Spring's Quartz scheduler integration, the scheduler and Quartz jobs are configured in the application context. While it is the Quartz scheduler, and not Spring itself, that actually creates new Jobs, it is easy to at least pass a reference to the application context, as part of the Job data, to the newly created job. So the Job does have to work with the container but doesn't have to worry about *how* to get the container.

However, consider the case of EJBs, which are created by the EJB container. There is simply no way to force the EJB container to somehow provide a newly created EJB with a reference to an existing Spring application context or bean factory. One option is for each EJB instance to create its own application context instance, and this is the default behavior of the Spring EJB base classes, as described previously. However, this is often not going to be an ideal solution. It is problematic when there are resources in the Spring container that have a relatively expensive (in terms of time) startup cost. Consider for example a Hibernate `SessionFactory`, which has to enumerate and initialize a number of class mappings. It is also problematic when the resources in the Spring container start using up significant amounts of memory. While EJBs are pooled by the container so Spring containers would not be continuously created in normal usage, it's clear that a solution for shared usage of a Spring container is needed.

Any scenario that has the same constraints as EJBs can also benefit from shared access to a Spring container. Spring provides a generic bean factory–accessing interface called `BeanFactoryLocator`:

```
public interface BeanFactoryLocator {

    /**
     * Use the BeanFactory (or derived class such as ApplicationContext) specified
     * by the factoryKey parameter. The definition is possibly loaded/created as
     * needed.
     * @param factoryKey a resource name specifying which BeanFactory the
     * BeanFactoryLocator should return for usage. The actual meaning of the resource
     * name is specific to the actual implementation of BeanFactoryLocator.
```

```
    * @return the BeanFactory instance, wrapped as a BeanFactoryReference object
    * @throws BeansException if there is an error loading or accessing the
    * BeanFactory
    */
   BeanFactoryReference useBeanFactory(String factoryKey) throws BeansException;

}
```

BeanFactoryLocator in and of itself does not imply singleton access to anything, but Spring does include a couple of almost identical "keyed" singleton implementations of BeanFactoryLocator, called ContextSingletonBeanFactoryLocator and SingletonBeanFactoryLocator.

ContextSingletonBeanFactoryLocator and SingletonBeanFactoryLocator

The basic premise behind ContextSingletonBeanFactoryLocator is that there is a shared application context, which is shared based on a string key. Inside this application context is instantiated one or more other application contexts or bean factories. The internal application contexts are what the application code is interested in, while the external context is just the *bag* (for want of a better term) holding them.

Consider that a dozen different instances of non-IoC configured, application glue code need to access a shared application context, which is defined in an XML definition on the classpath as serviceLayer-applicationContext.xml.

```xml
<?xml version="1.0" encoding="UTF-8"?>
<!DOCTYPE beans PUBLIC "-//SPRING//DTD BEAN//EN"
"http://www.springframework.org/dtd/spring-beans.dtd">

<!--
   Service layer ApplicationContext definition for the application.
   Defines beans belonging to service layer.
-->

<beans>

   <bean id="myService" class="...">
     ...
   </bean>

   ...     bean definitions
</beans>
```

The glue code cannot just instantiate this context as an XmlApplicationContext; each such instantiation would get its own copy. Instead, the code relies on ContextSingletonBeanFactoryLocator, which will load and then cache an outer application context, holding the service layer application context above. Let's look at some code that uses the locator to get the service layer context, from which it gets a bean:

```java
BeanFactoryLocator locator = ContextSingletonBeanFactoryLocator.getInstance();
BeanFactoryReference bfr = locator.useBeanFactory("serviceLayer-context");
BeanFactory factory = bfr.getFactory();
```

```
MyService myService = factory.getBean("myService");
bfr.release();

// now use myService
```

Let's walk through the preceding code. The call to `ContextSingletonBeanFactoryLocator`
`.getInstance()` triggers the loading of an application context definition from a file that is named (by
default) `beanRefContext.xml`. We define the contents of this file as follows:

beanRefContext.xml

```
<?xml version="1.0" encoding="UTF-8"?>
<!DOCTYPE beans PUBLIC "-//SPRING//DTD BEAN//EN"
        "http://www.springframework.org/dtd/spring-beans.dtd">

<!-- load a hierarchy of contexts, although there is just one here -->
<beans>

  <bean id="servicelayer-context"
        class="org.springframework.context.support.ClassPathXmlApplicationContext">
    <constructor-arg>
      <list>
        <value>/servicelayer-applicationContext.xml</value>
      </list>
    </constructor-arg>
  </bean>

</beans>
```

As you can see, this is just a normal application context definition. All we are doing is loading one context inside another. However, if the outer context (keyed to the name `beanRefContext.xml`) had
already been loaded at least once, the existing instance would just have been looked up and used.

The `locator.useBeanFactory("serviceLayer-context")` method call returns the internal application context, which is asked for by name, `serviceLayer-context` in this case. It is returned in the form
of a `BeanFactoryRef` object, which is just a wrapper used to ensure that the context is properly released
when it's no longer needed. The method call `BeanFactory factory = bfr.getFactory()` actually
obtains the context from the `BeanFactoryRef`. The code then uses the context via a normal `getBean()`
call to get the service bean it needs, and then releases the context by calling `release()` on the
`BeanFactoryRef`.

Somewhat of a complicated sequence, but necessary because what is being added here is really a level of
indirection so that multiple users can share one or more application context or bean factory definitions.

We call this a keyed singleton because the outer context being used as a bag is shared based on a string
key. When you get the `BeanFactoryLocator` via

```
ContextSingletonBeanFactoryLocator.getInstance();
```

it uses the default name `classpath*:beanRefContext.xml` as the resource location for the outer context definition. So all the files called `beanRefContext.xml`, which are available on the classpath, will be combined as XML fragments defining the outer context. This name (`classpath*:beanRefContext.xml`) is also the key by which other code will share the same context bag. But using the form:

```
ContextSingletonBeanFactoryLocator.getInstance(<resource name>);
```

for example:

```
contextSingletonBeanFactoryLocator.getInstance("contexts.xml");
```

or

```
contextSingletonBeanFactoryLocator.getInstance("classpath*:app-contexts.xml");
```

allows the name of the outer context definition to be changed. This allows a module to use a unique name that it knows will not conflict with another module.

Note that the outer bag context may define inside it any number of bean factories or application contexts, not just one as in the previous example, and because the full power of the normal XML definition format is available, they can be defined in a hierarchy using the right constructor for `ClasspathXmlApplicationContext`, if that is desired. The client code just needs to ask for the right one by name with the `locator.useBeanFactory(<id>)` method call. If the contexts are marked as `lazy-init="true"`, then effectively they will be loaded only on demand from client code.

The only difference between `SingletonBeanFactoryLocator` and `ContextSingletonBeanFactoryLocator` is that the latter loads the outer bag as an application context, while the former loads it as a bean factory, using the default definition name of `classpath*:beanRefFactory.xml`. In practice, it makes little difference whether the outer bag is a bean factory or full-blown application context, so you may use either locator variant.

It is also possible to provide an alias for a context or bean factory, so that one `locator.useBeanFactory(<id>)` can resolve to the same thing as another `locator.useBeanFactory(<id>)` with a different ID. For more information on how this works, and to get a better overall picture of these classes, please see the JavaDocs for `ContextSingletonBeanFactoryLocator` and `SingletonBeanFactoryLocator`.

A Shared Context as the Parent of a Web-App Application Context

In Chapter 4, we examined how Spring's `ContextLoader` class, triggered by the `ContextLoaderListener` or `ContextLoaderServlet`, can be used to load an application context for the web-app. You may want to review that section of Chapter 4 at this time.

Especially when creating a J2EE application, with multiple web-apps (and possibly EJBs), it is often desirable to define a shared parent application context to one or more web-app application contexts. In this setup, all service layer code can move into the shared context, with the web-app contexts having only bean definitions appropriate to the actual web view layer. Note that this does potentially affect how you will package your Spring-based app because the Spring framework and all classes that are used across web-apps will have to live in a classloader shared by the web applications, such as any global EJB classloader or an application server classloader. Most J2EE appservers do support a number of class-loader setup variations, allowing this configuration to work.

It is relatively trivial to subclass the existing `ContextLoader` class, so that using `ContextSingletonBeanFactoryLocator`, it triggers the loading of a shared parent context (with any other web-app inside the same J2EE app, which is configured the same).

Note that the following customization of `ContextLoader` has actually made it into Spring itself, for version 1.1.4. Before using this customization, ensure that it is actually needed in your version of Spring.

Let's look at the necessary code to customize `ContextLoader`:

```
public class SharedParentLoadingContextLoader
        extends org.springframework.web.context.ContextLoader {

  // --- statics

  protected static final Log log = LogFactory.getLog(ContextLoader.class);

  /** servlet param specifying locator factory selector */
  public static final String LOCATOR_FACTORY_SELECTOR = "locatorFactorySelector";
  /** servlet param specifying the key to look up parent context from locator */
  public static final String BEAN_FACTORY_LOCATOR_FACTORY_KEY =
          "parentContextKey";

  // --- attributes

  protected BeanFactoryReference _beanFactoryRef = null;

  /**
   * Overrides method from superclass to implement loading of parent context
   */
  protected ApplicationContext loadParentContext(ServletContext servletContext)
          throws BeansException {

    ApplicationContext parentContext = null;

    String locatorFactorySelector = servletContext
            .getInitParameter(LOCATOR_FACTORY_SELECTOR);
    String parentContextKey = servletContext
            .getInitParameter(BEAN_FACTORY_LOCATOR_FACTORY_KEY);

    try {
      if (locatorFactorySelector != null) {
        BeanFactoryLocator bfr = ContextSingletonBeanFactoryLocator
                .getInstance(locatorFactorySelector);

        log.info("Getting parent context definition: using parent context key of '"
```

```
                       + parentContextKey + "' with BeanFactoryLocator");
          _beanFactoryRef = bfr.useBeanFactory(parentContextKey);
          parentContext = (ApplicationContext) _beanFactoryRef.getFactory();
        }
      }
    catch (BeansException ex) {
      throw ex;
    }

    return parentContext;
  }

  /**
   * Close Spring's web application definition for the given servlet definition.
   *
   * @param servletContext
   *             current servlet definition
   */
  public void closeContext(ServletContext servletContext)
          throws ApplicationContextException {
    servletContext.log("Closing root WebApplicationContext");

    WebApplicationContext wac = WebApplicationContextUtils
            .getRequiredWebApplicationContext(servletContext);
    ApplicationContext parent = wac.getParent();
    try {
      if (wac instanceof ConfigurableApplicationContext) {
        ((ConfigurableApplicationContext) wac).close();
      }
    }
    finally {
      if (parent != null && _beanFactoryRef != null)
       _beanFactoryRef.release();
    }
  }
}
```

The normal `ContextLoader` implementation already provides template methods, which subclasses may use to load a parent context to the web-app context, so all we are doing here is hooking into those methods to load the shared parent via `ContextSingletonBeanFactoryLocator`.

We also need a specialized version of `ContextLoaderListener` to call our variant of `ContextLoader`:

```
public class ContextLoaderListener
        extends org.springframework.web.context.ContextLoaderListener {
  protected org.springframework.web.context.ContextLoader createContextLoader() {
    return new SharedParentLoadingContextLoader();
  }
}
```

Finally, we modify the normal web-app `web.xml` configuration file to add parameters for the parent context:

```
<web-app>

<context-param>
        <param-name>locatorFactorySelector</param-name>
        <param-value>classpath*:beanRefContext.xml</param-value>
</context-param>
<context-param>
        <param-name>parentContextKey</param-name>
        <param-value>servicelayer-context</param-value>
</context-param>

...

</web-app>
```

For the `ContextSingletonBeanFactoryLocator.getInstance(String selector)` method call, we are specifying a value of `classpath*:beanRefContext.xml`. We are also specifying that inside of the context bag defined by `beanRefContext.xml`, we are interested in using the context with the ID of `servicelayer-context`.

Using a Shared Context from EJBs

We're now ready to find out how `ContextSingletonBeanFactoryLocator` may be used to access a shared context (which can also be the same shared context used by one or more web-apps) from EJBs. This turns out to be trivial. The Spring EJB base classes already use the `BeanFactoryLocator` interface to load the application context or bean factory to be used by the EJB. By default, they use an implementation called `ContextJndiBeanFactoryLocator`, which creates, as described in a previous section, an application context based on a classpath location specified via JNDI.

All that is required to use `ContextSingletonBeanFactoryLocator` is to override the default `BeanFactoryLocator`. In this example from a Session Bean, this is being done by hooking into the standard Session EJB `setSessionContext()` method:

```
// see javax.ejb.SessionBean#setSessionContext(javax.ejb.SessionContext)
public void setSessionContext(SessionContext sessionContext) {
  super.setSessionContext(sessionContext);
  setBeanFactoryLocator(ContextSingletonBeanFactoryLocator.getInstance());
  setBeanFactoryLocatorKey("serviceLayer-context");
}
```

First, because the Spring base classes already implement this method so they may store the EJB `SessionContext`, `super.setSessionContext()` is called to maintain that functionality. Then the `BeanFactoryLocator` is set as an instance returned from `ContextSingletonBeanFactoryLocator` `.getInstance()`. If we didn't want to rely on the default outer bag context name of `classpath*:beanRefContext.xml`, we could use `ContextSingletonBeanFactoryLocator.getInstance(name)` instead. Finally, for the `BeanFactoryLocator.useBeanFactory()` method that Spring will call to get the final application context or bean factory, a key value of `serviceLayer-context` is specified, as in the previous examples. This name would normally be set as a String constant somewhere, so all EJBs can use the same value easily.

For a Message Driven Bean, the equivalent override of the default `BeanFactoryLocator` needs to be done in `setMessageDrivenContext()`.

Testing Concerns

There is no question that bringing EJBs into the picture complicates the testing scenario because EJBs normally require a relatively heavyweight EJB container in which to execute. Whereas the build/deploy/test cycle for an in-appserver test can be anywhere from 30 seconds to as much as 10 minutes, an in-IDE unit test can be finished in several seconds. This is a tremendous difference in terms of potential productivity! There are several viable strategies for testing EJB-based code.

Implement Business Functionality in POJO Delegate

In the first Stateless Session Bean example in this chapter, you saw an example of an EJB that implements a business interface delegating to a POJO implementation of that interface, obtained from an application context. Aside from the fact that this strategy makes a future switch to a POJO-only implementation very easy, it also makes testing easier. Generally, the POJO service implementation, which is where all the business functionality is actually implemented, can be tested in an in-IDE unit or integration test, with a build/test cycle of only a few seconds. It is still worthwhile to also test the EJB in an in-application server integration test, but this may be done much less frequently because most development work will happen in the POJO service.

Because of the large time savings, the strategy of testing outside an application server is the most valuable, where it is feasible. (Hence, there is a strong motivation for *making* it feasible through appropriate design decisions.)

Use a Mock EJB Container

MockEJB (`www.mockejb.org`) is a framework that provides a mock or fake EJB container environment, such that at least some EJB classes can be tested as-is inside your IDE instead of having to deploy them into an appserver. The complete set of EJB interfaces and lifecycles is relatively complex, so MockEJB cannot provide a perfect emulation of a real EJB container, but it may be good enough to test most functionality in your EJBs from your IDE. Even if you can test most functionality out of the appserver while developing it, you should still regularly test in the appserver. No emulation of an environment is as accurate as the real environment, especially when we're talking about emulating something as complex as an EJB container.

In addition to providing a mock EJB environment for testing EJBs outside of the appserver, MockEJB also allows the creation of Mock EJBs, which may be deployed along with your real ones in the appserver, as a way of isolating EJBs under test from the rest of the application, or in order to provide test data.

The authors have not used MockEJB extensively, but it appears to be at the very least a valid approach worth investigating.

Integration Testing Inside the AppServer

The final strategy is to test EJBs via an integration test running inside the application server, or server-side. This is not the most attractive strategy from the point of view of total build/deploy/test time because deploying an entire application into an application server may take anywhere from 15 seconds to a number of minutes depending on how complex the application is and how heavyweight the application server is. On the other hand, there is the advantage that you are testing the real EJBs inside the real container they will ultimately run in. Even if this is not your primary testing strategy, it *should* be at least a test strategy used periodically.

There are a number of ways to kick off in-server integration tests. One of the most convenient approaches is offered by Jakarta Apache Cactus (http://jakarta.apache.org/cactus/index.html), which allows a command-line Ant build to transparently run a normal JUnit test remotely, inside the deployed test application in the application server. The other approach is to simply do integration testing by driving the view layer itself with a tool such as Canoo WebTest (http://webtest.canoo.com/webtest/manual/WebTestHome.html) to use view layer functionality, which will stress the classes that need to be tested. While tests of the view layer itself are very useful, if in-server integration testing of lower-layer code is actually needed, we feel an approach similar to that afforded by Cactus is much more convenient, as normal JUnit tests that directly drive the relevant code may be used.

Here's an example of a unit test that is run in appserver via Cactus:

```
public class ProxyBasedAccessTest extends TestCase {

  public static Test suite() {
    ServletTestSuite suite = new ServletTestSuite();
    suite.addTestSuite(ProxyBasedAccessTest.class);
    return suite;
  }

  public void testLocalSLSBProxyFactoryBean() throws Exception {

    ApplicationContext ctx = new ClassPathXmlApplicationContext(ClassUtils
        .addResourcePathToPackagePath(this.getClass(), "applicationContext.xml"));
    SimpleServiceClient client = (SimpleServiceClient) ctx
        .getBean("simpleServiceClient", SimpleServiceClient.class);
    client.useSimpleService();
  }
}
```

As you can see, it's just a normal JUnit test, except that JUnit's optional suite() method is defined to return the test suite as a Cactus ServletTestSuite. Alternately, the test case class could have just extended Cactus's CactusTestCase class instead of the JUnit TestCase class the preceding code extends. In any case, the test code is allowed to generally do anything a normal JUnit test is able to; the only difference is that it's running inside the application server.

Aside from writing Cactus-compatible test cases like this, the other thing that needs to be done is *Cactify* the WAR file or the EAR file for the J2EE application. This is a step in the build process where your Ant script can use a Cactus-specific task called <cactify> to insert a special redirector servlet inside the web-app. This redirector is what actually ends up redirecting tests specified from a client-side build file, to a test running in the server.

Running one or more server-side tests via Cactus is just a matter of deploying the J2EE application to the container, and then in a client-side Ant build file, using the `<cactus>` Ant task. This task is almost identical to the normal Ant `<junit>` task, except it runs server-side tests by talking to the redirector. You see any errors from the tests locally, just as if you were running JUnit locally.

Cactus also has a programmatic API, although most users control tests via the special Ant tasks it provides.

> *One important disadvantage of testing your EJBs or other server-side components inside the application server, as with Cactus, is that it's difficult to reproduce failure scenarios. For example, you can't easily verify behavior when a connection cannot be obtained to the database, in the context of a single test. Thus we recommend that you do not rely on this approach as the main basis of your unit testing strategy — which should certainly cover such failure scenarios.*

Summary

In this chapter, we've seen how, should you choose to use Spring together with EJBs, Spring can make accessing and implementing EJBs much easier. We've explored the use of convenient proxies for encapsulating access to EJB Home objects as well as the EJBs themselves, along with the use of Spring's abstract base classes for easily implementing Session Beans and Message Driven Beans, with access to an automatically loaded bean factory or application context. We've also learned about the `ContextSingletonBeanFactoryLocator`, useful for EJBs to access beans from a shared application context, and in fact useful for any glue code that has some of the same constraints as EJBs. Finally, we've discussed some strategies for testing your code when EJBs come into the picture.

12

Web MVC Framework

Spring provides a web framework based on the *Model-View-Controller (MVC)* paradigm. Although it is similar in some ways to other popular MVC frameworks such as Struts and WebWork, we believe that Spring Web MVC provides significant advantages over those frameworks. Spring MVC provides out-of-the-box implementations of workflow typical to web applications. It is highly flexible, allowing you to use a variety of different view technologies. It also enables you to fully integrate with your Spring-based, middle-tier logic through the use of the Dependency Injection features you've already seen.

You can use Spring Web MVC to make services created with other parts of Spring available to your users by implementing web interfaces. This chapter gives you an overview of the architecture of Spring's Web MVC framework as well as the implementation of concepts such as *model*, *view*, and *controller*. After studying some of the most important infrastructural components, we'll continue to guide you through a couple of practical scenarios in which we'll use most of the components explained earlier.

After reading this chapter you will have learned the basics about workflow in a Spring-based web application. You'll be able to implement your own controllers handling common tasks such as form submissions, validation, data binding, and uploading files. You will also have an overall insight into all of Spring's web-related functionality, including the way Spring MVC enforces best practices when using JavaServer Pages and how it can be used along with appropriate third-party libraries to generate Excel spreadsheets, PDF documents, and other content types.

A Simple Example

Before we dive into all of Spring's web-related features, let's get a simple page up and running that demonstrates some of the main concepts. We'll begin by creating a *controller* called `SimpleController`. This object will prepare a *model* and hand it over to the *view* (for example, a JSP). Our controller extends `AbstractController`, one of many built-in controllers predefining specific workflow when dealing with web interfaces. The `AbstractController` is one of the simpler ones. On receiving a request, `SimpleController` prepares a `ModelAndView` object, identifies the view (in this case called `welcome`), and adds a `Date` to the model. After returning the `ModelAndView` object, the controller has completed its work: having chosen a view and provided it with a model, based on information in the request that it can use to render the response.

```java
import org.springframework.web.servlet.mvc.ModelAndView;
import org.springframework.web.servlet.mvc.AbstractController;

public SimpleController extends AbstractController {

  public ModelAndView handleRequestInternal(HttpServletRequest request,
    HttpServletResponse response)
  throws Exception {

    // create a model-and-view using 'welcome' as the name of the view
    ModelAndView mav = new ModelAndView("welcome");
    // then, add an object to it and return it
    mav.addObject("date", new Date());
    return mav;
  }
}
```

You will need to wire up the controller in an `ApplicationContext`, as controllers and other web tier objects are configured using Spring's Dependency Injection. For objects responsible for handling web workflow, the application context must be an instance of the sub interface `WebApplicationContext`.

Like many other MVC frameworks, Spring's Web MVC framework is built around a generic servlet known as a *Dispatcher Servlet* or *Front Controller*. This pattern is explained in more detail by Crupi, Malks, and Alur in *Core J2EE Patterns* (Pearson Education, 2003). The `DispatcherServlet` is the end-point a user connects to with their web browser. For now, assume that you will need to define the servlet in your `web.xml` file of your web application and create a file called `[servlet-name]-servlet.xml` in the same directory as the `web.xml` file (`/WEB-INF/`). The `[servlet-name]-servlet.xml` file defines the beans in your `WebApplicationContext`; hence our `SimpleController` will be defined there. The `WebApplicationContext` will contain all our web-related components. Its parent will be the application context containing middle-tier services and necessary supporting objects such as data sources. We will highlight the use of parent and child application contexts later in this chapter.

For our example, the contents of the `[servlet-name].xml` file (excluding XML headers) will be as follows:

```xml
<beans>
  <bean name="/index.html"
    class="org.springframework.sample.web.SimpleController"/>

  <bean
    class="org.springframework.web.servlet.view.InternalResourceViewResolver">
    <property name="prefix"><value>/WEB-INF/jsp</value></property>
    <property name="suffix"><value>.jsp</value></property>
    <property name="viewClass">
      <value>org.springframework.web.servlet.view.JstlView</value>
    </property>
  </bean>
</beans>
```

The user connects to the web application through the DispatcherServlet, which delegates to the appropriate controller. The following piece of code is an excerpt from our web.xml file declaring the servlet and mapping all requests onto the DispatcherServlet:

```
<servlet>
  <servlet-name>sample</servlet-name>
  <servlet-class>
     org.springframework.web.servlet.DispatcherServlet
  </servlet-class>
  <load-on-startup>1</load-on-startup>
</servlet>

<servlet-mapping>
  <servlet-name>sample</servlet-name>
  <url-pattern>/*</url-pattern>
</servlet-mapping>
```

We need to create the actual JSP to display something to the user. The following JSP uses the *Java Standard Tag Library* to display the Date that the SimpleController adds to the model:

```
<%-- welcome.jsp --%>
<%@ taglib prefix="c" uri=http://java.sun.com/jstl/core %>

<html>
  <head>
    <title>Hello world!</title>
  </head>
  <body>
    <h1>Hello world</h1>
    <p>
      Right now, the time is <c:out value="${date}"/>.
    </p>
  </body>
</html>
```

As an alternative to JSP, you could equally implement the page using Freemarker or Velocity, or have iText generate a PDF, or POI generate an Excel file based on the model returned from the controller. Switching to Velocity templates, for example, would require changing the view class of the view resolver shown in the previous example to VelocityView and exchanging welcome.jsp for a welcome.vm Velocity template. It would *not* require any changes to controller or model, as Spring MVC cleanly separates model, view, and controller. We discuss a range of view technologies, including Velocity, JavaServer Pages, and XSLT in Chapter 13.

General Architecture

Let's begin by exploring the concepts involved with applying MVC to the web. If you've worked with WebWork or Struts or some other web MVC framework before, you will recognize many of the concepts discussed in the next few pages. However, even if the concepts are familiar, the following discussion should provide a useful insight into the rationale behind the architecture of Spring's Web MVC Framework.

Web MVC Concepts

The MVC architectural pattern aims to divide the layer implementing interactions with users into three different kinds of objects:

❑   **Model** objects represent data: for example, the orders a user has placed, or information about a user's account.

❑   **View** objects are responsible for displaying the data represented by the model: for instance, in a table, list, or form.

❑   **Controllers** are objects responding to the actions a user takes, such as a form submission or a link being clicked. Controllers are responsible for updating the data represented by the model or taking other appropriate measures related to the user's action. This might for example involve delegating a request to the business tier that in turn will process an order.

The traditional implementation of the MVC architectural pattern in GUI implementation (depicted in Figure 12-1) involves actions being taken, after which controllers update the model, with the changes being *pushed* back to the view, which updates itself (through for example the *Observer* pattern). Such an ideal implementation is not feasible for web applications because of the limitations of HTTP. Typically, a user issues a request, allowing the server to update the view, which is then sent back to the user's browser. It's impossible to propagate changes back to the client in between requests. This forces us to use an approach where instead of the model *pushing* changes to the view, on every request, the view *pulls* the relevant data from the model in order to display it in tables, lists, forms, or whatever user interface elements are required.

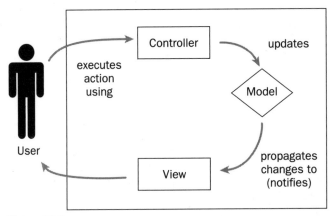

Figure 12-1

The MVC design pattern defines a clear separation between responsibilities and results in clean code. Fortunately, using a pull approach will not prevent you from using the MVC triad. It just changes the way things work a bit. So in Spring MVC you will still be able to separate logic accessing data from the data itself and the code that will render the view. The latter might be an HTML page generated by JavaServer Pages (JSP) or an Excel file generated by a class using Apache POI.

Generic Web MVC Using a Dispatcher and Controllers

Let's now take a closer look at web applications designed using the MVC pattern. A web browser uses an HTTP request to communicate a user's action to the server. The server does some processing and generates a view, which is communicated back to the client using an HTTP response.

The MVC pattern comes into play when the HTTP request reaches the server. Based on the information carried in the HTTP request, such as the URL and any parameters, the web application should be able to execute it. When it has finished processing the user's request, possibly creating or updating a model, it will hand over responsibility to the view. The view in its turn uses the HTTP response to transmit any data back to the client, such as pages marked up using HTML or raw data representing an Excel document.

A good web framework distinguishes between dispatching the request and processing it. In other words, the *dispatcher* determines what controller is needed to fulfill each request while the controller does the actual processing. This separation removes the need for unnecessary processing of the HTTP request when implementing controllers, making application code cleaner and less closely coupled to HTTP. Such decoupling increases testability and may allow for greater code reusability.

Figure 12-2 illustrates how a request will be handled by a web framework using the concepts described previously.

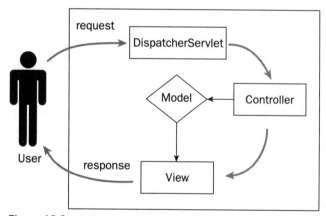

Figure 12-2

The MVC pattern applied to web applications is discussed in greater detail in Chapter 12 of *Expert One-on-One J2EE Design and Development*.

> Note that a true MVC pattern is based on event notification — it's a *push model* where changes to the model get propagated to the view using the *Observer* pattern. MVC applied to web applications is also known as the Model 2 architecture. Some purists argue that because of missing out on the push aspect of the true *Model-View-Controller* pattern, the Model 2 architecture shouldn't be called MVC. Nevertheless, the term "web MVC" is here to stay. What matters is that a good Model 2 implementation provides a clear and fixed decomposition of all the aspects involved with the creation of a web application. It provides the best separation of concerns possible within the limits of the push-based approach of modern-age browsers.

Requirements for a Good Web MVC Framework

Spring does not try to reinvent the wheel. It unites and integrates best practices and solutions: for example, Hibernate and iBatis, in the case of data access. However, Spring does provide its own MVC package. Given the existence of other popular MVC implementations such as Struts and WebWork, you might wonder why.

The rationale behind implementing yet another MVC implementation lies in the fact that we considered that other more traditional implementations didn't provide an elegant enough solution. Spring has clearly set a couple of goals for the MVC package (a more thorough discussion can be found in Johnson's *J2EE Design and Development*):

❏   An MVC implementation should be **non-intrusive**. Where possible, you shouldn't have to adopt practices or standards set by the developers of the MVC framework you are using. Typical examples here would include the requirement to extend framework-proprietary classes to be able to do dynamic binding of request parameters to domain objects. Also, you shouldn't have to do this to create controllers implementing your logic. Finally, validation shouldn't be tied to the front-end; you might prefer to do this in your business logic. Spring uses interfaces where possible; you will not be restricted to using functionality provided only by the framework, and you can easily implement additional behavior yourself.

❏   Across web applications developed over time, differences might exist with respect to a view technology being used, performance requirements, or the way the framework determines which controller is used to fulfill a certain request. An MVC framework **should be suited for environments having different requirements**. It should, for example, be possible to implement a high-performance controller that implements only the bare necessities as well as controllers that execute wizard-style workflow including validation, error-messaging, data binding, and detection for invalid form submissions.

❏   An MVC package should be **agnostic with respect to the view technology** being used. Controller implementations or the contents of a model shouldn't have to change when switching from JavaServer Pages to Velocity, or having both an HTML view as well as a view rendering a PDF file representing the data in the model. It should also be possible to easily include new view technologies being developed in the community.

❏   Complete freedom should be maintained with respect to HTML generation. Simple and small utilities (such as custom tag libraries) should be provided only for functionality the framework contains that can't be used without those utilities.

❏   The framework should be **highly configurable, consistent with the way this is done throughout the complete solution**. The way you manage and configure middle-tier services shouldn't be any different from wiring up controllers, views, and additional web-related functionality. All the benefits of Dependency Injection should be applied to the web tier.

❏   We encourage you to keep the MVC layer **as thin as possible**, by providing easy ways to delegate requests to the middle-tier and integrating with other services such as AOP.

These requirements partly came out of Rod Johnson's experience architecting demanding high-end web applications from 1999 to 2001. All were *practical*, rather than theoretical, requirements. They have proven to recur in many user requirements we have seen since.

Spring's Web MVC Equivalents

In the previous sections you have learned about models, views, controllers, and dispatchers. Spring provides equivalents to those that can be completely integrated with your middle-tier code using Spring's Dependency Injection features.

Executing Actions in Controllers

The components actually taking care of web-related processing (and eventually delegating tasks to your middle tier) are the controllers. Spring includes a variety of controllers, all targeted to solve specific problems in web applications such as form handling and doing wizard-style workflow. Most of the controllers Spring provides derive from the `org.springframework.web.servlet.mvc.Controller` interface, which specifies the following method:

```
ModelAndView handleRequest(HttpServletRequest req, HttpServletResponse res)
throws Exception
```

A controller is responsible for handling the request through either returning a `ModelAndView` relevant to the request (the normal case), or returning `null` if the controller has dealt with the request itself: that is, has written to the `ServletResponse` itself — generally not considered to be a good practice, but sometimes unavoidable. Spring provides several controller implementations, many of which don't work with the `HttpServletResponse` object. As a developer, you probably won't ever need to work with the servlet response, as the `ModelAndView` gives you all the control you need. But if you ever stumble upon a situation where you need more flexibility, you can always implement the `Controller` interface or extend one of the controllers somewhat higher up in the hierarchy (such as `AbstractController`).

Returning a ModelAndView

The `ModelAndView` class allows you to specify a response to the client, resulting from actions you have performed by the controller. This object holds both the view the client will be presented with as well as the model that will be used to render the view. `ModelAndView` objects can be created in a number of ways. The underlying structure of the model is a `java.util.Map`. A convenient constructor allows you to specify a model map directly, or you can construct an empty model and add objects through methods on the `ModelAndView` class itself:

```
// first create ModelAndView, along with the name of the view
ModelAndView mav = new ModelAndView("showDetailsTemplate");
// add the show which we'll be rendering in our view
mav.addObject("show", showDao.getShow());
return mav;
```

> A request in Spring, dispatched to a controller, should always result in a
> `ModelAndView` **object being created and returned, unless you've handled the request**
> **directly and do not wish the dispatcher to start rendering any view.**

One might ask why Spring incorporates its own `ModelAndView` type. Model elements are added to the map this type holds, and adding elements directly to the `HttpServletRequest` (as request attributes) would seem to serve the same purpose. The reason to do this is obvious when taking a look at one of the requirements we have set for the MVC framework: It should be as view-agnostic as possible, which means we'd like to be able to incorporate view technologies not bound to the `HttpServletRequest` as well. This could be, for example, XSLT where the model is contained by an XML document that is to be transformed using an XSL style sheet. Testability is also slightly improved by abstracting away from the Servlet API.

Rendering a View

To complete the picture, you should understand the `View` interface and the concept of *view resolvers*, although you'll probably never implement a `View` directly. Implementations of the `View` interface are responsible for rendering the response to the client, often being something like an HTML page. The `View` interface provides exactly one method stating its responsibility: rendering the view:

```
void render(Map model, HttpServletRequest req, HttpServletResponse res)
throws Exception
```

Implementations of the `View` interface will typically evaluate a template such as a JSP or Velocity template to generate actual content, rather than doing it in their own Java code. Thus `View` implementations are often generic, parameterized by their use with many different templates.

Spring uses a view resolution strategy involving *logical view names*. Views are identified by name, keeping controllers from having to specify identifiers specific to the view technology being used. A *view resolver* is responsible for delivering a view technology–specific view object, based on the logical view name. Using view technology–independent logical view names in conjunction with a view resolution strategy provides complete decoupling of controllers returning models and views rendering models. Switching from one view technology to another does not require you to change any controllers or other infrastructural code — merely configuration and files specific to the view technology being used such as JSPs or Velocity templates.

Completing the Picture: The DispatcherServlet

As we've discussed the general concept of web MVC, you've heard about requests being *dispatched* to controllers. Typically, web frameworks implement this behavior of dispatching the HTTP request using a *Front Controller Servlet*. So does Spring. The main entry point for any request a user is issuing is the `DispatcherServlet`. This will inspect it and determine what controller it needs to execute the given request. The `DispatcherServlet` models the workflow involved with executing a request. It dispatches requests to controllers and takes care of rendering the response, based on the model and view information the controller returns. All this is done using a couple of other features of Spring Web MVC, which you'll learn about later on.

Infrastructural Components

Now that you've learned about the basic concepts involved with implementing a web application using Spring Web MVC, let's get into the details.

Implementing a web application using Spring Web MVC involves building and setting up controllers, providing views and data to display in the views. All this is linked together using a `DispatcherServlet` in combination with an `ApplicationContext`. The `DispatcherServlet` provides a gateway to the server and acts as the manager of the workflow involved with HTTP-based request-response handling. A special type of context, the `WebApplicationContext` integrates with the dispatcher servlet and manages all web-related components such as controllers, views, mappings between URLs, and interceptors. The WebApplicationContext doesn't differ much from a "normal" ApplicationContext, and as a user, you'll hardly notice the difference.

Figure 12-3 lays out the basic architecture involved with a Spring web application. Next, we'll discuss the components in more detail.

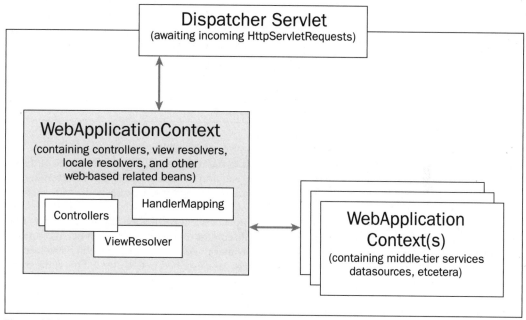

Figure 12-3

The DispatcherServlet

The org.springframework.web.servlet.DispatcherServlet is the main entry point of any request to a Spring MVC application. Like any other servlet, the dispatcher servlet must be declared in your web.xml file. This makes it available to the outside world (meaning it is accessible to applications using the HTTP protocol). The servlet can be configured to meet your needs and has the initialization parameters listed in the table that follows to control its behavior.

> Note that in all but exceptional situations the default parameters to DispatcherServlet will do. In addition, you shouldn't need to subclass **DispatcherServlet** to provide custom behavior. In the case of Spring MVC, like Spring generally, the framework provides a host of extension points in the form of interfaces that you can implement. We'll see most of these later in this chapter.
>
> You should *not* normally need to extend Spring infrastructure classes to customize behavior, which ties your code unnecessarily to the implementation of the framework itself.

Parameter	Description	Default Value
contextClass	Type of WebApplicationContext to use	XmlWebApplicationContext
namespace	The namespace of the WebApplicationContext to use	[name of servlet]-servlet
contextConfigLocation	Parameter to override the default value of location(s) to look for WebApplicationContext(s)	/WEB-INF/[namespace].xml
publishContext	Whether or not to publish to ApplicationContext in the ServletContext (making it available to other Servlets)	true

Each DispatcherServlet defined in a Spring web application will have an associated WebApplicationContext. As we've seen, by default its namespace will include the name of the servlet, and its scope is limited to requests mapped to that servlet only, meaning other servlets receiving a request won't be able to use objects defined in WebApplicationContext initialized by the first one.

To be able to share common functionality across multiple servlets within one application, upon initialization, the dispatcher servlet will first of all inspect its configuration (elements of type init-param elements from web.xml), and start looking for an "ordinary" ApplicationContext, initialized by a ContextLoaderListener or ContextLoaderServlet, as described in Chapter 3. This context might, for instance, contain the middle-tier services that you're going to use from your controllers. If you use Spring's built-in, web-oriented ContextLoader, such an application context must be located in the ServletContext of the web application. If such an ApplicationContext is found, it will be the parent of the WebApplicationContext that will be tied specifically to the servlet.

> **A Spring Web MVC application cannot exist without a** WebApplicationContext. **When using the** DispatcherServlet**'s default configuration, you must provide an XML file defining beans, place it in the** /WEB-INF **directory of your WAR file, and name it** [name of servlet]-servlet.xml **unless you specify otherwise.**
>
> **As already mentioned, it's possible to have multiple** DispatcherServlets **for one web application. This approach has a similar result as Struts modules. Think carefully about where to place your beans. The** xxx-servlet.xml **should always contain web-related beans, while the parent application context loaded by the** ContextLoaderListener, **for example, should contain middle-tier beans, such as datasources, data access objects, and service objects.**

You declare a Spring DispatcherServlet in your web.xml file as follows. This servlet will use default values for all configuration parameters, resulting in a web application context defining controllers and other web tier objects being loaded from /WEB-INF/sample-servlet.xml.

```
<servlet>
  <servlet-name>sample</servlet-name>
  <servlet-class>
```

```
        org.springframework.web.servlet.DispatcherServlet
    </servlet-class>
    <load-on-startup>2</load-on-startup>
</servlet>
```

To illustrate how to modify the behavior of the DispatcherServlet, you could have two XML files, together defining a WebApplicationContext. To do this, you would have to include an init-param in the declaration of the Servlet. Multiple locations can be included by separating those using commas, semicolons, or spaces.

```
<init-param>
    <param-name>contextConfigLocation</param-name>
    <param-value>/WEB-INF/ctx/controllers.xml /WEB-INF/ctx/utils.xml</param-value>
</init-param>
```

Next, you have to tell the Servlet container to direct requests you want handled by your Spring web application to the DispatcherServlet. You usually map a range of file extensions to the DispatcherServlet, for example all files ending with .view and .edit, in your web application context mapped to view controllers and form controllers. You map requests to the DispatcherServlet using Servlet mappings. The Servlet mapping that follows will tell the servlet container to map all requests ending with .view and all requests ending with .edit in the secure path to the DispatcherServlet. Note that this configuration step is required by the Servlet specification, not by Spring.

```
<servlet-mapping>
    <servlet-name>sample</servlet-name>
    <url-pattern>*.view</url-pattern>
</servlet-mapping>

<servlet-mapping>
    <servlet-name>sample</servlet-name>
    <url-pattern>/secure/*.edit</url-pattern>
</servlet-mapping>
```

The previously mentioned URLs clearly indicate what they're dealing with: editing and viewing. In addition to a clear separation based on functionality, a well-defined and logically grouped collection of URLs in your web application has more benefits. In one project one of the authors encountered a situation where he needed to apply a SiteMesh page decorator to all requests, except for the ones that were targeted to a new window (pop-ups). Using a clearly defined grouping, he could easily map the decorator to all requests, except for those ending with .popup.

Neither Spring nor the Servlet API forces you to use specific extensions or patterns in URLs. You are free to use whatever URLs you like. Even better, with Spring, matching of controllers need not be based purely on URLs — a capability not supported by most web MVC frameworks. For example, you could define a mapping based on parameters, or even HTTP session state.

Remember that exposing extensions such as .jsp or .asp — or even the .do used by convention in many Model 2 Java web applications — gives potential hackers immediate insight into what technology you're using. If you can't come up with a sensible extension, consider using .html instead.

After you have declared the `DispatcherServlet` and possibly modified it using Servlet `init-params`, you're finished as far as the `web.xml` file is concerned. Next, you will have to create a `WebApplicationContext` containing controllers and possibly other web-related components such as view resolvers, exception handlers, and locale resolvers. If you are happy with the defaults, most of these definitions are optional. However, by defining them you can achieve a high degree of customization of MVC framework behavior, if required.

Remember that initializing a separate application context containing your middle-tier services should be done by using the `ContextLoaderServlet` (or `Listener`). This is already covered in Chapter 3, but we'll include a short code snippet to refresh your memory:

```
<context-param>
  <param-name>contextConfigLocation</param-name>
  <param-value>
    /WEB-INF/applicationContext.xml
  </param-value>
</context-param>

<servlet>
    <servlet-name>context</servlet-name>
    <servlet-class>
      org.springframework.web.context.ContextLoaderServlet
    </servlet-class>
    <load-on-startup>1</load-on-startup>
</servlet>
```

> **Remember that if using the `ContextLoaderServlet`, don't forget to add the load-on-startup parameter. The parent application context (the one for your middle-tier services) should be loaded first (hence you have a lower load-on-startup figure), before the `DispatcherServlet`, which usually needs beans from the parent context!**

The WebApplicationContext

The `WebApplicationContext` contains all web-related beans responsible for making your logic accessible to users. These may include beans to handle multilingual websites and beans defining mappings from incoming requests to controllers. The `WebApplicationContext` will be initialized by the `DispatcherServlet`. When using default values, it will be of class `org.springframework.web.context.support.XmlWebApplicationContext`.

The `WebApplicationContext` is a child context of the `ApplicationContext`, which will contain middle-tier services such as transactional service layer objects, data sources, and data access objects.

> **It's a best practice to keep a clear separation between middle-tier services and web-related components. A web interface is just one way to access middle-tier services. Remoting or JMS might be another way. In the case of remoting, there will be an additional child context, containing all beans necessary to access the service by, for example, JAX-RPC.**

The XmlWebApplicationContext is used by the DispatcherServlet to model the workflow involved with web applications. The DispatcherServlet inspects the WebApplicationContext for declarations of some special beans used to execute the workflow. Some of them will have defaults; some of them you will have to provide yourself. You will learn more about those types of beans later, but let's now have a quick look at what they are:

- ❏ A HandlerMapping is responsible for determining the appropriate controller (or any other custom handler) to dispatch a request to. A criterion to base the decision on might be, for example, the URL of the request.

- ❏ A ViewResolver is capable of mapping logical view names to actual views, such as a JavaServer Page, a Velocity template, or an XSL style sheet to apply to the contents of the model.

- ❏ A LocaleResolver will resolve the locale to use when rendering a view or performing other language-dependent logic.

- ❏ A MultipartResolver provides support for uploading files with HTTP, for instance by using Commons FileUpload.

- ❏ ThemeResolvers provide support for themeable interfaces, for example, by using different style sheets and resource bundles.

- ❏ HandlerExceptionResolvers provide support for catching unexpected exceptions and, for example, informing the user by providing a predefined view displaying information about the exception.

- ❏ Controllers provide the interactional logic of your web application and access to collaborators from your middle tier, which provide actual business services, which should be independent of any particular interface type.

- ❏ HandlerInterceptors provide the capability to intercept incoming HTTP requests. Interceptors are useful to add additional crosscutting behavior to your web infrastructure, such as security, logging, and auditing.

> As you can see, Spring MVC offers a host of extension points — which, we feel, makes it uniquely flexible among web application frameworks. Note that you don't need to specify custom implementations of these extension points unless you need the extra power they provide. So don't worry if you're feeling a bit overwhelmed right now — you don't need to deal with all these concepts in simple applications, but you will be very grateful for the flexibility they offer as your web applications become more complex.

WebApplicationContext inherits all functionality of the ApplicationContext (as discussed in Chapter 2). Beyond that, it holds a reference to the ServletContext. In normal situations, you don't need access to the WebApplicationContext or the ServletContext from your controllers or other web-related beans. If it *is* necessary, you can extend the org.springframework.web .context.support.WebApplicationObjectSupport convenience class, which in turn extends ApplicationObjectSupport (see Chapter 2). WebApplicationObjectSupport provides the following methods:

```
WebApplicationContext getWebApplicationContext();
ServletContext getServletContext();
File getTempDir();
```

The first method returns the application context in which your web-related beans reside. In common situations you usually won't need access to the application context because wiring up collaborating beans should preferably be done in the file describing the `WebApplicationContext`.

The `getServletContext()` method provides access to the `ServletContext` through which you can reach web application–wide resources possibly stored in there by other servlets.

If you need a place to store temporary files, Servlet containers offer a standard facility and `getTempDir()` returns a directory where you can store your information. This is, for example, often used by utilities that enable users to upload files. The file is first stored in a temporary directory after which it sits there waiting to be processed by a controller.

Workflow Involved with Handling Requests

Now that you understand the `WebApplicationContext` and the `DispatcherServlet`, let's take a more detailed look at the flow that's involved with an incoming request. The flow is graphically explained in Figures 12-4 and 12-5. We'll do that using two flow diagrams. All concepts mentioned in the diagrams will be discussed in the next couple of sections.

The first phase involves determination of the path of execution by a handler mapping. The path of execution consists of zero or more *interceptors* and exactly one *handler*.

A *handler* is the component actually *handling* the request — in other words, taking appropriate action, considering the request. More specifically, it's the component that prepares the model.

> **The terms handler and controller are often used interchangeably. If you're using Spring's controller infrastructure there won't be any real difference between the two. In rare cases, however, you might have to plug in your own handler infrastructure. The important thing to remember is that controllers or handlers are used to prepare a model using incoming information from the servlet request.**

Interceptors are also components involved in the path of execution, intercepting the request, because they are given a chance to execute a piece of logic before and right after the handler does its work. Interceptors are a Good Thing (as is also proven by WebWork2) because they allow you to *add additional logic to the path of execution*, without affecting the handler itself. Interceptors resemble Servlet Filters a bit; those are also capable of intercepting the request to modify it or execute other behavior. Servlet Filters are part of the Servlet 2.3 specification. They differ from Spring `HandlerInterceptors` (as they are actually called) in that Filters are modeled on a more framework-independent level and allow for interaction with the request and the response at a lower level. Spring `HandlerInterceptors` are aware they're being executed in the context of the Spring Framework and allow for more framework-focused behavior, such as the modification of the `ModelAndView` or the inspection of an `ApplicationContext`. Just as Aspect Oriented Programming in general (covered in-depth in Chapter 4) greatly improves the degree of decoupling in your overall software design, `HandlerInterceptors` allow for adding behavior to the execution of a request without affecting the actual component handling the request.

> Those of you switching from Struts to Spring MVC should carefully study the concept of Spring HandlerInterceptors. At the time of writing, Struts does not offer something similar — at least, not as part of its core. (The *Struts Action Invocation Framework* is an independent initiative offering interceptor behavior, located at http://struts.sourceforge.net/saif.) Interceptors are a powerful and useful concept when implementing web applications. They can significantly simplify implementing many common requirements, and improve maintainability thereafter.

After the path of execution has been determined, any interceptors found will be given a chance to intercept the incoming request. Each one of the interceptors can decide to stop the framework from further processing the request. This is useful in, for example, an interceptor for security purposes. If an interceptor chooses to stop the framework from further processing the request, the framework won't allow the handler (determined by the path of execution) to process the request.

If none of the interceptors halts flow down the execution chain, Spring will hand over control to the handler and allow it to process the request.

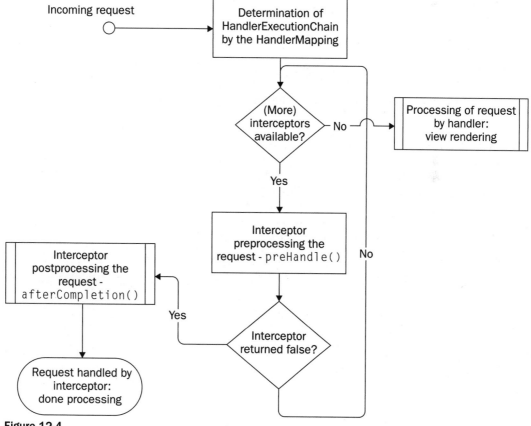

Figure 12-4

After a request has been preprocessed by the interceptors that were found (if any), Spring hands over control to the handler associated with the request. Such a handler should return a `ModelAndView` object. There are a couple of possible outcomes.

First of all, an exception might be thrown. In this case, Spring will inspect the `WebApplicationContext` for *exception resolvers*. Exception resolvers are components capable of inspecting an exception and determining an appropriate model-and-view relevant to the exception. If one of the resolvers results in a `ModelAndView`, this will be used to render a response to the client. Think of a warning to a user if a database connection couldn't be made or something similar. If the resolver(s) could not come up with an appropriate `ModelAndView`, the exception will be re-thrown, in which case the standard exception mapping mechanisms part of the servlet descriptor file (`web.xml`) might pick up on it.

> There are two ways to deal with errors in a web application. When errors arise that you can't avoid or deal with using Spring's exception resolvers, we tend to use the infrastructure the `web.xml` deployment descriptor offers to take appropriate actions. To take appropriate actions when business exceptions occur or when a Spring proprietary exception occurs, usually we use the Spring exception resolver infrastructure.

If no exception is thrown, Spring will use the `ModelAndView` returned by the handler to render a response to the client.

> Processing of the request should always result in a `ModelAndView`. If no `ModelAndView` is returned, Spring assumes that the handler itself has dealt with the request and no further action is taken (meaning Spring won't start rendering a view).

All interceptors available in the path of execution are allowed to post process the request, just before Spring starts rendering a response *and also* right after rendering has finished. Finally, Spring informs you of the fact that request execution has finished. It does so using the event notification infrastructure of the `ApplicationContext` (which is further explained in Chapter 3). The event thrown here is the `org.springframework.web.context.support.RequestHandledEvent`.

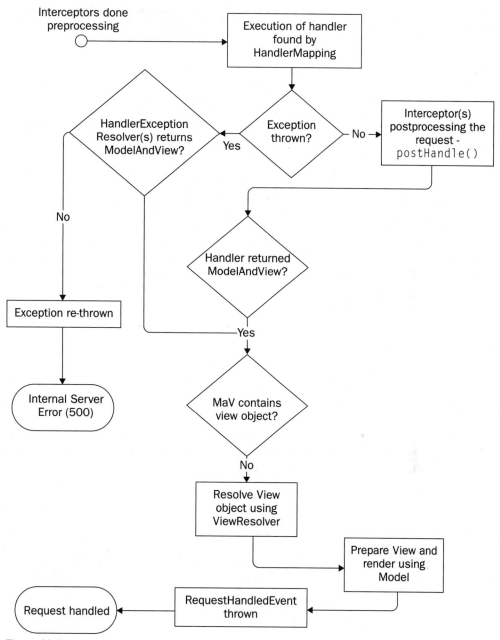

Figure 12-5

Common Layout of a Spring MVC Web Application

Spring MVC is an extremely flexible piece of technology. Most use cases don't require much customization or configuration, but that flexibility is likely to help you a great deal when you encounter tougher requirements. Up until now you've seen what is involved with a request being handled by Spring MVC. First, a `HandlerMapping` is inspected to return a handler (or controller). After the `Controller` has returned a `ModelAndView`, the `ViewResolver` provides a concrete view instance after which Spring lets the view do its job — render a response to the client. It's that simple.

The simplest configuration possible for a web application using Spring MVC is one where only controllers, views, and a simple view resolver are defined, all in the `WebApplicationContext`:

```
<bean id="/someRequest.html"
  class="org.springframework.prospring.web.SomeController"/>

<bean name="someView" class="org.springframework.web.servlet.view.JstlView">
  <property name="url"><value>/WEB-INF/jsp/someView.jsp</value></property>
</bean>

<bean class="org.springframework.web.servlet.view.BeanNameViewResolver"/>
```

This approach will not scale to larger applications. The following is a list of all types of components in Spring Web MVC along with their respective defaults and common bean names. You will learn about them shortly. For now it's important to realize Spring does not require you to know and use all of them. Most are intended for use only in more demanding applications requiring internationalization or the uploading of files. While reading the rest of this chapter, pick what you need and refer to this part of the chapter every now and then to see where the component you're reading about fits in.

> Remember that the most important parts of your web tier are the `Controllers` returning `Models` and the `View` returned to your client.

Component Type	Defaults To	Remarks
Controller	None	Controllers are the components providing the actual behavior. You will have to implement them yourself.
ViewResolver	InternalResourceViewResolver	Request will be dispatched using the `RequestDispatcher`, which causes the servlet container to pick it up again and redirect it to a servlet or JSP.

Component Type	Defaults To	Remarks
HandlerMapping	BeanNameUrlHandlerMapping	Provides elegant *in-context* resolving of controllers. Using this, you cannot specify interceptors, however.
LocaleResolver	AcceptHeaderLocaleResolver	Takes the locale from the client's request header. Others are available based on cookies, session storage, and so on.
MultiPartResolver	None	Needed only if you want to upload files. Implementations available for Commons and COS file upload packages.
HandlerExceptionResolver	None	Needed to provide appropriate responses to exceptions generated by Controllers. One implementation available: SimpleMappingException Resolver.

Note that the previous table lists only the most important concepts used in Spring Web MVC. Later in the chapter we will cover some of the more advanced functionality used only in rare situations.

HandlerMappings

You've seen a web.xml file defining URL patterns. All URLs matching those patterns will be routed to the Spring DispatchetServlet and picked by one or more HandlerMappings. A HandlerMapping is capable of determining a path of execution through the web application. As we've seen, the execution chain consists of one handler and possibly one or more interceptors.

The determination of the path of execution can be done using a variety of criteria. The most obvious way to determine which handler to use is to inspect the URL of the request. Using Spring, however, you're not limited to using the URL. If you want, you can implement a handler mapping yourself, which can be done by deriving from AbstractHandlerMapping and overriding getHandlerInternal (HttpServletRequest) or implementing the HandlerMapping interface.

In your application context, you can define more than one handler mapping if you need to. When doing this, Spring will inspect each one of them until an appropriate path of execution has been determined. The HandlerMapping implements the Ordered interface, meaning that at startup the context will inspect all handler mappings and order them using the OrderComparator (this is explained in more detail in Chapter 2).

> If after querying all `HandlerMappings` available, a `HandlerExecutionChain` still isn't found — that is, no matching handler is found — Spring will inform the client by sending it an HTTP 404 response code (Page Not Found).

Note that you don't necessarily have to define a handler mapping in your application context. If Spring doesn't find one in your context, it will use the `BeanNameUrlHandlerMapping`.

Spring provides handler mappings using typical criteria to determine the path of execution. Let's examine them.

BeanNameUrlHandlerMapping

Using the `BeanNameUrlHandlerMapping` you can map URLs to `Handlers` by using their names in the web application context. Consider the following (part of a) web application context:

```
<bean
  name="/account.edit /secure/*account.edit"
  class="example.AccountFormController"/>
```

This specific controller will be used to dispatch all requests targeted to `/account.edit`, `/secure/largeaccount.edit`, and `/secure/smallaccount.edit`.

> If you don't define a handler mapping in the web application context yourself, `BeanNameUrlHandlerMapping` will be used.

This controller is most similar to the behavior Struts provides for mapping URLs to Struts Actions. You can list more than one URL, and you can define URL patterns, using an Ant-style notation.

To use `BeanNameUrlHandlerMapping` effectively, you must understand Ant-style path expressions. To be able to match a path using a generic expression, Ant uses asterisks and question marks. When evaluating a path expression, the question marks act like wildcards and will cause a path to match, no matter what character is in place of the question mark as long as there is just one character in that specific place. This means that, for example, given the path expression `/secure/test.?sp`, both `/secure/test.jsp` and `/secure/test.asp` will match.

In addition to a question mark, you can use the asterisk, which also acts like a wildcard, but can be replaced by any given number of characters or even no character at all. This means that both `/secure/simpletest.jsp` and `/secure/test.jsp` will match when evaluating those paths using `/secure/*test.jsp` as the path expression. When using *two* asterisks, you indicate you want URLs in all paths to match. For example, when using `/**/test.jsp` as a path expression, both `/secure/test.jsp` and `/nonsecure/deeper/test.jsp` will match, as well as `/test.jsp`.

SimpleUrlHandlerMapping

In addition to `BeanNameUrlHandlerMapping`, Spring provides another handler mapping that can be configured in the application context, which will use the request URL to base a mapping on. Using Ant-style path expressions and the `SimpleUrlHandlerMapping`, you can create more complex URL structures that map to handlers and have other more advanced features available. Consider the following examples:

```
<bean id="accountEditor" class="example.AccountFormController"/>

<bean id="handlerMapping"
  class="org.springframework.web.servlet.handler.SimpleUrlHandlerMapping">
  <property name="urlMap">
    <map>
      <entry key="/secure/account*.edit">
        <ref bean="accountEditor"/>
      </entry>
    </map>
  </property>
</bean>
```

The above code snippet shows a controller responsible for editing accounts. The controller is mapped to all incoming requests URLs matching the given pattern (`/secure/account*.edit`).

In the preceding example, we're using the `urlMap` property to include a mapping of URL patterns to controllers. We could also have used the `mappings` property. The latter does not support references to a controller directly, as done in the preceding example. Instead it maps URLs or URL patterns to bean names using a `Properties` object. This gives you the ability to externalize the mapping in a file if you want to. Let's have a look at that:

```
<bean id="accountEditor" class="example.AccountFormController"/>
<bean id="accountViewer" class="example.AccountViewController"/>

<bean id="handlerMapping"
  class="org.springframework.web.servlet.handler.SimpleUrlHandlerMapping"
>
  <property name="mappings">
    <bean
      class="org.springframework.beans.factory.config.PropertiesFactoryBean"
    >
      <property name="location">
        <value>urlmap.properties</value>
      </property>
    </bean>
  </property>
</bean>

## urlmap.properties file located in /WEB-INF/
/secure/account*.edit=accountEditor
/**/account.view=accountViewer
```

> By default, **Spring treats all controllers as singletons. In some situations (where you explicitly reference beans, using** `<ref bean="XXX"/>`, **even setting the singleton property of the given bean to false won't result in multiple beans being created (for that specific reference). A solution to this problem in case of the** `SimpleUrlHandlerMapping` **is to use the** `mappings` **property, not referring directly to beans, but identifying a controller by name. Every time Spring needs a controller included in the mapping, it will ask the** `ApplicationContext` **for one (hence respecting the** `singleton` **property). In other words, if you want to model a controller as a prototype (which is generally discouraged), use the** `mappings` **property containing bean names and set the** `singleton` **property (of the controller) to false. This allows a single use controller — for example, one that may not be threadsafe.**

CommonsPathMapUrlHandlerMapping

Spring also provides a handler mapping that works with Commons Attributes, defined in your controllers. Metadata and attributes are more extensively covered in Chapter 9.

Using the `CommonsPathMapUrlHandlerMapping` removes the need to set up the mapping between controllers and URLs explicitly in the web application context. Instead you define attributes in the controllers themselves, which contain information about the URL those need to be mapped to. Using the Commons Attributes compiler and indexer, Spring will be able to look up your controllers automatically. Using Commons Attributes to wire your controllers can be handy when you have simple controllers you need in more than just one web application and when you don't want to worry about mentioning them in the web application context.

Let's have a look at an example. First of all, we'll write ourselves a controller:

```
import org.springframework.web.servlet.mvc.ModelAndView;
import org.springframework.web.servlet.mvc.AbstractController;

/**
 * A simple controller preparing the model for a webpage
 * welcoming the user and telling him the time.
 *
 * @@org.springframework.web.servlet.handler.metadata.PathMap("/showGenres.html")
 */
public GenreController extends AbstractController {

    private GenreDependency dependency;

    public ModelAndView handleRequestInternal(HttpServletRequest request,
      HttpServletResponse response)
    throws Exception {

      // create a model-and-view using 'welcome' as the name of the view
      ModelAndView mav = new ModelAndView("genres");
      // fill the model with the genres, retrieved using the dependency
      // ...
```

```
        return mav;
    }

    public void setDependency(GenreDependency dependency) {
        this.dependency = dependency;
    }
}
```

This controller prepares a model containing genres and returns the `ModelAndView` accordingly. As you can see, we've included a Commons Attribute in the JavaDoc section of the controller mentioning a URL. At runtime, Spring will use this attribute to map the controller to the specified URL, in this case `/showGenres.html`. As with the other handler mapping based on URLs, you can use the Ant-style path expression here also.

We've also included a dependency the controller needs satisfied to be able to retrieve the list of genres. Controllers wired up using Commons Attributes or other metadata facilities available (such as JDK 1.5 metadata) don't need to be mentioned in the web application context; they're discovered by Spring based on the attributes. Because often you still need middle-tier services to retrieve information from, say, a database, Spring auto wires the controller when it discovers it. Auto wiring can be done using constructors and setters; the latter is shown in the previous example. More on auto wiring can be found in Chapter 9.

> As you can see, we need to specify the fully qualified class name of the attribute (`PathMap`) in the JavaDoc attribute. We could also have imported the `PathMap` class, after which mentioning `@@PathMap("/showGenres.html")` would have sufficed. However, many IDEs detect unused imports and won't detect that in this case they may be used by a Commons Attributes `Attribute`. The *remove unused imports* features of those IDEs will remove the import statement mentioning the `PathMap` and compilation of the attributes using, for example, Ant will fail. We recommend using the fully qualified class name of the attribute you're using because errors that turn up after cleaning imports are hard to detect.

We've set up our controller but we still need to do two things. First of all, we need to mention the `CommonsPathMapHandlerMapping` in our context. This is pretty simple:

```
<bean class="org...servlet.handler.metadata.CommonsPathMapHandlerMapping"/>
```

The only thing left now is the compilation of the attributes using the Commons Attributes compiler and the indexing of the classes that contain attributes. This is explained in more detail in Chapter 9.

More Than One HandlerMapping

As a sophisticated IoC container, Spring allows you to define more than one instance of certain components. More specifically, this holds for `HandlerMappings`, `ViewResolvers`, and `ExceptionResolvers` (the latter two components are covered later in the chapter). In the case of handler mappings, the golden rule is that if a `HandlerMapping` does not deliver an appropriate `HandlerExecutionChain` (that is, it returns `null`), the next available `HandlerMapping` will be asked for one. Only if no appropriate result is found after inspecting all `HandlerMappings` will an exception be thrown.

If you define more than one handler mapping, Spring will inspect each one of them in the order resulting from sorting based on the `Ordered` interface. Customizing the order can be done by setting the `order` property on each of the handler mappings:

```
<bean class="org.springframework.web.servlet.handler.BeanNameUrlHandlerMapping">
    <property name="order"><value>1</value></property>
</bean>

<bean class="org.springframework.web.servlet.handler.SimpleUrlHandlerMapping">
    <property name="order"><value>2</value></property>
    <property name="mappings">
      <props>
        <prop key="/list*.html">listShowsController</prop>
        <prop key="/*">fallbackController</prop>
      </props>
    </property>
</bean>
```

The example shows how to define two handler mappings where the `BeanNameUrlHandlerMapping` takes precedence over the `SimpleUrlHandlerMapping`. This causes any controller that is defined in the application context directly to be used before the controller mentioned in the properties mapping of the second `HandlerMapping` is inspected.

HandlerExecutionChain and Interceptors

In the previous section you learned about the different handler mappings Spring provides. Handler mappings determine the path of execution for a request a user has issued, for example based on the request URL. When an appropriate mapping is found, the handler mapping returns a so-called `HandlerExecutionChain`, which instructs the dispatcher servlet on how to progress.

> The `HandlerExecutionChain` **consists of** *interceptors* **and exactly one handler (or controller), together providing all you need when it comes to accessing your business logic and other supporting services such as authentication, logging, and filtering.**

A `HandlerExecutionChain` always contains a handler taking care of the request (in other words, executing the actual logic). A handler can be of *any* type. There are no specific requirements to a handler, as long as it is capable of handling a request and there's an appropriate `HandlerAdapter` that knows how to use the handler in the `HandlerExecutionChain`. By default, Spring uses two `HandlerAdapters`, one for invoking handlers deriving from the `Controller` interface and one for invoking handlers of type `ThrowAwayController`. The different types of controllers are covered later in this chapter.

A `HandlerExecutionChain` might also contain one or more `HandlerInterceptors`, which are capable of intercepting incoming requests. Interception is especially suited for actions such as logging, security, and auditing. A more in-depth discussion about the concept itself can be found in Chapter 4.

We've already discussed the workflow involved with an incoming request. Let's review the interceptors:

1. Call to `preHandle(HttpServletRequest, HttpServletResponse, Object)` on any `HandlerInterceptor` available in the chain of execution. The `Object` in this case is the handler from the chain. This call allows to you execute any logic *before* the actual handler is allowed to do its job. Here you can check whether or not a user is allowed to issue this request, for example (this could be done using a `UserRoleAuthorizationInterceptor` explained a bit further on). Based on the return value of the call, Spring will decide to proceed with handling the request. When returning `false`, the dispatcher assumes the interceptor has handled the request itself (for example, when security constraints should prevent a user from issuing the request). In such a case Spring will immediately stop handling the request, which means the remaining interceptors, on which `preHandle()` hasn't been called, won't be consulted, just as the handler itself won't be consulted. Any interceptor, however, that *did* successfully return `true` before this moment will receive an `afterCompletion()` call.

2. Retrieve the handler from the `HandlerExecutionChain` and start looking for a `HandlerAdapter`. All available `HandlerAdapters` (registered in the `WebApplicationContext` or provided by default) will be inspected to see if one of them supports such a handler (usually determined, based on the class of the handler). In all except some complex and maybe rare situations there is no need to worry about the `HandlerAdapter`, its implementations, and the way they work. Spring's default behavior works just fine.

3. The next step is the actual execution of the handler. This will execute your actual business logic, or better; after some initial preparation such as data-binding, delegate the request to the middle tier. After the execution of the request has completed, you should prepare a `ModelAndView`, containing data that a JSP or, for example, a Velocity template needs to render an HTML page or a PDF document.

4. Next, all interceptors will be called again, using the `postHandle(HttpServletRequest, HttpServletResponse, Object, ModelAndView)` method. Here you can modify the `ModelAndView` (maybe add extra attributes to it or maybe even remove things). This is your last chance to execute logic *before* the view gets rendered.

5. Next, the view will be resolved and rendered. We will cover view resolving and rendering later in this chapter.

6. The last step involves calling `afterCompletion(HttpServletRequest, HttpServletResponse, Object, Exception)` on any interceptor available. The object is the handler that took care of the logic involved with this request. If an exception has occurred during the completion of the request, it will be passed in there as well.

WebContentInterceptor

Spring provides some `HandlerInterceptors` implementing functionality often needed in web applications. One of those is the `WebContentInterceptor`, providing functionality for easy modification of caching behavior of a web application and useful generic tasks such as limiting the methods (`GET`, `POST`, `PUT`) that are supported by the webapplication. Configuring this interceptor would be done as follows (note that the `UserRoleAuthorizationInterceptor` will be explained later):

```
<bean class="org.springframework.web.servlet.handler.SimpleUrlHandlerMapping">
  <property name="interceptors">
    <list>
      <ref local="contentInterceptor"/>
      <ref local="userRoleAuthorizationInterceptor"/>
```

```
      </list>
    </property>
  </bean>

  <bean id="contentInterceptor"
      class="org.springframework.web.servlet.mvc.WebContentInterceptor">
    <property name="cacheSeconds"><value>30</value></property>
    <property name="supportedMethods"><value>GET</value></property>
  </bean>
```

The following table shows the properties that are available for the content interceptor.

Property	Description	Default Value
cacheSeconds	The amount of seconds that is specified for content caching headers, if those headers are generated.	-1, which results in no caching headers being generated
supportedMethods	The HTTP methods associated with client requests that the interceptor will permit. If the request method is not allowed, a ServletException will be thrown.	GET and POST
requireSession	A ServletException will be thrown if a request without an associated session is found.	false
useCacheControlHeader	Indicates whether or not to use the HTTP 1.1 *Cache-Control* directive while generating content caching headers.	true
useExpiresHeader	Indicates whether or not to use the HTTP 1.0 *Expires* directive while generating content caching headers.	true

UserRoleAuthorizationInterceptor

Spring also features a simple authorization interceptor that checks a user's Principal with a set of roles you specify. Adding the interceptor to your handler mapping is done in the same way as when using the content interceptor. The UserRoleAuthorizationInterceptor features a property called authorizedRoles, which is an array of Strings. The interceptor directly delegates to HttpServletRequest.isUserInRole(String). When the user issuing the request is not in a role mentioned with the configuration of the interceptor, an HttpServletResponse.SC_FORBIDDEN is sent to the client, corresponding to status code 403. Using, for example, the error mappings in the web.xml descriptor, you can direct the user to an appropriate error page. You could also subclass the interceptor and override the handlerNotAuthorized(...) method to perform custom actions.

```
<bean id="userRoleAuthorizationInterceptor"
    class="org....web.servlet.handler.UserRoleAuthorizationInterceptor">
  <property name="authorizedRoles">
    <list>
      <value>administrator</value>
      <value>editor</value>
    </list>
  </property>
</bean>
```

> The `UsersRoleAuthorizationInterceptor` **can be used in combination
> with the JAAS features of an application server. Generally, the**
> `UserRoleAuthorizationInterceptor` **suffices in simple situations only: It does
> not aim to be a powerful general security solution. For more complete security solu-
> tions, including advanced features such as single-sign-on, we recommend Acegi
> Security System for Spring, discussed in Chapter 10.**

Other Handler Interceptors Provided by Spring MVC

Other handler interceptors provided by Spring MVC concern persistence and internationalization:

- ❑ `OpenSessionInViewInterceptor` and `OpenPersistenceManagerInViewInterceptor`: For use with Hibernate and JDO, respectively. Refer to Chapter 7 for a more in-depth discussion about those.

- ❑ `LocaleChangeInterceptor`: Use this to change the locale a web application uses on the fly. This specific interceptor will be covered later in the chapter.

Handlers and Their Adapters

Handlers are the actual components responsible for executing the logic in your web application, or dele-gating to another component executing the logic. Handlers should somehow be able to fulfill an incom-ing request and return an `org.springframework.web.servlet.ModelAndView` object containing the logical name of a view and the model the view will render. Out of the box, Spring provides two types of handlers.

All handlers that can inspect the `HttpServletRequest` and modify the `HttpServletResponse` by themselves derive from the `org.springframework.web.servlet.mvc.Controller` interface. Most of Spring's handlers are built using this interface.

There's a second type of handler Spring provides, which doesn't depend on the Servlet's request and response objects. This somewhat resembles the approach taken by the WebWork and Maverick web application frameworks, in that the information from the request the user issues is bound to the handler, which in its turn needs to create a `ModelAndView` and return it. The interface to implement when you like this approach is `org.springframework.web.servlet.mvc.throwaway.ThrowAwayController`.

We'll cover the different controllers later, together with some scenarios in which they are especially useful.

ModelAndView and ViewResolvers

Spring's MVC framework is built around the concept of a handler (controller) returning `org.springframework.web.servlet.ModelAndView` objects. The `ModelAndView` is named after what it contains, and with the model, the view should be able to render an appropriate response sent back to the client.

> The model is a map containing keys (Strings) mapped to values representing the actual value of the entry. While rendering the view, the map will be available specific to the view technology used (for example, in the `VelocityContext` when using Velocity or in the request context when using JSPs).

The handling of a request should result in a `ModelAndView` object being returned. The `DispatcherServlet` knows how to use `ModelAndView` object and in the end needs a concrete `org.springframework.web.servlet.View` instance that will be responsible for rendering the view: for example, a JavaServer Page or a Velocity template. Construction of a `ModelAndView` object is possible using either the concrete view object or a logical name. To get from a logical view name to a view, an `org.springframework.web.servlet.view.ViewResolver` is used. `ViewResolvers` manage a mapping between logical view names and their concrete `View` object counterparts. Different implementations of the `ViewResolver` interface have different behavior when looking at how the mapping is actually being done.

A `ViewResolver` resembles all other web-related components in that it also needs to be declared in the context of your web application and will be automatically picked up by Spring. Let's have a look at some of the different `ViewResolvers` Spring provides.

UrlBasedViewResolvers

The `org.springframework.web.servlet.view.UrlBasedViewResolver` maps logical view names directly to URLs that it hands over to the view class specified. The view class in turn uses the URL to render the response. The URL can, for instance, point to a JavaServer Page, a Velocity template, or an XSLT style sheet. You can configure the `UrlBasedViewResolver` in a couple of ways. First of all you *need* to specify a view class. The view class will eventually render your view (JSP, Velocity template, and so on). You can also tweak the way the URLs are created, using a prefix and a suffix.

The `UrlBasedViewResolver` comes in two shapes: `InternalResourceViewResolver` and the `VelocityViewResolver`, which have only minor differences between them. The `InternalResourceViewResolver` is a convenient resolver, already setting a specific view class (`InternalResourceView`), but still allowing you to override it. The `VelocityViewResolver` applies some Velocity-specific properties to all views it creates, also allowing you to override those. They include the `NumberTool` and `DateTool` objects, which allow for easy formatting of numbers and dates. Velocity features will be more extensively covered in the next chapter, when we discuss the integration of different view technologies.

An example:

```
<bean class="org.springframework.web.servlet.view.InternalResourceViewResolver">
  <property name="viewClass">
```

```
    <value>org.springframework.web.servlet.view.JstlView</value>
  </property>
  <property name="prefix"><value>/WEB-INF/jsps</value></property>
  <property name="suffix"><value>.jsp</value></property>
</bean>
```

This will result in a logical view name `welcome` being mapped to `/WEB-INF/jsps/welcome.jsp`. The `JstlView` class specified will result in a special Java Standard Tag Library object being merged into the request context, but again, this will be covered later in this chapter.

BeanNameViewResolver and XmlViewResolver

The `org.springframework.web.servlet.view.BeanNameViewResolver` and the `org.springframework.web.servlet.view.XmlViewResolver` both provide functionality to retrieve views from a `BeanFactory`. The latter uses a `BeanFactory` dedicated to views, which, once loaded, is not visible to the rest of the application. The `BeanNameViewResolver` queries only the `BeanFactory` in which it was declared.

An example:

```
<bean id="welcome" class="org.springframework.web.servlet.view.JstlView">
  <property name="url"><value>/WEB-INF/jsps/welcome.jsp</value></property>
</bean>

<bean class="org.springframework.web.servlet.view.BeanNameViewResolver"/>
```

Suppose you're using the configuration as specified. After returning `welcome` as the logical view name, the `BeanNameViewResolver` will retrieve the view bean from the context and use this to render the JSP.

As briefly mentioned in the preceding text, the `XmlViewResolver` basically has the same behavior with one difference: a `BeanFactory` dedicated to holding the views is instantiated and inspected when a view is needed. This means you will have to declare your beans in a separate file, for example `/WEB-INF/views/views.xml`, and wire up the `XmlViewResolver` as follows:

```
<bean class="org.springframework.web.servlet.view.XmlViewResolver">
  <property name="location"><value>/WEB-INF/views/views.xml</value></property>
</bean>
```

ResourceBundleViewResolver

The behavior of the `org.springframework.web.servlet.view.ResourceBundleViewResolver` resembles that of the `XmlViewResolver`, but when using the former, resource bundles containing bean definitions are used instead of XML files. The `ResourceBundleViewResolver` allows for localized views based on a locale from the user's request.

```
# /WEB-INF/classes/views.properties
index.class=org.springframework.web.servlet.view.JstlView
index.url=/WEB-INF/jsps/index.jsp

welcome.url=/WEB-INF/jsps/welcome.jsp
```

```
store.url=/WEB-INF/jsps/store.jsp

# /WEB-INF/classes/views_nl.properties
welcome.url=/WEB-INF/jsps/nl/welcome.jsp

<bean class="org.springframework.web.servlet.view.ResourceBundleView">
  <property name="baseName"><value>views</value></property>
  <property name="defaultParentView"><value>index</value></property>
</bean>
```

The preceding code sample shows two Properties files where one is the default containing three views and the second one overrides one view for a specific language. Note that it's better not to provide separate JSPs to do localization but instead localize the JSPs themselves, using the JSTL localization tags or the Spring message tag (more about that later). Just to show the behavior of the ResourceBundleViewResolver, we did it here anyway.

Upon startup, the ViewResolver will load the resource bundles, using the basename specified with the bean definition. The view will be resolved based on the locale associated with a request. Also defined with the bean definition of the view resolver is a defaultParentView. Because it would be annoying to specify the view class with every view you're defining, the default parent view will be used for any missing values (such as the view class). Overriding is of course always possible.

> Spring integrates with a variety of view technologies, some of which need a dedicated ViewResolver. The next chapter provides more insight into those view resolvers.

Chaining View Resolvers

While one view resolver will suffice in most cases, Spring offers the possibility to *chain* view resolvers. Chaining of view resolvers is ideal in situations such as those where you want to have fallbacks, if you want to provide support for different view technologies, or if you have stored your templates in different locations.

> Spring's contract for chaining of view resolvers is that if a view resolver returns null from the resolveViewName() method it starts looking for other view resolvers to allow those to try to resolve the view.

Before we show you an example of how to chain view resolvers, you should know that some view resolvers always attempt to resolve the view name and are not aware of whether or not the underlying resource exists. This is the case for all view resolvers that hand over control to an engine or other mechanism that doesn't inform the view resolver in case a resource does not exist. Specifically, this is the case for all UrlBasedViewResolvers: the InternalResourceViewResolver, the FreeMarkerViewResolver, and the VelocityViewResolver. As a result of this, these view resolvers must always be last in the chain.

Overriding One Specific View

The following example shows how to use two view resolvers: one based on bean names and one based on internal resources. This example shows how to override just one view. In this case, we want to present results of one specific request in an Excel file instead of an HTML page generated by a JSP.

```
<bean id="viewResolverOne"
  class="org.springframework.web.servlet.view.BeanNameViewResolver">
  <property name="order"><value>1</value></property>
</bean>

<bean id="viewResolverTwo"
  class="org.springframework.web.servlet.view.InternalResourceViewResolver">
  <property name="order"><value>2</value></property>
  <property name="prefix"><value>/WEB-INF/jsp/</value></property>
  <property name="suffix"><value>.jsp</value></property>
  <property name="viewClass">
    <value>org.springframework.web.servlet.view.JstlView</value>
  </property>
</bean>

<bean name="listShows"
  class="org.springframework.prospring.web.view.excel.ListShowsView"/>
```

We have to specify an order because the `DispatcherServlet` does not know in which order we want to have our view resolvers questioned. The `DispatcherServlet` detects all view resolvers, sorts them based on the `org.springframework.core.Ordered` interface (see Chapter 3), and inspects the one with the lowest order integer first. In this case, it's the `BeanNameViewResolver`, which causes an Excel view to be rendered if the view name is `listShows`, and a JSP to be rendered otherwise.

Disabling View Resolver Chaining

We've run into situations where users developed a controller that also implemented the `ViewResolver` interface. While it's questionable why that should be necessary, we've included a facility to *disable* view resolver chaining to support it. Chaining does not have an impact on performance, so if you don't need to disable it, you can leave the setting as is.

Enter the following in your `web.xml` file if you want to disable view resolver chaining:

```
<servlet>
  <servlet-name>chaining</servlet-name>
  <servlet-class>org.springframework.web.servlet.DispatcherServlet</servlet-class>
  <init-param>
    <param-name>detectAllViewResolvers</param-name>
    <param-value>false</param-value>
  </init-param>
</servlet>
```

> You can also disable the detection of multiple `HandlerMappings` and multiple
> `HandlerExceptionResolvers` if you need to. The same principles apply with only
> the initialization parameter differing. For exception resolvers, set the
> `detectAllHandlerExceptionResolvers` property to `false`. For `HandlerMappings`,
> do the same with the `detectAllViewResolvers` property. When you turn off the
> detection of multiple components of the same type, you are required to specify the
> bean name to tell Spring which of the bean definitions represents the one you wish
> to use. This is the common bean name, mentioned in the listing of all Spring MVC
> component types earlier in this chapter.
>
> Again, in most situations you shouldn't need to change the default setting, which is
> to detect all components of the same type available. Spring MVC's flexibility doesn't
> mean that you always need to use all the choices offered.

Locale Changing and Resolution

Using Spring locale resolution techniques, you can easily localize your web application. Locale resolution can be done in a variety of ways, based on all kinds of criteria, ranging from the accept header to a cookie placed at the client's machine.

The main component involved with localization is the `org.springframework.web.servlet.`
`LocaleResolver`. It has two methods: one to resolve the locale based on the incoming request and one to set the locale, using the `HttpServletResponse`, for example, thus making it persistent (using a cookie for `CookieLocaleResolver`, for example). The latter is optional because not all places in which locale information is stored are also writable (think of headers in an `HttpServletRequest`).

```
Locale resolveLocale(HttpServletRequest req);
```

```
void setLocale(HttpServletRequest req, HttpServletResponse res, Locale loc);
```

Using a `LocaleResolver` is simple; just define one in your application context and it will automatically be picked up by the MVC framework. The
`org.springframework.web.servlet.support.RequestContextUtils` has support for retrieving the locale using

```
Locale RequestContextUtils.getLocale(HttpServletRequest request);
```

and

```
LocaleResolver RequestContextUtils.getLocaleResolver(HttpServletRequest request);
```

Spring provides three `LocaleResolvers` and an additional `LocaleChangeInterceptor` capable of changing the locale based on HTTP request parameters associated with an incoming request. The three are as follows, and we'll discuss each in turn:

- ❑ AcceptHeaderLocaleResolver
- ❑ SessionLocaleResolver
- ❑ CookieLocaleResolver

AcceptHeaderLocaleResolver uses the accept-header field in the header sent by the client's browser to retrieve the locale. Retrieving the locale from the request simply corresponds to a call to HttpServletRequest.getLocale(). The AcceptHeaderLocaleResolver does not support setting the locale: It is intended to identify a specified locale.

SessionLocaleResolver inspects the HTTP session (if any) for a Locale object. If no session exists, or the Locale yesobject could not be found in the session, the accept header is used as a fallback. This LocaleResolver does support setting of the locale.

The third locale resolver Spring provides is the CookieLocaleResolver and we'll cover this one in more detail, together with the LocaleChangeInterceptor, which will allow for changing of the locale based on HTTP parameters sent along with the incoming request. First, let's get the CookieLocaleResolver up and running:

```
<bean class="org.springframework.web.servlet.CookieLocaleResolver">
  <property name="cookieMaxAge"><value>3600</value></property>
</bean>
```

If you need to, you can also tweak the cookie path, limiting the visibility of the cookie and the name of the cookie.

Next, using the LocaleChangeInterceptor, we will allow the user to (using links including parameters) modify the locale.

```
<bean class="org.springframework.web.servlet.handler.SimpleUrlHandlerMapping">
  <property name="interceptors">
    <list>
      <bean class="org.springframework.web.servlet.LocaleChangegInterceptor">
        <property name="paramName"><value>language</value></property>
      </bean>
    </list>
  </property>
  ....
</bean>
```

Using this handler mapping (of course along with some additional mapping of URLs to controllers), users will be able to change the locale when executing requests. In the following example, the locales will be changed to Dutch and English, respectively.

```
http://www.springframework.org/sample/editAccount.html?language=nl

http://www.springframework.org/sample/index.view?language=en
```

HandlerExceptionResolvers

In the beginning of this chapter we reviewed the single method specified on the `Controller` interface:

```
public ModelAndView handle(
   HttpServletRequest request, HttpServletResponse response)
throws Exception;
```

As you can see, while implementing this method, you can throw any exception you like. We've chosen to allow this—like most other web application frameworks—because we don't want to limit you while implementing controllers and force you to throw a Spring-specific exception. This does *not* mean that we regard *declaring* methods in your application to throw `Exception` as a good practice.

> The `handle` **method throws a** `java.lang.Exception`. **Good IDEs offer support for automatically overriding methods from a superclass and, while doing this, they often include the throws clause from the overridden method. Remember that you can, and normally should, narrow the throws clause for such a method. This is generally a good thing to do because it prevents you from throwing unspecified checked exceptions (if** `java.lang.Exception` **is not mentioned in the** `throws` **clause, compilation will fail). Second, including specific exceptions you throw in the throws clause of the method automatically documents your controllers. When reviewing the JavaDoc, for example, you can then easily collect information about all exceptions thrown from controllers, which will be useful in applying a consistent policy for dealing with them.**

Imagine a controller that has to reserve a seat for us in the performance venue. It's a simple controller that takes a request parameter identifying the show. It uses a service object to look up the show and throws a `ShowNotFoundException` if the show does not exist. In other words, the method signature of the controller looks like this (assuming the developer who wrote this code has correctly narrowed down the throws clause of the method):

```
protected ModelAndView handleRequestInternal(
   HttpServletRequest request, HttpServletResponse response)
throws ShowNotFoundException;
```

Maybe you can imagine that in other controllers, similar error conditions might arise where `ShowNotFoundExceptions` are also thrown. Because we probably want to deal with the error in the same way in our entire application, it's a good idea to separate the error handling from the throwing of the error itself.

Spring offers `HandlerExceptionResolvers` that allow for controller-independent behavior when an exception is thrown. `HandlerExceptionResolvers`, just as `LocaleResolvers`, `MultipartResolvers`, `HandlerMappings`, and some of Spring Web MVC's other infrastructural components are automatically picked up by the `DispatcherServlet`. The `HandlerExceptionResolver` offers one method:

```
ModelAndView resolveException(
   HttpServletRequest request, HttpServletResponse response,
   Object handler, Exception ex);
```

Note that this method is *not* allowed to throw an exception. The `handler` argument represents the controller or interceptor from which the exception originated and the exception is also passed to the method.

Of course, you can implement a `HandlerExceptionResolver` yourself, offering custom behavior when an exception is thrown, but before doing that, first have a look at the Spring `SimpleMappingExceptionResolver`. It offers you parameters to specify the status code and also can include the exception in the model while redirecting to a specific view that should be rendered.

Let's configure the `SimpleMappingExceptionResolver`. We'll of course begin with the class name:

```
<bean id="exceptionResolver"
  class="org.springframework.web.servlet.handler.SimpleMappingExceptionResolver">
```

We'll first set up the `exceptionMapping`. This is a properties object that contains class name patterns and view names. If the class name of the exception thrown matches the specified pattern, the corresponding view name will be used. The pattern does not support wildcards — merely a substring matching the class name. Therefore, you have to carefully think about what pattern you're going to use. Using "Exception" as the pattern will almost always match, as exceptions tend to have this string in their class name. Of course, using the FQCN is also possible and will always produce the expected result. In the following example, a `ShowNotFoundException` will result in the `shownotfound` logical view name being used.

```
<property name="exceptionMapping">
  <props>
    <prop key="ShowNotFoundException">
      <value>showNotFound</value>
    </prop>
  </props>
</property>
```

Next, we'll tell the resolver to include the exception in the model. The exception attribute is customizable. All of this, by the way, resembles the error handling mechanism offered by the Servlet specification. The difference is that it's more tailored to the environment you're developing your web application in. For instance, it gives you access to the object (handler) the exception originated from.

```
<property name="exceptionAttribute">
    <value>showNotFoundException</value>
</property>
```

We'll also set the status code. This is the response code the client will get if an exception is thrown. Furthermore, we'll set the default error view. If none of the mapped patterns matches the class name of the exception thrown, this is the view name that will be used, as some kind of a last resort.

```
    <property name="statusCode"><value>500</value></property>
    <property name="defaultErrorView"><value>genericError</value></property>
</bean>
```

Providing two error JSPs (or Velocity templates, FreeMarker macros, or Excel views if that's what you like) is the last thing we need to do. We'll show you one here:

```
# /WEB-INF/jsp/showNotFound.jsp

<h1>Ooops, an exception has occurred</h1>
```

```
<p>
  It seems you have selected a show that does not exist (anymore).
  Just to be sure, we'll provide you with the exception message:
 <c:out value="${showNotFoundException.message}"/>
</p>
```

The last thing you need to know about the `HandlerExceptionResolvers` is that you can add more than one of them to your application context, and order them, using the `order` property. The `SimpleMappingExceptionResolver` adds an additional feature in case you define multiple resolvers: the `mappedHandlers` property, which is a collection of all handlers this exception resolver should be applied to. If the `mappedHandlers` property is *not* set, it will apply to all handlers in your application. This feature is especially useful in a complex application where multiple `HandlerMappings` are used. Generally, one exception resolver is tied to one handler mapping.

> You should be able to see the consistency in Spring MVC's overall approach to extension points such as exception resolves, view resolvers, and so forth. The Spring project probably places more emphasis on consistency than any other application framework: partly the result of Spring's genesis from *Expert One-on-One J2EE Design and Development*, which provided a consistent overall vision, but also due in large part to the thoroughness of Spring co-lead Juergen Hoeller, who always strives for consistent naming and usage patterns throughout the framework.
>
> This consistency will benefit you as you work with all parts of the framework — for example, by enabling you to build on the Spring understanding you've previously gained as you come to grips with framework features that are new to you.

Controllers

We've discussed locale resolution, model-and-view classes, view resolution, and mapping URLs to handlers, but what about the controllers themselves? Spring provides a variety of controllers that will meet your needs when implementing important common requirements in web applications. For example, Spring features form controllers allowing you to do form workflow, command controllers, and multi-action controllers, comparable to Struts `DispatchActions`. We'll discuss the most important controllers before covering usage scenarios in which we'll not only discuss the controllers, but also all the other features you've learned about earlier in this chapter.

WebContentGenerator

Spring's most important controllers implement the `org.springframework.web.servlet.support` `.WebContentGenerator` interface. The `WebContentGenerator` also serves as a basis for the `WebContentInterceptor`, which has already been discussed along with the `HandlerMapping` earlier in this chapter. There you can also find a detailed explanation of the parameter the `WebContentGenerator` offers.

AbstractController

Spring's most basic controller is the `org.springframework.web.servlet.mvc.AbstractController`. It provides an abstract implementation of the `Controller` interface mentioned earlier in this chapter. Common functionality shared across all controllers is implemented here, and together with the `org.springframework.web.servlet.support.WebContentGenerator`, it provides a good foundation for controllers, in the end resulting in web pages or other HTTP-related content. Remember that often you can use a controller further down the hierarchy that offers behavior more targeted at a specific requirement. There will, however, be situations in which you need to extend `AbstractController`. The only method you need to implement returns a `ModelAndView`:

```
protected ModelAndView handleRequestInternal(
   HttpServletRequest request, HttpServletResponse response)
throws Exception;
```

> Remember that you can also return `null` from your controller, in which case Spring will assume you have dealt with the request yourself (for example by writing to `HttpServletResponse`). This feature should be used with caution, however. You typically don't want to end up outputting HTML in your controller. Use this feature only if you want to redirect the user to a different page in rare cases where you can't handle the situation with an exception resolver—or perhaps, if you want to generate binary content in the controller itself. (Note that the latter is not usually necessary, as a View would normally be a better choice. The Spring view abstraction can cope with generating *any* content type, including binary content types, as it is not tied to JSP or HTML.)

UrlFilenameViewController

Let's start with simple controllers, which do not involve logic such as form handling. As we've seen, a `Controller` should return an appropriate `ModelAndView` after processing a request. The `View` will be used to render a response to the client; the model is data relevant to the request. In some cases no model data is required, and you simply want to render a view (a plain JSP or Velocity template not incorporating any dynamic data). In this case you can use the `org.springframework.web.servlet.mvc` `.UrlFilenameViewController`. It transforms the virtual filename in the URL to a logical view name that will be included in the `ModelAndView`, returned, and then picked up by any `ViewResolver` you're using. This is a convenient controller to let all requests go through Spring, and, for example, expose JSPs located in your `/WEB-INF` directory indirectly to your users. We'll see an example of using the `UrlFilenameViewController` in the next chapter when we discuss Tiles integration.

> Using the `UrlFilenameViewController` can be especially convenient in case you have static resources such as HTML pages but still need every request intercepted by a `HandlerInterceptor`. In any case, try to avoid calling JSP pages directly; here the `UrlFilenameViewController` comes in handy as well.

Let's have a look at an example:

```
<bean id="staticViewController"
  class="org.springframework.web.servlet.mvc.UrlFilenameViewController"/>

<bean class="org.springframework.web.servlet.handler.SimpleUrlHandlerMapping">
  <property name="interceptors">
    <list>
      <ref bean="loggingInterceptor"/>
    </list>
  </property>
  <property name="urlMap">
    <map>
      <entry key="/*.html"><ref local="staticViewController"/></entry>
    </map>
  </property>
</bean>

<bean class="org.springframework.web.servlet.view.InternalResourceViewResolver">
  <property name="suffix"><value>.jsp</value></property>
  <property name="prefix"><value>/WEB-INF/jsp/</value></property>
  <property name="viewClass">
    <value>org.springframework.web.servlet.view.JstlView</value>
  </property>
</bean>
```

Using an `InternalResourceResolver` in combination with a `UrlFilenameViewController` will map all requests for HTML files to the JSPs in the `WEB-INF/jsp` directory. In the example, we apply a logging interceptor to every request.

ParameterizableViewController

The `org.springframework.web.servlet.mvc.ParameterizableViewController` is a simple controller that allows easy configuration of the view to return. It defines a template method called `handleRequestInternal()` that does the actual work, which is not much. On its own, the controller does no more than just returning the view you've been configuring using the `viewName` property. Of course, you can extend the controller if you like and implement different behavior in an overridden `handleRequestInternal()` method. The advantage this controller has over the `AbstractController` is that is decouples the view from the controller:

```
<bean name="/simple.html"
  class="org.springframework.web.servlet.mvc.ParameterizableViewController">
  <property name="viewName"><value>welcome</value></property>
</bean>
```

On the one hand, it's convenient to be able to configure your view outside the controller itself, but on the other hand, if you forget to configure it, the view name will be "null," which is not allowed!

MultiActionController

The `MultiActionController` provides a component with which you'll be able to group certain functionality mapped to different requests and request types in one controller. The `MultiActionController` resembles (and is indebted to) the Struts 1.1 `DispatchAction` and `MappingDispatchAction`, but in true

Spring fashion, it is more configurable and interface-friendly. Remember that a `MultiActionController` is not the only way of preventing common functionality to be duplicated. Other options to allow for reusable functionality used by multiple controllers include simply using plain old inheritance where shared functionality is put in superclasses.

The multiple actions in a `MultiActionController` are modeled as methods in any deriving controller. An example:

```
import org.springframework.web.servlet.mvc.multiaction.MultiActionController;

public class TicketController extends MultiActionController

  public ModelAndView reserve(HttpServletRequest request) {
    // perform logic to reserve a ticket based on the
    // request coming in...
  }

  public ModelAndView cancel(HttpServletRequest request) {
    // perform logic to cancel a reservation based on the
    // request coming in...
  }
}
```

The `MultiActionController` works only in combination with a `MethodNameResolver`. Based on the incoming HTTP request, the resolver will decide what method of the `MultiActionController` will take care of the actual processing and creation of a `ModelAndView`. Built-in `MethodNameResolvers` include the `ParameterMethodNameResolver`, inspecting the `HttpServletRequest` for a preconfigured parameter containing the name of the method to call, and the `PropertiesMethodNamesResolver` that uses a `Properties` mapping and Ant-style expressions to resolve a method name. Configuring a method name resolver in combination with a `MultiActionController` would be done as follows:

```
<bean class="ticketReservationController"
  class="org.springframework.sample.web.TicketController">
  <property name="methodNameResolver">
    <ref local="reservationActions"/>
  </property>
</bean>

<bean id="reservationActions" class="org.springframework.web.servlet.mvc...
                                    multiaction.PropertiesMethodNameResolver">
  <property name="mappings">
    <props>
      <prop key="/reserve/*.ticket">reserve</prop>
      <prop key="/cancel/*.ticket">cancel</prop>
    </props>
  </property>
</bean>
```

Data Binding

In addition to the simpler controllers such as the ones we discussed just before, Spring features some advanced data binding controllers. Using those, you can model form workflow in your web applications and other interactions that require binding of request parameters to objects specified up front. To explain the concept, let's look at an example. Consider the following request:

```
http://www.springframework.org/sample/sendToFriend.action?
  show=The+Lion+King&
  email=friend@springframework.org
```

Data binding will allow us to "bind" the request parameters (show and email) to the following command object:

```
package org.springframework.prospring.sample.actions.SendInfo;

public class SendInfo {

  private Show show;
  private String email;

  public void setShow(Show show) {
    this.show = show;
  }

  public void setEmail(String email) {
    this.email = email;
  }
}
```

The incoming request contains a movie title and an email address of someone a user thinks is interested in the movie. Using the SendInfo object, we can easily send the person an email. The request contains all information already, so the only thing we need to do is actually map the incoming information onto a SendInfo object and take care of the emailing (for which, of course, we've got another component wired up). The mapping is taken care of by Spring's data binding controllers.

> **Spring won't limit you to binding data of only primitives or framework-specific types. Complete freedom to bind to a complex domain model will be maintained without forcing you to implement specific superclasses or interfaces. Most of this is done using PropertyEditors, discussed in Chapters 2 and 3. Custom binding is also possible. We'll discuss this later.**

In Chapters 2 and 3 you learned about PropertyEditors and validation. Those concepts are heavily used when leveraging data binding with Spring, not only when using the web framework. Please familiarize yourself with those concepts if necessary before reading on.

We won't explain each and every data-binding controller in detail. First of all, you'll learn about some special features Spring includes to ease the pain of working with forms and binding parameters to requests and validation data. After that, we'll have a look at some use cases that will show you how to use the Spring MVC framework in combination with some of the components we've just described and functionality you've already seen (reserving a seat, for example).

Convenient Functionality When Working with Data Binding

You learned the basics about data binding in the previous section. Also, you've seen the notion of a `Validator` earlier in this book. This section discusses the features Spring includes for working with those two concepts in the web tier. We'll discuss possible problems you might encounter when working with checkboxes, the solutions Spring provides, and also cover indexed and mapped properties.

Checkboxes and Radio Buttons

Checkboxes have a nasty habit of sometimes getting lost in translation because of a quirk in HTML. When a checkbox in an HTML page is *not checked*, its value will not be sent to the server as part of the HTTP request parameters once the form is submitted. Most of the time you *do* want your domain objects to reflect the state of the unchecked checkbox. Lists modeled using radio buttons have the same behavior. Spring has support for resetting unchecked checkboxes, even though these are not communicated back to the server.

To tell Spring to set the value of a checkbox to `false` if no parameter is found in the request for the specific checkbox (in other words, if the checkbox is unchecked), include an extra (best left hidden) parameter prefixed by an underscore ("_"). By doing this, you're saying: "The checkbox was visible in the form and I want my object that the form data will be bound to, to reflect the state of the checkbox no matter what!"

It's possible to remove this behavior if you need to. In the `initBinder()` method of your controller(s), simply set the `fieldMarkerPrefix` property of the `ServletRequestDataBinder` to `null`.

Indexed and Mapped Properties: Maps, Lists, and Arrays

Spring has simple support for binding indexed properties on collections such as arrays, lists, and maps. As much as possible, the support conforms to existing notations such as the ones used by the JSTL Expression Language (EL) and the Object Graph Navigation Language (OGNL). The table that follows offers a list of examples of how you would bind properties to a collection of objects of the following type:

```
public class Person {
    private String name;
    public String getName() { return this.name; }
    public void setName(String name) { this.name = name; }
}
```

Collection	Expression	Explanation
Map (existing in the model under the name map), containing String mapped to Person objects	map[k1].name map['k1'].name map["k1"].name	All three notations are valid; k1 in this case is the key under which the object in question is stored
Array or List containing Person objects, stored in the model under the name array	array[0].name array['1'].name array["2"].name	0, 1, and 2 are the (obviously zero-based) indices of the elements in the list

Real-World Examples of Using Controllers

The sample application featured is more extensively described in Chapter 15. This section will show you how we'll be implementing some of the use cases mentioned in Chapter 15. Using a simple controller, we'll allow users to view information about a specific show. Also, we'll create a form controller with which bookings can be made, and last but not least, we'll create a wizard-style process to add shows to our box office.

Viewing a List of Performances Using the AbstractController

Users can select a show from the list of shows the welcome screen presents them with. The show the user selects will then be displayed along with the performance and availability data. Let's implement an `AbstractController` modeling this behavior.

> **When one of the other controllers Spring offers doesn't suit your needs and you're planning to implement the `Controller` interface directly, consider extending the `AbstractController` instead. It offers many convenient configuration parameters enabling you to customize the controller's behavior.**

Workflow of the ViewShowController

Let's first review the workflow the controller will be responsible for:

1. The user will arrive at the welcome screen where he or she will be presented with a list of genres and corresponding shows. Each show is represented by an identifier that is placed in a link on the screen. Clicking on one of those links will trigger our controller.

2. The controller will inspect what show the user selected by retrieving the identifier from the `HttpServletRequest`.

3. Using the identifier, the middle tier will have to retrieve the show corresponding to the identifier.

4. Our controller will have to determine a logical view name and the contents of the model with which, for example, a JSP can render the view (the show, including data availability).

Step 2 mentions a request. Assume the request to be the following:

```
http://www.springframework.org/sample/viewshow.html?id=1234
```

Implementing the Controller

First, we'll implement our controller. We'll do this using two possible approaches. The first approach starts with extending the `AbstractController`. Implementing the template method provided by the superclass is all you need to do.

```
import org.springframework.web.servlet.mvc.AbstractController;
import org.springframework.sample.boxoffice.logic.BoxOffice;
....
```

```
public class ViewShowController extends AbstractController {

    /** The boxoffice domain object we'll be using to retrieve shows with */
    private BoxOffice boxOffice;

    /** And a setter to be able to wire it up in our application context */
    public void setBoxOffice(BoxOffice boxOffice) {
        this.boxOffice = boxOffice;
    }
}
```

The following template method will retrieve the show the user selected and return an appropriate model:

```
protected ModelAndView handleRequestInternal(
    HttpServletRequest request,
    HttpServletResponse response) {

    // first, inspect the request for an identifier
    long showId = RequestUtils.getRequiredLongParameter(request, "id");

    Show show = boxOffice.getShow(showId);

    return new ModelAndView("showdetails").addObject("show", show);
}
}
```

We're using Spring's `RequestUtils` convenience class (located in the `org.springframework.web.bind` package) to retrieve the show identifier. This is a useful class to use in simple cases where advanced data binding is overkill. If the required request parameter isn't present, the `getRequiredLongParameter()` method will throw an exception, which you should preferably handle by adding a `HandlerExceptionResolver` to your application context (discussed later in this chapter).

> **Note that we're creating and returning the `ModelAndView` in a single line of code. In general, you should be careful with this because it makes debugging more difficult. If `NullPointerException`s are thrown, it's difficult to see what the cause is. In this case it's obvious, however, that this code won't throw any exceptions.**

> **Another note about exceptions: In the previous example we're not including any exception in the throws clause of the `handleRequestInternal()` method. Most methods in Spring Web MVC are allowed to throw arbitrary exceptions. However, as noted in the discussion of exception signatures earlier in this chapter, we recommend using the narrowest throws clause you can, in accordance with good Java style.**

We could have also chosen to use the `ThrowawayController` approach to implementing the functionality. The `ThrowawayController` offers more of a command-style approach in that for each request, a controller is instantiated and populated with the values from the request, after which the controller should have enough information to proceed and return a `ModelAndView`. The advantage when using these kinds of controllers is that you won't be tied to the Servlet API because all information from the

`HttpServletRequest` is already transferred to the command object (the controller itself) by the framework and no reference to the request itself is given to the controller. This means testing outside a container without mock objects. For example, the `HttpServletRequest` is pretty easy.

```java
import org.springframework.web.servlet.mvc.throwaway.ThrowawayController;
import org.springframework.sample.boxoffice.logic.BoxOffice;

public class ViewShowController implements ThrowAwayController {

    private Long id;

    /** upon execution, the HTTP request parameter 'id' will be passed in here */
    public void setId() {
        this.id = id;
    }

    /** method to implement, specified by ThrowawayController interface */
    public ModelAndView execute() {
        if (id != null) {
            Show show = boxOffice.getShow(Long.parseLong(showId));
            ModelAndView mav = new ModelAndView("showdetails");
            mav.addObject("show", show);
            return mav;
        } else {
            return new ModelAndView("error", "message", "unexpected.noshowid");
        }
    }
}
```

Wiring Up the Controller

Now that we've created our controller, we're going to wire it up using our application context located in the WEB-INF directory of our web application.

```xml
<bean name="/viewshow.html"
        class="org.springframework.sample.web.ViewShowController">
    <property name="boxOffice">
        <ref bean="boxOffice"/>
    </property>
</bean>
```

This is all you need to do to be able to retrieve shows using your middle tier and allow the view technology of your choice to render an HTML page or perhaps create PDF, Excel, or other content.

Making a Reservation

The application allows users to reserve seats and purchase tickets. From the screen presenting the show and corresponding performances and availability, the user can select a specific performance, reserve a certain number of seats, and purchase the actual tickets. Before we go on, let's have a more detailed look at what workflow is involved with doing the actual purchase:

1. From the screen presenting the user with the details of the show, he can select a specific performance and a price band. This will take the user to a screen where he can select the number of seats he wants to reserve.

2. At this moment, the application will present the user with the number of seats available. The user will be taken to a form that will allow him to purchase the tickets.

3. The form will be presented alongside some details about the performance the user is purchasing tickets for. The form consists of text fields and checkboxes and other widgets with which the user will be able to fill in his personal information (first name, last name, and so on) and payment details (credit card number, type of credit card).

4. Submitting the form will trigger some additional processing, and after that, validation will be performed. If errors are encountered, the form will be redisplayed, now containing error messages. The user will then be able to fill in the fields that contained errors.

5. After the validation succeeds, the actual payment will be done and the tickets will be purchased. The user will then be taken to another page telling him the purchase has been completed successfully.

SimpleFormController

In a typical form-editing and -submission process, users are first presented with a form, which they can fill out and submit, after which data binding and validation will be done. If all goes well, the application might, for example, store something in a database after which it tells the user everything went just fine.

The `org.springframework.web.servlet.mvc.SimpleFormController` does exactly this. It is one of the most useful and often-used controllers Spring provides and can be almost completely configured using Spring's Dependency Injection features.

The process of implementing a simple form controller can be summarized as follows (items between parentheses are not always necessary):

❑   Extend `org.springframework.web.servlet.mvc.SimpleFormController`.

❑   Set the `formView` and `successView` properties used in your application context.

❑   Add a setter for your service object capable of, for example, storing the form object in the database.

❑   (Override the `referenceData()` method to dig up some options to display in a drop-down box or choices as part of a group of checkboxes.)

❑   (Override the `formBackingObject()` method to get rid of Spring's default behavior of instantiating a simple command class or set the `commandClass` property if you just want an empty command object backing your form.)

❑   (Add a couple of validation objects using the `validators` property.)

❑   Implement the `doSubmitAction()` method to manage a fully processed, validated, and ready-to-store object.

There is, however, a lot more to tell. Before we begin, let's review the properties and some of the callbacks and other customization possibilities involved with the `SimpleFormController`.

> Don't let the flexibility of the command controllers and form controllers scare you off! The authors usually find themselves overriding only three methods: `formBackingObject()`, `referenceData()`, and `doSubmitAction()`; however, we often come across requirements where the construction of a command object is so expensive that doing it twice is just too much. That's where the `sessionForm` property comes into play. You'll find that working with Spring's controller infrastructure is easy if you don't have complex requirements, and extremely powerful otherwise.

Properties to Configure the Controller With

The `SimpleFormController` inherits a lot of its functionality from the `AbstractFormController` and the `BaseCommandController`. To tweak its behavior, the following properties are at your disposal:

❑ `commandClass`: This class will by default be instantiated and used as the object that *backs the form*, meaning the binding of properties will be done on this object. By default, Spring will just instantiate a new object using the default constructor (if available) of the command class specified. Often you don't want just a new class being created, but instead, you want to load an object from the database, for example. In this case you don't need to set the command class, but override `formBackObject()` instead. This method is discussed later in this chapter.

❑ `formView` and `successView`: Logical view names pointing to the view containing the form and the view rendering after the form has successfully been submitted, validated, and processed. The `SimpleFormController` exposes the `success` and the `form` view as properties; if you need custom selection of those views, extend the `AbstractFormController` instead. One of the typical problems with forms is the after-POST problem. If you have done a POST request and you try to refresh it in the browser, it will typically ask you if you want to resubmit the data. Often you don't want to do this. Spring offers you a way to issue a GET request immediately after a POST request has occurred. This feature involved prefixing the view name with `redirect:`. This feature is discussed in more detail in the next chapter.

❑ `sessionForm`: Based on whether or not this property is set, Spring will instantiate a new object the first time the form is shown and store it in the user's session. Upon form submission, the form will be retrieved from the session and used to bind the incoming data. Of course, upon form submission, the form object will be removed from the session. By default, this property is set to `false`. If you leave it like that, each and every time the controller services a request (both requests to show the form as well as form submission requests), a new command object will be looked up. Instantiating a simple command class using the default behavior (in other words, if you haven't overridden `formBackingObject()`) isn't really costly. If you, however, retrieve an object backing the form from the database, you might consider enabling this property because not doing so might have some impact on performance.

❑ `bindOnNewForm`: Property indicating whether or not to bind request parameters when a request for a new form is being processed. If you set this property to `true` (the default is `false`), all parameters available in the `HttpServletRequest` will be bound to the command object when a new form is shown. This can be extremely handy when you want to pre-populate a form.

❑ `validators`: To be used after databinding has been done. Validators are of type `org.springframework.validation.Validator` and are explained in more detail in Chapter 3.

❑ validateOnBinding: By default this property is true; if you set it to false, validation will
   not occur.

❑ commandName: The last property allows you to tweak the name under which the command
   object (backing the form) will be put in the model. It defaults to command. Not all view technologies have to access the model directly when using a form controller because, for example, the
   form macros and custom tags provide convenient ways to render form fields and values, but in
   certain circumstances you might need to access it. The command name defaults to command.

Callbacks and Template Methods for Custom Behavior

There are several callback methods you can implement to get custom behavior or to extend Spring's
default behavior. These include methods called right before and after validation and methods to be
implemented when you want to perform custom logic involved with the submitting of a form.

❑ Map referenceData(HttpServletRequest request, Object command, BindException
   errors): This method can be used if your form does not only need the command object, but
   additional data such as options to be displayed in a drop-down box, choices a user can make
   using checkboxes, and so on. All elements in the map will be merged in the model and thus be
   available for the view to render.

❑ initBinder(HttpServletRequest request, ServletRequestDataBinder binder):
   Perhaps the most important method in the controller, except for one of the submit actions you
   need to override to actually do something with the command object. This method allows you to
   add custom property editors (see Chapter 2 for more information on those) to the binder. The
   DataBinder is used in the Spring tags to transform domain property (such as a Date, but also
   domain-specific property such as a Show's Genre to Strings), which after submitting the form
   can be transformed back again into the original object. This method gives you complete decoupling of the web-specific form controllers and your domain object and is something Struts mim-
   ics, using the ActionForms. Because the form controller is completely stateless, this method is
   called both while issuing the form view request as well as the submit request.

❑ onBind(HttpServletRequest request, Object command, BindException errors) and
   onBind(HttpServletRequest req, Object command): Use this method in case you want to do
   custom binding. This method is called right after databinding, *but before validation.* Imagine you
   have a form containing three input fields together making up a date (one field for the year, one
   for the month, and one for the day). Using PropertyEditors, you can't bind the three form
   fields easily to one domain property. You could use a little JavaScript that (on submitting the
   form) transfers the three properties to a hidden input field and use a property editor to transform
   the hidden input parameter to a date instead of the three separate fields. Another (and maybe
   better) approach would be to override onBind() and do the custom binding here yourself.

❑ onBindAndValidate(HttpServletRequest req, Object command, BindException
   errors): Use this method if you need to do custom validation that cannot be performed by the
   normal validators you've specified with the controller. Usually validators don't have access to the
   servlet request, so if you want to do validation that cannot do without the request, this is the place.

❑ ModelAndView onSubmit(HttpServletRequest req, HttpServletResponse res, Object
   command, BindException errors) and their simpler forms onSubmit(Object command,
   BindException errors) and onSubmit(Object command): These methods all return a
   ModelAndView object (or null if you don't want the framework to continue with request handling) and are supposed to be overridden to do custom processing involved with form submission. These methods are called after databinding, validation, and only if after validation, the
   BindException object did not contain any errors. If you want to redisplay the form (for example

when errors arise saving the object), you can use the `showForm(HttpServletRequest request, HttpServletResponse response, BindException exception)`.

❑ `void doSubmitAction(Object command)`: This method is the simplest form of the submit method. You don't have to bother to return a `ModelAndView` object; the `SimpleFormController` automatically creates one for you using the `successView` property. This is where you can, for example, store the command object in the database using the persistence technology of your choice.

❑ `isFormChangeRequest(HttpServletRequest request)`: This method is called by the controller to identify situations in which it should redisplay the form, without doing any validation. This is especially useful in situations where you do an intermediary submit and want to change the data (and maybe the form) itself, based on a selection a user has done. An example could be a form with two select boxes, one filled with countries and one with cities where the one with the cities needs to be updated after a user selects a country. A little JavaScript could trigger the submit action after selecting a country. `referenceData()` can be used to add the list of corresponding cities to the model. By default, this method returns `false`, which tells the controller to proceed with the normal workflow involved with form submission.

❑ `suppressValidation(HttpServletRequest request)`: This method by default delegates to the `isFormChangeRequest()` method. In some situations, however, you might want to suppress validation in certain cases. Returning `true` from this method will do exactly this.

❑ `handleInvalidSubmit(HttpServletRequest request, HttpServletResponse response)`: The default implementation of the controller tries to resubmit the form with a newly created form object (retrieved by `formBackingObject()`). Override it if you want to add custom behavior, such as not allowing users to submit a form when no object is found in the session. The default behavior, by the way, should also work okay when the Back button is clicked after the form has already been submitted.

> Whenever doing things such as custom binding, for example in the `onBind()` method, you probably need to access the `HttpServletRequest`. Your best option to do so is using the `org.springframework.web.bind.RequestUtils`, offering methods such as `getIntParameter()`, `getBooleanParameter()`, and corresponding variants that will throw an exception if the parameter does not exist. Using the `HttpServletRequest` directly is tedious and you need to do lots of checking that can better be avoided (or moved to a utility class).

Form Workflow

The form workflow is graphically laid out in Figures 12-6 and 12-7. Figure 12-6 explains the workflow involved with requests that need to display a form.

> When a form controller services a request, based upon the outcome of the `isFormSubmission()` method, it starts the form submission process or the workflow for showing a new form. By default, all GET requests are associated with new forms; all POST requests are treated as form submission requests. You can always modify the behavior by overriding the `isFormSubmission(HttpServletRequest)` method.

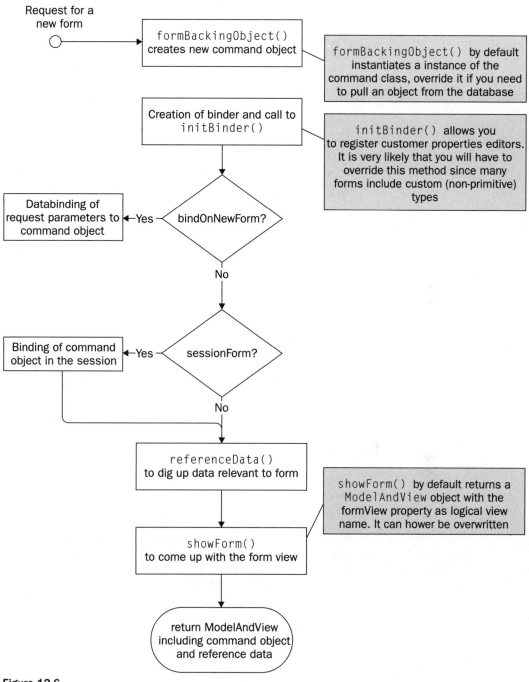

Request for a
new form

formBackingObject()
creates new command object

formBackingObject() by default
instantiates a instance of the
command class, override it if you need
to pull an object from the database

Creation of binder and call to
initBinder()

initBinder() allows you
to register customer properties editors.
It is very likely that you will have to
override this method since many
forms include custom (non-primitive)
types

Databinding of
request parameters to
command object ◄─Yes─ bindOnNewForm?

No

Binding of command
object in the session ◄─Yes─ sessionForm?

No

referenceData()
to dig up data relevant to form

showForm() by default returns a
ModelAndView object with the
formView property as logical view
name. It can hower be overwritten

showForm()
to come up with the form view

return ModelAndView
including command object
and reference data

Figure 12-6

1. The form display process starts with the creation of a new command. The method called to do this is `formBackingObject()`. By default, it instantiates a new instance of the command class you have configured. If you override this method, you might instead retrieve an object from the database. For example, include an additional parameter in the request that identifies a certain object you want to edit. Retrieve this parameter in the `formBackingObject()` method and load the corresponding object using a service object or DAO.

2. The binder is created and you're allowed to further customize it (add additional property editors, and so on) in the `initBinder()` method.

3. The form displaying process continues by determining whether or not binding needs to be done. Binding when displaying a new form can be turned on by setting the `bindOnNewForm` property to `true`.

4. The next thing is to store the object in the session (but only if `sessionForm` is set to `true`).

5. The last thing the controller does is create the model. It actually does so by calling `BindException.getModel()` or `Errors.getModel()`. The `BindException` wraps the actual command object and can create an appropriate model for you. You will probably do this yourself as well once in a while, as we'll see while reviewing the submit process.

The process of submitting a form (laid out in Figure 12-7) is slightly more complicated. It involves checking for the command object, invocation of the callbacks, validation (if needed), and the actual calling of the submit methods.

```
import org.springframework.web.servlet.mvc.SimpleFormController;

public ConfirmBookingController extends SimpleFormController {

    public void initBinder(
        HttpServletRequest request, ServletRequestDataBinder binder)
    throws Exception {

        binder.registerCustomEditor(new ShowEditor());
    }
```

As you can see, the binder now knows how to convert shows to String and String back to show — all because we've registered the `ShowEditor`.

1. When a form is submitted (usually this is the case when a POST request is done to the controller), the controller first determines whether or not `sessionForm` is set to `true`. If so, it retrieves the command object from the session. If none is found, it will call `handleInvalidSubmit()`, which by default resubmits the form. Overriding is of course possible.

2. If `sessionForm` was set to `false`, the controller will call `formBackingObject()` again to retrieve a command object.

3. After the binder has been created (see the preceding code example), binding and validation will be done and the corresponding callbacks will be called to allow for custom processing. Validation, by the way, can be turned off by setting `suppressValidation` to `true`.

4. After the binding has been done and validation succeeded, the `onSubmit()` callbacks will be called. By default, if you override none of them, the last method called is `doSubmitAction()`, which returns `void` and uses the `successView` configured with the controller.

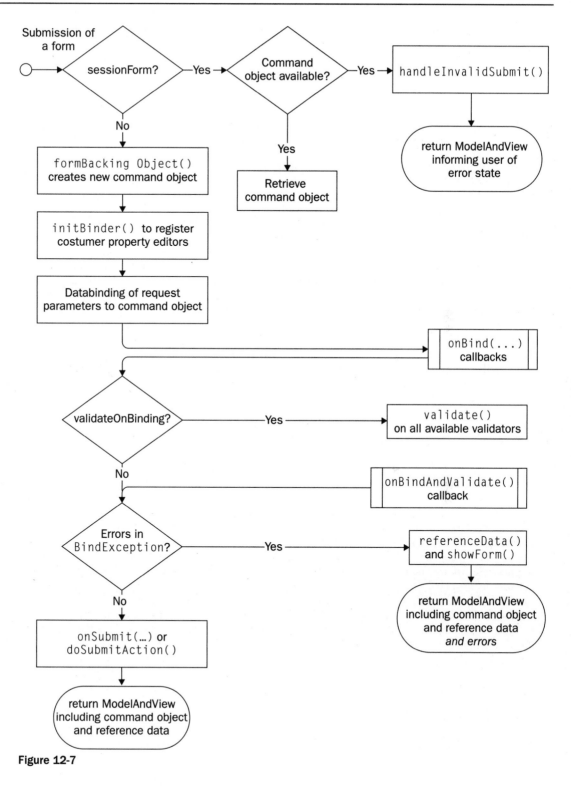

Figure 12-7

When validation fails, the process is, of course, a bit different because we have to show the form again, including validation errors. The process somewhat resembles the displaying of the form for the first time. As you know, all Spring controllers result in a `ModelAndView` being created and so do the form controllers. The model a form controller returns consists of three things:

❑   The command object (under the key configured using the `commandName` property or "command" if you don't configure it)

❑   The errors (if any) wrapped by a special utility object

❑   The referenced data returned from the `referenceData()` method, which is merged into the model.

The fact that Spring maintains binding errors separately from the form object means that domain objects can be used for form objects — a contrast with Struts, which requires the use of `ActionForm` subclasses to hold both form information and any accompanying errors.

When overriding one of the callbacks such as `onSubmit()`, you have the option to return to the form view (in case of errors during saving or other situations that might require it). You can do so by calling `showForm(HttpServletRequest request, BindException errors, String viewName)`. In its turn this will trigger the reference data method and return the appropriate view. One thing to keep in mind is that the `BindException` actually *wraps* the target (or command) object and if you capture the model returned from the `showForm()` call and go and meddle with the model yourself, you'll run into trouble. Replacing the command object somewhere during the process of submitting the form should be done prior to the `onSubmit()` callbacks, or by creating a new `BindException`, wrapping the new target in it, and passing it to the `showForm()` method.

Wizard Functionality

The `SimpleFormController` supports single-page forms. When going through an order or signup process, you probably need multiple pages including forms that together fill a certain domain object: one page that fills the personal details, one that contains address data, and one that contains payment information. Spring offers a controller specifically designed to support wizard-style forms. The `org .springframework.web.servlet.mvc.AbstractWizardFormController` supports multiple pages including finish and cancel actions and events that change the page in the wizard. As with any other controller, you can adjust it to your needs using Spring's Dependency Injection features. Also, as the name implies, it's abstract, so you will have to extend it to add behavior to it such as the saving of objects.

The `AbstractWizardFormController`'s workflow resembles the workflow of the `AbstractFormController` a lot, but where the latter works for "one pagers," a wizard of course has multiple pages. To support this, the callback and template methods offered by the `AbstractFormContoller` are all mirrored to include a page number. It contains, for example, a `referenceData()` method that does not include the request and the command object, but also an integer representing the page number to allow you to return reference data specific to the page that is currently being displayed to the user.

Basic Configuration

Let's first review the properties the wizard controller supports:

❑ pages: A String array, representing the logical view names of the wizard's pages. To have everything work correctly with arrays, page numbers in a wizard are zero-based. The view names in this array are used in the ModelAndView objects returned from the processXXX methods we'll be reviewing later.

❑ allowDirtyBack and allowDirtyFoward: Because navigation through the wizard and moving from one page to another is regarded as a form submission, data binding and validation will always take place. The default behavior of the wizard controller is to prevent the user from going to the next or the previous page if validation errors occur. In such a case, the controller will redisplay the current page, allowing you to display the error messages. allowDirtyBack and allowDirtyForward allow you to modify this behavior in which the controller will ignore validation errors when moving to the previous and to the next page respectively. As said, the default value is false.

❑ pageAttribute: If you set this parameter, the controller will put the current page number (as an integer) in the model, using the String you specify. You need this in case you have one view that renders multiple view pages (we'll review the different options to render pages in a minute).

The wizard controller derives from AbstractFormController, so parameters such as sessionForm, commandClass, commandName, and bindOnNewForm are all at your disposal.

Template Methods

As already mentioned, the wizard mirrors the different callback and template methods from the AbstractFormController. In addition to passing the request and the command object around, the page number is often also given to you when overriding such methods. Let's briefly review those before diving into the flow of the wizard controller:

❑ referenceData(HttpServletRequest request, Object command, Errors errors, int pageNumber): Method you can override to add page-specific reference data to the model.

❑ onBindAndValidate(HttpServletRequest request, Object command, BindException ex, int pageNumber): Page-specific data binding and validation can be done if you override this method.

❑ processCancel(HttpServletRequest request, HttpServletResponse response, Object command, BindException errors): Called in case the user indicates he wants to cancel the wizard using a cancel button, for example. You can trigger the cancellation process by including a request parameter keyed _cancel. This method should return a ModelAndView object that will be used to render the cancellation page.

❑ processFinish(HttpServletRequest request, HttpServletResponse response, Object command, BindException errors): Called in case the user indicates he wants to finish the wizard. You can trigger the process of finishing the wizard by including a request parameter while submitting keyed _finish. This method is called only if all pages will have been successfully validated (which is done by calling the validatePage() method for all pages).

❑ validatePage(Object command, Errors errors, int page) and validatePage(Object command, Errors errors, int page, boolean finish): Template methods to override if you want to do validation. You have to decide yourself here how you are going to do validation. One option is to append the page number to the validate() method of the Validator, and call it using reflection.

Flow of a Wizard

The typical flow of a wizard and the interaction with the `AbstractWizardFormController` is displayed in Figure 12-8. As you can see, the finishing and cancellation of the wizard will result in calls to `processFinish()` and `processCancel()`, respectively.

Page Changes, Numbering, and Other Actions

A wizard consists of multiple pages and hence needs to maintain state between individual HTTP requests. Most importantly, we need to keep track of what page is currently showing. In addition to that, we also need to trigger actions that change the page. This section briefly discusses how to change pages and trigger the finish and cancel actions.

The `AbstractWizardFormController` keeps track of page numbers using either the user's session or a request parameter. It's best to choose which to use based upon the actual project you're using the controller in. Often we'll turn on the session support when using this controller because keeping the actual state of the domain object across multiple requests and with partial elements filled in throughout the wizard can prove to be a hassle.

Back to what we were discussing: the page numbers. To be able to call the correct methods including the correct page numbers (for example the `referenceData()` method, but also the `validatePage()` method) with session support disabled, we need to include a request parameter in our HTML page, containing the current page. The `AbstractWizardFormController` will automatically pick this up when you submit the form. In fact, it's a good thing to do this anyway because we need to ensure the controller picks up on the right page also when the user clicks the Back button. Including a request parameter alongside a session attribute guarantees we'll always get the right page communicated to the controller. The parameter has to be keyed _page and include the current page number, nothing more.

> Note that you can expose the current page as an attribute in the model. Configure the `pageAttribute` parameter of the controller in your context (for example, with `currentPage`) and after that simply output it, like this:
>
> ```
> <input type="hidden" name="_page" value="${currentPage}">
> ```

Triggering the finish and cancel actions is a matter of including a `_finish` or `_cancel` parameter in your request, such as this:

```
<input type="hidden" name="_cancel" value="value">
```

The `AbstractWizardFormController` will pick up on these and trigger the right processes. As you might know, image buttons don't communicate the name of the input element itself, but the coordinates at which it has been clicked, prepended *with* the name of the input element. `<input type="image" src="submit.gif" name="_cancel">` will result in a _cancel.x and _cancel.y parameter being communicate through the request. The `AbstractWizardFormController` fortunately supports this.

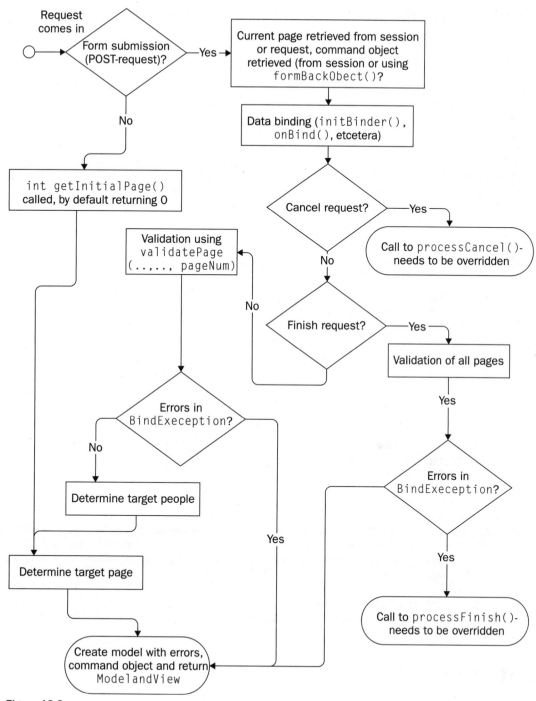

Figure 12-8

Extending Spring's Handler Infrastructure

When using Spring Web MVC in complex projects, you might run into situations where you need to extend the handler infrastructure itself. This can be done in one of two ways: by extending the Spring Controller interface (or by subclassing one of the classes implementing it), or by writing a new `HandlerAdapter`. This section covers the latter option. This is really an infrastructural feature of Spring MVC that is seldom used in normal applications because of the many other extension points offered by the framework. However, it's worth covering to round out your knowledge of the framework's architecture.

An `org.springframework.web.servlet.HandlerAdapter` defines exactly *how*, when, and if at all controllers are executed. Two `HandlerAdapters` exist, which are automatically supported when using the Spring `DispatcherServlet`. The first is the `HandlerAdapter` supporting the `org.springframework.web.servlet.mvc` controller infrastructure (all classes implementing the `Controller` interface). The second is the one supporting the `org.springframework.web.servlet.mvc.ThrowayControllerHandlerAdapter`.

The `HandlerAdapter` interface has the following methods:

❑ `boolean supports(Class clzz)`: Identifies if the `HandlerAdapter` supports this type of handler. In case of the common Spring Controller infrastructure, this class returns `true` for all classes implementing the `org.springframework.web.servlet.mvc.Controller` interface.

❑ `ModelAndView handle(HttpServletRequest request, HttpServletResponse response, Object handler)`: Should handle the actual request. Only called if the `HandlerAdapter` returned `true` for when it was asked if it supported the handler class (using the previously explained method). This call should return a `ModelAndView` or `null`. The latter indicates the handler has dealt with the request itself.

❑ `long getLastModified(HttpServletRequest request, Object handler)`: Should return -1 if there is no support for determining the last modification date or an appropriate long value if it does. This method is called only if the `HandlerAdapter` supports the Handler's class and adheres to the same contract as defined for the `HttpServletRequest.getLastModified()` method.

As mentioned previously, two handler adapters are installed by default: the `ThrowAwayControllerHandlerAdapter` and the `SimpleControllerHandlerAdapter`. Additional handler adapters can be installed to fully customize Spring's behavior if needed, by adding them to the `WebApplicationContext`. They are automatically picked up by Spring, just as with the `LocaleResolver` or `MultipartResolver` beans.

While we recommend using Spring's Web MVC default Controller infrastructure, there might be situations in which you need to customize the handling of *all requests* in your web application.

Uploading Files

It's quite easy to upload files using Spring. You can choose between the Jakarta Commons FileUpload package (`http://jakarta.apache.org/commons/fileupload`) and the O'Reilly Servlet (COS) package (`http://servlets.com/cos/index.html`) where the latter can be used under the terms of the

Buy-A-Book license. (Be sure to read and understand the terms of that license before using COS.) Whichever package you will be using, accessing files uploaded using a browser is done in a consistent way; the only difference between the two is the way the so-called *multipart resolver* is configured in your application context. The resolver detects whether an incoming request is a multipart request containing uploaded files, and, if so, Spring wraps the complete `HttpServletRequest` in a `MultipartHttpServletRequest` offering methods to retrieve the uploaded data.

This consistent approach is ensured through the `org.springframework.web.multipart` `.MultipartResolver` interface, which is implemented for both these third-party frameworks and could equally be implemented to work with any other technology for multipart handling.

Configuring the Multipart Resolver

Two multipart resolvers exist: one based on the COS package and another one based on Commons FileUpload. Both resolvers have properties you can modify to customize the resolver's behavior. Those properties include the limit of the file size that can be uploaded and the temporary storage location. More information on which parameters are available can be found in the Spring JavaDoc.

The following code snippets show how to configure both the multipart resolver that uses Commons FileUpload and the one that uses COS:

```
<bean class="org.spfw.web.servlet.multipart.commons.CommonsMultipartResolver">
  <!-- maximum file size (1 megabyte) -->
  <property name="maxUploadSize"><value>1048576</value></property>
</bean>

<bean class="org.spfw.web.servlet.multipart.commons.CosMultipartResolver">
  <property name="maxUploadSize"><value>1048576</value></property>
</bean>
```

You do not need to worry about wiring the resolver to controllers or the dispatcher servlet; Spring automatically detects it and will start using it to inspect requests immediately.

Creating a Form to Upload a File

File can be uploaded using a form, but there are some special requirements when constructing such a form. First of all you need to include an `<input type="file">` element and you also need to specify the encoding of the form in which you include the input element. A complete example:

```
<form method="post" enctype="multipart/form-data">
  File: <input type="file" name="file"/>
</form>
```

This is all you need to do to allow users to upload files using a web browser, although of course you still need to develop a controller that takes care of the data uploaded.

Handling Uploaded Data

There are two ways to retrieve the data that has been uploaded by users. As mentioned previously, Spring automatically wraps the `HttpServletRequest` in a `MultipartHttpServletRequest` to allow retrieval of the data. Every controller that has access to the `HttpServletRequest` can cast it to the latter:

479

```
public class UploadSeatingPlanController extends AbstractController {

  protected ModelAndView handleRequestInternal(
    HttpServletRequest request, HttpServletResponse response) {

    // if uploaded data is available, the request is a MultipartHttpServletRequest
    // so let's check that
    if (!(request instanceof MultipartHttpServletRequest)) {
      return new ModelAndView("error", "message", "unexpected.noseatingplan");
    }

    MultipartHttpServletRequest mpRequest = (MultipartHttpServletRequest)request;
    // the map containing file names mapped to files
    Map m = mpRequest.getFileMap();
    // an iterator iterator over all files
    Iterator it = mpRequest.getFileNames();

    // code that handles the file(s) uploaded
  }
}
```

While it is pretty straightforward, Spring provides an even more elegant way to retrieve the data from the request, almost without any custom code, with the domain model object containing, for example, a `byte[]` property:

```
public class SeatingPlan {
  private byte[] file;

  public void setFile(byte[] file) {
    this.file = file;
  }

  public byte[] getFile() {
    return this.file;
  }
}
```

Using a custom editor, we don't need to cast the request to `MultipartHttpServletRequest`. Instead, Spring does the binding for us (if, of course, we configure the form controller correctly) and we just have to take care of saving our domain object. Note that an additional editor (the `StringMultipartFileEditor`) is available to automatically convert the file to a String and bind it to the domain object. Also, you could use the `MultipartFile` type in your domain object, but this creates an unnecessary dependency to the `MultipartFile` class and is discouraged.

```
public class UploadSeatingPlanController extends SimpleFormController {

  protected void initBinder(
    HttpServletRequest request,
    ServletRequestDataBinder binder)
  throws ServletException {

    // bind the custom editor that will take care of the uploaded data
    binder.registerCustomEditor(byte[].class,
```

```
        new ByteArrayMultipartFileEditor());
    }

    protected ModelAndView doSubmitAction(Object sp) {

        // Spring has bound the file to the seating plan
        SeatingPlan seatingPlan = (SeatingPlan)p;

        // do something with the seating plan... e.g. save it!

        // and then... return the success view
    }
}
```

Note that the name of the input element (file) in the form described previously corresponds to the name of the property in the domain object.

Testing Your Controllers

As with any other component in your application, you will naturally want to unit test your controllers as well. While we've left discussion of testability until late in this chapter, the topic is very important, and testability is by no means an afterthought in the design of Spring MVC!

Spring provides a collection of *mock* classes that may be used to unit test your controllers. These *mock* classes are included in the Spring distribution and are located in the spring-mock.jar. There are mocks for the ServletContext, HttpServletRequest, HttpServletResponse, and other core Servlet API interfaces. These mocks go beyond the capabilities of those available from MockObjects.com, and thus are provided by Spring. (They are extensively used in testing Spring itself: Mock objects are used widely in Spring's own unit tests.)

You can test your controllers in a couple of ways, but directly instantiating the controllers and calling the controller's handle method is the easiest. To do more extensive testing of the controller's behavior (including verification of the calling of methods on business objects), you can use EasyMock. If your application context is more complex and the dependencies of your controller include components available only in the application context and hard to construct in a unit test, you might want to test the controllers after instantiating the application context itself. We'll cover both approaches in the following examples.

Testing Without the Application Context

In the following example we'll assume the following:

❑   We want to test the ViewShowController, as explained in the first part of the *usage scenario* section.

❑   We've implemented a dummy of the BoxOffice interface, delivering data we can use for testing purposes. This prevents us from having to create a database.

481

```java
import javax.servlet.http.HttpServletRequest;
import javax.servlet.http.HttpServletResponse;

import org.springframework.mock.web.MockHttpServletRequest;
import org.springframework.mock.web.MockHttpServletResponse;

import org.springframework.sample.boxoffice.DummyBoxOffice;

public class ViewShowControllerTest extends TestCase {

  private ViewShowController vsc;

  public void setUp() {
    vsc = new ViewShowsController();
    // use our previously create MockBoxOffice
    vsc.setBoxOffice(new DummyBoxOffice());
  }

  public void testCorrectModel() {
    // construct request and add the parameter for the show id
    MockHttpServletRequest request = new
      MockHttpServletRequest("GET", "/listshows.html");
    request.addParameter("id", "1");

    // construct the response
    MockHttpServletResponse response = new
      MockHttpServletResponse();

    // retrieve the model
    ModelAndView mav = vsc.handleRequest(request, response);

    // and do some tests
    assertEquals(1, mav.getModel().size());
    assertEquals(Show.class, mav.getModel().get("show"));
  }

  public void testNoShowId() {
    MockHttpServletRequest request = new
      MockHttpServletRequest("GET", "/listshows.html");
    // no parameter in this test, since we want to test if the
    // model will contain a correct error message

    MockHttpServletResponse response = new
      MockHttpServletResponse();
    ModelAndView mav = vsc.handleRequest(request, response);

    assertEquals(1, mav.getModel().size());
    assertEquals("unexpected.noshowid",
      mav.getModel().get("message"));
    // the correct message was available
  }
}
```

More Extensive Testing Using Mock Objects

Remember that in the previous example we're constructing the controller ourselves, so we don't actually test the behavior of the complete configuration, including, for example, `HandlerMappings` and the `DispatcherServlet`. Another way of testing would be to use a mock objects library such as EasyMock (`www.easymock.org`) to test if the controller actually performs as expected. We won't explain EasyMock in detail here; however, the following example should give you a decent enough idea. We'll modify the test shown in the previous example to include verification of the actual calls to the `BoxOffice` object:

```
import org.easymock.MockControl;

public class ViewShowControllerTest extends TestCase {

  public void testCorrectModel() {
    // construct the mockcontrol, the mock
    MockControl control =
      MockControl.createControl(BoxOffice.class);
    BoxOffice office = (BoxOffice)control.getMock();

    // and the controller
    ViewShowController controller = new ViewShowController();
    Controller.setBoxOffice(office);

    // record the (expected) behavior
    office.getShow(1);
    control.setReturnValue(new Show());

    // finished recording, now replay and execute the
    // appropriate method
    control.replay();

    MockHttpServletRequest request = new
      MockHttpServletRequest("GET", "/listshows.html");
    request.addParameter("id", "1");
    MockHttpServletResponse response = new
      MockHttpServletResponse();

    ModelAndView mav = vsc.handleRequest(request, response);

    assertEquals(1, mav.getModel().size());
    assertEquals(Show.class, mav.getModel().get("show"));

    // verify the calling sequence (is the getShow() method actually called)
    control.verify();
  }
}
```

EasyMock, which we used in this example, is just one of several mock object libraries available. Others include jMock, which can be found at `http://jmock.codehaus.org`.

Testing Using the Complete Application Context

There are two reasons for testing controllers with a completely instantiated application context. First, it might be too difficult or complex to test a component in complete isolation. While you should always try to mock every collaborator a component has, in some cases it might take too much time or be too much of a hassle. The second reason is to *test the application context itself*. Personally, we feel the latter should be done while executing an integration test only. Testing using an application context might result in strange behavior. It's not just your controllers (or whatever components) you're testing; you're testing a complete application.

If you need to test using a concrete application context, you have to start using the `org.springframework.web.context.support.XmlWebApplicationContext` directly. Use the context in combination with the `org.springframework.mock.web` classes geared toward testing Servlet API–dependent components without a servlet container. Remember that not all functionality of a servlet container will be available. Rendering JSPs, for example, will not be possible! First instantiate an `org.springframework.mock.web.MockServletContext` and pass it to the `XmlWebApplicationContext`. The context will be loaded from the `resourceBasePath` specified while constructing the `MockServletContext`, although omitting it will also work (the classpath will be used as your WAR root). Any additional application context files you normally specify using the `contextConfigLocations` initialization parameter in the `web.xml` file will now have to be specified using the `XmlWebApplicationContext` programmatically:

```
MockServletContext servletContext = new MockServletContext("./war");
XmlWebApplicationContext webContext = new XmlWebApplicationContext();
webContext.setServletContext(servletContext);

// initialize parent contexts (e.g. applicationContext.xml)
ApplicationContext context = ...
webContext.setParent(context);

// results in servletname-servlet.xml being loaded from WEB-INF
webContext.setNamespace("servletname");

webContext.refresh();
```

After you've initialized your web application context, it's a matter of *getting* your controller bean and executing a request:

```
Controller controller = (Controller)webContext.getBean("controller");
MockHttpServletRequest request =
  new MockHttpServletRequest("GET", "/listShows.html");
MockHttpServletResponse response = new MockHttpServletResponse();
ModelAndView mav = controller.handleRequest(request, response);

// do asserts
```

Note that Spring includes some very useful abstract test classes that facilitate testing of Spring contexts. They are located in the `spring-mock.jar` that comes with the distribution. One of those is the `org.springframework.test.AbstractSpringContextTests`. This class does not support the loading of `WebApplicationContexts` as shown above when using it out-of-the-box. However, you can easily extend it and load the `WebApplicationContext` yourself. One important advantage of the Spring test support classes (besides the fact that they eliminate the need for you to write lookup code) is that some of them cache the application contexts across multiple test methods. This can significantly speed up the running of tests, improving productivity. It is possible that web-specific test superclasses will be added to the `org.springframework.test` package in future releases of Spring.

Other Ways to Test a Web Application

While testing units of your application in the most isolated form as possible is good practice, executing integration tests is also vital. JUnit in its raw form does not offer a convenient way to test static or dynamic websites as a whole. To do such HTTP-based integration tests, you can choose from several tools:

- ❑ **jWebUnit** and **HttpUnit** are both hosted on SourceForge and offer JUnit extensions to easily set up a web conversation and test the flow of a web application programmatically.

- ❑ **TestMaker** is created by Push2Test (`www.pushtotest.com/ptt/testmaker`) and offers an advanced application to perform testing of web applications by using a scripting language.

- ❑ **Canoo WebTest** (`http://webtest.canoo.com/`) uses an XML syntax to express expected behavior of a web application.

We recommend using automated testing techniques when building web interfaces. In general, as much testing as possible should be automated, in all layers of an application. Automated testing of web interfaces is particularly valuable in that it gives you a strong set of regression tests, eliminating the need for tedious (and error-prone) clicking through pages to verify that a change hasn't broken previous functionality.

Summary

In this chapter you've seen most of the features of the Spring Web MVC framework.

We've reviewed the architecture of Spring Web MVC, including its `DispatcherServlet` and the concept of a `ModelAndView`, and strongly typed controllers such as the `AbstractController` and the `SimpleFormController`. Together, with features such as `HandlerMappings`, `HandlerInterceptors`, and `ExceptionResolvers`, you can control the flow of your web application and respond to errors.

`LocaleResolvers` and `MultipartResolvers` complete the picture.

One of the major advantages of Spring's MVC framework is that it clearly separates all responsibilities in a web application. Models contain data to be rendered to the response; views perform the actual rendering; while controllers process user interaction, invoke the middle tier to obtain the model data to display, and choose the appropriate view to generate the response for the user. If you're familiar with Struts, you should be able to map these concepts onto those used in Struts: Models correspond to JavaBeans, exposed by JSPs in a Struts action; Spring views correspond to JSPs used in a Struts application; and a Spring controller corresponds to a Struts Action. But you should note that Spring provides an elegant decoupling of these three concepts, and expresses the concepts in a way that is more independent of JSP or the Servlet API, maximizing potential for reuse.

We've seen that Spring Web MVC is completely view agnostic. Spring's *model and view* abstraction is independent of the Servlet API, and is equally suited to generating HTML, XML, other text, or binary content.

Spring Web MVC is an extremely flexible solution to building web applications. Although we've covered the most important topics in this chapter, you can easily extend Spring Web MVC to fully match your requirements in more complex projects.

While you may be feeling a bit overwhelmed with all the information in this chapter, remember that you don't need to use all the advanced features that Spring MVC provides unless you are writing a sophisticated application — in which case you will be grateful for using a web application framework that can cope with complex, unusual scenarios.

In the next chapter, we'll cover some of the view technologies integrated with Spring. One of the unique features of Spring's web infrastructure lies in the fact that it's completely agnostic to views. You can use Velocity, JavaServer Pages (JSPs), and Velocity as well as Freemarker templates and even convenience classes to generate PDF and Excel documents.

13

Web View Technologies

In the previous chapter you learned how to use Spring's Web MVC Framework. We explored how to implement controllers, how to create models, and how to map incoming requests to relevant controllers. This chapter will show you how to render views based on the models your controllers return.

We reviewed the requirements for a well-designed MVC package. One of the most important is that the controller infrastructure should be view-agnostic. You've seen how Spring achieves this by using *logical view names* in combination with components called *view resolvers*.

This chapter explores the view resolvers that Spring provides. Each one of them offers a unique way to transform logical view names to resources capable of rendering the view itself (such as a JSP or Velocity template). It's also possible to implement custom view resolves for additional view technologies.

First, we will introduce some of the basic concepts through an example. Then we will explain some of the view technologies Spring integrates with, such as JavaServer Pages, Velocity, and iText PDF. We'll also cover the features included to simplify the creation of HTML forms. You can use this functionality when writing JSPs and FreeMarker and Velocity templates.

After working through this chapter, you will know how to use the view technologies integrated with Spring to create a flexible, maintainable user interface for your web applications, not only using HTML-based views, but also variations such as those that can produce reports in Excel or PDF format.

The next chapter will discuss how to integrate Spring with other web frameworks such as Struts and Tapestry. Together with the previous and the next chapter, this one completes the trio of chapters detailing Spring's support for building clean but powerful web tiers based on your needs and preferences, with the technologies of your choice.

An Example

Each and every view technology has its pros and cons. Spring does not favor any particular view technology or implement one itself. It aims to work with any view technology, supporting the most popular options out of the box and enabling the implementation of custom view integration if required.

The fact that Spring's web MVC framework is view agnostic is a major strength, compared to competing frameworks such as Struts. This gives you complete freedom of choice when it comes to developing the front-end of a web application.

In Chapter 12, we discussed logical view names and how to resolve views using `org.springframework` `.web.servlet.view.ViewResolvers`. You've also briefly read about the `View` interface with its `render()` method. We will review the different implementation of the `View` and `ViewResolver` interfaces. For now, let's stick with a simple example. Consider the following objects shown in Figure 13-1.

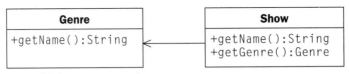

Figure 13-1

The controller that follows (resembling the `ViewShowController` we saw in Chapter 12) retrieves a specific show and encapsulates it in a `ModelAndView` object. The logical view name used by the controller is `show`. This name will then be linked to a JavaServer Page and a FreeMarker template, the two view variations.

```
Show show = boxOffice.getShow(Long.parseLong(showId));
ModelAndView mav = new ModelAndView("showdetails");
mav.addObject("show", show);
return mav;
```

The model has been created; the logical view name is specified. We will now review the basics of rendering a view displaying the name of a show. This involves the following steps:

❑   Linking the logical view name to a view resource (JSP, FreeMarker template) using a `ViewResolver`

❑   Creating the actual resource (the JSP or the `.fm` file)

We will also show you how to generate a PDF document using iText.

General Configuration

Regardless of the view technology being used, Spring will always use an `org.springframework` `.web.servlet.ViewResolver` to link the logical view name (in this case `show`) to that view technology, and to any resources needed to render the view (when combined with the model). This resource could, for example, be a JavaServer Page or a Velocity template. It could, however, just as well be a class in which you generate a PDF file.

The view listing all shows will contain links such as the following. These will allow users to select a specific show they want more information about:

```
http://www.springframework.com/boxoffice/viewshow.html?id=254
```

We haven't defined a `HandlerMapping` in our application context, which results in the default `BeanNameUrlHandlerMapping` being used. If we name our controller after the URL, it will be mapped correctly:

```xml
<bean name="/viewshow.html"
    class="org.springframework.sample.web.ViewShowController">
  <property name="boxOffice"><ref bean="boxOffice"/></property>
</bean>
```

JavaServer Pages

To construct a view using JavaServer Pages, we first define a view resolver in the web application context. The resolver here mentions a view class also supporting JSPs using the Java Standard Tag Library (JSTL):

```xml
<bean id="viewResolver"
  class="org.springframework.web.servet.view.InternalResourceViewResolver">
  <property name="prefix"><value>/WEB-INF/jsp</value></property>
  <property name="suffix"><value>.jsp</value></property>
  <property name="viewClass">
    <value>
      org.springframework.web.servler.view.JstlView
    </value>
  </property>
</bean>
```

After we've declared a view resolver that will transform view names to JSP files (here located in the `WEB-INF/jsp` directory), we create a JSP called `showdetails.jsp` and we're done.

```jsp
<%@ taglib prefix="c" uri="http://java.sun.com/jstl/core" %>

<h1>Hi user!</h1>
<p>
  You've selected <c:out value="${show.name}"/>, which happens to be
  in the genre called <c:out value="${show.genre.name}"/>.
</p>
```

FreeMarker

We could easily switch our view technology to FreeMarker. Some view technologies need a special configurer to set up the templating engine rendering the pages. FreeMarker can be configured using the `FreeMarkerConfigurer`. After you have defined the configurer, you need to mention a view resolver and specify the view class:

```xml
<bean id="freeMarkerConfigurer"
  class="org.sprfr.web.servlet.view.freemarker.FreemarkerConfigurer">
```

```
  <property name="templateLoaderPath">
    <value>WEB-INF/fm/</value></property>
  </property>
</bean>

<bean id="viewResolver"
  class="org.springframework.web.servlet.view.UrlBasedViewResolver">
  <property name="viewClass">
    <value>
      org.springframework.web.servlet.view.freemarker.FreeMarkerView
    </value>
  </property>
</bean>
```

Together with the following FreeMarker template called showdetails.fm, located in the /WEB-INF/fm directory, the view will render a similar output to the original JSP:

```
<h1>Hi user!</h1>
<p>
  You've selected ${show.name}, which happens to be in the genre called
  ${show.genre.name}.
</p>
```

Velocity configuration closely resembles the FreeMarker configuration in this example.

Generating PDFs Using iText

One of the libraries available to generate PDFs is iText (www.lowagie.com/iText). It supports the programmatic construction of PDF documents and has a capable and intuitive API. To include PDF views in your application, code a view class generating the PDF:

```java
import com.lowagie.text.Document;
import com.lowagie.text.Paragraph;

import org.springframework.web.servlet.view.document.AbstractPdfView;

public class ViewShowPdf extends AbstractPdfView {

  protected void buildPdfDocument(
    Map model, Document doc, PdfWriter writer, HttpServletRequest request,
    HttpServletResponse response)
  throws Exception {

    Show show = (Show)model.get("show");

    StringBuffer buffy = new StringBuffer();
    buffy.append(
      "Hello user, you've selected ").append(
      show.getName()).append(
      " which happens to be in the genre called ").append(
      show.getGenre().getName());

    doc.add(new Paragraph(buffy.toString()));
  }
}
```

The class needs to be defined in the application context as follows:

```
<bean name="showdetails"
  class="org.springframework.sample.web.ViewShowPdf"/>
```

To complete the picture, the `showdetails` view name must be linked to the bean we just defined. We define a `BeanNameViewResolver` to do so as follows:

```
<bean id="viewResolver"
  class="org.springframework.web.servlet.view.BeanNameViewResolver"/>
```

You've seen that all there is to changing a view is implementing the actual view resources themselves and changing the view resolver. There is no need to change controller or model, whatever the view: a key value proposition of Spring MVC. Before we move on and start exploring more of the functionality Spring provides to ease development of views, we'll discuss some things you must understand when choosing a view technology for a particular project.

Considerations When Choosing a Technology

We don't want to favor any particular one of the technologies presented in this book. The Spring philosophy is that this is *your* choice, which you should make based on your application's requirements and your team's skillset. You should realize that choosing one of the technologies for one or more projects will have an impact. Not only during, but also *after* development, business requirements will dictate changes to the interface of an application. Experience with the view technology chosen should be spread over a team, and although the greater part of the development of interfaces is often done by HTML designers and programmers, the Java developers themselves should also be familiar with it.

> Be pragmatic when choosing a view technology. Look at how well the technology in question fits in the overall technical architecture. However it's often more important to review the knowledge of your project team and the amount of effort required to implement and (often most importantly) *maintain* an application's web interface.

Spring enables you to choose whichever view technology you prefer. If your team is more experienced in using Velocity, nothing is preventing you from implementing your application using it. Even better: It's possible—quite easy in fact—to use multiple view technologies at the same time. For example, you can use both FreeMarker as well as JavaServer Pages in the same application. We'll see how to do that in this chapter.

A more thorough discussion of view technologies and what aspects and criteria to keep in mind when deciding on one can be found in *J2EE Development without EJB* by Johnson and Hoeller.

View Objects and Models

In the previous chapter you read a short discussion on the Model-View-Controller paradigm. In the MVC triad, a view is responsible for rendering the model prepared by the controller. Also, through the view, users might be able to execute further actions—for example, by clicking a link. Because achieving view independence is one of the major requirements we've set for Spring, controllers don't know what view will be rendered. This is a Good Thing, as it allows controllers to be reused with different view technologies if necessary — and it often *is* necessary in complex applications. Controllers indicate only a logical view name; the framework takes further responsibility to resolve the JSP or Velocity template in question and renders it.

> Keep in mind that a view is *just rendering* the model. It should access the model only in read-only fashion. In other words, avoid calling setters. In addition, you should avoid calling methods that throw exceptions — the last thing you want to do is *debug* your JSP to look for a potential method call that throws an exception. Related to that, avoid using try-catch blocks (either using inline Java code or by using the JSTL tags). They make code unreadable to HTML programmers and it often results in situations where exceptions get silently swallowed.
>
> The Open Session in View pattern (see Chapter 7) creates a situation where exceptions can be thrown all over the place. Carefully assess the situation to see if you really need this construct. It lengthens the lifetime of your session, causing more (maybe unnecessary) resources to be consumed, but it can also result in error-prone situations. Do not forget to set up a proper error handling mechanism in web.xml using error pages or the like — once the view has started rendering, Spring has handed off control, so HandlerExceptionResolvers won't suffice.

Views render models, so must have access to them. The way views access model data isn't the same across all view technologies. JSPs use data in the HTTP request context along with session- or application-scoped data. Velocity, on the other hand, doesn't have the notion of application-scoped data. In fact, it doesn't even rely on HTTP-specific constructs to access the model. This is one of the main reasons that models in Spring Web MVC are plain and simple instances of java.util.Map. Tying a view technology to transport-specific constructs, such as HTTP request context, should ideally always be avoided if possible. A graphical layout of the preparation of the view is displayed in Figure 13-2.

In the case of a JavaServer Page or a Velocity template, the template file embodies the actual markup of what should be rendered to the client. In the case of an Excel file (which is just as much a view on model data as a JSP is), we will need to write a Java class implementing the logic to create and output the spreadsheet. That said, we can distinguish between preparing the model so that the logic rendering the response (be it a JSP file or a piece of Java code creating rows and cells in an Excel file) will be able to access it, and the actual rendering of the response to the client. In the case of the Excel file, both the preparation of the model as well as the actual rendering is done by Java code. In the case of a JSP, a view object (Java code) prepares the request context — merges the model into it — and the JSP file renders it.

We've seen that all views in Spring Web MVC are implemented by a View object, all having a render(Map, HttpServletRequest, HttpServletResponse) method. As we continue, we will review the most common view technologies used in applications built with Spring Web MVC and we'll see how to use, among others, the AbstractExcelView, the JstlView, as well as the Tiles Configurer and corresponding TilesView. We will also cover how to use some of the macros and custom tags Spring comes with and how to use tag files and JSP fragments to simplify the creation of forms.

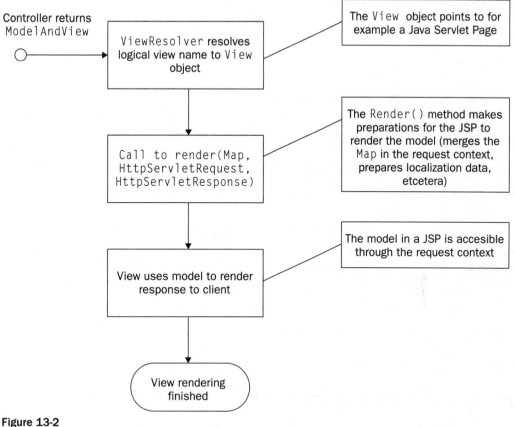

Figure 13-2

Features Offered by the AbstractView

All views Spring features extend `org.springframework.web.servlet.view.AbstractView`. Except for some basic features, such as a parameterizable content type, it offers *static attributes*. Through the use of those static attributes, you can add additional attributes to the model returned by any controller, without the controller knowing. This is especially suited for customizing your views, without having your controllers implement any additional logic.

Attributes can be specified in one of two ways. When using the `XmlViewResolver` (which loads an XML file containing beans that represent views), you can add any arbitrary object to the static attributes. When using the `ResourceBundleViewResolver`, you can use a comma-separated value (CSV) format to specify them.

```
<bean id="viewResolver"
  class="org.springframework.web.servlet.view.ResourceBundleViewResolver">
  <property name="basename"><value>views</value></property>
</bean>
```

The following are three view files, each containing different attributes for the view defined:

```
# /WEB-INF/classes/views.properties
index.class=org.springframework.web.servlet.view.InternalResourceView
index.url=/WEB-INF/jsp/index.jsp

# /WEB-INF/classes/views_en.properties
index.attributesCSV=title={title},content={/WEB-INF/jsp/content-en.jsp}

# /WEB-INF/classes/views_fr.properties
index.attributesCSV=title={titre},content={/WEB-INF/jsp/content-fr.jsp}
```

Along with everything added to the model by a controller, when returning the index view, the title and the content attributes are also merged into the model, making them available to the view renderer. Using JSTL tags, we can now create our view:

```
<html>
  <head><title><c:out value="${title}"/></title></head>
  <body>
    <jsp:include page="${content}"/>
  </body>
</html>
```

Issuing a New Request Using the RedirectView

A special and in some situations often used view is the RedirectView, which redirects the user to a different URL, rather than rendering the view itself. One of the many situations where you will be using the RedirectView is when you want to issue a GET request after the posting of a form. This way, you won't run into awkward *repost data* warnings shown by several browsers.

The RedirectView has two features. After specifying a URL, it will first append all model data to the URL—as request parameters. When this is done, the RedirectView will use the response to send the browser a redirect.

When you indicate you don't need to maintain HTTP 1.0–compatible redirects, Spring will send a 303 status code with an accompanying Location header. Refreshing of a POST request is in principle not possible because a POST request is considered to be a *non-repeatable* transaction (consider making a reservation); RFC2616 states that a 303 status code has to redirect the browser to the URL specified by the Location header, without any questions being asked in the case of a POST request. The RedirectView essentially solves the problem of refreshing after a POST request because a GET request is inserted right after it. The user will no longer receive warnings. Refer to http://ppewww.ph.gla.ac.uk/~flavell/www/post-redirect.html for more information on redirects after POSTs. The following is an excerpt from a SimpleFormController:

```
public void onSubmit(Object command)
throws Exception {
  // save the command object
```

```
RedirectView rv = new RedirectView("/confirm.action");
rv.setContextRelative(true);
rv.setHttp10Compatible(false);
return new ModelAndView(rv);
}
```

Of course, wiring up RedirectViews can also be done using the ResourceBundleViewResolver in combination with a resource bundle containing view definitions:

```
# views.properties
confirm.class=org.springframework.web.servlet.view.RedirectView
confirm.http10Compatible=false
confirm.url=/confirm.action
```

As you read before, the RedirectView adds any additional objects from the model as request parameters to the URL it redirects the client to. Instead of confirming for the user the successful execution of the action, we could also show him the show, using a ViewShowController (using a DAO to load a show and add it to the model):

```
public void onSubmit(Object command)
throws Exception {
  Show show = (Show)command;
  //save the show
  ModelAndView mav = new ModelAndView("showdetails-rd", "show",
    new Long(show.getId()));
  return mav;
}

# views.properties
showdetails-rd.class=org.springframework.web.servlet.view.RedirectView
showdetails-rd.http10Compatible=false
showdetails-rd.url=/show.view
```

Returning the view like this will result in the following URL being set as the Location header and sent back to the client: http://host.com/show.view?id=<showid>.

Remember that Spring just adds all model attributes to the URL, using the toString() method of the object in the model. With complex toString() implementations, this might result in problems with the length of the URL. Spring encodes the URL so issues with invalid characters in the URL won't arise.

One solution to prevent lengthy URLs is to post process the model. Often objects included in the model come from the database. Looking them up again is no real issue if caching is involved. We've seen people implement a handler interceptor that switched all domain objects in the model for their respective primary keys (of course only when a redirect was issued). Another solution is to derive from RedirectView and create one specific to your application. Removing items from the model that don't make sense and replacing domain objects with their primary keys can then be done if you override the queryProperties() method.

Using View Prefixes to Issue Forwards or Redirects

As an alternative to returning RedirectViews from your controllers, Spring also supports prefixes you can add to the view name that will trigger redirects or forwards. By prefixing the view name, you remove the need to specifically instantiate the RedirectView and you decouple your controller from it. An excellent example of this mechanism is when using it in combination with the SimpleForm Controller. When using a RedirectView directly, we'd have to implement onSubmit() as follows:

```
public ModelAndView onSubmit(Object command) {
    Show show = (Show)command;
    // do something with the show here

    return new RedirectView("success.html");
}
```

If we use the redirect prefix, we can change this to the following:

```
public void doSubmitAction(Object command) {
    Show show = (Show)command;
    // do something with the show here
}
```

and configure the URL to redirect using the successView property:

```
<bean class="example.RedirectingFormController">
    <!-- other properties here -->
    <property name="successView"><value>redirect:success.html</value></property>
</bean>
```

The redirect: prefix issues a redirect; in other words, it calls HttpServletResponse .sendRedirect(). The second prefix Spring offers is the forward: prefix that can be used to forward to another controller (or other Servlet resource) using the Servlet RequestDispatcher. Using the forward: prefix for JSPs is discouraged; Spring offers the InternalResourceView to do this. Use the forward: prefix to forward to yet another controller.

JavaServer Pages

The most common view technology in Java web applications nowadays is JavaServer Pages (JSPs). This is partly because JSP is part of the J2EE specification, which means it's guaranteed to ship with the application server or web container of your choice. JSP dates back to 1999, and the latest version is JSP 2.0. JavaServer Pages 2.0 is part of the J2EE 1.4 specification, and hence is already supported by many vendors at the time of this writing.

As did version 1.2, the JSP 2.0 specification improves a lot upon previous versions with respect to clean JavaServer Pages not requiring any Java code and simplifying the way web pages can be authored. JSP 2.0 enhancements include the incorporation of the Expression Language, which was previously part of the Java Standard Tag Library and JSP fragments that allow you to create reusable pieces of JSP code. More information about JavaServer Pages and the changes since 1.2 can be found in *Pro JSP Third Edition* by Simon Brown et al. (Apress, 2003) or in a series of articles by Hans Bergsten on ONJava (www.onjava .com/pub/a/onjava/2003/11/05/jsp.html).

> JavaServer Pages allow you to incorporate Java code in your view files. This should, however, always be your *last resort*. Using Java code in your JSPs increases the risk of including non–view-specific functionality, preventing you from easily migrating to another view technology if needed. Furthermore, graphic designers and HTML programmers don't know Java code and won't know how to handle it. Use the Java Standard Tag Library and the expression language instead of Java scriplets as well as the other new features in JSP 2.0 where possible. Last but not least, there are always third-party tag libraries available that might already do what you have in mind.

Note that you can prevent the use of scriptlets by including a JSP property in your `web.xml` file. The following example disables scriptlets for *all* JavaServer Pages:

```
<jsp-property-group>
  <url-pattern>*.jsp</url-pattern>
  <scripting-invalid>true</scripting-invalid>
</jsp-property-group>
```

Configuring Your Application to Use JSP

To use JSP in your web application, you will have to configure a `ViewResolver`, just as you would when using any other view technology. There are two view classes you can choose when using JSP. Both take care of preparing the model for the JSP to render. More specifically, this means they merge the model contained by the `ModelAndView` into the request context, providing the JSP access to it. The first view class provides basic support for old-fashioned JavaServer Pages, not using the Java Standard Tag Library (JSTL). It may or may not be a surprise to you, but for a Servlet container, a JSP is no different from any other request for a resource in the web application — hence the name `InternalResourceView` (in the package `org.springframework.web.servlet.view`). The second view class (`org.springframework.web.servlet.view.JstlView`) has more added value in that it does not merely merge the model in the request context as request attributes, but also prepares the localization context for the JSTL tags dealing with i18n. More specifically, this means you will be able to use the `MessageSource`(s) defined in your `ApplicationContext`.

> In order to use the tags from the Java Standard Tag Library, you should use the `JstlView`. Remember that in Servlet containers implementing the JSP 2.0 specification, you're not limited any longer to using the expression language only in tags — you can use expressions anywhere now. You can now, for example, write `<input type="${person.name}"/>` instead of having to encapsulate the `${person.name}` fragment in a `c:out` tag. Where possible, try to use JSP 2.0 features — they increase maintainability and readability of your JSPs dramatically!

Creating Forms Using Custom Tags

In the previous chapter we reviewed some of the command controllers and form controllers with which you can create validating forms. Spring provides some custom tags that facilitate the creation of forms using those controllers. The primary goal of Spring's tags is to *reduce duplication*. Before we look at an example using all the tags, here's a list of those available:

❏   spring:bind: Creates a BindStatus object and binds it in the request context making it available to JSTL and custom tags. The BindStatus object holds all relevant information about a specific property of the command object, indicated by the path attribute. Spring:bind is to be used when creating forms and displaying complex properties in a web page without knowing the format of the properties up front.

❏   spring:transform: A tag supporting the transformation of properties from other sources than the command object, based on property editors exposed by the spring:bind tag. Spring:transform is especially suited for rendering reference data, such as options in a drop-down box.

❏   spring:hasBindErrors: A tag exposing the org.springframework.validation.Errors object for a specific request.

❏   spring:message: A Spring equivalent of the JSTL fmt:message tag. The JSTL fmt:message tag cannot be used in certain environments — Spring still allows you to internationalize your application using the spring:message tag.

❏   spring:htmlEscape: A tag supporting the escaping of text in HTML. All Spring tags support HTML escaping through the Boolean htmlEscape attribute.

The tags in the preceding list are best explained by example. Let's first review how to create a form:

```
public class Reservation {

  public void setShow(Show show) { ... }
  public Show getShow() { ... }

  public void setDate(Date d) { ... }
  public Date getDate() { ... }

  public void setNumberOfPersons(int p) { ... }
  public int getNumberOfPersons() { ... }
}
```

We will be using the bean shown in the preceding code in our form, having getters and setters for both the date and the show properties. Next, we'll review our form controller.

```
public class ReservationFormController {

  // non-relevant methods left out

  protected void initBinder(HttpServletRequest request,
      ServletRequestDataBinder binder)
  throws Exception {
    binder.registerCustomEditor(Show.class, new ShowEditor(...));
    binder.registerCustomerEditor(Date.class,
        new CustomDateEditor("yyyy-MM-dd", true);
  }

  protected Map referenceData(HttpServletRequest request)
  throws Exception {
    Map refData = new HashMap();
```

```
      List shows; // lookup shows
      refData.put("shows", shows);
   }

   public ModelAndView onSubmit(Object command) {
      Reservation r = (Reservation)command;
      // do something with the reservation
      return new ModelAndView(getSuccessView());
   }
}
```

The ShowEditor in this example can transform a Show object to a String representing the name of the show, as well as the reverse (looking up Show objects by name). After we've configured the form controller with an appropriate form view, success view, and command class, we're ready to implement the JSP.

Let's review a fragment of a JSP in which we create a form to allow the user to select a show as part of the reservation. (This view is rendered after a controller has added the list of shows to the model using the referenceData() method.)

```
<form method="post">
   <select name="show">
      <c:forEach items="${shows}" var="show">
         <option value="${show.name}">${show.name}</option>
      </c:forEach>
   </select>
   <input type="text" name="date"
      value="<fmt:formatDate value="${reservation.date}" pattern="yyyy-MM-dd"/>"/>
   <input type="text" name="numberOfPersons"
      value="${reservation.numberOfPersons}"/>
</form>
```

As you can see, in this example we need to format the date using a pattern also specified when creating the property editor in our controller. Also, we need to pass the name of the show as the value of the options we're creating. Again it's kind of tightly coupled to the property editor we've created in our controller. You can see how this duplication will result in a lot of hassle when you need to change things in your web application (for instance change the property editor to use an identifier instead of a name to resolve shows). Fortunately, Spring provides custom tags so that we don't need to implement JSPs like that in the previous example.

BindStatus and spring:bind

Each and every command controller (that means also the SimpleFormController and the Wizard FormController) has built-in support for the creation of a binding object that facilitates command validation. We've reviewed the functionality of this binding object (org.springframework .validation.Errors) in Chapter 12. In the view layer, you can reuse this object implicitly to retrieve property values from the command object your controller deals with. You can do this through using the <spring:bind> tag. Let's start off with a small example:

```
<spring:bind path="command.numberOfPersons">
   <input type="text" name="${status.expression}" value="${status.value}"/>
</spring:bind>
```

> Note that by default, Spring binds the command object (in this case the reservation) in the model (resulting in the object being bound as an attribute to the HttpServletRequest when using JSP) using the identifier command. You can change this behavior by setting the commandName property in your WebApplicationContext. We generally encourage people to do so and to change it to something more sensible. It increases the readability of your JSPs. If we had modified the command name to show, the preceding example would have to be changed to <spring:bind path= "show.numberOfPersons">. More information on the command controllers and ways to modify the command name can be found in Chapter 12.

As you can see, we've surrounded the input element by a spring:bind tag. By doing so, we're telling Spring to create a BindStatus object and make it available under the name status. This object contains information about the property mentioned in the path attribute (in this case numberOfPersons), such as the actual value of the property but also error messages. The most important properties (getters) the BindStatus object provides are as follows:

❑   status.expression: Returns the expression identifying the property. While submitting the form, Spring will use this expression (after all, it will be communicating back to our controller using HTTP request parameters) to bind the value of the input field to our command object. Use this attribute to set the name property of your HTML input field.

❑   status.value: Returns the value of the property (not transformed by any property editor registered for the property). Ideally suited for comparing the property with other objects (to compare a selection and see which object is selected, for example).

❑   status.displayValue: Returns the value of the original property, *already transformed* by the property editor registered for this property. This accessor returns a String, usable in input fields and so on.

❑   status.error: Determines whether or not the currently bound property has an error message attached to it (returns a Boolean, so it's easily usable in JSP expressions).

❑   status.errorMessages: Retrieves an array of error messages. The error messages are the ones you created in your controller or that were created by any validators associated with your controller.

❑   status.errorMessage: Gives you the first error message available.

❑   status.errorCode and status.errorCodes: Give you the first available error code and all error codes as an array, respectively. Note that these are the *not-localized* codes. The other properties such as status.errorMessage return already localized codes.

Because the status.displayValue method not only looks up the value of the property but transforms it to a String using the property editor bound in the controller, you can use this method to remove formatting issues from your form elements:

```
<spring:bind path="command.date">
  <input type="text" name="${status.expression}"
    value="${status.displayValue}">
  <c:if test="${status.error}">
    <font color="red"><c:out value="${status.errorMessage}"/></font>
  </c:if>
</spring:bind>
```

As you can see, it's easy to incorporate error messages created during the validation stage (in your controller) and also to remove the patterns needed to format dates. They have to be mentioned only in one place, alongside your property editor.

> Be careful when outputting properties using embedded EL expressions, such as `<c:out value="${status.errorMessage}"/>`. Often they include user input, which might result in problems when not escaping. Use `<c:out value="${status.errorMessage}"/>` instead, which by default does character escaping.
>
> Furthermore we could have rewritten the above code fragment to include a conditional operator and make it look something like this:
>
> ```
> ${status.error ? status.errorMessage : ''}
> ```
>
> We've encountered numerous cases where less experienced developers didn't understand how a conditional operator works. Try to imagine what an HTML programmer thinks when she sees such an expression! Use the conditional operator cautiously because often it doesn't increase readability of your JSP code.

spring:nestedPath

Sometimes you might have forms including lots of data as well as data spread across a more complex object model. The `spring:nestedPath` tag helps limit the amount of JSP code you need to type. The `nestedPath` tag simply tells any nested bind tags to use the nested path mentioned with the parent tag. We can rewrite the preceding example as follows:

```
<spring:nestedPath path="command">
  <spring:bind path="date">
    <input type="text" name="date" value="${status.displayValue}"/>
    ...
  </spring:bind>
</spring:nestedPath>
```

> This tag is especially useful when writing JSP fragments and reusing those across multiple form JSPs.
>
> Also, if you're using a complex domain model with lots of nesting, you will greatly benefit from the `nestedPath` tag.

spring:transform

In the example where we allowed the user to select a show from a list, we created the following piece of JSP:

```
<select name="show">
  <c:forEach items="${shows}" var="show">
    <option value="${show.name}">${show.name}</option>
  </c:forEach>
</select>
```

Of course, we can rewrite this to a JSP code using the `spring:bind` tag as well, but we will still have to specify what value our property editor will use when transforming the input text back to a show object:

```
<spring:bind path="command.show">
  <select name="${status.expression}">
    <c:forEach items="${shows}" var="show"
      <option
        <c:if test="${status.value == show}">selected</c:if>
        value="<c:out value="${show.name}"/>">
          <c:out value="${show.name}"/></option>
    </c:forEach>
  </select>
</spring:bind>
```

The `spring:transform` tag provides you with support for transforming properties not contained by a *command* using property editors associated with the *command*. The shows rendered in the preceding example need to be transformed in the same way the `spring:bind` tag does the transformation. The `spring:transform` tag provides this support, internally using the same property editor as the `spring:bind` tag.

Note that the `spring:transform` tag can be used only *inside* a `spring:bind` tag:

```
...
<c:forEach>
  <option value="<spring:transform value="${show}"/>">
    <c:out value="${show.name}">
  </option>
</c:forEach>
...
```

The `spring:transform` tag also supports the storing of the transformation result in a variable, using the `var` attribute.

> All Spring tags extend `HtmlEscapingAwareTag` **by the way, offering the** `htmlEscape`
> **Boolean property, allowing you to switch HTML escaping on or off for all output**
> **generated by the corresponding tag. By default, HTML escaping will always occur.**
> **You can set defaults by using the** `HtmlEscapeTag` **or by specifying a**
> `defaultHtmlEscape` **property in your** `web.xml`.
>
> **HTML 4.0 is compliant with several character sets, such as ISO Latin-1. You can use**
> **whatever characters are available in the character sets supported by HTML 4.0. Parts**
> **of Unicode are also supported by HTML 4.0. Special characters, such as the German**
> **ü character and the symbol for the European currency, €, can be expressed only in**
> **Unicode. Transforming those characters from ASCII to Unicode is what the HTML**
> **escaping functionality does. You can find a full list of what characters are supported**
> **at** `www.w3.org/TR/REC-html40/sgml/entities.html`.

spring:message

The `spring:message` tag is the Spring equivalent of the `fmt:message` tag from the Java Standard Tag Library. We felt the need to implement our own tag supporting internationalization because not everyone has the opportunity to use the JSTL. The `spring:message` tag has three properties (plus the standard `htmlEscape` all tags offer): one for specifying the message code, one for a default message that will be used if the code can't be resolved to a message, and one for storing the message in a page scoped variable.

```
<spring:message
  code="reservation.show.select.label"
  text="Select your show">
```

While the preceding code snippet will directly output the result (after the tag has looked up the actual message using the `MessageSource` registered), you can also store the result in a variable for future use:

```
<spring:message
  code="reservation.show.select.label"
  text="Select your show"
  var="messageVariable"/>
```

Using `${messageVariable}` in you HTML now will result in the resolved message being output. If the message cannot be resolved, the `spring:message` tag will output the string specified by the `text` attribute.

> Note that most of Spring's tags support scoping, through the `scope` attribute. Variables can be stored in one of four scopes: page (exposed to the *current* JSP only), `request` (exposed for all pages rendered in the current request), `session` (stored in the session), and `application` (stored in the application's memory, hence visible to all consecutive requests, for all users). Keep in mind that storing a variable in a user's session will cause the variable to be left hanging there for the entire lifetime of his or her session (unless you remove it). In applications with a large number of concurrent users, this can result in a dramatic increase in the amount of memory used by the application.

Spring's message tag relies on the `ApplicationContext` for its messages. The `ApplicationContext` itself is an `org.springframework.context.MessageSource`, and will be able to resolve messages if you specify a message source with it (refer to Chapter 4 for information on `MessageSources`).

A Final Note on Spring Tags

Since JSP 2.0, all tags are EL-enabled, which means that you can use the expression language everywhere to pass objects to tags (for example by doing `<pref:tag value="${date}"/>`). This wasn't the case in JSP 1.2, where tag developers had to provide EL-enabled versions of their tags themselves. As a result, lots of tag libraries provided both versions of their libraries for the old-school request-time expressions (rtexprvalue) using scriptlets (for example `<pref:tag value="<% show.getDate() %>"/>`) as well as EL versions supporting the expression language. With the latter you could rewrite the preceding example to `<pref:tag value="${show.date}"/>`.

All Spring tags support the expression language. We strongly recommend you not use the runtime expressions anymore because they severely impact the readability and maintainability of your JSP code.

Because the tags support EL, you are allowed to do something like this:

```
<c:set var="bindPath" value="firstName"/>

<c:if test="${showLastName}">
  <c:set var="bindPath" value="lastName"/>
```

```
    </c:if>
```

```
<spring:bind path="${bindPath}"/>
    <input type="text" name="${status.expression}" value="${status.value}"/>
</spring:bind>
```

Using Tag Files to Create Reusable Elements

In the previous sections we've been reviewing the Spring tags facilitating data binding, error messages, and i18n. You may have noticed that each time we introduced a tag, the level of coupling and duplication got reduced, but at the same time, we had to write more and more JSP code. We can prevent writing lots of JSP code with `spring:bind` tags littered all over the place in a couple of ways. First of all, we can write our own custom tags generating HTML input fields. This is the approach Struts has been taking with its `html:XXX` tags. Except for the normal HTML attributes such as `style`, `id`, and `name`, these include Struts-specific attributes that will facilitate data binding. By including `<html:text style="width: 150px;" property="name"/>` we could, for example, let Struts generate a text field with a preset width, which will be bound to the `name` property of the associated `ActionForm`.

With Spring, we explicitly decided not to include a tag library for generating markup as the preceding example shows. It limits the ways the developer can create markup, and in addition, HTML programmers need to learn an additional (and rather large) tag library. Last but not least, with the newly added features in JSP 2.0, we don't even have to create those tags anymore.

We'll show you how to code a form with a simple text field where the user has to enter his name — all this using JSP tag files. Note that JSP 2.0 (of which tag files is one of the new features) isn't implemented yet by all major Servlet container vendors. At the time of this writing, Jetty and Tomcat both support the latest JSP specification.

Tag files are ordinary pieces of JSP, placed in a directory and mentioned in the JSP using normal tag library declarations. Once set up, you can use them just as you would use any other tag. First, we'll have to create a new directory beneath `WEB-INF`, called `tags`. This is where the JSP fragments will be placed. Second, we'll mention the `tags` directory in our JSP creating the form:

```
<%@ taglib prefix="form" tagdir="/WEB-INF/tags" %>
<html>
  <body>
    <h1>Please enter your name</h1>
    Name:
    <form:text path="command.name"/>
  </body>
</html>
```

The `form:select` tag file will render an HTML select element for us and the `form:text` tag will render an HTML input field. Let's review these tag files:

```
<%-- partial text.tag, located in /WEB-INF/tags --%>
<spring:bind path="${path}">
  <input type="text"
    name="${status.expression}"
    value="${status.value}"/>
  <c:if test="${status.error}"><font color="red">${status.errorMessage}</c:if>
</spring:bind>
```

As you can see, we've again decreased the level of duplication in our JSP; we don't have to mention the `spring:bind` tags in numerous places and we've refactored the code for the input field to a separate tag file. More resources on Spring and how to use tag files can be found online at the Spring Wiki site (`http://opensource.atlassian.com/confluence/spring/display/DISC/Minimize+Typing+with+nestedPath+Tag`).

Velocity and FreeMarker

FreeMarker and Velocity are templating tools with different aims than JSP. Both tools offer a sophisticated templating language, entirely based on a proprietary engine, written in Java. As opposed to JavaServer Pages, both FreeMarker and Velocity promote the separation of logic from presentation as much as possible, not even offering the possibility of including Java code in the template. We won't go too deeply into the advantages and disadvantages of the two approaches here. In a team where responsibilities are strictly separated and where you have one or more graphical designers and HTML programmers, you might be better off choosing FreeMarker or Velocity because it offers a more HTML-oriented templating language and there's no danger of Java developers putting Java code in templates.

Spring offers support for both FreeMarker-based views as well as views created using Velocity, through the `org.springframework.web.servlet.view.freemarker` and `org.springframework.web.servlet.view.velocity` packages, respectively. We'll cover Velocity and FreeMarker together, as the features Spring offers for integrating them are very similar. Please refer to the section "JavaServer Pages" earlier in this chapter as necessary, as some of the concepts are more thoroughly explained there. Pointers will be offered where necessary.

> Note that both Velocity as well as FreeMarker can be used to do email templating, for example. Using Velocity to send emails is covered in-depth in Chapter 9.

Configuring the View Resolver

As you've seen in the example right at the beginning of this chapter, configuring Spring to work with Velocity is a matter of adding a view resolver to your web application context alongside a so-called *configurer*. To start working with FreeMarker you'd have to do the same thing.

Configuring Velocity

Velocity templates created with the Velocity Template Language (VTL) are rendered using the `VelocityEngine`. Configuring the engine has to be done using the `org.springframework.web.servlet.view.velocity.VelocityConfigurer`. The simplest configuration of them all is the following, where using the `resourceLoaderPath`, you can indicate where your Velocity templates are placed:

```
<bean id="velocityConfigurer"
  class="org.springframework.web.servlet.view.velocity.VelocityConfigurer">
  <property name="resourceLoaderPath"><value>WEB-INF/views/</value></property>
</bean>
```

After adding this bean to your context, the VelocityEngine will be configured for you. As you might know, configuring a VelocityEngine happens using a Properties file. With the Spring VelocityConfigurer, you can specify the properties inline or reference them using the configLocation property. More information on the properties available to configure the engine can be found in the JavaDoc of the org.apache.velocity.runtime.Runtime class and in the Velocity Developers guide (http://jakarta.apache.org/velocity/developer-guide.html#Velocity Configuration Keys and Values).

```
<bean id="velocityConfigurer"
   class="org.springframework.web.servlet.view.velocity.VelocityConfigurer">
   <property name="configLocation"><value>WEB-INF/velocity.properties</property>
</bean>
```

After adding the configurer, you will have to add a ViewResolver to complete the integration of Velocity in your application. Here's how to create the view resolver:

```
<bean id="viewResolver"
   class="org.springframework.web.servlet.view.velocity.VelocityViewResolver">
   <property name="suffix"><value>.vm</value></property>
</bean>
```

This bean indicates that all your Velocity templates end with a .vm extension. Using the resource LoaderPath, we already specified where the view resolver will get its templates from.

Velocity has a built-in capability to provide your templates with so-called *tools* to format dates and numbers, for example. The Velocity documentation includes a detailed section on a set of generic tools that come with the Velocity distribution and how to use them. The documentation can be found at http://jakarta.apache.org/velocity/tools/.

The VelocityViewResolver class provides two properties to enable the inclusion of tools to format dates and numbers. (The tools from the Velocity distribution by default use the default system locale; Spring's LocaleAwareDateTool and LocaleAwareNumber tool use Spring's built-in locale resolution strategies to format dates and numbers using the user's locale.) The following example enables the inclusion of the date tool and number tool in the Velocity context:

```
<bean id="viewResolver">
   class="org.springframework.web.servlet.view.velocity.VelocityViewResolver">
   <property name="numberToolAttribute"><value>numbertool</value></property>
   <property name="dateToolAttribute"><value>datetool</value></property>
</bean>
```

Suppose your model (returned from your controller) includes a date, identified by the key currentDate; you can format it in a Velocity template as follows:

```
$date.format("yyyy-MM-dd", $currentDate)
```

Configuring FreeMarker

FreeMarker configuration closely resembles the configuration of the Velocity engine. Including the org.springframework.web.servlet.view.freemarker.FreeMarkerConfigurer and the org.springframework.web.servlet.view.freemarker.FreeMarkerViewResolver in your application context is all you need to do to add FreeMarker support to your web application:

```
<bean id="freemarkerConfigurer"
  class="org.springframework.web.servlet.view.freemarker.FreeMarkerConfigurer">
  <property name="templateLoaderPath"><value>/WEB-INF/templates/</value></property>
</bean>
```

```
<bean id="viewResolver"
  class="org.springframework.web.servlet.view.freemarker.FreeMarkerViewResolver">
  <property name="suffix"><value>.ftl</value></property>
</bean>
```

Templating tools are often used not only to generate HTML pages displayed in a browser, but also to programmatically send template-based emails. Spring's FreeMarker support features a `FreeMarker ConfigurationFactoryBean`, which allows developers to externalize the `freemarker.template .Configuration` object and use it, for example, for both email templates and templates used in a Web MVC application. In the following example, `TemplateMailSender` is responsible for sending emails using Spring's mail sending infrastructure and using the `freemarker.template.Configuration .getTemplate()` and `freemarker.template.Template.process()` methods. For more information about how to programmatically use the FreeMarker template engine, have a look at the FreeMarker documentation at `www.freemarker.org`.

```
<bean class="example.mail.TemplateMailSender">
  <property name="freemarkerConfiguration">
    <ref bean="freemarkerConfig"/>
  </property>
</bean>

<bean class="viewResolver"
  class="org.springframework.web.servlet.view.freemarker.FreeMarkerViewResolver">
</bean>
```

```
<bean id="freemarkerConfig"
  class="org.sprfr.web.servlet.view.freemarker.FreeMarkerConfigurationFactoryBean">
  <property name="templateLoaderPath"><value>/WEB-INF/templates/</value></property>
  <property name="dateFormat"><value>MM/dd/yyyy</value></property>
  <property name="timeFormat"><value>MM/dd/yyyy HH:mm</value></property>
</bean>
```

You might wonder why we don't need to pass the configuration (the `freemarkerConfig` bean shown earlier) to the configurer. Spring automatically picks up factories creating FreeMarker configurations and processes them for you.

Using the Form Simplification Macros

Spring's support for Velocity and FreeMarker comes with a set of form simplification macros that facilitate the creation of forms and working with Spring's command controllers. The form simplification macros to some extent resemble the custom tags described in the preceding section on JSPs. However, there are a few extras. Both macros and the custom tags simplify the binding of command objects edited or created by form controllers. For more information on concepts such as `BindStatus` and binding, please refer to the section "Creating Forms and Using Custom Tags."

Configuring Your FreeMarker and Velocity Templates to Use Macros

FreeMarker as well as Velocity includes ways to enable macros in specific templates. Spring allows you to specify whether or not to include the macros using the `exposeSpringHelperMacros` property on both the `FreeMarkerView` and the `VelocityView`. For example, using a `ResourceBundleViewResolver`, you can specify for each individual template whether or not to include macros:

```
<bean id="viewResolver"
    class="org.springframework.web.servlet.view.ResourceBundleViewResolver">
    <property name="basename"><value>views</value></property>
</bean>
```

Along with a `views.properties` file in `/WEB-INF/classes`, the preceding view resolver would do the job and turn on form simplification macros for both the `showForm` view and the `confirmReservation` view. The other view won't have them included.

```
showForm.class=org.springframework.web.servlet.view.velocity.VelocityView
showForm.url=show-form.vm
showForm.exposeSpringMacroHelpers=true
```

```
confirmReservation.class=\
    org.springframework.web.servlet.view.freemarker.FreeMarkerView
confirmReservation.url=confirm-reservation.ftl
confirmReservation.exposeSpringMacroHelpers=true
```

```
login.class=org.springframework.web.servlet.view.velocity.VelocityView
login.url=login.vm
login.exposeSpringMacroHelpers=false
```

> As you can see, this example also shows you how to use both Velocity and FreeMarker in one web application. Using the `ResourceBundleViewResolver` (but also using the `XmlViewResolver`) you can use many different types of views at the same time, a requirement often encountered in applications that need to export to Excel or PDF, for example.

Note that by default the `exposeSpringMacroHelpers` property is set to `false`. You can either turn it on per bean, or you can use the notion of parent bean definitions. Consider the following:

```
showForm.class=org.springframework.web.servlet.view.velocity.VelocityView
showForm.url=show-form.vm
```

```
showDetails.parent=showForm
showDetails.url=show-details.vm
```

The view class of the `showDetails` view is now automatically inherited from the `showForm` view. Of course, specifying a parent for every view is somewhat of a hassle, so it's also possible to specify a default parent bean, which all views will inherit:

```
defaultParentView=showForm
showForm.class=org.springframework.web.servlet.view.velocity.VelocityView
showForm.url=show-form.vm
```

It is also possible to indicate that you want form simplification macros to be included in *all* your Velocity- or FreeMarker-based views. Setting the same property (exposeSpringMacroHelpers), but this time on either the VelocityViewResolver or the FreeMarkerViewResolver, is all you need to do; for example:

```
<bean id="viewResolver"
    class="org.springframework.web.servlet.view.velocity.VelocityViewResolver">
    <property name="exposeSpringMacroHelpers"><value>true</value></property>
</bean>
```

Using Velocity or FreeMarker Macros to Create a Form

To illustrate the Velocity and FreeMarker macros, we'll use a Reservation class (as we did with the examples for using the JSP custom tags) for which we will create a form. The end-user will be placing a reservation using the form and the associated form controller.

```
public class Reservation {

    public void setShow(Show show) { ... }
    public Show getShow() { ... }

    public void setDate(Date d) { ... }
    public Date getDate() { ... }

    public void setNumberOfPersons(int p) { ... }
    public int getNumberOfPersons() { ... }
}
```

The form controller is shown here:

```
public class ReservationFormController {

    // non-relevant methods left out

    protected void initBinder(HttpServletRequest request,
        ServletRequestDataBinder binder)
    throws Exception {
        binder.registerCustomEditor(Show.class, new ShowEditor(...));
        binder.registerCustomerEditor(Date.class,
            new CustomDateEditor("yyyy-MM-dd", true);
    }

    protected Map referenceData(HttpServletRequest request)
    throws Exception {
        Map refData = new HashMap();
        Map shows; // lookup shows
        refData.put("shows", shows);
    }

    public ModelAndView onSubmit(Object command) {
        Reservation r = (Reservation)command;
        // do something with the reservation
        return new ModelAndView(getSuccessView());
    }
}
```

As you can see, we're binding a custom editor to be able to transform shows to Strings (usable in an HTML form) and one to transform dates to Strings (and of course the other way around when the user submits the form). The `referenceData` shows the inclusion of a list of shows a user will be able to choose from. The property editors will be used by the macros and the helper class `BindStatus`. The following example shows how to use the `springFormSingleSelect` and `springFormInput` macros. We're passing the `springFormSingleSelect` macro a `Map` of shows (identifiers mapped to show names) bound in the request by the controller where the `springFormInput` macro just needs a path (`command.date`) to generate an input with type text. Using the last parameter of both the `springFormInput` as well as the `springFormSingleSelect` macro, you can pass any additional attributes that will be included in the `input` and the `select` tags respectively.

```
<form method="post">
    Shows:  #springFormSingleSelect("command.show", $shows, "style='width:100px;'")
    <br>
    Date:   #springFormInput("command.date", "style='width:100px;'")
    <br>
    People: #springFormInput("command.numberOfPersons", "")
    <br>
    <input type="submit"/>
</form>
```

We've just shown the Velocity markup while using macros. FreeMarker resembles the Velocity syntax a lot.

The following list shows all macros that are available since Spring 1.1:

❑   `formInput`: Generates a standard input field with type text. The only parameter except the attributes parameter available for all macros is the command path you're binding on.

❑   `formTextArea`: Generates a text area using the command path specified. This macro also allows for passing in attributes such as `style`.

❑   `formSingleSelect`: Generates a select box where the user will be able to select only one of the options available. As always, the first parameter is the command path you're binding on. The second parameter is a `Map` of options that will be included in the drop-down box. The key is used later to bind the property (in our example controller, this would be the show identifier, used by the property editor to look up the correct show). The last parameter again has to include any additional HTML options you wish to pass along.

❑   `formMultiSelect`: Has the same syntax as `formSingleSelect`, except for the fact that this macro generates a drop-down box where the user can select more than just one option.

❑   `formCheckboxes` and `formRadioButton`: Two macros that facilitate the creation of a list of checkboxes or radio buttons. The first parameter is again the command path and the second parameter a `Map` of options to include. Often, you want each checkbox to be placed on a single line in your web page. The third parameter allows you to specify a separator character that will be included after rendering a checkbox or radio button. With the last parameter you can pass additional HTML attributes to the checkboxes and radio buttons.

More information about the Velocity macros can be found online at `www.springframework.org`.

Tiles

Web applications often require a layout including items or elements appearing on many pages. Think of menus or a shopping cart. Almost all major view technologies include a way to decompose the layout of one HTML page into different parts, which can then be included (sequentially) in one main template. But mostly the main template itself describes what to include. When considering a page that requires a menu besides some other content, for example welcoming the user, we could (using JSPs) do the following:

```
<html>
  <head><title>Welcome</title></head>
  <body>
    <jsp:include page="menu.jsp"/>
    <h1>Welcome <c:out value="${user}"/>!</h1>
  </body>
</html>
```

There are a couple of disadvantages to this approach:

❑ We can't parameterize the menu. We might, for example, want to highlight a specific option in the menu but we can't indicate that alongside the include directive.

❑ If the menu.jsp file changed (it might become a static HTML file, maybe a different view technology is used or, even simpler, the location changes), we would need to change a lot of pages including this file.

With respect to the second drawback, you could argue that using a dynamic inclusion (`<jsp:include page="${menu}"/>`) we could achieve what we want, but then we have to put the menu attribute in our model somehow, which might involve extra work being done in our controller. Spring has an elegant solution for this problem. Using static attributes, you can dynamically include additional data in your model, independently from the controller.

A somewhat more advanced solution to the problem is Struts Tiles, a template-centric framework. Struts Tiles involves tile definition defined in an XML file together with templates defined in JavaServer Pages or the Velocity Template Language. Here, think of a template as a collection of rectangles on a web page where each box is a tile. It's best to explain things with an example. We'll first create our menu in a file called menu.jsp:

```
<tiles:importAttribute name="highlighted"/>

<a href="home.html"
  <c:if test="${highlighted == 'home'}">class="highlighted"</c:if>>
  Home
</a>
  |
<a href="contact.html"
  <c:if test="${highlighted == 'contact'}">class="highlighted"</c:if>>
  Contact
</a>
```

You can see we've implemented our menu now using a `highlighted` attributed that represents either the home menu item or the contact menu item (we'll discuss the `importAttribute` tag later in this chapter). Using JSTL, we decide what item should be highlighted.

Next, let's implement our template (`template.jsp`):

```
<html>
  <head><title><tiles:put name="title"/></title></head>
  <body>
    <tiles:insert name="menu"/>

    <tiles:insert name="content"/>
  </body>
</html>
```

As you can see, using the `tiles:insert` tag and the `tiles:put` tag, we're adding a title, a menu, and a piece called `content` to the page. The magic involved here is a collection of *tiles definitions*, defined in an external XML file as shown here:

```
<!DOCTYPE tiles-definitions PUBLIC
  "-//Apache Software Foundation//DTD Tiles Configuration 1.1//EN"
  "http://jakarta.apache.org/struts/dtds/tiles-config_1_1.dtd">

<tiles-definitions>

  <definition name="welcome" page="/WEB-INF/jsp/template.jsp">
    <put name="title" value="Welcome" type="string"/>
    <put name="menu" value="menu-home" type="definition"/>
    <put name="content" value="/WEB-INF/jsp/content.jsp" type="page"/>
  </definition>

  <definition name="menu-home" page="/WEB-INF/jsp/menu.jsp">
    <put name="highlighted" value="home"/>
  </definition>

  <definition mame="menu-contact" extends="menu-home">
    <put name="highlighted" value="contact"/>
  </definition>

</tiles-definitions>
```

In the template JSP, you saw that we're including something called menu and something called content. As you might have noticed, those things are tiles and the tiles definitions file shown defines them. When including `<tiles:insert name="menu"/>` in our JSP, we're actually including the tile named menu-home because that's the tile we've linked to when defining the tile called `welcome`. As you can see, we've separated the definition of our templates from the actual implementation and we can also parameterize them by extending already defined tiles and changing attributes of those tiles.

Tiles comes with good documentation so we won't go into more detail on the Tiles definition language and the way to extend, parameterize, and configure tiles. Instead, please refer to the Struts user guide and the specific section on Tiles (`http://struts.apache.org/userGuide/building_view.html#includes`).

Spring's integration with Tiles consists of a Tiles configuration utility and two Tiles view implementations. The concept of configurers is also used with Spring's support for Velocity and FreeMarker. A configurer typically loads configuration files and sets up the technology Spring integrates with.

> Classes such as the `TilesConfigurer` and the `VelocityConfigurer` implement an `org.springframework.beans.factory.InitializingBean`. All classes implementing this interface and registered in an `ApplicationContext` will automatically be picked up while loading the context, to allow for initialization to be done.

In the case of Tiles, the configurer loads the definition files and sets up a `TilesDefinitionFactory`, to be used by the `TilesView` and the `TilesJstlView`. The latter is the view class you will have to use for Tiles-based views.

```
<bean class="org.springframework.web.servlet.view.tiles.TilesConfigurer">
  <property name="definitions">
    <list>
      <value>/WEB-INF/definitions/definitions.xml</value>
    </list>
  </property>
</bean>

<bean class="org.springframework.web.servlet.view.InternalResourceViewResolver">
  <property name="viewClass">
    <value>org.springframework.web.servlet.view.tiles.TilesJstlView</value>
  </property>
</bean>
```

The preceding example shows how to wire up a definitions file in `/WEB-INF/definitions` and how to use the `TilesJstlView` to render Tiles-based views. When not in need of JSTL (although we can't imagine why someone would ever *not* include JSTL in his JSPs), you can also use the `TilesView`, which doesn't include the localization context for use by JSTL formatting tags.

To render a Tiles view, the only thing you have to do is return the tile definition name from your controller:

```
protected ModelAndView handleRequestInternal(
  HttpServletRequest request, HttpServletResponse response) throws Exception {\
  return new ModelAndView("welcome");
}
```

The Tiles view will automatically search for a definition named `welcome` and render it. When the welcome definition cannot be found, a `ServletException` will be thrown. Using a `HandlerException Resolver`, you let Spring resolve this to a view and render an appropriate response to the client.

> There are many ways to design and set up a request-driven web application using a template structure. Another elegant solution is SiteMesh, which is based on the Decorator pattern. We strongly recommend that you check out SiteMesh (www.opensymphony.com/sitemesh) as well when choosing between technologies to include templates in your application. Although integrating SiteMesh is not necessary (it's *really* easy to set it up), integration classes *are* available. There is a custom SiteMesh factory and Spring-compatible decorators. More information on how to integrate SiteMesh with Spring can be found at http://wiki.opensymphony.com/display/SM/Integration+with+Spring.

Views Based on XML and XSLT

With the increasing use of XML as an encoding standard to transfer business-related data with, we often need to transform XML to HTML using the *eXtensible Stylesheet Language* (*XSL*). Spring offers a view implementation taking away the need to set up an XSLT transformer yourself, leaving you with only one task: the creation of the source for the transformer, an `org.w3c.dom` document. This is achieved through the use of an abstract method, via the *Template Method* design pattern.

The following example shows how to use Spring `AbstractXsltView` to transform an XML file with a Spring bean definition to a simple HTML page:

```
public void BeansView extends AbstractXsltView {

  protected Node createDomNode(
    Map model, String root,
    HttpServletRequest request, HttpServletResponse response)
  throws Exception {

    // get resource from model
    Resource resource = (Resource)model.get("resource");

    // create document builder
    DocumentBuilderFactory factory = DocumentBuilderFactory.newInstance();
    DocumentBuilder docBuilder = factory.newDocumentBuilder();
    docBuilder.setEntityResolver(new BeansDtdResolver());

    // get the resource
    InputStream is = resource.getInputStream();
    try {
      Document doc = docBuilder.parse(is);
    } finally {
      is.close();
    }
    return doc;
  }
}
```

The `AbstractXsltView` has three properties that you can use to customize its behavior. The view needs a style sheet to transform the XML document with. (If you don't specify a style sheet, the view will throw an exception telling you it's incorrectly configured.) The second is a URI resolver you might need to register to resolve URIs. No URI resolver will be registered if you do not specify it. URI resolvers are used in `xsl:include` and `xsl:import` tags included in your XSL style sheet. (Most XSLT libraries such as Saxon provide concrete `URIResolver` implementations, and there are also resolvers that use an XML database to look up included resources.) The last property is a `String` identifying the root in the document. This root String is passed to the `createDomNode()` method as implemented in the preceding example. It gives the view a bit of flexibility, allowing you to specify which part of an XML document you want to transform. (You will have to take care of returning the node related to the root property yourself, by the way.) The root property isn't used in this example:

```
<bean class="org.springframework.web.servlet.view.BeanNameViewResolver"/>
```

```
<bean name="beansView" class="org.springframework.prospring.view.xsl.BeansView">
  <property name="stylesheetLocation"><value>/WEB-INF/beans.xsl</value></property>
```

```
    </bean>

    <bean name="contextController"
      class="org.springframework.prospring.controller.ShowContextController"/>
```

The last thing to do is implement a controller. The example controller retrieves a Spring `Application Context` file (taken from the virtual filename in the user's request), loads it, and adds it to the model. Using this controller, `http://host.com/path/applicationContext.xml` will result in the `application Context.xml` file from `/WEB-INF` being loaded and added to the model:

```java
public class ShowContextController extends AbstractController {

  protected ModelAndView handleRequestInternal(
    HttpServlerRequest request, HttpServletResponse response)
  throws Exception {

    // get the filename:
    String uri = request.getPathInfo();
    String filename = uri.substring(0, uri.lastIndexOf("."));

    Resource res = getWebApplicationContext().getResource(res);
    if (!res.exists()) {
      throw new FileNotFoundException(
        "ApplicationContext '" + filename + "' does not exist");
    }
    ModelAndView mav = new ModelAndView("beansView", "resource", res);
  }
}
```

We can now map the `ShowContextController` using a `SimpleUrlHandlerMapping` to present all application contexts available to the user, using a simple XSL style sheet.

```xml
<bean class="org.springframework.web.servlet.handler.SimpleUrlHandlerMapping">
  <property name="urlMap">
    <map>
      <entry key="/**/*.xml"><ref bean="contextController"/></entry>
    </map>
  </property>
</bean>
```

Remember that catching exceptions (such as the `FileNotFoundException` thrown in the preceding example) can be resolved to an appropriate view by registering a `HandlerExceptionResolver` in your web application context.

Excel and Other Document-Based Views

We've seen how to use FreeMarker, Velocity, and JavaServer Pages to render HTML-based views. However, web applications oftentimes not only require web pages, but also document-based views, such as PDF documents or reports in Excel format. While designing Spring, it was clear that it should not be necessary to make any changes to a controller to switch between an HTML-based view and, for example, a view that generates PDF files. The solution should be the cleanest possible implementation of the MVC architectural pattern.

Generating an Excel File from Our List of Shows

One of the controllers in our application allows the user to select a show from a list. The controller creates a `ModelAndView` and adds a list of shows to the model. The following example shows how to create an Excel file that lists all shows, instead of an HTML page. Excel is widely used in many industries, including the financial industry.

The technology used here is Jakarta POI (`http://jakarta.apache.org/poi`), one of the Java APIs used to generate Excel files. Another API is `jExcelApi`, available from `www.jexcel.org`. Both integrate well with Spring, through the `org.springframework.web.servlet.view.document` `.AbstractPoiExcelView` and `org.springframework.web.servlet.view.document` `.AbstractJExcelView`, respectively. Both view classes are based on the Template pattern and require you only to subclass the Spring class and implement the code that generates the actual Excel content. The view class allows for the loading of templates, and if no template is specified (using the `url` property), a new and empty workbook is created for you.

```
public class ListShowsView extends AbstractExcelView {

  public void buildExcelDocument(
    Map model, HSSFWorkbook wb,
    HttpServletRequest request, HttpServletResponse response)
  throws Exception {

    HSSFSheet sheet = wb.createSheet("shows");
    HSSFCell titleCell = getCell(0, 0);
    setText(titleCell, "All shows");

    List shows = (List)model.get("shows");
    Iterator it = shows.iterator();

    for (int i = 0; it.hasNext(); i++) {
      Show show = (Show)it.next();
      HSSFCell nameCell = getCell(sheet, i +2, 0) {
      setText(nameCell, show.getName());
      setText(nameCell, show.getGenre().getName());
    }
  }
}
```

As you can see, it's not so difficult to generate an Excel document while reusing the same controller we're using to present the user with an HTML page listing all shows. The only thing left to do is the wiring up of the view and the view resolver. We can, for example, include the view in our `views` `.properties` file mentioned alongside a `ResourceBundleViewResolver`.

```
### boxoffice-servlet.xml

<bean class="org.springframework.web.servlet.view.ResourceBundleViewResolver">
  <property name="basename"><value>views</value></property>
</bean>

### /WEB-INF/classes/views.properties
listShows.class=org.springframework.prospring.web.view.excel.ListShowsView
```

Returning `listShows` as the view name from your controller is all you need to do to trigger the `ListShowsView`.

> Be careful when deciding on an API to use for your Excel views. Jakarta POI has the most active user community, but when you need to include images in your Excel files, jExcelApi is your only option at the time of this writing. Of course, Spring MVC decouples your controllers and models from the particular view generation library you choose in any case.

Using a Template as a Basis for Your Excel File

Both the `AbstractJExcelView` and the `AbstractExcelView` (where the latter uses Jakarta POI and the former jExcelApi) support the loading of templates. Using templates, you can let someone else design an Excel template including formulas and images while you're filling in the live data. By setting the `url` property on the view class, Spring will load the template using Spring's `Resource` classes. While including a template in a web application context, Spring will search in your `/WEB-INF` directory. The template mechanism supports localization, based on the locale, resolved by the `LocaleResolver` mentioned in your context. Last but not least, Spring will itself append `.xls` to the URL you're providing. This means that using the following example, users with an English locale will get the template from `/WEB-INF/example_en.xls` whereas Dutch users will be presented with an Excel file filled from the template located in `/WEB-INF/example_nl.xls`.

```
listShows.class=org.springframework.prospring.web.view.excel.ListShowsView
listShows.url=example
```

When using templates, nothing changes in the way you fill your Excel file: The template is loaded and will be passed along with the model and the servlet request and response in the `buildExcelDocument()` method.

Other Document-Based Views

Besides the `AbstractExcelView` and the `AbstractJExcelView`, Spring also features two view classes to generate PDF files. The first resembles the Excel view classes a lot, in the sense that you'll have to create your PDF file programmatically, using iText. The second uses Apache FOP. More information about generating PDF files can be found online in the reference manual.

Using a HandlerInterceptor to Distinguish Between HTML and Excel

A neat technique to allow the user to specify what format he likes to have his results displayed in is to use a `HandlerInterceptor` to change the view name based on an input argument provided by the user. Bear with us while we explain this through the use of an example.

First, we're going to provide the user with a search page where she can enter a search query, based on which a list of shows will be retrieved. We'll also provide the user with two options to choose from, output in Excel or using HTML.

```
Search for:
  <input type="text" name="query"><br>
Output in:
```

```
     <input type="radio name="format" value="xls"/>Excel or
     <input type="radio" name="format" value="html"/>Html<br>
```

```
<input type="submit"/>
```

Our controller will search for shows matching the search query somehow and return the `ModelAndView`.

```
protected ModelAndView handleRequestInternal(
   HttpServletRequest req, HttpServletResponse response {

   String query = RequestUtils.getRequiredStringParameter("query");
   List shows; // retrieve shows matching the query

   ModelAndView mav = new ModelAndView("listshows", "shows", shows);
   return mav;
}
```

> `org.springframework.web.bind.RequestUtils` **is a convenience class that
> includes methods to retrieve parameters of different primitive types. The**
> `getRequired*` **methods all throw a** `ServletRequestBindingException` **if the
> parameter does not exist in the request.**

As you can see, the view name we're returning is `listshows`. The next thing we're going to do is attach a `HandlerInterceptor` to the `UrlHandlerMapping` and let it `postHandle()` the request:

```
public class OutputFormatModificationInterceptor
extends HandlerInterceptorAdapter {

   private String parameter;
   private String defaultSuffix = "";
   private Properties suffices;

   // setters and getters omitted

   public void postHandler(
      HttpServletRequest request, HttpServletResponse response,
      Object handler, ModelAndView mav) throws Exception {

      String format = request.getParameter("parameter");
      String suffix = suffices.getProperty(format);
      // modify view name if exists
      if (suffix != null) {
        mav.setViewName(mav.getViewName() + suffix);
      } else {
        mav.setViewName(mav.getViewName() + defaultSuffix);
      }
   }
}
```

When wiring it up as follows, all requests to the controller with the format parameter set to `xls` will output using the Excel view we've created. The other requests will result in an HTML page.

```
<bean class="org.springframework.web.servlet.handler.BeanNameUrlHandlerMapping">
  <property name="interceptors">
    <list>
      <ref bean="formatInterceptor"/>
    </list>
  </property>
</bean>

<bean id="formatInterceptor"
  class="org.springframework.prospring.web.OutputFormatModificationInterceptor">
  <property name="suffices">
    <props>
      <entry key="xls">-xls</entry>
      <entry key="html">-html</entry>
    </props>
  </property>

  <property name="parameter"><value>format</value></property>
  <property name="defaultSuffix"><value>-html</value></property>
</bean>

<bean name="/listShows.action"
  class="org.springframework.prospring.web.controller.ListShowsController">
  ...
</bean>
```

Of course we still need to define our views. We'll use a `ResourceBundleViewResolver` and a `views.properties` (in `/WEB-INF/classes`) file again:

```
listShows-html.class=org.springframework.web.servlet.view.JstlView
listShows-html.url=/WEB-INF/jsp/listShows.jsp

listShows-xls.class=org.springframework.prospring.web.view.document.ListShowsView
listShows-xls.url=showListingTemplate
```

> **Note that** `ResourceBundleViewResolver` **supports localization, so you can even distinguish between views in different languages.**

Implementing Custom Views

Although Spring provides view classes and view resolvers for a variety of view technologies, you might run into a situation where you need to implement a custom view. One of the authors once came across a requirement where he needed to implement an ultra-high performance application, largely based on XML. Instead of implementing an `XSLTView` using a style sheet, he chose to implement a new view, based on `SAXHandlers` that rendered the (simple) views. Because the `SAXHandlers` could stream the HTML back to the client, it greatly improved the performance of the application.

View and AbstractView

Implementing a custom view begins with implementing the `org.springframework.web.servlet.View` interface. The view interface specified just one method:

```
void render(Map model, HttpServletRequest request, HttpServletResponse response)
throws Exception;
```

The `Map` is the model returned from the controller. Because Spring Web MVC is a web-oriented framework, and clients will always access your controllers with an HTTP client (such as a browser), rendering the view will be a bit difficult if we're not passing along the `HttpServletRequest` and the `HttpServletResponse`.

For convenience purposes, Spring implements an `AbstractView` class, offering some common functionality shared by all view implementations. This includes the following:

❑ `requestContextAttribute` property, when there is a need to expose the Spring `Request Context` object. By default this is null, which will result in no `RequestContext` being bound to the request.

❑ `staticAttributesMap` property and `staticAttributesCSV` setter (parsing static attributes into the `staticAttributesMap`), allowing users to specify attributes that will be bound to the request independently of the model.

❑ `contentType` property, to specify the content type of the view. In many cases this will be `text/html`, but in the case of the `AbstractPDFView`, it's set to `application/pdf`. View implementations typically set this property in a hard-coded fashion (still allowing developers to override it if needed).

❑ Overridden `render()` method, taking care of the creation of the `RequestContext`, the binding of the static attributes to the request, and the calling of the Template Method `renderMerged OutputModel()`.

❑ Extension of `WebApplicationObjectSupport`, offering access to the `WebApplicationContext`.

When implementing a custom view, you can either extend `AbstractView` or `AbstractUrlView`, where the latter adds a `url` property to consistently model URL-based views (such as `RedirectView` or the `InternalResourceView`).

Implementing a View Generating XML from a Data Object

The following example shows how to implement a view that outputs Hibernate XML generated by the Hibernate `Databinder` (www.hibernate.org/hib_docs/api/net/sf/hibernate/Databinder.html). We're using the XMLDatabinder in this case, which unfortunately requires a `SessionFactory`.

```
public class HibernateDataView extends AbstractView {

    /** needed by Hibernate Databinder */
    private SessionFactory sessionFactory;
    /** transformer */
    private Transformer transformer;
    /** model attribute to use (if null, all objects will be bound and output) */
    private String modelAttribute;

    public void setSessionFactory(SessionFactory sessionFactory() {
```

```
      this.sessionFactory = sessionFactory;
    }

    public void setModelAttribute(String modelAttribute) {
      this.modelAttribute = modelAttribute;
    }

    protected void initApplicationContext()
    throws Exception {
      TransformerFactory factory = TransformerFactory.newInstance();
      this.transformer = factory.newTransformer();
    }

    protected void renderMergedOutputModel(Map model,
      HttpServletRequest request, HttpServletResponse response)
    throws Exception {

      XMLDatabinder dataBinder = new XMLDatabinder(this.sessionFactory);
      dataBinder.initializeLazy(false);
      if (modelAttribute != null) {
        dataBinder.bind(model.get(modelAttribute));
      }
      else {
        Iterator it = model.values().iterator();
        while (it.hasNext()) {
          dataBinder.bind(it.next());
        }
      }

      PrintWriter writer = response.getWriter();
      writer.write(dataBinder.toGenericXML());
      writer.close();
    }
  }
```

Using a `ResourceBundleViewResolver` (or any other view resolver), we can now wire up and use our newly created `HibernateDataView` to render Hibernate-persisted objects to our users:

```xml
<bean id="hibernateShowView"
  class="org.springframework.prospring.view.HibernateDataView">
  <property name="modelAttribute"><value>show</value></property>
</bean>
```

If, in a controller, we're returning a `ModelAndView`, as shown in the following code, the user will be presented with an XML representation of the `Show` loaded by our data-access object.

```
    private ShowDao showDao;

    protected ModelAndView handleRequestInternal(
      HttpServletRequest request, HttpServletResponse response)
    throws Exception {
      Long id = WebUtils.getRequiredLongParameter("id");
      Show show = showDao.loadShow(id);
      return new ModelAndView("hibernateShowView", "show", show);
    }
```

> Hibernate's Databinder infrastructure can be used to generate XML for any object registering with the Hibernate **SessionFactory**. In combination with an XSL style sheet, you can use this to generate PDFs, for example, using Apache FOP.

Considerations When Implementing Custom Views

Many of Spring's view resolvers include a caching facility. Spring maintains an internal cache of logical view names mapped to `View` instances. If possible, design your view implementation to be threadsafe in order to make it reusable across more than just one request. If this is not possible, you can disable caching by setting the `cache` property of the view resolver to `false` (caching of views is available only on the `AbstractCachingViewResolver` and its subclasses).

Before embarking on the implementation of your own custom view, check for already existing implementations. It's very likely that the team that created the view technology can implement a Spring view class in no time, if they haven't done this already.

Summary

In this chapter, we've reviewed some of Spring's integration facilities you can use when developing the front-end of a web application using Spring MVC. One of the important things to keep in mind when developing an application that might, in the future, require more than just one view technology is to design your controllers in such a way that they don't include any view-dependent elements. Tie your views to your controller using the logical view name only, available in the `ModelAndView` class. View resolvers will determine what view will be used to render the model returned from the controller. This separation allows for application including several view technologies.

We've also seen why Spring chose a model implementation that has been completely decoupled from the `HttpServletRequest`: to allow seamless integration of view technologies such as the document-based PDF and Excel views that are not aware of the Servlet API. This clean decoupling of model and controller from view is one of the key strengths of Spring MVC.

The last thing we've reviewed is how to implement your own view. Although you will hardly ever need this (Spring integrated with numerous view technologies out-of-the-box), it's good to know that it's possible.

The next chapter will focus on integrating other MVC and web-oriented frameworks with Spring, such as Struts, WebWork, Tapestry, and JSF. Spring MVC is a flexible and lightweight solution for building request-driven web applications, but in some situations, there might be an existing investment in another web framework such as Struts. Sometimes it's better to be pragmatic about what solution to use. Leaving your front-end alone and refactoring your backend infrastructure to use Spring is a perfect way to start modernizing your application.

Integrating with Other Web Frameworks

In the previous two chapters you've learned about Spring's MVC framework. Spring MVC is a flexible MVC framework with the benefit of complete integration with Spring's Dependency Injection features.

In general, Spring doesn't try to lock you in to one specific solution. For example, there are integration facilities for several data access technologies; Spring can expose your business objects via Hessian, Burlap, and HttpInvokers but also with RMI and JAX-RPC. The same holds for web application frameworks. Spring aims to give you freedom to choose the technology you think is best for your requirements.

This chapter focuses on ways to integrate with existing applications and with popular Web MVC frameworks. You will learn how to integrate with front-ends based on Struts, WebWork, Tapestry, and JSF (JavaServer Faces), four of the most popular incarnations of the MVC pattern applied to web applications.

We'll start with a brief conceptual introduction to these four frameworks. We'll suggest guidelines to help you choose between the solutions available (including Spring MVC). Next, we'll explore techniques to integrate web applications with a Spring middle tier. We'll conclude by giving examples of how to integrate each of the four frameworks into a Spring application.

Considerations When Choosing an MVC Framework

While Spring provides its own Web MVC framework, several reasons might force you to use a different web application framework. For example, your team might have an existing investment in another framework. We believe the learning curve for Spring Web MVC is less steep than some of the other frameworks, partly because it reuses Spring's Dependency Injection features. However, adopting a new framework will always have a cost. Alternatively, you might be working on an existing application, built with a particular MVC framework. Often when doing an overhaul of such an application, there's no time to refactor each and every layer. Bottlenecks and problems more often than not occur in the backend, and when you're choosing Spring to facilitate refactoring, it may be prudent to keep the MVC layer in place and integrate it with a newly created Spring-based backend. With respect to JSF: This relatively new technology uses an entirely different approach and resembles ASP.NET in many respects.

Comparing the Traditional Web MVC Frameworks

In Chapter 12, we discussed the requirements of a successful MVC framework. Key values we identified included non-intrusiveness, flexibility, testability, and being agnostic with respect to view technologies. It's important to consider how frameworks meet these requirements in the following areas:

❏ Form submission is vital to most web applications. Data from a form on an HTML page, posted by the user, is accessible via the `HttpServletRequest`. Most MVC frameworks allow for transformation of the parameters in the request to a Java object (where, for example, `postForm.html?name=Spring` will result in a `setName("Spring")` calls on a preconfigured form object). The process of doing so is called *data binding*. To what extent data binding is supported and whether or not transformation of primitives to objects is implemented by the framework of your choice will significantly influence the way you will be working with it and how efficiently you can build pages containing forms.

❏ Validation is done by every framework we discuss here. It's important to know how the framework you're choosing implements validation. Ideally, the validation mechanism shouldn't be tied to the Servlet API; validation of domain objects can just as well be part of the service layer. If the validation mechanism is tied to the Servlet API, you can't move it to a Servlet-independent service layer.

❏ In many projects — especially for large projects — specialist HTML developers create the layout of the website and even individual pages. Some HTML developers will know JSP; some will know only Velocity or XSLT; many lack programming skills altogether, yet have valuable knowledge of HTML layout issues. In some projects, it might be necessary to create Excel files or PDF documents. Those documents are just as much views as HTML pages are. Thus it's important not only to design for a clean separation between Java code and presentation elements, but for a web application framework to support more than one view technology, ideally in a fully transparent fashion independent of how your controllers will be delivering the actual input for the view. In other words, typically a framework that best supports the *Model-View-Controller* patterns is preferred.

❏ Controllers are the components handling the user's actions. Two things are important about the way a framework supports controllers:

❏ To what level the controllers can be tested in isolation. Controllers are excellent candidates for being unit-tested; some frameworks, however, don't allow this because it's not possible to use the controllers without the framework itself.

❏ Web applications often include some aspect-oriented behavior, which you don't want to embed in each and every controller. Using web interceptors, you can separate those things from your controllers. If your framework supports interceptors, you will see that it increases the efficiency of the development of your web application.

The following sections discuss four of the most popular MVC frameworks — WebWork, Struts, Spring MVC, and JSF — in the context of these criteria.

Struts is one of the older MVC frameworks. It has been available since late 2000 and has been the de facto standard for building Web MVC applications since 2002. Struts is hosted by Apache and can be found at `http://struts.apache.org`. As of January 2005, the current Struts 1.2.*x* series can be considered relatively stable and not likely to change significantly. Work on Struts 2.0, codenamed "Shale," has been announced. This line of the codebase is still very much in the preliminary planning stages, and not much is known about it other than the fact that it will probably not be backward compatible with Struts 1.*x*, but rather will be primarily a layer meant to handle workflow around base UI handled by JSF.

WebWork is hosted by Open Symphony. Version 2 is based on XWork, a library implementing the command pattern. WebWork actions (controllers) are not tied to the Servlet API, greatly increasing testability. WebWork is a relative newcomer but widely considered to be one of the better alternatives to Struts. WebWork can be found at `www.opensymphony.com/webwork`.

Tapestry is an Apache Jakarta project. Like JSF, Tapestry uses a more component-oriented, event-driven approach than Spring MVC, Struts, or WebWork, and works at a higher level of abstraction in terms of mapping web UI elements to Java code. While Tapestry is not as well known as Struts or perhaps even Spring MVC, it can be considered mature, and is in use in a number of production applications. As of January 2005, Tapestry 3.0 is the current version, with work on the next major release, to be called 3.1 or 4.0, at a relatively advanced stage. Tapestry can be found at `http://jakarta.apache.org/tapestry`.

JSF is an emerging technology based on specification by Sun. Compared to Spring MVC, Struts, and WebWork, it has a more component-oriented, event-driven approach and a much higher level of abstraction. While a promising technology, there are some drawbacks, including its immaturity, which we'll discuss later in this chapter. JSF is a specification, with potentially multiple implementations. The best known are the Reference Implementation created as part of the specification process, and MyFaces, available at `www.myfaces.org`.

Data Binding and Validation

Editing data is an often seen use case in web applications. All of the frameworks under discussion offer their own way of binding request parameters to objects created on the server. To what extent each framework facilitates data binding is covered in this section.

WebWork

WebWork has advanced features for working with request parameters and binding:

❑ WebWork can bind form data to objects in one of two ways: in a completely command-oriented fashion, where the action (controller) represents both the data as well as the behavior (it implements the GoF command pattern). You also have the option to use a `ModelDriven` action, which binds data to a separate object (for example your domain model, implemented as Hibernate objects).

❑ WebWork uses OGNL to convert primitives to objects (for example `'2004-10-12'` to a `java.util.Date` object). Predefined converters are available, and implementing your own converter for a custom type is not difficult. Although OGNL is not a standard of any sort, it's easy to learn and has the same characteristics as, for example, the Expression Language from JSP 2.0. However, compared to the latter, it's generally more advanced, with less limitations, and as such more usable in practice. Conversion errors are treated in a consistent manner. The XWork `ActionContext` contains a `conversionErrors` map, and using a `ConversionErrorFieldValidator` you can display errors to the user. Customization of the error messages is possible using i18n.

❑ Validation can be done in one of two ways: either by implementing your own `validate()` method where you programmatically validate the input of a user, or by using XWork's more sophisticated validation framework. The latter allows for validation contexts with which you can validate a certain object in different ways, depending on the context you've specified. This is an advanced feature that will help in more complex applications. The XWork validation framework is partly configured in XML.

Struts

Struts uses `ActionForms` to implement data binding. It integrates tightly with the Commons Validator, which offers you advanced XML-based validation.

❑ Data binding with Struts is done using `ActionForms`. For every form, you have to extend the concrete `ActionForm` class, which prevents you from reusing your domain model and working with it directly in your HTML forms. This requirement is widely considered to be one of the major design flaws in Struts. After the form data is transported to an `ActionForm` object, you have to extract it yourself and modify your domain model accordingly — an extra step that isn't required by WebWork and Spring. Dynamic forms (introduced in Struts 1.1) make the whole data binding process less painful, but you still have to extend a concrete class.

❑ Struts `ActionForms` are supposed to be JavaBeans to convert expressions to setters and getters. They use almost the same expression language as Spring does: `user.name`, for example, will result in `getUser().setName("value")`. Indexed properties, however, are treated differently: `user[2]` will result in `getUser(2)`, `setUser(2, "value")` respectively.

❑ Transformation of user input to objects other than primitives or Strings is not supported by Struts. Even though Struts allows you to parse integers and such, when parsing fails, there is no standard mechanism for informing the user about parsing errors. Although Transformation of objects other than Strings or primitives can be done in the transformation code you have to implement anyway (because of the `ActionForm`), it's still a major shortcoming. Struts does have support for binding files to `ActionForms` (as `FormFile` objects), which means uploading files is easy.

❑ Validation in Struts is done using Commons Validator (`http://jakarta.apache.org/commons/validator`), an XML-based declarative approach to validating `ActionForms`. Commons Validator is the most mature validation framework available in the open source community. This, however, tells us more about the state of validation in general than about the quality of the Commons Validator. We feel that configuring the Commons Validator with the XML format provided is awkward and unintuitive.

Spring MVC

Spring's data binding and validation is quite similar to WebWork's features. Furthermore, Spring has a pluggable validation mechanism, based on the Spring `Validator` interface.

❑ Data binding in Spring is done in a similar fashion as WebWork. Spring has a wide variety of controllers and supports the WebWork command-oriented way of development as well. Indexed properties are supported (so you will be able to bind a list of objects to your domain model), as are nested properties. Just as with WebWork, with Spring it's possible to reuse your domain model in your entire application and seamlessly bind user input to it.

❑ Transformation of user input to objects (note the previous example: transforming `2004-10-12` to an appropriate `java.util.Date` object) is supported via the use of the `PropertyEditor` infrastructure from the JavaBeans standard. There are a lot of property editors available with the

Spring distribution, and building your own custom property editors is easy enough. As opposed to Struts, conversion errors are handled in a consistent, easy manner.

❑ Conversion errors that occur during the transformation of properties are treated in a consistent manner. The `DataBinder` treats them as any other validation errors, adding error messages to the `Errors` class. Standard i18n keys are provided, which you can easily customize. Think of a `NumberFormatException` thrown after parsing a number or some other exception being thrown if the invocation of a setter failed or in case the setter simply didn't exist (the `DataBinder` JavaDocs explain all this in more detail).

❑ Validation in Spring is done using the `org.springframework.validation.Validator` interface. Spring does not provide a concrete validation implementation. There are, however, utility classes available to do programmatic validation (`org.springframework.validation.ValidationUtils`). The community has already implemented validator classes that integrate with Commons Validator. A rule-based validation framework is also on its way.

Tapestry

Tapestry also provides sophisticated data binding support.

❑ Tapestry data binding works at a relatively high level of abstraction, handled at the component level. In its simplest form, a component such as a `TextField`, in the page template, will specify an OGNL expression that is the binding path for the data. This may be a relatively simple, nested JavaBean access, but also include arbitrary method calls as also allowed by OGNL. The binding path is also the path used to obtain the data for display when the page is output.

❑ Conversion of types is usually handled by the component itself. For example, the `DatePicker` component produces a drop-down calendar on the web page and will transparently handle binding the result of the user selection to a `java.util.Date` property as specified via a property path. There are components for most HTML elements, for example checkboxes (the latter component binding to a Boolean property). There is no built-in mechanism (such as Spring MVC's registration of `PropertyEditors`) to handle binding text fields to arbitrary user-specific types. Because OGNL allows arbitrary method calls, it is fairly simple for this use case to call custom setter methods that perform conversion, although at the disadvantage of being able to transparently use existing domain objects.

❑ Validation is handled by using validator objects of type `IValidator`. For each page component that needs to be validated, another component of type `ValidField` is defined and essentially exists to associate the page component with a particular validator instance, and to handle rendering. A related object with page scope, called a *Validation Delegate,* coordinates all the validation for the entire page. Validator exists for common types, such as Strings, Numbers, Email addresses, and Dates. They can check for common validity aspects such as input not being empty or null, the minimum size, and so on, and also aspects specific to the type, as in the case of the email validator, which checks whether the input is a valid email address or not. Additionally, there is a regex validator which will validate based on a regular expression pattern. Client-side JavaScript validation code can be set to be automatically generated. If used, it will work in addition to the server-side code. Server-side validation errors get collected by the Validation Delegate, to be displayed in a consistent fashion.

❑ There is no concept of a pluggable validation object such as Spring's `Validator`, meant to validate the content of the entire page or a domain object backing the page, although it's easy to add additional custom Java code to a page lifecycle method to do additional validation, which can combine any errors with those produced by field level validation.

JavaServer Faces

❏ JSF takes a different approach to binding data. With JavaServer Faces, binding can be done to a JSF-managed bean (sometimes also called code-behind file—similar to the ASP.NET code-behind page). A slightly modified version of the JSTL Expression Language is used. Instead of writing `${user.name}` with the JSF Expression Language (JSF EL), you will have to write `#{user.name}` where `user` has to be a JSF-managed bean and `name` represents the name property.

❏ Conversion of types in JSF can be done by using the `Converter` interface. JSF delivers converters for most standard types. The `Converter` interface much resembles the `java.beans.PropertyEditor` interface. The former, however, is tailored for use within JavaServer Faces. Conversion methods can also be directly implemented in your code-behind file (backing bean).

❏ Validation of user input is done by built-in validation support that is easily extensible by adding custom `Validator` implementations. This resembles Spring's validation support except for one thing: JSF positions validation *before* the user input is converted and bound to the (domain) model whereas Spring first binds the data and then calls any validator available. This results in Spring validators being usable in the middle tier as well, whereas JSF validators are tied to the Faces API and can be used only in the front-end (more on the JSF lifecycle can be found later in this chapter).

❏ Display of validation and conversion errors is standardized through the `FacesMessage` type and the `ValidatorException` and `ConverterException`, respectively. `FacesMessages` are typically associated with a specific component in the view. JavaServer Faces supports internationalization of `FacesMessages` through the `Application.getMessageBundle(String)` method.

Dealing with the Presentation Layer

Spring offers tag libraries, as we discussed in Chapter 13. WebWork and Struts both offer convenient tag libraries as well. We'll also compare the frameworks based on which view technologies they integrate with.

WebWork

❏ Support is offered for Velocity, FreeMarker, and JavaServer Pages. Of course the latter is natively supported by Servlet containers. For Velocity and FreeMarker, you will have to add a custom WebWork servlet.

❏ Just as binding of data from forms happens using the data binding features, you can retrieve data from objects in your view templates as well. In WebWork this is done using the OGNL expression language embedded in WebWork JSP tags, similar to JSTL `<c:out value="${person.name}"/>` tags.

Struts

❏ Struts offers support for JavaServer Pages only. There are, however, external libraries available for Velocity as the view technology (hosted by the Velocity project, also part of Apache), and it's possible to use a "bridge servlet" to work with other view technologies.

❏ Struts has a rich set of tag libraries that support the retrieval and displaying of data bound in the model in all kinds of HTML widgets (select boxes, text fields, and so on). The `html:XXX` tags are a convenient way to limit the amount of HTML you need to type. It is, however, not a standard and chances are that HTML developers don't know how to work with those.

Spring MVC

❑ Spring seamlessly integrates with JSP, Velocity, FreeMarker, and XSLT and it's also possible to generate document-based output in Excel or PDF format. Spring completely decouples the view from the controller, aiming for an easy transition to a different view technology if needed.

❑ Spring features a set of tag libraries that facilitate binding of values (transformation of object to displayable String values and vice-versa, using the before mentioned property editors). In release 1.2, a set of JSP tag files is available that will make it easier for you to create HTML widgets such as text fields and select boxes. All tag files and custom tags reuse and support the JSTL Expression Language. Macros for FreeMarker and Velocity are also available, resembling the custom tags. The Spring tags are fundamentally different from Struts' tags, for instance. Spring's tags are focused entirely on integration with existing presentation tier technologies such as JSTL. They do not focus on providing easy ways to render checkboxes and other widgets. That's what HTML and other tag libraries will probably do better.

Tapestry

❑ Tapestry page templates are simply HTML source files. A Tapestry-specific `jwcid` attribute added to an HTML element specifies the corresponding Tapestry component to use to render that section of the web page. The component is a high-level construct, which knows how to render itself, is backed by Java code, and deals as needed with the page or other components it is embedded in. Depending on the component itself, and how much configuration information it needs, the component reference and attributes specified in the HTML page may be enough, or additional configuration information may need to be specified in a separate `.page` file. Components exist that correspond to most lower-level HTML elements such as input boxes or checkboxes and radio buttons, as well as higher level constructs such as a date picker.

❑ It is very easy to construct new components, generally more so than in JSF.

❑ Because templates are essentially plain HTML files, they may be edited in close to WISIWYG fashion in any standard HTML editor, much more so than for other view technologies such as JSP or Velocity/FreeMarker, where the markup interferes in terms of getting an idea of the final output.

❑ Tapestry is intrinsically tied to its templating format, based on components. It is essentially impossible to access Tapestry components or pages from another view technology such as JSP or Velocity/FreeMarker, although Tapestry does include code for handing off to JSP pages or allowing JSP pages to hand off to Tapestry pages.

JavaServer Faces

❑ JavaServer Faces includes a set of core components and render kits that facilitate the rendering of standard widgets such as text boxes and radio buttons. The implementation of those components (usable in JSP as tags) is left to the vendor providing the JSF implementation. Where Spring and WebWork do not focus on providing tags generating HTML widgets (text fields, radio buttons, and such), JSF much more resembles Struts in this respect. This is also related to the higher abstraction level JSF tries to achieve. Communication between components and how input and validation tie together is part of the technology — you don't have to implement all this yourself, whereas with the other command-oriented frameworks (but not Tapestry) you might end up doing more coding.

❑ JavaServer Faces defaults to JavaServer Pages, but depending on the implementation of the specification, other templating technologies might be supported as well.

Controller Infrastructure and Interception Handling

Of course any MVC framework requires controllers or a similar mechanism to sit between the view layer and the business services layer. Struts, WebWork, and Spring all offer a controller hierarchy, although there are significant differences. JSF and Tapestry both take a different, more event-driven approach.

WebWork

❏ WebWork has the most advanced interception infrastructure of these frameworks. Interceptors are fully configurable to be executed against any given set of URLs (so it's possible to apply only interceptors to all URLs with the .html extension, for example). WebWork interceptors are heavily used in the framework itself: for example, to do data binding and validation.

❏ WebWork actions are completely decoupled from the Servlet API, which greatly increases testability. Theoretically, you could reuse your actions in a fat client as well. However, we're a little skeptical about whether it really makes sense to use the same approach for a rich client application and the heavily constrained HTTP interaction model.

❏ The controllers are modeled as command objects, holding both the data and the behavior related to a user's action. As the command objects hold data as well, a new command object needs to be created for every request.

❏ WebWork does not include a wide variety of prebuilt controllers that model often-used processes in web applications (displaying a form, submitting it, returning to the form because of validation errors, and so on).

Struts

❏ Controllers in Struts are called actions. Your actions always have to extend an abstract base class. This and the fact that actions need the framework to work correctly seriously limits the possibility to test your actions in isolation. A separate project is available on SourceForge (offering the StrutsTestCase). Using this, you can test Struts Actions without a Servlet container.

❏ Struts actions are tied to the Servlet API, just as Spring's Controller interface is (unless you're using the Spring ThrowAwayController).

❏ Struts actions are required to be threadsafe. For each type of action, only one instance is maintained. Although it's a good practice to create threadsafe components, there might be situations where you simply cannot do without an object per request because of resource management, for example.

❏ Struts includes a small collection of actions that facilitate trivial tasks, such as forwarding to a different page. Struts has a large user base and a big community. Many extensions are built for Struts, so for a lot of usage scenarios, actions are probably available.

❏ Struts does not feature an interceptor mechanism. Common behavior spread over multiple actions will have to be implemented in abstract action classes or delegates that you call in every action. This increases coupling between functionality and behavior in your web application and results in higher maintenance costs (code spread over more classes, difficult to remove a specific functionality, and so on).

Spring MVC

❏ Spring features HandlerInterceptors, which you can configure just as you configure any other component in Spring. Spring supports so-called *before* and *after* advice: You can implement custom behavior before a controller is executed (or stop the execution if you like) and after the controller has finished executing.

❑ The most often used Spring controllers all implement the `Controller` interface. Spring also provides a WebWork-style controller that is created on every request. This is the `ThrowAway Controller`. Because the top-level types are interfaces, with Spring it's possible to implement your own controller infrastructure if you like — you don't have to extend a concrete class as with Struts.

❑ Although most of Spring's controllers *are* tied to the Servlet API (unless you're using the `ThrowAwayController`), you can test them in complete isolation. No container is needed if you want to execute your controllers. Spring's test classes that mock the Servlet API are a convenient way to test.

❑ By default, there's only one instance for each controller bean. If you want, you can define the controllers to be prototype, resulting in one controller for every request.

❑ Spring's controller infrastructure suits many common scenario's encountered in web application development. For example, there are controllers to do ordinary form workflow (displaying the form, submitting it, and so on) and to implement a wizard-like flow.

❑ Spring's controllers are fully configurable and allow for overriding specific parts of the request flow (data binding, validation, everything can be customized or overridden). Spring controllers are largely based on the Strategy and Template Method design patterns.

Tapestry

❑ Tapestry does not have the notion of a strongly typed Controller. Rather, components and pages are coded to respond to lifecycle callbacks and events from user interactions. The pages and components are completely Tapestry-specific, extending special interfaces, and it is generally expected that page and component code deals, for the most part, with user interface concerns, and relies on a lower-level service layer for non–UI related aspects.

❑ It is not easy to completely unit test Tapestry 3.0 pages and components because of the complex lifecycle that they embody. Proper delegation to a service layer for non-UI concerns, together with the small amount of code needed to produce UI because of this high-level nature of Tapestry, does mean that there is relatively little UI code to test compared to some frameworks such as Struts, for equivalent functionality. Tapestry versions 3.1and 4 aim to significantly reduce the difficulty of unit testing pages.

❑ There is no easy method to transparently intercept event and lifecycle callbacks, short of bringing in an AOP framework, or subclassing pages and components.

JavaServer Faces

JavaServer Faces does not have the notion of a strongly typed controller. Instead, any ordinary object (preferably a JavaBean) can act as a handler and has to be defined in the configuration of the application as a managed bean. JSF managed beans can be scoped (per application, session, or request). Handlers can contain conversion and validation code as well as code to save the data a user submitted (or references to service objects doing this).

As opposed to the other frameworks under discussion, JavaServer Faces has a much higher level of abstraction. When developing an application with JavaServer Faces, you don't necessarily have to know about the difference between GET and POST and the way user input is communicated using HTTP query parameters. While this may sound like an advantage, the result is a less flexible technology that might limit you in some situations. Also, to fully understand why things work the way they work, you might end up getting into some of the lower-level details anyway.

> **"All non-trivial abstractions, to some degree, are leaky."**
>
> Joel Spolsky – www.joelonsoftware.com

Other Characteristics

Let's quickly note a few other characteristics of these frameworks, good and bad. These include non-technical reasons that you might consider when choosing a framework.

WebWork

❑ WebWork is built on top of XWork, a implementation of the GoF *Command* pattern. It allows you to create configurable command objects and use them in its web framework.

❑ WebWork doesn't seem to have generated a lot of press yet. It still remains to be seen whether it will become a popular framework used by the masses.

❑ Documentation for the WebWork MVC framework is not extensive and largely conceptual. Pragmatic usage of the framework is not covered in the documentation. We feel that the weak documentation of WebWork is a major gap.

❑ WebWork is supported by Open Symphony, a healthy open source community. WebWork is also used in a number of complex, public web applications (including the Confluence Wiki product from Atlassian, which also uses Spring), so it is proven to be able to meet challenging requirements.

Struts

❑ Struts has been available since 2000 and has been adopted by many big corporations as their preferred web application framework. Whatever the technical arguments, Struts won't go away any time soon.

❑ Struts has a large user base and a healthy community. The mailing list generates a huge amount of traffic — sometimes over 100 emails per day.

❑ Struts development has traditionally progressed at a slow pace, especially when compared to the Spring project. Recently, Struts announced a separate, more JSF-oriented project. The Struts 1.*x* branch continues and will focus on providing backward-compatible releases without any major redesigns.

❑ Because of its popularity, there are many books and other resources on Struts.

❑ Because of its popularity, Struts has better tool support than other web application frameworks.

❑ Struts is hosted by Apache, a healthy open source community.

Spring Web MVC

❑ Spring Web MVC integrates seamlessly with its Inversion of Control container so you do not have to learn a new way to configure your controllers. Furthermore, it's easy to link your presentation tier to your middle tier.

❑ Although Spring is relatively new, its Web MVC framework is already widely used in both large and small projects. The flexibility the Web MVC framework gives you has already led to a wide variety of applications, ranging from applications with a custom-built controller infrastructure to facilitate extremely high loads to rich business applications with a complex interface.

- ❏ Spring is a project with a *release-early-release-often* philosophy. Since the 1.0 release in March 2004, two major releases have been done, as well as almost ten minor releases — including bug fixes, maintenance work, and minor enhancements.

- ❏ There is an Eclipse plug-in for Spring that manages and visualizes application context files. There is also a documentation tool called BeanDoc that generates HTML reports of your contexts.

- ❏ As of mid 2005, there are a significant number of books on Spring (besides this one), and more books are on the way. Spring also features an extensive reference guide, in HTML format as well as PDF. While Struts is still ahead of all other web frameworks in this area, the gap is narrowing between Struts and both Spring MVC and JSF.

- ❏ Spring, as an independent project, is hosted at SourceForge and has an active mailing list, forum, and user community.

Tapestry

- ❏ For developers used to a traditional command-oriented *Model 2* framework such as Struts, Tapestry, because of its component-oriented nature with fairly complex lifecycles, will have a relatively steep learning curve (which it shares with JSF) for new developers, compared to the learning curve to pick up another command-oriented framework. For smaller projects where there is already a team of developers experienced in a traditional framework, the time investment may not be worth it. For larger projects, or with the expectation of ongoing work, the time investment is generally worth it.

- ❏ Tapestry 3.0 applications produce URLs that are generally considered ugly. While there is a patch available that reworks the URL strategy even for Tapestry 3.0, if this is a concern it may be best to wait for Tapestry 3.1 or 4.0, which offer additional URL generation options out of the box, including a much friendlier format.

- ❏ There is no high-level concept of flow between pages in Tapestry, such as afforded by Spring MVC's `SimpleFormController`. However, any of the frameworks mentioned in this chapter are well served by adding some sort of more powerful, higher-level, web flow framework.

- ❏ Although Tapestry is more mature than JSF right now, and generally considered more usable than JSF without special tools, the fact that JSF is backed by a JCP standard probably means that JSF will become more popular than Tapestry. However, there is no sign that either will disappear. There is a Tapestry book available and a vibrant user community.

JavaServer Faces

- ❏ JavaServer Faces is a relatively new technology based on the assumption that multiple vendors will provide an implementation of it. There are a couple of open source implementations available, such as Smile (`http://smile.sourceforge.net`) and MyFaces (`http://myfaces.sourceforge.net`). The Apache initiative is also starting a JSF implementation, dubbed Struts Shale.

- ❏ Although JSF is a promising technology, opinions are mixed. Combined with an appropriate implementation and tool support, it should be a powerful technology. Note, however, that because of the high level of abstraction JSF tries to achieve, you might end up with a less flexible application framework. An often-heard argument is that if your primary focus is performance, you shouldn't choose JSF to serve as your MVC framework.

- ❏ There are already a significant number of books published on JSF and of course you can download the specification, which provides a wealth of information as well.

- ❏ Many big vendors are enthusiastic about JSF. Thus it is likely that it will benefit from excellent tool support.

533

Integrating with Spring: Core Concepts

In Servlet-based web applications, the ServletContext is *the* place to store application-relevant data. Each Servlet-based application has exactly one Servlet context object where you can store, for example, configuration data. The Servlet context can be accessed by any of the Servlets declared in your application by means of many of the javax.servlet specific types such as ServletRequest, ServletResponse, ServletConfig, and FilterConfig. When developing a web application, the ServletContext is also the place where Spring stores the application context(s) for your application (have a look at Figure 14-1).

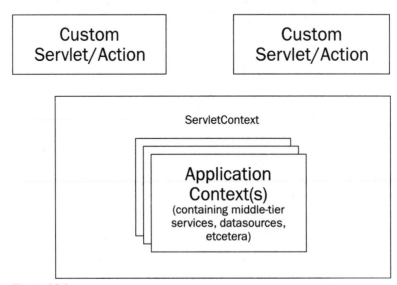

Figure 14-1

The examples shown in this chapter all use the org.springframework.prospring.ch14.OrderService interface, declaring exactly one method:

```
public Order getOrder(String orderId);
```

In our application, we've implemented the OrderService and defined it in an application context (located in /WEB-INF/applicationContext.xml) as follows. Note that for this example we've chosen to leave out any dependencies on data-access objects and such.

```
<bean id="orderService"
    class="org.springframework.prospring.ch14.ShowOrderAction" />
```

You might remember from earlier chapters that loading an application context in a web application can be done using the ContextLoaderListener (or in non–Servlet 2.4–compliant environments using the ContextLoaderServlet). We'll load the application context with our order service as follows. Note that you can tweak the location of the application context by setting the contextConfigLocation at context parameter level. This way you can include more than one context or override the default name (/WEB-INF/applicationContext.xml).

```
<web-app>

  <listener>
    <listener-class>
      org.springframework.web.context.ContextLoaderListener
    </listener-class>
  </listener>


  ...
</web-app>
```

To show you how to retrieve an `ApplicationContext` from the `ServletContext`, we'll develop a small Servlet:

```java
public class ShowOrderServlet extends HttpServlet {
  private OrderService orderService;

  public void init() throws ServletException {

    ServletContext sContext = getServletContext();
    ApplicationContext appContext =
      WebApplicationContextUtils.getRequiredWebApplicationContext(sContext);

    orderService = (OrderService)appContext.getBean("orderService");
  }

  protected void doGet(HttpServletRequest req, HttpServletResponse res)
  throws ServletException, IOException {

    String id = RequestUtils.getParameter(req, "orderId");
    Order order = orderService.getOrder(id);
  }
}
```

The `WebApplicationContextUtils` class is part of Spring and resides in the `org.springframework.web.util` package. Using this class you can retrieve the application context stored in the `ServletContext` from anywhere in a web application, provided that you have the `ServletContext` available. There are two variants of retrieving the application context. One is to just call `getWebApplicationContext()`, which will return `null` if no context was found. The `getRequiredWebApplicationContext()` method throws a `java.lang.IllegalStateException` if no context could be found. The latter is perfectly suited for retrieving an application context during an initialization phase and when the context is absolutely required.

Of course this is not the way you would like to develop web applications in general (developing a Servlet per action) and certainly not the way you would like to retrieve your dependencies. The following sections describe how to retrieve (or rather inject) dependencies in your Struts or WebWork actions using more advanced mechanisms.

One interesting thing still left to mention here is the auto wiring capabilities of Spring's application contexts. We'll look into using the auto wiring features in more detail while discussing the Struts integration, but after you've looked up a Spring `WebApplicationContext`, one of the things you can do is auto wire the object from which you have looked up the context. Although the object isn't wired in a Spring context, this way it can still benefit from Spring's IoC features. Use the following line of code to auto wire your object by type, where this could of course be replaced by any arbitrary object. Dependencies expressed in the form of setters will now automatically be satisfied, based on the argument type of the setter.

```
context.getBeanFactory().autowireBeanProperties(this,
    AutowireCapableBeanFactory.AUTOWIRE_BY_TYPE, true);
```

WebWork Integration

Integration with WebWork is possible using the XWork SpringObjectFactory. This object factory is part of the XWork-optional package and resolves any dependencies for your actions, before WebWork takes over control and executes your actions.

You can initialize a SpringObjectFactory in one of two ways: by using a Servlet listener or by using an initializing bean defined in your Spring application context. The former relies on the fact that the Spring application context(s) are already loaded by, for example, a ContextLoaderListener, as explained in the next section.

Setting Up the ObjectFactory

Enabling the SpringObjectFactory using a listener is quite simple:

```
<web-app>

    <listener>
      <listener-class>
         org.springframework.web.context.ContextLoaderListener
      </listener-class>
    </listener>

    <listener>
      <listener-class>
         com.opensymphony.spring.xwork.SpringObjectFactoryListener
      </listener-class>
    </listener>

</web-app>
```

The first listener loads the Spring application context(s), just as we've seen in other parts of this book. The second listener initializes the XWork object factory. XWork manages all WebWork actions and XWork creates these actions using the specified object factory. The SpringObjectFactory inspects the Spring application context to look for actions. After the actions are created, XWork passes them on to WebWork.

> Note that we've defined the Spring listener before the XWork listener. This is important because the XWork listener relies on Spring context(s) being loaded first! The order in which you define listeners in web.xml is also the order in which they are executed, so in this example, the XWork listener is executed after the Spring one.

The second option we have to configure in the `SpringObjectFactory` is to define it in the Spring application context. Which option to use is essentially a matter of taste. A Spring-managed `SpringObject Factory` has to be defined as follows:

```
<bean id="springObjectFactory"
  class="com.opensymphony.xwork.spring.SpringObjectFactory"
  init-method="initObjectFactory"/>
```

If you get all this set up, defining WebWork actions is a matter of including the action reference in your `xwork.xml` file and defining the actual action itself in the Spring context.

```
# xwork.xml
<action name="showOrder" class="showOrderAction">
  <result name="success">showOrder.jsp</result>
</action>

# applicationContext.xml
<bean name="showOrderAction"
  class="org.springframework.prospring.ch14.ShowOrderAction4" singleton="false">
  <property name="orderService">
    <ref bean="orderService"/>
  </property>
</bean>
```

Note that the name of the XWork defined action matches the bean name of the action defined in Spring and is no longer reflecting the action's class name. Furthermore, you have to make sure the Spring-defined action is declared to a prototype (`singleton="false"`) because WebWork demands all actions to be non-singletons.

Struts Integration

Developing the MVC layer of an application using Struts involves developing `Actions`. In Struts, `Actions` are mapped to URLs in a configuration file. Wiring an `Action` typically looks like this:

```
<action path="/showOrder"
  type="org.springframework.prospring.ch14.ShowOrderAction">
  <forward name="success" page="/showOrder.jsp"/>
</action>
```

As we've seen, acquiring an application context is quite easy. Developing a Struts `Action` using a Spring-defined resource is easy as well:

```
public class ShowOrderAction extends Action {

  private OrderService orderService;

  public void setServlet(ActionServlet servlet) {
    super.setServlet(servlet);

    ServletContext sContext = servlet.getServletContext();
    ApplicationContext appContext =
```

```
        WebApplicationContextUtils.getRequiredWebApplicationContext(sContext);

    orderService = (OrderService)appContext.getBean("orderService");
}
```

```
    public ActionForward execute(ActionMapping mapping, ActionForm form,
        HttpServletRequest req, HttpServletResponse res) throws Exception {

        String orderId = RequestUtils.getRequiredStringParameter(req, "orderId");
        Order order = orderService.getOrder(orderId);
        req.setAttribute("order", order);

        return mapping.findForward("success");

    }
}
```

As you can see, we're acquiring an application context as the Action initializes. We're reusing Spring's `WebApplicationContextUtils` class and the action won't initialize correctly if there is no context available.

Using ActionSupport

The class shown in the previous section is a simplified version of a utility base class Spring also provides: the `org.springframework.web.struts.ActionSupport` class. Using this class results in the following, slightly more compact, code:

```
    public class ShowOrderAction2 extends ActionSupport {

    private OrderService orderService;

    protected void onInit() {
        orderService =
            (OrderService)getWebApplicationContext().getBean("orderService");
    }

    public ActionForward execute(ActionMapping mapping, ActionForm form,
        HttpServletRequest req, HttpServletResponse res) throws Exception {

        // same as above

    }
}
```

The ActionSupport class offers access to the Spring-defined `MessageSources` through the `getMessageSourceAccessor()` method. Furthermore, you can do custom initialization and destruction (acquiring and releasing of resources for example) by overriding the `onInit()` and `onDestroy()` methods.

Using DelegationRequestProcessor and DelegationActionProxy

Using the `ActionSupport` class, we're still not able to fully utilize Spring's Dependency Injection features in our Struts Actions. We still have to acquire resources ourselves, something you should not want to do anymore, after having played with other parts of Spring.

Fortunately there are several solutions. Using the `DelegatingRequestProcessor` exposes the full power of Spring's DI features in combination with Struts Actions. You will be able to wire up your actions in an application context. There are two things you need to do. First you will have to enable the `ContextLoaderPlugIn`, which loads a `WebApplicationContext` from the `/WEB-INF` directory (just as the Spring `DispatcherServlet` does). You will also have to define a simple delegating proxy action for each of the Struts actions you've defined in the Spring application context.

A second option would be to create a simple autowiring Struts baseclass that loads the Spring application context and autowires itself. This concept is also used in several other parts of the Spring Framework — for example in the `AbstractDependencyInjectionSpringContextTests` base unit test class. We'll first discuss the `DelegationActionProxy`.

Defining the Struts ActionServlet and the ContextLoaderPlugIn

A typical Struts configuration consists of an `ActionServlet` and a Struts configuration file, containing your actions, global forwards, and so on. The plug-in has to be defined in your `struts-config.xml` file as follows:

```
<struts-config>

  <!-- action mappings -->

  <!-- message resources -->

  <plug-in className="org.springframework.web.struts.ContextLoaderPlugIn"/>

</struts-config>
```

The plug-in closely resembles the classes used to set up a Spring `DispatcherServlet`. In Chapter 12, we reviewed all the configuration parameters available for you to tweak the context class, the namespace, and so on. All these parameters and the concepts explained there also apply to the `ContextLoaderPlugIn`. In short, the plug-in loads a `WebApplicationContext` named after your Struts `ActionServlet` and takes any contexts loaded by the `ContextLoaderListener` (or Servlet) as its parent.

```
<web-app>

  <listener>
    <listener-class>
      org.springframework.web.context.ContextLoaderListener
    </listener-class>
  </listener>

  <servlet>
    <servlet-name>struts</servlet-name>
```

```
    <servlet-class>org.apache.struts.action.ActionServlet</servlet-class>
  </servlet>

  ...
</web-app>
```

If the preceding code is your `web.xml` file, the `ContextLoaderPlugIn` loads a web application context for you located in the `/WEB-INF` directory and named `struts-servlet.xml` (named after your action servlet). The listener we've defined loads an additional application context from `/WEB-INF/applicationContext.xml` (in our case the context containing the `OrderService`).

> **The** `WebApplicationContext` **named** `[servlet-name]-servlet.xml` **is *the* place to define your Struts actions and other web-related beans. Keep your middle-tier beans separated from any of the beans dealing with MVC functionality. This facilitates testing and keeps the structure of your application clean.**

We're almost done setting up the environment. The last thing we need to do is define a custom Struts `RequestProcessor`. The request processor is what Struts uses to process requests; in other words, it's how Struts looks up your actions and calls them. Spring provides a custom processor to allow you to define your beans in a Spring application context instead of in a Struts configuration file. This way you can fully use the Spring Dependency Injection features. A custom request processor can be defined in the Struts configuration file:

```
<struts-config>

  <!-- action mappings -->

  <controller
    processorClass="org.springframework.web.struts.DelegatingRequestProcessor"/>

  <!-- message resources -->

  <plug-in className="org.springframework.web.struts.ContextLoaderPlugIn"/>

</struts-config>
```

The next thing we need to do is define a `WebApplicationContext` containing our Struts actions, wired up using Spring:

```
# struts-servlet.xml
<bean name="/showOrder"
  class="org.springframework.prospring.ch14.ShowOrderAction3">
  <property name="orderService"/>
    <ref bean="orderService"/>
  </property>
</bean>
```

This action is implemented as follows:

```
public class ShowOrderAction3 extends Action {
  private OrderService service;

  public void setOrderService(OrderService service) {
    this.service = service;
  }

  public ActionForward execute(ActionMapping mapping, ActionForm form,
      HttpServletRequest req, HttpServletResponse res) throws Exception {
    String id = req.getParameter("orderId");

    Order order = service.getOrder(id);

    req.setAttribute("order", order);
    return new ActionForward("/showOrder.jsp");
  }
}
```

As you can see, we're fully utilizing Spring's Dependency Injection features and don't have to bother with retrieving an application context anymore.

The final thing is to declare the Struts action in a Struts configuration file. Basically we're duplicating the action here. Unfortunately, this is what the Struts integration code needs to work correctly.

> Remember to keep your `struts-config.xml` files (or whatever they are named) up-to-date and to copy the bean name as the action name.

In the Struts configuration file, we can also mention the action forwards to use:

```
<action name="/showOrder">
  <forward name="success" path="/showOrder.jsp"/>
</action>
```

By doing this, we can change the return statement to the following:

```
return mapping.findForward("success");
```

There are a few things you might need to know when integrating Spring with Struts:

❑ If you have your own custom Struts request processor, which conflicts with the Spring `DelegatingRequestProcessor`, you can also use the `org.springframework.web.struts.DelegatingActionProxy`. Define this in your `struts-config.xml` file as an ordinary action (along with forwards and so on) and it will delegate all calls to the action to a Spring-defined one. An example of how to use this can be found in the sample code with this chapter.

❑ Spring's `DelegatingActionProxy` and `DelegatingRequestProcessor` are aware of Struts modules. If the `ShowOrderAction` would have to live in a module called "ordermodule," the only thing we'd have to do would be to name our action `/ordermodule/showOrder` instead of `/showOrder`.

❑ If you need to work with Tiles, use the `TilesDelegatingRequestProcessor` instead of the normal delegating one. It provides the same functionality of the original Struts `TilesRequestProcessor`.

❑ If you ever need to write your own `RequestProcessor`, you should definitely have a look at the `org.springframework.web.struts.DelegatingActionUtils` class. It provides convenience methods that will determine the Spring bean name for a given action mapping.

Using an Auto Wiring Base Action

As noted before, there are other options as well to have your actions dependency injected. An approach also used in other places in the Spring Framework is to auto wire a certain object. Auto wiring is a concept explained earlier and the only thing you need to do to auto wire an object you've created is to pass it to the `BeanFactory`:

```
ApplicationContext context; // retrieve application context;
SomeClass toAutoWire; // create object somehow
```

```
context.getBeanFactory().autowireBeanProperties(toAutoWire,
   AutowireCapableBeanFactory.AUTOWIRE_BY_TYPE, true);
```

Remember the different auto wiring types: by name, by type, using a constructor, or automatic. We usually prefer to use auto wiring by type or by name because the automatic option often is a bit too magical and not sufficiently transparent. But let's get back to what we came for: auto wiring of our Struts action!

Remember `OrderAction2` from a few pages back? It used the following code to retrieve a dependency:

```
orderService = (OrderService)getWebApplicationContext().getBean("orderService");
```

The fact that in this example we're going to use auto wiring removes the need to wire the action in the Spring context as we did with `DelegationRequestProcessor` and `DelegationActionProxy`. We'll refactor our action and let it extend `AutowiringActionSupport`, a Struts base class that we'll have to create ourselves.

```
public class ShowOrderAction3 extends AutowiringActionSupport {

  private OrderService orderService;

  public void setOrderService(OrderService orderService) {
    this.orderService = orderService;
  }

  public ActionForward execute(ActionMapping mapping, ActionForm form,
    HttpServletRequest req, HttpServletResponse res) throws Exception {

    // same as in previous examples

  }
}
```

The new base class we're about to create will pick up the setter. It will auto wire the action by type and pass the action itself to the auto wiring facility.

```
Public class AutowiringActionSupport extends ActionSupport {

  protected void onInit() {
    getWebApplicationContext().getBeanFactory().autowireByType(this,
      AutowireCapableBeanFactory.AUTOWIRE_BY_TYPE, true);
  }

}
```

Of course, you can extend other ActionSupport classes as well as create an auto wiring base class.

Tapestry Integration

Integrating a Tapestry Web UI layer with a Spring-provided services layer is relatively simple. This section describes how to use Tapestry and Spring together, but does assume you are already familiar with how Tapestry works and how to use the Spring application context.

We're going to show a sample of how to integrate by taking the existing Spring sample application called JPetStore, and by implementing a Tapestry page that is essentially fairly similar to the existing item detail page. The Tapestry page, however, has an input field allowing the item ID to be specified, and once the user has submitted a valid ID, the page will display the details for the specified item.

Getting Beans for Tapestry

The ItemView.java page class we're going to create is going to need access to the PetStoreFacade service object from the Spring application context, stored under the bean ID petStore. The most obvious mechanism to get at the application context is through the standard Spring static utility method WebApplicationContextUtils.getApplicationContext().

In the Tapestry page's Java code, we could just do something like this:

```
WebApplicationContext appContext =
      WebApplicationContextUtils.getApplicationContext(
      getRequestCycle().getRequestContext().getServlet().getServletContext());
PetStoreFacade petStore = (PetStoreFacade) appContext.getBean("petStore");
```

This works but is not an ideal solution as the Java code is aware of Spring; it's not IoC in style. Instead, we rely upon the fact that Tapestry already has a mechanism to declaratively add properties to a page. In fact, especially when the properties need to be persistent, this declarative approach is the preferred approach to managing all properties on a page, so that Tapestry can properly manage their lifecycles as part of the page and component lifecycle. The automatic handling of persistent page properties is one of Tapestry's strongest points.

The Page Class

Let's examine our `ItemView.java` page class:

```
public abstract class ItemView extends PetStoreBasePage {

  public abstract Item getItem();
  public abstract void setItem(Item item);

  public abstract String getItemIdFilter();

  public abstract PetStoreFacade getPetStore();

  /**
   * handle form submissions, which let an item be specified
   **/
  public void formSubmit(IRequestCycle cycle) {

    if (getItemIdFilter() != null) {
      Item item = getPetStore().getItem(getItemIdFilter());
      setItem(item);
    }
  }
}
```

There's not actually very much going on at the level of Java code. We have declared three abstract properties: `item`, `itemIdFilter`, and `petStore`. The accompanying page definition file, `ItemView.page`, will also declare these all as page properties, and at runtime Tapestry actually generates a final version of the class, which implements these values and initializes them properly as per the page definition.

When the user submits the request to view an item, the item ID input box is going to come in as the `itemIdFilter` property. The code then uses the instance of the `PetStoreFacade` service, which is stored in the `petStore` property, to read in the item, which is then stored in the `item` property, to be displayed to the user. This simple implementation will not warn the user of an invalid item number. An invalid number will simply result in a null `item` being set, which the page template will check for.

The Page Definition

Now we need to create the page definition file, `ItemView.page`. First, however, we want to make it easier for *any* page to get at the application context. As a convenience, we extend the normal Tapestry `BaseEngine` class with our own implementation, which gets the context and puts it in an easier-to-access location:

```
public class BaseEngine extends org.apache.tapestry.engine.BaseEngine {

  public static final String APPLICATION_CONTEXT_KEY = "appContext";

  // see org.apache.tapestry.engine.AbstractEngine#setupForRequest(
  //        org.apache.tapestry.request.RequestContext)
  protected void setupForRequest(RequestContext context) {
    super.setupForRequest(context);

    // insert ApplicationContext in global, if not there
```

```
    Map global = (Map) getGlobal();
    ApplicationContext ac = (ApplicationContext)
            global.get(APPLICATION_CONTEXT_KEY);
    if (ac == null) {
      ac = WebApplicationContextUtils.getWebApplicationContext(
              context.getServlet().getServletContext());
      global.put(APPLICATION_CONTEXT_KEY, ac);
    }
  }
}
```

What the preceding code does is obtain the Spring application context and put it in the Tapestry application's `Global` object, where it's easier to get at from page definitions.

Now let's look at the actual page definition:

```
<?xml version="1.0" encoding="UTF-8"?>
<!DOCTYPE page-specification PUBLIC
  "-//Apache Software Foundation//Tapestry Specification 3.0//EN"
  "http://jakarta.apache.org/tapestry/dtd/Tapestry_3_0.dtd">

<page-specification
        class="org.springframework.samples.jpetstore.web.pages.ItemView">
```

```
  <property-specification name="error" type="java.lang.String"/>
  <property-specification name="item"
        type="org.springframework.samples.jpetstore.domain.Item" persistent="yes"/>
  <property-specification name="itemIdFilter" type="java.lang.String"/>
  <property-specification name="numberFormat" type="java.text.DecimalFormat">
    new java.text.DecimalFormat("$#,##0.00")
  </property-specification>
  <property-specification name="petStore"
        type="org.springframework.samples.jpetstore.domain.logic.PetStoreFacade">
    global.appContext.getBean("petStore")
  </property-specification>
```

```
</page-specification>
```

A number of properties are defined here, including the three properties previously mentioned. The other two, `error` and `numberFormat`, are used by our page's base class and by the HTML template, respectively.

The only interesting definition for our present purposes is for the `petStore` property, which, using the OGNL expression language, specifies an initial value for this property as `global.appContext` `.getBean("petStore")`. In this expression, the application context that was put into the `Global` object by the custom engine class is asked for the `PetStoreFacade` bean, which has the ID `petStore`.

The Page Template

Now let's look at the page template itself, `ItemView.html`:

```
<html jwcid="$content$">
```

```
<body jwcid="@Border">

<h1>Item View</h1><hr/>

<span jwcid="@ShowError"/><span jwcid="@ShowValidationError"
      delegate="ognl:valDelegate"/>

<form jwcid="@Form" listener="ognl:listeners.formSubmit"
      delegate="ognl:valDelegate">
  Enter a valid item id to view its details:
  <input jwcid="@TextField" value="ognl:itemIdFilter" size="20" maxlength="20"/>
  <br/>
  <input type="submit" jwcid="@Submit" value="Show Item"
         style="background: #cccccc none;"/>
</form>

<span jwcid="@Conditional" condition="ognl:item != null">

  <table align="center" bgcolor="#008800" cellspacing="2" cellpadding="3"
         border="0" width="60%">
    <tr bgcolor="#FFFF88">
      <td bgcolor="#FFFFFF">
        <span jwcid="@Insert" value="ognl:item.product.description" raw="true"/>
      </td>
    </tr>
    <tr bgcolor="#FFFF88">
      <td width="100%" bgcolor="#cccccc">
        <b><span jwcid="@Insert" value="ognl:item.itemId"/></b>
      </td>
    </tr>
    <tr bgcolor="#FFFF88">
      <td>
        <b><font size="4">
        <span jwcid="@Insert" value="ognl:item.attribute1"/>
        <span jwcid="@Insert" value="ognl:item.attribute2"/>
        <span jwcid="@Insert" value="ognl:item.attribute3"/>
        <span jwcid="@Insert" value="ognl:item.attribute4"/>
        <span jwcid="@Insert" value="ognl:item.attribute5"/>
        <span jwcid="@Insert" value="ognl:item.product.name"/>
        </font></b>
      </td></tr>
    <tr bgcolor="#FFFF88"><td>
      <font size="3"><i><span jwcid="@Insert"
            value="ognl:item.product.name"/></i></font>
    </td></tr>
    <tr bgcolor="#FFFF88"><td>
      <span jwcid="@Conditional" condition="ognl:item.quantity lte 0">
       <font color="RED" size="2"><i>Back ordered.</i></font>
      </span>
      <span jwcid="@Conditional" condition="ognl:item.quantity > 0">
       <font size="2"><span jwcid="@Insert"
            value="ognl:item.quantity"/> in stock.</font>
      </span>
    </td></tr>
    <tr bgcolor="#FFFF88"><td>
      <span jwcid="@Insert" value="ognl:item.listPrice"
```

```
                    format="ognl:numberFormat"/>
      </td></tr>
    </table>
  </span>

  </body>
</html>
```

The page template is mostly a simple conversion of the original JSP template for viewing an item, `item.jsp`. However, an input box has been added at the top so that the user may enter an item ID and submit it. Showing the item detail is handled by the last two-thirds of the template, but this is wrapped in a conditional so that the item is shown only if the `item` page property is not null. Therefore, on the initial view of the page, it will display only the input box asking for an item ID, and on subsequent views, assuming the item could be successfully looked up, the item detail will also be shown.

Tapestry Integration Final Thoughts

As you've seen, the point of integration between Tapestry and Spring is very thin, and the mechanism is not too complicated. It is also not very intrusive. Tapestry's page definitions with the property declarations are already a form of IoC. Java code implementing a page class just declares abstract properties and uses them; it doesn't care how those properties are actually initialized. This makes it easy to declare all services that need to come from Spring as page properties, and then in the page property definition declaratively set the initial values of those properties as beans obtained from a Spring application context. The one small annoyance with this mechanism is that while this is still IoC for the Java code (which is what really matters), it's not IoC for the page definition files; that is, OGNL expressions in the page definitions are actually responsible for pulling beans from the context, instead of the context itself specifying properties for pages, as if those pages were any other bean.

JavaServer Faces Integration

Special thanks to Arjen Poutsma for preparing content for this section.

Both Spring and JSF have their own specific format to define beans: Spring uses <bean>; JSF uses <managed-bean> blocks. Although the format is somewhat different, the concepts underlying both are quite similar. This can be seen by looking at a typical JSF-managed bean definition:

```
<managed-bean>
  <managed-bean-name>myJsfManagedBean</managed-bean-name>
  <managed-bean-class>example.MyJsfManagedBean</managed-bean-class>
  <managed-bean-scope>session</managed-bean-scope>
</managed-bean>
```

This block defines a JSF-managed bean named `myJsfManagedBean`, which is of class `example.MyJsfManagedBean`. Because the scope of this bean is defined as `session`, only one instance of the JSF-managed bean will be created per HTTP session.

Integrating Spring with JSF centers around the concept of bean resolution, meaning that you can refer to Spring-managed beans within a JSF-managed bean or a JSF page. This is done using the `DelegatingVariableResolver`, provided by Spring. This is a standard JSF `VariableResolver` that delegates to the original JSF resolver first, and then to the Spring root `WebApplicationContext` (loaded by the `org.springframework.web.context.ContextLoaderListener`). Spring also provides the `org.springframework.web.jsf.FacesContextUtils` with which you can get a reference to the Spring `WebApplicationContext` yourself. This class resembles the `WebApplicationContextUtils` a lot and a `getWebApplicationContext()` and a `getRequiredWebApplicationContext()` method, but using a `FacesContext` to look up the Spring context.

To use the Spring `VariableResolver`, put the following in your `faces-context.xml`:

```
<application>
  <variable-resolver>
    org.springframework.web.jsf.DelegatingVariableResolver
  </variable-resolver>
</application>
```

Let's say you have a Spring-managed bean in your `applicationContext.xml`:

```
<bean id="mySpringManagedBusinessObject"
  class="example.MySpringManagedBusinessObject">
  <!-- additional details omitted -->
</bean>
```

You can now refer to this bean in your JSF-managed beans and pages using the standard JSF expression `#{mySpringManagedBusinessObject}`. The `#{}` notation is specified by JSF and resembles the `${}` notation used in JSP a lot. The difference here is that when using the JSF notation, the bean will be looked up in your `FacesContext`, whereas using the JSP notation, the `PageContext` will be inspected. The expression language principles used in JSTL and JSP 2.0 apply to JSF expressions as well, by the way, so you can use the `#{mySpringManagedBusinessObject.users}` expression to retrieve a collection of users from a `getUsers()` method. The following is an example of how you can refer to the Spring-managed bean from within your JSF configuration:

```
<managed-bean>
    <managed-bean-name>myJsfManagedBean</managed-bean-name>
    <managed-bean-class>example.MyJsfManagedBean</managed-bean-class>
    <managed-bean-scope>session</managed-bean-scope>
    <managed-property>
      <property-name>mySpringManagedBusinessObject</property-name>
      <value>#{mySpringManagedBusinessObject}</value>
    </managed-property>
</managed-bean>
```

Note that it's also possible to refer to your Spring-managed bean from within a JSF page:

```
<h:inputText value="#{myJsfManagedBean.mySpringManagedBusinessObject.name}" .../>
```

Note that there is a SourceForge project (jsf-spring) that makes it possible to refer to JSF-managed beans within your Spring context and to configure Spring beans in a JSF configuration file. This project also provides functionality to scope Spring beans in the same way you can scope JSF beans, giving you the additional session and request scopes. This project provides more advanced and tighter integration with JSF. You can find out more about it at `http://jsf-spring.sourceforge.net`.

Summary

In this chapter we've reviewed some of the integration facilities that come with Spring to facilitate the development of an MVC layer based on a framework other than Spring MVC. It's often wise to preserve existing investments; hence such integration facilities are important. Always decide what's best for your team and try to strike a good balance between reusing existing knowledge and introducing new concepts that will help your team get those projects done more effectively while creating highly flexible and maintainable solutions.

We've seen how to integrate with Spring's `ApplicationContext` classes in general, using the `Servlet Context`: the place where web applications generally store application-wide data. We've also seen how to make Struts actions behave like Spring beans, allowing you to reuse your existing knowledge of Dependency Injection with Spring. We've also seen how to use the WebWork `SpringObjectFactory` to wire up XWork actions using Spring.

In this chapter, we covered the leading Java web tier technologies (besides Spring's own MVC framework): Struts, WebWork, Tapestry, and JSF.

In the future, we expect that many more open and closed source software packages will provide libraries to integrate with Spring. If you encounter another solution that you need to integrate with, be sure to check if there is something available already. You can consult the Spring forum or the people who originally developed the solution you want to use. If you need to write web tier integration yourself, the examples in this chapter of integration with Struts and other technologies should provide a good starting point.

15

The Sample Application

In the previous chapters we have covered a lot of functionality provided by the Spring Framework. It is now time to put the pieces together in a complete application. We will use the example from *Expert One-on-One J2EE Design and Development* by Rod Johnson, with some minor adjustments in the requirements. If you don't have the book, you can find the updated requirements in Appendix A of this book. Some of the solutions have already been used as examples in earlier chapters explaining how to use Spring for a specific technology, but this chapter will show how it is all tied together.

Spring covers such a large set of technologies that most applications will use only a part of what Spring has to offer. This is also true for our sample application. We have chosen to limit the application to certain technologies that we feel are the most commonly used, but this does not limit the applicability of the approach to include other technologies if your projects have different needs or requirements.

One value that a sample application provides is the opportunity to show a *complete* example with all configuration files and all Java code — complete and in a deployable form. This allows you to see all the relationships between the files and it also allows you to investigate a fully functioning example in full detail.

The primary focus of this chapter is to explain how this application is designed and implemented. We will cover the major architectural features and present the reasoning behind the choices made, but not necessarily cover all the technical details because this has already been covered in the preceding chapters.

When you read this chapter, you should have the source code for the sample application at hand. It can be downloaded from the "Download Code" section of the Wrox "Programmer to Programmer" website located at www.wrox.com.

Choice of Server Technologies

The example application is a web-based application, and the first choice we have to make is what application server to target. Although most J2EE servers provide compatible implementations, the deployment steps and configurations vary between them. The original implementation of this sample application used an EJB container, which we now consider unnecessary for this type of application. Back in 2001, EJBs provided the only available solution for declarative transactions in Java/J2EE applications, and this was the motivation behind implementing parts of the application as EJBs. Spring's transaction framework now provides an attractive alternative solution, so we have chosen not to use EJBs. This not only simplifies the code we will need to write but gives us more options when it comes to picking an application server.

We think that the Apache Tomcat server provides a good starting point for our sample application. It is widely used, so you may well be familiar with it already, and it provides a stable environment for development and for production use.

Next up is the choice of a database server. We primarily used MySQL 4.1 to develop this sample application, but the code should work against other SQL databases. We have tested the application on PostgreSQL 8.0 and Oracle 9i/10g and we provide database scripts for these databases as well. You will not be able to use older MySQL versions, however, because we make use of sub-queries, which were not supported in version 4.0 or earlier.

In the rest of this chapter we will look at the completed application starting with the database layer and working our way up via the DAO layer, to the Service layer, and finishing with the Web layer.

Application Layers

The application is layered to limit any dependencies to a single layer if possible. This is a generally accepted practice and one that we always recommend. Figure 15-1 shows the different layers of the sample application together with the Spring- and non-Spring–related configuration files that are associated with each layer.

One thing you will notice once you start working with Spring is that you write considerably less code in your business classes. Most "glue" code is now unnecessary, as configuration is now handled by the framework. You will also be able to use AOP for crosscutting concerns such as transactions and security. This usually amounts to a considerable amount of code that can be eliminated by using Spring-provided AOP solutions.

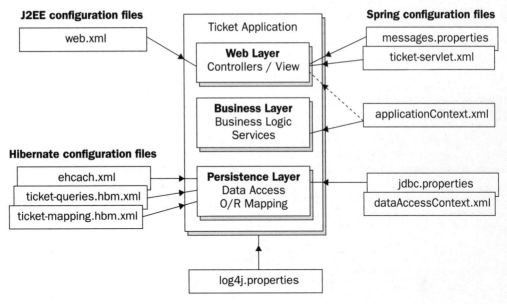

Figure 15-1

The downside to this Java code saving is that it all has to be configured, so you end up with some additional XML files. This is, however, a one-time problem as you start developing the application and it is far more than made up for by the time saved on writing repetitive "plumbing" code. It's also important to note that virtually all applications of real-world complexity that we've seen face the need to externalize configuration from Java code in one way or another. Thus the XML configuration in a Spring application is typically a consistent alternative to ad hoc configuration that would otherwise be scattered — perhaps less visible in a single place, but often amounting to *more* total configuration, and a greater maintenance burden.

You will notice the biggest difference later on when you have to maintain the application. When you go back into your application to make changes, you will have a much easier time understanding and modifying the code. This is because all this extra code cluttering your core business logic code is no longer there. Finding the right location in the code where you need to make changes is much easier. Also, the configuration files give a high-level "road map" of the application, and the highly coherent, loosely coupled classes that IoC and AOP encourage are easier to maintain.

Persistence Layer

The persistence layer is a very important part of your application design. This is where you define how your data is going to be stored, potentially for years to come. This usually involves a relational database as well as some technology to ease the mapping between the relational model and your Java classes.

Data Model

We will begin the exploration by looking at the data model. You have already seen parts of this model in Chapter 5 when we explored the JDBC Framework. Now we will look at the entire data model in full detail. You can refer to the Entity/Relationship model shown in Figure 15-2.

It's important to note that this is an existing data model that we have inherited from the previous book *Expert One-on-One J2EE Design and Development* by Rod Johnson. This means that a lot of design decisions already have been made for us, which is not an uncommon situation.

There are a couple of different categories of tables in this data model. First we have the reference data that contains information about some fairly static entities. There are items added here, but they don't change frequently. Tables in this category are Shows, Genre, Performance, Price_Structure, Seating_Plan, Seat_Class, Price_Band, and Seat. The Seat_Class defines seating classes that a seat belongs to—an example is "AA," "Premium Reserve." The next table is the Seating_Plan table that lets us define different plans for different types of performances—an example is "Standard Opera Seating." The Price_Structure table adds similar flexibility for the pricing information—an example is "Standard Opera Pricing." The last table in this category is the Price_Band, which links the Price_Structure and Seat_Class with a specific price.

Next, we have some tables that contain information relating to the relationships between these reference tables. Tables in this category are Seat_Status and Seat_Plan_Seat. The Seat_Status table will allow us to query for available seats—seats that don't belong to any booking. The price_band reference in this table is not necessary but it provides a convenient shortcut to the pricing information. Then there is a Registered_User table to keep track of users registering on the site. Finally we have some tables that contain reservation data such as Booking and Purchase.

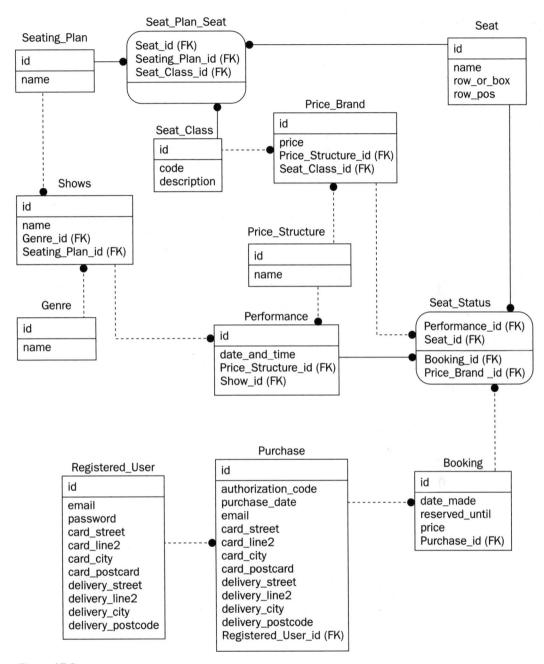

Figure 15-2

Domain Object Model

Now, let's look at the object model shown in Figure 15-3. This is the model that we will map the data model to. Just like the data model, this model is also mostly inherited from the previous implementation of the sample application.

For the most part, this object model is very close to the data model and the mapping is straightforward between the database tables and the domain classes. The exception here is the relationship between a Seat, a SeatingPlan, and a SeatClass. This is modeled in the database as an *Association Table Mapping* (see page 248 in *Patterns of Enterprise Application Architecture* by Martin Fowler or the accompanying website www.martinfowler.com/eaaCatalog/associationTableMapping.html for more on this pattern). The consequence of this is that the table holding the associated keys does not contain any additional information beyond the relationships and we will not create a corresponding class in our domain model. We will simply refer to the table Seat_Class_Seat in our queries, but the domain objects themselves do not have explicit references to each other. If this table contained some additional data elements, then we would add a class to map this data to. With our solution, we need to use an SQL query rather than an HQL query, to query this association. However, Hibernate provides good support for using SQL queries, and hence there is no reason at this point to add an additional mapped object, which would add more complexity overall.

There is one additional association table mapping between the Seat and Performance tables. This table contains additional information regarding the seat's availability for a certain performance and we have included a SeatStatus class that we map this table to. There are, of course, two additional classes that we have not mentioned yet. They are RegisteredUser and Payment that are referenced by the Booking class. We don't show the attributes in the UML diagram, but they are all the columns of the corresponding table mapped to their corresponding Java data type.

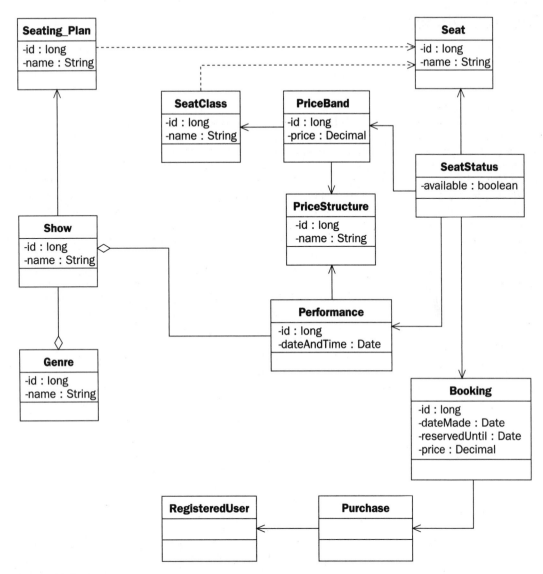

Figure 15-3

Object/Relational Mapping

We use Hibernate for our Object/Relational mapping. Choosing an O/R mapping solution can be a difficult task especially considering the recent introduction of the early draft of the new EJB 3.0 specification. Spring supports all the popular O/R Mapping solutions and it will also support the new EJB 3.0 persistence specification when it is finalized. Hibernate was the first O/R Mapper to be supported by Spring and it still remains the most popular one, so it was the most logical choice for our sample application. In addition to this, it is an excellent product and we knew it could handle our requirements.

In this section, we will take a look at some of the more interesting parts of the mapping definitions. The class/table mapping file is named `ticket-mapping.hbm.xml` and it is located in the `/src/orm` folder.

The mapping definitions start out by defining the mapping and relationships between the Genre, Show, Performance, and Seat domain objects. A Genre has a number of Shows associated. Each Show has a number of Performances and each Performance has a reference back to the Show and it also has a reference to the PriceStructure that it is associated with. The Seat class has a reference to the Seat to the left and right of it.

Hibernate's XML mapping metadata is quite intuitive, so you should find the following listing easy enough to understand even if you are not familiar with Hibernate. If necessary, please refer to the Hibernate reference manual or a book on Hibernate for an explanation of the meaning of the required elements.

```xml
<class name="Genre" table="Genre">
  <cache usage="read-only"/>
    <id name="id" column="id" type="long">
      <generator class="identity"/>
    </id>
    <property name="name" column="name" type="string"/>
  <set name="shows" lazy="true" inverse="true" order-by="name">
    <key column="Genre_id"/>
    <one-to-many class="Show"/>
  </set>
</class>

<class name="Show" table="Shows">
  <cache usage="read-only"/>
    <id name="id" column="id" type="long">
      <generator class="identity"/>
    </id>
    <property name="name" column="name" type="string"/>
  <set name="performances" inverse="true" order-by="date_and_time">
    <key column="Show_id"/>
    <one-to-many class="Performance"/>
  </set>
</class>

<class name="Performance" table="Performance">
  <cache usage="read-only"/>
    <id name="id" column="id" type="long">
      <generator class="identity"/>
    </id>
    <property name="dateAndTime" column="date_and_time" type="timestamp"/>
  <many-to-one name="show"
    class="Show"
```

```
      column="Show_id"/>
  <many-to-one name="priceStructure"
    class="PriceStructure"
    column="Price_Structure_id"/>
</class>

<class name="Seat" table="Seat">
  <cache usage="read-only"/>
    <id name="id" column="id" type="long">
      <generator class="identity"/>
    </id>
    <property name="name" column="name" type="string"/>
    <property name="rowOrBox" column="row_or_box" type="int"/>
    <property name="rowPosition" column="row_pos" type="int"/>
  <many-to-one name="leftSide"
        cascade="none"
        outer-join="false"
        foreign-key="fk_left_Seat">
    <column name="left_Seat_id"
        not-null="false"/>
  </many-to-one>
  <many-to-one name="rightSide"
        cascade="none"
        outer-join="false"
        foreign-key="fk_right_Seat">
    <column name="right_Seat_id"
        not-null="false"/>
  </many-to-one>
</class>
```

These definitions are sufficient for retrieving the populated Genre objects including references to Show, which in turn references all the Performance objects associated with a specific Show. The HQL query we use for retrieving all genres that do have some performances is as follows:

```
select g from Genre g
join fetch g.shows s
group by g
having size(g.shows) > 0
order by g.name
```

Again, HQL should be fairly intuitive, especially if you already know SQL (a necessity for enterprise Java developers).

We are using join fetch to ensure that the lazy-loaded collection of shows in the Genre class is populated. A Hibernate "fetch join" allows lazy relationships (including collections) to be retrieved along with their parent objects (Genre objects in this case) in a single query. It is particularly useful in cases like this, where we want to eagerly load a relationship that is marked as lazy in the static metadata.

This HQL query and a couple of additional ones are stored in the mapping file ticket-queries.hbm.xml as named queries. The use of "named" queries is a good practice in most ORM tools, including TopLink and Hibernate, when queries are complex. For example, it allows for query tuning in a well-defined location, without changing Java code. Named queries can also be reused in multiple DAO implementations, which guarantees consistency.

```
<query name="currentGenres">
  <![CDATA[
      select g from Genre g
      join fetch g.shows s
      group by g
      having size(g.shows) > 0
      order by g.name
  ]]>
</query>

<query name="availabilityForPerformance">
  <![CDATA[
      select new
          org.springframework.samples.ticket.dao.hibernate.AvailabilityDetail(
          pb, p, count(ss.seat), count(ss.booking))
    from Performance p, PriceBand pb, SeatStatus ss
    where ss.performance = p
    and ss.priceBand = pb
      and p.show = :show
    group by p.id, pb.id
  ]]>
</query>

<query name="costOfSeats">
  <![CDATA[
      select pb.price from PriceBand pb, SeatStatus ss
      where pb.id = ss.priceBand
      and ss.performance = :performanceId
      and ss.seat in ( :seatIds )
  ]]>
</query>

<query name="getSeatStatusForBooking">
  <![CDATA[
    from SeatStatus
    where Performance_id = :perfId
    and Seat_id in ( :ids )
  ]]>
</query>
```

The next item in the mapping file is a query that will return all available seats for a specific performance. This query relies on some information in the Seat_Plan_Seat table. Because this table is not mapped to an object, we have to use a named SQL query here. The mapping to the Seat object is straightforward; it's just the selection of the available seats that is a little tricky. We include only those seats that don't have a reference to a booking instance. We also include a "for update" clause, which will lock the selected rows in the database. This will prevent other users from booking these seats until our booking transaction has completed.

```
<sql-query name="availableSeatsToBook">
  <![CDATA[
    select {seat.*} from Seat seat
    where exists
      (select * from Seat_Status ss
      where ss.Seat_id = seat.id
      and ss.Performance_id = :perfId
```

```
        and ss.Booking_id is null)
    and exists
        (select * from Seat_Plan_Seat sps
    where sps.Seat_id = seat.id
    and sps.Seat_Class_id = :seatClassId)
    for update
    ]]>
    <return alias="seat" class="Seat"/>
</sql-query>
```

Note the use of the `seat.*` syntax to automatically select all mapped columns from the `seat` table. This is a Hibernate convenience that greatly simplifies the SQL query we need to write and ensures that our query will not break if we change the mappings for the `Seat` class. The only downside to using an SQL query here is that it depends on specific table and column names, which are otherwise concealed from application code using Hibernate metadata. However, this is usually an acceptable small price to pay. In cases where queries are highly complex, there may be an important advantage in using SQL queries, as it enables DBAs to tune them.

As we can see, Hibernate — like other leading ORM tools — can actually *help* us in some cases if we need to work at an SQL level.

DAO Implementation

The data access logic is not overly complex when it comes to the Java code. Most of the complexity is contained in the queries that are part of the Hibernate mapping file. We are using a Data Access Object (DAO) to separate the data access–specific code from the rest of the application. All the required methods are specified in the `BoxOfficeDao` interface and any implementation class must implement this interface. The implementation for Hibernate, which we are using here, is named `HibernateBoxOfficeDao`.

This DAO implementation extends the `HibernateDaoSupport` class and this allows us to use Spring's Hibernate support to execute all of our Hibernate queries. This amounts to just a few lines of code for each method. The only exceptions are the `reserveSeats` and `getAvailabilityForPerformance` methods that do involve more complex processing or multiple calls to the database to retrieve and update the relevant objects.

A typical call to execute a named query looks like this:

```
public Seat[] getAvailableSeatsToBook(Performance performance, SeatClass seatClass)
                        throws DataAccessException {
    List seats =
        getHibernateTemplate().findByNamedQueryAndNamedParam(
            "availableSeatsToBook",
            new String[] {"perfId", "seatClassId"},
            new Object[] {new Long(performance.getId()), new Long(seatClass.getId())});
    return (Seat[])seats.toArray(new Seat[seats.size()]);
    }
```

The parameters for this query — the `Performance Id` and the `Seat Id` — are passed in as named parameters in an array.

Note the code that we do *not* need to write. (This will be particularly obvious if you have used Hibernate without Spring in the past.) Spring's Hibernate integration is taking care of important issues such as obtaining the correct Hibernate `Session` to use, opening and closing it as necessary, and translating Hibernate exceptions into Spring's informative, persistence API-agnostic `DataAccessException` hierarchy. Code using this DAO via its interface is not tied to Hibernate. We could implement this DAO interface using another persistence API such as TopLink or JDO (or JSR-220 persistence, when it is finalized).

The code that we *do* need to write is not obscured by such mundane but important issues: It is focused on providing the necessary data to run the query and return strongly typed results.

The `getAvailabilityForPerformance` method is a bit more complicated and it starts out by getting the available performances together with availability and price information in the form of an `AvailabilityDetail` helper class. The next step is to populate an extension to the `Performance` class named `PerformanceWithAvailability` with these availability data. These two steps are highlighted in the program listing.

```
public PerformanceWithAvailability[] getAvailabilityForPerformance(Show show) {
    List availability =
        getHibernateTemplate().findByNamedQueryAndNamedParam(
        "availabilityForPerformance",
        "show",
        show);
    List performanceWithAvailability = new LinkedList();
    long lastPerformanceId = -1;
    PerformanceWithAvailability perf = null;
    for (int i = 0; i < availability.size(); i++) {
        AvailabilityDetail curr = (AvailabilityDetail)availability.get(i);
        if (lastPerformanceId != curr.getPerformance().getId()) {
            perf = new PerformanceWithAvailability(
                curr.getPerformance().getId(),
                curr.getPerformance().getDateAndTime(),
                curr.getPerformance().getPriceStructure(),
                curr.getPerformance().getShow());
            performanceWithAvailability.add(perf);
            lastPerformanceId = curr.getPerformance().getId();
        }
        PriceBandWithAvailability pb = new PriceBandWithAvailability(
            curr.getPriceBand().getId(),
            curr.getPriceBand().getPrice(),
            curr.getPriceBand().getPriceStructure(),
            curr.getPriceBand().getSeatClass(),
            curr.getAvailableSeatCount());
        perf.add(pb);
    }

    return (PerformanceWithAvailability[])performanceWithAvailability.toArray(
        new PerformanceWithAvailability[performanceWithAvailability.size()]);
}
```

This DAO class needs a reference to the Hibernate `SessionFactory` that we have defined in our configuration file. Naturally, this dependency is resolved in our sample application using Spring's Dependency Injection features. However, the DAO implementation is not tied to or aware of Spring IoC, and could be used programmatically without the Spring container. The content of the necessary configuration file is explored in the next section.

Data Access Context

The data access context is defined in a configuration file named `dataAccessContext.xml`. This is a regular Spring bean definition file with the beans needed for the DAO along with a transaction manager to provide transaction management for the data access technology that we are using. In this case it is, of course, a `HibernateTransactionManager`, but if we had used JDO instead, then we would just swap out the transaction manager for a `JDOTransactionManager`.

```xml
<bean id="transactionManager"
  class="org.springframework.orm.hibernate.HibernateTransactionManager">
  <property name="dataSource">
    <ref local="dataSource"/>
  </property>
  <property name="sessionFactory">
    <ref local="sessionFactory"/>
  </property>
</bean>
```

The data source configuration details are provided in a separate Properties file to allow an administrator to easily modify these setting at deployment time. If they are in a separate file, the administrator does not have to worry about accidentally altering any other configurations. Figure 15-4 shows the basic structure of this configuration.

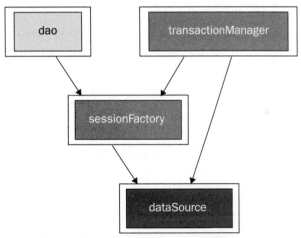

Figure 15-4

The graphs in Figures 15-4, 15-5, and 15-7 showing the structure of the configuration files were prepared using *SpringViz*, a utility for visualizing Spring's configuration files developed by Mike Thomas. It can be downloaded from `www.samoht.com/wiki/wiki.pl?SpringViz`.

Business Service Layer

The Business Service Layer is perhaps the most important part of the application. Business logic will normally reside here, and it is important to avoid any dependencies on surrounding layers and implementation technologies (including Spring!) in order to increase reusability and maintainability.

Business logic that is shared across multiple use cases, that does not imply delimitation of a transaction, and that depends only on relationships with other domain objects, rather than service layer objects, may best be coded in persistent domain objects. Follow normal OO design criteria here.

Services

All business logic is contained in the two service classes, and the Web Layer will access this logic via two interfaces. The first one is `EventsCalendar`, which provides information regarding available shows and scheduled performances. The primary methods are:

```
public abstract Collection getCurrentGenres();

public abstract Collection getAllGenres();
```

The second interface is `BoxOffice`, which provides services geared toward booking available seats, making payments, and so on. The most important methods for this interface are:

```
public abstract PerformanceWithAvailability[] getAvailabilityForPerformance(Show s)
    throws NoSuchPerformanceException;

public abstract Reservation allocateSeats(ReservationRequest request)
    throws RequestedSeatNotAvailableException, NotEnoughSeatsException,
        InvalidSeatingRequestException;
```

The majority of the business methods simply make a call to the DAO to retrieve the requested information. The `allocateSeats` method does include a lot more processing, however, so we have chosen to discuss it a bit further here.

```
public Reservation allocateSeats(ReservationRequest reservationRequest)
    throws RequestedSeatNotAvailableException, NotEnoughSeatsException,
        InvalidSeatingRequestException {

Performance performance = reservationRequest.getPerformance();
SeatClass seatClass = reservationRequest.getSeatClass();

// Get the available seats for this performance and seat class
Seat[] seats = boxOfficeDao.getAvailableSeatsToBook(performance, seatClass);
if (seats.length < reservationRequest.getNumberOfSeatsRequested()) {
  throw new NotEnoughSeatsException(seatClass.getId(),
      seats.length, reservationRequest.getNumberOfSeatsRequested());
}

// Pick the correct number of seats
Seat[] seatsRequested =
    new Seat[reservationRequest.getNumberOfSeatsRequested()];
System.arraycopy(seats, 0, seatsRequested, 0,
    reservationRequest.getNumberOfSeatsRequested());

BigDecimal price = boxOfficeDao.getCostOfSeats(performance, seatsRequested);

// New booking
Booking booking = new Booking();
booking.setDateMade(new Date());
```

```
        booking.setPrice(reservationRequest.getBookingFee().add(price));
        booking.setReservedUntil(reservationRequest.getHoldUntil());
        // Add booking and update seat status
        boxOfficeDao.reserveSeats(seatsRequested, performance, booking);

        // Create a Reservation object
        Reservation reservation = new Reservation(seatsRequested, booking);

        return reservation;
    }
```

We start by getting the available seats for the performance and seat class requested in the `Reservation Request`. If there aren't enough seats available, a checked exception is thrown, forcing the caller to deal with this situation. As we noted in other chapters, checked exceptions are often inappropriate for infrastructural exceptions. However, they are excellent in cases like this, when the situation definitely *is* recoverable, rather than a fatal system error. If we have enough seats, then we copy the requested number of seats to an array for further processing. These seats are used to create a booking that is used in the call to the `reserve Seats` method of the DAO. Finally we create a `Reservation` object that is returned.

Application Context

The service layer is configured in the `applicationContext.xml` file. Figure 15-5 shows the structure of this file.

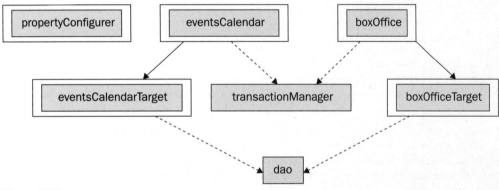

Figure 15-5

One of the most important aspects of the service layer is the definition of the transaction semantics. This is expressed in `applicationContext.xml` via a transactional proxy for the business object targets and transaction attributes. The transactional proxy is given the name of the target object, and the web layer will not have to be aware of any of the transaction management that is handled behind the scenes.

We have chosen the `TransactionProxyFactoryBean` as it is easy to use and provides all the functionality we need for this application. All `get*` methods are executed in a read-only transaction if one is already started. The `allocate*` methods will require a transaction because we want to eliminate any chance of double booking seats in the `allocateSeats` method. This method does its work in a couple of steps and it is essential that no other transaction reserves any of the requested seats until we are done processing. We have chosen to rely on a database lock via a `select ... for update` statement; for more detail, see the Hibernate query definition mentioned earlier in the section covering the O/R Mapping. This strategy will work well as long as we can control all applications that book seats.

565

```
<!-- Transactional proxies for the primary business objects -->
<bean id="boxOffice"
  class="org.springframework.transaction.interceptor.TransactionProxyFactoryBean">
  <property name="target">
    <ref local="boxOfficeTarget"/>
  </property>
  <property name="transactionManager">
    <ref bean="transactionManager"/>
  </property>
  <property name="transactionAttributes">
    <props>
      <prop key="get*">PROPAGATION_SUPPORTS,readOnly</prop>
      <prop key="allocate*">
   PROPAGATION_REQUIRED, ISOLATION_READ_COMMITTED,timeout_60,-
ApplicationException
      </prop>
    </props>
  </property>
</bean>

<bean id="eventsCalendar"
  class="org.springframework.transaction.interceptor.TransactionProxyFactoryBean">
  <property name="target">
    <ref local="eventsCalendarTarget"/>
  </property>
  <property name="transactionManager">
    <ref bean="transactionManager"/>
  </property>
  <property name="transactionAttributes">
    <props>
      <prop key="get*">PROPAGATION_SUPPORTS,readOnly</prop>
    </props>
  </property>
</bean>
```

The transaction definitions are then configured to work together with the data access layer in the form of a transaction manager. The transaction manager is defined in the `dataAccessContext.xml` file that we saw earlier and can easily be altered depending on the data access technology being used. The transactional proxy does not need to know what type of transaction manager is in use.

Web Layer

We are finally getting closer to the part of the application that the end user will see and interact with. The technology used for this layer is Spring's MVC Framework. One important feature of this MVC Framework is the lack of dependency between the controllers and the views. You could switch view technology without having to modify your controllers.

Flow Through the Application

As discussed previously, the sample application is based on the sample application from *Expert One-on-One J2EE Design and Development*. We'll implement the presentation layer using Spring MVC, but before we begin, let's first revisit the flow through the actual application, when looking at it from a client's perspective as shown in Figure 15-6.

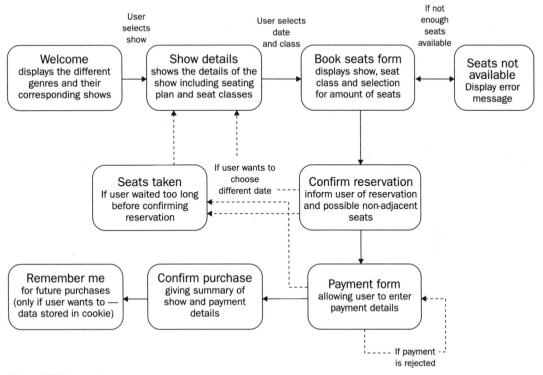

Figure 15-6

1. The user enters the main page and is presented with a list of drop-down boxes, containing shows. The shows are all grouped with the genre they belong to.

2. After the user has selected a show, she will be presented with a range of dates for which seats are available. The calendar shows the dates, as well the seat classes for which seats are still available.

3. After selecting a seat class and a date, a form is displayed containing information about the price of each seat. The user can choose a number of seats here.

    a. If the number of seats chosen is available, the user will skip to the next step.

    b. If not enough seats are available, an error message will be displayed, after which the user will go back to Step 2

4. The next screen displays a confirmation about the reservation. If the seats are not adjacent, the user will be informed.

5. After the user indicates she wishes to purchase the tickets, a check is performed as to whether or not another user has reserved the seats in the meantime. (Seats are automatically reserved for five minutes for each user, so if a user waits for longer than that, there is a possibility that somebody else may take her seats.) The next screen displays a form where the user can fill in her personal details and payment information (credit card info). The personal data of the user is automatically filled in if during a previous purchase the user chose to store that information in a cookie on her local computer.

6. A successful payment request (with the credit card data entered by the user) results in a confirmation screen being displayed where the user can optionally choose to fill in a password to store the personal data on her computer using a cookie.

Configuring the Application via web.xml

The web application will, upon startup, use information provided in the standard J2EE web.xml file for the initial configuration. In this file we specify the context location for the application contexts used by this web application.

We also specify the class that will be used to load these application contexts. In a server that follows the initialization order specified in the Servlet 2.4 specification, you can safely use a ContextLoader Listener. More and more application servers do adhere to this new specification. For older servers, you might have to substitute this listener with a servlet loaded as the first one on startup. In that case you would use a ContextLoaderServlet.

Another important configuration item is the declaration of the dispatcher servlet. We are using a standard DispatcherServlet here. See Chapter 12 for more information regarding these startup options.

```xml
<?xml version="1.0" encoding="ISO-8859-1"?>
<!DOCTYPE web-app
    PUBLIC "-//Sun Microsystems, Inc.//DTD Web Application 2.3//EN"
    "http://java.sun.com/dtd/web-app_2_3.dtd">

<web-app>

    <context-param>
        <param-name>contextConfigLocations</param-name>
        <param-value>
            /WEB-INF/dataAccessContext-local.xml   /WEB-INF/applicationContext.xml
        </param-value>
    </context-param>

    <listener>
        <listener-class>
            org.springframework.web.context.ContextLoaderListener
        </listener-class>
    </listener>

    <servlet>
        <servlet-name>ticket</servlet-name>
        <servlet-class>
            org.springframework.web.servlet.DispatcherServlet
        </servlet-class>
        <load-on-startup>1</load-on-startup>
    </servlet>

    <servlet-mapping>
        <servlet-name>ticket</servlet-name>
        <url-pattern>*.html</url-pattern>
```

```
    </servlet-mapping>

    <welcome-file-list>
      <welcome-file>listShows.html</welcome-file>
    </welcome-file-list>

  </web-app>
```

This bootstraps the Spring container, and ensures that no application objects are required to load a Spring context or explicitly look up other objects. Instead, Dependency Injection is applied to all application code.

Web Controllers

The `ticket-servlet.xml` file contains the URL-to-servlet mappings that the dispatcher servlet needs. This is expressed as a regular bean definition using the name attribute to define the URL such as `/listShows.html`. This URL is mapped via the class attribute in this case specifying `org.springframework.samples.ticket.web.ListShowsController` as the controller class. We include only the relevant parts of this file here to show how these options are defined. In addition to the controller, we also specify the view resolver class—in our case this is a JSTL resolver to be used with our JSPs. Please refer to Chapter 12 for more detailed discussion.

```
    <?xml version="1.0" encoding="UTF-8"?>
    <!DOCTYPE beans PUBLIC "-//SPRING//DTD BEAN//EN"
    "http://www.springframework.org/dtd/spring-beans.dtd">

    <beans>

      <bean name="/listShows.html"
          class="org.springframework.samples.ticket.web.ListShowsController">
      <property name="eventsCalendar"><ref bean="eventsCalendar"/></property>
      </bean>

      <bean name="/displayShow.html"
        ...
      </bean>

      <bean name="/reserveSeats.html"
        ...
      </bean>

    ...


      <bean id="viewResolver"
        class="org.springframework.web.servlet.view.InternalResourceViewResolver">
      <property name="prefix"><value>/WEB-INF/jsp/</value></property>
      <property name="suffix"><value>.jsp</value></property>
      <property name="viewClass">
        <value>org.springframework.web.servlet.view.JstlView</value>
      </property>
```

```
    </bean>

    ...

</beans>
```

The graphic in Figure 15-7 shows the relationships between the three main controllers and the classes in the service layer that they refer to. Each controller is represented by the URL that it is mapped to.

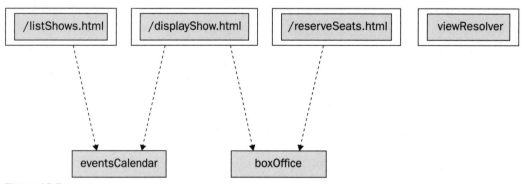

Figure 15-7

We will end the exploration of the controllers by briefly looking at the ListShowsController. The logic is very simple: Retrieve the data for the current genres from the eventsCalendar service and then pass this on in the form of a ModelAndView. All dependencies have already been configured via Dependency Injection and most of the request/response code is part of the AbstractController, so there is very little code in this servlet class.

```java
public class ListShowsController extends AbstractController {

    /** the eventscalendar to use */
    private EventsCalendar eventsCalendar;

    protected ModelAndView handleRequestInternal(
        HttpServletRequest httpServletRequest,
        HttpServletResponse httpServletResponse) {
      Collection genres = eventsCalendar.getCurrentGenres();
      logger.debug("Genres: " + genres.size());
      ModelAndView mav = new ModelAndView("showlist", "genres", genres);
      return mav;
    }

    public void setEventsCalendar(EventsCalendar eventsCalendar) {
      this.eventsCalendar = eventsCalendar;
    }

}
```

View Technology

We have chosen to implement the views as JSPs, as this is the technology that most of our readers are familiar with. We could just as easily have implemented the views using a templating solution such as Velocity or FreeMarker.

We are not going to look at each individual screen in the application, but we will take a closer look at one screen to highlight some of the features we have taken advantage of: the welcome screen.

This screen (see Figure 15-8) has a very simple layout. A drop-down box for each genre that has shows with some performances is presented together with a button to initiate a transition to the next screen for the selected show.

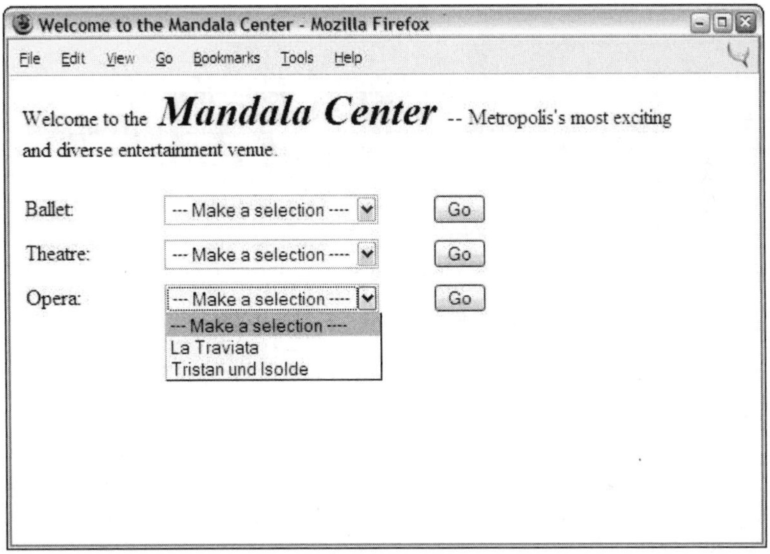

Figure 15-8

The following code example shows the JSP used to generate this screen. There are very few decorative features included because we recommend using a separate decorator layer for this. SiteMesh and Tiles are excellent choices here. We are using JSTL 1.1 syntax to provide better compatibility with the variety of application servers that you might want to try to deploy this application on. We strongly recommend using JSTL if you are using JSP.

```
<%@ taglib prefix="c" uri="http://java.sun.com/jstl/core" %>
Welcome to the <font size="+2">Mandala Center</font>
-- Metropolis' most existing and diverse entertainment centre.
<table border="0">
<c:forEach items="${genres}" var="genre">
  <c:if test="${not empty genre.shows}">
    <tr>
      <td><c:out value="${genre.name}"/>: </td>
      <td>
```

```
            <form action="<c:url value="/displayShow.html"/>" method="post">
              <select style="width: 150px;" name="showId">
                <c:forEach items="${genre.shows}" var="show">
                  <option value="<c:out value="${show.id}"/>">
                    <c:out value="${show.name}"/>
                  </option>
                </c:forEach>
              </select>
              <input type="submit" value="Go"/>
            </form>
          </td>
        </p>
      </c:if>
    </c:forEach>
```

Comparison with the *J2EE Design and Development* Implementation

As we already noted, the requirements for our sample application are essentially the same as for the sample application presented in *Expert One-on-One J2EE Design and Development* by Rod Johnson. This book introduced an *Interface21* application framework that has been greatly enhanced to become the Spring Framework. Because these two implementations have much in common, it is informative to compare them and to note some of the differences.

Simpler Technology

The biggest differences stem from the fact that the framework has undergone some important enhancements that allow us to use simpler technology. There is no longer a good reason to use EJBs for this type of application. The framework now provides declarative transaction management, which was one of the advantages of using EJBs in the past.

Hibernate simplifies the data access layer and there is no need to provide a custom caching solution for infrequently changing data. We simply enable Hibernate's second level cache for the appropriate classes.

Because we are not using EJBs or other more advanced J2EE features, we can deploy our application as a WAR file to any servlet container that is compatible with the Servlet Specification version 2.3 or later. This greatly simplifies the deployment step, and tends to improve portability between servers.

Yet we could still take this application and run it in a high-end application server using JTA. We haven't ruled out any options here.

Database Changes

We are also using an open source database instead of the proprietary Oracle database that was used earlier. This eliminates any use of stored procedures because the target database, MySQL, does not currently support stored procedures. They will be available in an upcoming 5.0 release, but we have decided to use the production-ready 4.1 version. We are also using Hibernate as the O/R mapping framework and this allows us to move any custom caching from the application layer to the O/R mapping layer. This also eliminates the need for the Message Bean that was used to invalidate some of this caching in the earlier implementation.

The data model is essentially the same as it was. We are treating this as a "legacy" database and any existing data can safely be imported into the new database. It has been adjusted for MySQL and we are using the INTEGER datatype for the keys instead of NUMERIC. The reason for this is that the INTEGER datatype clearly defines this as a number without any decimals, while the NUMERIC datatype is defined to receive a default precision and scale unless one is provided. This does not have an impact for Oracle because Oracle uses a proprietary NUMBER datatype internally, but it could have some impact for other databases.

Server Configuration

You are going to need both a database server and a Java application server. We have developed and tested the sample application using MySQL version 4.1 and Apache's Jakarta Tomcat server version 5.5.

MySQL

You can download both software and installation instructions for the MySQL server from www.mysql.com. You also need to download the MySQL Connector/J version 3.1 JDBC driver from the MySQL site.

Once you have installed this database server, there are a few steps involved in configuring it to be used for the sample application.

You need to create a new user account and a new database for the MySQL server. All commands that follow assume that you have made the MySQL installation directory your current directory. We also assume that you have added a password to your "root" user account. If not, just run this command (after replacing the question marks with your new password):

```
Windows:  bin\mysqladmin -u root password ????????
Linux:    ./bin/mysqladmin -u root password ????????
```

To create the Spring database, we execute this command—you will now be prompted for the root password before your command is completed:

```
Windows:  bin\mysqladmin -u root -p create spring
Linux:    ./bin/mysqladmin -u root -p create spring
```

Finally we need to add the "spring" user and grant access to the spring database. For this step we start the command-line client and enter the commands at the mysql prompt. To start the command-line client enter:

```
Windows:  bin\mysql -u root -p
Linux:    ./bin/mysql -u root -p
```

You will again be prompted for the root password. Then at the mysql> prompt enter the following commands:

```
use mysql;
grant all on spring to spring@localhost identified by 't1cket';
exit
```

You should see a couple of messages saying "Database changed" and "Query OK, 0 rows affected."

Tomcat

You can download the Jakarta Tomcat server software and installation instructions from http://jakarta. apache.org/tomcat/index.html.

Installing Tomcat is very simple — either unzip the distribution to the desired location, or if you are on Windows, you can use the download that provides a regular Windows installer that you should execute.

There are no specific steps to prepare the Tomcat server to be able to run the sample application.

Build and Deployment

Building and deploying the application is very easy. We assume that you already have your system configured with a Java SDK version 1.4 or later and also that you already have Apache Ant installed. You can download the source code for the sample application from the "Download Code" section of the Wrox "Programmer to Programmer" website located at www.wrox.com. Just unzip the downloaded archive in a location of your choice.

You will also need to download a recent production release of the MySQL Connector/J JDBC driver from the MySQL website located at www.mysql.com. Unzip the downloaded archive and copy the JAR file named mysql-connector-java-x.x.xx-xxxx.jar (the exact name will vary depending on the downloaded version) to the lib yesdirectory in the directory where you have unzipped the sample application.

Creating and Loading the Database Tables

We are assuming that you have created the spring database following the preceding instructions. To create the tables we need to run the sample application, copy the create-ticket-mysql.sql file from the db directory of the sample application, and download to the directory where you have MySQL installed. Now you can run the following command:

```
Windows:  bin\mysql -u spring -p spring < create-ticket-mysql.sql
Linux:    ./bin/mysql -u spring -p spring < create-ticket-mysql.sql
```

You will be prompted for the password for the "spring" user—it was earlier set to be "t1cket". After this script completes, you can perform the same procedure for `load-ticket-mysql.sql`. This script file will load the necessary test data. There is also a `clear-ticket-mysql.sql` to delete the test data and a `drop-ticket-mysql.sql` script for dropping all the tables.

Building the Application and Deploying It to the Tomcat Server

The build script that we are using is a standard `build.xml` script. To build the application, change to the directory where you have unpacked the downloaded sample code. Then simply run `ant build`.

There is another Ant target named "warfile" that will build the application and pack everything into a WAR file located in the `dist` directory. This WAR file can be deployed directly in your application server. For Tomcat, simply copy this file to the `webapps` directory that is part of your Tomcat install. When Tomcat is started, you should be able to open `http://localhost:8080/ticket` in your web browser.

Summary

In this chapter we have seen an example of how Spring can be used to ease the development of web-based J2EE applications. We looked at the different layers and the associated configuration files. We also looked at some of the code and discussed some of the choices we had to make while developing the application.

We covered the steps necessary to prepare MySQL for hosting the database used by this application. With the database in place we showed how to build and deploy the application to the Tomcat Server.

Finally, we noted some differences between our current implementation and the original implementation presented in *Expert One-on-One J2EE Design and Development*.

We hope that after reading this chapter, you will have a feel for how a Spring application is implemented, and configured, as a set of logical layers with clear responsibilities.

16

Conclusion

Let's now look back over what we've learned so far, and discuss some guidelines that will help you succeed in your Spring-based projects.

Problems Solved by Spring

The original motivation for Spring was to simplify J2EE development. It does this by providing sophisticated configuration management services that remove the need for developers to write their own lookup code; by providing an AOP framework that provides declarative services to POJOs; and by abstracting developers from complex J2EE APIs. Together, this enables a POJO programming model, in which POJOs typically don't need to call enterprise services explicitly, but can do so by accessing well-defined interfaces, with no "implicit" dependencies such as JNDI.

To enjoy maximum benefit from this approach, you should never write any JNDI or other lookups; use fewer singletons and custom factories; and have no need for ad hoc configuration techniques such as parsing your own XML documents or parameterizing objects from Properties files. The core of Spring is one powerful, extensible factory to end all factories.

The Spring approach is also beneficial in non-J2EE environments. Spring's Dependency Injection and AOP capabilities are equally relevant in J2SE applications. All nontrivial applications tend to need some externalization of configuration, and using a container such as Spring is a much better approach than ad hoc approaches. Spring's JDBC and other data access capabilities are also valuable in non-J2EE environments, as is its integration with numerous popular products and APIs that can be used in a range of scenarios.

> **Spring can provide a consistent architectural backbone in both J2EE and non-J2EE (even client-side or standalone) applications. Spring largely decouples your application code from its runtime environment, meaning that you can maximize code reuse and enjoy a consistent programming model wherever your code executes.**

The Spring Solution

Spring essentially has three elements:

❏ **IoC container:** The Spring core, which provides highly sophisticated capabilities for configuration management.

❏ **AOP framework:** A proxy-based AOP framework that works in conjunction with the Spring IoC container to provide declarative services to POJOs and allow the use of custom aspects.

❏ **Consistent service abstraction and integration:** This provides a basis for a POJO application model delivered using IoC and AOP. It also allows Spring to integrate with numerous other products within a consistent conceptual framework.

Let's quickly review some of the major modules in the framework, as shown in the following table.

Module	What It Does	Why and When to Use It
IoC container: bean factory	Basic Spring IoC container. Provides powerful and extensible Dependency Injection capabilities.	If you need a small-footprint IoC container — for example, in use in an applet.
IoC container: application context	More advanced IoC container. Adds resource loading, event publication, and other capabilities.	Normal usage of Spring IoC container. An application context *is* a bean factory so the usage model is consistent.
AOP framework	Allows sophisticated interception to be applied to any object managed by a Spring container, or programmatically using a proxy factory. Supports core AOP concepts such as pointcuts, making it much more than a simple interception mechanism.	As an enabling technology for Spring enterprise services such as declarative transaction management — in which case there is no need for developers to be consciously aware of the use of AOP. To enable application developers to implement custom aspects to modularize code that would otherwise be scattered throughout an application's object model.

Module	What It Does	Why and When to Use It
Data access abstraction	Provides a common approach to resource management and exception handling, regardless of which of the supported data access technologies you use. Spring supports the following data access technologies out of the box: Hibernate, JDO, TopLink, iBATIS, and Apache OJB. The framework provides a strong conceptual basis for supporting other APIs. JSR-220 POJO persistence will be supported as soon as the specification and binaries are released in mature form. It is also possible for users to implement support for proprietary or other unsupported data access APIs, while building on Spring's key data access concepts.	We recommend that you use Spring's data access abstraction, whichever data access technology you use. We recommend that you use Spring's data access support to implement persistence framework–agnostic *DAO interfaces*, meaning that your business service layer is decoupled from the persistence framework.
JDBC abstraction framework	Provides an API layer over JDBC that simplifies exception handling, greatly reduces the amount of code that needs to be written in typical JDBC operations, and reduces the likelihood of making common errors.	Use instead of direct use of JDBC whenever you need to perform SQL-based relational operations.
Transaction abstraction	Integrates with Spring's data access framework to provide a transaction abstraction that works in any environment and can provide declarative transaction management without EJB — even, without JTA.	To decouple application code from the underlying transaction management infrastructure. To provide simpler, more easily testable programmatic transaction management than JTA or local transactions. To provide more powerful and portable declarative transaction management than EJB CMT, *for any POJO*.

Table continued on following page

Module	What It Does	Why and When to Use It
MVC web framework	Spring's own web MVC framework.. Conceptually most similar to Struts.	Use if you prefer a request-based web framework (as opposed to a component-based framework such as Tapestry or JSF) and want a highly flexible, customizable framework that has a clean separation of model, view, and controller responsibilities and can accommodate a wide variety of view technologies.
JMS	Supports publication of JMS messages. *Support for message-driven objects — an alternative to message-driven beans — is planned for future releases of Spring.*	Use to make sending JMS messages much easier, regardless of how you consume messages.
J2EE integration	Integrates with the core container to avoid the need for JNDI lookups and to make EJBs easier to implement and access.	To decouple application code from the JNDI environment, making it easier to test and use in non-J2EE environments, and making the intent clearer by focusing on the relevant *business interfaces* providing application functionality, not J2EE API details. Greatly reduces the amount of code you need to write — for example, by wholly eliminating the need to write JNDI lookups or obtain an EJB reference via the EJB's home interface.
Lightweight remoting	Provides remoting support to export POJO services across a range of remoting protocols.	Use to export remote services based on any Spring-managed objects.
JMX support	Provides JMX management to Spring-managed objects. Spring does not provide its own JMX MBean server: Its JMX support integrates with that provided with your application server, or a standalone JMX server.	Use to manage your application objects at runtime with JMX.
Scripting support	To enable any object managed by a Spring container to be written in a scripting language instead of Java.	We discuss when you might choose to implement an object in a language other than Java later in this chapter.

Together, these modules make a coherent whole. Dependency Injection is used consistently within the framework, as is AOP (where necessary). Once you understand the core Spring concepts, you will be able to leverage that knowledge in all parts of the framework.

Guidelines for Spring Development

This book has covered both the *how* and the *why* of Spring development. Let's summarize some of the most important criteria in the *why* category that will help you develop successful Spring applications.

Technology Choices

Let's begin by looking at some of the key technology choices you might make in typical applications.

Spring Versus "Old J2EE"

If you're reading this chapter, you've presumably decided to use Spring. However, you still may be considering *where* you should use Spring: in particular, how your Spring usage should relate to the traditional EJB component model.

> **Spring provides a compelling alternative to the EJB programming model in a large proportion of J2EE applications. If you're implementing a web application — even a high-end transactional web application — you're probably better off without EJB. If it uses a single database, you can probably do perfectly well with a servlet engine such as Tomcat or Jetty, without the added complexity of an application server. Spring's declarative transaction management provides a programming model that is portable between low- and high-end environments, so you can always switch to a full-blown application server if you ever need to, while doing the simplest deployment that can possibly work in the meantime.**

Even if you have multiple transactional resources, you may well not need EJB. You can use Spring's declarative transaction management over JTA as a replacement for EJB CMT, although in this case we recommend that you *do* use a high-end application server that provides robust distributed transaction management (although a standalone transaction manager such as ObjectWeb's JOTM is an option).

> **Spring gives you a choice as to whether you need to use a full-blown application server. If you *really* need an application server, Spring will let you get at its full power; if you *don't* really need its capabilities, Spring will help you dispense with the unnecessary complexity and baggage it brings, but without closing off the option of deploying your code to a full-blown J2EE application server in the future if you ever need to.**

If you do choose to use EJB — or if it is imposed on you by managerial fiat — you can still use most of Spring's capabilities behind an EJB facade. It is good practice in EJB 2.*x* applications to make EJBs only coarse-grained facades, with the bulk of the work being done by POJOs behind them. Spring provides an excellent way of managing those POJOs, and its superclasses for implementing EJBs both make this good usage practice easier and help to catch some common EJB programming errors, such as failure to honor the implicit contract required of EJBs but not expressed in any interface (such as the need for an `ejbCreate()` method). A Spring application is likely to be much closer to the eventual EJB 3.0 model than an EJB 2.*x* architecture.

As using EJB 2.*x* entity beans is hardly a viable architectural choice, you will still want to use Spring's data access integration behind an EJB facade if you choose to use EJB. Note that this will work perfectly if you choose to use EJB container-managed transactions.

Distributed Versus Local Objects

Minimize unnecessary calling out of process. It adds complexity and performance overhead. It does not usually increase scalability. Co-locate business objects and their callers if possible.

This is, of course, a matter of prudent design rather than a consequence of using Spring. Spring in fact provides a powerful *lightweight remoting* infrastructure that supports multiple protocols.

As with transaction management, Spring remoting can increase potential for code reuse, by isolating callers from dependency on specific remoting infrastructures — they need simply to express a dependency on the business methods interface of the potentially remote service, and leave Spring's client-side infrastructure to perform the necessary lookup and remoting service steps. Of course, it's still dangerous to rely on location transparency: There are many issues to be considered in transferring object graphs over the wire.

> **Distribution should be seen as a facade layer on top of a well-defined service layer. Distribution considerations should not infect the whole of your design, as has traditionally occurred with transfer objects and orthodox J2EE architecture.**

Java Versus Other Languages?

As of Spring 1.3 you can use a variety of languages, including Groovy and Beanshell, to implement any object managed by a Spring container. As other objects depend on that object by interface, they are unaware of its implementation language. (Yet another example of the benefits of the pluggability that an IoC container provides.) You can configure a scripted object using Spring Dependency Injection or Setter Injection, and you can also apply the full power of Spring's AOP framework to any scripted object — for example, providing it with declarative transaction management or custom auditing.

Why would you choose to implement an object in a language other than Java? Some indications are:

- ❑ **You need dynamic reloading.** Spring's support of scripting languages allows this, *so long as the external contract (interfaces) of the script doesn't change.*

- ❑ **The code is naturally much more concise in the scripting language than in Java, or the intent is much clearer.** For example, if you can use Groovy closures to good effect, there may be a real case for writing an object in Groovy instead of Java.

On the other hand, reasons *not* to use another language are:

- ❑ **Better IDE support for Java, such as code completion:** This gap may narrow in the future as Eclipse plug-ins and other IDE support are developed for Groovy and other languages.

❑ **Better performance:** Even scripting languages that compile to Java byte code are likely to impose more performance overhead than pure Java objects. Spring's dynamic scripting support also means that any scripted object will be an AOP proxy, with a number of introductions, although this amounts to only a modest overhead.

❑ **Consistency:** Clearly the expectation will be that objects in a Java platform application will be written in Java. You need to have good reason to cut against that expectation.

The choice is up to you: As usual, Spring doesn't constrain you.

Layer by Layer

Let's now look through the architectural tiers of a typical Spring application, discussing best practices in organizing whole applications and the individual tiers.

A Layered Architecture

We recommend — and Spring facilitates — the use of a *layered architecture*. Note that while *logical* layering is essential to clean application design, *physical* layering is not.

In a typical Spring application, the layers will be as follows:

❑ **Presentation tier:** Most often a web tier, but a good architecture should accommodate a choice of different presentations. We include remoting as a form of presentation in the present discussion.

❑ **Business services layer:** The entry point for the application's services. The business services layer is typically responsible for delimiting transactions within which code in lower architectural tiers will execute.

❑ **DAO interfaces:** A layer of interfaces used to find and save persistent domain objects. This is called the *Repository* in Eric Evans' *Domain Driven Development* (Addison-Wesley, 2003).

❑ **Persistent domain objects:** Persistent objects such as *Product* or *Performance* that make up a model of the application domain, and may contain behavior as well as state.

❑ **Databases and other EIS tier services:** The application uses these for persistence and integration.

Of course such layering is not Spring-specific; it reflects good architectural practice. However, Spring significantly helps to *facilitate* good practice.

Let's summarize best practices for each layer, beginning closest to the database.

Data Access and Integration

The most common requirement is working with one or more relational databases — usually, with *one*. The key choice here is between the use of O/R mapping and a relational approach to data.

> **In general, if you can use O/R mapping, you should probably do so, as it will save time and effort by freeing you from the significant effort of writing SQL to load and store your objects, and may help to give you a better domain model. (Application developers should spend time on their domain, rather than plumbing concerns such as writing mundane SQL.) However, you should not be dogmatic, and insist on using O/R mapping where it's a poor fit.**

Indications that O/R mapping won't work in a particular application include:

❑ A complex legacy data model, where there is no natural O/R mapping

❑ The need to use stored procedures heavily (for example, because of a requirement to update the database only through stored procedures)

❑ Many set-based operations

❑ Limited scope for caching

If these considerations apply, you are probably better off using a relational, SQL-based approach, with Spring JDBC or iBATIS SQL Maps.

In some applications you will need to mix both SQL-based and O/R mapping approaches. If you do mix and match, remember the following issues, which are crucial to preserving data integrity:

❑ JDBC updates or deletes can invalidate the first- or second-level cache of the ORM product.

❑ ORM updates that have not been flushed to the database can result in JDBC queries returning stale results. Explicitly flush the ORM tool's first-level cache if you need to query. But where possible, if you must query the same data, do it within the ORM tool, which should manage flushing automatically.

If an ORM tool and JDBC code are used to access different tables — as often happens — these issues are not a concern.

Although the application developer is responsible for ensuring correct semantics, Spring does help significantly with the plumbing of mixing and matching: for example, making it easy to use the same JDBC connection in JDBC and Hibernate code, even without the use of JTA.

> **Never use JDBC directly. Consider an ORM tool, or iBATIS SQL Maps. If you need low-level relational access, use Spring JDBC. Avoid direct use of the JDBC API, which will cost time and allow greater potential for errors.**

Whatever O/R tool you choose — and the choice is up to you, not imposed by Spring — we recommend that you use Spring's data access integration and the recommended DAO interface approach to work with data. This has many benefits:

❑ It decouples business service objects from API details, meaning that business objects operate at a higher level of abstraction and are more testable.

❑ It insulates your application against changes in data access technology. For example, if you want to migrate from Hibernate 2 today to JSR-220 persistence once it is released, you will be able to do so without extensive change: While you will inevitably need to take semantic differences into account, the bulk of the work will be limited to reimplementing a well-defined layer of DAO interfaces.

❑ Spring's data access exception hierarchy is not only a key element in the decoupling, but helps to clean up your code through being highly informative.

We recommend that you configure your O/R mapping tool using Spring's local factories, rather than through JCA (which adds complexity without adding real value in this case). For example, it's usually best to configure Hibernate using Spring's `LocalSessionFactoryBean`.

Persistent Domain Model

Persistent domain objects model things and concepts in your domain. Because J2EE has a poor history on object orientation, it's important to make the following notes about domain objects:

❑ Remember the *object* part. Don't fall into the traditional J2EE trap of viewing them as dumb bit buckets. They *should* encapsulate their state, and may contain behavior.

❑ Domain objects should use inheritance as necessary. Forget another antipattern from the dark days of EJB 1.*x* and 2.*x* entity beans, where inheritance was off-limits.

Your domain model is inevitably partly determined by the capabilities of your persistence strategy. For example, *some* use of inheritance is often appropriate, but *deep* inheritance may well pose a problem for O/R mapping solutions — at least, if you care about having an idiomatic relational model, rather than tables that contain data for several subclasses. (Database views may sometimes help here.)

If you can, try to avoid making your persistent domain objects depend on your persistence strategy — for example, by implementing callback interfaces such as Hibernate's `net.sf.hibernate.Lifecycle` or JDO's `javax.jdo.InstanceCallbacks`. (For example, if you are using Hibernate, *user types* are valuable in such cases, externalizing Hibernate-specific code from domain objects themselves.)

Business Services Layer

In a traditional J2EE architecture, this layer would be implemented in stateless session beans. In a Spring application, it will be implemented as POJOs, which can enjoy a variety of declarative services — both from Spring, and custom.

The major issues here are transaction management and thread management.

Transaction Management

There are a number of important choices around transaction management. With a Spring-based solution you can make any of these choices, in any combination. However, as transaction management is a crucial architectural issue, you need to understand the issues behind the decisions you make.

Programming model

There's a fundamental choice between *programmatic* transaction management (writing code to drive transactions through some API) and *declarative* transaction management (using a framework that can automatically delimit transactions around methods or other boundaries). Spring supports both.

> **We recommend declarative transaction management in most cases. If you can avoid writing code to handle the transaction aspect, it's a win. Given appropriate design, most things can be done with declarative transaction management.**

If you choose programmatic transaction management, Spring's transaction abstraction — and especially the `TransactionTemplate` helper class — will significantly simplify the programming model whatever underlying transaction infrastructure you use.

If you've chosen declarative transaction management, you have the choice between two major implementing technologies: EJB CMT and Spring transaction management. EJB CMT works well, but of course incurs the various negatives attached to EJB as a technology overall.

> In general, we recommend Spring's declarative transaction management, rather than EJB CMT. It's simpler to set up and more powerful (through the unique *rollback rule* concept), and it decouples your code from JNDI and JTA, maximizing potential for reuse and testing.

If you want to use MDBs, using CMT makes more sense: In this case, you can get message acknowledgment.

Spring's own message consumption capabilities should eventually provide an additional choice here.

Underlying infrastructure

There is also a choice of underlying infrastructure for your transactions: for example, JTA *global* transactions, or JDBC, Hibernate, JDO, or other *local* transactions on a specific API.

If you choose to use EJB, you are tied to JTA. If you choose Spring transaction management — whether programmatic or declarative — you have a consistent programming model over any supported transaction infrastructure (including all those just mentioned).

> Don't automatically use JTA. Far fewer applications need distributed transactions than J2EE developers have traditionally assumed. Distributed transactions have a high cost in complexity and performance, so it's wise to avoid them if possible.
>
> While JTA is not intended purely for distributed transactions — and using JTA won't make your transactions distributed if you're using just a single database — it is a relatively complex API and infrastructure combination, and using local transactions may be more appropriate.
>
> Fortunately, with Spring you don't need to make a permanent choice between local and global transactions. You can preserve the same programming model, changing only configuration, not code, and confidently start with a simple transaction infrastructure until it's proven that you need greater power and complexity.

Threading Issues

Another important issue to consider in business services is the threading model.

> Choose the simplest threading model that can possibly work. Given that service layer objects are normally stateless, this is *a single shared instance*. Normally this is not difficult to achieve, as instance variables will be configured via the IoC container before the object's business methods can be invoked, and thus are not read-write at runtime. Instance variables of types such as DAOs — such as the `DataSources` and `Session` factories that DAOs use — are normally threadsafe, although of course you need to be aware of the issues.
>
> It's normally necessary only to pool *resources*, such as database connections, rather than instances of business objects.

We believe that the traditional insistence on using a pool of service objects, which EJB enforces in the case of stateless session beans, is not necessary. Unnecessary pooling can actually be harmful if you want a single instance rather than a pool of instances — which, for example, may all have their own copies of reference data. It also typically slightly reduces performance, without increasing scalability.

However, you can add pooling transparently if you find a valid case for it, using Spring's *pooling target sources*, discussed in Chapter 4.

Presentation Tier

The presentation tier should sit on a well-defined business object layer. When this is the case, the complexity of the presentation tier is reduced, and it becomes feasible to have multiple different presentation tiers on one application, which may be a business requirement.

> The presentation tier should be thin. It should contain only the code required to process user interactions, invoke business services, and display the results of processing to the user.

Web Application Presentation

All web applications should use a web application framework to provide structure and encourage best practice.

Choose between Spring MVC's other web technologies based on merit and how they fit your requirements. While Spring MVC is a good, flexible MVC solution, if there are compelling reasons for choosing another framework — such as substantial in-house experience with Struts, or the existence of an in-house library around another web framework — you can easily integrate with a Spring-managed middle tier, and still enjoy the bulk of the benefits that Spring offers. Choice of web application framework is not always a purely technical choice.

> Remember that you can pick and choose what Spring modules you wish to use: Although Spring is potentially a one-stop shop, it's also a set of modules that you can choose individually.

Approach the choice between view technologies, such as JSP and Velocity, using similar decision criteria as when choosing between web application frameworks. Don't automatically choose JSP. Remember that in any large project, web tier views are likely to be maintained by HTML developers rather than Java developers, and their preferences are also very important. One of the key benefits of using Spring MVC is that it is designed to make controllers and models independent of any view technology. Thus, with it, you could reasonably expect to be able to mix JSP and Velocity views within an application without introducing any architectural inconsistency, and you can add different types of views (such as PDF generators) without affecting controller or model code.

Remoting

Don't build remoting concerns into the fabric of your application — for example, propagating transfer objects through multiple architectural layers.

Instead, think of remoting as a layer over a well-defined service model. In some cases, you may simply want to export the services represented by the service layer objects. Spring enables you to export remote services from any POJO it manages, over a range of protocols. However, in many cases, you will need to add a remote facade to address issues such as the following:

❑ **Serializability:** Remote arguments and return values must be serializable. Alternatively, you may want to transform data into XML representation, for example for SOAP document literal encoding.

❑ **Granularity:** "Chatty" remote calling is very harmful to performance and must be avoided. Thus you may want to offer coarse-grained operations that replace multiple fine-grained operations.

❑ **Data disconnection:** There may be issues in "disconnecting" or "detaching" persistent objects from the persistence store. These issues vary between APIs such as Hibernate and JDO, but with any API you will need to consider the amount of associated data that has been retrieved because some degree of lazy loading is usually essential for performance.

Spring's remoting services are accomplished using its AOP framework under the covers. This can be particularly useful if you want to add an interception chain around remote invocation — a concept offered by many remoting technologies (although in a less flexible way), but lacking in EJB.

You can also export remote services using remote EJBs, with a Spring context behind the EJB facade. This is a good choice if you want RMI-based remoting — and it is significantly facilitated by using Spring to help consume the EJB services on the client side, without the need for any EJB or JNDI-specific code.

Web Tier Design Principles

Ensure clean separation of the different types of objects in your web tier.

— Controller objects should process user input and invoke the necessary business services.

— Model objects contain data necessary to display the results of this processing — they do not perform processing themselves.

— Views are responsible purely for rendering model data.

Structuring Applications

Let's now look at some issues relevant to all architectural tiers.

Overall Issues

We recommend the following guidelines in general:

- ❏ **Practice good OO design.** Spring is primarily an *enabling* technology from the design perspective. You are responsible for using a good OO design; Spring is less likely to get in your way than traditional J2EE APIs and the EJB component model. In particular:

  - ❏ Follow best practice by **programming to interfaces rather than classes.** While, unlike some IoC containers, Spring doesn't enforce this, doing so does make it easier to leverage the full power of Spring's AOP framework. But more importantly, programming to interfaces is an OO best practice that an IoC container such as Spring makes very much easier. You will no longer lose some of the value of using interfaces because you need to code singletons and factory objects; Spring eliminates the need for such code, and you should reap the full benefit.

  - ❏ Thus, the **Strategy** design pattern becomes easy to use and is often a good choice. Such use of delegation is usually better and more flexible than reliance on concrete inheritance.

- ❏ **Don't use your own configuration mechanisms such as XML files, database lookups, or properties files.** Spring provides a wide range of configuration choices: not just XML, but the ability to define objects in Java, database tables, and so on.

- ❏ **Avoid unnecessary dependence on Spring APIs.** There should normally be no need to depend on Spring APIs for *configuration*. (Using Spring abstractions, such as data access APIs, is a different matter.) Part of the point of Dependency Injection is to minimize the need for dependency on any container. Become familiar with capabilities of Spring's IoC container that can help to minimize such dependencies, such as Method Injection (discussed in Chapter 3).

Spring Configuration Issues

Let's now look at some issues specific to Spring usage.

Different Styles of Dependency Injection

Spring supports three types of Dependency Injection:

- ❏ **Setter Injection**, in which objects are configured using their JavaBean properties.

- ❏ **Constructor Injection**, in which objects are configured using constructor arguments.

- ❏ **Method Injection**, in which the container overrides abstract or concrete methods, typically to perform a container lookup, without the need to write Spring-specific code.

It's even possible to mix and match all three of these — for example, using Constructor Injection to populate mandatory dependencies, and using Setter Injection to populate optional dependencies.

The choice between these is up to you. Making a wrong initial choice for a particular object is of no great consequence, as you can always refactor, and Spring will localize the impact of that so that it doesn't affect any objects that depend on the refactored object.

Most of the Spring team tend to prefer Setter Injection in general, but the choice is really up to the application developer.

Method Injection is typically used only to avoid container dependence — for example, when obtaining unique instances of non-threadsafe objects. Method Injection requires dynamic byte code generation using CGLIB, so it adds a degree of complexity at runtime that is not incurred by the other forms of Dependency Injection.

Autowiring

As we discussed when we talked about Dependency Injection, Spring can do the work of resolving the *object* dependencies of any object.

Auto wiring can be done *by name*, in which case properties are resolved by method name (for example, a `dataSource` property would be satisfied by a bean with name `dataSource`); or *by type* (for example, all dependencies of type `javax.sql.DataSource` are satisfied by a single bean definition of that type).

Autowiring by type tends to be more useful and intuitive. However, it works only in cases where there is a single object implementing each target type. For example, if there are two `DataSources`, auto wiring by type will not work.

Auto wiring by name can cope with multiple instances of the target type (such as `transactionalDataSource` and `readOnlyDataSource`).

You can set autowire mode at the individual bean definition level, or at the context definition level, and still retain the ability to override the default for individual bean definitions. Spring's default is for no autowiring, requiring explicit wiring.

On the plus side, autowiring:

❑   Is less verbose than explicit configuration.

❑   Keeps itself up to date. For example, if you add more properties, they will automatically be satisfied without the need to update bean definition(s) of that class.

On the negative side, autowiring:

❑   Is somewhat magical. The container's behavior at runtime isn't described in your configuration, merely implied. However, Spring's policy of raising a fatal error on any ambiguity means that unwanted effects are unlikely.

❑   Is less self-documenting than explicit wiring.

❑   Cannot be used for simple configuration properties, rather than object dependencies. However, you can still explicitly set configuration properties on autowired beans.

The Spring team tends to use explicit configuration in general. However, it is a matter of personal preference, and you and your team should at least be aware of the autowiring features Spring offers. The Spring philosophy is to make good practices easy to follow but to avoid imposing choices on developers using Spring.

As with choice of Dependency Injection style, this is a choice that doesn't need to be permanent. Bean definitions can be changed in isolation without impacting other bean definitions. (You can adopt autowiring at context level, however.) However, a degree of consistency is normally a good idea in a project, in this area, as with most others.

Autoproxying

One of the most important decisions you can make is whether you will use "autoproxying" rather than per-bean AOP configuration. Autoproxying allows you to specify a single interceptor chain for use with multiple objects. It supports per-instance and shared instance models, so this does not automatically mean the same interceptor instances for all autoproxied objects.

The most obvious win here concerns J2SE 5.0 annotations, which can be used to drive Spring declarative transaction management and other features, as of Spring 1.2. Released only in late 2004, J2SE 5.0 is too new to be an option in typical enterprise projects in early 2005, but its acceptance will gradually increase. If you *are* using J2SE 5.0, we recommend using autoproxying for transaction management.

Even if you are not using J2SE 5.0, you should understand how Spring's autoproxying features work and use them where appropriate. Essentially, autoproxying enables you to apply consistent AOP advice to a number of objects. The objects themselves will be defined as POJOs.

Use of autoproxying works particularly well in a team, as a few aspect or infrastructure experts can deliver the necessary aspects and autoproxy configuration, leaving application developers to get on with the job of implementing business objects as POJOs. This is a clean separation of responsibility, as well as concerns.

Again, however, autoproxying is slightly magical. It is, however, possible to control ordering of autoproxied advisors, by making them implement the `Ordered` interface. Thus ordering can also be addressed by an infrastructure team within a larger application development team.

Inheritance of Bean Definitions

Another powerful means of simplifying Spring configurations is to "inherit" bean definitions. This can help greatly to reduce the volume of configuration. For example, you might:

❑ Use an inherited definition to set common properties on a `View`.

❑ Use an inherited definition to set up AOP proxying information.

We strongly encourage understanding and using this mechanism. Duplication — whether in configuration or code — is bad and should be minimized.

Breaking Up Configuration

Try to avoid having one large XML configuration file. This will create unnecessary contention in your source control system, and is likely to become unwieldy.

Another powerful motivation for breaking up XML configuration is that you can isolate those parts of your configuration that may change in different environments. For example, if you have DataSource and transaction manager definitions in a single file, you could then have two versions: a test one that uses a local DataSource and local transaction manager, and a production one that uses a JNDI DataSource and Spring's JTA transaction manager. These definitions will have the same bean names in each file. On the other hand, the definitions of your application objects, such as DAOs and business objects—which of course will depend on such configuration—will be the same in all environments. Thus you can test the bulk of your configuration even outside the eventual deployed environment, which will help speed up testing.

You can also use a base context definition to apply declarative services such as autoproxy infrastructure. For example, the Spring jPetStore sample application shows the use of attributes to drive transactions. This is accomplished through a base context definition *that does not normally need to be edited as the application is enhanced.* Consider such base definitions as defining the services of your container. You are effectively creating your own container, and Spring gives you the tools—and examples—to do it.

What Should Be an Aspect?

As Spring provides an AOP framework, you now have the choice between implementing some types of functionality using OOP or AOP.

> *This not purely a Spring issue: There are a variety of other AOP frameworks that will also give you this choice. Hence this section is not really Spring-specific.*

Declarative middleware is an obvious application for AOP, especially transaction management and declarative security checks. We believe that AOP is clearly the best way to address such requirements in most applications.

The trickier problems concern custom aspects. And here you are not dealing purely with technical considerations. You should consider the following:

❑ **Will your team understand an AOP approach to this problem?** The flip side of this is that sometimes using AOP can localize tricky problems and simplify the job of many developers.

❑ **Is the AOP approach clearly superior to the OOP approach?** Does it modularize a large amount of code that would otherwise be scattered and duplicated? In this case, any "risk" around using AOP may be far outweighed by the inevitable development and maintenance effort associated with a non-AOP approach.

❑ **Is my object model to blame?** Will refactoring improve things, without AOP?

If you have a compelling case for using AOP, don't allow fear about a new paradigm to stop you. But don't model things as aspects just because you can.

> **Code duplication is a good indication that you *should* use AOP. Through modularizing crosscutting concerns, AOP provides a powerful way to address such code duplication.**

Testing Your Applications

With Spring, you can test your applications as follows:

❑   Unit testing

❑   In-context testing

❑   Higher-level forms of testing that you would traditionally perform in any case

> **Appropriate use of Spring greatly enhances testability compared to traditional J2EE design.**

Let's look at these stages of testing in turn, and how Spring can affect them (for the better).

Unit Testing

Unit testing means *testing objects in isolation*. The essence of unit testing is what it leaves out. If your unit tests unnecessarily rely on *real*, rather than mocked or stubbed, collaborators, they will be unduly complicated, and you are almost certain to encounter duplication when there isn't a clear match between a unit test and the code it tests.

> **Unit testing should be done without any container, Spring or other, and without any further dependencies such as a database or JNDI environment. Part of the point of Dependency Injection and AOP is to enable true unit testing; you should take advantage of that important bonus of this programming model.**
>
> **You should unit test Spring applications using plain JUnit tests. You do not need infrastructure such as Cactus that is designed to run inside an application server or other special runtime environment.**
>
> **Your unit tests should be designed for speed. Your entire unit test suite should be automated, and you should be able to run all unit tests in a few minutes at most. It should be realistic to run *all* unit tests before committing any change to source control.**

Please see *J2EE without EJB* for a thorough discussion of unit testing techniques for lightweight J2EE applications.

> *Contrary to some widely held misconceptions, commitment to thorough unit testing — and design to facilitate it — does not mean reduced commitment to other forms of testing.*

In-Context Integration Testing

There are two problems with the traditional reliance on testing inside an application server in traditional J2EE: It's not true unit testing (if that's what is intended) and it's too slow. Deployment to a container takes precious time; doing it every time you make a code change is a huge obstacle to productivity. The cumulative effect of many interruptions — even relatively short interruptions — is a huge loss of productivity.

With Spring or another Dependency Injection container that offers a non-invasive programming model, the first of these issues is taken care of. You can and should do true unit testing without any container in sight.

The second issue can also be addressed with Spring. What if you want to do a form of integration testing where you test objects working together in a subsystem, working against either stub resources or real resources such as databases? In this case, you can start a Spring container in an ordinary JUnit test case. Starting a Spring container requires very little overhead: Spring is merely a class library from the point of view of a JUnit test. There is a huge difference between the sub-second startup time of a typical Spring context and the seconds required to start up an application server and the deployment units needing testing.

Spring provides support for such test-time context startup in the `org.springframework.test` package. This enables you to create JUnit test cases that are themselves configured by Dependency Injection, being populated by objects from a Spring IoC container. Even better, there is a superclass (`org.springframework.test.AbstractTransactionalSpringContextTests`) that automatically creates a transaction for each test method before rolling it back after completion. This can be a very powerful technique when you want to do integration testing, actually hitting your database, but don't want the overhead of deployment to a J2EE application server or traditional setup and teardown scripts to keep your database clean. The overhead of running such tests is modest, as by default the application context will be cached throughout the execution of your own test suite, in the event that initializing of certain objects or frameworks such as Hibernate is a noticeable startup cost. (While the startup cost of the Spring container itself will be negligible, that may not be the case for some of the application objects and framework objects it may contain.)

Higher Levels of Testing

Of course there is much more to testing than unit testing and integration testing. Later stages of testing are beyond the scope of this book. In this case, you will do what you would have done without using Spring: Spring can't help you too much, beyond simple things such as making it easier to invoke remote services to drive tests against a deployed container. For any project, you need a proper test plan and, usually, a testing team to ensure it's executed. While thorough unit testing is extremely important to success, it's not the be all and end all of testing.

Related Projects

Spring has created an increasingly rich ecosystem because of its popularity and (even more) its extensible design, which makes it easy for other projects to integrate with Spring without being coupled too tightly to it.

Let's look at some of the most important related projects, which you may find valuable in your Spring development.

Acegi Security for Spring

Acegi Security System for Spring (`http://acegisecurity.sourceforge.net/`) provides comprehensive security services for Spring-powered projects. Acegi Security handles the typical security requirements of complex applications, including authentication, authorization, run-as replacement, and domain object instance-level security.

Acegi Security is structured around a `ThreadLocal` object known as `ContextHolder`. Stored in the `ContextHolder` is an `Authentication` object, which identifies the principal and an array of `Granted Authoritys`. In keeping with Spring's philosophy, Acegi provides a consistent abstraction over pluggable authentication mechanisms. A number of authentication mechanisms are included in the project to populate the `Authentication`. The most commonly used is the DAO-based authentication provider (backed by an RDBMS), although also popular is the Yale CAS integration, which is an open source project that provides enterprise-wide, single sign-on for a wide variety of web languages (Java, Apache, Python, ColdFusion, PHP, ASP, and so on). Authentication details can be collected from HTTP forms,

BASIC authentication (RFC 1945) headers, and even from the web container itself (support is currently provided for Tomcat, Jetty, Resin, and JBoss). The BASIC authentication allows the direct use of Acegi Security with all standard web services protocols.

At runtime, Acegi Security intercepts invocations that need to be secured, terming these intercepted invocations "secure objects." There are secure object handlers currently provided for web requests (the equivalent of using servlet specification security), AOP Alliance `MethodInvocations` (for use with standard Spring business object proxies), and AspectJ `JoinPoints` (useful if you're using AspectJ for domain object security). AOP provides a more general and flexible method of securing method calls than the EJB declarative security model.

Acegi Security provides a number of filters to ease integration with typical web-app projects.

Acegi is effectively the "official" security project for Spring. Spring will never offer its own security framework, and we recommend that users with non-trivial security requirements look first at Acegi, rather than implementing their own security framework. Acegi Security's close relationship with Spring is indicated by the fact that it has its own forum space on the main Spring Framework forums.

If you need to implement a web application with simple security requirements, you can of course use the security features defined by the Servlet specification in Spring applications.

Other Projects

Other projects directly associated with the Spring framework include:

❑ **Spring IDE for Eclipse** (`http://springide-eclip.sourceforge.net/`): A set of plug-ins for the Eclipse platform designed to ease working with Spring XML configuration files, including adding visualization support for dependencies.

❑ **The Spring Modules project** (`www.springmodules.org`): A set of Spring integrations for various technologies, such as the Lucene search engine, OSWorkflow, and Drools rule engine.

❑ **The Spring Framework.NET** (`www.springframework.net/`): A .NET implementation of Spring's core concepts, providing IoC and AOP support on the .NET platform that offers a consistent programming model to Spring Java. Note that this project is not merely a port of Spring (which would not be idiomatic on .NET) but adapts key elements to the .NET environment.

Other Spring-related projects, not directly associated with or endorsed by the Spring project itself, include:

❑ **Aurora MVC** (`http://sourceforge.net/projects/auroramvc/`): An alternative MVC framework, built on Spring concepts and designed for use with a Spring middle tier.

❑ **JSF-Spring** (`http://jsf-spring.sourceforge.net/`): Integration between JSF and Spring, for users who require a more customizable integration than Spring provides for JSF out of the box (which should be sufficient for most users).

❑ **Wanghy Cache** (`http://jsf-spring.sourceforge.net/`): Provides declarative caching services for Spring applications, using Spring AOP.

❑ **Spring XMLDB** (`http://sourceforge.net/projects/springxmldb/`): Framework to aid the integration of XML databases and XML database access into the Spring Framework.

This is by no means a complete list at the time of this writing, and new projects appear frequently.

Numerous other frameworks also ship Spring integration, including:

❑ **WebWork** (`http://wiki.opensymphony.com/display/WW/WebWork`): Popular MVC web application framework.

❑ **Mule** (`http://wiki.muleumo.org/display/MULEPROJ/Home`): An Enterprise Service Bus messaging framework.

❑ **Cayenne** (`http://objectstyle.org/cayenne`): Open source O/R mapping framework.

Spring in Non-J2EE Environments

The Spring IoC container and AOP framework is equally at home in a J2SE environment as in a J2EE environment. So are many of the Spring service abstractions because they decouple from the J2EE APIs. This is valuable, as many concepts are far more general than J2EE or server-side applications.

Thus you can use Spring not just in a simple web container such as Tomcat, but in standalone applications or rich clients. Some users even use the basic Spring IoC container in applets.

The *Spring Rich Client (RCP)* project is the most important initiative in this space. It is a framework for developing Swing-based desktop applications. The Spring RCP project was launched in March 2004 in response to increasing interest in Spring in J2SE environments, and the project lead is Keith Donald, who is also a core Spring developer.

Spring Rich aims to simplify the Swing programming model by building abstractions over low-level Swing APIs; to promote the implementation of well-layered applications, with a clean separation between presentation and business services; and to provide an integration point for diverse UI frameworks. Thus it is fully in keeping with core Spring Framework values.

Spring Rich provides abstractions for managing the lifecycle and configuration of desktop applications, such as windows, editors, and toolbars; a command framework building on Swing's base action support, but adding much more power; a powerful data binding and validation framework; and support libraries for common requirements such as wizards, preferences, progress monitoring, and property sheets.

> **If you are developing a rich client for a server-side application, or a standalone Swing application, Spring Rich deserves consideration. It adds significant convenience to managing UI elements, and is particularly compelling if you need to access server-side services using remoting, as you have access to the full Spring remoting support.**

To Find Out More

Let's conclude with a quick summary of where you can go to learn more about some of the material covered in this book.

Books and Articles

This has predominantly been a practical book, and although we've covered some theory, we haven't had space to describe all the concepts in detail. We recommend the following books for further reading on some of the major topic areas in this book:

- ❑ **Dependency Injection:** Chapter 3 should have you well up and running. If you want more theoretical and conceptual background, you can refer to the coverage of IoC and Dependency Injection in Chapter 6 of *J2EE without EJB*. However, you should not need to do any further reading to be productive with the Spring IoC container. You can best build your understanding of Dependency Injection through practical experience.

- ❑ **AOP:** Ramnivas Laddad's excellent *AspectJ in Action* (Manning, 2003) gives a good introduction to AOP, and is particularly relevant if you're considering using AspectJ along with Spring. Adrian Colyer's *Eclipse AspectJ: Aspect-Oriented Programming with AspectJ and the Eclipse AspectJ Development Tools* (Addison-Wesley, 2005) includes an example of AspectJ/Spring integration from an AspectJ perspective, and is a good practical guide to AspectJ, from its lead developer. Chapter 8 of *J2EE without EJB* ("Declarative Middleware Using AOP Concepts") provides a conceptual background on the motivation of using an AOP approach to solve common middleware problems.

- ❑ **OO design:** The classic text here is *Design Patterns* (Gamma, Helm, Johnson, and Vlissides, [Addison-Wesley, 1995]). Every OO developer should read this book. Spring makes it easier to apply many of the best practices described here. Chapter 4 of *Expert One-on-One J2EE Design and Development* (Johnson, 2002) is also helpful in discussing issues around OO design in J2EE applications. We also recommend *Domain Driven Design* by Eric Evans (Addison-Wesley, 2003).

- ❑ **Web frameworks:** *Spring Live* by Matt Raible (SourceBeat, 2004) has good coverage of using Spring with different web frameworks.

- ❑ **O/R mapping:** Both Hibernate and iBATIS have excellent reference documentation that is available from the projects' respective home pages. There is also a range of books available on Hibernate, JDO, and other O/R mapping products.

Online Resources

There is much useful information about Spring online. You should refer to the Reference Manual and the JavaDoc available from `www.springframework.org`.

The Spring forums (`forum.springframework.org`) are active and a good place to go to ask questions. Be sure to use the search facility first, in case the question has been asked — and answered — before!

The Spring-developer mailing list is the place to go if you want to contribute ideas or patches to Spring, or discuss implementation issues with the core team. Subscribe by following the mailing list links from the Spring home page. Note that the Spring developer list is not intended for asking questions about how to use Spring, unless the questions concern framework implementation and design issues.

Sample Applications

In addition to our box office sample application, we recommend that you study the following sample applications included in the Spring distribution.

These applications are suitable for use as templates. You can get them running quickly, and then keep the basic structure as you change the implementation to your own domain.

jPetStore

This is a good example of a web application using Spring and iBATIS. The comparison with Sun's EJB-based Java Pet Store is particularly illuminating.

Note the alternative configurations that show use with a JNDI-bound, container-managed datasource with JTA, and local JDBC transactions for use in a simple web container with a single database. There is also an alternative configuration showing the use of annotations, rather than XML metadata, to drive declarative transaction management.

This application includes good examples of the use of Spring's lightweight remoting, exporting services over a range of protocols without any change to the core business model.

The web tier includes both Spring MVC and Struts implementations. This is an excellent place to look if you are already familiar with Struts and want to see what Spring MVC has to offer.

PetClinic

This is a simple web application using Spring's data access abstraction with a variety of underlying persistence technologies. Hibernate, Spring JDBC, and Apache OJB are supported, demonstrating how the use of DAO interfaces we recommend can successfully isolate business objects from the persistence layer. The PetClinic also illustrates use of the `org.springframework.test` package for quick, effective integration testing outside an application server.

ImageDB

This is a web application showing more advanced use of Spring's JDBC abstraction. The principal functionality concerns BLOB writing and reading.

This application also demonstrates Spring's integration with the popular open source Quartz scheduler.

The web tier is implemented using Spring MVC.

> There are also a number of sample applications using Spring on the web, such as Matt Raible's AppFuse, although these are not authored or endorsed by the Spring team.

The Future

Spring is the most advanced implementation of the "post EJB" vision, and it's hard to see that changing in the near future. The Spring team is advancing at a rapid pace. (The fact that Spring is a moving target has made the writing of this book more of a challenge.) Crucially, Spring's design is highly adaptable: It is possible to add many new features without modifying the core container because of the hooks the container offers.

Spring's momentum continues to grow, so you can rest safe in the knowledge that your project's investment in Spring is safe for the foreseeable future.

> **Despite the rapid pace of Spring's evolution, you can rely on backward compatibility. Because of Spring's design, and the use of IoC and AOP, your code is not coupled tightly to the Spring internals — indeed, it's often not coupled to Spring APIs at all. Thus, as Spring evolves, your applications need not be broken.**

EJB 3.0 is being heavily hyped by Sun and — especially — some application server vendors. (Given the vested interests in keeping EJB alive, at least as a name, this is hardly surprising.) But it's unclear what benefit it will offer.

The EJB 3.0 specification (still in early draft at the time of this writing) seems set to offer a small subset of Spring's Dependency Injection capabilities. This offering may look compelling to those who have never used a Dependency Injection container. But it is far from innovative.

We believe that the day of the EJB container is coming to a close. The concept of a monolithic container that offers a fixed set of services is clearly dated. It will be replaced by more lightweight containers that are not J2EE-specific or restricted to use on the server side, and which deliver services to POJOs through Dependency Injection and AOP. Spring already offers such a model, in mature, battle-tested form.

It is, however, important to note that Spring will provide support for users who choose to use EJB 3.0, as it has always supported EJB 2.*x* usage. And Spring of course offers many valuable features not addressed by EJB 3.0, as well as features that EJB 3.0 is also attempting to deliver. But there seems little compelling case for EJB today.

> *The POJO persistence specification to be released by the JSR-220 Expert Group, distinct from the EJB 3.0 specification, is a different matter. We expect that this will become an important API, and Spring will provide full support for it as soon as it is released.*

However, as the next few years play out, it's certain that the lightweight container movement has changed the face of J2EE development forever, and that open source projects — particularly, Spring — have played a huge role in defining and popularizing new features. This innovation is likely to continue. As part of the Spring community, we hope that you will help us make Spring better and better. Spring is what it is today partly because of the community spirit of its developers and users — we welcome you to participate in that!

Requirements for the Sample Application

This chapter specifies the requirements for an application that is realistic enough to show how the Spring Framework can be used to develop a modern web application. If you have read *Expert One-on-One J2EE Design and Development* by Rod Johnson, you will recognize this example. We are using the same example, with some minor adjustments, to show the progression from the *Interface21* framework presented in Rod's earlier book to today's Spring Framework.

The sample application has been designed from a business perspective. We will show you how to translate these business requirements into a fully functioning web application using features provided by the Spring Framework.

Overview

The requirement is for an online seat reservation system for the Mandala Center, an arts and entertainment complex that presents shows in a range of genres such as opera, concert, theatre, and comedy. The Mandala Center currently has three performance halls. Each hall has a default seating plan, used for most performances, but occasionally a particular show may vary this slightly. For some shows there might be a need to remove a portion of the seats to make room for equipment or add additional stage area and so on. This also affects which seats are considered adjacent.

The Mandala Center is owned by the Z Group, an international entertainment company that owns many other entertainment venues. The Z Group views the online booking system for the Mandala Center as a pilot and hopes to use it as a basis for systems for its other venues. The new system must allow for re-branding—it must be possible to change the presentation of the site without changing the basic functionality.

Some of the Z Group's other venues are in non–English speaking countries, so although there is no immediate requirement for internationalization, it will be necessary if the system is successful. Some venues are in multilingual countries such as Switzerland, so if the system is adopted in these venues, it must allow users to choose their own language.

The following business requirements do not attempt to describe every functional aspect of a real-world ticket reservation system.

User Populations

The application must support three groups of users: public Internet users (customers); box office users (employees of the Mandala Center who assist customers who have chosen not to purchase online); and in a later phase, administrators (employees of the Mandala Center responsible for posting and updating data).

Public Internet Users

These users are customers accessing the service through a web browser. Most connect using a modem at speeds of up to 56K, and it is important that the system has acceptable response times over a modem connection. Customers wish:

- ❑ To find out what shows are offered and access information about shows and performances
- ❑ To find out what performance dates still offer seating availability
- ❑ To book seats online, using a credit card

Registration will be offered only as a convenience to save users from having to re-enter their billing address. The priority is for a positive user experience so users will not be forced to register because that risks alienating them.

In order to fulfill these requirements, the system should offer a simple, usable, and fast web interface. It is important for this interface to work on as many browsers as possible. Browser-specific functionality should be avoided. Applets, Flash animations, and the like are considered likely to deter users and should not be used.

Box Office Users

These are employees of the Mandala Center who work within the Mandala Center itself, and are on the local network. Some employees may work from home, in which case they will have access to a broadband Internet connection. Box office users perform the following activities:

- ❑ Respond to phone and over-the-counter inquiries by members of the public, principally on the availability of seating. To support this task, box office users must be given powerful query functionality unavailable to public Internet users, to enable them quickly to respond to questions such as, "What is the first date on which I can have 25 adjacent B reserve seats to *Carmen*?"
- ❑ Sell tickets to members of the public who wish to see a show.

❑ Supply tickets to customers who booked online but chose to collect the tickets from the box office instead of having them delivered by mail. This is also necessary for late bookings, when there isn't time to send out tickets.

❑ Occasionally, cancel reservations on phone requests.

These users are primarily concerned with service reliability and usability. They receive a constant flow of inquiries from customers who expect efficient service when they call.

Box office users must be given a powerful system that offers a quick way to perform common tasks. As the box office interface is for internal use only, there should be less emphasis on its branding and cosmetics.

The Mandala Center management team wishes to maximize their IT investment and so believes that the same online ticket reservation system should service public Internet users and box office staff. Box office users, like customers, will use a web interface. This interface will be protected from Internet users via role-based security and will have a separate entry point from the public Internet application. The system will automatically grant the appropriate privileges, based on username and password.

Administrators

These are employees of the Mandala Center, where the ticketing system will be in operation. Admin users must be located within the Mandala Center itself, accessing the local network. They fulfill a variety of clerical, marketing, and management functions:

❑ Add new shows and performances.

❑ Run management information and financial reports.

❑ Configure settings of the ticketing system; such as the maximum number of tickets that can be purchased in one transaction, and the period of time tickets can be reserved before payment is made.

The Mandala Center's management has decided to defer requirements gathering and design of this interface until Phase 2. The current design must take this additional functionality into account and provide a design that is extensible.

Assumptions

Let's now consider the following assumptions:

❑ Internet users will not be required to accept cookies, although it is expected that most will.

❑ Seats for each show will be divided into one or more seat types, such as Premium Reserve. Seating plan and the division of seats into types will be associated with shows, not individual performances.

❑ All seats within the same class for the same performance will be the same price. However, different performances of the same show may have different price structures. For example, matinees may be cheaper than evening performances, to attract families.

- Users will request a given number of seats of a chosen type for a specified performance, and will not be allowed to request specific seats. Users will not be allowed to provide "hints" for seat allocation such as "toward the front of A Reserve" and "on the right rather than the left."

- Users requesting seats will be assumed to want adjacent seats, although they will be offered whatever is available if sufficient adjacent seats cannot be allocated. Seats are not considered to be adjacent if they are separated by an aisle.

- Internet customers will not be able to cancel a booking once payment has been processed. They must call the box office, which will apply the Mandala Center's policies regarding cancellation and refunds, and use the box office interface to cancel bookings when this is allowed.

Scope Limitations

As it is to serve as an example rather than a commercial application, some areas have been ignored. However, these are essentially refinements, and do not affect the system architecture:

- No security will be implemented for credit card purchasing. HTTPS would be used in a real application, but the details of setting this up vary between J2EE servers.

- A real system would connect to an external payment processing system to process credit card payments. In the sample application, this is replaced by a dummy component that blocks for a varying period of time and randomly decides whether to approve or reject transactions.

- No allowances will be made for special seating requirements such as wheelchair access, although this is an important consideration in most ticketing systems.

Delivery Schedule

The Mandala Center's management has determined that having a true online ticketing solution is a business priority. Thus they have determined a delivery schedule to ensure that the public system becomes available online as soon as possible. This schedule calls for the application to be delivered in three phases:

- **Phase 1:** Core Internet user interface, as described in the next section, and the box office interface.

- **Phase 2:** Admin interface. In Phase 1, no GUI will be available to Admin users; they will need to work with the database using database tools.

- **Phase 3:** More sophisticated Internet interface. This will offer registered users premium services and add internationalization support.

The sample application will extend only to Phase 1. The whole of the core Internet user interface, and part of the box office interface (which won't be fully defined in this chapter), will be implemented. However, the sample application must define an architecture that will provide a basis for the later phases, so their requirements that are known ahead of time will be considered in the current phase.

Internet User Interface

Let's look in detail at the public Internet user interface. This illustrates many common issues in building web applications.

Basic Workflow

Although we've used UML-like graphics, each box represents a screen presented to a user successfully choosing a performance and purchasing a number of tickets, rather than a state. The diagram in Figure A-1 shows an Internet user successfully booking seats.

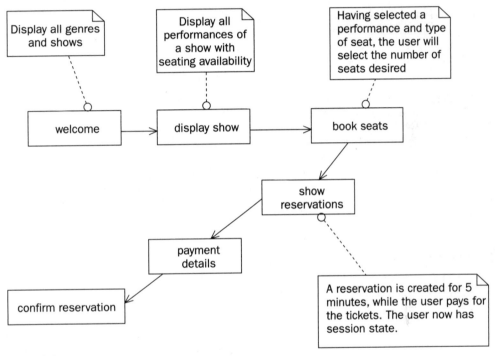

Figure A-1

Users are initially presented with the "welcome" screen, a list of all genres (such as Opera) and shows (such as Wagner's *Tristan und Isolde*), playing at the Mandala Center (see Application screens that follow for screenshots). Users can then proceed to the "display show" screen, which shows all performance dates for a given show, along with the types and prices of seats on sale and the availability of each type of seat. This screen should indicate only whether each type of seat is available or sold out, not the number of seats remaining. This meets the needs of most users while avoiding disclosure of sensitive business information—for example, which tickets to a particular show might be selling poorly. Users can request a number of seats of a given type for a particular performance, in which case these seats are reserved to allow time for online credit card payment.

The system distinguishes between the concepts of reservation and confirmation/purchase in the booking process. The user can reserve seats for a performance for a period of time (typically 5 minutes), which will be held in system configuration. Reservation protects these seats from being shown as available to other users. Confirmation occurs when the user provides a valid credit card number, at which point a reservation becomes an actual purchase. Reservations are held in the database and in the user's session state. Reservations must either:

- Progress to bookings as a result of confirmation.

- Expire, if the user fails to proceed to purchase in the given time. These seats will then be available to other users. However, the user who made the reservation may still purchase the seats without seeing an error message if they are still free when (s)he submits the payment form.

- Be cleared, as the result of user activity other than continuing on to purchase. For example, if a user makes a reservation but then navigates back to the "display show" screen, it is assumed that (s)he does not want to proceed to purchase these seats, and that they should be returned to fully available status.

Error Handling

In the event of a system error (such as the J2EE server failing to connect to the database), the user should be shown an internal "error" screen consistent with the current branding. This should advise the user to try again later. Support staff should be notified by email and through the log file record in the event of serious problems. The user must never see a screen containing a stack trace, "500 Internal Error" or other technology or server-specific error message. A user requesting an invalid URL should see a screen consistent with the current branding, advising that the requested page was not found and containing a link to the "welcome" page.

Application Screens

Let's now take a closer look at workflow in the public Internet interface. The diagram in Figure A-2 is a more detailed version of the previous diagram, and shows all screens available to the Internet user, and the transitions between them.

The additional detail concerns failures to complete a booking and the optional user registration process. The user can fail to proceed to reservation or confirmation under the following circumstances:

- The user requests the "display show" screen and leaves a long delay before following one of the links to the "book seats" screen. By the time the user proceeds to this screen, many more seats have been sold and the requested type of seat is no longer available.

- The only seats that can be offered to the user are not adjacent. The user does not wish to accept this, and follows the "try another date" link back to the "display show" screen. The unwanted reservation should be cleared and the user must begin the booking process again.

- The user made a registration, but failed to submit a credit card number in the lifetime of the reservation. This is not a problem unless the seats have been reserved or purchased by another user. In this case, the problem is explained to the user, who is reassured that their credit card was not debited and offered a link to the "display show" screen.

- The user enters a credit card number in a valid format, but the transaction is declined by the credit card processing system. In this case, the user will be informed that the credit card payment was declined and that the reservation has been lost. The reservation is cleared, and the user must begin the reservation progress from scratch.

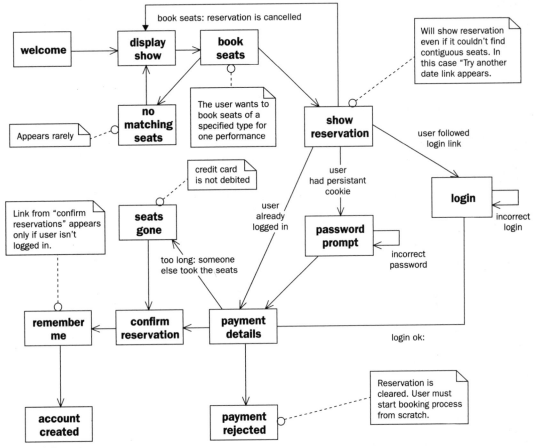

book seats: reservation is cancelled

Will show reservation even if it couldn't find contiguous seats. In this case "Try another date link appears.

Appears rarely

The user wants to book seats of a specified type for one performance

user followed login link

credit card is not debited

Link from "confirm reservations" appears only if user isn't logged in.

user already logged in

user had persistant cookie

incorrect login

too long: someone else took the seats

incorrect password

login ok:

Reservation is cleared. User must start booking process from scratch.

Figure A-2

The registration process is optional. It allows users to enter a password to create an account that will save them from having to enter their billing address and email with each purchase. Users should not be forced to register to purchase tickets because the management feels that this may reduce sales.

Registration will be offered after a user who is not logged in, and who has provided an email address not already associated with a registered user, has made a booking. The user's username will be her email address, which is entered in the course of the booking process. When a user registers and the application detects that the user's browser is configured to accept cookies, her username will be stored in a persistent cookie enabling the application to recognize her registration status on subsequent visits and prompt for a password automatically. This prompt will be introduced into the registration process through a distinct screen between the "reservation" and "payment details" screens. The following rules will apply:

❑ If the user is logged in, billing address and email address (but not credit card details, which are never retained) will be pre-populated on the payment details form.

❑ If a persistent cookie containing the user's email address is found but the user is not logged in, the user will be prompted to enter a password, before proceeding to the payment details form. The user can choose to skip password entry, in which case the persistent cookie will be deleted and the user will see an empty "payment details" screen.

If the user isn't logged in and doesn't have a persistent cookie, there should be a link on the "show reservation" page to allow the user to try to log in by entering both username and password before seeing the "payment details" screen. In the event of successful login, a persistent cookie will not be created.

The screenshots that follow present all the controls and information required on each page. However, they do not fully define the presentation of the application: For example, these screens might have a custom header and some side columns added. There may be more than one such branding: It is a business requirement for the technical architecture to allow this flexibility.

Welcome Screen

This page, shown in Figure A-3, provides an index of all shows and performances currently available. It may also include static information and links about the Mandala Center. The aim is to minimize the number of pages the user has to work through to perform common tasks, so this page allows direct progress to information about each show, without making the user browse intervening pages.

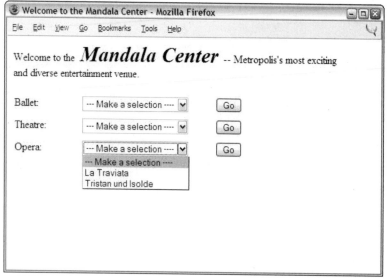

Figure A-3

The page must be dynamic: Genres and shows must not be hard-coded in HTML. The number of genres will not be so great in the immediate future that having a separate drop-down for each genre is likely to become unworkable. However, the system architecture must support other interfaces, such as splitting this page by having a separate page for each genre, if the number of genres and shows increases significantly. The user's first impression of the system is vital, so this page must load quickly. Requirements for this page are summarized in the following table.

Screen Name	Welcome
Purpose	Display all genres and shows. If there are no current shows in a genre, that genre should not be displayed.
Alternative screens	None
URL	`/welcome.html`. This should be the default page if the user does not specify a URL within the application.
Data displayed	Dynamic genre and show listing from database; static information determined by HTML presentation (such as photograph of the Mandala Center).
Requires existing session state?	No
Effect on existing session state	None
Effect on refresh/resubmission	Page should be marked as cacheable by the browser for 1 minute. Requests received by the web server should result in the generation of a page.
Effect on back button	Irrelevant. The user has no session state for the application.
Parameters required	None
Effect of invalid parameters	Parameters to this page will be ignored.

Display Show Screen

This screen, shown in Figure A-4, will allow the user to choose a performance date for a show in which she is interested, and proceed to make a booking. It will also provide information about the show in question such as the history of the work being performed and cast information. It is expected that some users, reluctant to use their credit cards online, will use the Internet interface only to this point, before calling the box office to purchase tickets on a given date; this is an additional reason for providing comprehensive information on this page.

No support is required for pagination in Phase 1 (although this is a potential refinement later); the user many need to scroll down to see all performances. For each performance, there is typically a hyperlink from each type of seat to the "booking" page. A superscript is used in place of a hyperlink to indicate that the given class of the given performance is sold out.

Screen Name	Display Show
Purpose	Display information about the show. Display a list of all performances of the show, with availability (available/sold out) of each seating type. Include a legend explaining the cost of each type of seat.
Alternative screens	None
URL	`/show.html`

Table continued on following page

Screen Name	Display Show
Data displayed	Dynamic performance and seat availability information from database.
	HTML-format information about the show the user is interested in. This must be legal HTML within the content well, and may contain internal and external hyperlinks. This will be maintained by non-programmers with HTML skills. The URL of this document within the web application should be associated with the show in the database. If no URL is specified in the database, the seating plan for the performance should be displayed in place of the show information.
Requires existing session state?	No
Effect on existing session state	Any existing reservation will be cleared without notifying the user. However, any existing user session will not be destroyed.
Effect on refresh/resubmission	Page should be regenerated by the server.
Effect on back button	Irrelevant. The user has no session state for the application.
Parameters required	id (integer): The unique id of the show.
Effect of invalid parameters	Parameters other than the show id should be ignored. If no show id is supplied or if the show id is non-numeric or out of range, a generic "invalid request" page will be displayed, with a link back to the "welcome" page. This cannot happen within normal operation, as the user should arrive at this page only as a result of hitting one of the Go buttons on the "welcome" page.

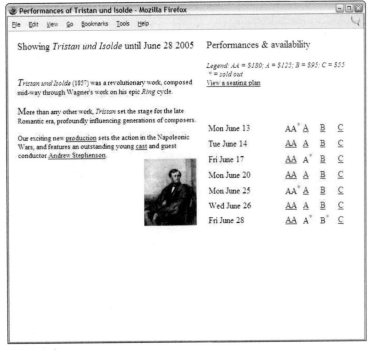

Figure A-4

Book Seats Screen

To arrive at the screen shown in Figure A-5, the user selects a performance date and ticket type by following a seat type link—one of the AA, A, B, or C links shown in Figure A-4.

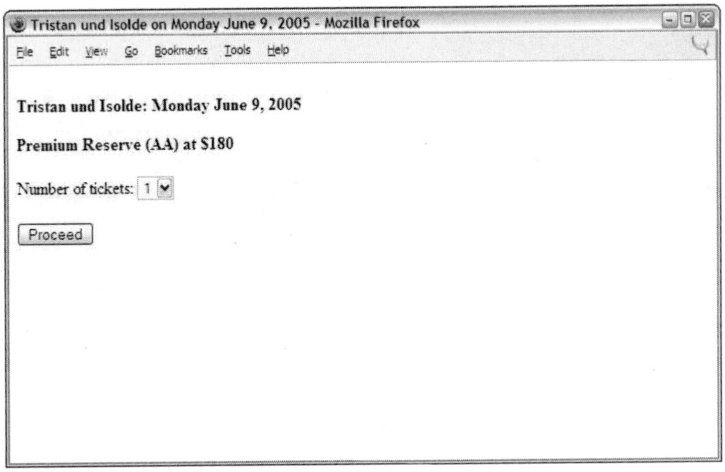

Figure A-5

Screen Name	Book Seats
Purpose	Provides a form enabling users to request a number of seats of a given type for their selected performance.
Alternative screens	If no tickets are available for this performance, a simple screen should say that that type of ticket is sold out and provide a link back to the "display show" screen.
URL	`/bookseats.html`
Data displayed	The name of the show and the date of the performance.
	The name of the ticket type (such as Premium Reserve) and its unit price.
	A drop-down box with a default number of tickets selected. The default value can be set by the Administrator, and should be configured to 6 seats in the applications factory settings. The value initially displayed in the drop-down should be the lower of the default value and the number of tickets of the requested type left (for example, if the default value has been set to 8 and only 7 seats are left, the selected value will be 7). The range of values in the drop-down should be from 1 to the lower of the number of tickets left and a default maximum set by the Administrator. A typical value of the default maximum for seats purchased in the same transaction might be 12, to discourage scalpers.
Requires existing session state	No
Effect on existing session state	Any reservation will be cleared. However the session will not be destroyed.
Effect on refresh/resubmission	Page should be regenerated by the server. It is important that this page always provide up-to-date information on seat availability (implicit in this screen appearing at all, and shown in the values in the drop-down), so no caching is permissible.
Effect on back button	Irrelevant. The user has no session state for the application.
Parameters required	`id` (integer): The unique id of the show.
	`type` (integer): The unique id of the seat type.
Effect of invalid parameters	Parameters other than the show id should be ignored. If either parameter is missing, is non-numeric, or is out of range, a generic "invalid request" page will be displayed, with a link back to the "welcome" page.

Show Reservation Screen

The screen in Figure A-6 results from the successful reservation of the number of seats requested. This is the first operation resulting in the creation of session state.

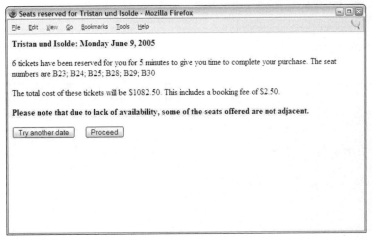

Figure A-6

Screen Name	Show Reservation
Purpose	Informs the user that (s)he has successfully reserved a number of seats.
Alternative screens	If no seats are available (because the user delayed in submitting the form and the performance filled up), display a screen explaining the problem and prompting the user to try another date. In this case, no reservation will have been created, and the user will not have session state.
URL	`/reservation.html`
Data displayed	The name of the show and date of the performance selected.
	The number of seats requested.
	The total cost of the tickets.
	Whether or not the seats are adjacent. If the seats are not adjacent, this should be explained to the user and a link should be provided to allow the user to try another performance date. The seating plan will enable the user to work out how close these seats are (for example, B25 to B28 may be an acceptable gap; A13 to Y40 may not).
	Seating plan (including all seat classes) to enable the user to work out the position of the seats. This seating plan will not be dynamic in Phase 1: There is no need to highlight the position of the reserved seats.
	"Remember me" link if the user doesn't have a persistent cookie and isn't logged in. This will enable the user to log in before proceeding to the "payment" screen.

Table continued on following page

Screen Name	Show Reservation
Requires existing session state	No. The generation of this page will create session state if none exists.
Effect on existing session state	If the user has an existing reservation, it is cleared before processing the new seat request. It should be impossible for the user to have more than one simultaneous reservation in his/her session state or in the database.
Effect on refresh/resubmission	On resubmission, the application should notice that the reservation held in the user's session matches the request. An identical screen (except that the expiry time of the reservation should be shown rather than the length of the reservation period) should be returned without any updates in the database. The lifetime of the reservation will not be prolonged.
Effect on back button	Invalid
Parameters required	id (integer): The unique id of the show.
	type (integer): Type we wish to reserve seats for.
	count (integer): Number of seats requested.
Effect of invalid parameters	Parameters other than these should be ignored. A generic "invalid request" page will be displayed, with a link back to the "welcome" page if any of the required parameters are missing or invalid, as this should not happen in normal operation.

Payment Details Screen

Note that the "password prompt" or "login" page may appear before the page shown in Figure A-7, and may result in the pre-population of address and email fields for logged-in users. Credit card details will always be blank, as they are not retained under any circumstances.

Screen Name	Payment Details
Purpose	Allows a user who has successfully reserved seats to pay for tickets and provide an address to which they can be mailed.
Alternative screens	A user who isn't logged in but has a persistent cookie will be directed to the "password prompt" page before arriving here.
URL	/payment.html
Data displayed	Name of show and performance.
	Number of seats reserved.
	Price of seats.
	User profile data if the user is logged in. Otherwise all fields will be empty.

Screen Name	Payment Details
Requires existing session state	Yes. This page should be shown only if the user has a reservation in her session. Requesting this page without a session or without a reservation should result in a generic "invalid request" page.
Effect on existing session state	None
Effect on refresh/resubmission	Page should be regenerated by the server. If the reservation held in the user's session expired, the user should be shown a page indicating this and providing a link back to the "display show" page.
Effect on back button	Invalid
Parameters required	None. This page depends on session state, not request parameters.
Effect of invalid parameters	All parameters will be ignored.

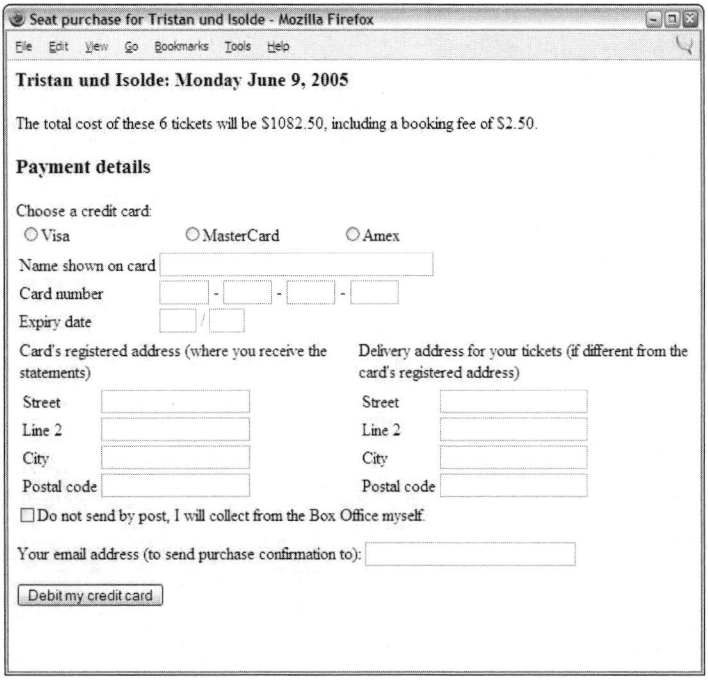

Figure A-7

On an invalid submission, this page will be redisplayed with the missing or invalid field values highlighted and an error message for each field explaining the problem. The exact means of highlighting errors is a detail to be decided later. However, the system should support different styles of highlighting.

All fields are mandatory except line 2 of this address. The following validation rules are to be applied on submission of the form on this page:

❑ Credit card number is 16 digits.

❑   Credit card expiration date is 4 digits.

❑   Postal code is a valid UK postcode format (for example SE109AH0). However, no attempt will be made to check that this is a real postal code. (Submissions that look like UK postcodes may be syntactically correct but semantically meaningless.) It is the user's responsibility to enter their address correctly. In subsequent releases, other countries must also be supported, and postal code validation must be implemented based on the country selected from a drop-down. Only a fixed subset of countries will be supported, as the cost and reliability of posting tickets to some countries is considered unacceptable.

❑   Email address must pass simple validation checks (that it looks like an email address, with an @ symbol and dots in the right place). However, the transaction can still succeed even if the email address does not prove to work; ticket purchase should not block while a test email is sent.

No attempt will be made to validate the credit card number's checksum. This is a matter for the external credit card processing system.

Confirm Reservation Screen

The screen in Figure A-8 confirms the user's ticket purchase and provides an electronic receipt.

Screen Name	Confirm Reservation
Purpose	Confirm the user's credit card payment. Provide a reference number. Allow the user to register if the user isn't logged in (a logged-in user will not see the content under the ruled line).
Alternative screens	If the credit card is in an invalid format or if mandatory fields are missing or invalid, the "payment" screen is shown again, populated with the rejected values.
	If the credit card is in a valid format but payment is rejected by the credit card processing system, the user should be sent to the "payment rejected" screen and the reservation cleared. This is treated as the end of the reservation process. The attempt to use a questionable credit card number should be prominently logged for the system administrator to see.
	If the user's reservation has expired but the tickets are still available, payment will be processed as normal. If tickets have been sold to another user, the user will be redirected to the "seats gone" page, and the expired registration cleared from the user session. The user's credit card will not be debited.
URL	`/confirmation.html`
Data displayed	Seats reserved; booking reference; price paid; user's email address (the email address will not allow modification if the user is logged in). Only the last four digits of the credit card number should be displayed. For security reasons, the credit card number should never be held in the user's session or in the database.
Requires existing session state	Yes. A reservation must be found in the session, and the price must match the payment offered.

Screen Name	Confirm Reservation
Effect on existing session state	The reservation will be removed from the session object, as it will have been converted to a confirmed booking in the database. The user profile object will be retained in the session, which must not be destroyed. A logged-in user will remain logged in.
	If a logged-in user changed his profile (either of the addresses), the database should be updated automatically with the new information.
Effect on refresh/resubmission	Resubmission of this form must be prevented, to avoid any risk of debiting a user's credit card twice.
Effect on back button	Resubmission of this form will be impossible, so the back button should cause no problem.
Parameters required	Parameters described under discussion of "payment" screen.
Effect of invalid parameters	See discussion of "payment" screen.

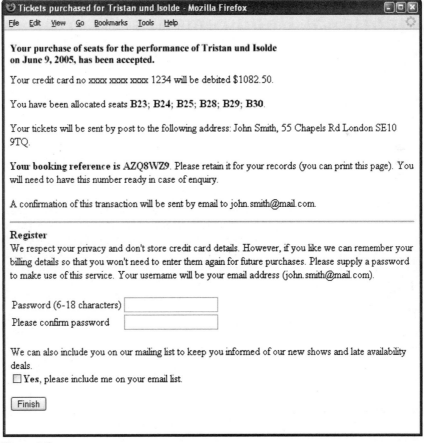

Figure A-8

Box Office User Interface

The box office interface should enable queries and operations such as the following:

❑ For a given show, display the total number of seats of each type available for a given date, as well as the five longest runs of adjacent seats (for example, this would enable a box office user to tell a caller that they couldn't have 18 adjacent seats, but could have groups of 16 and 2 or 10 and 8).

❑ For a given show, show the first date on which a given number of seats (adjacent or non-adjacent) of a given type is available.

❑ Cancel a booking, given the booking reference (the box office user can first view the booking data).

The box office interface's "welcome" page (after mandatory login) should offer immediate access to all common queries.

Each screen in the box office interface should prominently display the time at which it was rendered, and the box office interface must not implement caching of seating availability: Box office staff must always have access to up-to-date information. Each screen in the box office interface relating to a show or performance must display the relevant seating plan. Only those features of the box office interface described previously need to be implemented for the sample application.

Non-Functional Requirements

Normal activity is fairly modest. However, at peak times (such as when a new performance by a major star is listed), the site may experience sharp peaks of user activity. Such activity will often center on a single show, meaning that the performance requirements for the "show" page are almost the same as the "welcome" page. The following table shows the minimum performance requirements for the most performance-critical pages of the public Internet interface.

Page	Hits Per Second	Time (secs) to Render Page (Discounting Network Transfer)	Average Time (secs) to Retune Page over 56K Modem
Welcome	2	1	3
Display Show	2	2	5
Book Seats	2	3	5
Show Reservations	1	3	5
Payment Details	1	3	5
Process payment details[a]	1	30	30

[a]Performance will partly depend on the speed of the external credit card processing system.

These are the minimum targets that will meet the immediate business requirements. The aim should be to far exceed them with a single Intel-based server running the application server, demonstrating the potential of the system for wider use within the Z Group (the database will be running on a separate machine).

Special attention must be paid to performance characteristics under concurrent access, and especially to the following scenarios:

❑ **Heavy activity for one show or even one performance:** This is a realistic possibility — for example if a movie star makes a guest appearance on a single night during the run of a play.

❑ **Supporting concurrent requests for seats when a performance is almost full:** This may result in multiple users trying to reserve the same small groups of seats. It is vital that this does not seriously impair overall performance, and that the reservation database cannot be corrupted.

❑ **Effect on the box office interface of heavy load on the public Internet interface:** It is vital that box office staff are able to do their job without being hampered by slow response times.

If necessary to achieve adequate performance, the following tradeoffs are acceptable:

❑ A new show or performance added by an Administrator may take up to 1 minute to show up on the web interface. However, the system must not require a restart.

❑ The availability, or lack of availability, of seating for a particular class (as shown to public Internet users on the "display show" page) may be up to 1 minute out of date, although any time lag should be avoided if possible.

As cancellations are fairly rare, the remote possibility of a user failing to book a seat because the desired class was marked as sold out, when in fact availability reappeared within 1 minute of the user requesting the "display show" page, is deemed to be acceptable in the interests of performance. The slightly greater possibility that the performance may have sold out after the data was cached is not considered a serious problem: After all, the user could have answered the telephone or discussed the performance dates with friends and family prior to following the link for a given performance date and seat type. Such delays will often be much longer than 1 minute.

Hardware and Software Environment

The target application server will be Apache Tomcat 5.0. Management is keen to minimize licensing costs, especially as the application may be deployed on a number of sites. The application may need to be ported to another application server in the future, so the design must not be dependent on Tomcat. Should such porting be required, a small budget will be allocated for any code changes required and for testing on the new platform. If possible, the application should be verifiable as J2EE-compliant to reassure management that portability is achievable.

The Mandala Center does not presently have its own web-facing hardware. Appropriate hardware will need to be purchased based on performance analysis; management is keen to minimize cost by maximizing performance per cost of hardware.

The application should support clustering if this becomes necessary as demand increases, but management expects that the performance figures described can be exceeded on a single server. All machines in any server cluster would be within the same network.

The database will initially be MySQL 4.1. It is possible that the database will be ported to an Oracle 10g database at some point. Management feels that current O/R mapping technologies will allow for an easy migration if it becomes necessary. Care should be taken when designing SQL queries to avoid using proprietary extensions. The database server and application servers(s) will run on the same local network, so rapid connectivity can be assumed.

There are no other constraints regarding technology to be used. Management has made a strategic decision to adopt J2EE technology because it believes it offers the best chance of successful integration with the legacy booking systems at the other venues with the X Group, but management has no preconceptions on how J2EE should be used. Whether to use technologies such as EJB, JSP, and XSLT is a technical decision. As the project will involve building a team, no constraints regarding existing J2EE expertise (such as "strong servlet experience, no EJB experience") need be considered.

A number of the Mandala Center's staff have HTML skills, but are non-programmers. Therefore it is important that HTML content and site presentation can be controlled, as far as possible, without the need for more than a superficial understanding of J2EE technologies.

Index